THE
NATIONAL
TRUST
GUIDE

THE NATIONAL TRUST GUIDE

compiled and edited by
ROBIN FEDDEN
and
ROSEMARY JOEKES

JONATHAN CAPE
THIRTY BEDFORD SQUARE LONDON

FIRST PUBLISHED 1973
© 1973 BY THE NATIONAL TRUST
REPRINTED 1973, 1974, 1975
SECOND EDITION © 1977 BY THE NATIONAL TRUST
REPRINTED 1979, 1980

JONATHAN CAPE LTD, 30 BEDFORD SQUARE, LONDON WC I

British Library Cataloguing in Publication Data

National Trust
 The National Trust guide. – 2nd ed.
  1. National Trust   2. England – Description and
 travel – Guide-books
 I. Fedden, Robin   II. Joekes, Rosemary
 914.2 ′04 ′857   DA632

ISBN 0–224–01486–2

PRINTED IN GREAT BRITAIN BY JOLLY & BARBER LTD, RUGBY

Acknowledgements

The preparation of a comprehensive Guide to a complex organization such as the National Trust inevitably involves many people, and the editors have received generous help and co-operation. They gratefully acknowledge their debt.

Scholarly contributions on matters relating to particular aspects of the Trust's properties and collections have been made by Geoffrey de Bellaigue, Brand Inglis, John Kenworthy-Browne, J. L. Nevinson, Anthony Rye, Peter Thornton, and Kenneth Woodbridge. The editors were also fortunate in being able to draw on the expert advice of Miss Phyllis Ireland, the Trust's Archaeological Correspondent, and of Miss Clare Fell, Honorary Archaeological Adviser. Graham Thomas, besides writing much of the entries on gardens, was of great help on a wide range of botanical and horticultural matters, as was D. J. Sales.

The section on the coast and country properties has in the main been the work of the Trust's Regional Staff and Gervase Jackson-Stops. Both the latter and Michael Trinick made a major and invaluable contribution. Special thanks are also due to Sir Dawson Bates, I. F. Blomfield, M. J. Rogers, and C. A. Page. The chapter on houses owes much to the contributions of Dudley Dodds, Martin Drury, Julian Gibbs, Anthony Mitchell, John Sutcliffe and Merlin Waterson.

Contents

FOREWORD by the Earl of Antrim   9

HOW TO USE THIS BOOK   10

GENERAL INTRODUCTION by Viscount Norwich   11

I HOUSES   21
Introduction *by Nigel Nicolson*
Picture Collecting in England *by St John Gore*   39

II GARDENS AND LANDSCAPE PARKS   227
Introduction *by Miles Hadfield*

III FOLLIES, MONUMENTS, VILLAGES, DOVECOTES,
CHAPELS, AND BUILDINGS OF USEFUL INTENT   263
Introduction *by Barbara Jones*

IV MEDIEVAL BUILDINGS   305
Introduction *by John Harvey*

V INDUSTRIAL MONUMENTS   359
Introduction *by J. M. Richards*

VI ARCHAEOLOGICAL SITES   389
Introduction *by Jacquetta Hawkes*

VII COAST AND COUNTRY   417
Introduction *by C. H. D. Acland*

MAPS   551

GLOSSARY   569

NATIONAL TRUST PROPERTIES NOT DESCRIBED IN THE TEXT   577

PICTURE CREDITS   593

INDEX   596

Foreword

by the Earl of Antrim, Chairman of the National Trust

When *The National Trust Guide* was first published in 1973, it was an immediate and lasting success and has proved a standard work of reference.

The duty of the National Trust is unlike that of many organizations concerned with the preservation and care of our national heritage. Its work is a continuing process. The time has come, therefore, to revise *The National Trust Guide* and bring it up to date to include properties which have come to the Trust in the last five years and to mark the changes which time has wrought. Amongst these, sadly, was Robin Fedden's death in the spring of 1977. In him the Trust lost an invaluable and irreplaceable servant, a unique personality whose many talents contributed perhaps more to the Trust than any man of his time. Luckily he had been able to discuss and approve the revisions and to imprint his own standards of scholarship upon the work before his last illness, leaving Rosemary Joekes to continue and finish. I should like to think that this new edition of *The National Trust Guide* will stand as a tribute to Robin Fedden. I should also like to congratulate Rosemary Joekes on the high standard which has been achieved.

How to Use this Book

The Guide covers all the important properties of the National Trust in England, Wales and Northern Ireland. Each chapter deals with a particular type of property and is prefaced by an introductory essay followed by a gazetteer.

The National Trust, as the biggest private landowner in the country, is responsible for rather over one acre in every hundred. Naturally in a single volume it is impossible to include a description of all the Trust's open spaces. Those of lesser importance, and also buildings that may be visited only by written appointment or by special arrangement, are omitted from the Guide, but will be found in the list at the back of the book. Covenanted properties are not included.

The maps, on pages 551–568, show the distribution of properties described in the Guide according to the classification adopted by the editors. Visitors may find it helpful to use the Guide in conjunction with the National Trust's *Places to Visit Atlas, The National Trust Map*, and guidebooks to individual properties. A complete register of the Trust's holdings is to be found in *Properties of the National Trust*, to be reissued in 1978.

Opening times vary from property to property and are subject to change. Houses described may be closed for repair or other reasons. Opening arrangements will be found in the list of *Properties Open*, published annually by the Trust, which also gives information on admission fees, nature trails, information centres, shops, restaurants, picnicking, car parks, and guided parties.

Any inquiries about properties, publications or membership should be addressed to: The National Trust, 42 Queen Anne's Gate, London SW1H 9AS.

General Introduction
by Viscount Norwich

The National Trust is now eighty-three. It was born on 16 July 1894, in Grosvenor House, Park Lane – kindly made available by the Duke of Westminster of the day – and received its formal baptism six months later when it was registered under the Companies Act, on 12 January 1895, as 'The National Trust for Places of Historic Interest or Natural Beauty'. Though never in any real sense a sickly child, it proved a slow developer; indeed, only after its fiftieth birthday was it to get fully into its stride. Perhaps it has not even now reached its ultimate maturity; it is certainly still growing, faster than ever. But that is just as well. It will need all its strength, and more, if it is to meet the challenge of the years to come.

Fortunately the Trust's three progenitors were ideally equipped for the task they had set themselves, and the principles which they chose to guide them have been over the years triumphantly justified. Octavia Hill could already look back on a lifetime of dedication to the cause of housing reform, in which field her achievement can be compared only with that of her contemporary Florence Nightingale in the sphere of nursing. She combined, as all successful pioneers must, the qualities of far-sightedness and down-to-earth practicality. No one saw more clearly the dangers with which the spread of industrialization and commercialism were already threatening town and countryside alike; no one knew better how to galvanize others into thinking as she did, how to raise money by appealing simultaneously to generosity and to conscience, how to make herself heard in the right quarters – how, in short, to get things done.

The Sidney Herbert to Miss Hill's Florence Nightingale, the professional administrator to whom she turned for advice and through whom she worked, was Sir Robert Hunter. He too had something of the visionary about him; the original spark of the idea seems in fact to have been his. But he was also solicitor to the Commons Preservation Society and to the General Post Office, a man with long first-hand experience both of charitable institutions and of government departments; he was thus superbly qualified to draw up the Articles of Association and to mould the nascent Trust into the shape best suited to its needs.

Finally there was the Reverend Hardwicke Rawnsley, Canon of Carlisle and Honorary Secretary of the Trust from its inception until his death in 1920. Archaeologist, athlete, journalist, traveller, lecturer, social worker, founder of the Lake District Defence Society and passionate conservationist, Canon Rawnsley thundered out the gospel of the Trust from a thousand platforms and pulpits up and down the country, and for a quarter of a century constituted a one-man public relations and fund-raising machine of formidable efficiency.

The fundamental precept on which this remarkable trio were agreed from the outset was that their new organization must, at all times and at all costs, preserve its independence; and that, while working as closely as possible with the government of the time, it should never accept subsidies from public funds in such a way as to inhibit its freedom of action. This has remained, up to the present day, the cornerstone of the Trust's philosophy. Inevitably, it has brought its own problems, among them that eternal paradox which cannot fail to strike anyone coming into contact with the Trust for the first time: the fact that an organization so fantastically rich in property – the largest private landowner in the country, possessing more than one per cent of all the land in England, Wales and Northern Ireland and some ten miles of coastline in every hundred – should at the same time be perennially short of cash. There is nothing really surprising about this. Clearly the Trust cannot sell its possessions; many of the endowments accompanying gifts of properties have since, with rising costs and inflation, proved hopelessly inadequate; and apart from the income produced by admission charges and rents (themselves almost invariably tied to specific estates) it must rely, for its freely expendable income, almost entirely on the generosity of the public. This, over the years, has been immense; one of the most moving aspects of the Trust's work is the way in which it has been supported, from its earliest beginnings, by those who can ill afford to do so. In 1902, when Canon Rawnsley launched an appeal for the Brandlehow woods on Derwentwater, one subscription arrived with a note: 'I am a working man and cannot afford more than 2s. but I once saw Derwentwater and can never forget it.' That same spirit still lives; it is doubtful whether the people of any other country in the world would have continued, year after year, to respond with such enthusiasm, and the Trust is endlessly grateful. But it remains impecunious and always will.

Poverty, however, is a small price to pay for independence. There has always existed in these islands a rooted prejudice against anything resembling a Ministry of Fine Arts, and it is anyway debatable whether any government department could, or even perhaps should, by its very nature possess the sensibility and flexibility required for so broad and sweeping a range of conservation projects. The Trust sees each one of its thousand properties as an individual, with its own character to be preserved. To recapture the spirit of some long-neglected house or the particular elusive flavour of a stretch of water-meadows is no easy task, and one which seldom falls within the abilities of a bureaucracy, however enlightened it may be. In such matters there is an inner logic to be followed, often imperceptible to the untrained eye and probably indefensible in Parliament as well.

On the other hand, the Trust's relations with succeeding administrations have grown ever closer over the years. At the beginning of the century the public was still for the most part apathetic towards the whole question of conservation – in 1905, after ten years' work, total income amounted to just £837 – and its elected representatives tended to reflect the general indifference. The only real sign of government confidence during this early period – though that a vitally important one – was the passing of the National Trust Act of 1907 which made the Trust a statutory body, at the same time empowering it to declare its land and buildings inalienable and to create by-laws for their protection. This principle of inalienability has been the key to much of its subsequent success. Briefly, it means ownership in perpetuity, immunity from sale, surrender to, or compulsory purchase by, government departments or any other authority, unless by special resort to Parliament. Thus it provides potential donors with a virtual guarantee that their house or land will be safe for ever – an assurance without which many a property would have been lost to the Trust, with possibly disastrous results.

But despite this early sign of confidence, it was only just before the Second World War that the conscience of the nation really began to awake. By now the first and most immediately obvious threat was to the larger country houses. At that time the Trust possessed only two; during the first decades of its existence the owners of such houses were usually quite capable of maintaining them on their own account, and until a second National Trust Act, passed in 1937, enabled it to hold land and investments to provide for the upkeep of its properties it was in any case ill-equipped to do so. This new legislation, however, made possible the 'Country House Scheme', whereby the owner of an historic house could transfer it to the Trust, together with its contents and a suitable endowment, while he himself and his heirs and assigns after him could continue to live in it, subject to certain conditions which included opening it to the public on regular and specified days. Blickling in Norfolk, whose owner, Lord Lothian, had long been the leading proponent of the scheme, was the first great house to come to the Trust in this way; but after its transfer in 1940 others followed thick and fast – Wallington and Cliveden, Great Chalfield and Polesden Lacey, Speke Hall and Gunby Hall, West Wycombe and Lacock Abbey and half a dozen more before the war ended.

Peace inevitably brought its own problems. Robin Fedden, who knew as much about the Trust as any man, described in his book *The National Trust, Past and Present* the grim new pattern that was beginning to emerge:

> An increase in wages that was overdue, a sharp increase in taxation, the impact of higher death duties which often seemed to fall with ironic weight when owners died on active service, imperilled [the] future [of the country houses]. Mansions which had survived the cannonades of the Civil War, the financial panic of the South Sea Bubble, the changes of the Industrial Revolution, and even the accession of profligate or incompetent heirs, were gravely threatened. Maintenance was neglected; dry rot and the insidious beetle set about their work. As owners grew hard-up, mortgages were called in and banks foreclosed. Fine houses were sold for their marble chimneypieces and the lead on their roofs. Timber merchants in a week mercilessly denuded parks which had taken two centuries to mature. A national asset, unique and irreplaceable, was wasting.

More and more owners of houses turned in despair to the Trust. And since many people, not altogether surprisingly, find it hard to understand just what prompts a man already in financial straits to surrender a property which may easily be worth a million pounds or more without receiving any payment in return, and even then only on the condition that he makes over a substantial lump of capital, perhaps tens of thousands, into the bargain, it may be worth while at this point to explain the workings of the Country House Scheme in a little more detail.

The first and most important advantage to the donor is that, once the transfer has been completed, he is relieved from that moment of all further anxiety and responsibility for the upkeep of his house. It is safe at last for posterity, and he can sleep soundly at night in the knowledge that it will be maintained and cherished for all time. Not only can he go on living there; he will be encouraged to do so, and his children after him. His house, like all houses, needs the breath of life within it, and the Trust would always prefer it to continue as a family home rather than be fossilized into a museum. He will have the satisfaction too of knowing that he, or rather it, is receiving full value for money. Both the property and its endowment will be exempt from death duties; and since the Trust, as a charity, will pay no tax on the endowment income, every penny of this will be available to maintain the house and its contents, the garden and the estate. To be sure, there will be drawbacks. It is no pleasant experience to find oneself living in a family house that is no longer one's own, no easy task to reconcile oneself to the loss not only of ownership but of a large measure of control. Henceforth the former owner, now merely the occupier, will have forfeited his free hand in matters affecting improvements, redecoration or repair; and although it will always go as far as it reasonably can to meet his wishes, the final decision on all such questions will in future rest with the Trust alone. He may, too, initially resent the tramp of strangers' feet through the principal rooms – and, worse still, the garden – on summer afternoons; but occasional public access has after all been a feature of English country life for some 300 years, and many a disgruntled donor, faced with the prospect of relearning his house's history for the benefit of the visiting hordes, has found himself falling in love with it all over again and actually looking forward to opening days.

In 1946 the Chancellor of the Exchequer, Dr Hugh Dalton, announced his intention of taking advantage of the government's little-used powers to accept houses and land in payment of death duties and of turning such properties over to the Trust, where appropriate. Another floodgate was opened; some sixty new acquisitions, including several houses of real importance and distinction, have since passed through it into Trust hands. Here again the question of the endowment can prove a problem; it happens from time to time that a donor or a body of executors simply cannot raise sufficient capital to enable the Trust to maintain the property. In such an event there are several other possible sources of funds. If the quality of the house merits it, the Historic Buildings Council may recommend a government grant. Sometimes, too, one of the great charitable foundations may agree to make up the deficit; there may even, in very exceptional instances, be a case for a public appeal. Furthermore the Trust has received increasingly sympathetic consideration in recent years, and increasingly generous financial support, from local authorities. Occasionally the solution consists of a combination of these; Sudbury Hall, for example, one of the most beautiful houses to have come to the Trust in recent years, owes its present superb restoration to a generous grant from the Historic Buildings Council and its maintenance to an annual subsidy from the Derbyshire County Council, who have now converted its Victorian wing into a Museum of Childhood. The system, alas, is not foolproof; it could happen that all these sources proved dry and that a lovely old house had to be left to await disintegration or demolition. But in the last quarter of a century at least, Heaven be praised, it seldom has.

In view of Nigel Nicolson's masterly article in the pages which follow, little more need be said here about country houses *per se* – except, perhaps, a brief word of caution. The National Trust must never be thought of as a collector of these houses. When a building is offered to it – and the Trust would not dream of making an unsolicited approach – the first question it asks is the simplest: Is the building in danger? If it is not, if it can still be maintained in private ownership, or if its continued existence is not in some way threatened, then whatever its architectural or historical distinction the chances are that it will be refused. The Trust is not a predator. What it is, and what for owners of historic houses it is determined to remain, is a lifeline, to be used in emergencies only.

Where coast and countryside are concerned, however, very different considerations apply. Here, by contrast, the danger lies not in the changing times but in a continuation of the old regime of liberty and *laissez-faire*. Up to the turn of the century this system worked well enough; boundaries between town and country had not yet been blurred by ribbon development, most seaside resorts still preserved a Regency or early Victorian elegance, and the word 'pylon' remained unfamiliar to all but Egyptologists.* It comes as something of a surprise to learn that, as early as 1908, the Trust was calling a conference 'to consider the question of the disfigurement of roads by telephone and telegraph posts' – not, alas, one of its most successful initiatives; for the most part, however, England was still green and pleasant. Then came the motor car, first by itself and later with a caravan swaying behind, and all was changed. The speed and extent of the transformation can best be judged from the heartbreaking fact that, by the middle of the 1950s, out of more than 3,000 miles of coastline in England, Wales and Northern Ireland only 900 were considered sufficiently unspoilt to be worthy of preservation.

In such circumstances the Trust clearly cannot sit back and await offers; it must itself take the initiative. And so it has – most notably by means of Enterprise Neptune whose avowed object at the time of its launching in 1965 was to capture as many of those 900 miles as it could. Twelve years later, thanks to Neptune and, as always, to the generosity of the public response to its appeal, some 350 of them are safe for posterity.

*The sense it bears today appears from the *Oxford English Dictionary* to date back only as far as 1923, when Edward Shanks wrote in *The Richest Man* of how 'a cable, a thin black line, traversed the crystal air, borne up on pylons'.

But with operations of this kind it is not only in terms of overall mileage that the Trust has to think; there is also the size of the individual properties to be considered. Those days are past when the offers of small parcels of land would be gratefully accepted, without thought for what lay beyond. A once-beautiful copse becomes little more than a refuse-dump if, like Maggoty's Wood in Cheshire, it is subsequently overshadowed by a modern housing estate. It follows that the Trust must not be content with keeping a constant watch for any remaining tracts of open country or coast that can still be rescued from the clutches of speculator or developer; it must also seize every opportunity of enlarging existing properties threatened by encroachment on their immediate surroundings. Thus its agents and representatives must pay particular attention to these areas, noting any potential acquisition, nursing it as a prospective Member of Parliament might nurse his constituency, winning the confidence of the present owner, and trying to ensure that, if in future it is at any time to come on the market, the Trust will be given first refusal. To see the full force of this argument one need only compare the two neighbouring counties of Dorset and Devon. In Dorset, much of the coast and its hinterland has traditionally formed part of large estates; these have been their own protection, and the land remains comparatively unspoilt. South Devon, on the other hand, has not enjoyed similar advantages. There, the properties have always tended to be small and numerous. The result is sad – and all too evident.

On the north coast of Devon and in Cornwall things are better again, but for a different and even more cogent reason – the lack of easy access by motor car. And this brings us to another of those fundamental paradoxes with which the Trust has to contend. It exists to preserve beautiful, peaceful and unspoilt land for the benefit of the public; at the same time, if too much of the public takes advantage of that land – and particularly if it arrives, as it almost always does, by car – the land loses those very qualities for which it was acquired. How, then, are the two key principles which underlie the whole philosophy of the National Trust to be reconciled – the principles of preservation and access?

It occasionally happens that, for a limited period, the two are in fact irreconcilable. In such an event, preservation must always come first since, as a past Chairman of the Trust once put it, 'Preservation may always permit of access, while without preservation access becomes for ever impossible.' Fortunately, the problem seldom arises in so drastic a form; but it has not yet in every case been satisfactorily solved, and every year it looms larger. Car and even caravan parks do not usually cause too much difficulty; for these the question can normally be reduced to one of proper siting and, where necessary, screening – the secret being not to set them too close to the areas which they serve and may otherwise spoil. The odd tourist may cavil at having to walk the last few hundred yards, but most will agree that this is a small price to pay for the preservation of the character and beauty of the area. The real headache comes when a given property can no longer bear the pressure not of cars but of the visitors themselves. This can be serious enough in an historic building; in gardens and the countryside it can be a catastrophe. During the summer the gardens at Stourhead and at Sheffield Park are each visited by 120,000 people, occasionally receiving over 4,000 in a single Sunday afternoon. No garden can stand this sort of invasion for long. Not only will it lose the atmosphere which is its whole *raison d'être* – the serenity and tranquillity that can be engendered by a vista of far-off trees, a perfectly-sited bank of flowers, or a temple reflected in the waters of a lake – but its very fabric will be damaged, sometimes irreparably: grass trampled and uprooted, ornamental bridges weakened, lawns carpeted with bottles and polythene bags (serried rows of litter-bins are not very much better). Even the birds become bloated with left-over sandwiches. This is not conservation, it is wholesale destruction. The Trust is naturally loath to close, without prior warning, a garden which many people may have driven many miles to see; it is even more reluctant to limit visitors by high admission charges – a measure which would tend to discourage those very sections of the public least likely to possess gardens of their own. But it cannot, at moments such as these, sit back and do nothing.

Even in the open countryside the same problem can arise, as anyone who has been ill-advised enough to visit a famous beauty-spot on a summer Bank Holiday will know to his cost. In such places the overriding danger is ecological. Most English plants and grasses are fairly resilient – they have to be. But if they are trodden and trampled too often, even their powers of recovery fail them. The result is erosion: land formerly covered with a rich sward becomes bare and sterile, a morass in wet weather, a barren dust-bowl in dry. But here, at least in the larger properties, there may be an easier solution. The load, with any luck, can be spread. For every area where the burden of visitors threatens to become intolerable there are usually several others which lie ignored. The public can then be gently persuaded, perhaps by a new car park, perhaps even by one or two tactful signboards, to head off in other directions and along fresh paths, leaving the old ones time for regeneration before it is too late.

Yet this technique must be employed with caution. Of all the qualities of landscape that this country can boast, solitude is already one of the rarest and consequently one of the most vitally important to preserve where it exists. It follows that those stretches of countryside or coastline whose magic resides in their loneliness and wild desolation must never be too clearly indicated.

Enjoyment of them, by their very definition, can be given only to a few; it should therefore by right belong to those who will take the time and trouble to find them for themselves. Too much signposting, in other words, can be as disastrous as too little. For those moderately sound of wind and limb, possessed of an Ordnance Survey map and a stout pair of shoes, the rewards will be immense. But they must be earned.

Conclusions of this kind, set out baldly in black and white, may seem self-evident. They are not. They are lessons learnt, sometimes painfully and only after endless discussions, over long years of trial and, all too often, error. And for every such lesson learnt a dozen problems remain intractable and countless new ones arise. For times not only change; they change faster and faster and, as Octavia Hill sternly pointed out some eighty years ago, 'New occasions teach new duties.' The basic precepts of the Trust may remain firm, but its policies are in a state of constant evolution. Nor is the question simply one of challenge and response; since every one of the Trust's properties has its own individuality, the same challenge may call for a thousand different responses.

It is this constant need for imagination, sensitivity and flexibility of approach that makes association with the National Trust so infinitely rewarding. And – if a member of the Executive Committee may be permitted the reflection – it is the extent to which these qualities have been demonstrated over the years that distinguishes the Trust, time and again, from its foreign counterparts. During 1970 I made an exhaustive tour of a country that boasts an artistic, scenic and archaeological heritage as rich and varied as any in the world, a heritage of which it is rightly proud and which it is assiduous in its efforts to preserve. Those to whom the work of conservation is entrusted perform it with enthusiasm, knowledge and considerable expertise. Only the sensitivity is lacking. Snow-white notice boards, the height of a man, stand in front of every ancient monument, right in the centre, killing it, for all aesthetic purposes, stone-dead. Ancient temples, meticulously reconstructed piece by piece, fail utterly to recapture their former glory when each stone has been numbered, not discreetly in one corner, but in figures daubed six inches high in thick black paint across its face. Sites justly famous for their natural beauty are slashed through with new roads which, given a moment's thought for landscaping, could have followed a slightly different line which would have rendered them invisible. And everywhere, clamped to every corner column, festooned over every façade, the most remorseless visual bane of the century – wire. Telephone wires, telegraph wires, electrical supply wires, wire-fencing, wire-netting, barbed wire, even desultory coils of wire left lying about because the festooners found that they had too much of it or that it might come in handy later – there is no relief from it, no escape. How, one wonders, can the authorities, so conscientious in some respects, be so blind in others? For the trouble is not that they do not care; it is that they do not see.

Dismal amid the desecration, I thought longingly of the National Trust; of how differently it would have approached the task, of how carefully it would have considered the mood of each site and the ways in which its character and atmosphere, as well as its fabric, could best be preserved. Only after deciding this would it have turned its attention to questions of amenity and access – which, however, it would then have studied with precisely the same thoroughness. The result would have been a single coherent plan, reconciling the interests of both property and public, showing the one to its best advantage and giving the other the facilities that it required.

This is not to say that the Trust is infallible. How could it be? It is faced with thousands of decisions every day. Not all can be right; besides, decisions that seem right when they are taken may well prove wrong in the different circumstances prevailing ten years later. But its failures have been relatively few, while its successes can be stunning. Its achievement, taken as a whole, is by any reckoning immense. I know of no organization, public or private, that has done more to make this country what it surely is – the most agreeable in the world to live in.

This book gives an insight into and a description of that achievement. It is certainly not a final report; for the Trust's work will never be finished. As mechanization, industrialization and population continue to increase, its responsibility to future generations becomes ever clearer. So does our own: to back it to the hilt, secure in the knowledge that it will continue as it has for eighty-three years to protect and preserve whatever is loveliest in the kingdom, to maintain and to cherish it, and – above all – to care.

I
Houses

Introduction *by Nigel Nicolson*

The National Trust owns many hundreds of inhabited buildings, of which about ninety fall into a class so special that their preservation is seen by many as the Trust's greatest achievement. These are houses, mainly in the country but a few in towns, which for their architecture, their contents, their associations, or all three, are of such importance that if a catastrophe were to destroy all others of their kind, future historians could still assess from them the character and quality of our civilization.

Ninety may not seem a large number in a country renowned for its historic buildings. The number accounts for about one in four of such houses open to the public, and a small part of all those worth preserving. But it is a highly important part, assembled in less than fifty years and increasing at the rate of one or two a year. Never since the dissolution of the monasteries has a single body had in its charge so remarkable a group of habitable buildings. Not even the Crown at any stage of its long history, nor any equivalent organization in any free country of the world, can rival the National Trust in its ownership of great houses. It is owing to the coincidence that, at the very moment when many of them faced destruction, Government and people became as deeply aware of their importance as their owners, and all three found in the National Trust an instrument of salvation.

It is worth imagining the argument of anti-preservationists, if such exist, in order to restate the answer to it. It could be said that a house, like a tree, has a natural life beyond which it is absurd to prop it up further, and that once the social circumstances which created it have vanished, a large country house becomes an anachronism, a burden upon the State, and little more than a sentimental reminder of an imagined golden age, robbing us of valuable land which should be used for agriculture or for housing more people more fittingly. It benefits a fortunate few at the cost of many, and is the symbol of a snobbish and unregretted past. Its contents are of value, certainly, but, being portable, they are not in danger. They can be sold, or rehoused in museums where more people can see them. The house itself is not worth preserving, since, once it can no longer be lived in as intended, it is a mere carcass. Besides, the constant process of repair and modernization has altered it beyond recognition, and it has become a monstrosity, like a Rembrandt which has been frequently overpainted, with the difference that the Rembrandt can be cleaned but the house cannot.

The best answer to this foolish argument was given by Kenneth Clark in an address to National Trust members in 1970:

> The world of great houses and peaceful village streets and decent market towns once seemed absolutely inviolable. Now it has largely vanished, and is continuing to vanish at an incredible speed. But a great part of us – our laws, our language, our lyric poetry – belongs to that world. What a misfortune if these parts of our life were without visible confirmation. The National Trust not only provides a great pleasure – and pleasure isn't to be sneezed at: it also plays an important part in stabilizing and unifying our society.

To think otherwise is to assume, in the melancholy words of the American master mind Herman Kahn, that 'everything we create is eventually garbage. So all we have in the world is a huge garbage-making machine.' A vast amount of what has been created and even more of what we create today is undoubtedly and deservedly garbage. But obsolescence depends upon what lies in the mind of the creator. These great houses were built to last, not merely as the memorials of a single man or a single family but as ornaments to the country and as expressions of a whole attitude to life. The builders knew that their houses would eventually seem old-fashioned, but to say that for this reason they are expendable is as absurd as to argue that Michelangelo was 'superseded' by Bernini.

The English people, perhaps more than any other, perhaps even to a fault, are conscious of their past. It is important to us that our country, which includes its buildings as well as its fields and coasts, should remain a palimpsest upon which many hands have written. The French anthropologist Claude Lévi-Strauss has spoken of 'the powerful mental brake which has saved the English from destroying continuously their past history and their natural environment, unlike the French who have cheerfully spent so much of their time destroying the former and are now engaged in destroying the latter'. Americans can happily boast of 'Chicago's ever-changing skyline'. For us that description, if applied to London, would be a matter for self-reproach. How much more so if applied to a market town or the complex of buildings which form a great country estate!

Many of these houses are architectural masterpieces, collectively the greatest contribution which Britain has made to the visual arts, and comparable in their sustained variety to the body of English poetry. To permit their destruction, wilfully or through neglect, would be as great a crime as to burn half Shakespeare's works. Indeed it would be greater. For while poetry is constantly renewable, the great house will never be recreated in modern times. The art form itself has disappeared. Never again, unless one day it is decided to rebuild Buckingham Palace, will domestic architecture on this scale be possible. It is literally irreplaceable.

Our architectural heritage is due to two strokes of good fortune. At the only time when people could build houses like this, they did build them like this. Their taste matched their opportunity. And succeeding generations, long before preservation became national policy, instinctively acknowledged their trusteeship. During the three centuries, the 16th to the 18th, when great affluence was concentrated in the hands of very few, those few had the energy, the knowledge and the audacity to raise these huge houses to their own and their country's glory. They borrowed ideas from each other, adapted ideas taken from abroad, and created by a bold series of experiments a style, or rather an architectural attitude, which is unmistakably English. The great house, not the small, was the unit for experiment. It was there that major innovations were introduced, where the most original architects and the finest craftsmen practised. Repeatedly by their example they lifted the standards and transformed the style of smaller buildings throughout the country, suggesting new ideas of comfort and refinement which within a few years would be reproduced on a more modest scale in innumerable towns and villages. This influence was not confined to England alone. It spread to the European Continent, to the Americas, and through our Empire to the whole developing world. Visit almost any of the older towns of the eastern United States and you will find embedded in their centres a group of 18th-century houses which might have been lifted from an English cathedral close. Visit so minute a Caribbean speck as the Cayman Islands, and you will find there a Governor's house which is recognizably English Palladian. The historical importance of English domestic architecture is a reason for its preservation which will be applauded by millions beyond our shores, not in theory alone but by actual pilgrimage, since amongst all the attractions of Britain cited by foreign visitors our great houses rank high. They rightly see in them their architectural ancestry.

Other countries can boast the same heritage, but not quite to the same degree, since fewer of their houses survive intact with their parks, gardens and collections. The French, Italians and Germans have often been kinder to their old towns than we have, but one has only to recall the disenchantment experienced at a beautiful house like Azay-le-Rideau, furnished from museum stock and devitalized by bored uniformed attendants, or the deplorable state of some of Palladio's finest villas, to realize how much we owe to the love which owners and curators have bestowed on our houses. But we must not boast too freely. We have enjoyed several advantages which other countries have not: freedom from invasion, and a relatively stable society; the system of primogeniture which prevented the splitting up of great estates; and the tradition that these houses were not mere residences for the nobility but centres of agriculture, and once of local justice and administration. The English country house, unlike many on the Continent, was a permanent home, not a summer refuge from the metropolis. Childhood associations with a single place, the slow revolution of generations of the same family and their servants, the very portraits on the walls which gave the house a second and watchful set of occupants – all this created a gentle momentum which safeguarded the house and made sacrifices on its behalf as natural as a father's devotion to his child.

It is true that the houses were continually changing. As we shall see, very few National Trust houses exhibit today the unaltered conceptions of their first builders. New methods of heating, lighting, cooking, washing and walling remedied functional faults. New fashions altered the shapes, the decoration and the use of rooms. Sometimes the house was found too large, sometimes too small. New wings were grown, or old ones amputated. The entrance was switched to the garden front or vice versa. Until the 19th century such changes were made in sympathy with the older work, and time obliterated the scars and lines of juncture. The character of a house develops much like character in a human face. It is a record of changing fortunes, but it also reveals changing attitudes. What arrangements were made at different periods to eat, to sleep, to alternate rooms for display with rooms for daily use? When was the bathroom invented, the corridor, the smoking room? How were the servants treated, how were they lodged and fed and organized for work? Were guests encouraged? Was there a nursery for the children, a compound for their pets? And let us not forget the improving services of the house, its intestines, its drains and flues, and the way it was plugged in to the outside world by stabling and carriageways, storerooms and greenhouses and eventually by electricity and the telephone. It is the visible adaptation of old houses to new needs and habits which makes them so fascinating a commentary upon social history. If all other arguments for preservation were scrapped, this would remain decisive, that no evidence of the past is more revealing. These houses are historical documents of priceless value.

There is one other reason for keeping them in the manner of the National Trust, complete with contents and, if possible, the family. The furnishing of a house, from the tapestries of the saloon to the kitchen-stove, is even more important as a record of changing taste than the structure itself. Disperse them through sale and you will be left with a mere husk. The rooms will be undressed, uninteresting, lifeless. However rich the gilding of the cornices, however glossy the floors, rooms demand movable furnishing, and without it they are robbed of their function, and of much of their design, like a library without books. The contents tell the story of the building's many past inhabitants: what they acquired and from where, how much importance they attached to contemporary work and how much to antiques, what journeys they made, what careers they pursued, what works of art they bought or commissioned or tried amateurishly to create for themselves, what toys, utensils and gadgets they accumulated, what books they read, what mistakes they made – in short, how they lived, and therefore how they thought. Art history may be learnt more easily in museums, because only the choicest pieces are exhibited there and they are chronologically arranged. But it is the juxtaposition in a house of objects of different periods, quality and origin, that humanizes both it and them. Like a fireplace or hall-screen, they have their proper context, and to separate them from it is an act of dismemberment. The National Trust does not regard its function as one of mere salvage, like a dealer's. It is concerned with the integrity of a house as a home.

National Trust houses are spread so widely throughout the country that one is seldom beyond half a day's drive from a dozen of them, but in density unequally owing to chance and the concentration of great houses in the south-east and the Midlands. Chance again (for the Trust does not 'collect') has given it the ownership of excellent examples of all the main periods and architects except Vanbrugh. It is particularly rich in the work of the Elizabethans and the late 17th and late 18th centuries. Every house mentioned in this survey is a property of the Trust.

The earliest of them were havens of comfort and security in a difficult and alarming world. The effort of hauling stone, brick and timber over unmetalled trackways to build Hardwick on its Derbyshire hilltop or Oxburgh in the Norfolk marshes or Cotehele in the steep valleys of Cornwall, magnifies their achievement. Once the house was completed, there was little to tempt its owners and retainers to wander from it. It was built self-sufficient, as if to stand a siege. Today it wears a less isolated look. Its park is a refinement of the surrounding fields, its lake the village pond writ large. Every visitor to Trust properties is familiar with the sudden tightening of the landscape which announces the neighbourhood of a great house. A wall or fence of unusual solidity bows inward to frame an entrance gateway, and there is a glimpse of fine trees rising from rolling grassland, through which the unfenced road winds to the house. Knole, Osterley, Tatton, Clandon, Saltram, Lyme, Trelissick, Ickworth, Shugborough, all have parks of this type, and the list could be prolonged. It is only rarely that a big house like Petworth rises cliff-like from its village, or, like Blickling and Attingham, is sited to astonish the traveller on the public road. The English habit is to lead by serpentine approach to sudden display.

The first sight of a house must make a tremendous impact; not a cluster of casually dropped remarks, but a single statement. It must mark the end of a journey, as if all travail has led up to this point, and it must express the status and ambition of its founder, whose motive was to spend new wealth in the most effective and enduring manner possible, to please his family, excel his neighbours, amaze his friends, and perpetuate his name and line. 'When men sought to cure mortality by fame,' wrote Sir Francis Bacon, 'building was the only way.' It must promise seclusion and hospitality within, but these things must be implicit in the shape of the whole. It must have symmetry and nobility. Its intention is not to overawe, nor to charm, but to impress and delight. It must belong to the countryside from which it has emerged, but not hug it closely like an animal its den, for it is a proud building 'in daytime on every side glittering by glass,' as Robert Laneham, Gentleman Usher to Lord Leicester, wrote, 'at night by continual brightness of candle, fire and torchlight'.

These intentions remained constant, from 15th-century Oxburgh to 19th-century Cliveden. In the earlier period there was always a series of barriers to penetrate, to hold off the unwanted intruder and to dignify, by guarded admission, the expected guest. Perhaps it was nothing more than a wall with central piers and a gate, but more often a gatehouse, of which two lovely examples survive at Lanhydrock and Charlecote, or a tower flanked by octagonal turrets, sometimes the central feature of the entrance range, like Oxburgh's, or free standing as at Sissinghurst. Coughton Court in Warwickshire illustrates the development of the style. Built in 1509 by Sir George Throckmorton, this magnificent structure, mullioned and transomed and four-turreted, is still basically a Gothic building, but with its organ-like golds and recessions, its dazzling display of many faceted windows, it clearly belongs to a house and not to a castle, for it is indefensible and was conceived as much for the outlook from within as for the splendour it gave to the house when seen from the far end of its avenue.

Once admitted through the gatehouse, the visitor confronted the bulk of the house. Outhouses were tucked behind it or to one side, for not yet was everything that belonged to the house forced into it: the 'splendid' parts lay separate from the 'useful' parts. For the former there were two variations. Either the house was extrovert, rising direct from park and garden with short wings and a porch (a famous early example is Barrington Court, the first large house to pass into the Trust's ownership, and two later ones, Trerice and Melford Hall), or the rooms looked inward across a courtyard, after the style of a college. Sometimes the outward-looking and the inward-looking were combined, as with charming effect at Cotehele.

Knole illustrates a favourite plan for a house of the largest size. The courts were placed one behind the other, with the hall in one of the crosswings, forming a succession of enclosures, a progressive withdrawal from the outside world, increasing in seclusion as the womb of the house is reached. Knole's five quadrangles provide still centres for the buildings around them. The open spaces multiply the number of external façades, creating new architectural opportunities and many subsidiary entrances. They are courts to cross, treading on grass or gravel or paving stones or cobbles, and courts to look into from upstair windows, remaining part of the house though open to the sky. The area covered by actual buildings is thus increased fourfold or more, adding to their importance when seen from a distance, and making the management of the house convenient and self-centred. Knole is partly castellated, but nobody could call it austere. It has a controlled romanticism. Variety is added to impressiveness by its bays and gables topped by the Sackville leopard, and the horizontality of the whole is relieved by great chimneys, a clock tower and a roof of russet tiles which slips and slides, dips and rears, in a frenzy of protection. It is a vast house, more like a medieval Umbrian town, but those who have lived in it know how intimate it can seem when gentle moonlight floods its courts, and the distant sound of a piano or laughter from the kitchen dispels childhood fears.

Hardwick is the greatest example in England of the extrovert house, and the most adventurous building to survive from the Elizabethan age. It was begun by Elizabeth, Countess of Shrewsbury, in 1591 when she was already past seventy years old. The core of the house was finished in under three years, and it was fully habitable in seven. Though she was helped by Robert Smythson, Hardwick is an expression of her dominating personality and of an inventiveness amounting to genius. Living to the age of ninety, Bess of Hardwick spent her life, 'proud, furious, selfish and unfeeling, a builder, a buyer and seller of estates, a money-lender, a farmer, and a merchant of lead, coals and timber'. The very site of Hardwick proclaims her character. Mounted on a hilltop within a hundred yards of the old hall (which she also transformed) where she was born, it stands fretted against the skyline like a castle, but the imagined battlements are found on closer approach to be parapets enclosing her initials, 'E.S.', in stones four feet high. It is a house which stares at the beholder. It takes courage to knock at its single external door. The huge expanse of glass seems from outside more like armour-plating than a means of lighting the interior. Six towers ride the roof line, forming bold angles and receding planes, a triumph of architectural pageantry. Its grace is achieved without decoration – a balustrade along the roof, a Tuscan colonnade below, that is almost all. The impact of the building is its combination of strength (stone) and delicacy (glass). Ladderlike the mullions climb the façade, the windows increasing in height as they mount upwards, as if to emphasize the risk taken with their fragility.

A third Elizabethan house of the noblest sort is Montacute. Like Hardwick, its exact contemporary, and like the great majority of houses of this period, it is the amateur creation of its first owner, Edward Phelips, who had made money in the Law. Untutored in architecture but assisted by a master mason, William Arnold, he built his house of the local Ham Hill stone, the most radiant of our native materials, honey-coloured, absorbing the sun and exuding it. By the devices of shallow recessions, bays, columns, gables, statues, he gave his house a liveliness which does not impair its placidity. Window matches window, gable answers gable, but the symmetry of Montacute is not mechanical. It rises high to a serrated roof line, topped by chimneys in pairs which make virtues out of awkward necessities. The house was not allowed to straggle. It expresses a conscious will, the taste and purpose of one man, its beauty emerging from its constructional propriety. In the forecourt of what was once the entrance front two pavilions or gazebos frame the house at an exactly calculated distance. If any critic feels tempted to accuse the Elizabethans of clumsiness, let the Montacute gazebos be his answer. They are pieces of confectionery in stone, playful reminders of medieval turrets, but constructed with a lightness, a swirl, a feminine extravagance which can only be paralleled in music.

These superb houses have their less sophisticated counterparts in all quarters of the country. Bateman's, Kipling's Sussex home, is an example of the Elizabethan tradition extending well into the 17th century, a modest stone-built house with brick chimneys, a good illustration of the truism that country craftsmen working in their native materials were in that age incapable of offence. Another is Snowshill in the Cotswolds, and a third, Benthall Hall. In the north, the Trust owns two remarkable houses which reproduce in whitened plaster and blackened timber the Elizabethan features which were executed more regularly in brick and stone elsewhere. At Speke Hall the builders made no concessions to symmetry, allowing the house to grow new arms as freely as an amoeba, and using the walls as canvases for monochrome designs round its exterior and with even greater lavishness in its inn-like courtyard. Little Moreton Hall in Cheshire is lifted straight from a fairy story, a gingerbread house, its bays and porches and gables jostling each other for space, turning this way and that as if in conversation. Along one roof the Moretons (as an afterthought, for no gentleman's house was complete without one) balanced a Noah's Ark of a long gallery with perilous disregard for the laws of gravity and construction, but it has stood there for four hundred years.

An important group of Trust houses originated as castles, another group as monasteries. Rarely in the 16th century would a castle serve its original function, garrisoned like Lindisfarne against the Scots. To most Elizabethans the feudal castles seemed little more than outworn fortifications, forbidding in site, construction, internal arrangements and associations, expressing and imposing a spartan way of life, cramped, crouched and wary. Sometimes, when necessity or family attachment outweighed convenience, they chose to inhabit them unchanged, like the vast brick keep at Tattershall, which was occupied as late as 1693. Sometimes a little castle like Scotney would have an Elizabethan wing added. But occasionally they would choose to prise open these huge stone boxes, and to create from them fine houses, as if liberating a butterfly from its chrysalis. The most dramatic of them is St Michael's Mount, in turn monastery, fortress and house, standing on a pyramidal rock cut off from the Cornish mainland at high tide by twenty feet of water. Another is Powis Castle in Wales, where the huge border fortress still stands as solidly as it did in the 13th century, but has been softened by windows and resculpted internally to admit a long gallery and later a monumental staircase and a suite of state rooms which accommodate themselves with a struggle to curving walls and barrelled ceilings. Compton Castle, built in about 1320 to defend the Devonshire coombs against French raids, is a fortified manor house which still wears the look of an illustration torn from a medieval Book of Hours, with its portcullis entrances, machicolations, and the house flag of the Gilberts asserting its proud origins. Croft Castle slipped more easily into modern times because it was built low and foursquare. Rooms could be created naturally behind the flat curtain walls, the turrets forming circular bowers off them, and the central courtyard was roofed in the 18th century to win space for a hall and a gallery. Sizergh in Westmorland, basically a pele tower but now a mansion, has walls nine feet thick, containing 14th-century fireplaces and windows.

Those are the main habitable castles. The religious houses are even more remarkable for the skilful re-use of thick walls raised for totally different purposes. Lacock Abbey was a 13th-century nunnery, of which parts were preserved when other parts were converted in 1550 by Sir William Sharington, who had travelled in Italy and brought back some of the first Renaissance motifs to be seen in an English house. Here we are far from houses built all of one piece to astonish and delight, but for all the botchiness of its architecture, Lacock illustrates another characteristic of English builders, their improvisation, their romanticism, and their attachment to visible reminders of the past. They set themselves apparently impossible tasks. At Buckland Abbey, Sir Richard Grenville of the *Revenge* made the abbey church into the hall of his new house, which Drake was later to inhabit. At Anglesey Abbey, rebuilt after the Dissolution as a manor house, the Canons' Parlour, dating from 1236, still does duty as a dining room. At Mottisfont, Lord Sandys, who already owned The Vyne, undertook in his declining years the ambitious conversion of the priory church into a self-contained house, which was later given on one side an elegant Georgian façade. There one can sleep suspended at the roof level of an Augustinian nave, and be comfortably unaware of it; play scrabble in Rex Whistler's wonderfully cool Music Room, supported by the vaulting of a 13th-century cellarium; or take an alfresco tea beside an artificial cut of the River Test, flowing swift and transparent, a stream in which Ophelia might have drowned herself but where for centuries monks fished for their supper. There are few houses where the past is more charmingly contained.

Very different from the swept and polished rooms which visitors see today in the Trust's Elizabethan houses were the conditions in which their creators lived. The stench of garlic mingled with the stench of open drains. The multitude of servants brought into the house the muck and refuse of the yards. A wooden tub before the bedroom fire served as a bathroom. The kitchen was more like a charnel-house. The servants slept in every part of the house on straw pallets, gathering up their beds, as in a battleship, before the master made his rounds. The main rooms, because size was proof of status, were enormous, such warmth as could be generated in them by wood fires escaping to lofty ceilings and through warped window frames. It was a man's world, of politics, business and sport, a place for ringing footsteps and shouted commands. They strode their galleries like quarterdecks, and their houses were controlled, not by women but by officers. The very gardens were planned like parade grounds, the flower-beds drawn up in battalions, the surrounding walks as regular as Roman ramparts. The splendour of their clothes matched the armorial glass in their windows. Their vanity was synonymous with their pride, and their houses expressed their determination to leave behind them not merely a tomb and a portrait, but a monument to their fame.

For all the uncouthness of their manners and of much of their fiendish decoration, there was a growing sense of style. The lord of the house no longer needed to banquet daily with his men. Henceforward withdrawal marked his authority, not a six-inch dais separating the high table from the crowd in the body of the hall. The Great Hall was indeed retained – wonderful examples can be seen at Cotehele, Speke, Trerice, Charlecote and, supremely, at Rufford Old Hall – but it came to be used more for ceremonial entry and reception than for meals, except in the grandest houses like Knole, where until the 18th century some place for feeding 300 servants was essential. At Knole, one can see the first open staircase, providing a three-dimensional stage for ladies ascending and descending in their broad farthingale skirts, which replaced the bleak flights of stone or timber around a solid core, like that at Montacute, and was soon to be copied in a joyful *tour de force* of carpentry and carving as the main feature even of so modest a house as Benthall Hall.

The staircase led eventually but invariably to a long gallery (Knole has three of them), the most striking of Elizabethan rooms, the least explicable and the most difficult to adapt to modern usage. They were rooms in which to take gentle exercise in winter (the Elizabethans were great hibernators), rooms for hanging pictures against tapestry, rooms for music and dancing, and rooms where, in the farthest recesses, children could play. In the earliest versions, like the famous long gallery at The Vyne, the great length was diversified only by intricate panelling. Then fireplaces were introduced centrally or towards each end, and wide window-embrasures served as miniature lobbies of their own, recesses for business, madrigals or flirtation, where cushioned seats overlooked the garden. The galleries were terribly cold, and later, less hardy generations were forced to flee to smaller rooms, like the sixth 'Bachelor' Duke of Devonshire who was 'driven to habitation of the Library [at Hardwick] by a vain attempt we made to pass some evenings in the Long Gallery, although surrounded by screens and sheltered by red baize curtains'. Some of them, like Blickling's and Lanhydrock's, became libraries; Montacute's (the longest of all) recently became a picture-gallery, and Hardwick's has always been the loveliest picture-gallery in the kingdom; that at Ham House was completely redecorated in 1639 for show and exercise rather than comfort; at Mottisfont the gallery became the Georgianized central corridor; but some remain quite unaltered, like that at Lyme Park, 120 feet long by 18 broad, lined from end to end with panelling which incorporates in its chimneypiece the arms and supporters of Queen Elizabeth. That the fashion did not completely die is shown at Polesden Lacey, where the wide corridors filled with splendid works of art are its 20th-century equivalent, as is Packwood's gallery, constructed as late as 1932.

For the finest of Elizabethan Great Chambers one must return to Montacute, to Hardwick, to Knole, to Blickling, to Speke, and above all to Lyme Park, where the wainscoting is one of the most intricate examples of Elizabethan joinery to survive. It was here that the family sometimes ate and received important guests, a combined dining and drawing room, but in the largest houses the suite of ceremonial rooms – hall, long gallery, and Great Chamber – was closed in winter, and the family would live in a nest of smaller rooms opening off them. A small dining room was usual by the end of the 16th century, a parlour, a breakfast room, a study, day and night nurseries – in fact almost all the specialized rooms found in houses of two centuries later. At the other end of the house servants' rooms multiplied. In great houses, like The Vyne, Knole, Petworth and Cotehele, there was a chapel. Thus the house grew. Rooms of widely different length and height and function were boxed together within a symmetrical casing, and privacy was won from these capacious shells as well as areas for parade.

The National Trust houses of Tudor, Elizabethan and Jacobean date form a sequence which lacks only an example of the flashier piles like

Burghley, or of the most classical like Longleat, but Longleat is unique. These houses have their critics. Osbert Lancaster has written of them: 'The old medieval restraints have been abandoned, but nothing as yet had appeared to take their place, so that the architects with a number of new processes at their disposal were at a complete loss as to how best to apply them.' This is undeniable as regards decoration, inside and out. But the argument cannot be upheld when challenged by such a house as Blickling, a lovely composition of brick and stone which owes nothing to the classical revival and little to medievalism, but pleases by its colour, its grace, its originality, its wavy gables and helmeted cupolas, its central tower which from a distance foreshadows Wren, its perfect accomplishment of what Robert Lyminge, its architect, set out to do. Blickling was built in about 1620, just in time to demonstrate the ultimate possibilities of the Elizabethan style before Inigo Jones crushed it.

Until the last decade of the 17th century the Trust has only two major examples of the architectural revolution to offer, if one excepts internal remodelling and the portico which John Webb attached so boldly on the Tudor garden front of The Vyne. But those two, Ham House and Ashdown, are exquisite.

The core of Ham House is Jacobean, but its present character owes everything to the Duke of Lauderdale and his wife, Elizabeth Dysart, who enlarged and modernized it in the 1670s; and of the two it was the Duchess whose will was dominant. Those who believe that houses, like dogs, reveal the character of their owners, will be disillusioned when they visit Ham, and fortunately so, for we have it on the authority of the Duchess's contemporary, Bishop Burnet, that 'she was restless in her ambition, profuse in her expense, and of a most ravenous covetousness; nor was there anything she stuck at to compass her end, for she was violent in everything – a violent friend, and a much more violent enemy'. Ham suggests nothing of this except her extravagance. She and her unamiable husband created a restful house, peaceful in its situation on a great bend of the Thames near Richmond, and wonderfully calm in its interlocking suites of rooms. The entrance hall, paved in black and white marble, with a gallery running all round it, links the two main storeys in a manner quite foreign to the house which the Lauderdales inherited, and off it, at both levels, run rooms which alternate between large and small, so that every door opens upon a surprise, each richly decorated but none flamboyantly, the smallest, the Queen's Closet, carrying the heaviest load of wainscoting and hangings in crimson and gold. Ham is the perfect evocation of the best the 17th century could offer.

Ashdown is as courageous in its architecture as is Ham in its decoration. It stands in a part of the Berkshire Downs so empty that even a cottage would seem obtrusive, but far from crouching in scale to the rounded hills, it rises five storeys high and only five windows wide, its proportions heretical, its arrogance improper, but its effect so delightful that even a photograph of it makes one start with pleasure. From the platform of its steeply hipped roof rises an octagonal cupola, crowned by a copper ball.

Then suddenly, between 1690 and 1710, we come upon a bouquet of National Trust houses, representative of what to many people is the climax of English domestic building, our only truly indigenous style apart from the Elizabethan. Some call it loosely 'Queen Anne', others 'Wren', but it is misleading to label it as an architectural period at all, since it was highly diverse and boldly experimental, the period of Vanbrugh and Hawksmoor, of huge wall-paintings and Grinling Gibbons, of the Baroque and a strong influence from France, but also of decent, gentle building which in town and country seems at last to have found the ideal answer to what Sir Henry Wotton in the 16th century had advocated as the essentials of good building, 'commoditie, firmness and delight'.

One such house is Antony, its very name suggesting its masculine grace. One façade is the mirror-image of its opposite (apart from a Victorian *porte cochère*), and when dissected one finds them to be composed of many elements: the pediment Greek, the windows French, the dormers Dutch, the porch Italian, but the whole as English as the view over Repton's park, teaching a visual lesson in proportion which could not be put into words. Another is Mompesson House in Salisbury Close, a princess of a house, built in 1701 of creamy stone in a row of smaller brick and stone buildings which it does not overshadow, being a well-mannered neighbour and its serenity that of a beautiful woman in a crowd. Or Tintinhull, a house of 1600, refaced a hundred years later to alter its entire character, a clumsy toy which became a miniature work of art, again a matter of exquisite balance between windows, roof, pediment, doorway and pilasters. This is the house and garden which most people of sensibility and modest means, leafing through an illustrated guide to National Trust houses, would choose for their own. Or, if of slightly grander taste, they might prefer Wallington, the Trevelyan house in Northumberland, well-knit and unexclamatory; or Hanbury Hall, possibly the work of William Talman, where in a favourite style of the period two broad and shallow wings advance a fraction to frame a pedi-mented centre topped by a cupola. This house, like Sudbury Hall and many others, even the latest transformation of Powis Castle, has interior painting on ceilings or stairwell walls by Thornhill, Verrio or Laguerre, a short-lived foreign fashion which to our eyes consorts ill with the refined simplicity of the exteriors. In the more direct Wren tradition is Gunby Hall, whose three bays (ignoring a 19th-century wing) might be three separate houses in Cheltenham or London's Inns of Court.

Uppark, Dyrham and Petworth are more splendid versions of those so far mentioned. Of the three Uppark, though the smallest, is queen, for its situation on the South Downs overlooking the English Channel from a great distance is regal, and the foursquare set of the house, the marriage of plain roseate brick to embellished stone, the equal windows tall as grenadiers, give it the dignity of a medallion struck true from its die. Inside it is no less superb, but not in a palatial way, for its rooms are companionable, ivory walls fondled by straying tendrils of gilded wood and curtains looped in the 18th-century manner to the window tops. How strange a setting for the youth of Emma Hamilton and H. G. Wells, who for a time occupied in their different capacities the master's bedroom and his kitchen!

The east front of Dyrham, designed by Talman in 1698, is one of the most satisfying compositions in stone to be seen in England. While Uppark could be said to raise the English manor-house to its zenith, Dyrham is the transplantation, as the Trust's guide-book suggests, of a Genoese palace to the setting of a great English park. Rich classical elements are combined with strong horizontal lines to create the nearest approach to the full Baroque which the English could tolerate without violating our vernacular tradition. The opposite front is the work of a Frenchman, S. Hauduroy, simpler as a flat piece of scenery but enlivened by a stone external stairway and one-storey galleries leading on one side to a medieval church, and on the other to a stable block, a vigorous building which provided for twenty-six horses accommodation as splendid as for the occupants of the house.

Petworth, in contrast, is disfigured by the destruction of its central feature, a flattened dome, soon after it was built. When viewed from its park, the house appears too unemphatic for its great length, and only when examined from the terrace are the subtlety and quality of its mouldings and recessions apparent. The glory of Petworth is its interior, not only for the art collection which is discussed elsewhere in this volume, but for the rooms which extend *en suite* along the garden front, including the cool centre of the house, the Marble Hall, and the famous room where Grinling Gibbons mounted his carvings around and between the paintings, less effectively as a form of decoration in the mass (for they can appear scabby) than in detail. The intricate ingenuity of representing in limewood, his single material, flowers and animals, leaves curled by autumn, cherubs pillowed cheek against cheek, violin strings, a lace handkerchief, fish threshing their tails in death agony, is beyond emulation.

We are now launched upon the 18th century, and National Trust houses crowd so profusely that only outstanding examples can be mentioned. The Trust is fortunate to possess in Stourhead not only the most remarkable garden of its age, but a Colen Campbell house which was one of the first to employ the Palladian style which soon swept the country. The greatest example in the Trust's ownership is the new front by which the Venetian architect, Giacomo Leoni, transformed the Elizabethan house at Lyme Park. The huge Ionic portico with its matching bays is one of the boldest Palladian achievements to survive. The same architect built Clandon for Lord Onslow, incorporating an enormous entrance hall, a forty-foot, two-storeyed cube encrusted with plasterwork, and a lovely suite of rooms around it which the Trust reopened in 1971 after extensive redecoration and refurnishing. Shugborough is a magnificent 18th-century house, but here the classical convention is less evident, for the house, of three architectural periods brilliantly unified, is low and undemonstrative in spite of its great size. Rounded pavilions rising to roof level at each end and Samuel Wyatt's porch of 1794 give it a Regency look from outside, and provide within a splendid set of rooms equally fit for royalty or a children's Christmas party. At West Wycombe the flexibility of the Palladian style is shown by the superimposition of two colonnades along the south front, Corinthian over

Tuscan, more reminiscent of southern American classical architecture than of British. The rooms, particularly the small Tapestry Room, are so perfectly disposed and proportioned that it is difficult to conceive of an aristocratic style of living translated into more agreeable architectural terms.

Claydon, of which only part survives, expresses a totally different taste. It contains what James Lees-Milne has called 'the most astounding rococo suite of rooms in Great Britain', considered by their contemporaries to be as imbecile as their creator, Luke Lightfoot, but to our eyes a triumph of graceful carving, having no parallel in Trust houses except the overmantel of the drawing room at Peckover.

With Attingham we return to Palladian normalcy, though internally it is less successful, since the central room, a high picture-gallery, is squashed between the entrance hall and the stairs. Its huge outside portico, almost the only decoration on a rectangular central block, makes an unforgettable impression when first seen from the Shrewsbury road, and for once explains and almost excuses that lamentable phrase, 'a stately home'. The classical style lingered on in England until the turn of the century, as seen at Tatton Park, Buscot, Berrington and Philipps House, Dinton, but it was an Irishman, the Bishop of Derry and 4th Earl of Bristol, who produced at Ickworth its last and most staggering manifestation. He had already built in Ireland a great domed and winged house which no longer survives, and the lovely Mussenden Temple (also a property of the Trust), a drum pinioned by engaged columns. Having inherited his brother's Suffolk estates, he began in 1794 to reproduce there a vast enlargement of his temple with curving wings, in which he intended to house his art collection. He did not live to see it finished, and his collection was dispersed, but his son, with remarkable fidelity to his father's plan, completed the building in 1830, by which time it must have seemed a gigantic anachronism. Ickworth is huge – one end of one wing now serves the present Marquess of Bristol as a splendid country house – and the domed Rotunda, as magnificent as a papal tiara, is on such a scale that from within one is barely conscious of the curvature of the walls until one tries to hang a picture against them, forgetting that these great rooms are contained within an egg.

This is the moment to introduce the Trust's houses in Northern Ireland. For although two of them, the simplest, Ardress and Springhill, are basically 17th-century (though much improved during the 18th), three major houses were all built between 1760 and 1790. The earliest is Florence Court, a severe main block relieved by low pavilions joined to it by long stone arcades, and animated internally by delightful plasterwork, with which nearly all the Trust's Irish houses are enriched. Castle Coole is the greatest of them, and its splendour is enhanced by its preservation from any subsequent alteration, inside or out, and its retention of much of the original furniture and all the fittings. It is the work of James Wyatt in the grand late-18th-century manner, which demanded delicate wings attached to a firm body. Never was the style better executed than at Castle Coole, but it is in the interior (in such details as the landing at the top of the staircase) that the architect's distinction is best revealed. Finally comes Castle Ward, for which I must confess a particular affection, for no family disagreement ever resulted in a more charming compromise. The first Viscount Bangor favoured the classic style, his wife the neo-Gothick. So each designed half the house. On the Viscount's side we see a perfect Georgian house touched with rustication and a pedimented group of four half-columns. Walking round to the opposite front in expectation of its near-duplicate, we find the Countess's much more original contribution in spidery Gothick, windows with pointed arches and careful tracery, shallow battlements like the hemming of a neckline, and three tiny crocketed finials pricking the sky. The compromise extends indoors. A classical hall leads to a Gothick saloon, and the sitting room has a ceiling of fan-vaulting.

In describing some later houses in the Palladian tradition, I have by-passed the short but lovely period of Robert Adam. The Trust is rich in examples of it. It owns the earliest of all, Hatchlands, where the young Adam, soon after his return from Italy in 1758, designed the main decoration for the living rooms and two bedroom ceilings. They are rather coarse compared to the graceful filigree which he soon developed, and the chief beauty of the house is its staircase which owes nothing to him. But at three great houses, among the most important owned by the Trust, Nostell Priory, Osterley and Saltram, where Adam was working simultaneously, flying from one end of the country to the other in execution of his extravagant commissions, we can see his genius brilliantly displayed.

At Osterley he added a Roman portico to an Elizabethan house and raised the internal courtyard to the level of the first floor, taking an amazing liberty with an ancestral house, as much a tribute to the courage of his patron, Francis Child, as to the youthful architect's, for the conception, described in words, needs the reality of its execution to prove its possibility. At Nostell Priory Adam built an extra wing and also designed the stables. At Saltram he made extensive changes to the east wing.

But it is the interior of these three houses which colours the memory. Adam considered heavy entablatures and coffered ceilings inappropriate to private houses, and drew his new inspiration from what he imagined to have been 'the delicacy, gaiety, grace and beauty' of Roman decoration, adapting their variety of light mouldings, friezes, pilasters, grotesque stucco and 'fanciful figures and winding foliage', to create the sort of elegant frivolity that goes with weddings. His rooms, of which the Saloon at Nostell Priory is a good example, were further softened by apses and coved ceilings to cushion the occupants. The ceilings were as intricate as the patterned floors, and the walls, as in the entrance hall at Osterley, often became tableaux for low relief. There the colouring is gossamer cool, needing flunkies in scarlet livery to make shifting splashes of a deeper colour against the white and powder blue of the walls. Indeed, people are essential to Adam décors – animated people in fine clothes, rising in a rustle of silk from silk-covered chairs. The pictures, tapestry, and Adam's tiptoe furniture, which he often designed himself down to the very fire-irons, were all considered in advance in relation to the total effect. So his rooms remain unaltered, nobody ever having had the temerity to introduce a discordant object into such a place as the dining room at Saltram. The completeness of Adam's work is its best protection.

He had many imitators, but the best adaptation of the style is to be seen in the interior of Henry Holland's Berrington Hall. Berrington has an inner staircase hall, which, like The Vyne's of thirty years before, creates within a confined space a sense of the theatre, so ingenious are its levels and so dramatic the effect of the gallery-openings on three sides of the upper floor.

The Trust's 19th-century houses need no apology for the contrast between them and what has gone before. There are certain rooms which appal, like the gilded drawing room at Polesden Lacey, but Mrs Greville's house is otherwise a lovely enlargement of a Regency villa, surrounding a courtyard which suggests Spain more than the flowing Surrey hills outside, and containing works of art and furniture which are in such perfect condition that we owe almost as great a debt to their present curator as to their original makers. Utterly different is Penrhyn, a fantasy castle in North Wales, Norman outside, 'Oriental' within, built in the 1830s by Thomas Hopper, an early Victorian addition to the Trust's repertoire of great houses which may represent a collapse of taste but not of invention or energy. Later exercises in romanticism are Cliveden, the Astors' Italian *palazzo* by Sir Charles Barry; Waddesdon, the French Renaissance *château*; Ascott, another Rothschild house, this time half timbered; Dunster Castle, a 17th-century house developed from a medieval fortress, restored and altered by Anthony Salvin, the highly successful specialist in military architecture; Cragside, the fairy palace on a Northumbrian moor, built in the 'Old English' style by Norman Shaw, and not least Castle Drogo, one of Lutyens's most inspired buildings, not finished until 1930. The last concludes the chronicle of more than four hundred years of English domestic architecture and the Trust's contribution to its preservation.

There remain a few houses which have been accepted by the Trust more for their associations than for their architectural value. There is Washington Old Hall, the home of George Washington's ancestors; Moseley Old Hall, where Charles II hid after the battle of Worcester; Woolsthorpe, Isaac Newton's birthplace; Quebec House, the childhood home of General James Wolfe; Carlyle's house in Chelsea, Wordsworth's at Cockermouth, Coleridge's at Nether Stowey, and the thatched cottage where Thomas Hardy was born and grew up. There is Smallhythe, where Ellen Terry lived and died; Clouds Hill, which must be the tiniest habitable possession of the Trust, the cottage where T. E. Lawrence sought refuge and music; Hughenden, which Disraeli loved; Shaw's Corner, exactly as G. B. Shaw left it on his death; Lamb's House at Rye. And finally Chartwell, which bursts the bounds of a mere list, as Winston Churchill did of his century. This once undistinguished Victorian house was acquired by him for its view over the Weald of Kent, was transformed by him into a home and place of work which for a decade became the country's heart, brain and conscience, and is today the one property of the National Trust which every Englishman, if he visits no other, must wish to see.

This is not the place to describe the successive Acts of Parliament which permit an owner to transfer his house to the National Trust in exchange for certain benefits, nor to outline the Trust's own rules of acceptability which must be satisfied before a bargain can be struck. Robin Fedden has set out the conditions fully in his book on the Trust, *The National Trust, Past and Present*. The ex-owner, whom the Trust continues generously to call 'the donor', is surrendering his patrimony, but he is receiving back the promise of much more, the inviolability of his house and its contents for all time. He is honouring by a 20th-century compromise his ancestral obligation. In return, he opens his house to the public, who help maintain it by buying tickets at the gate.

It is nothing new for an owner to show his house to interested strangers. When George III let it be known that he would like to visit Ham House, Lord Dysart replied, 'Whenever my house becomes a public spectacle, His Majesty shall certainly have the first view.' Other owners were less ungracious, and an intrepid traveller like Celia Fiennes in the 1690s found little difficulty in gaining admission to almost any house she wished to see. Some of them are still lived in by the families whom she would have found there. Oxburgh, Knole, St Michael's Mount, Coughton, Petworth and Compton Castle are examples which come to mind. There were Lucys at Charlecote from 1189 to 1945, and Leghs at Lyme Park from 1346 to 1946. To many such families it was a natural wrench to part with their freehold to the National Trust, to admit tourists to familiar rooms, and to become responsible to a large organization for the management of an estate so long and so recently their own. In these circumstances it might be imagined that a house without family attachments would be more acceptable to the Trust than one where the Trust and the donor were obliged to watch each other warily until mutual confidence could grow. But the opposite is true. The Trust always encourages the family to remain in the house. If that is not possible, the Trust seeks a sympathetic tenant.

A lifeless house can become soulless – can, but not necessarily must. A family's personality, like the Devonshires' at Hardwick or the Ansons' at Shugborough, often impregnates a house long after they have ceased to occupy it, and always we shall say the same of Chartwell. Nor should we pity too much a house which has become nominally a museum, like Buckland Abbey or Polesden Lacey. Ham House itself (*pace* Lord Dysart) and Osterley are wonderfully cared for by the Victoria and Albert Museum. It is only when houses become quarters for a migrant population, like Cliveden (an extension of an American university) or Philipps House, Dinton (a Y.W.C.A. holiday home), that something is inevitably lost; or when the house is left empty of furniture, a rare misfortune which the Trust is quick to remedy by gifts and loans from elsewhere, as at Montacute, Paycocke's, Beningbrough Hall and, supremely, owing to Mrs Gubbay's legacy of magnificent furniture and china, at Clandon Park.

As the Trust's purpose is conservation, its prime task is to make sure that the structure of a house is sound. This normally raises few problems except financial. Not many people would quarrel with the careful repair of a classical cornice, the rebuilding of a shaky wall with its own bricks, the brilliant redecoration at Clandon, which far from destroying old work uncovered much that had been hidden, or the restoration, on the most exact evidence, of the hall windows at Compton Castle. But there could be disagreement about the wisdom of demolishing part of a building which alters the original architect's intention. Which is best – to remove Lewis Wyatt's ugly boxlike structure from the top of Leoni's garden-front at Lyme Park, or to preserve it as a part of the history of the building which future generations may not consider ugly at all? As Leoni himself had slighted a fine Elizabethan house to create his new façade, we could be wrong about Wyatt. The Trust's policy in such cases is to remove later additions 'only when they are clearly haphazard'. Thus a shoddy and disfiguring wing was demolished at Benthall, and two Victorian staircases at Trerice. At Spring-hill, Ardress and Derrymore in Northern Ireland, and at Ashdown, the Trust has cleared away 'valueless accretions'. But Lyme Park remains untouched.

The National Trust, though the greatest instrument of preservation, is not unique, nor is it the only agency through which the State acknowledges its trusteeship of the past. Some of the finest houses in the country – Chatsworth, Hatfield, Longleat, Woburn, Syon, Blenheim, Castle Howard, Althorp, Wilton, Holkham, Houghton – are still owned and occupied by the descendants of the men who built them. The Historic Buildings Council, a great benefactor of the Trust, has spent huge sums of public money in saving others. Many local authorities have done the same for what they call 'Pre-Planning Act structures'; and voluntary organizations, such as the Georgian Group and the Mutual Households Association, have made their own valuable contribution. But the committees, staff and members of the National Trust can claim to have done more for our old domestic buildings than any other group of people in our history, except the most important group of all, those who built them and cared for them over the centuries.

Picture Collecting in England *by St John Gore*

In order to appreciate the phenomenal achievement of the English collector it is necessary to bear in mind two facts. The first is that the majority of the paintings in our museums and galleries today were once in private owner- ship in this country; the second is the extent of the losses that the country has sustained as a result of sales to overseas buyers.

As long ago as 1838 Johann Passavant, the German historian, when staying on a visit to England with Sir Charles and Lady Eastlake – whom he bemused by locking his bedroom door and handing the key to the butler, and then by sitting down to dinner in his overcoat – deplored the export of works of art from this country. It was a process that was to be greatly accelerated on the arrival of the transatlantic buyer at the end of the century. The 20th century opened in this context as the century of thoughtless dispersal. In 1952 the country's concern was given effect by the establish- ment of the Waverley Committee. In its initial report on the situation the Committee published a list of paintings that had been exported since 1913. This list included, in addition to the names of famous artists represented by no more than a few paintings, forty-five works by Rembrandt, forty by Rubens, ten by Velasquez, twelve by Holbein, and twenty-eight by Gains- borough.

It is not the century of dispersal but the centuries of acquisition that concern us here: the 17th century, which saw the emergence of classical collecting; the 18th century, during which this taste was intensified; and the 19th century, which was the century of expanding sympathies and compre- hension.

The moment of the recognition of an idea or attitude that subsequently becomes a commonplace can sometimes be determined with a fair degree of accuracy. An example of this is the revolutionary change that occurred in England in the approach to collecting during the early years of the 17th century. This change was from a collection formed for dynastic purposes to a collection based on an understanding of works of art. The typical col- lection of the 16th century consisted in the main of portraiture: portraits of the family, of royalty, of notabilities. The widening horizon of appreciation in the early 17th century followed the discovery of European painting by a small group of connoisseurs, foremost among whom were Thomas, 2nd Earl of Arundel in the Howard line, Prince Henry, and his younger brother, Charles I. In their knowledge of pictures these men inhabited a different world to their predecessors and indeed to most of their contemporaries. During the same period there evolved the conception of the collector as a virtuoso. The development can be seen as an echo of Italian humanism, and the analogy can be taken further if it is remembered that this was the precise moment of Inigo Jones's introduction of Palladianism into England.

The greatest of all English collectors was Charles I. More even than the quality and quantity of his acquisitions, it is the wide range of his interests that so astonishes us today. Not only did he buy classical works, in which context his purchase of the greater part of the collection of the Duke of Mantua was his most famous single *coup*, but he also bought early Northern pictures. He owned, for instance, examples by Dürer and by Geertgen, as well as the Wilton Diptych, and this was a taste which would have seemed advanced at any period during the next 200 years. The names of Rubens, Gentileschi and, pre-eminently, Van Dyck testify to his activities as a patron. In all he owned 1,387 paintings, of which the majority were dispersed at the Commonwealth sale. Many of these today form the greatest treasures of the Louvre, the Prado, and the Kunsthistorisches Museum in Vienna.

The sheer physical feat of accumulating so vast a collection compels our admiration. Collectors such as Charles I, Buckingham and Arundel, whose agents travelled over Europe in search of works of art, must often have tensely awaited their latest acquisitions, conveyed across Italy and France on the backs of mules and on occasion manhandled over the Alps. The transport of the Mantegna *Triumphs*, which Charles I bought from Mantua in 1629, can hardly have failed to arouse his anxiety.

Horace Walpole described the Restoration as bringing back the arts but not taste, and there can be no gainsaying this if comparison is made between the fastidious elegance of Van Dyck and the inflated Baroque court portraiture of Lely. But Lely himself was a discriminating collector of drawings, and that the second half of the century was not entirely devoid of collectors in the newly founded classical tradition is clear if the collections of the 2nd Lord Sunderland at Althorp and the 5th Lord Exeter at Burghley are recalled. As memories of the Caroline court receded, so Horace Walpole's view of the situation deteriorated; and by the reign of George I he had to admit that the arts had sunk to their lowest ebb in England. Yet this was only a few years before his father, the Prime Minister, began to amass at Houghton what was soon regarded as the most eminent of all 18th-century picture collections. In 1779 it was sold *en bloc* to Catherine the Great. Wilkes demanded in Parliament that it should be bought by the state to form the basis of a National Gallery, but in the end it was the National Gallery of Russia, the Hermitage at Leningrad, that benefited by Houghton's loss.

The contents of the great collections of the first half of the 18th century, such as those at Blenheim, Chatsworth or Holkham, were dominated by Italian classical painting: by the artists of the High Renaissance, by the 16th-century Venetian masters, by the Bolognese and Roman painters of the early 17th century, and by the idealized landscapes of Italy seen through the eyes of Claude and Poussin. The Baroque style was represented primarily by the work of the most highly admired of all Northern artists, Rubens. Despite the irreconcilable views of the purists who wrangled over the respective merits of colour, as represented by Rubens, and design, as represented by Nicolas Poussin, and who became known from the opinions they professed as *Rubénistes* and *Poussinistes*, the work of both these artists or of their followers would have found a place in the majority of collections of this period. That collectors of smaller means acquired the lesser school pictures is a truism

Left: *Sir Anthony van Dyck (1599–1641): Thomas Wentworth, 1st Earl of Strafford; 52¾ × 43 in., Petworth House.* Right: *Claude Lorrain (1600–82): The Landing of Aeneas, 1675; 69 × 88 in., Anglesey Abbey.*

that underlines the importance that was attached to conformity in the 18th century. This passion for conformity had two opposite effects: on the one hand, it encouraged duplicity on the part of dealers, usually in Rome, who manufactured the old masters and antiquities that they knew the Englishman wanted; on the other, it led to the collector's complacent acquisition of a copy if an original work of art was unavailable. In 1763 a visitor to Lord Tilney's collection at Wanstead reported that he had seen there nothing but copies.

The society of the Augustan age was on occasions a despotic one. Rules were prescribed for most aspects of life and correct taste was one of them. The connoisseur, having assimilated the relationship of art and morality – Lord Shaftesbury, writing as Thomas Gray said 'with a coronet on his head', equated a virtuoso with a man of virtue – was provided with a list of the best artists and was even instructed as to what types of painting were most deserving of respect. In the forefront was subject painting or history painting, the so-called 'grand manner', which comprised ancient history, mythology and scripture.

It was axiomatic that subject pictures had to come from abroad. England possessed neither a Catholic Church nor the artistic tradition of Italy. British artists were embittered by the lack of patronage devoted to them in the most venerated type of painting and Hogarth was particularly caustic on the subject. His satirical print depicting the English connoisseur as a foppish monkey watering dead plants is a case in point. The dead plants, of course, represented the old masters.

Henry James once observed that 'whether or no the English people have

41

painted, the rest of the world has painted for them'. But whatever the scope and interests of collectors (and if the interests at this period were restricted, the opportunities were practically limitless), it is the result of the patronage of British artists, even if until the 19th century this meant little else than portrait commissions, that forms the backbone of nearly all collections. One qualification must, however, be made: in the 17th and early 18th centuries the majority of artists working in England whose names first come to mind are of foreign origin. It is through their foreign eyes that we picture today the society of the past.

Portraits by these artists throng the walls of many houses: the Caroline age, distilled so evocatively and with such sensitivity by Van Dyck during the nine years he spent in England; the florid world of the Restoration summarized by Lely; and the later Stuarts and early Hanoverians who stare at us with benumbed equanimity from the canvases of Kneller and Dahl. It was not until the second half of the 18th century that there emerged a distinguished national school of portraiture. It did not lack encouragement. Not only did owners commission portraits for their houses but, as Rocquet, a French visitor to London in 1755 who published his observations in *The Present State of the Arts in England*, explained, 'It is the polite custom, even for men, to present one another with their portraits.' And he added: 'As soon as a race horse has acquired some fame, they have him immediately drawn to the life.' The part played in English collections by animal painting, in which this country produced one man of genius, Stubbs, must be remembered in a history of collecting; but, measured by 18th-century standards, its position was not a high one.

The seal of royal and official approval was stamped upon the arts in England by the foundation of the Royal Academy in 1768. The first president was Reynolds and his *Discourses* – the lectures he delivered on the occasions of prize-giving to the Academy students – are still today among the truest expressions of a practical aesthetic theory. In so far as Reynolds's advice was aimed at encouraging the patronage of British artists in the production of subject pictures its effect was negligible; it was said at the time with some truth that while Barry followed Reynolds's precepts on what he should paint and starved, Reynolds ignored them and prospered. Ironically it was the American, Benjamin West, who in one respect and in a limited way broke the barrier imposed by collectors. His *Death of Wolfe* gained an immediate popularity. It conflicted with the canon laid down for history painting in that its heroes appeared in modern dress; and as a result it could be interpreted as reportage rather than as true, i.e. ancient, history painting. The new taste for the portrayal of contemporary incidents was exploited by West's compatriot Copley.

If British artists failed to find patrons in the most 'important' branch of painting, their success in the 'lesser' category of landscape painting was little better. In most collections the school of pure topography is represented, but in relation to imaginative landscape painting this plays much the same role as portraiture does in relation to history paintings. The landscapes of imagination were sought in Italy; and above all in the works of Poussin,

Left: *Sir Joshua Reynolds (1723–92): Theresa Robinson, Mrs John Parker, 1772;* *92 × 56 in., Saltram House.* Right: *Thomas Gainsborough (1727–88): Augustus Hervey, 3rd Earl of Bristol (exh. 1768); 91¼ × 60 in., Ickworth.*

Claude and Salvator Rosa. The comparative neglect of Wilson appears to have stemmed from no other reason than his British birth.

The 18th-century traveller took a subjective and literary view of nature. Surely at no other time would it have appeared apposite to observe, as Gilpin did when praising Gray for his appreciation of nature, that no man admired it with better taste. The introduction of the so-called 'Claude glass', a small convex mirror, slightly darkened, which compressed a view into a smaller compass, was typical of the doctrinaire approach of the period.

It was inevitably of his transalpine journey that the traveller wished to be reminded. The paintings of Claude and Poussin epitomized a classical world and at the same time recalled the scenery of the Roman Campagna. The stormy and hostile landscapes of Salvator Rosa, which led to the concept of the sublime, brought back memories of the hazardous crossing of the Alps. Nature was admired for its picturesque qualities – when it was like a picture. The culmination of this attitude is when the paintings in which Nature is transfigured are themselves reproduced in Nature. The Arcadian scenes of Claude were reconstituted in the Wiltshire landscape at Stourhead; and when Kent planted a dead tree he was imitating the wild scenes of Salvator Rosa.

The Grand Tour was the 18th-century collector's obligatory and generally richly rewarded journey to Italy. Lord Burlington, it is said, returned from this experience with 900 packing cases filled with works of art. During the second half of the century Venice was increasingly to rival Rome as the most important centre. In Rome it had generally been the custom to buy the

George Stubbs (1724–1806): Five Mares; 39 × 74 in., Ascott.

works of the old masters. But in Venice the purchase of contemporary painting in the form of views of the city became the fashion. As a result, *vedute* by Canaletto or from his studio are to be found in numerous collections of the period. (The presence in English houses of pictures by Guardi, whose loose and impressionistic style was not understood by his contemporaries and who at that time was regarded as a feeble imitator of Canaletto, is seldom owed to 18th-century collectors. It was not in fact until the revival of interest in the *dixhuitième* during the latter part of the 19th century that his style came to be appreciated.)

While the 18th-century collector directed his attention in the main to the classical world of Italy, this is not to say that landscapes by Northern artists were ignored. The role played by Rubens as a Baroque master has already been mentioned, and earlier both Charles I and Buckingham had owned landscapes from his hand. It is evident from the sale catalogues of dealers who visited the Low Countries and returned to London with their prizes that there was a ready market for 17th-century Dutch landscape paintings. To begin with, it was the Italianate Dutchmen such as Both and Berchem who were most in demand. But half-way through the century a taste developed for the more naturalistic painters, Ruisdael or Hobbema for example. The Northerners, however, did not storm every classical strong-hold; and Horace Walpole voiced an existing antipathy when he described the Dutch masters as 'drudging mimics of nature's most uncomely coarse-ness'. In the next century this would have been regarded as reactionary.

In company with the 19th century's gradual assimilation of hitherto neglected schools of painting, the appreciation of Dutch art became firmly established. Collectors like the Prince Regent, Sir Robert Peel and the 3rd Marquess of Hertford accumulated superb examples of this school. As well as buying landscapes, they developed a taste for the small genre scenes possessing a high degree of finish – 'drolleries', as they had formerly been termed, and cabinet pictures, as they came to be called. It was an interest that was to expand. The early period of the Industrial Age had witnessed the rise of a newly rich and educated class of people. These people, lacking the classical upbringing and background of the ruling families of the 18th century, did not necessarily, one can suppose, share an appreciation of grand and classical works of art. When they bought a picture they were perhaps more likely to think in terms of familiarity, homeliness or verisimilitude. It was not, therefore, surprising if their tastes turned to the Dutch School.

Partly as a result of these tendencies, the patronage extended to British artists underwent a change. Collectors began to go to them for subject pictures and particularly for subjects which showed a Dutch influence. It was neither Constable nor Turner – although paradoxically Turner as a romantic had a far higher reputation than Constable as a natural painter – who were the most admired artists in their lifetime; it was Wilkie, and among other reasons for his success was his resemblance to Jan Steen. The change that had taken place by the end of the first quarter of the century is illustrated by the catalogues of the Royal Academy exhibitions. Until then they had consisted mainly of portraits; now for the first time subject pictures were to preponderate.

Concurrently the relationship between artist and patron began to change. In the past a picture was generally painted as the result of a commission and its size and subject were predetermined. Now artists were increasingly in the position of being able to sell to the public pictures that had already been executed. A consequence of the end of the contractual system is a loss in the unity of design that could be imposed upon the decoration of a room.

Naturally enough there had always been a high degree of empiricism in the matter of interior decoration, perhaps to some extent proportionate to the scale of the collector's purchases abroad. In the early 19th century there

Left: *Salomon van Ruysdael (c. 1600–70): River Estuary 1647; 20½ × 32¾ in., Polesden Lacey*. Right: *Abraham Storck (1630–1706): View in Amsterdam, 1692; 25½ × 21½ in., Dyrham Park*.

Sir David Wilkie (1785–1841): Knox preaching before the Lords of the Congregation, 1822; 19½ × 24½ in., Petworth House.

was to be no reduction in such purchases. Indeed, at the end of the 18th century a fresh impetus had been given to collecting by the number of French collections thrown on to the English market as the threat of Revolution increased. Later other Continental owners, in the tide of the advance of Napoleon's armies, were forced to follow this example. The most notable of all such collections was that of the Duc d'Orléans, which was bought in 1792 by a syndicate consisting of the Marquess of Stafford, the Earl of Carlisle and the Duke of Bridgewater.

Sir Osbert Sitwell once wrote that 'those untoiling butterflies [i.e. the 18th-century Grand Tour collectors] accomplished more for English art than all the labouring stage elephants [the professors and historians] of the next century'. But this should not blind us to the fact that because of its diverse interests the 19th century is our supreme age of picture collecting. The restricted precepts of the 18th century had expanded into the wider comprehension of the 19th. When in 1857 the first great exhibition of privately owned works of art was held at Manchester, it contained a representation of European painting that would have been unthinkable fifty or even twenty-five years earlier. The significant fact was that out of the 1,200 paintings that were exhibited one-third were painted before 1500.

To a great extent this was due to a recognition of early Italian painting. Before the second quarter of the 19th century it was exceptional to think of Italian art otherwise than in terms of the 16th and 17th centuries. Anything earlier was dismissed as 'primitive'. But now its very lack of sophistication, or what seemed so at the time, led to its being regarded in Tractarian minds as specifically Christian art. The change in attitude was due to the influence of collectors such as Gambier Parry, Davenport Bromley, William Young

46

Otway and the Prince Consort, to the writings of Lord Lindsay and the dissemination of the Arundel Society prints, the purpose of which was to preserve the record of early paintings and to 'wean public taste from puerile and meretricious art'. This esteem for the Primitives, which at the outset was in part pietistic, led by easy stages to an admiration for early Northern painting. It led also to the beginning of the decline in popularity of the more worldly paintings of the *seicento*.

At the same time other schools of painting were emerging from obscurity. Only limited attention was paid to Spanish art, for although a few Spanish paintings had been brought back to England after the Peninsular War, little was known about Spain, and until the publication of Richard Ford's *Handbook* in 1845 few people had visited the country. The taste for the French 18th century was to become a far more prominent feature of English collecting.

Before about 1850 practically no consideration was given in England to French 18th-century painting. The Englishman abroad occasionally sat to French artists; in the second half of the 18th century he was most likely to wait until he had reached Rome, there to be painted by Batoni. In France itself the post-Revolutionary taste for the neo-classical style had completely eclipsed any regard for the art of the *dixhuitième*. Appreciation for it was re-established by, *inter alios*, the Goncourts, and shortly afterwards this appreciation was to cross the Channel, there to find its most enthusiastic supporter in the 4th Lord Hertford. By the 1860s French 18th-century works of art were being bought by the Rothschilds and other great banking families.

Left: *Pompeo Batoni (1708–87): Sarah Lethieullier, Lady Fetherstonhaugh, 1751; 39 × 29 in., Uppark.* Right: *Nicolas Lancret (1690–1743): Les Noces de Village c. 1735–7; 17 × 22½ in., Waddesdon Manor.*

One of the most magnificent of all concentrations of such works of art was accumulated by Baron Ferdinand de Rothschild at Waddesdon. But this is not the latest of the collections for which the National Trust has responsibility. Those at Upton and Polesden Lacey, and Buscot in part, were formed during the present century. More than three centuries earlier certain pictures were already furnishing the walls of Hardwick and Knole which still hang there today. Nowhere in England can an example of a Caroline collection be seen better than at Petworth, one of the houses owned by Van Dyck's first patron, the 10th Earl of Northumberland. At Dyrham there is an unusual collection, mainly of contemporary Dutch paintings, of the second half of the 17th century. Saltram, Uppark, Stourhead and Tatton are characteristic of 18th-century classical collections, and examples of 19th-century patronage are to be seen at Stourhead and, outstandingly, at Petworth. The visitor to these and other houses will find examples of most European schools of painting and of most periods, safeguarded and, to quote Henry James once more, 'beautifully passive under the spell of transmission', in the custody of the National Trust.

Houses

For houses built mainly before 1550, see Chapter IV

Antony House, Cornwall

5 miles west of Plymouth via the Torpoint car ferry, 2 miles north-west of Torpoint

No great house in the West Country is more vividly associated with Cornish history than Antony, which first came into the possession of the Carew family in the late 15th century. Richard Carew, the historian and author of *The Survey of Cornwall*, who succeeded to the estate in 1564, saw the Armada moving slowly up the coast and reported a Spanish raid on Newlyn. Despite the troubled times, his book and his portrait – both are still at Antony – reveal a serene and contented man.

There was to be little serenity or content for his grandsons. The elder, Sir Alexander Carew, was one of the most tormented and tragic figures of the Civil War. After initially supporting Parliament – which so shocked his family that they cut his portrait out of its frame and hid it – he began to have doubts of the justice of the Roundhead cause. His doubts were guessed, and he was executed in 1644. Sixteen years later, his younger brother, John Carew, a staunch Republican and one of the regicides, suffered a similar fate at the Restoration.

More tranquil times followed. Even so Sir Alexander's grandson, Sir William Carew, an ardent Stuart supporter, was placed under preventive arrest in 1715. Happily this did not hinder the building of Antony, which he finished in 1721. Early in the 19th century the estate passed through the female line to Reginald Pole, fourth son of Sir John Pole of Shute. Under him and his successors Antony entered its golden age. The estate prospered and the garden and park were enlarged and improved. Throughout the 19th

Antony House; Entrance front

century the masters of Antony continued to take an active interest in the affairs of the Duchy and represented East Cornwall in Parliament for many years. The tradition of public service continues today, and Sir John Carew-Pole, who lives at Antony and gave the house to the Trust in 1961, is lord-lieutenant of the county.

Commanding the medieval ferry between Devon and Cornwall at Antony Passage over the river Tamar, Antony must always have been a place of strategic importance. The house of silvery grey Pentewan stone is entered through a forecourt between cupolas and brick arcaded pavilions. The central block is typical of the ordered compositions of the time and school of James Gibbs, who was responsible for such familiar buildings as the Radcliffe Camera at Oxford and the church of St Martin-in-the-Fields in London. The architect of Antony is unknown, although it has been suggested that the dignified and deceptively simple composition may have been the work of a naval architect from Plymouth.

The rooms are panelled in Dutch oak or pine and contain many pieces contemporary with the house. The furnishings, china, books, embroideries, family relics, and above all the portraits, illustrate the way the lives of the family touched events in English history. A portrait of Richard Carew, a first edition of his *Survey of Cornwall*, a few pieces of English Renaissance furniture, and some panelling, survive from the Tudor house which preceded the existing mansion. Bowyer's moving portrait of Charles I at his trial, the painting of the ill-fated Sir Alexander Carew, the crude stitches clearly visible with which the picture was restored after he had become a martyr in the eyes of his Royalist family, and Hudson's portrait of Sir Watkin Williams-Wynn (which commemorates his pact with Sir William Carew to raise Wales and Cornwall for the Stuarts in the rising of 1715) all demonstrate the family's dangerous involvement in Stuart affairs.

Ardress House, Co. Armagh

7 miles from Portadown on the B28 Portadown/Moy road

Ardress would probably have remained a simple, undistinguished, mid-17th-century manor-house, had not the heiress to the property, Sarah Clarke, married the successful Dublin architect, George Ensor, in 1760. Ten years later Ensor transformed his wife's house into a pleasant Georgian country mansion.

The long pink-washed face of Ardress first appears framed by giant beech trees. The original front of five bays with steeply pitched roof is immediately distinguishable, flanked by Ensor's extensions. On the garden front he added two curved screen-walls with alcoves for statuary which contain marble busts. These curved screens frame Ensor's new rooms which include a picture-gallery (his original decoration disappeared in the last century) and the drawing room, a room of outstanding elegance. For the decoration of this room, the most important feature of Ardress, Ensor enlisted the

Ardress House;
Entrance front

The drawing room

services of the celebrated Dublin stuccoer, Michael Stapleton. The ceiling is an intricate design of circles and segments round a central plaque with classical figures. Similar plaques occur on the walls, festooned by formalized yet fanciful husk chains. The manner is very much that of Robert Adam, but with an element of naturalism and individuality which characterizes the work of the Irish plasterers. The room has been repainted in the original shades of muted blue and green.

The other rooms are smaller and simpler, with little of the urban sophistication of the drawing room. Robust in character, they are furnished with good English and Irish pieces of the 18th century. Most of the pictures are on loan from the Earl of Castle Stewart.

Arlington Court, Devon

7 miles north-east of Barnstaple, on east side of A39

The Chichesters had been at Arlington for over five and a half centuries when Miss Rosalie Chichester, the last of her line, died in 1949 at the age of eighty-four. She was an unusual woman, a prolific water-colourist, a fervid collector of objects such as shells and ship models that caught her fancy, and a lover of birds and beasts who turned her estate into an embattled nature reserve, ringing it with a high iron fence eight miles long. Living in the remoteness of Arlington surrounded by its dense woods, the old lady, who seemed a survival from another age, became a local legend in her lifetime.

The estate of 3,500 acres, which Miss Chichester left to the Trust, is a magical enclave of pastures, lakes and hanging woods. It is preserved as she left it, and the green walks beneath giant trees and above shadowed waters seem as remote as ever they were.

Arlington Court

The house itself was built in about 1820 by Thomas Lee, a local Barnstaple architect who was also responsible for the Wellington Monument (see p. 283). It is an uncompromising limestone block in the severest neo-Grecian style. The only concessions to ornament are the giant order of Tuscan pilasters at each corner and the pleasant semicircular Doric porch. The mid-19th century, which ruined the central hall and added a disastrous wing, cannot easily be forgiven for slighting so harmonious a building.

The interior of Arlington is distinguished for the rooms on the south front linked by shallow arches – it may be noted that Thomas Lee worked briefly in Sir John Soane's office – where the progression from room to room is emphasized by pairs of Ionic columns and scagliola pilasters. But the attraction of the interior is due less to the architect than to the personality of Miss Chichester. Against a background of furniture and pictures, some of the 18th century, which she inherited, the rooms reflect the tastes and predilections of her long tenure. Though there are few works of art of the first importance, apart from a mystical water-colour by William Blake, discovered on the top of a bedroom cupboard when the Trust moved in to Arlington, almost everything that Miss Chichester collected or arranged has its interest. In her vast collection of seashells may be heard the murmur of the seven oceans on which sailed the originals of her innumerable ship models, and exotic birds and butterflies recall the landscapes of the tropics. Victorian and Edwardian Devon is none the less firmly present. Throughout the house showcases and cabinets are filled with the little decorative objects that Miss Chichester loved: fans, vinaigrettes, snuff boxes, jewelled animals, Bilston enamels, endless family treasures and trinkets. A collection of the dresses worn by the ladies of the Chichester family between 1830 and 1910 leads to bedrooms of perfect 19th-century flavour. In one of them Miss Chichester was born in 1865.

Ascott, Buckinghamshire

½ mile east of Wing, 2 miles south-west of Leighton Buzzard, on south side of A418

Ascott is one of the few country houses accepted by the Trust on other than architectural merits. Acquired by Leopold de Rothschild in 1874, it is in the main a 'black and white' 19th-century building. Its interest lies in the garden and, above all, in the outstanding collection of works of art – in particular, paintings, porcelain and French furniture – owned by Leopold de Rothschild to which his son, Anthony de Rothschild, who gave Ascott to the Trust in 1949, made important additions. The collection is not least interesting for the similarities and contrasts it offers to that other great assemblage of Rothschild works of art only a few miles away at Waddesdon.

Though there are notable Italian paintings – an Andrea del Sarto *Madonna and Child with Infant St John*, a Tiepolo *Assumption*, and a Lorenzo Lotto portrait, the paintings are chiefly remarkable for the varied examples of the Dutch 17th-century school. These include representative works by Hobbema, van Mieris, Maes, Jan Steen, the Ostades, Berchem, Wouverman, van der Heyden, and a beautiful view of Dordrecht by Cuyp. The paintings of the English school, though fewer in number, are remarkable for their quality. They include two striking full-length portraits by Gainsborough, a glowing Turner of his late period, portraits by Reynolds and Romney and, pre-eminently, Stubbs's *Five Mares*, which probably portrays the Duke of Cumberland's stud at Virginia Water.

Ascott; The garden front

Ascott; View from the garden over the Vale of Aylesbury

Ascott; Thomas Gainsborough: Mary, Duchess of Richmond

The porcelain chiefly reflects the taste of Anthony de Rothschild, who gathered at Ascott, besides wares of the earlier dynasties, an unusual collection of Ming and K'ang-Hsi. Indeed in the so-called three-colour wares of the late Ming dynasty the Ascott collection is hardly rivalled in this country.

The work of the great French *ébénistes* of the 18th century is represented by a number of signed pieces – commodes, tables, *bonheurs du jour* – of which the most noteworthy is perhaps a Louis XV black lacquer writing table. Its lines, its gold decoration, and chased ormolu mounts, beautifully epitomize the rococo spirit. There are also fine examples of the more sober English mahogany furniture of the 18th century.

The thirty-acre gardens that look to the Chilterns across the Vale of Aylesbury were laid out in the late 19th century, on the advice of Sir Harry Veitch, the famous Chelsea horticulturist, and are a blend of the formal and the natural. Botanically they are remarkable for their specimen trees and shrubs. Golden yews are planted as single specimens, groups or hedges; and golden elms, Japanese maples and Arbor-vitae mingle with dark-leaved copper beeches and with a variety of rare specimens. A series of grass terraces lies below the house. At the end of one terrace there is an evergreen sundial, the Roman figures of the clock upon the grass being of box. Forming a circle round the figures, and likewise in box, is the legend: *Light and shade by turn, but love always*.

West of the terraces lies a sunken flower-garden of delightfully Victorian character. To the north of the house is a lily pond. When in flower, the white and coloured varieties of water-lily make an impressive display.

Ashdown House, Oxfordshire *(See colour plate facing p. 224)*

2½ miles south of Ashbury, 3½ miles north of Lambourn, on west side of B4000

The architect and the precise date of this unusual and remote house on the Berkshire Downs are unknown. We only know that it was built for William, 1st Earl of Craven, one of the richest, and one of the most chivalrous, figures of the 17th century, who devoted his life and fortune to the house of Stuart and in particular to Charles I's unlucky and brave-hearted sister, Elizabeth, Queen of Bohemia. Without hope that his love would be returned, he followed the Queen's fortunes with a constancy to which history offers few parallels.

When the 'Winter Queen' returned to England at the Restoration, without a kingdom or a husband, William Craven as a last gift – he had already given £31,000 to her son, Prince Rupert – consecrated to her the building of Ashdown. She never lived to see it, dying in Craven's London house and bequeathing him her papers and her pictures, some of which today hang at Ashdown. William Craven survived her for thirty-five years and died a bachelor at the age of ninety. The house, built in such sadly romantic circumstances, came to the Trust in 1956 as the gift of Cornelia, Countess of Craven.

The date of Ashdown must be about 1665. Possibly the builder was William Winde, soldier and amateur architect. Brought up among the exiled royalists in the Low Countries, he returned to England at the Restoration and became Gentleman Usher to the Queen of Bohemia. His Dutch up-bringing may account for the marked Netherlands flavour of Ashdown. In its downland setting the strangely tall house, built of dressed chalk with Bath stone quoins and window architraves, has more than distinction. Some would say it has magic. Its effectiveness depends largely on a widely projecting cornice and a steep hipped roof which is surmounted by a balustraded platform carrying an octagonal cupola.

Ashdown House; The west front

In a sense Ashdown is an inspired freak, a doll's house writ large. Too tall and narrow for a country house, it seems to have been transported from a Dutch canal and stranded – yet so felicitously stranded – on the surrounding chalk uplands. Its isolation is to some extent relieved by two detached pavilions, built some twenty years later, which lend a more conventional breadth and balance to the composition.

The most impressive feature of the interior is the monumental staircase which rises from hall to attic and occupies one quarter of the house. It is hung with twenty-three portraits, the majority by Honthorst or Miereveldt, depicting the Queen of Bohemia and her circle. They include likenesses of the Queen herself, of Frederick, Elector Palatine and King of Bohemia, and of their children; not least, they record the appearance of the faithful William, 1st Earl of Craven.

Apart from the cove-like acanthus plaster frieze on the ground floor, the rooms have lost most of their original features. So too had the 17th-century garden when Ashdown came to the Trust. It seemed proper, when the house was restored, to provide it with a formal garden such as William Winde might have designed and Lord Craven have approved.

Attingham Park, Salop

4 miles south-east of Shrewsbury, on north side of A5

Tern Hall, a modest Queen Anne house built in 1701, was transformed some eighty years later into the classical mansion of Attingham Park by Noel Hill, 1st Baron Berwick, a great-nephew of the original builder.

Noel Hill inherited it in 1783, and almost at once began to realize his ambitious plans to build a country seat on an extravagant and imposing scale. He changed the name of the house to Attingham, calling it after the medieval name of the parish of Atcham in which it stands, and he commissioned George Steuart as his architect. A Scotsman of considerable individuality of whose career little is known, Steuart was responsible for several houses and churches in Shropshire. A condition of his engagement was that the old Tern Hall should be incorporated in the new mansion. His solution was to build a central block, immediately in front of the existing structure, and to balance the unusual height and depth of the resultant building with twin flanking pavilions linked by colonnades. This huge façade is nearly 400 feet long and is given emphasis and cohesion by a central pedimented portico with four tall columns. Built of grey Grinshill ashlar and seen from the Tern bridge across the wide parkland that was landscaped by Humphry Repton, Attingham's pale and stately shape dominates the gentle Shropshire landscape in almost alien fashion.

Attingham's internal arrangement is both unusual and unusually theoretical for an English country house. Two sets of rooms, one primarily masculine and the other feminine, lie on each side of the entrance hall. Lord Berwick's octagonal study and ante-room on the west side of the central

Attingham Park; The portico

block are balanced by Lady Berwick's drawing room and ante-room to the east. Her boudoir, with its delicate wall-painted decoration, is one of the best preserved of the period.

Lord Berwick did not long enjoy his grand new mansion, for he died suddenly in 1789, leaving three sons who succeeded him in turn. The 2nd Lord Berwick travelled to Italy when he came of age in 1792. It was a momentous journey not only for him but for Attingham, as he spent lavishly on pictures and works of art. Ten years later, he commissioned Nash to make alterations to the house and to build a picture gallery. In the early 19th century, picture galleries in English houses were rarities – Stourhead has one – and those that existed were primarily for sculpture. Technically the Attingham gallery is interesting, for the ceiling is the earliest in which cast-iron window frames were used. They were made by the Coalbrookdale company a few miles away on the Severn. The result is an interesting exercise in Regency taste, with a hint of the later industrial influences so apparent in much mid-19th-century architecture. The collection housed in the gallery today was mostly acquired after the 1827 sale.

Unhappily Lord Berwick's costly works of art and his improvements to the house and park, coupled with his general extravagance, impoverished the estate. In 1827 many of the contents of Attingham were sold and Lord Berwick retired to Italy, where he died in 1832. His successor, the 3rd Lord Berwick, had been Ambassador in Sardinia, Savoy and Naples, and like his elder brother had a passion for all things Italian. He bought Italian paintings, sculpture and furniture, particularly in Naples, and he was thus able to refurnish Attingham splendidly. The painted and gilt Neapolitan pieces, many associated with the Bourbon Queen, Maria Carolina, and her Bona-

parte successor, Caroline Murat, are well suited to Steuart's elegantly proportioned rooms. A Parisian dinner service made by Bugoty, who was employed by the Empress Josephine, may well have belonged to her. Attingham's splendid ambassadorial silver by Paul Storr came as a perquisite, as was often then the custom, on Lord Berwick's retirement from the diplomatic service.

The youngest of the 1st Lord Berwick's three sons succeeded in 1842, and his descendant, the 8th Lord Berwick, inherited Attingham in 1897. He renewed the family tradition both of diplomatic service and love of Italy, and he and his wife made Attingham their home for fifty years. In 1947, Lord Berwick bequeathed Attingham to the Trust. Most of the first and second floors are leased to Concord College.

Bateman's, East Sussex

½ mile south of Burwash on the A265 Hawkhurst/Heathfield road

Ironworking was a highly profitable industry in East Sussex in the 17th century and there can be little doubt that Bateman's was built by a wealthy ironmaster. Solid and self-assured, the house was put up in 1634, as the date on the porch records. The design is thoroughly traditional and indicates the work of a local builder uninfluenced by the new classical fashions of the metropolis. Though one wing has been demolished – the house was originally of the familiar E shape – Bateman's has otherwise been remarkably little altered. The three-storeyed porch, the mullioned windows with dripstones, the gables with finials, and the grouping of the chimneys for decorative effect into a great central stack, are all characteristically Jacobean. So, inside the house, are the stone four-centred doorways, the simple oak wainscoting, and the staircase with strapwork newel-post and turned balusters.

Rudyard Kipling, with whom Bateman's is now so closely associated, bought the house in 1902. He has described his first sight of Bateman's:

> We had seen an advertisement of her, and we reached her down an enlarged rabbit-hole of a lane. At very first sight the Committee of Ways and Means [Mrs Kipling and himself] said: 'That's her! The Only She! Make an honest woman of her—quick!' We entered and felt her Spirit—her Feng Shui—to be good. We went through every room and found no shadow of ancient regrets, stifled miseries, nor any menace, though the 'new' end of her was three hundred years old.

Bateman's was to be Kipling's home until his death in 1936 and the interior

Bateman's; From the garden

remains today very much as he left it. Though Kipling's affection for the Orient is reflected in silk embroidery, porcelain and bronzes, the furnishings are mainly 17th-century English or Continental: solid oak pieces, Mortlake or Brussels tapestries, and a dining room 'papered' in the finest Spanish painted leather. Kipling's study is inevitably the focus of interest. Here, surrounded by his library, he wrote many of his books, including *Puck of Pook's Hill*, the hill itself being visible from the windows of the house. His writing chair is of walnut, an early 18th-century piece, and under the club feet blocks have been fitted so that it is precisely the right height for his table. The latter, patterned with a wealth of inkstains, is of 17th-century chestnut. The generous proportions of the waste-paper basket beneath recall the scrupulous care with which Kipling revised and rewrote his work. On the table lie blocks of the 'large off-white blue sheets' which he preferred, his pens, and all the paraphernalia of a writer's desk.

Bateman's; Kipling's study

The garden, through which flows the little Dudwell stream, was in part designed by Kipling. His plan for the pool and rose garden hangs in the house, and he planted the yew hedges and laid out the quiet lawns early in the century. Under the wall of the house grows the Maiden's Blush rose which has flowered in English gardens since at least the 15th century and is a coloured form of the White Rose of York. It seems particularly appropriate in a garden which conveys such a sense of timelessness.

Beningbrough Hall, North Yorkshire

$5\frac{1}{2}$ miles north-west of York, 3 miles west of Shipton, on the A19 York/Northallerton road

There are few rural landscapes less inviting than the flat plain of York. In such a monotonous expanse rise the massive red-brick façades of Beningbrough, a surprise and an architectural enigma.

In the 16th century Beningbrough passed by marriage to John Bourchier, the bastard son of Lord Berners, who had made the first English translation of Froissart's *Chronicle*. It was to descend by inheritance until 1917. At the time of the Civil War Sir John Bourchier, who had been imprisoned by Thomas Wentworth, Earl of Strafford, proved one of the King's most implacable enemies and on 27 January 1649 he was among those who passed sentence of death on Charles I. The silver seal which he impressed on the death warrant is preserved at Beningbrough. He escaped retribution by a timely death soon after the Restoration.

Surprisingly enough his heirs were re-established in their estates and it was the regicide's grandson who built Beningbrough in 1716, economically re-using panelling from the older family house in some of the top-floor bedrooms. It was his only concession to economy. The quality of the workmanship at Beningbrough, from the carving of the stonework on the exterior to the woodwork inside, is invariably of outstanding excellence and its chief distinction.

The tall rectangular building, of two storeys with attic floor and basement, is linked by screen walls to balancing pavilions. Its mellow brick, with very fine pointing, is set off with quoins of dressed and rusticated stone, and there is no trace of the classical orders, except on the porches of the two principal façades. Yet the exterior of this large, plain house has surprisingly Baroque features, and these recur in the treatment of the interior. The roof is supported by a continuous frieze with paired wooden brackets, scaled and scalloped, and in the frieze are set the attic windows in highly unorthodox fashion. Again, above the entrance porch is a central window, with strange curving ears and scalloped keystone, copied from a window by Bernini in Rome.

Who can have been Bourchier's architect? Vanbrugh was at one time suggested, but may be dismissed. Perhaps Thomas Archer, who owed so much to Italian Baroque, supplied a design which was carried out by a local man. At all events the building, inside and out, incorporates foreign elements that are strangely unconventional in the English countryside.

The outstanding features of the interior are the two-storey hall and the great staircase. The former, with its round-headed doorways and massive mouldings, has Vanbrugh overtones, while its coved ceiling recalls William Wakefield's Gilling Castle not far away. The staircase is a miracle of virtuosity. The stair treads, no less than seven feet wide, are parquetried, and most remarkably the balustrade, which is wholly in carved wood, simulates the delicate wrought ironwork of Tijou.

The same craftsmanship is echoed elsewhere in the scrolled acanthus carving of cornices, overmantels and overdoors. In particular the carving in the state bedroom, with its handsome William and Mary bed and elaborately framed overdoor portraits of forgotten Bourchiers, would do credit to Grinling Gibbons. Though an architecturally enigmatic house, there can be no question of its unusual quality.

In 1978 the National Portrait Gallery established a permanent exhibition of 17th- and 18th-century portraits in Beningbrough, as had first been done at Montacute in Somerset.

Benthall Hall, Salop

4 miles north-east of Much Wenlock via B4376 and B4375, 6 miles south of Wellington, 1 mile north of Broseley

The ancient family of Benthall, who were in sympathy with the Old Faith and later suffered for their support of the Stuart cause, built the Hall in the late 16th century. It is a fine example of domestic building of the time, and the general style of the architecture points to a date about 1580. Though the house was embellished in the second and third decades of the 17th century, when a new staircase, panelling, and plasterwork were added, it is otherwise very much of a piece.

The south front, with its gabled roof line, moulded brick chimney stacks, and mullioned and transomed windows, is unaltered. Its charm derives a good deal from the asymmetry of the composition and from the pair of

Benthall Hall

glazed octagonal bays which rise through two storeys. A third bay of this decorative and unusual type is situated on the west front.

The entrance porch contains a hiding place, like many houses in this Catholic part of the country, and five stone tablets form a quincunx above the door. This pattern, perhaps alluding to the five wounds of Christ, was probably meant, at houses like Benthall and Boscobel, to assure the initiated that the house was owned by Catholic sympathizers.

The decorative features of the interior speak chiefly of the first half of the 17th century, when a Lawrence Benthall married a Katherine Cassy of Gloucestershire, placed their coat of arms in the overmantel in the entrance hall, and made many improvements. The panelling in the entrance hall is 18th-century, but that in the oak dining room is of about 1610, and the elaborate staircase with pierced strapwork incorporating heraldic beasts must date from about ten years later. The panelled west drawing room, of about 1630, is also elaborately treated with plasterwork ceiling, frieze, and overmantel. The frieze is unusually rich and represents a variety of beasts set in roundels with birds supporting the drapery that forms the scrollwork. There is much good 17th-century furniture, including an oak refectory table of about 1640 that was probably made for the entrance hall, where it stands.

That intriguing Shropshire architect, Thomas Pritchard, who worked at Croft Castle, Powis Castle and Tatton, and who designed the celebrated iron bridge at near-by Coalbrookdale, added rococo chimney-pieces in the 1760s.

The Benthalls left the Hall in the mid-18th century. Their return is a happy story. They tried in vain to buy the estate back in 1844; managed to rent it for a few years early in the 20th century; and at last in 1934 obtained possession. Sir Paul Benthall, who lives in the hall, is twelfth in descent from the 16th-century builder. The property was given to the Trust in 1958.

Berrington Hall, Hereford and Worcester

3 miles north of Leominster, on west side of A49

Thomas Harley, when staying at Eywood with his brother, the 4th Earl of Oxford, drove over with a fellow guest to inspect the Berrington estate soon after he had acquired it in 1775. The fact that his fellow guest was none other than the illustrious and persuasive 'Capability' Brown was to determine the future character of Berrington. With his eye for a good setting, there can be little doubt that Brown chose the site for the house with its great panoramic view stretching to the distant ridge of the Black Mountains; a year or two later he supplied the plans for the park and artificial lake which transformed the surroundings of Berrington into one of the most graceful landscapes of the 18th century. It can also hardly have been a coincidence that in 1778 Harley received an estimate of £14,500 for the building of his house from Brown's son-in-law, Henry Holland, the fashionable and talented Whig architect. The house, which was finished in 1781, must in fact have cost a

great deal more, but cost was hardly a consideration to an ex-banker and an ex-Lord Mayor who had held the lucrative government contract to pay and clothe the British forces in America.

The rectangular house, which at first sight seems almost plain, exhibits the simplicity of line, the elegance and restraint, which are the hallmarks of Holland's work. The narrow-jointed, pinkish ashlar comes from sandstone quarries a mile distant, and a horse tramway was specially constructed to carry the stones. The principal feature of the entrance front is a pedimented Ionic portico, reached by a sweep of shallow steps. The doorway, almost

Above:
Berrington Hall; The entrance front
Left: *The staircase*

austere, is flanked by reliefs of urns under drooping garlands, a characteristic Holland device. The roof is discreetly hidden behind a balustrade and dentilled cornice. At the rear, quadrants link the house to three pavilions of Grecian simplicity which form a service courtyard, containing the original dairy and a fully equipped Victorian laundry.

The interior of the house forms a marked contrast, for the reception rooms are elaborately decorated. The stucco work, the painted panels (reputedly by Biagio Rebecca), and such features as chimneypieces, curtain boxes, bookcases and door furniture, are of exceptional quality. The treatment of the rooms is interesting in that it foreshadows Holland's development. Thus the drawing room, though most sensitively executed, is almost in the conventional Adam manner, while the boudoir and the hall anticipate Holland's chaster, more linear style. In architectural terms the staircase hall is Holland's masterstroke at Berrington; a brilliant and dramatic exercise in spatial design, it is related to the effects which Sir John Soane was later to achieve so successfully.

This faultless house, which seems coolly and effortlessly to express the canons of late-18th-century taste, was bought by the Cawley family in 1900 and came to the Trust in 1957.

Blickling Hall, Norfolk *(See colour plate facing p. 96)*

$1\frac{1}{2}$ miles north-west of Aylsham, on north side of B1354, 15 miles north of Norwich

The builder of Blickling, Sir Henry Hobart, Lord Chief Justice, was among the first baronets created by James I in 1611. He bought Blickling five years later and at once began to build. After his death in 1625, his son, Sir John, completed the work. Blickling continued in the Hobart family, who became Earls of Buckinghamshire in 1746, until the death of the 2nd Earl in 1793. The property then passed through the female line to the Marquesses of Lothian. The 11th Marquess, who died as ambassador in Washington in 1940, left the estate of 4,500 acres, the Hall, and its contents, to the National Trust.

The architect of the Jacobean house was Robert Lyminge, who died at Blickling in 1628. He had built Hatfield House twenty years earlier and there are marked similarities between the two buildings. The first sight of Blickling satisfies the most romantic conception of an historic country house. The warm red-brick façade, approached between great yew hedges, presents above its mullioned and transomed windows a splendidly dramatic roof line of turrets, curved gables and central cupola. Though old-fashioned even when first built, it must have satisfied Sir Henry both for its position in a well-wooded valley and for its symmetry and richly modelled surfaces.

Despite one's first impression of an early-17th-century house, much of the Jacobean interior has vanished. Thus, while the exterior reflects the best of the early building, the interior contains convenient and attractive rooms

Blickling Hall

of the Georgian period. During the 18th century John, 2nd Earl of Buckinghamshire, carried out many alterations and improvements, employing Thomas and William Ivory, father and son. From his time date the remodelling of the great hall and staircase, the ground-floor rooms on the east, and almost all of the north and west fronts. The temple, the castellated grandstand in the park, and indeed the park itself, also reflect his activity.

The 2nd Earl was ambassador at St Petersburg in the 1760s, and brought back, as a gift from Catherine the Great, the tapestry depicting Peter the Great at the battle of Poltava. To house this enormous object, he had William Ivory design a grand neo-classical room hung with apricot-coloured damask. Next door, to house the royal bedhangings acquired at the time of George II's death by virtue of the Earl's position as Lord of the Bedchamber, William Ivory designed a white and gold state bedroom. The Chinese bedroom, with its plasterwork and attractive 18th-century Chinese wallpaper, was the work of Thomas Ivory.

The long gallery contains Blickling's finest Jacobean ceiling. Dating from the 1620s, it is in the form of interlaced cast ribs enclosing panels modelled after illustrations in Henry Peacham's *Minerva Britanna*, a book of emblems published in 1612. The late-19th-century oak bookcases with painted frieze above contain the library of Sir Richard Ellys acquired by the 2nd Earl. This extensive library, the collection of an 18th-century scholar and bibliophile, is a complete and fascinating survival, containing the largest number of books published before 1500 in any National Trust house.

When the Earl died in 1793, his widow had Bonomi design a pyramidal mausoleum, which was built in the park on one of the avenues which were by then about a hundred years old. Here lie the bodies of the 2nd Earl and his two Countesses.

The next alterations at Blickling were due to John Adey Repton, son of Humphry Repton. He built the arcades, clock tower and the delightful orangery, and probably re-erected the fountain in its present position. He also, possibly with his father, landscaped the park, and designed some estate cottages. The crescent-shaped lake was then enlarged and stretches for a mile northward, and clumps of splendid oaks and beeches were planted.

In 1777 Hannah More wrote: 'The situation is highly pleasing: more so to me than any I have seen in the East. You admire Houghton, but you wish for Blickling; you look at Houghton with astonishment, at Blickling with desire ... the park, wood and water of this place, are superior to those of any of the neighbouring estates.' Her words still hold true for many visitors, for in addition to its setting and its architectural distinction, Blickling has an accumulation of paintings, tapestries and furniture that reflect the occupation of Hobarts and Lothians over more than 300 years.

The garden like the house has a long history and is of interest to the garden historian. The fifteen-foot-wide hedges on the entrance front probably date from the late 17th or early 18th century. Surrounding the house is a moat which may have been constructed before the present building; it is dry, and contains a variety of plants and shrubs delighting in the hot sun or cool shade which its walls provide.

Blickling Hall; The hall and Jacobean staircase

The great formal layout on the east side of the hall, with a broad central walk leading to a late-18th-century temple, dates from before 1729. The walk divides two wooded areas, each with a cartwheel-like pattern of rides within its squares, and the whole area is surrounded by a rectangular raised walk and ditch, and punctuated by stone urns. The ha-ha, of which this ditch is an example, was an innovation of the early 18th century; the raised walk is a feature of earlier days. Within these woodland rides are early daffodils, primroses and bluebells, azaleas, and early and late rhododendrons. Near the south verge of the terraced walk stands the orangery dated 1820.

The main parterre and lawns are a modern adaptation (about 1930) of a Victorian design, though the topiary is earlier. There are four large square beds of hardy flowers, surrounded by ribbons of dwarf roses edged with catmint: the two beds closest to the house are subdued and the two others are of bright colours. A fine traditional herbaceous border runs round two sides of the lawn. Farther from the house are other borders, where the Portland rose has grown for many years. On another lawn an immense Oriental plane grows; its branches in the past have layered and thus the original trunk is surrounded by younger trees. Very large limes and Turkey oaks are near by, and there are selections of conifers and magnolias. Autumn cyclamens are naturalized in the grass.

Bridge House, Cumbria

At the foot of Chapel Hill, Ambleside

This unique structure, the smallest dwelling owned by the Trust, was associated with an old Ambleside family, the Braithwaites, who were prominent in the town for some two hundred years until, in 1723, Lady Elizabeth Otway, niece and heiress of the last of the family, sold old Ambleside Hall. With this went the 'Brig House'. Later, and under successive owners it was used for various purposes, including a teahouse and a weaving shop. About 1843 'Chairy' Rigg and his wife were living there and reputedly brought up six children in this tiny dwelling. Later it became a cobbler's shop with a pigeon loft in the upper room. In 1926 it was bought by local subscription and handed over to the National Trust, which opened it in the same year as its first information and recruitment centre.

The Bridge House probably dates from the middle of the 17th century. It may have been built as a summer house or even as an apple store, and was converted into a dwelling sometime in the late 18th century. The flagged roof, and 'wrestler' slates along the ridge and the pinned timber bearers are typical of early stone buildings in the Lake District. Although it would seem as precariously poised as a mountain boulder, the Bridge House has, for some 400 years, withstood wind, rain and the occasional onslaught of the spate waters of the stream beneath.

Buscot Park, Oxfordshire

2 miles south-east of Lechlade on the A417 Lechlade/Faringdon road

From the Moray Firth to the Devonshire coast, at any date during the last quarter of the 18th and the first decade of the 19th centuries, houses in the Adam style with the discreet tranquillity of Buscot Park were being erected. Buscot, however, is not precisely what it seems, but is the result of a most careful restoration in the 1930s, by the 2nd Lord Faringdon, of a house built about 1780 and radically changed in the 19th century by the addition of a vast wing and an elaborate carriage porch of a kind to which the later Victorians were much addicted. The removal of these accretions and their replacement by flanking pavilions has revealed the broad flight of steps leading to the front door on the *piano nobile*.

The early history of Buscot is sketchy. In the 16th century the manor belonged to the Stonors of Oxfordshire, a staunch Catholic family, from whom it passed in 1557 to the Lovedens. The present house was built by a certain Edward Loveden Townsend, probably acting as his own architect. By 1859 the large estate, spanning the young Thames and covering nearly 4,000 acres of valley pasture and downland, had become almost derelict. It was bought by a rich Australian gold trader and landowner, Robert Campbell, who proceeded to initiate schemes for agricultural industrialization far ahead of his time.

Campbell's primary object was the large-scale production of sugar beet and its various by-products. He built, on an island in the Thames still called Brandy Island, an extremely expensive distillery to make spirit from sugar. French workers were brought over, and it operated successfully until the Franco-Prussian War of 1870. A narrow-gauge railway running round the

Buscot Park

estate, large-scale irrigation schemes, a nine-hour working day – all contributed to an imaginative project, but one which, in the long run, overreached Campbell's resources. After his death, the estate was sold to Sir Alexander Henderson, later created Baron Faringdon, financier and connoisseur. In 1948 it was acquired by Ernest Cook, who bequeathed it to the Trust. The 1st Lord Faringdon's notable collection of works of art was transferred to the Faringdon Collection Trustees in 1962, to ensure its permanent retention in the house.

The chief interest of Buscot is as a setting for this collection which reflects the catholic taste and the judgement of the 1st Lord Faringdon and his successor. The interior of the house has been sympathetically restored to display the paintings, furniture, porcelain and *objets d'art*.

The Italian paintings mostly date from the 15th and 16th centuries. The 17th century contributes Murillo's *Faith presenting the Eucharist*, removed from a Seville church during the Peninsular War, but the outstanding painting at Buscot is a Rembrandt portrait of a man, possibly Clement de Jongh, one of the first collectors of Rembrandt's graphic art. The three Rembrandt drawings at Buscot would have appealed to him. Paintings of the 18th century include a Gainsborough landscape (in an unusual technique using water-colour to simulate oil), Reynold's *Mercury as Cutpurse*, and a portrait by him of Lady Coventry.

The 1st Lord Faringdon patronized the English artists of his own time also. The collection includes works by Rossetti, Madox Brown, and G. F.

Watts. The paintings in the saloon, which depict *The Legend of the Briar Rose*, were bought from Sir Edward Burne-Jones in 1890 and are among the most ambitious achievements of the later Pre-Raphaelite period.

There is notable furniture of the late 18th and early 19th centuries. It includes elaborately carved side-tables designed by Robert Adam, a quantity of painted and inlaid satinwood, a fine Empire suite, and a number of Thomas Hope's rare and extravagant creations.

Silver, porcelain, and minor works of art – the things of lesser scale which so effectively determine the character of a house – all reflect the discrimination of the connoisseur: silver by Paul Storr, 'Egyptian' candelabra, Blue John vases, Renaissance ivories, bronzes and Chinese porcelains, from the simplest early ware to the elaborate armorial dishes of the *Compagnie des Indes*.

Carlyle's House, Chelsea, London

24 Cheyne Row

'A government should sustain intellect. It elevates and sustains a nation.' So wrote Disraeli to Thomas Carlyle in 1874, offering both an honour and a pension. The historian-philosopher's reply was equal to the occasion. He thanked the Prime Minister for his concern 'for my practical behoof', but declined both, declaring that 'after years of rigorous and frugal but never degrading poverty' he was now possessed of a superabundance of fortune.

The loftiness of thought and expression, the confidence typical of 19th-

Carlyle's House; The upstairs drawing room

century liberalism, is eloquently illustrated in this early-18th-century London terrace house in which the Carlyles lived for over thirty years from 1834 until their respective deaths in 1866 and 1881. Carlyle's own description of the house, written to his wife in Scotland, holds good still:

> The House itself is eminent, antique; ... Three storeys besides the sunk storey; in every one of them *three* apartments in depth ... a front dining-room (marble chimney piece, &c.); then a back dining-room ... out from this a china-room or pantry, ... fit to hold crockery for the whole street ... every bedroom with a dressing-room. Red Bed will stand behind the drawing-room; ... the height of this storey is 10 feet; ... of the kitchen (where is a Pump ...) about the same.

The annual rent was £35; it remained unaltered throughout their tenancy. As much as Carlyle's, his wife's vivid personality permeates the little house: portraits, photographs, caps, shawls, letters, chairs and second-hand sofa, the unregarded trivia of daily life. The pump in the basement kitchen remains with the kitchen range, made in Scotland in 1852 for £7 3s. Here Carlyle and Tennyson would retire to smoke their pipes up the chimney to avoid offending Mrs Carlyle's susceptibilities.

The original 'broad staircase' with its Queen Anne pine panelling, papered over and painted and grained in dark glossy Victorian brown, leads up from the drawing room, furnished mainly with the Carlyles' own undated, unfashionable pieces from Scotland, to the famous attic study added in 1853, at great cost to Mrs Carlyle's fractured nerves; an early attempt at sound-proofing was not successful and produced a room with no pretensions to beauty. Nevertheless Carlyle used it as his study for the twelve years in which he wrestled with the composition of his epic biography of Frederick the Great. It contains today relics of many eminent Victorian figures, cards from Goethe, Mazzini's signature on a lease witnessed by Carlyle, manuscripts, prints, books and – described by Carlyle as his most precious possession – his writing table with its pewter inkstand and reading lamp.

Fourteen years after his death, the house was bought by public subscription. Furniture and possessions were returned to the house and in 1936 it was transferred to the Trust.

Castle Coole, Co. Fermanagh *(See colour plate facing p. 96)*

1 mile south-east of Enniskillen on the A4 Belfast road

Set in a lush green landscape, among wooded hillocks, and above the still waters of a lough haunted by greylag geese, the white stone of Castle Coole, its Grecian repose, its balanced lines, evoke an immediate response. One of the most beautiful and architecturally satisfying of late Georgian houses, it is among the finest achievements of James Wyatt.

The Corry family had owned the Castle Coole estate since 1656, and the

Castle Coole; From the park

man who so magnificently expended his fortune on the creation of a masterpiece was Armar Lowry-Corry, 1st Earl of Belmore. He embarked on the building of his new house in 1788, nine years after his succession. No expense was spared. Portland stone came the long route by sea to Ballyshannon, whence the blocks were transported ten miles overland by bullock cart to Lough Erne and thence again by water to Enniskillen. Joseph Rose, the finest contemporary craftsman, was employed for the plasterwork, and Richard Westmacott, among the most eminent sculptors of his day, was later called in to design the marble chimneypieces. For the scagliola work the Earl summoned from across the water an Italian expert. The joinery, as appears in the doors and shutters, was also of superb quality, and no doubt correspondingly expensive. The joiners were brought over from England.

But it was Wyatt's genius, the architectural sensibility which in England created Heveningham and Heaton, that gave Castle Coole its distinction. His ground-floor plan employs a scheme common enough in the latter half of the 18th century: an oblong central block, flanked by colonnades having small terminal pavilions, the centre of the main front being emphasized by a pedimented portico, and that of the rear elevation by a semicircular bay. A Palladian note is struck only in the roof balustrade and the Venetian windows of the terminal pavilions. In all else Wyatt gave to the house the pruned simplicity and the severe Attic grace which, with the growth of neo-classicism, was becoming the ideal of enlightened architectural taste.

The entrance hall, like the other rooms of reception, shows the restraint of Wyatt's treatment. A screen of porphyry scagliola columns and niches, containing life-size casts from the antique, emphasize its architectural character. The same note is struck in the elliptical saloon beyond, though here grey scagliola pilasters contrast with gilt furniture of distinctly Continental flavour (*c.* 1855), and with crimson silk upholstery and hangings, to create an effect of richness.

Castle Coole; The saloon

In the dining room Wyatt's decoration, as it appears on the ceiling, the frieze, the lunettes over the windows, and the doorcases, exhibits his characteristic elegance. It would be difficult to cite a better example of the restrained taste of the 1790s. Much of the furniture, including the pier tables, sideboard, pedestals and urns, and a great wine cooler, was made for the room by the English joiners in 1797 and 1798. Though in the drawing room such furniture as the rosewood inlaid sofa tables and the massive Empire clock speaks largely of a later period, the plasterwork, the colour of the walls, and the draped hangings, are as Wyatt planned them. So too are the bookcases in the library, with their delicate reeded mouldings and fluted architraves.

Nothing at Castle Coole better illustrates the architect's talent than the staircase and the highly original lobby to which it leads on the first floor. The latter, in which hang portraits of the Corry family, is lit by a dome and surrounded at second-floor level by a gallery whose ceiling is supported by coupled columns. Stoves set in semicircular alcoves, and surmounted by casts of Greek poets from the antique, are contemporary with the rest of the Wyatt decoration. The state bedroom, giving on the lobby, was done up in 1821, when it was hoped that George IV might visit the house, and the flock wallpaper, the curtains and pelmets, and the state bed in flame-coloured silk, date from this period. On the same floor the Bow Room has been converted into a museum. Here is much of interest relating to the history of Castle Coole and the Lowry-Corry family, and not least the drawings of the architect who was employed to such good purpose by the 1st Earl.

The venerable avenue of oaks and the aged beeches south-east of the

74

house were planted in about 1700, probably by a Colonel James Corry who at about the same time introduced the flock of greylag geese which ever since has bred on the shores of the lough. The park, which provides so worthy a setting for the house, must have been landscaped by the 1st or the 2nd Lord Belmore between 1790 and 1840. It may well have been the latter, as he owned a copy of Repton's *Observations on the Theory and Practice of Landscape Gardening*.

Castle Coole was acquired from the 7th Earl of Belmore in 1951 with funds made available by the Government of Northern Ireland.

Castle Drogo, Devon

At Drewsteignton, 2 miles north-east of Chagford, 1 mile south of A30

Though built in the reign of George V, and thus historically the latest of the Trust's houses, Castle Drogo is architecturally among the most remarkable. It is also likely to be the last private house conceived on such a scale in this country. Built by Sir Edwin Lutyens between 1911 and 1930, it is not only one of his finest achievements, but a tribute to the understanding and co-operation of architect and client. The latter was Julius Drewe, who as a young man in the 1880s had made a fortune in launching the business which became a household word under the name of 'The Home and Colonial Stores'. It is to his descendants, the late Anthony Drewe and his son Dr Christopher Drewe, that the Trust is indebted for the gift of Castle Drogo and of 600 acres protecting the dramatic landscape that surrounds it.

Julius Drewe chose the splendid situation, a granite bluff that commands the deep defile of the river Teign immediately below. The site was appro-

Castle Drogo; From the north-east

Castle Drogo; The entrance hall

priate to the idea he had in mind, nothing less than the erection of a noble castle on land once owned by his putative medieval ancestors, the Drogos or Drus, whose name is preserved in the near-by village of Drewsteignton. No doubt he chose Lutyens not only for his competence as an architect, but because he recognized in him a fellow romantic who would appreciate his conception. Previously Lutyens's work had been domestic in scale and character, and the imperial pomp of New Delhi lay in the future, but at Lindisfarne Castle on Holy Island (see p. 137) he had transformed a small medieval fortress in masterly fashion, creating his architectural effects by calculated asymmetry and the sensitive relation of simple masonry to the rocky site. At Drogo, Lutyens gave monumental expression to the talents he had first exercised at Lindisfarne.

Set on the very lip of a heather-clad bluff, with the ground falling away precipitously on either side, the castle was firmly anchored to the underlying rock and built of finely dressed local granite. As the architect intended, it possesses the mass and assurance of a medieval stronghold. Yet it is in no sense a pastiche, but a building very much of its own time. The lines are clean, the planning unusual and the detail, though related to an earlier tradition, is applied with the originality and sensitivity that are the hall-marks of Lutyens's best work.

Over the entrance to the castle is a splendidly designed relief of a heraldic lion, the Drogo crest. The interior, with massive granite arches, bare granite walls and unpainted timber, strikes a note of simplicity and authority that both client and architect were determined to achieve. The hall and library are hung with tapestries that look particularly well in such a setting. The drawing room, flooded with light from great mullioned and transomed windows, is exceptional in that the woodwork is painted, the wainscot being

76

in soft stippled green such as Lutyens often used; the room thus provides a deliberate foil to the austerity of the rest of the interior.

The terraced garden to the north of the house is notable for a rectangular lawn edged with yew and topiary 'tents' in each corner, roofed with weeping elm (*ulmus glabra Camperdownii*). At a higher level there is a great circular lawn, also enclosed by yew hedges. There was once a tennis court here; few in England can have been situated at such a height, just under a thousand feet above sea level.

Castle Ward, Co. Down

7 miles north-east of Downpatrick, off the A25 Downpatrick/Strangford road

With its dells and wooded eminences, and its entrancing views over Strangford Lough, Castle Ward is perhaps the most beautifully situated house in Ulster. It seems as though nature herself had enthusiastically subscribed to the theories of 'picturesque' landscape which came into fashion soon after the house was built. Time and the wet mild climate have favoured the long life of giant oaks and beeches, or rarer foreign growths, and of the exotic palm. On every side man and nature have co-operated to pleasing effect.

This favoured demesne came into the possession of the Ward family in the second half of the 16th century, but it was 200 years before the present house was built. The builders were Bernard Ward and his wife Anne. For many years M.P. for Co. Down, Bernard was created Baron Bangor in 1770, and a Viscount before he died in 1782. Lady Anne, the daughter of the 1st Earl of Darnley, was, in the opinion of that indefatigable gossip-writer Mrs

Castle Ward; The classical entrance front

Delaney, so 'whimsical' that she lacked judgement. To her whimsy, and the fact that she had less conventional views than her husband, we owe the curious architectural character of Castle Ward.

Among the architectural fashions current in England was the Gothick, and this was the style favoured by the whimsical Lady Anne. Her husband preferred a less daring classical idiom. The result was a compromise that even in 1770 cost £40,000 to build and produced a house having the somewhat bizarre feature of contemporaneous fronts in both the Gothick and classical styles. Perhaps this already reflected marital incompatibility, for it was not long before the couple separated and Lady Anne exchanged the wild shores of Strangford Lough for the social delights of Bath. The house remained in the Ward family until the death of the 6th Viscount Bangor in 1950, when it was acquired by the Government of Northern Ireland and presented to the National Trust.

The adaptable architect of Castle Ward is unknown: his plan was a simple rectangle with an hexagonal bay at each end. The entrance front, an exercise in the Palladian manner, with rusticated ground floor and a central order under a pediment, expresses a conventional mid-Georgian taste. By contrast Lady Anne's front with its battlements, pinnacles and ogival windows, is eccentric, to say the least. Though the spidery yet decorative forms of Gothick had been popular in England for some time – Sanderson Miller's hall at Lacock Abbey (see p. 342) was finished in 1755 – they were slow to cross the Irish Channel. Castle Ward is one of the first houses in Ireland to exemplify the style.

Castle Ward; The Gothick front

Some 150 years ago, during the insanity of the 2nd Lord Bangor, the contents of Castle Ward were dispersed. Thus, few of the furnishings, apart from the family portraits, are original to the 18th-century house. On the other hand, the elaborate and contrasting decorative schemes devised by Bernard and Anne have survived almost unaltered. Bernard contributed, in particular, the hall with a Doric screen of scagliola columns and flowing plasterwork that incorporate panels, ribboned bows, and trophies (all no doubt by Dublin plasterworkers); the dining room, with 18th-century entablature and panelling grained and parcel-gilt by the 3rd Lord Bangor in about 1827; and the elegant staircase whose mahogany rail is inlaid with satinwood and ebony.

Lady Anne's taste is reflected in the saloon, morning room and boudoir which in their every detail celebrate the Gothick spirit. It is at its most fanciful in the fan-vaulted boudoir whose gaiety, so far removed from the seriousness of its distant medieval prototype, Lady Anne no doubt fully appreciated.

The domestic arrangements at Castle Ward are unusual. It seems that no servants, except possibly a valet and a lady's maid, slept in the house. An underground passage leads to a courtyard which contains both the servants' living quarters and those ancillary buildings necessary to the life of a large establishment, such as stables, bakery and laundry. The last has been reinstated with its ironing and airing rooms, ironing boards, flat irons and triangles and examples of laundered linen and clothes of the late 19th century. It is an evocation of a feature indispensable to the houses of the past.

In the grounds of Castle Ward stands a tower house, the Irish equivalent of the pele tower, a massive and defensive three-storeyed building erected by Nicholas Ward in 1610.

Beyond, and approached by an ancient lime avenue, lies an ornamental lake called the Temple Water, dating from the first half of the 18th century. A collection of wildfowl, representative of the species to be found on Strangford Lough, has been established on the lake. A little pedimented temple, a *plaisance* to which we may imagine Lady Anne resorting to read Thomson's *Seasons*, overlooks its tranquil waters. It is placed with that unfailing sense of situation which characterized the civilized gentry of the 18th century.

Charlecote Park, Warwickshire *(See colour plate facing p. 97)*

4 miles east of Stratford-upon-Avon, 6 miles south of Warwick, on the B4086 Stratford/Banbury road

The Lucy family owned Charlecote from the 13th century until 1945, when Sir Montgomerie Fairfax-Lucy presented the house and park to the Trust. Sir Thomas Lucy, who pulled down an older house in about 1558 and built the present house, was a man of substance, a magistrate and Knight of the Shire, and important enough to entertain Queen Elizabeth to breakfast in

Charlecote Park; The gatehouse

1572 on her summer progress to Kenilworth. But Sir Thomas is better
remembered for the long-established legend that in 1583 he fined a young
poet for poaching deer in his park. It is said that after being arraigned before
Sir Thomas in the great hall at Charlecote Shakespeare wrote ribald verses
on the gatehouse wall and in consequence was obliged to leave for London.
Later he took off Sir Thomas as Justice Shallow in *Henry IV, Part Two* and
the *Merry Wives of Windsor*, mocking the knight's pride in his ancestry by
references to a 'dozen white luces' in his coat of arms.

Charlecote was inherited in the direct male line until the death of George
Lucy in 1786. This much travelled and cultivated bachelor altered and
improved the house, and about 1760 he commissioned Capability Brown,
for £525, 'to alter the slopes of the park and give the whole a natural easy
corresponding level with the house'. Charlecote is the only park touched by
Brown's hand where he was expressly forbidden to cut down the avenues of
trees. Nor did he touch the meadow bordering the Avon where Charles I
camped with his army the night before the battle of Edgehill in 1642.

In the second quarter of the 19th century another George Lucy, who had married a Welsh heiress, made extensive alterations and additions to the house. Little was left unchanged of the 'goodly dwelling and rich' that Shakespeare knew, except the pink brick gatehouse. This beguiling structure, its twin octagonal turrets crowned with ogival cupolas, belongs to a transitional period of 16th-century architecture when Renaissance influence was impinging on the native English Gothic. It has even been attributed to John of Padua, Henry VIII's architect, who died in 1540.

Beyond the gatehouse, the forecourt is bounded by a gabled stable block and brewhouse to the south, and a long raised brick wall to the north, which shelters flower borders, embellished by an 18th-century lead shepherd and shepherdess. Straight ahead lies the house. At a distance its romantic skyline seems typical of the reign of Queen Elizabeth, yet the only surviving 16th-century feature is the fine two-storeyed Renaissance porch. Expressive of French rather than Italian influence, the doorway is flanked by Ionic pilasters, and surmounted by the arms of Queen Elizabeth and topped with a balustrade.

The great hall was renovated in 1833, but the heraldic glass survives from 1558. The adjoining library and dining room exemplify interior decoration of the time of William IV, which was carried out with immense assurance by the designer Thomas Willemont. The gigantic oak sideboard in the dining room was bought in 1858, after it had been declined as a gift by Queen Victoria. Mrs George Lucy described it as a 'masterpiece of genius and skill, throbbing with life'.

Less touched by Victorian enthusiasm, the tapestry room is furnished with a suite of ebony and ivory furniture in English Restoration style, probably made in Madras in the last quarter of the 17th century.

The house contains a library of early-17th-century books, collected by a bibliophile Lucy who died in 1640, and a series of historical and family portraits covering a span of 350 years. Among the family portraits is an early Gainsborough of George Lucy for which the painter charged eight guineas. But perhaps Charlecote's greatest treasure is a rare silver-gilt Tudor wine-cup dated 1524.

The scale of the ancillary buildings at Charlecote gives an impression of the needs of a large country establishment in the late 18th and early 19th centuries. The brewhouse, with its huge copper vats and wooden casks, retains much of the original machinery capable of producing large quantities of beer and ale. A valuation made in 1845 reveals that over 4,000 gallons were then standing in the cellars under the house. The Victorian kitchens are equipped with their original utensils, including a copper *batterie de cuisine*, complete from vast stewpans to tiny custard moulds. The coach house contains a number of 19th-century carriages, including a barouche and wagonette, and the superbly appointed travelling coach in which the whole family crossed the Alps during a two-year tour of the Continent in the 1840s.

Chartwell, Kent

2 miles south of Westerham, forking left off B2026 after 1½ miles

It was the wooded, watered, smoothly pastured coomb with its clear spring, the Chart Well, that captivated Churchill. He bought the house for its setting and its views. This was in 1922. It was to be his home for over forty years, and no other place meant so much to him.

The Victorian country house, which Churchill completely remodelled, has little architectural pretension. Its interest is in its close association with the great man who lived there. Its contents may be read like an intimate and fascinating biography, for they reflect Churchill's preoccupations, trials and achievements from the age of forty until he left Chartwell for the last time, shortly before his death.

Each room tells something of the man and his life at Chartwell: the library with the books he collected over a lifetime; the drawing room with its easy chairs and the table set for bezique; the dining room, where over the brandy his imaginative and often provocative conversation, and his wonderful sense of phrase, created an unforgettable impression on his listeners; and not least the studio, where an unfinished canvas stands upon the easel and the walls are hung with the work that was such a solace and pleasure to him.

The study is, however, the heart of Chartwell. It is exactly as Churchill left it in October 1964 and bears his authentic imprint. It was in this room that he contemplated his political future when re-elected to Parliament in 1924; here that he pondered policy as Chancellor of the Exchequer; and here

Chartwell; From the garden   *Sir Winston Churchill's study*

that in the 1930s, when out of office and favour, he desperately reflected on the progress of events in Germany. To the study he returned, famous but rejected, after the electoral defeat of 1945, and here, after relinquishing the office of Prime Minister in 1954, he passed much of his old age, reading and writing.

The study was part of the statesman's life, but it was also the author's workshop. At the wide mahogany table he wrote or dictated *The World Crisis, Marlborough*, and *The Second World War*. The pictures and photographs with which Churchill surrounded himself in the study movingly reflect his affections and friendships. On the writing table itself are photographs of his wife 'Clemmie', his children, and his grandson Winston. There are also a photograph of Smuts, and busts of Napoleon and Nelson. On the walls hang a view of Blenheim where he was born, and portraits of his talented father, Lord Randolph Churchill, and the mother to whom he was so devoted.

A long terraced lawn, its line broken by one or two old yews, stretches in front of the house. Below, the land falls away to the coomb and the lakes which Churchill created. By contrast, the flower garden was Lady Churchill's province. Its charm relates to its simplicity. She preferred, and achieved, direct effects. The plants are unpretentious. Such things as potentillas, fuchsias, and lavender predominate. A love of cool colour finds expression in massed white geraniums, white tulips, and cherry-pie. The horticultural flavour is that of any pleasant country garden. The difference lies in the taste and skill of the planting and the layout.

In 1945 an anonymous group of Churchill's close friends bought Chartwell and gave it to the Trust so that the nation should own the home of the foremost statesman of his age.

Clandon Park, Surrey

At West Clandon, 3 miles east of Guildford. On A247, south of A3 and north of A246

About 1730, Thomas, 2nd Lord Onslow, decided to rebuild his Elizabethan family home at Clandon, and commissioned the Venetian architect Leoni to draw up the plans. The square red-brick house with stone dressings which rose during the next decade was very far from the strict Palladian formula which was by this time *de rigueur* among English architects; instead, its external design and decoration are a strange hybrid of Baroque and Palladian, with French, Italian and English motifs. The effect is one of exuberant grandeur and at the same time endearing *naïveté*.

The formal gardens, canals and courtyards which originally surrounded the house have disappeared, and the exterior of Clandon is no preparation for the Baroque splendour that lies within. A 19th-century porch and *porte cochère* have also transformed Leoni's entrance front. But once inside the house, its glory is revealed in the magnificent marble hall, rising through two

Clandon Park; The hall   *The Palladio room*

storeys, one of the most imposing of 18th-century rooms. The plasterwork is
almost certainly by the Italian stuccoers Artari and Bagutti, mythological
scenes framed in an astonishing medley of broken cornice, trophies, *putti*,
masks and ribbons. The two superb marble chimneypieces, here as elsewhere
in the house, are the work of Rysbrack.

In recent years two generous gifts have breathed life into the series of
state rooms that had long lacked most of their original contents. First the
late Mrs David Gubbay bequeathed her famous collection of furniture and
porcelain to Clandon; and secondly, a benefaction from Mr Kenneth Levy
made extensive redecoration possible. The state rooms were restored,
wherever feasible, in their exact 18th-century colours and materials, and
now form an unparalleled succession of Augustan interiors.

Most striking, perhaps, are the saloon with its original ceiling colours,
blue, pink and pale yellow, discovered under layers of whitewash; the
Palladio Room covered in a French flock wallpaper of 1780; and the Green
Drawing Room – all of which have Artari and Bagutti plasterwork. Smaller
and more intimate are the Hunting Room, filled with Mrs Gubbay's
collection of Chinese porcelain birds climbing the walls on gilt rococo wall-
brackets, and the Morning Room, with neoclassical satinwood furniture and
Chelsea porcelain. A highly ornate and tasselled state bed of about 1700 with
a set of chairs *en suite*, and five large paintings of birds by Francis Barlow, are
amongst the treasures original to the house, to which Mrs Gubbay's bequest
has added commodes by Langlois, a marquetry dressing-table attributed to
Chippendale, Nymphenburg figures by Bustelli, and a collection of early
Staffordshire pottery.

Claydon House, Buckinghamshire

At Middle Claydon, 3½ miles south-west of Winslow, 13 miles north-west of Aylesbury

Though the Verneys have been in Buckinghamshire since the 13th century, it was not until 1620 that Sir Edmund Verney became the first of his family to live at Claydon House. We know more of Sir Edmund and his family than of almost any group of people in the 17th century, thanks to the Verney Papers which record life at Claydon in his time. Sir Edmund was a noble and ultimately a tragic figure. Having served in Charles I's household when the latter was Prince of Wales, he was appointed Knight Marshal of the Palace when Charles succeeded to the throne. He was also for many years Member of Parliament for Wycombe. On the outbreak of the Civil War, although convinced of the rightness of the Parliamentary cause, his loyalty to Charles did not waver. 'I have eaten his bread,' he wrote, 'served him for near thirty years and will not do so base a thing as to forsake him, but choose rather to lose my life (which I am sure I shall do) to preserve and defend those things which are against my conscience to preserve and defend.' He was created Standard Bearer to the king and, as he had predicted, lost his life. His body was never recovered after the battle of Edgehill, but his severed hand was found clutching the royal standard.

At the Restoration, Sir Edmund's eldest son returned to Claydon and lived to see the family fortunes restored before he died in 1696. Two years later, his son John, a wealthy Levant Company merchant, was created Viscount Fermanagh, and an earldom was added to the family honours in the next generation. It is with the 2nd Earl Verney, who succeeded in 1752, that the architectural history of Claydon is chiefly concerned. He was a man of taste, generous and attractive, but sadly improvident. Music and the arts were an obsession, and politics an abiding and expensive interest. The Earl

Claydon House; The staircase

The Chinese room

combined the two in rebuilding and enlarging Claydon on a monumental scale to rival Stowe, the mansion of his political opponent, the Tory Earl Temple. The enterprise beggared him. The contents of Claydon were sold and he fled to France. Later, when the huge unfinished house was shut and empty, a stable boy discovered the Earl wandering in the shuttered rooms. He fed and cared for the old man and concealed him for weeks in the house.

On the Earl's death, his successor sensibly, but regrettably, pulled down two-thirds of the vast edifice, which in due course passed through the female line to Sir Harry Calvert, a Peninsular general. His son took the name of Verney and married in 1858, as his second wife, Parthenope Nightingale, elder sister of the formidable Florence. His descendant, Sir Harry Verney, made over the property to his son, who gave Claydon House to the National Trust in 1956.

Of Lord Verney's ambitious extensions, begun about 1754, only the west wing remains. Its restrained classical exterior conceals an astonishing suite of rococo rooms. The work of Luke Lightfoot, an eccentric craftsman-contractor, 'with an austere look, fierce as an eastern Monarch', of whom little is known but that he was both talented and difficult, these rooms are decorated with a freedom of fancy and a liveliness of rhythm unparalleled in this country.

The Pink Parlour and the adjoining North Hall, a double cube of fifty feet, are decorated with wood carving of the greatest virtuosity. Ceilings and cornices, *chinoiserie* niches, panels and overmantels, embodying flowers, fruit, birds, beasts, medallions, swags, wreaths and flowing tracery, create an effect of uninhibited exuberance and invention.

Lightfoot's most extraordinary legacy is the Chinese Room on the first floor which marks the height of English *chinoiserie*, so much in fashion about the middle of the 18th century. The room is a rare, perhaps a unique, realization of the fantasies so often to be found in textbooks of the period. One wall is transformed into a pagoda-like alcove with tiny bells hanging from the roof, in which a Chinese couple are taking tea. Carved in high relief, their rococo and *chinoiserie* setting is a miracle of light-hearted precision.

Such extravagances were not to the taste of all Lord Verney's contemporaries. Some approved rather the saloon, whose decorations were in a restrained Palladian style. The coffered plaster ceiling and the cornice were executed by Joseph Rose, the eminent plasterer so often employed by Robert Adam. He was also responsible for the well of the staircase. The latter may have been designed by Sir Thomas Robinson, Yorkshire squire, dilettante, and sometime director of Ranelagh Gardens. He wrote that it 'will be very noble and great, Mr Rose's part very beautiful indeed and when completed it will be one of the great works of Claydon'. So it proved. The mahogany treads and risers are inlaid with parquetry of holly, ebony and ivory, and the ironwork balustrade incorporates scrolls and garlands of husks and ears of corn, so delicately wrought that they rustle when anyone goes up the stairs.

A century later, these stairs were trod by inhabitants of a world very different from that of the extravagant Whig nobleman, with his passionate patronage of the arts. Parthenope Verney and her sister Florence Nightingale, who lived for many years at Claydon, have both left the impress of their powerful personalities on the house. Florence Nightingale's bedroom, its Victorian treatment and furnishings effectively eclipsing the original 18th-century decoration, adjoins a room devoted to relics of her Crimean mission and other memorials of the military history of the Verney family. The hand of her sister, Parthenope, is to be seen in the friendly 19th-century library which she created from the 18th-century drawing room. The elegance of an earlier age survives in its plaster ceiling and Ionic doorcases.

Cliveden, Buckinghamshire *(See colour plate facing p. 97)*

On the left bank of the Thames, off B476, 2 miles from Taplow

The first house at Cliveden was built in 1666 by William Winde for the 2nd Duke of Buckingham, playwright and member of the Cabal:

> A man so various that he seem'd to be
> Not one, but all mankind's epitome.

It underwent additions and alterations in the early 18th century – both Archer and Leoni were employed – and was evidently a very grand mansion, for Frederick, Prince of Wales, father of George III, rented it from 1739 to 1751. Forty-four years later it was burnt to the ground, little surviving except Winde's great terrace on which it stood.

A new house which rose on the same site was also burnt down in 1849. In the following year the then owner of Cliveden, the Duke of Sutherland, called in Sir Charles Barry. His vast balustraded pile, 150 feet long, with nine bays on the garden front and an Ionic order embracing the two upper storeys, is in its self-confident way something of a masterpiece. Unfortunately Barry's interior decoration was largely swept away after 1870, when Cliveden passed into the ownership of the Duke of Westminster. Perhaps the finest things inside the house today are the immense French Renaissance fireplace, the handsome Brussels tapestries from the set known as *The Arts of War* (both in the Hall), and the Louis XV panelling in the dining room which came from the Château d'Asnières, once used by Madame de Pompadour as a hunting box.

In 1893 Cliveden was bought by the Astor family, an event which introduced not the least interesting period of its history. Between the two World Wars when the 2nd Viscount Astor and his American wife – Lady Astor was the first woman to enter parliament – ruled at Cliveden, the house became one of the major social and political centres in the country. The 2nd Viscount gave the property to the Trust in 1942, and the house is today the English home of Stanford University, an arrangement which happily prolongs an Anglo-American association.

The garden and grounds at Cliveden require no panegyric. The natural

Cliveden; The shell fountain

site, the wooded slopes falling steeply to the Thames, the famous prospect down the 'Cliveden Reach', have offered designer and gardener a unique opportunity.

The entrance drive winds through the Rhododendron Valley to a Victorian marble fountain of monumental proportions, whence a broad formal avenue of limes stretches to the house. The forecourt is curtained by yew hedges, dating from the end of the 17th century, and in front of them stand sculptured Roman sarcophagi. Ancient mulberries and two fastigiate oaks stand on the lawns.

William Winde's great achievement in designing the terrace to the south of the house is clearly apparent. The scale is immense. One stands well above the vast lawn, which is set with a parterre of low box hedges, enclosing triangular beds which contain grey foliage plants. The design probably dates from Barry's time. From Winde's terrace steps lead to a lower terrace and a notable early-17th-century balustrade brought from the Borghese Gardens in Rome.

Half-way down to the river is the Italian garden, later adapted as a cemetery for those who died in the Cliveden War Hospital, 1914–18. Thence a woodland walk leads to the Canning Oak, the great leaning tree under which the statesman is said to have lingered, enjoying the views. Above and beyond lie the glades of ilex which are a remarkable feature of the grounds and provide so satisfactory a setting for urns and statuary. At the end of one glade is a group of *Rhododendron macabeanum*, its great leaves contrasting with the dark oaks. From the rhododendrons a stretch of greensward, known as Queen Anne's Walk, leads to the Blenheim Pavilion designed by Leoni in about 1735.

Three further features call for special mention. West of the monumental fountain that looks down the formal avenue to the house lies the Long Garden, a mown walk flanked by box hedges, topiary, and 18th-century statuary; to the east of the fountain lies a complex water garden with a 'Japanese' pagoda bought at the Great Exhibition of 1851. Finally just north-west of the house is a rose garden of novel design laid out by Geoffrey Jellicoe in 1956.

Clouds Hill, Dorset

9 miles east of Dorchester, $1\frac{1}{2}$ miles east of Waddock crossroads on B3390, 1 mile north of Bovington Camp

That complex personality, Lawrence of Arabia, perhaps the outstanding legend to emerge from the First World War, and the author of one great book, *Seven Pillars of Wisdom*, was disguised as 'Private Shaw' in the Tank Corps when he first rented the derelict and undistinguished cottage at Clouds Hill. As he wrote to a friend, 'I covet the idea of being sometimes by myself near a fire.'

He used the cottage at such times as he could escape from duty. 'I don't sleep here', he wrote from Clouds Hill, 'but come out at 4.30 p.m. till 9 p.m. nearly every night, and dream, or write, or read by the fire, or play Beethoven or Mozart.' He lived mainly upstairs, and the sitting room, as E. M. Forster described it, 'a brownish room – wooden beams and ceiling, leather covered settee', is as Lawrence left it, the ascetic home of a strange and enigmatic man. The gramophone and the old 78 r.p.m. records are still there, as are photographs relating to his Arabian campaign (a model of strategic imagination), and the dour furniture he made or bought. It is an interior far from sympathetic, yet bearing the authentic impress of one of the most unusual men of his age.

Early in 1935 Lawrence, who meantime had spent many years in the Air

Clouds Hill; The sitting room   *The book room*

Force away from his cottage, was discharged from the Services and returned to live at Clouds Hill. 'Everything, inside and outside my place', he wrote, 'approaches perfection.' On 8 May he told Lady Astor, 'Wild mares would not at present take me away from Clouds Hill. It is an earthly paradise and I am staying here until I feel qualified for it.' Five days later, returning from Bovington Camp, he had a fatal crash on his motor cycle.

Coleridge Cottage, Nether Stowey, Somerset

8 miles west of Bridgwater, on south side of A39

Late in December 1796, Coleridge, with his wife Sara and his infant son, moved into what was then a pretty, low, thatched cottage with a clear brook running before the door. He was to stay three years and to write in the cottage most of his best verse: *The Ancient Mariner*, the first part of *Christabel*, and *This Lime-Tree Bower my Prison*.

Coleridge Cottage; The sitting room

Though the cottage was much altered in the 19th century, and only four rooms remain that existed in Coleridge's day, it was here that the poet, as opposed to the later prosewriter, found his deepest inspiration. William and Dorothy Wordsworth, established in 1797 at Alfoxden, often came over to Stowey and Charles Lamb was a welcome visitor. It was during a walk with Wordsworth that the idea of *The Ancient Mariner* took shape, and the poem contains direct references to places in the neighbourhood.

Coniston Hall, Cumbria

1 mile south of Coniston, off A593

Rising with some drama on the western edge of Coniston Water, the hall was probably built by William Fleming (described as 'a gentleman of great pomp and expense') in the latter half of the 16th century. Houses of the date and consequence of Coniston are rare in the heart of the Lake District, where long after Elizabethan times even the rich lived rough, and moreover the hall exhibits unusual architectural features.

Its survival is something of a miracle, for Coniston was abandoned early in the 18th century and fifty years later had become an ivy-clad ruin. Its conversion in about 1815 to serve as a barn and farmhouse saved but disfigured it. The Trust is undertaking extensive restoration.

Built of the sombre local stone, with a thin covering of roughcast, the building is crowned by the tall conical chimneys which give presence to many old houses in the north-west. It was essentially a hall-house with a transverse wing at either end. The western wing has been a tenanted farmhouse for 150 years; the shorter eastern wing has been derelict since the 18th century. The original hall is now entered through a 19th-century door, up a ramp for farm wagons. The ramp was necessary when this part of the building was converted into a barn, for the hall was situated, not in the usual fashion at ground level, but on the first floor. This novel disposition was no doubt intended to place it comfortably above the surface mists of the lake, as well as rising water at times of flood. Inside the barn, to the right, sections of the original oak screens survive; behind lay the screens passage giving access to the kitchens and offices in the west wing. The hall was warmed by the substantial arched fireplace of dressed pink sandstone on the south wall opposite the present entrance. The other sandstone fireplace at the east, or left, end of the barn served William Fleming's withdrawing room, which was separated from the hall by a wooden partition that has disappeared, though leaving evidence of its exact position. Thus both the hall and the withdrawing room were comprised within the dimensions of the present barn. The mullioned windows in both rooms were of oak and some of the original framing survives.

Coniston Hall

The squat east wing, when its four walls stood, must have looked much like a pele tower, though there is no reason to think it served as such. It probably contained the solar and still has a 16th-century garderobe. Placed in the thickness of the wall between this wing and the withdrawing room there survives a newel staircase with solid oak blocks for treads; it gave access from ground level to the private apartments above.

When the National Trust acquired Coniston Hall in 1971, this interesting and picturesque building looked on a caravan camp. The caravans have now been sited in woodlands to the south.

Coughton Court, Warwickshire

9 miles west of Stratford-upon-Avon, 2 miles north of Alcester, on the A435 Redditch road

Coughton stands in richly timbered countryside close to the forest of Arden. The magnificent Tudor gatehouse dominates the late-18th-century Gothick wings on either flank. Described by the 17th-century historian Dugdale as a 'stately castle-like Gate-house of freestone', it is three storeys high with mullioned oriels and octagonal battlemented turrets, and soars above the entrance archway which is surmounted with the Royal Arms of Henry VIII and the arms of the Throckmorton family. From 1409, when the heiress to the property married Sir John Throckmorton (Under-Treasurer of England in the reign of Henry VI), until 1946, when the 11th baronet, Sir Robert Throckmorton, made over the property to the Trust, the family remained in undisputed, though not untroubled, possession. The Throckmortons have been distinguished above all by their tenacious allegiance to Roman Catholicism.

Sir George Throckmorton built the gatehouse soon after 1518 and surrounded the house with a wide moat. Unusually for its period, the gatehouse was incorporated into the main structure of the house, the tall room on the first floor becoming the principal chamber. The gatehouse archway, with delicate fan-vaulting, leads to a courtyard on a less ambitious scale. The gabled wings, typical of early-16th-century half-timber work, were once linked by a chapel forming the fourth side. It was damaged by a Protestant mob in 1688 and later demolished.

After a steady growth in prosperity in the 15th and early 16th centuries, through public service and provident marriages, the Throckmortons, like other leading Catholic families, paid a high price for recusancy throughout Elizabeth I's and later reigns, suffering frequent fines and imprisonment. None the less, the secret celebration of mass continued at Coughton, and hiding places and chambers were contrived to conceal the priests, many of them Jesuits, who slipped illegally in and out of the country. It is ironic that the family's own apostate has become its most widely known member. Nicholas, whose Protestantism was said to wax and wane with his health, was the father of Bessie Throckmorton, maid of honour to Queen Elizabeth,

*Coughton Court;
The gatehouse and entrance
front*

who secretly married Walter Raleigh to her mistress's great displeasure. Nicholas was courtier, statesman and ambassador to France and Scotland. Curiously enough, the diplomat who fussed about the effect that the Queen's conduct towards Leicester might have on her reputation, later supported the passionate career of the Queen of Scots; in 1586 the family was involved in the Babington plot to place her on the English throne.

It was nearly twenty years later, on the night of 5 November 1605, that the most famous episode in Coughton's history took place. In the gatehouse drawing room an anxious group, including the wives of the conspirators, awaited the outcome of the Gunpowder Plot. A manservant brought news from London of its miscarriage, whereupon the disappointed party hastily dispersed. Thomas Throckmorton, head of the family, whose sister was married to Catesby, was discreetly absent and survived unscathed, dying in 1618. His grandson was created a baronet in 1642.

The Civil War brought fresh trouble to Coughton, which was besieged and captured by Parliamentary troops in 1643; they withdrew a year later, after looting and damaging the house. The estates were sequestrated, but later restored. Though the Catholic Throckmortons could take no part in public life during the remainder of the 17th–18th centuries, they quietly prospered, intermarrying with leading Catholic families and acquiring estates from Berkshire to Devon.

In the 1780s, the 4th baronet, whose brilliant and lively portrait by Largillière hangs in the Tudor gatehouse drawing room, was responsible for remodelling the west front, and building the charming Gothick staircase. His grandson filled in the moat about 1795, cleared away the remains of the chapel – thus opening one side of the courtyard – and refashioned the south wing as a new chapel. Sir John, who died in 1819, was a well-known sporting squire. In 1811, as a result of a thousand-guinea wager, the famous Throckmorton coat was made for him 'between sunrise and sunset of a summer's day' from the shearing of the sheep to the finished garment: '... illustrative of manufacturing celerity', says the poster which hangs behind the coat on display in the house.

By 1835, the 17th baronet, Sir Charles, added the final touch to the appearance of the house as we see it today. He removed the attractive Jacobean gables on the west front and added the present battlements and dun-coloured stucco. Inside, he restored and uncovered the splendid panelling in the dining room, which with its noble Caroline marble and timber chimneypiece, and its rare combination of Tudor with early and late Caroline panels and mouldings, is perhaps the most notable room at Coughton.

About 1910, the 9th baronet converted the chapel into a large saloon, dominated by the early-16th-century staircase taken from Harvington Hall. The 11th baronet's mother, who lived at Coughton until her death in 1955, was responsible for much of the beautiful embroidery in the house. Her son, Sir Robert Throckmorton, continues the family tradition at Coughton today.

The interior of Coughton possesses a singular charm. The juxtaposition of periods, the feeling of casual growth rather than of planned design, the series of rooms decorated and furnished by successive generations and containing the natural accumulation of centuries, and not least the unparalleled collection of Catholic relics, puts Coughton in a class apart.

Cragside, Northumberland

1 mile east of Rothbury, entrance from B6344, Morpeth to Rothbury road

In 1863 Sir William Armstrong took a much needed holiday at Rothbury in Upper Coquetdale, which he had known as a small boy. It was to be a momentous occasion for he decided to buy as much land as he could in the Debdon valley and build a weekend house and shooting lodge. William Armstrong was well able to indulge his fancies since he was a very rich man, the leading industrialist of the north-east and owner of the largest arms manufactory in England. His career was as remarkable as his talents. Son of a prosperous Newcastle merchant and amateur mathematician, young Armstrong began his working life as a solicitor and practised law for ten years. He also had a passion for scientific experiment and was an ardent and skilful fisherman. One day, fishing on the Coquet, he was struck by the

Cragside; The entrance front

inefficient use of water power made by the waterwheel on the river. He thereupon began to study hydraulics and by 1847 left the legal profession to start an engineering works specializing in hydraulic cranes and lifts. This prospered after a slow start and he made a fortune. The Crimean War turned Armstrong's active mind to the problems of armaments and resulted in the invention of the Armstrong breach-loaded gun, whose patents he gave to the nation. However, the gun still brought him a second and much greater fortune; the demand from overseas was so great that by the time of his death, the Elswick works on the Tyne rivalled the Krupps factories in Germany as the largest in the world.

This outstanding Victorian industrialist was a complex character; inventor, scientist, he ran his business with a practical and benevolent paternalism. His native city of Newcastle owed much to his philanthropy. Yet Armstrong was by nature a countryman and to the Cragside estate he devoted nearly forty years of energy and enthusiasm, transforming the landscape and building a house which has been described as the 'quintessence of later Victorian romanticism'.

All this lay in the future. Twenty acres of hillside between the Debdon Burn and the river Coquet were Armstrong's initial purchase, and half-way up the steep slope an undistinguished stone villa was built whose only important feature was a central tower. Such houses were repeated by the thousand throughout northern England and Scotland, in city suburbs and small Highland towns. But Cragside was ultimately to be very far from an ordinary house, as unusual as its owner.

95

The landscape of inland Northumbria is beautiful, with shallow, thinly-wooded dales that run forty miles from the central spine of England down to the coast, and sparsely-covered moors and rounded hills stretching rank upon rank to the Cheviots and the Scottish border. There is fine fishing in the clear streams bordered by birch and scrubby alder. The water is cold, the air clear, spring comes late and summers can be short and glorious. Here William Armstrong worked to realize his dream. He extended his property from 20 to 1,700 acres. He made roads, dammed streams, cleared some part of the surrounding moors of heather and scrub so that over 7,000,000 trees, mostly conifers, could be planted. The house gradually arose from their midst. Today Wagnerian is the inevitable epithet that springs to mind, so un-English is the medley of towers, chimneys and gables rising from the sea of dark, magnificent conifers. And yet it remained stubbornly Victorian with its disregard for local architectural style, its romantic mixture of Gothic and Elizabethan, deliberately irregular, picturesque, 'quaint'. Labelled 'Old English' by its highly successful creators, Norman Shaw and his partner W. E. Nesfield, the supreme merit of this style lay perhaps in its adaptability.

At Cragside Shaw was faced with formidable problems, which were solved with considerable ingenuity. When the future Lord Armstrong (he was ennobled in 1897) decided to make Cragside his principal home, he laid down certain criteria which the architect had to fulfil. The original holiday house was to be incorporated into the new scheme, a large picture gallery was required, the house was to be made suitable for entertaining on a very grand scale the many distinguished clients who came from all over the world to purchase armaments. At the same time, it was to be a comfortable home for Armstrong and his wife when they were alone. Technically it was a remarkable achievement considering the difficulties of the site, which had to be hacked out of the rocky hillside. Cragside grew piecemeal over twenty years, though by 1875 the outline of the house as it now stands was complete, with the exception of the drawing room wing. (The work had all been carried out by estate workmen, many of whom were housed in a row of cottages built by Shaw for the purpose in Rothbury.)

Yet for all its size and heroic grandeur, Cragside is curiously homely. Perhaps the absence of a cohesive overall internal design contributes to this effect, which seems to be at odds with the scale of the principal reception rooms. Of these the drawing room is the most impressive. Designed as a gallery for Lord Armstrong's collection of contemporary paintings (most of which were sold in 1919), it was built into the rock, and lit from above and from one large recessed bay window. The room is dominated by an enormous marble and alabaster overmantel-cum-inglenook carved from ceiling height to fireplace with exuberant detail in a style which owes much to 'Renaissance at its fruitiest'. The effect is as if a rock temple had been moved indoors. The drawing room was inaugurated by the visit of the Prince and Princess of Wales in 1884, which is most delightfully illustrated in an album of water-colours still on view in the house. Another striking feature of the drawing room – and one which must have been most inconvenient for the hosts – is the fact that it is separated from the rest of the house by 165 feet of

Blickling Hall, Norfolk; c. 1620; East front from the formal garden

Castle Coole, Co. Fermanagh; c. 1790; The entrance front

Charlecote Park, Warwickshire; Dining room, restored and refurnished 1830–40

Cliveden, Buckinghamshire; 1850; Terrace front

passages, lobbies and stairs, the dining room and library being at the northern end. The library is one of Shaw's most successful rooms, low ceilinged and comfortable. He designed most of the furniture, including some interesting cane and ebonized chairs. Four cloisonné vases converted to lamps are of note for they were first reconverted from gas to electricity in 1880 and were the first domestic electric lights in the world. Cragside was the first English country house to be lit by electricity, beating Hatfield by a few months. Power was supplied by a water turbine and the forty-five Swan lamps were made in Newcastle by Joseph Swan, a friend of Lord Armstrong. There are other technical innovations at Cragside: hydraulic lifts, hot and cold Turkish baths. A fitted washbasin in Lady Armstrong's bedroom and bath in her husband's dressing room were advanced features at that time. The kitchen was fitted with a hydraulic spit, though few other concessions were made to domestic efficiency. It is situated very close to the dining room, which is a rather dark high-ceilinged room facing north-west with an inglenook fireplace behind a massive stone arch with little Pre-Raphaelite stained-glass windows from the Morris works. The master of the house was depicted here by the painter H. H. Emmerson, reading his newspaper with a couple of dogs at his carpet-slippered feet.

While the house and some of its furnishings may have appeared exotic to the Shah of Persia, the King of Siam and other Oriental potentates who were entertained here, there were traditional English shooting parties, picnics on the moors and strolls through the miles of woodland paths and the magnificent azaleas and rhododendron shrubberies above the river. Since Cragside was acquired by the National Trust in 1977 the grounds have been made into a country park.

Croft Castle, Hereford & Worcester

5 miles north-west of Leominster, 9 miles south-west of Ludlow; on the B4362 Presteigne road, $2\frac{1}{2}$ miles from turning off the B4361 Leominster/ Ludlow road

The 'famous and very Knightly family of the Crofts' were for 400 years styled 'de Croft'. They may have come to England from Normandy even before the Conquest. At all events they were persons of consequence from the Middle Ages until the 18th century. When their fortunes declined they were compelled, shortly before 1750, to sell their ancient castle. Their return to Croft in 1923 is thus a romantic story, and Lord Croft, who now lives in the castle, represents one of the oldest territorial links in the country.

Croft Castle has the charm attaching to buildings of martial intent which in more settled times acquired domestic grace. Originally a Marcher castle– a Croft married the daughter of Owain Glyndwr – the plan of Croft is roughly square, enclosing a courtyard, with a tower at each corner. Walls and towers probably date from the 14th or 15th century, and for some 400 years there was a gate in the centre of the entrance front giving carriage

Croft Castle

access to the open courtyard, an arrangement resembling that found in medieval castles and the colleges of Oxford and Cambridge. It disappeared in the 18th century when much else was happening at Croft and the building was in process of transformation from castle to country house. To the 18th century we owe the politer sash windows, which create so pleasant a contrast with the random medieval masonry, the parapets which screen the roofs, and the two delightful Gothick bays on the entrance front.

The association of Croft at this period with the Knight and Johnes families, who were connected with the Gothick movement, may account for some of the most engaging features of the interior such as the Gothick staircase with its delightful plasterwork, the rococo detail of the ceilings and blue and gold painting of the panels in the Blue Room, and the painted bookcases in the library. In such a setting Lord Croft's remarkable collection of Gothick furniture looks particularly well. This includes a pair of elbow chairs of about 1770, whose design derives from a Robert Adam drawing. Other rooms of interest are the Oak Room, with 17th-century panelling, and the drawing room with early-18th-century panelling and a series of family pastel portraits in attractive Baroque frames.

The church that lies across the lawn is roughly contemporary with the castle, and its most notable feature is the early-16th-century altar tomb to Sir Richard Croft and his wife. Sir Richard captured the unfortunate young Prince of Wales at the battle of Tewkesbury and eventually became Treasurer of the King's Household.

The grounds at Croft offer an interesting contrast to the classic 18th-century parkland associated with the work of Capability Brown. The great avenues, which are the splendour of Croft, were flourishing a century before Brown was born. Happily they escaped the axe of the Georgian 'improvers', so that Croft boasts some of the finest oaks in the country, with girths of forty feet, and an avenue of sweet chestnuts stretching nearly half a mile and perhaps 350 years old.

If Croft was largely spared the attentions of Brown and his followers, its Fish Pool Valley clearly reflects the later 'picturesque' movement and the reaction against the earlier school of landscape. Uvedale Price and Richard Payne Knight, who between them may be said to have invented the 'picturesque', were not only Herefordshire squires but on terms with the contemporary owners of Croft. The Fish Pool Valley is a direct expression of their theories.

Victorian additions to Croft are the splendid wellingtonias, Deodar cedars, redwoods, Monterey pines and other trees in the garden and park.

A Gothick arch, another legacy of the 'picturesque', gives access to the garden adjoining the house. Beyond stretches a pastoral countryside.

Derrymore House, Co. Armagh

$1\frac{1}{2}$ miles north-west of Newry on A25

Derrymore is a rare survival, for time seems to have spared none of the other single-storeyed and thatched houses built by the Ulster gentry in the 'cottage' style towards the end of the 18th century. Combining a traditional Irish idiom with elements of the fashionable 'picturesque' taste, it was described in 1803, some twenty-five years later, as 'the most elegant summer lodge'. Such indeed it is.

Three small pavilions are linked to form a U-shaped building that acquires a rhythm from the thatch which sweeps upwards over the gable ends, and derives a light-hearted fantasy from archaistic features such as

Derrymore House

labels over window heads and trefoil lunettes. The front door, with one of those wide and shallow fanlights so characteristic of late-18th-century work in Ulster, leads to the Treaty Room, which is surprisingly large for so modest a house.

This room is by tradition associated with the considerable role that Isaac Corry, the builder of Derrymore, played in the stormy Irish politics of his time. One of the most distinguished politicians of his day, he was M.P. for Newry almost continuously from 1766 to 1806. A devoted servant of the administration, he became Chancellor of the Irish Exchequer in succession to Sir John Parnell. It was said of him:

> For the loss of Sir John we need not be sorry,
> For his place is well filled by the keen Isaac Corry,
> Who the art of financing has brought to its height,
> Our taxes being heavy he laid them on light.

The financier was at the same time a man of marked spirit and was involved in various 'affairs of honour', including a duel with the patriot, Henry Grattan, in which he received a ball in the arm. None the less Grattan was among the friends – such as Corry's close associate, Lord Castlereagh, and the enlightened Lord Charlemont – who were guests at Derrymore, which was something of a political *foyer*. Indeed it was more than this, for in the Treaty Room, under its unpresuming thatch, is traditionally said to have been drafted the Treaty of Union between England and Ireland. Though Corry was the best and most generous of landlords, his carriage not surprisingly was subsequently stoned as he passed through Newry. His association with the hated Union was well known.

In 1859 Derrymore was acquired by the Richardson family, and nearly a century later Mr J. S. W. Richardson presented it to the National Trust.

Dunster Castle, Somerset

In Dunster village, 2 miles south-east of Minehead, on A396

Close to the border of Somerset and Devon, where the little river Avill runs to the sea at a point where the Quantock and Bredon Hills meet the northernmost tip of Exmoor, a wooded mound dominates the mouth of the valley. For a thousand years there has been a fortress on this site. In the Domesday Book it is mentioned as Torre, a tower belonging to Aluric the Saxon. After the Norman invasion Dunster and various other manors were granted to William de Mohun and a castle was erected. In 1376 Lady Joan de Mohun sold the castle and estate to Lady Elizabeth Luttrell for 5,000 mercks. The redoubtable vendor retained the life interest and had the best of the bargain for she outlived the Lady Elizabeth by thirty years, dying in 1404. Sir Hugh Luttrell quickly took possession, although the de Mohun heirs contested the transaction and brought him to court. The Luttrells remained at Dunster for over five hundred years (except for an interregnum

Dunster Castle from the south

of some thirty years during which the estates were forfeited in the Wars of the Roses) until 1976, when Lt. Col. Walter Luttrell gave the castle and park to the National Trust.

Of the Saxon tower and Norman castle nothing remains; the oldest feature is the 13th-century gateway to the lower ward. The castle then comprised an upper ward on the summit of the Tor and a lower ward with a curtain wall and semicircular bastions. When Sir Hugh Luttrell moved in he built the gatehouse (now known as the Tenants' Hall) over the gateway and repaired the castle. His direct descendant, John Luttrell, who inherited in 1538, was a picturesque figure. He fought with Henry VIII's armies in the struggles against the Scots and was knighted after the sack of Edinburgh in 1554. His famous allegorical portrait by Hans Eworth hangs in the hall. In 1617 his nephew, George Luttrell, contracted with William Arnold who built Montacute for 'a house or parcell of buildings to be sett up and built within the Castle of Dunster'. There were wrangles between the two but the work was done and the castle transformed into a Jacobean house with the conventional H-shaped ground plan. George Luttrell also built the octagonal yarn market in the centre of Dunster which lies directly beneath the castle.

During the Civil War Dunster Castle was a focal point in the struggle in the west. Thomas Luttrell inclined to the Parliamentary cause and refused access to a Royalist force in 1642. The next summer a stronger force returned and he immediately surrendered. A garrison under Colonel Wyndham took over the castle. Two years later the young Prince of Wales was sent to Somerset to rekindle support for the King and spent a fortnight at Dunster. In November 1645 Colonel (later Admiral) Blake surrounded the castle and the siege lasted until April 1646 when Colonel Wyndham surrendered with honour. After Charles I's execution in 1649 the war was over but the country was still troubled and Royalist risings were feared. Dunster was felt to be a potential threat, so orders were given for it to be demolished leaving only the house and gatehouse.

After the Restoration the family fortunes revived. In 1680 Francis Luttrell married an heiress and the young couple brought life and gaiety back to Dunster Castle. To them we owe the great staircase with its magnificently carved balustrade, the fine plaster ceilings above it and in what is now the dining room. Francis Luttrell raised a regiment of foot soldiers for William of Orange which subsequently became the Yorkshire regiment, the Green Howards. He died suddenly and in debt. To save the contents of the house from creditors, his widow bought them and took them to London, where they were all destroyed in a fire. Little of the 17th-century furniture in the house today, therefore, has been in Dunster since that time.

In the early 18th century the estates suffered but after the marriage of Margaret Luttrell, sole heiress to her father's property, to her cousin Henry Fownes, things gradually improved. He created the deer park, improved the steep approach road and made some modest alterations to the interior including a breakfast and withdrawing room on the first floor. Dunster remained untouched for the next ninety years while the family were busily engaged in local affairs. The Luttrells had two seats in Minehead in their pockets and the family were Members of Parliament themselves for nearly forty years.

In 1867 George Fownes Luttrell inherited Dunster from his uncle. The estates were in good order and ranked the fourth largest in Somerset, extending to over 15,000 acres. The house however was not and George Luttrell, enjoying a comfortable income, set about remedying matters. He engaged the highly successful and experienced Anthony Salvin, a specialist in medieval architecture, amongst whose many commissions were restorations and improvements at Windsor Castle. The wonderful natural setting and the ancient history of the place fired his imagination and Dunster may be numbered amongst his most successful exercises. His designs included building two battlemented towers and a low service wing grafted on the Jacobean house. He remodelled the main entrance and the great hall, added a drawing room and conservatory and created a typically Victorian 'male domain' of gun room, business room, muniment room, billiard room and library. On the first floor he altered what had been a banqueting hall to show the magnificent set of 17th-century Spanish leather hangings depicting the tale of Antony and Cleopatra. On the lower ground floor new domestic offices included stillroom, larders, innumerable storerooms and a large kitchen with views over the park and towards the sea, not commonly the lot of 19th-century indoor servants.

Wonderful views are the rule not the exception at Dunster: over the magnolia and mimosa trees, the tropical garden and the luxuriant evergreens which flourish in the gentle climate, seaward towards the Bristol Channel and the Welsh coast, and inland to the summit of Dunkery Beacon. Its picturesque skyline rising above the treetops of the mound, set against the background of wooded hills, makes Dunster Castle a most successful and romantic amalgam of the architecture of four centuries.

Dyrham Park, Avon

7 miles north of Bath, west of the A46 Bath/Stroud road, 2 miles south of M4

Evelyn's description of William Blathwayt, the builder of Dyrham, matches his portrait in the Great Hall: 'This gentleman is Secretary of War, Clerk of the Council, etc., having raised himself by his industry from very moderate circumstances. He is a very proper, handsome person, very dextrous in business, and, besides all this, has married a great fortune.'

Blathwayt had married Mary Wynter in 1686 in the church at Dyrham. It was after her death, five years later, that he began to rebuild the old Tudor home of the Wynters. He started by adding the west front, to the design of a French architect, S. Hauduroy, whose correspondence is preserved, together with the building accounts, but who is otherwise unknown. This simple front, built of local Cotswold stone, is flanked by one-storey pavilions. Despite the English domestic character of the elevation, it betrays distinct French overtones in such features as the close fenestration, while the scrolled consoles of the balcony over the door are probably inherited from the Hôtel Lauzun in Paris. Moreover the west terrace, enclosed on three sides, resembles a *cour d'honneur*, and gives the building something of the flavour of a town house of the period.

By 1698 Blathwayt was at the height of his career and by reason of his senior rank in the royal service had access to a royal architect and royal craftsmen. For the east front he commissioned a design of some architectural importance from William Talman; though built between 1700 and 1704, it belongs rather to the school of Wren and is innocent of the Vanbrugh-Hawksmoor style. This monumental façade of warm Bath stone is surmounted by a richly carved classical cornice and balustrade and is reminiscent of a Genoese town palace. The decoration includes sophisticated festoons, 'carved by Mr Harvey of Bath', side by side with archaic strapwork from engravings in Rubens's *Palazzi de Genova*. The orangery or greenhouse is attached in unusual fashion to Talman's front, and its massive coupled Tuscan columns are an echo of Versailles. It is balanced by arcading

Dyrham Park; East front and orangery

on the north which runs into the hillside 'in a curious collusion between symmetry and geography'.

There have been fallow deer at Dyrham since Saxon times at least, but the present aspect of the 263-acre deer park dates from the end of the 18th century. Talman's front looked on to elaborate pleasure grounds laid out by George London, the most famous gardener of William Blathwayt's time, with terraces, parterres, a canal, fountains and a cascade, 'the finest in England except for the Duke of Devonshire's', streaming down the steep hillside from the statue of Neptune. He is the sole surviving witness of this formal scene that was set under the enclosing Cotswold escarpment and engraved by Kip.

Entering the house today, we walk into Blathwayt's sensible late-17th-century rooms, not rich and extravagant, but satisfying in their sense of solid craftsmanship. Little change has taken place over nearly three centuries of family occupation. On a fine afternoon we are drawn through the house to the open west doors and the terrace above the garden. Here the framework of the 17th-century garden that Kip depicted has suffered less change, and the great lawns are overlooked, as they have always been, by the medieval church containing the Blathwayt monuments and hatchments.

The sparsely furnished West Hall is reminiscent of Holland, and we have only the dummy-board company of 'A Woman a-pareing of an apple' which she has been doing since 1710, according to the housekeeper's inventory of that year. The Dutch taste was familiar to Blathwayt, who had known the Netherlands from the earliest stages of his career. When acting as Secretary of State, he accompanied William III to Holland each summer in the years when he was building Dyrham.

Throughout the house, the blue and white Delftware, particularly the pyramid tulip holders, the collection of minor Dutch pictures, the bird paintings by Hondecoeter, and such things as the leather Blathwayt brought home from The Hague to hang on the walls, reflect Dutch influence. The New World has also made its contribution. Blathwayt's connection with the American colonies enabled him to obtain fine cedarwood for one of the staircases and Virginian walnut to panel the Diogenes Room. In this room, with its Mortlake tapestries, there is still, as there was in 1710, 'a Delft flowerpot in ye chimney'.

The Balcony Room on the first floor, which was Blathwayt's sitting room, has elaborate panelling which Hauduroy marbled and gilded in 1696. The blackamoors belonged to Blathwayt's uncle who brought him up, Thomas Povey, the man of taste and fashion now known only from the pages of Pepys and Evelyn. Povey also sent to Dyrham the two perspective paintings by Hoogstraeten much admired by Pepys, and the bookcases similar to those made by Sympson for Pepys in 1666 to his 'most extraordinary satisfaction', and now at Magdalene College, Cambridge.

Later Blathwayts acquired the elegant furniture in the drawing room made by Linnell and by Gillow, and commissioned Gainsborough to copy the *Peasant Woman and Boy* by Murillo which now hangs at Dyrham with the original.

East Riddlesden Hall, West Yorkshire

$1\frac{1}{2}$ miles north-east of Keighley on the A650 Keighley/Bradford road

Fined, imprisoned and excommunicated, the Murgatroyds of Riddlesden were a byword for profanity and debauchery, and by popular tradition the river Aire below the house changed its course in protest at their doings. None the less, to James Murgatroyd, who first acquired the property in 1638, we owe a house of unusual interest.

The hall is first seen across a fishpond, the 'Stagnum de Ridlesden' from which the Canons of Bolton were obtaining fish in the 14th century. Though the ashlar masonry has been sadly darkened by the polluted atmosphere of the last 150 years, the mullioned windows, the gables, the great porch with finials and battlements, create much the same impression as they must have done at the end of the 17th century. The most notable feature is the two-storeyed porch, its doorway flanked by columns of vaguely Corinthian character, and with a circular window of eight lights above (of a type said to be unique to the West Riding of Yorkshire).

The porch, the main body of the house on the left, and the so-called Banqueting Hall on the right, are Murgatroyd buildings and date from about 1640. The western addition, distinctly classical in inspiration, of which only the façade with pedimented windows survives, was built by the Murgatroyds' more respectable successors and dates from 1692. Adjoining this wing are four curious stone hutches with arched openings that were probably mews for hawks.

The isolated building with battlements immediately in front of the hall on the left is also Murgatroyd of about 1640. On the battlements are rudely executed reliefs of Charles I and his Queen and the motto 'Vive Leroy'. Whatever their failings, Murgatroyds were not afraid to show where their allegiance lay.

East Riddlesden Hall

East Riddlesden Hall; Kitchen

The interior of the hall offers several rooms with unaltered Murgatroyd panelling and plasterwork. In the last few years the Trust has furnished them with suitable 17th-century paintings, pewter, Delftware, and oak furniture.

In the grounds is one of the finest barns in the north of England. A hundred and twenty feet long, it has a pair of gabled porches in each flank and a splendidly timbered roof.

Erddig, Clwyd *(See colour plate facing p. 128)*

1 mile south of Wrexham, off A483

Though built in the 1680s, it is to John Meller, a successful London lawyer who acquired the property in 1715 and enlarged the house soon after, that Erddig owes much of its character today. The new owner, no doubt setting out to impress his Welsh neighbours, bought (besides such things as tapestries, oriental porcelain and silver) a quantity of early 18th-century furniture from the most distinguished London cabinet-makers. Much of this has survived with its original upholstery. The very plainness of the oak wainscot in the state room sets off the brilliance of Meller's gilt and silvered pieces. In the saloon there is silvered seat furniture covered in crimson Spitalfields velvet; sumptuous gilt girandoles are reflected in the no less splendid pier glasses of 1726, carved with grotesque heads, splayed feathers and falcons' beaks. The famous Erddig state bed, upholstered in embroidered Chinese silk, is of the same period and was made in London in 1720. An inventory compiled six years later not only reveals the quantity of fine furniture that John Meller bought, but has enabled the Trust to identify the very silks and cut velvets that he chose for pelmets, seat covers and hangings.

But Erddig is much more than a repository of works of art. Between 1735, when Meller left the house and its collections to a nephew, Simon Yorke, and 1973 when the latter's direct descendant Mr Philip Yorke gave them to the Trust, Erddig has been the home of a single family of country squires, content to cherish everything and throw nothing away. Herein lies the unique interest of the house.

However, the Philip Yorke who inherited in 1767 and whose sympathetic portrait by Gainsborough hangs in the dining room, was not averse to change. He bought Chinese wallpapers and porcelain, employed James Wyatt to reface the west front and, in the 1770s, William Emes to landscape the park with its magnificent hanging beechwoods and the striking circular waterfall known as 'The Cup and Saucer'. A passionate antiquarian, it was his strong historical sense, rather than apathy, that prompted him to preserve the character of the earlier state rooms and to retain the then unfashionable formal garden. The bones of the garden layout – formal walks, canal, pond and lime avenue all in the Dutch manner – have happily survived. Recent restoration and replanting have scrupulously preserved the original conception. Apart from a few Victorian features reflecting the revival of formal gardening in the last century, such as a parterre with stalagmite fountains, the gardens are much as they appear in an engraving of 1740.

Erddig is no less exceptional for the portraits which preserve the likenesses of successive generations of family servants. The portraits begin in the late 18th-century with the house carpenter, 'spider-brusher' and gamekeeper, and are continued in daguerreotypes and photographs until the whole system of domestic servants collapsed in this century. This fascinating insight into the workings of that complex organization, an English country house, is complemented by the survival of all the service and estate buildings – the blacksmith's shop, sawpit, wet and dry laundries, the

Erddig; The Saloon 	*The drying room*

bakehouse and kitchens – which can now be seen by visitors much as they were in Erddig's heyday.

The recent restoration of the house, outbuildings and gardens, which all had suffered great damage from subsidence following coal mining, was the most ambitious ever undertaken by the Trust.

Felbrigg Hall, Norfolk

3 miles from Cromer, west of B1436

Of the original Felbrigg, house of the family of that name, nothing now remains above ground. The present house, built by the Windham family, dates from the 17th–19th centuries.

The Jacobean entrance front, which was building in the 1620s at the same time as near-by Blickling Hall, remains unaltered. In 1665 William Samwell was called in to add a new brick wing on the south for William Windham, a keen forester, to whom we owe the fine chestnuts in the park. The next changes occurred when William Windham II, a few years after returning from the Grand Tour in 1741, began to refurbish the house in the mid-18th-century taste. Samwell's wing was partly gutted and James Paine, with Thomas Rose acting as his plasterer, created a new dining room, staircase and Gothick library. The cabinet was fitted out to receive Windham's Grand Tour acquisitions, such as views of the Campagna and Dutch School pictures. Paine retained, however, the superb plaster ceilings in the drawing room and in the cabinet. That in the drawing room is dated 1687 and bears the monogram 'WW', for William Windham I.

Felbrigg Hall;
The cabinet

William Windham II was followed by his extremely able son William Windham III, 'Weathercock Windham' the politician, who made further improvements and additions. In 1863 'Mad Windham', a bankrupt, sold Felbrigg to a local merchant, John Ketton. His grandson, the late Robert Wyndham Ketton-Cremer, a scholar and writer of distinction, left Felbrigg Hall to the National Trust in 1970.

What we now see at Felbrigg is the result of 300 years' growth. Though one gets the impression of slow change occasioned by convenience and aesthetic sense, the Georgian rooms remain wonderfully unaltered, the decoration and the contents faithfully reflecting the taste of William Windham II in the years after his return from the Grand Tour.

Nowhere is the effect of the quiet passage of time better seen than in the landscape around Felbrigg and its undulating parkland. The Great Wood of 600 acres or more that protects the house and the grazing of the park from the North Sea winds, was planted in the 17th century, but successive generations, and in particular William Windham III in the early 19th century, have developed it and have watched over the growth of the forest. At Felbrigg even the trees are rooted in history.

Fenton House, Hampstead, London

On west side of the Grove, north of Hampstead Underground station

With the discovery of mineral springs at the end of the 17th century, Hampstead developed into something of a spa, and London merchants and lesser gentry began to build substantial houses in and near the salubrious village on the heights. But it was still rural. In the 1820s, when Keats walked the six miles from Guy's Hospital to the Heath, it was largely along country roads, a long uphill pull from the city. Only in the second half of the 19th century was the village absorbed by the 'Great Wen' of London.

Built in the reign of William and Mary, Fenton House was among the most substantial houses of the early development. Neither the name of the family who built it, nor that of the architect they employed, are now known, but by 1793 the house had become the property of a Baltic merchant, a Mr Fenton, from whom it derives its name.

The house, built of deep brownish brick, stands in a large garden that still has almost a rural air. But for a Regency colonnade connecting the two bays on the east side, the exterior remains unaltered. There is a simple pediment on the main front, and a wooden dentilled cornice, painted white, supports a roof with widely projecting eaves. It is a simple, seemly design. Inside, some of the robust bolection (moulded panelling, typical of the late 17th century) survives.

The principal interest of Fenton House lies, however, in its contents: firstly, the furniture, and above all the porcelain owned by the late Lady Binning, who acquired the house in 1936, and left both the house and her collection to the Trust; and secondly, the collection of keyboard instruments

Fenton House; Garden façade

bequeathed by the late Major Benton Fletcher.

The Fenton House porcelain is chiefly notable for many examples of fine 18th-century German ware: there are pieces from the factories at Meissen, Fürstenberg, Nymphenburg, Frankenthal and Höchst, including Meissen figures and groups of the Commedia dell'Arte modelled by Kändler. Outstanding are a delicately modelled harlequin dated 1743, and a splendid green parakeet of 1741.

English 18th-century ceramics include representative pieces from the Chelsea, Bow, Derby, Plymouth and Bristol factories. Notable are a fine Chelsea red anchor group, 'Winter and Spring', a lovely shepherd and shepherdess from Plymouth, and sets of the Classical and Rustic Seasons

Fenton House; Virginal by Robert Hatley, 1664   *'Scaramouche' Meissen, c.1743*

from Bristol. By way of contrast there are charming Staffordshire pottery figures of the same period.

Oriental ceramics are well represented and include some fine early Sung, Korean, and Ming ware. There are also a large number of Chinese pieces made for the European export market during the K'ang-Hsi period between 1662 and 1722.

Among the musical instruments in the Benton Fletcher collection are a fine concert harpsichord made by Burkat Shudi in 1770, the largest model made in 18th-century England, and a single-manual harpsichord. Shudi, the partner and father-in-law of John Broadwood, was one of the best-known makers of his day. Jacob and Abraham Kirckman, partners in a rival firm, were the builders of two smaller two-manual instruments at Fenton House. There is also one of the few surviving 17th-century virginals, made in London in 1664 by Robert Hatley.

Spinets and clavichords are well represented, as are early pianos by Broadwood and, perhaps as a tribute to the pioneer of modern early keyboard instrument makers, a harpsichord by Arnold Dolmetsch dated 1925.

Florence Court, Co. Fermanagh

7 miles south-west of Enniskillen, 1 mile west of Florence Court village on A32

The first Cole settled at Enniskillen in 1607, but it was not until the early 18th century that the property acquired its romantic name. It was called after Florence Cole, who died in 1718, wife of John Cole, M.P. and High Sheriff. She was pronounced 'a virtuous young lady, of great renown'. She was also a considerable heiress and it was her wealthy son, another John Cole, created Lord Mountflorence, who built the present house in about 1760. The earldom of Enniskillen was conferred on his successor, and it was the 5th Earl, a much loved man of distinctly idiosyncratic character, whose son, Viscount Cole, gave Florence Court to the Trust in 1953.

The house, in surroundings that are romantic and wild, stands below the mournful mountains of Cuilcagh, whose bogs and savage wastes form at this point a formidable barrier between Northern Ireland and Eire. Majestic beeches, oaks and sycamores, planted some 200 years ago, complete the setting. In the demesne grow the famous Florence Court yews (*Taxus baccata* 'Fastigiata'), descendants of a pair found in the neighbourhood in 1770. These yews can only be propagated from cuttings, and seedlings revert to the common female berry-bearing type.

The tall three-storeyed mansion is linked by corridors with open arches to low flanking pavilions. The central bays of the main façade break forward and the centre of the house is given further emphasis by a pediment over the doorway and a Venetian window with flanking niches on the floor above. The windows have fat stone consoles, massive keystones, and heavy, toothed surrounds. Such features recall the work of James Gibbs, and the

elevation has a pronounced early Georgian flavour. Early Georgian no doubt it would be in London or Dublin, but this is remote Enniskillen and the date is after the middle of the century.

The entrance hall has the same *gravitas*, and its treatment – Doric order, frieze with triglyphs, pedimented doorway, solemn Gibbsian fireplace, and panels with swags of drapery – echoes the front elevation. After this the fanciful and spirited rococo plasterwork of the ceilings in the drawing room, dining room, and Venetian room, comes as a surprise. These ceilings and the plaster panels of the staircase hall – the staircase has fluted balusters and a handrail of tulipwood – are the great feature of the interior of the house. Nearly all the designs have their prototypes in Dublin houses decorated between 1745 and 1770, and the work was undoubtedly carried out by expert craftsmen from the capital.

Gawthorpe Hall, Lancashire

Off A671, on the Burnley side of Padiham

At the end of the 16th century, English domestic architecture, though still dependent on the past, was about to enter an exciting phase. The Palladian designs of Inigo Jones were no more than twenty years ahead, and a new class of professional architects was emerging, amongst whom is numbered Robert Smythson. For stylistic reasons it is thought possible to consider Gawthorpe Hall his work, thus linking this Lancashire house (built between 1600 and 1605 by a clergyman, the Rev. Richard Shuttleworth) to a group of nationally important houses, including Hardwick (see p. 118), Longleat and Wollaton. Gawthorpe is important architecturally in one other respect. The great hall does not lie parallel to the main axis of the house and is not entered directly from the porch as was usual in medieval and early Tudor houses, but is placed at right angles and to the side with the kitchen and offices below.

The drawing room with its fine plaster ceiling, panelling and fireplace is still in its original state, as is the ceiling of the long gallery on the top floor. However, the remainder of the house is substantially the work of Sir Charles Barry, who remodelled Gawthorpe for the Shuttleworth family between 1850 and 1852. The tower was heightened, an open-work parapet added, new pinnacles installed to accommodate extra chimney flues and some of the windows altered. Inside Barry constructed a new staircase, altered the entrance lobby and remade ceilings. Walls were given new wainscots and more fireplaces were added. The roof was repaired and the whole property modernized. An ambitious garden layout was prepared but not carried out until the 1890s; two of Barry's park lodges remain.

The Shuttleworth family had owned land in Lancashire since the 15th century but it was not until after the Reformation and through the practice of law that they became wealthy, as was the case with many newly-rich Elizabethans. Richard Shuttleworth, born in the early 1540s, became a successful London lawyer. Serjeant-at-Law in 1584, he was knighted and became Chief Justice of Chester in 1589. He invested his fortune in land, buying estates in Lancashire, Westmorland and Yorkshire. He married a daughter of Sir Peter Legh of Lyme (see p. 139) but died childless in 1599. The estates were inherited by his brother, Lawrence, Rector of Whichford in Warwickshire. Lawrence Shuttleworth was the builder of Gawthorpe but he died a bachelor and was succeeded by his nephew Richard, perhaps the most distinguished member of the family. High Sheriff for Lancashire,

Gawthorpe Hall; The entrance front

Member of Parliament, he became a colonel in the Parliamentary Army and fought an action in 1643 which put Lancashire decisively on Cromwell's side. Colonel Shuttleworth lived at Gawthorpe for sixty years and it was here that all his eleven children were born.

For the next 150 years the history of Gawthorpe was muted, as the house was rarely occupied by the family, who lived either in the south or elsewhere on their estates. Not until Janet Shuttleworth, heiress to Gawthorpe, returned to her ancestral home in 1836 at the age of eighteen, did its fortunes revive. Her husband, Dr James Kay, later Sir James Kay-Shuttleworth, Bt, commissioned Sir Charles Barry to renovate the house. Their son Ughtred was created a peer in 1902. The late Lord Shuttleworth presented the house to the National Trust in 1972. Gawthorpe is now let to Lancashire County Council and is used as part of a local College of Further Education. The remarkable collection of textiles, embroideries and lace made by the late Miss Rachel Kay-Shuttleworth is displayed in the house.

Grantham House, Grantham, Lincolnshire

In Castlegate, opposite the parish church

Within a stone's throw of the parish church, yet with its tranquil garden sloping down to the willow-fringed river Witham, Grantham is that agreeable phenomenon, a country house in a town – *rus in urbe*.

Though both Princess Margaret, daughter of Henry VII, and Cardinal Wolsey lodged at Grantham House, little remains of the medieval building except some 15th-century windows now situated on an internal staircase. The house we see today dates mainly from the 16th–18th centuries. The asymmetrical entrance front has a certain picturesque charm; features dated 1574 and 1737 speak of a mixed history. It is the garden front, however, which gives the house architectural distinction. This dignified façade is basically later-17th-century. The mullioned and transomed windows on

Grantham House; The garden façade

either side of the central pedimented doorway survive unchanged, though sashes and narrow glazing bars were inserted in the other windows in the late 18th century, when probably the stone front was rendered.

The panelling inside the house again tells of a mixed architectural history. The oak wainscot in the panelled room is of early 17th-century date and may be contrasted with the painted 18th-century panelling in the drawing room.

Ham House, Richmond, Surrey

South bank of the Thames, west of A307 at Petersham

Houses which strike, clear as a bell, the individual note of their times, have a special appeal. None strikes such a note with more precision, or with richer timbre, than Ham. Here in the house 'at the banks of the Sweetest River in the World', the late 17th century convincingly survives: gods and goddesses in parley on painted ceilings, Lely's court beauties on the walls, sumptuous damasks and velvets, repoussé silverwork, Delft tulip vases and K'ang-Hsi porcelain, lacquer chests on giltwood stands, ebonized and C-scrolled furniture, and *putti* everywhere. The rich and slightly raffish world of the Restoration and of the devious Cabal is wonderfully evoked.

We owe all this to the Duke and Duchess of Lauderdale, among the least attractive couples of their age. Lady Dysart, the heiress of Ham, though beautiful, quick and well-informed, was violently ambitious, 'and of a most ravenous covetousness'. Lauderdale, the powerful member of the Cabal, whom she married in 1671, was 'the coldest friend and the most violent enemy that ever was known'. Yet for all their faults, both had tremendous drive, and a love of the rich and luxurious. The results are apparent at Ham.

The house which the heiress inherited was built in 1610. The plan was the familiar H, with a large hall in the centre lit by windows on both sides and with a staircase at one end. Her father had already made alterations, and in 1637 had replaced the original staircase by the splendid staircase which exists today and which is an early example of a type more usual after the Restoration. Two years after marriage the Lauderdales, who must have found the Jacobean character of their house very old-fashioned, embarked on extensive changes. Among other things they doubled the depth of the central block by filling in the space between the uprights of the H on the south front, so providing new suites of rooms. When they had finished, Ham, inside and out, looked much as it does today, though in about 1730 the 4th Earl of Dysart, the great-grandson of the Duchess, was to rebuild the bays with Venetian windows on the south front and to introduce some splendid Georgian furniture.

On the interior of the house the Lauderdales expressed their taste and their wealth in a profusion of lavish decoration. Ham is nothing if not sumptuous, and the celebrated silver chimney furniture in many of the rooms – silver-mounted tongs, shovels, bellows and so on – are in keeping with the spirit of the house. Plaster ceilings, chimneypieces, grained panel-

Ham House; The entrance front

ling and parquetry floors, were all designed to contribute to the total effect and were executed by the finest craftsmen.

Verrio, who was working for Lauderdale's master at Windsor, was called in to paint a ceiling, and there are eight portraits by Lely's hand in the long gallery. Many of the other pictures, mostly by Dutch artists, were specially commissioned for the house. Dutch craftsmen were also employed on the furniture, and many pieces have a distinctly Netherlands flavour. What is unusual is that in room after room the Lauderdales would today recognize the furniture that figures in their 17th-century inventories. This fortunate survival is partly due to the fact that it was stored for long periods in the 18th

Ham House; Sir Peter Lely: The Duke and Duchess of Lauderdale

116

century. The total effect, the sense of warmth and colour, owes much to the splendid hangings, the tapestries, silk damasks, and cut velvets, in which Ham is probably richer than any other contemporary house.

The garden, too, is a rare survivor of a formal 17th-century layout, with terrace, parterre and wilderness. Generous benefactions from Mr Kenneth Levy, the Stanley Smith Horticultural Foundation, and an anonymous donor enabled the Trust to undertake its restoration in 1975, to mark European Architectural Heritage Year. Today it appears once again much as it did when it delighted Evelyn on a visit in 1678.

Hanbury Hall, Hereford & Worcester

2½ miles east of Droitwich, 1 mile north of the B4090 road to Alcester

This essentially English house speaks clearly of the Age of Wren and was built, as the date on the entrance front proclaims, in 1701. The owner was Thomas Vernon (1654–1721), an eminent barrister who sat as Member of Parliament for the City of Worcester. Though he employed as his architect a certain William Rudhall, of whom almost nothing is known, the style of Hanbury strongly reflects the influence of William Talman who was so prolific a designer of country houses towards the turn of the century (see pp. 33, 103).

The red-brick house with hipped roofs, rises, orderly and dignified, across a Victorian forecourt. The five-bay centre of the entrance front carries a pediment on giant columns, and is flanked by projecting wings of three bays. A porch with Corinthian columns, set below a window with Baroque volutes that are very much in Talman's manner, gives directly on the large entrance hall. The hall and staircase are the important internal

Hanbury Hall from the forecourt

features of Hanbury. The hall ceiling is painted in monochrome *trompe l'œil*, emblematic of the seasons, probably by an assistant of James Thornhill, while the walls and ceiling of the open well staircase are decorated with murals executed by Thornhill himself. They represent scenes from classical mythology, and surprisingly enough the figure of Dr Sacheverell about to be torn by the Furies. The trial of the notorious doctor, who was found guilty of preaching a seditious sermon, occurred in 1710, and the painting must have been commissioned soon after.

Such painted ceilings and staircases were in the height of fashion in grand houses between the Restoration and the death of Queen Anne in 1714, and were nearly all carried out by a trio of master decorators – Verrio, Laguerre, and Thornhill (see p. 32) – who worked in the exuberant manner of the later Italian Baroque. Thornhill had risen to sudden fame when commissioned in 1708 to paint the great hall at Greenwich, and Thomas Vernon was fortunate to have been able to persuade him to execute his spirited murals in the remote Worcestershire countryside.

Hardly any original Vernon furniture survives in the house, apart from the excellent bust of the founder in the hall. However, the drawing room has been brought to life again and furnished by the Merrill Trust in the United States. The fine Watney collection of porcelain and flower paintings is displayed in the Long Room.

In the early 18th century there was a large formal garden to the west of the house. This has disappeared, but the orangery survives. A carved basket of flowers adorns the pediment, and the orangery is a delightful example of a type of building which first became fashionable in the reign of William and Mary.

Hardwick Hall, Derbyshire

6½ miles north-west of Mansfield, 9½ miles south-east of Chesterfield, south of Glapwell on A617

In writing of Hardwick it is difficult to avoid hyperbole. Its architecture, atmosphere and contents set it apart from other houses. A nonpareil that history and chance have miraculously preserved, it evokes the end of the Elizabethan era and the early 17th century with complete authenticity.

Built between 1591 and 1597 by Bess of Hardwick, that tough and talented Elizabethan with a passion for architecture and a flair for marrying rich husbands, it is one of a small group of houses of the period which have no Continental parallel. For once, English architecture pays no tribute to France, Italy, or Holland. Our original native contribution to Gothic was the Perpendicular style; after the Reformation when fewer churches were built, craftsmen were still familiar with the idiom, and the Perpendicular found domestic expression in a handful of houses such as Hardwick, Wollaton, and Wotton. The great façade of Hardwick, its symmetry, its huge expanse of window ('Hardwick Hall, more glass than wall') is only understandable in terms of the last and wholly English phase of Medieval Gothic.

Bess of Hardwick employed Robert Smythson to design her mansion, but she no doubt influenced him as firmly as she seems to have influenced everyone who came within her orbit. The inside is as remarkable as the exterior, and the plan has one strikingly original feature. The two-storeyed entrance hall, the late-16th-century equivalent of the medieval great hall, is not situated parallel to the façade but, for almost the first time in the history of English architecture, at right angles to it. This hall, entered at the end of its long axis through a screen of stone pillars, the vestigial remains of the medieval screens, runs across the building from front to back. The innovation greatly facilitated the symmetrical planning which the Renaissance had made fashionable.

The elaborate chimneypiece of painted plaster strapwork in the hall is the first of a series of contemporary chimneypieces in stone, marble and plaster, and the entrance hall is a worthy introduction to the sequence of state apartments culminating in the Long Gallery and the High Great Chamber. The latter with the light flooding through the huge windows and with its deep painted frieze and 16th-century tapestries must surely be one of the most satisfying rooms of its period in Europe.

But the appeal of Hardwick is in something more than its architecture, its friezes, chimneypieces and panelling. Time has laid little hand on it. Bess of Hardwick's formidable eye would not find much changed. Her favourite second son was created Earl of Cavendish in 1618, and well before the end of the century the great mansion of Chatsworth had become the family seat. On the hilltop above its quiet parkland, Hardwick, a secondary residence or a dower house, was providentially isolated from the currents of taste and fashion.

Hardwick Hall; The south façade

Hardwick Hall; The High Great Chamber   *Long Gallery*

In her eighty-first year, and four years after she had moved into her new home, Bess of Hardwick compiled an inventory in which were listed all the important rooms and their contents. After over three and a half centuries many of the things she prized still remain in the house. Thus in the High Great Chamber there are half a dozen 16th-century pieces, astonishing survivals, including such things as a card table with parquetry inlay top of about 1580.

But it is for its 16th- and 17th-century tapestries, and above all for its collection of 16th-century embroideries, that Hardwick is justly famous. No comparable collection of Elizabethan embroidery survives. The majority of pieces can undoubtedly be attributed to the workrooms, if not to the needle, of Bess herself, and many can be identified from the inventory she made in 1601. In the entrance hall are hangings unique in England; patchworks depicting allegorical subjects, they were probably made out of rich copes and altar frontals from the dissolved monasteries. Many of the finest embroideries were table-carpets, made at a time when carpets were more often draped over tables than spread on the floor. Others are cushions, pillow cases, and hangings for state beds. The beauty and virtuosity of the work, no less than its quantity, are breathtaking.

Time has also spared the setting of the house. The gnarled stag-headed oaks of the park are rooted as deeply in history as in the Derbyshire soil. The walled entrance court with its elaborate cresting, though once paved, survives from the 16th century, and the garden on the south front, though it has lost the formal elaboration of knots and parterres, retains its original shape and axial avenues. The 18th-century improvers who created the great landscapes at Chatsworth were never summoned to Hardwick and the ghost of the Elizabethan garden survives. The Trust has recreated a herb garden such as must once have existed and of which Francis Bacon would have approved.

Hardy's Cottage, Higher Bockhampton, Dorset

3 miles north-east of Dorchester, ½ mile south of A35

> It faces west, and round the back and sides
> High beeches, bending, hang a veil of boughs,
> And sweep against the roof.

So Hardy wrote of the modest thatched cottage, built by his great-grandfather in 1800, where he grew up. Architecturally the cottage has little to distinguish it from others of the period, though there is a squint in the porch said to have been inserted to enable Hardy's grandfather, who sometimes smuggled brandy, to watch the lane for the excisemen, and there is also a little office with barred windows where Hardy's father, a master builder, kept his money and ledgers, and paid his men through a pay window opening on to 'Egdon' Heath.

Hardy's Cottage

The interest of the place is in its associations: the room where Hardy was born in 1840; the room where, at a table by the window, he wrote *Under the Greenwood Tree* (1872) and *Far from the Madding Crowd* (1874), when abandoning his career as an architect he returned to his birthplace to write; and the sitting room, where for parties a barrel of cider was brought in from the woodshed and four fiddlers played in the corner.

Hatchlands, Surrey

East of East Clandon, on north side of the A246 Guildford/Leatherhead road

Admiral of the Blue the Hon. Edward Boscawen, a naval hero in his day, began this pleasant red-brick house in 1756. Though the architect is unknown, the Admiral two years later engaged for the interior decoration the services of a young man just returned from the Grand Tour, by name Robert Adam. The special interest of Hatchlands derives from his work in the library, drawing room, and staircase hall. It was Adam's first recorded commission as a decorator, and although the style is unlike the Adams' late manner it has already moved some way from the masculinity of conventional Palladian.

Both the library and drawing room retain Adam's sculptured marble chimneypieces, and elaborate plaster ceilings. The latter, which incorporate nautical symbols in honour of the Admiral, are models of sensitive yet robust design. Adam's staircase was modified in the 1790s when Giuseppe Bonomi, who also altered the little entrance hall that gives on the garden, introduced a large window on the half-landing. A large music room was added in 1888–90 to designs by Halsey Ricardo.

H. S. Goodhart-Rendel, the distinguished architectural historian, who was tenant for life of Hatchlands, gave the property to the Trust in 1944.

Hatchlands;
Drawing room chimney-
piece and overmantel,
designed by Robert Adam

Hill Top, Near Sawrey, Lancashire

Between Esthwaite Water and Windermere, 2 miles south-east of Hawkshead

Unpretentious, with rubble walls, slate roof, and 'cottage' garden, Hill Top is a good example of a typical 17th-century Lakeland farmhouse. Chance, which brought Beatrix Potter as a young woman to Sawrey village in the summer of 1896 and enabled her to buy the house soon after, has also made it something different, for her imaginative genius peopled the house she loved with the creatures of her fancy, creatures which half a century later have acquired for children and grown-ups a reality that is absolute. Hill Top, a modest dwelling in the Lake District, belongs to the timeless world of the imagination. It is not even Beatrix Potter's house, but the farm of Jemima Puddleduck and Tom Kitten's home; Cousin Kitty knocks at the front door, and up the narrow garden path comes the policeman looking for Pigling Bland.

Beatrix Potter was nearly thirty before her animal fantasies began to take shape and before the publication of her first book, *The Tale of Peter Rabbit*. Hill Top she found 'as nearly perfect a place as I ever lived in'. After a constricted and conventional upbringing, it spelled self-expression and release, and it was intimately associated with the years in which she produced her series of minor masterpieces. In 1913 at the age of forty-seven, on her marriage to William Heelis, she moved across the road to Castle Cottage. The move and the marriage coincided with the end of her truly creative period. Perhaps this was one reason why she kept Hill Top as a sort of private sanctuary, and could not bring herself to sell or alter it. The house was too closely associated with her first independence from her authoritarian parents and her discovery of a unique literary talent.

With its little windows and creaking stairs, its beams, nooks and corners, the angular shadowy cottage is as she left it. This is its fascination. Moreover, the contents of Hill Top are not only the things with which she surrounded herself in the years when she lived there – modest 'cottagey' things, pottery ware, oak furniture, and the vernacular art of the Lake District – but often enough they provide the background material, the stage properties, as it were, for the delicate and sensitive illustrations to her books. In the doll's house is the very food that Tom Thumb and Hunca Munca stole, and throughout the house are simple objects which have acquired familiarity and distinction in her drawings.

Next door, the small pub – the Tower Bank Arms – is now also owned by the Trust. It is illustrated in *The Tale of Jemima Puddleduck*. Beatrix Potter left Hill Top to the Trust in 1944. But she left much more. For many years she had been vigilant and active in the conservation of the Lake District. She ensured that over 4,000 acres in the country that she loved, including estates at Troutbeck, Tilberthwaite, and Monk Coniston, came into the Trust's keeping.

Hughenden Manor, Buckinghamshire

$1\frac{1}{2}$ miles north of High Wycombe on the A4128 Great Missenden road

Disraeli had been in Parliament for ten years when, in 1847, feeling that the time was ripe for the future leader of the Conservative Party to become a landed proprietor, he set out to acquire the Hughenden estate. The purchase price of £35,000 was raised with difficulty, but in the summer of 1848 he was able to write to his devoted wife, Mary Anne: 'It is all done, you are the Lady of Hughenden.'

The house which Disraeli bought was a stuccoed building of simple appearance and characteristic of many country houses of about 1800. Under Mrs Disraeli's direction Hughenden was clothed in brick and wholly re-modelled, with the addition of parapets and finials, in what can best be described as Victorian Tudor.

The house, surrounded by a sweeping park and set off by a new terraced garden 'in the Italian style', was delightfully situated. Almost every year when Parliament was in recess Disraeli and his wife retreated there. He cared particularly for the autumn woods and one year noted 'the limes all golden, the beeches ruddy brown, while the oaks and elms and pines are still dark and green ...' The Disraelis were happy at Hughenden, and it became a sadder place on his wife's death in 1872. But Disraeli remained devoted to the house and in the last few months of his life was often there alone. He chose to be so. A young secretary coming into the library where the ageing statesman seemed to be dozing in front of the fire heard him murmur: 'Dreams ... dreams'. Though he died in London, he gave instructions that his body should return to Hughenden. He is buried with his wife in the graveyard beside the church in the park.

Though Disraeli's nephew, Coningsby, made certain alterations, the interior of Hughenden with dark panelling, fan-vaulting, moulded plaster-work and Tudor overtones, still strikes a note of which Mary Anne Disraeli would have approved, and its furnishings, so many of which Disraeli himself

Hughenden Manor; The entrance

*Hughenden Manor;
Disraeli's study*

*Benjamin Disraeli
as a young man*

knew, movingly evoke the statesman and his times. There are the portraits of his family, friends and political associates, and in the drawing room, looking out across the terraced garden as the young couple themselves must often have done, are portraits of Disraeli and his bride by Alfred Edward Chalon. In the library are the books that reflect the literary tastes of a great man who was at the same time politician and novelist. 'I have a passion', Disraeli wrote, 'for books and trees. I like to look at them. When I come down to Hughenden I pass the first week in sauntering about my park and examining all the trees, and then I saunter in the library and survey the books.' Other rooms – the Disraeli Room, the Politician's Room, the Berlin Congress Room – illustrate further aspects and predilections of a man whose character remains as fascinating and enigmatic today as it was to his contemporaries. Perhaps most evocative is Disraeli's study, where portraits of his father and mother hang over the fireplace. On the writing table is the paper heavily edged with black that he always used after his wife's death, and on the bookshelves stand his wife's diaries, his schoolbooks, and some of the novels which he wrote in this room.

Ickworth, Suffolk

3 miles south-west of Bury St Edmunds, on west side of A143

The extraordinary creation of a far from ordinary man, Ickworth must be one of the most unusual houses in England. Although a local architect, Francis Sandys, was employed, the inspiration for Ickworth must have come from its creator, Frederick Augustus Hervey, 4th Earl of Bristol and Bishop of Derry. In 1775 the Earl-Bishop had built Downhill in Co.

Ickworth

Londonderry and in 1787 Ballyscullion on the shores of Lough Beg. The latter, in which he lost interest soon after it was roofed, together with Belle Isle on Lake Windermere, the Pantheon, Bernini's Colonnades at St Peter's and his S. Andrea at Quirinale, served as the model for Ickworth. Building started in the 1790s and on the Earl-Bishop's death in 1803 was interrupted for some twenty years. Parts of the interior remain unfinished even today.

Now chiefly remembered as a notable dilettante, it is well to recall that Frederick Hervey, on his elevation to the see of Derry in 1768, proved not only a conscientious prelate but a ready friend to both Catholics and Protestants. In the acerbated religious and political climate of 18th-century Ireland, the Earl-Bishop was on the side of humanity and good sense. He was also an inveterate traveller and collector. Ickworth was intended to house the spoils of his continental tours. He planned a collection of 'few pictures but choice ones', and 'to have my galleries to exhibit an historical progress of the art of painting both in Germany and Italy, and that divided into its characteristical schools – Venice, Bologna, Florence, etc.' But in 1798 the French invaded Italy, occupied Rome and confiscated his collections. The Earl-Bishop himself was imprisoned for nine months and on his release remained in Italy where, on the road to Albano, he died of gout.

The great house that he left embodies the standard Palladian plan of centre-block, wings and pavilions, but the centre-block at Ickworth is an ellipse of three storeys with two orders of columns, topped with a frieze by Flaxman illustrating themes from Homer, and is crowned by a dome which rises a hundred feet to the balustraded parapet that surrounds the central skylight. Semi-elliptical wings sweep forward to join the rotunda to the large rectangular pavilions.

The interior of the rotunda is mainly of the 1820s, and the large rooms with their strangely shaped external walls contain paintings by Reynolds and Gainsborough, fine 18th- and 19th-century French and English furniture and silver. As a sculptural centrepiece, lit by the dome skylight a hundred feet above, stands Flaxman's 'Fury of Athamas'. The statue was commissioned by the Earl-Bishop in Rome in 1790 for 600 guineas and illustrates, as well as anything can, the energy, enthusiasm and tastes of one of the most eccentric figures of the late 18th century.

The astonishing collection of Ickworth silver we owe mainly to the Earl-Bishop's predecessors. The 1st and 2nd Earls of Bristol bought extensively and with great discrimination from many of the leading silversmiths of the day, and the 1st Earl was clearly much taken with the elaborate designs introduced by the Huguenot craftsmen from France. The Ickworth collection, ranging from the works of late-17th-century makers to those of Paul Storr, comprises outstanding examples by the hand of such famous silversmiths as Pierre Platel, Philip Rollos, Paul de Lamerie, Paul Crespin, and Frederick Kändler.

Knightshayes Court, Devon

2 miles north of Tiverton

Inventor, mill owner and philanthropist, John Heathcoat, born in Derbyshire in 1783, was one of the giants of the Industrial Revolution. He was also a man who took unexpected decisions. After his lace mill in the Midlands was wrecked by Luddites in 1816, he moved, lock, stock and barrel, to Tiverton, where he re-established the thriving business which still

Knightshayes Court; The north front

Knightshayes Court; The terrace garden

operates as John Heathcoat and Company. It was his grandson John Heathcoat-Amory, Liberal M.P. for Tiverton, a baronet (1874) and a famous master of foxhounds, who built Knightshayes Court in the 1860s, employing William Burges, one of the most talented of Victorian architects. The exterior of the house exemplifies Burges's uncompromising and highly personal style, though unfortunately he was never able to carry out his elaborate decorative scheme for the interior. The house contains a small collection of old master paintings.

However it is for the remarkable garden developed since the Second World War by the late Sir John Heathcoat-Amory (grandson of the builder) and his wife that most people visit Knightshayes today. Though the entrance drive, the large lawns near the house and the terrace below the south front were part of Burges's original design, the garden assumed its present character and extent after 1950 to reach some twenty-five acres by the time of Sir John's death in 1973. They had begun by planting and extending the garden within the framework of the first Sir John's woodlands. Close to the house the elaborate 19th-century layout of the terrace was simplified and replanted. The pool garden with statues set against the hedges (the yew hedges east of the house date from the 1880s) and the formal paved garden adjoining were complete by 1959. Steps lead to the garden-in-the-wood, developed in the early 1960s with bulbs, flowers and shrubs beneath the light shade. To the north and east more woods were developed encompassing the glade overlooking a recently planted arboretum. West of the drive a large, mature planting of mollis azaleas and rhododendron was thinned and a pool enlarged in 1972 to make a setting for a new willow garden. In all parts of the garden at Knightshayes there are fine trees, especially chestnut, limes and oak, including an exceptional specimen of Turkey oak in the park below the house.

Erddig, Clwyd; East front from the garden

Little Moreton Hall, Cheshire; 16th century

*Montacute House, Somerset; 1688–98;
West front*

*Smallhythe Place, East Sussex; Late
15th century; Ellen Terry's house*

Knole, Kent

At the Tonbridge end of Sevenoaks on A21

This great, grave house, its jumbled pile set on the contours of the rounded hill or knoll from which it takes its name, is one of the largest private houses in England. Here is no unified concept or overall design, rather an organic growth, so that in essence Knole is the 'grand relation of those small manor houses which hide themselves away so innumerably among the counties'. Seen from any angle, what impresses is the vast size. The four acres of buildings of grey-brown Kentish stone, the irregular roof lines with brown-red tiles topped by slim brick chimneystacks, the battlemented towers, the turrets and gables, seem more like a fortified medieval town or collegiate establishment than the home of a single family – save perhaps a royal or princely one. In the course of its long history, Knole was indeed both a king's and an archbishop's palace before becoming the home of the Sackville family for ten generations.

Knole is first referred to in 1291, but its history is obscure until 1456, when Sir William Fiennes, Lord Saye and Sele, sold the manor for £266 13s. 4d. to Thomas Bourchier, Archbishop of Canterbury. The Archbishop built much of the present house, transforming the rough medieval manor into a palace fit for the Primate of England. Though it is hard to determine exactly what parts of Knole date from his time and that of his successor, Cardinal Morton, Bourchier was responsible for extensive alterations and additions, including the gatehouse named after him, the great hall, and the original solar, on which the Jacobean 'ballroom' was grafted. In 1538 Henry VIII obliged the reluctant Cranmer to 'deliver his house up into the King's hands'. Henry spent considerable sums but little time at Knole.

Knole

In 1566 Queen Elizabeth gave Knole to her cousin Thomas Sackville but it was not until 1603 that he was able to buy out the sitting tenants. Thomas Sackville, created Lord Buckhurst in 1567 and Earl of Dorset in 1604, was the son of Richard Sackville, descendant of a Sussex family of Norman origin, a man so wealthy that he was known as 'Fillsack'. His son has a small but respectable place in literary history as the author of *Gorboduc*, the earliest English tragedy in blank verse. He deserted poetry for politics when young and held various high offices of state under Elizabeth and James I. He spent enormous sums on enlarging and adorning Knole – no less than £40,000 in ten months; bills survive showing payments to masons, glaziers, plasterers and upholsterers, and upwards of three hundred Italian workmen were imported. To him we owe very largely the existing silhouette of the house and much of the interior, including the long galleries, with panelled walls and richly plastered ceilings, a type of room so characteristic of large Elizabethan houses. But, again, what makes Knole so exceptional is its scale. Where most great Elizabethan houses have one long gallery, Knole has three, each with an adjoining state bedroom.

The state apartments are largely furnished with the original Jacobean and Caroline furniture for which Knole is renowned, many of the pieces being literally unique. Rows of cross-legged wide-backed chairs, upholstered in their original velvets and brocades and many with their attendant stools, line the panelled walls.

The 2nd Earl succeeded his father in 1608, but lived only a year, and the 3rd Earl proved a disaster. He sold or mortgaged much of the London property which was the basis of the Sackville fortune. He is remembered principally for his marriage to the strong-minded Lady Anne Clifford, heiress of the Earl of Cumberland, who left a remarkable diary describing her quarrelsome, unhappy years at Knole. The Civil War affected the Sackvilles more than many royalist families, for the wife of the 4th Earl was governess to the children of Charles I. Knole was plundered by Parliamentary cavalry, the 4th Earl's younger son was captured and executed in Abingdon, and the estate was sequestered. The 5th Earl, Richard Sackville, married another heiress, Lady Frances Cranfield, daughter of the Earl of Middlesex, who brought another title, money and furnishings into the family. Their son Charles, the 6th Earl, is described by Dryden as 'the best good man, with the worst-natured Muse'. He was a courtier of the Restoration, poet and patron of poets, a 'munificent, rakish, witty and florid figure'. Wycherley, Prior and Dryden were his guests, Kneller painted his portrait, and Pope wrote his epitaph. But the end of his life was sad, his mind gave way and his third wife kept him 'in a sort of captivity in Bath'. The 7th Earl, who succeeded in 1706, was created Duke of Dorset and served George I and II in various high offices. The 3rd Duke, John Frederick, was a resplendent figure with talent and charm in plenty. He had excellent taste and added silver, paintings, and furniture to the splendid collection of his forebears. He was the friend and patron of Reynolds (in all he owned twenty-two paintings by this artist) and he contributed the best-known piece of sculpture at Knole – the nude plaster of his Italian mistress who

Knole; Giannetta Baccelli, mistress of the 3rd
Duke of Dorset

Sir Joshua Reynolds, P.R.A.:
John Frederick Sackville,
3rd Duke of Dorset

now lies demurely and comfortably prone at the foot of the great staircase.
This gay and gifted peer was British ambassador in Paris from 1783 to 1789.
He married at forty-five and died nine years later in the same sad condition
of mind as his father and great-grandfather, leaving a five-year-old heir.
When he was killed coursing hares in Ireland just after his twenty-first
birthday, the dukedom went to a cousin and became extinct on his death.

Knole was eventually inherited through the female line by a descendant
of the 4th Duke. He succeeded to the title of Baron Sackville, created in
1876, and was the grandfather of Victoria Sackville-West, the writer and
creator of Sissinghurst (see p. 252). On the death of her father in 1928, the
title and the property were inherited by Major-General Sir Charles
Sackville-West, 4th Baron Sackville, through whose generosity Knole
passed into the keeping of the National Trust in 1946.

Knole stands in a large and beautiful park, with clumps of broad oaks, tall
beeches, coverts of bracken, low hills and valleys. The deer-cropped turf
laps the entrance front and the massive Elizabethan wall which encloses
twenty-six acres of garden. The long, low entrance front has 'a beautiful
decent simplicity', as Horace Walpole wrote, 'which charms one'. Jacobean
gables flank the gateway tower, known as the Wicket, leading to the Green
Court, which is strongly reminiscent of the quadrangle of an Oxford college.
Beyond this and entered under the archway of Bourchier's gatehouse lies
the Stone Court. Here the hand of several generations is represented.
Bourchier's late-15th-century work is topped by Thomas Sackville's early-
17th-century gables; an Ionic colonnade dated 1743 which supports a
balcony bears the initials of Lionel, 1st Duke of Dorset. Above the balcony
is a stone wreath brought from another family property in the reign of
Charles II. One side of the Stone Court, so called from the flags which pave
it, is taken up by Bourchier's great hall, much altered by Thomas Sackville.

Knole; The Great Hall   *The Cartoon Gallery*

He added oak panelling, plaster ceiling, and the elaborately carved oak
screen two storeys high. Victoria Sackville-West relates in her history *Knole
and the Sackvilles* how 'it has sometimes happened that I have found a stag
in the banqueting hall, puzzled but still dignified, strayed in from the park'.

Beyond the hall, the stairs, decorated with typical Jacobean grisaille
murals and curiously small in scale, lead to the incomparable series of
galleries and state rooms above. The Brown Gallery, longest and narrowest
of the galleries, lined with 17th-century chairs and stools, leads to the suite
known as Lady Betty's Rooms. Here Lady Betty Germaine, a prim widow
and friend of the family, lived in the time of George II. The Spangled
Bedroom (which takes its name from the particular kind of appliqué strapwork embroidery found on the bed hangings and furniture) also gives off the
Brown Gallery, and in turn leads to the Leicester Gallery, with its Charles I
billiard table and the famous Knole settee. The adjoining Venetian
Ambassador's bedroom, with a William and Mary window and fireplace,
strikes a later architectural note. The huge four-poster, carved and gilded,
with green velvet hangings, is one of the most sumptuous in the house and
bears the cypher of James II. It is one of the two royal state beds acquired –
together with other furniture from Whitehall – by the 6th Earl as 'per-
quisites' of the Lord Chamberlain. The gilt furniture is probably by
Thomas Roberts at the turn of the 17th century; the Flemish tapestries are
very fine late-16th-century work.

The Ballroom, large and very grand, is in fact a structure of the late 15th
century, but the panelling and decoration are early-17th-century. The
panelling below a richly carved frieze is painted white. The ceiling is in
elaborate plasterwork, and the floor-to-ceiling marble mantelpiece, engraved with the Sackville arms, adds to the generally ornate effect. The
furniture too is richly ornamented, being an amalgam of many periods. On
the walls hang portraits of all the Sackville owners of Knole.

The 18th century is recalled in the crimson drawing room, with paintings by Gainsborough, Hoppner and Reynolds of notable figures like Dr Johnson and Garrick, and the 3rd Duke's Chinese servant boy, as well as family portraits.

The richest of all the state rooms is, however, the adjoining Cartoon Gallery, its name deriving from the copies of Raphael's cartoons which almost cover the faded rose-red velvet walls. The surrounds of the tall Jacobean windows are elaborately carved, coloured and gilded; the ceiling is embellished with delicate floral plasterwork; the splendid marble mantelpiece is the equal of that in the Ballroom. The furniture dates from Charles II's time, as does that in the adjoining King's Bedroom. The latter, sometimes called the Silver Room, contains a unique state bed, of the second half of the 17th century, with hangings of gold and silver thread, all topped by ostrich plumes, and said to have cost the equivalent of £40,000. The famous silver furniture is also Caroline, comprising chased and ornamented sconces, tables and mirrors. The simpler Georgian dressing set, complete down to a silver eye-bath, is dated 1743.

From all these great rooms, through Tudor mullions or Georgian sash windows, the gardens may be glimpsed – formal walks and beds, fruit trees and roses, shrubs and tree plantings. Beyond lies the park, a landscape that has hardly changed since Thomas Sackville first saw it some four centuries ago.

Lamb House, Rye, East Sussex

In West Street, facing west end of the church

The Lambs, who were the greatest power in Rye for a century and a half, would be surprised to learn that the house they built was famous as the home of an expatriate American novelist. James Lamb completed Lamb House in 1723, a residence befitting the town's chief burgess, for in the same year he was chosen mayor for the first time. Three years later George I, returning from Hanover to open Parliament, was driven ashore on Camber Sands and lodged, snowbound, for four nights at Lamb House. Mrs Lamb, who had to give up the best bedroom, was delivered of a boy on the night of the King's arrival. The latter acted as godfather at the christening and the boy naturally received the name of George.

It cannot have been an easy visit, for His Majesty spoke almost no English and the Lambs had no German. But James Lamb was equal to most occasions. He was to be elected Mayor of Rye thirteen times – the mayoralty was to become almost a family appanage and his son held the office for twenty terms – and to found the family dynasty which controlled the corporation and managed the return of the rotten borough's two Members of Parliament in the interests of the Dukes of Newcastle and of the Whigs until the Reform Bill of 1831. As so often happened, the rotten borough filled a useful role and sent to Parliament two future Prime Ministers, Robert Jenkinson and Arthur Wellesley, later respectively Earl of Liverpool and Duke of Wellington.

In the 1860s the Lambs sold Lamb House. Thirty years later Henry James saw it when visiting Rye and was captivated. He first took a lease and two years later, in 1899, bought it for £2,000. The brick-fronted early Georgian House remained, and still remains, little altered. It has one or two pleasant panelled rooms and a good staircase with twisted balusters, all characteristic of its period.

When Henry James moved in, he had just celebrated his fifty-fifth birthday and was already an established literary figure on both sides of the Atlantic. He spent much of the last eighteen years of his life in the house and wrote there the complex novels of his final period. *The Awkward Age* (1899) was the first to be written at Lamb House, and among its famous successors were *The Wings of the Dove* (1902), *The Ambassadors* (1903) and *The Golden Bowl* (1904). In the autumn and winter he wrote in the green room on the first floor, but in the summer months he resorted to a charming pavilion in the garden whence his rich voice could be heard through the open window booming to his amanuensis as he dictated, and she took down on the typewriter, his endless involuted periods. (The garden-pavilion, con- temporary with the house, was destroyed by an enemy bomb in 1940.)

After 1899 Lamb House became a place of resort or pilgrimage for most of the distinguished literary figures of the time. Wells, Beerbohm, Belloc, Chesterton, Conrad, Ford Madox Ford, Gosse, Kipling, and not least Edith

Lamb House

Wharton who was a frequent visitor, were entertained there. The longer he lived at Lamb House, the more James came to love it. 'All the good things that I hoped of the place', he wrote, 'have, in fact, properly blossomed and flourished'; and again, 'the quiet essential amiability of Lamb House only deepens with experience'. One of his greatest delights was the large tranquil garden, though he left its management strictly to his competent gardener and never attempted to establish an intimate relationship with his plants. He was at Lamb House, in failing health, for the last time in the autumn of 1915, a few months before he died.

In 1950, Mrs Henry James Jr, the widow of James's nephew (son of his philosopher brother William James), presented Lamb House to the Trust. The small white-panelled Henry James Room contains some of the novelist's furniture and part of his library, together with many of the known likenesses of James, including the Sargent portraits, in original or reproduction. These enable the visitor to form a clear idea of how Henry James looked from boyhood to old age.

Lanhydrock, Cornwall

$2\frac{1}{2}$ miles south of Bodmin on B3268

In 1620 Richard Robartes, merchant and banker of Truro, bought the manor of Lanhydrock. Though briefly sequestered by the Royalists in the Civil War, it was to remain in the family until his descendant, the 7th Viscount Clifden, gave the property to the Trust in 1953.

Richard Robartes did not live to see his new house at Lanhydrock, which

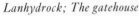
Lanhydrock; The gatehouse

was completed by his son about 1640. The foursquare granite mansion built round a courtyard – the east side was demolished in 1780, giving the house its present plan – made no concession to modernity and followed the sober pattern of many Cornish houses of a generation earlier. By contrast the charming little two-storeyed gatehouse, not finished until 1651, with its gay proliferation of obelisks, strikes an almost Renaissance note.

A disastrous fire in 1881 destroyed most of the house, sparing little beyond the porch with its coat of arms and the north wing. The long gallery in the north wing was fortunately undamaged, and the plasterwork in this fine barrel-vaulted room – it is 116 feet long – enables one to appreciate the robust work of the local craftsmen who in the 17th century must have decorated much of the house.

Lanhydrock was rebuilt to the original plan after the fire. Some of the rooms as reinstated have a considerable period charm. The smoking room, and the billiard room with all its appointments, are particularly evocative of a recent but vanished age. The kitchen quarters, planned on a splendid scale and complete with all their fittings, conjure up visions of the *haute cuisine* practised there until 1969, when the last Miss Robartes of Lanhydrock died in the house. There is some good furniture, such as a fine upholstered suite of the time of George II and two Louis XIV *Boulle* writing tables, and tapestries of Brussels and Mortlake manufacture. The collection of family portraits includes works by Kneller, Hudson, Romney and Richmond.

Protected by ageing beechwoods that surround the park, Lanhydrock

Lanhydrock; The long gallery

with its church and charming gatehouse are approached by a famous avenue of beeches and sycamores, some of the latter planted as long ago as 1648. Probably the original garden round the house was swept away, as so often happened in the 18th century, when the park was brought up to the walls. The formal garden that now precedes the forecourt dates from Victorian times. The low enclosing wall carries finials resembling those on the gatehouse, and there are several bronze vases by Ballin, goldsmith to Louis XIV, which came from Bagatelle, embellishments for the new scheme laid out in 1857. The lawns, set with sentinel yews, contain rosebeds, and boxhedges treated in the knot-garden style. (There is a second garden near the fine old barn, which has been replanted with unusual herbaceous plants for summer interest.)

The first Lord Robartes started the collection of trees before 1634, but his descendant, Lord Clifden, was the creator of the informal plantings – extending from the church and house around the hillside – from 1930 onwards. There are many large magnolias, such as *M. campbellii, M. mollicomata, M. veitchii, M. obovata* and *M. kobus*. Azaleas and rhododendrons are grouped along the walks, on the sloping lawns and in the woodland areas; the emphasis is on hardy hybrids, though a number of other species are also present. Tulip trees, flowering ash, copper beeches, swamp cypresses and other trees grow well, and many hydrangeas and summer-flowering shrubs have recently been planted.

Lindisfarne Castle, Northumberland

On Holy Island, 5 miles east of Beal across the sands

Lindisfarne, or Holy Island, derives the latter name from its association with St Aidan, who established a community of monks on the island in the 7th century. Both St Aidan's monks and the Benedictines who followed in 1082 built on the sheltered ground to the south-west of the island where the ruined abbey still stands. On such a wild coast they needed protection from

Lindisfarne Castle; From the west

Lindisfarne Castle; The Ship Room

the North Sea gales and they left undisturbed the dramatic outcrop of rock which was later to carry Lindisfarne Castle.

It seems that no building stood on the crag before 1548 when the site was fortified by the government as a defence for the harbour of Holy Island. The Castle, which was briefly and dramatically seized for the Stuarts in 1715, played a useful role for over 200 years, but after its guns were removed in 1819 it fell into disuse as a fort, and was used by coastguards.

Edward Hudson, the founder of *Country Life*, found it in sorry condition when he bought it in 1902. He summoned Lutyens, already established as the leading country house architect, to restore it and fit comfortable modern quarters within the ramparts. Lutyens excelled at romantic reconstructions, and the effects he achieved at Lindisfarne have been well described as 'romance without period'. The castle illustrates Lutyens's subtle use of materials (stone, brick, slate, and cobble), of differing floor levels, and of angled building patterns. Not least it shows his ability to establish a poetic relationship between a building and its setting.

In spring fulmar petrels nest on the ledges of the crag, and in summer the rock face is bright with stonecrop, thyme, spur valerian, mallow and gillyflower. The stepped ramp leads up – and at each step the views widen – to what is surely the most enchanting of miniature castles. It is also a tribute to the genius of a leading English architect of the early 20th century.

Little Moreton Hall, Cheshire *(See colour plate facing p. 128)*

4 miles south-west of Congleton, on east side of the A34 Manchester/ Newcastle-under-Lyme road

Rising high above the surrounding fields and reflected in the waters of its quiet moat, Little Moreton is the most picturesque half-timbered house in the country. Top-heavy, with leaning walls and sagging roofs, it seems like some vast unstable doll's house. The air of fragility is deceptive, for the strength of a good timbered building is that over the centuries it can 'give' comfortably to stresses and strains. The crazy structure has lasted for over 400 years, and is as sound at heart as on the day it went up.

The house was built by the ancient Moreton family at two or more periods in the 16th century. The stone bridge that crosses the moat, and is the only means of access, leads to the gatehouse with jutting upper storeys and an oriel window under the gable. To the left is a garderobe projection which drained into the moat. The carving of the gatehouse entrance exhibits naïve Renaissance motifs and, like the long gallery which runs at roof level right across this front, probably dates from as late as 1570.

The gatehouse gives access to a cobbled courtyard. To the left lies the garden, with a recently planted knot-garden, laid out to a 17th-century design in Leonard Meager's *The English Gardener*, and immediately opposite rises the astonishingly fretted and gabled north front with its wealth of carving. This highly romantic façade assumed its present appearance in 1559 and the date is inscribed on one of the bay windows.

Though almost unfurnished, the interior of Little Moreton conveys an authentic sense of period. The work of 16th-century timber craftsmen – panelling, moulded beams, and moulded mullions and transoms – speaks for itself. The great hall, which in customary fashion must have dominated the house when it was first built, underwent alteration in the mid-16th century and perhaps afterwards. Today the most impressive rooms are the withdrawing room, with its noble ceiling and bold panelling, and the long gallery. The latter, a concession to fashion in the Elizabethan age when no gentleman's seat was complete without a gallery, was daringly added over the existing south front in about 1570. The almost continuous fenestration, which makes it so light and sunny, is unusual, as is the plasterwork decoration of the two gable ends. The chapel contains tempera painting of Renaissance character which must date from the end of the 16th century.

In the garden are two curious mounds. These were never defensive works, but ornamental features which no doubt originally carried seats and perhaps arbours from which a view of the surrounding countryside could be obtained. Such lookouts occur in several 16th- and 17th-century gardens, and in at least one other Cheshire garden, that at Dunham Massey.

Lyme Park, Cheshire

On west outskirts of Disley, 6½ miles south-east of Stockport

In 1346 Sir Thomas Danvers captured the Constable of France at Crécy and in the same year Edward III rewarded him with lands at Lyme. His only daughter soon after married Sir Piers Legh and founded the race of the Leghs of Lyme. Exactly 600 years later, in 1946, the direct descendant of the hero of Crécy, Richard Legh, 3rd Lord Newton, gave the Lyme estate to the Trust.

Lyme Park; From the south-east, with Leoni's portico

Lyme probably stands at a higher altitude than any other great house in England. The park, nine miles in circumference, rises to 1,220 feet, and was already walled in the reign of Queen Elizabeth and famous for the breed of red deer that were hunted by successive generations of Leghs. In this noble setting Sir Piers Legh VII, soon after 1550, built a Tudor mansion to replace a medieval hall-house which had stood at least since the middle of the 15th century. The most notable feature of the entrance front of Lyme is still his towering Tudor gateway incorporating the four classical orders, and one of the earliest examples in England of such a composition. Though the other elevations reveal no trace of the 16th-century mansion, it reappears inside the house, notably in the splendid long gallery and drawing room.

Externally Lyme now reflects the genius of Giacomo Leoni (see p. 33), the Palladian architect who in the early 1720s was commissioned by Peter Legh to give the older house an imposing classical dress. Imposing it certainly is, and the south front that faces the lake and the moorland beyond is one of the boldest achievements of Palladian architecture in this country. A vast Ionic portico rests on a basement of rusticated arches, the pediment surmounted by giant lead figures of Neptune, Venus and Pan. Six bays on either side carry pilasters that rise from the rusticated basement through two storeys to support the cornice. An internal courtyard, repeating the theme of rusticated arches, and with the chief apartments set on a *piano nobile* and distinguished by tall pedimented windows, recalls the gravity of an Italian *palazzo*.

The interior delectably combines 16th-century work with Leoni's measured statements. The gallery, 120 feet long, and the drawing room, both

Lyme Park; The saloon: carved motifs attributed to Grinling Gibbons

with arcaded panelling, are outstanding examples of 16th-century decoration. The drawing room has a deep plaster frieze and a plaster ceiling
studded with bosses and spiral pendants – the whole room is a triumph
of elaboration. Leoni's most notable contributions are the entrance hall
hung with early Mortlake tapestries, the grand staircase – the ceiling by
Francis Conseiglio and Joseph Polfreman, the carving by a local craftsman, James Moore – with family portraits lining its walls, and the saloon,
which is perhaps the most successful of all the rooms at Lyme. Corinthian pilasters divide the oak-panelled walls and each panel is decorated
with limewood carvings that represent the seasons, painting and music.
These brilliant carvings have been convincingly attributed to Grinling
Gibbons.

The contents of the house, most of them on loan from the 4th Lord
Newton, include not only tapestries and furniture of outstanding quality but
much that speaks of the long history of Lyme and the Leghs. There are
chairs with coats of arms that record dynastic alliances, early Chippendale
chairs covered with the cloak which Charles I wore to the scaffold, and such
curiosities as the portrait of Joseph Watson, the great huntsman who for a
wager drove twelve brace of stags from Lyme to Windsor Forest – what a
different countryside this conjures up – and at the age of a hundred and two
'hunted a buck, a chase near six hours long'. No less evocative in this house
is a copy of Velasquez's *Las Meninas*, for the dog portrayed in the familiar
picture is a Lyme mastiff. This famous breed, which died out in the 19th
century, was prized throughout Western Europe and the forebear of the
mastiff painted by Velasquez was reared at Lyme and presented to Philip II
in 1604.

Maister House, Hull

In High Street

As John Taylor, the 'Water Poet', wrote in 1622, a good Hull merchant lived 'as he were Neptune's son'. The houses of such merchants, many rebuilt or redecorated in the 18th century, were splendid examples of the taste of their time and rich in the skills of the plasterer and woodcarver. Most of them were situated in High Street and the adjoining area where, from medieval times to the 19th century, the more important merchant families lived over their counting houses and near their private wharves. As so many of these houses have disappeared in the last fifty years, the acquisition and transfer to the Trust by the Georgian Society for East Yorkshire of Maister House, one of the finest survivals, is particularly welcome.

The Maister family, who were to play a prominent role in the history of the city for nearly 300 years, settled in Hull – or Kingston-upon-Hull, as it has been officially designated since the reign of Edward I – in the mid-16th century. Little is known of their old town house in High Street which was destroyed by fire in 1743. The present house built by Henry Maister on the same site – work was already under way in 1744 – shows the strong influence of Lord Burlington who knew Henry Maister, and whose Yorkshire house, Londesborough, was only some twenty-five miles from Hull.

Maister House; The staircase

Opposite:
Melford Hall; The entrance front

The plain brick façade, capped with a stone parapet, displays the Palladian *gravitas* advocated by Lord Burlington. Its severity, relieved only by a fine pedimented doorcase, is a foil to the richness of the hall and staircase within. The splendid stone staircase with wrought-iron balustrade rises round three sides of the square hall, and the walls are elaborately ornamented with stuccowork. A gallery with richly coffered soffits surrounds the staircase well, and at roof level a coved and plastered ceiling supports a glazed octagonal lantern which lights the staircase and hall. No expense was spared. Robert Bakewell, the famous Derby ironsmith, was employed on the wrought-iron balustrade to the stairs, and a statue of Ceres was commissioned from Cheere, the London sculptor. The whole triumphant conception is thoroughly Palladian, and both in design and detail reflects the work of a highly competent architect and craftsman.

Melford Hall, Long Melford, Suffolk

3 miles north of Sudbury on A134

Melford is one of the prettiest villages in Suffolk. The main street, which is wide and long, and at its northern end rises through an expansive green to the church and the Cordell Almshouses, is lined with fine prosperous-looking buildings. Melford Hall is separated from the green by a high brick wall surmounted by an octagonal gazebo decorated with gables and pinnacles. More pinnacles, cupolas and twisted chimneys are glimpsed beyond the wall. They condition one's first response to the house.

The builder of Melford Hall was William Cordell, a successful and ambitious lawyer who rose to be Speaker of the House of Commons, a Knight and Master of the Rolls. His house, of which there is a plan in the *Book of John Thorpe* at the Soane Museum, is of brick, with stone embellishments and a fine stone porch. It is now U-shaped in design, but originally was a hollow square. Although partly re-fenestrated at a later date, the Hall with its chimneys and turrets is a typical mid-16th-century building. The house must have been largely complete by 1578, when Sir William Cordell entertained Queen Elizabeth at Melford in great state and magnificence. A contemporary account of the visitation records that 'there was in Suffolk suche sumptuous feastinges and bankets as seldom in ani parte of the worlde there hath been seen afore'. Melford was sacked by the Parliamentarians in the Civil War, while in the ownership of the Savages, but having passed again to the Cordell family it was redecorated by Sir Cordell Firebrace in the 1730–40s, and finally sold in 1786 to Sir Harry Parker, the 6th baronet.

The Parker family, related closely to the Parkers of Saltram (see p. 176), was distinguished for its seamen. The 5th baronet, Sir Hyde Parker, Vice-Admiral of the Blue, commanded the fleet at St Lucia in 1780, and his son Hyde, Sir Harry's brother, gave Nelson the famous signal at Copenhagen. The third Hyde Parker, son of the second, became First Sea Lord and fought in the Napoleonic wars. His son, Captain Hyde Parker, was killed during the Crimean campaign, and the Captain's nephew, the last Admiral Hyde Parker, served during the First World War.

The 7th baronet, Sir William, filled in the recesses between the turrets on the west side and built a library at much the same time as his cousins at Saltram were creating their library. This elegant Regency room contains Romney's portrait of Admiral Sir Hyde Parker, the 5th baronet, and a series of pictures by Dominic Serres. These illustrate the naval engagements of the 5th baronet and his son Admiral Sir Hyde Parker, Kt, whose portrait, also by Romney, hangs over the Regency staircase. In the house are various pieces of Chinese porcelain captured in 1762 by Admiral Sir Hyde Parker from the Spanish galleon, *Santissima Trinidad*, laden with gifts from the Emperor of China.

The north wing of the house was gutted by fire during the Second World War and restored by the 11th baronet, after whose death Melford was transferred to the National Trust. His son Sir Richard lives at the Hall.

Mompesson House, Salisbury

In the Cathedral Close

No cathedral is blessed with as harmonious and well-bred an architectural setting as Salisbury. Many generations have made their contribution to the Close, and with one regrettable post-war exception, not a single building in this exclusive assembly is out of key. Yet even in such company Mompesson House has unusual distinction, the fairest of many fine houses.

The Mompessons, an old Wiltshire family, are first recorded in the Close in 1635. Thomas Mompesson, a Royalist who raised a hundred men to support that heroic fiasco, John Penruddock's rising against the Commonwealth in 1655, found favour and fortune at the Restoration. By 1680 he had acquired the leases of the houses on the site now occupied by Mom-

Mompesson House

pesson House. His son, Charles Mompesson, however, built the house and nearby stable block when he inherited the property in 1701; his coat of arms is set over the front door and the date 1701 occurs on the rainwater heads. The façade is a carefully balanced composition. Ornament is confined to the dentilled cornice, the doorway with broken pediment and the curving scrolls that frame the window above. The narrower windows on either side of the doorway lend a subtle variation to the architectural rhythm. The restrained dignity of the composition makes many more decorated houses seem a little vulgar.

The interior decoration, executed in about 1740, comes as something of a contrast, and is contemporary with the brick wing that links the house with the stables. Though some of the panelling is a sturdy survival from about 1700, and the finely carved staircase may be of the same date, the elaborate plaster ceilings and overmantels are in a mixed manner that speaks both of Palladio and the Baroque. The effect, in a relatively small house, is one of great richness. The house was thoroughly restored by Mr Denis Martineau, who gave it to the Trust in 1952.

Montacute Somerset House *(See colour plate facing p. 129)*

4 miles west of Yeovil, on north side of A3088

By the late 15th century a Phelips owned land at Montacute, the Somerset village that derives its name from the conical hill – *mons acutus* – which rises near by. During the 16th century the Phelips accumulated property in the village; Thomas Phelips probably lived in a modest house on the site of the present stables. His son, Edward, was an ambitious and successful lawyer;

he was knighted by James I, became Speaker of the House of Commons in 1604 and later Master of the Rolls. About 1588, he set about building the most magnificent house of its time in Somerset. Montacute was meant as a demonstration of his wealth and importance. In contrast to the priory and most medieval houses, it was symmetrical and of a towering height; at the same time it made great play of the large windows then fashionable – Elizabethans like modern architects had a passion for immense areas of glass – and not least it incorporated a wealth of Renaissance detail copied from the Continent and thought to be the hallmark of good taste.

The strange thing is that Montacute though meant primarily to impress – most grand Elizabethan houses were self-advertisement – is so poetic a building. Perhaps its secret lies in the fantasy of its finialled gables, obelisks, turrets and pavilions, or in its honey-coloured stone which sometimes seems to make the house give off a rich golden glow. Perhaps time and disappointed hopes have something to do with it. The Phelips family lost their impetus by the middle of the 17th century, and the imposing mansion, outside the current of affairs, became for nearly three centuries a quiet country house in a quiet village.

Montacute has undergone only one major architectural change. The entrance front was once on the east and there the builder concentrated his Renaissance novelties: classical entablatures, pedimented windows, shell-headed niches, chimneys shaped like columns, and the Nine Worthies, clumsy but charming figures, in full Norman dress. In 1786 Edward Phelips, the fifth Edward to live at Montacute, changed the entrance to its present position on the opposing west front, and at the same time built a two-storey addition between the projecting wings to contain corridors. This made the place more liveable, for the original plan, as so often in earlier houses, made no provision for corridors, and many of the rooms, bedrooms included, had to serve also as passages.

Architecturally such additions are often disastrous, but Edward Phelips, clearly a man of taste, bought part of the stonework façade of Clifton Maybank, a remarkable Dorset house of 1550, then being demolished. It fitted in perfectly. The porch, a fascinating mixture of Gothic and Renaissance ornament, is one of the most agreeable features of Montacute, and the addition as a whole is an interesting example of mid-16th-century building when Gothic forms still co-existed with the new fashions imported from abroad.

The interior of the house offers surprises and delights. The heraldic stained-glass in the great parlour and great hall is as good as or better than any surviving from the Elizabethan period, and forty-seven coats of arms celebrate the Phelips family, their connections, and West Country neighbours. The depth of the spirited plaster friezes in some of the rooms is also distinctive, and the walls below them are once again hung with rich tapestries. In the great hall with its 16th-century panelling – one of the most engaging halls of the period – the elaborate screen is in stone with rusticated arches and flamboyant strapwork cresting. The dais end of the hall is decorated with unselfconscious plasterwork, a long relief by a Somerset

Montacute House; Left: *The west front* Right: *The east front, boundary walk and garden*

Brueghel, telling the story of an idle husband and his punishment at the hands of the parish. Though its detail is 19th-century, the long gallery at the top of the house, a characteristic feature of great Elizabethan and Jacobean mansions, is 172 feet long, the longest surviving gallery of the period. It now houses the impressive exhibition of 16th and early 17th century portraits from the National Portrait Gallery.

When Montacute came to the Trust in 1931, through the generosity of Mr Ernest Cook, it was empty. It has since been furnished largely with Sir Malcolm Stewart's splendid bequest, and with generous gifts and loans. There are some particularly fine fabrics, among them a 15th-century Tournai tapestry of an armed and mounted knight and a Gobelin tapestry from the *Nouvelles Indes* series.

On the original entrance front, the balustrades and pavilions and the raised boundary walks on the north survive from the 16th-century Elizabethan garden. The layout to the north dates from the 19th century, but with its yew hedges and calculated formality it successfully evokes the spirit of a garden such as Edward Phelips, Master of the Rolls, would have approved.

Moseley Old Hall, Staffordshire

4 miles north of Wolverhampton, east of the A449 Stafford road

Now on the sad outskirts of Wolverhampton, this house sheltered Charles II for two days and a night after the disastrous battle of Worcester. Charles after the Restoration dictated the story to Samuel Pepys, telling how at dawn on 8 September, five days after the battle, he arrived with the Penderel

147

Moseley Old Hall

brothers, faithful retainers of the Catholic Giffards of near-by Chillington. In the half-light Mr Whitgreave, the owner of Moseley, and Father Huddleston, had difficulty in recognizing the King disguised as a woodcutter. Upstairs they took off his worn shoes and stockings and washed his feet, brought clean clothes, and some 'biskett' and a glass of wine, and the fugitive was able to sleep in a bed for the first time since the battle. Next day a posse of Commonwealth troops arrived to question Whitgreave, but the King's presence was undetected. In the evening Charles went up to the oratory at the top of the house with Father Huddleston and the latter spoke of the sad condition of the persecuted Catholics. Thirty-four years later, as Charles II lay dying in London, it was John Huddleston, the fugitive priest of Moseley, who administered the last rites and received him into the Catholic Church. After dark, with the faithful Lord Wilmot, the King left on the hazardous journey that was to take him across the channel to Fécamp and safety.

So Moseley Old Hall became part of one of the most compelling stories of adversity and adventure in English history. After the Restoration Thomas Whitgreave, very properly, received an annuity of £200 a year, a large sum in those days. The Old Hall remained in the possession of the family until 1925. In the meantime, the half-timbered exterior, encased with brick in the 19th century, had been roughly treated. Fortunately little damage was done to the interior. The King who arrived in the half-light on 8 September 1651 would recognize it today. The front door opens on the main hall; on the opposite side is the orchard door with heavy iron studding through which

Charles unobtrusively entered. To the left is the parlour with original oak panelling. On the first floor is the bedroom and the four-poster in which, exhausted, he must have spent so welcome a night. Adjoining is the secure but restricted hiding place, devised initially for itinerant Catholic priests such as Father Huddleston, where the King took refuge when the Commonwealth soldiers paid their unwelcome visit. Off Mr Whitgreave's room on the same floor, with contemporary panelling and the original wide floorboards, there is a little chamber over the front porch where the King, with feelings that may readily be imagined, watched many of his soldiers struggling northward along the road. The oratory which he visited with Father Huddleston – surely a visit of profound significance – is discreetly situated in the attics.

Portraits of the Whitgreaves and the Penderels recall the exciting aftermath of Worcester, and there is Charles's letter to Jane Lane, who helped him to escape to France. Most of the furniture is not original to the house, but it is, like the Dutch and Lambeth porcelain, mainly of the 17th century and such as might have been at Moseley when the King found refuge there.

The garden and orchard round the hall have been restored by the Trust to a design of 1640, and the plants are only such as existed in English gardens in the 17th century.

Mount Stewart House, Co. Down

On east shore of Strangford Lough 5 miles south-west of Newtonards

The gardens (p. 245) came to the Trust over twenty years ago; but not the house. This divided ownership promised difficulties if the house ever passed from the ownership of the Londonderry family and fell into unsympathetic hands. The transfer of the mansion to the Trust in 1976, with many of the important contents, was therefore particularly welcome. The gift was made possible by the generosity of Lady Mairi Bury, who had inherited from her mother, Lady Londonderry, and by a substantial endowment from the Ulster Land Fund.

The house, named after Alexander Stewart who bought the property in 1744, began to assume its present form in the 1780s when his son, 1st Marquess of Londonderry, called in James Wyatt (who started work on Castle Coole, p. 72, a year or two later). Wyatt designed the west front, originally the entrance front, and an attractive entrance hall. This (now the breakfast room) has mahogany doors inlaid with satinwood, and an octagonal ceiling with plaster decoration of typical Wyatt design that is repeated in the parquetry floor (not unlike Stuart's Temple of the Winds, p. 246; no doubt the same craftsmen were employed).

The Down election of 1790, which resulted in the return to Parliament of Robert Stewart, later to become Lord Castlereagh, cost the family £60,000 and brought a temporary halt to building activities. When work was resumed early in the 19th century, it was to the designs of George Dance,

Mount Stewart House; South front

whose happiest contribution was the spacious staircase.

A new entrance front on the north was also begun by Dance, but this façade did not assume its present form, with a large Ionic pedimented portico, until the 1820s. It has been suggested that Vitruvius Morrison was the architect. If so, he was at the same time responsible for the large hall and saloon, with their marbled pillars and somewhat ponderous grandeur. Further extensive additions were made to the east end of the house about the middle of the century.

Mount Stewart House; The dining room

Mount Stewart contains fine furniture, silver-gilt, and porcelain. There are one or two outstanding paintings, notably *Hambletonian*, an equestrian study by Stubbs. However the special interest of the interior lies in its associations with Lord Castlereagh, the eminent Foreign Secretary (1812–22) who played a decisive role at the Congress of Vienna and soon after died by his own hand in tragic circumstances. A set of early 19th-century giltwood chairs used at the Congress, and subsequently embroidered with the arms of the plenipotentiaries, are preserved at Mount Stewart, as is a version of Castlereagh's full-length portrait by Lawrence. The latter hangs above the Empire desk at which he wrote his dispatches from Vienna, and on the desk stands a massive inkstand fashioned – an odd fancy – from the gold snuff boxes presented to him by the Pope and no less than fifteen European sovereigns. The library in Wyatt's west wing is to become a museum dedicated to the memory of the statesman.

Nostell Priory, West Yorkshire

6 miles south-east of Wakefield, north of A638

The fertile plain of east Yorkshire lifts gently towards the upland moors of the Pennines in a series of long straight valleys. Approaching the industrial area round Leeds and Bradford, the landscape becomes more austere, the horizon punctuated by chimneystacks, deserted slag heaps and collieries. Here, where the finger of industrial grime touches the stonework etching its contours, stands Nostell Priory.

The main block, based on a design by Palladio for the Villa Mocenigo, was begun by Sir Rowland Winn in 1733. It is almost certain that the originator of this idea was an amateur gentleman architect in Lord Burlington's circle, Colonel James Moyser of Beverley, who was also a close friend of Sir Rowland. But the executant of his scheme was the young James Paine, soon to prove one of the most successful architects of the 18th century, and it is clear that Paine alone was responsible for modifying Moyser's plan and for the rococo decoration of much of the interior.

Apart from the central block only one of the four corner pavilions in the original plan now survives, for in 1765 Sir Rowland died and his son, the 5th baronet, decided to employ Robert Adam rather than Paine to complete the house. The north wing, with a portico more Roman than Palladian in feeling, is by Adam and was intended to be balanced by a similar wing to the south; perhaps initially postponed whilst Adam was working on the graceful stable block, it was never built. The exterior has been little altered since 1785, when the 5th baronet died.

The Winn family have owned Nostell since 1654. Centuries before they came to Nostell, a Priory was established on the estate, one of the first houses of Austin canons in England. It was dedicated to St Oswald early in the 11th century and was occupied by the industrious friars – who even turned to opencast coal-mining – until the Priory was confiscated in 1539 and given to

Dr Leigh, 'fattest and most pompous' of the King's Commissioners. It passed through various hands before its acquisition by Rowland Winn, Alderman of the City of London. His brother was created a baronet at the Restoration. The 4th baronet, Sir Rowland, and his son between them built the great house which exists today. A later Sir Rowland (1820–93), created Baron St Oswald, was for many years an M.P., becoming Chief Whip and Lord of the Treasury. His great-grandson, the present Lord St Oswald, lives today at the Priory, and it was through him and the trustees of the estate that Nostell was conveyed to the National Trust in 1953.

The interior of Nostell reflects the taste of successive generations, and above all the fine quality of English craftsmanship of the 18th century. The decoration is splendid both in concept and execution. The plasterwork, much of it by Joseph Rose, the wall and ceiling paintings by Antonio Zucchi and his wife Angelica Kauffmann, all so closely associated with Robert Adam, and the superb furniture fashioned by Thomas Chippendale to Adam's designs, make Nostell outstanding among country houses of the period.

Paine and Adam each contributed their share to the interior. Paine was responsible for the general disposition, but Adam, though leaving untouched the staircases and many of the bedchambers, contributed to several of the state rooms his characteristic neo-classical decoration. Thus to Paine's charmingly exuberant rococo dining room, its swirling lines and gaiety of design in striking contrast to the robust and massive masculinity of the exterior, he added panels of delicate grotesques. In particular, Adam was responsible for decorating the central and northern part of Paine's block (his own north wing was only completed in the 19th century). The central hall, giving on the terrace, is one of his best rooms, with a particularly fine coved ceiling by Joseph Rose the younger; his library, a smallish square room, with bookshelves and furniture all by Adam, achieves a striking architectural unity. The large writing desk in this room is among Chippendale's most impressive pieces.

The Chippendale furniture at Nostell is justly famous, and it is one of the three houses in England where his complete accounts survive and each piece can be identified. Harewood, Nostell and Osterley are outstanding examples of houses possessing a quantity of the great cabinet-maker's work based on original Adam themes. Though many fine pieces are associated with his Director style – for example a set of beautiful ribbon-back chairs – there are a number of significant neo-classical pieces, notably a set of lyre-backed chairs in the library. English neo-classical furniture, directly attributable to Robert Adam's influence, was a striking innovation in the 1760s and antecedes its appearance in France in the next decade as Louis-Seize. Perhaps the most obviously beautiful pieces at Nostell are the two inlaid serpentine-fronted commodes in the saloon, their double doors superbly inlaid, and the veneered drawers treated to resemble shimmering watered silk. The tall pier-glasses in the hall, and the side tables beneath them, are also striking examples of the collaboration between architect-decorator and cabinet-maker. The accounts show the thoroughness of Adam's approach,

Nostell Priory; The dining room, designed by James Paine

The Chinese bedroom, designed by Robert Adam

and alongside the charges for this magnificent furniture are such modest items as '5s. for taking down window curtains, cleaning them and putting up a bed' and '34 yards of printed cotton at 6s. 6d.'

Illustrative of the tradition of splendid craftsmanship at Nostell is the remarkable longcase clock made in 1717 by John Harrison, son of the estate carpenter. Its works are made almost entirely of wood and the pendulum rod is the earliest recorded use of mahogany in England. The clock still keeps perfect time, and Harrison was later to invent a timekeeper exact enough to determine longitude at sea, for which he was awarded, but never received, £20,000. Tradition maintains that it was he, or another member of the Harrison family, under whom Chippendale received his training, and on whose instructions Chippendale may have made the famous Nostell doll's house, perhaps his earliest extant work. Chippendale was born at Otley, not far away, and the quality of the fragile and miraculous miniature furniture in the doll's house reveals the work of an exceptionally gifted cabinet-maker, faithfully copying the early-18th-century furniture that must once have existed at Nostell. The costumes, silver, and decoration of the doll's house vividly portray the life of the Winns in the time of George II, as the family house in which it stands displays the taste of their successors later in the 18th century.

Nunnington Hall, North Yorkshire

In Ryedale, 4½ miles south-east of Helmsley, north of B1257

Nunnington already had a long history when it became Crown property in the middle of the 16th century. Two of the people who subsequently lived there deserve special mention. One was Robert Huicke, physician successively to Henry VIII, Edward VI and Elizabeth. He was the doctor to whom fell the unwelcome task of telling the Queen that she could never

Nunnington Hall; The south front

expect to have children. He was perhaps responsible for some of the Tudor work on the west side of the house.

The other distinguished name is that of Lord Preston. An ardent supporter of the Stuart cause, he was Charles II's ambassador to Louis XIV and enjoyed the close confidence of James II. After the latter fled the country, he set out in a fishing boat to bring him back, was captured and barely escaped with his life. He subsequently retired discreetly to Nunnington where he died in 1695.

In retirement he was not inactive. Besides translating Boethius, he planted the ancient avenue of sycamores in the village, and remodelled the south side of the house. This late-17th-century elevation, with the rooms immediately behind it, lends Nunnington its architectural distinction. A classical doorway with a broken pediment leads into Lord Preston's hall. His arms and those of his wife appear in the elaborately carved chimneypiece, and his boldly moulded panelling, and doorcases with broken pediments, are characteristic late-17th-century work.

Lord Preston was responsible also for an adjoining room with painted wainscot, for painted canvas panels on the ceiling which repeat the Preston arms, and for the distinguished staircase with its wide, almost leisurely, treads and turned oak balusters. The staircase, now hung with Flemish 17th-century tapestries after designs by Rubens, leads to the drawing room, which is also of Preston's creation and contains 15th-century French 'verdure' tapestries in which figures are depicted against a formal background of flowery meadows; these he may have acquired when he was ambassador in Paris.

Lord Preston's architectural setting owes much to the furniture, porcelain and paintings collected by the late Mrs Ronald Fife who left the house to the Trust in 1952.

154

Ormesby Hall, Cleveland

3 miles south-east of Middlesbrough, south of A174

The Pennyman family acquired the manor of Ormesby in 1600. Probably the low quadrangular block which stands to the east of the Georgian mansion was built soon after. Though the block was long since converted into kitchen and service quarters, a remarkable Jacobean doorway survives with entablature, rusticated arch and coat of arms.

The main house was built by Dorothy, widow of Sir James Pennyman, in about 1750 and her nephew, another Sir James, a spendthrift in the best 18th-century manner, added the elegant stables and redecorated the dining room and drawing room in the Adamesque style of the 1770s. Though not very grand by 18th-century standards, both the design and decoration of the house reflect taste and craftsmanship of a high order.

The architect of Ormesby is unknown but he was clearly of a conservative cast of mind for the high plain block with hipped roof, heavy cornice, and pediments on the two main fronts, has the flavour of a building earlier than the mid-18th century. The entrance hall, where the decoration of Lady Dorothy's time is unaltered, is screened by Ionic columns at both ends and incorporates characteristic Palladian motifs, such as the oak wreaths on the frieze and doorcases, and Vitruvian scrolls on the dado. The adjoining library is of the same period. By contrast, in the dining room and drawing room, redecorated by Sir James, the influence of the Adam brothers is clearly apparent and the intricate design of the plasterwork ceilings has been attributed to Carr of York. The portrait of Sir James, painted by Reynolds in 1762 for £20, hangs over the dining room fireplace.

Perhaps the most distinguished feature of Ormesby is the first-floor gallery that runs across the middle of the house. The walls have mid-18th-century panelling, and the doors curved or broken pediments; the columns were probably inserted in the 1770s. Some of the bedrooms are decorated in an equally lavish fashion.

Ormesby was bequeathed to the Trust by the late Colonel J. B. W. Pennyman in 1962.

Ormesby Hall

Osterley Park, Middlesex, London

Just north of A4, beyond Osterley station

Originally a 'faire and stately building of bricke' built about 1577 by Sir Thomas Gresham, founder of the London Royal Exchange and Gresham College, Osterley Park was transformed into a monument of 18th-century classicism by Robert Adam between 1761 and 1780 for the grandsons of the founder of Child's Bank, Francis and Robert. The latter's daughter and heiress, Sarah Anne, eloped at the age of eighteen to Gretna Green with the 10th Earl of Westmorland in 1782. She was soon forgiven by her mother, but her father left Osterley and the Child fortune to her second child, Sophia, who married the Earl of Jersey in 1804. Their descendant, the 9th Earl of Jersey, gave the property to the Trust in 1949.

Little at Osterley, other than the mellow brick stable block, is clearly of Sir Thomas Gresham's time, the ghost of the older house being imprisoned in Adam's splendid mansion. Adam was called in to remodel and redecorate an Elizabethan house built round a courtyard with towers at the corners. He respected this arrangement which survives in 18th-century disguise. In accordance with Italian principles he set the chief apartment on the first floor. The approach was perhaps his masterstroke: a high flight of steps leads to an Ionic portico which spans one side of the courtyard.

The interior of the house, as we see it today, is almost wholly Adam's creation, and many of his plans and designs survive to illustrate his style as it matured over twenty years. His magnificent series of state apartments occupies three sides of a square, and his superb decoration, furnishings and fittings, 'all delicacy, grace and beauty', remain unchanged. Apartments such as the hall, the library, the eating room, and the drawing room – 'worthy', Horace Walpole thought, 'of Eve before the fall' – are among the purest examples of the neo-classical style. The painted Etruscan room is an

Osterley Park

interesting experiment in that type of interior decoration inspired by the Greek vases found at Pompeii in the mid-18th century which Adam and his contemporaries were pleased to call Etruscan. Adam conceived his rooms as complete entities; he took as much care, and often showed as much originality, in the design of furniture, carpets and fittings as in his treatment of walls and ceilings. His furniture at Osterley includes many examples of the finest cabinet-making of the second half of the 18th century. The library chairs and desks are outstanding, as are a pair of commodes in the drawing room, while the state bed is one of his most ambitious exercises in furniture design. In the tapestry room, hung with Gobelin tapestries after Boucher which strike at Osterley a profoundly rococo note, a gilt side-table with inlaid marble top, and a pair of gilt and painted tripod stands, well exemplify his versatility.

Steps lead down from the long gallery to a broad lawn beyond which lies a chain of lakes enlarged from the ponds mentioned in 1596 and bordered by a group of enormous cedar trees. In the grounds are a Doric temple of about 1720 and a semicircular conservatory built by Adam against the faded brick wall of Sir Thomas Gresham's Elizabethan kitchen garden.

Owletts, Cobham, Kent

1 mile south of A2 on B2009

Brick-built and unpretending, Owletts is a pleasant Charles II house. It was raised by husbandry of corn, hops, and cherries, derived from the adjoining estate of 600 acres. A single feature distinguishes it from other and less important houses of the period: its spacious staircase, an unexpectedly grand feature, with a ceiling of 1684 that is beautifully and opulently

Owletts; The staircase ceiling

plastered with a formal design of wreaths and leaves characteristic of the finest craftsmanship of the period. Such richness and elegance in so simple a house are unexpected and wholly effective.

When Owletts passed to the Baker family early in the 19th century, the casement windows had already been replaced, as so often in the 18th century, by sashes, but happily much of its wide timber flooring had survived. Sir Herbert Baker, the well-known architect who left Owletts to the Trust, was responsible for minor alterations, and also designed or introduced much of the furniture. He invoked the help of Gertrude Jekyll in laying out the garden.

Packwood House, Warwickshire

14 miles north of Stratford-upon-Avon, 11 miles south of central Birmingham, 1 mile east of Hockley Heath, off the A34 Birmingham/Stratford road

Though internally much altered in the 20th century, Packwood House is a rewarding example of domestic Tudor architecture with mid-17th-century additions. Above all it is remarkable for its topiary garden, a reminder of the sombre days of the Puritan Commonwealth when even a garden might have biblical associations. It is thought to have been laid out in about 1655 by John Fetherston, and represents the Sermon on the Mount. Crowning the Mount is 'The Master', a single large yew tree surrounded by a box hedge; other venerable yews symbolize the Evangelists and the Apostles; and finally groups of smaller trees represent the listening 'multitude'. Nearly all the 19th-century yews survive and their dark conical symbolic shapes are dramatically impressive. Every summer it takes a month for three men to clip them.

A ha-ha surrounds the yew garden and separates it from the more conventional flower garden and its long terraced herbaceous border, full of

Packwood House; Stable block and outbuildings

colour in midsummer; the latter is sheltered by red-brick walls, with a gazebo at each corner, the earliest built by John Fetherston, the others later, at intervals of a hundred years. The walls incorporate two unusual features: one wall has a row of niches or 'bee-holes' to hold bee skeps, and another has internal pipes for hot water which were installed in the late 18th century, making in effect an outdoor greenhouse, with peach trees trained along the wall.

The contrast between the early house, its Tudor timbering stucco-rendered in the 19th century, and the rich plum-coloured Staffordshire brick of the 17th-century additions is striking. So is the disparity in size, as the house, originally a modest farmhouse, is considerably smaller than the stable block and outbuildings.

Little remains of the original interior, for extensive alterations were carried out by the donor of the house, Mr Baron Ash, after the First World War, and by his father earlier in the century. This part of Warwickshire is rich in timber construction, and there are many fine examples in the house of features such as flooring and panelling brought to Packwood from other old houses in the neighbourhood. The rooms are notable for fine fabrics (French and Flemish tapestries, a rare painted canvas arras, Italian and other embroideries), and for furniture that includes a 14th-century refectory table, 17th-century pieces of English and Continental provenance, a suite of George I walnut chairs and other good English 18th-century furniture. In time the interior of Packwood will come to have increasing significance as the reflection of the taste of a rich and knowledgeable amateur in the period before the Second World War.

Peckover House, Wisbech, Cambridgeshire

On the north bank of the river Nene

Peckover House is associated with the rise to prosperity of one of those Quaker families which have played so notable a role in the history of East Anglia over the last 250 years. In the second half of the 18th century Jonathan Peckover bought what is now Peckover House and, in association with the Gurneys, another prominent Quaker family, established the local Wisbech bank which retained its independence until merged with Barclays in 1896. The family acquired a peerage in 1907, and the last representative of the family gave the house to the Trust in 1948.

The solid merchant houses which flank the river Nene are witness to the consequence of Wisbech when it was a port and the river still navigable for substantial vessels. Peckover House, built in 1722, is the most imposing of the mansions. Though the exterior, very properly, eschews aristocratic airs, it achieves an effect by its Georgian sense of proportion and the varied texture of its brickwork. Below a brick cornice and parapet, brick pilasters flank the main elevation on the river, and brick panels below the windows add a welcome decorative touch.

Peckover House; The drawing room, overmantel

The interior comes as a surprise. Inside the house, merchant reticence gives way to a wealth of elaborate decoration. The rooms, including the bedrooms, are panelled and have fireplaces with carved overmantels. The plasterwork, some of 1722 and some dating from the middle of the century, is of the greatest elegance. These rooms, amost untouched, show what wealth and the best provincial craftsmanship could achieve in the first half of the 18th century.

Among the happiest features of the house are the staircase of 1722, with plasterwork perhaps some thirty years younger, the exuberant mid-18th-century rococo overmantel in the drawing room, and the beautifully carved dado and doorcases in the morning room.

The garden is a rare survival of a Victorian layout, complete with summer houses, beds, borders, and evergreens. The maidenhair tree (*Ginkgo biloba*) is one of the largest in the country, and there are good specimens of the tulip tree (*Liriodendron tulipifera*) and the cut-leaved beech (*Fagus sylvatica* 'Heterophylla').

Penrhyn Castle, Gwynedd

1 mile east of Bangor between A5 and the coast

Thomas Hopper (1776–1856) was ready, and able, to build almost anything. He had already executed a Gothick conservatory for the Prince Regent at Carlton House and the restrained classical front of the Carlton Club in St James's Street, when in 1827 G. H. Dawkins Pennant, the immensely wealthy owner of the Penrhyn slate quarries, commissioned him to build the gigantic neo-Norman castle at Penrhyn. The work took a decade and, whether one likes it or not, the building is something of a masterpiece. With his previous essay in a similar style at Gosford in Northern Ireland, it firmly establishes Hopper as the outstanding figure of the strange and short-lived Norman Revival.

The scale of Penrhyn, constructed of Mona 'marble' from Anglesey, is cyclopean, and the exterior, with its own convincing architectural unity, conveys an overpowering sense of mass. The castle is not, of course, the uncompromising Norman which Hopper's contemporaries believed it to be. It possesses, very properly, a strong early 19th-century flavour. At the same time the treatment of walls and towers, elaborately crenellated and machicolated, often recalls the military architecture of the later Middle Ages, while the lavish, almost frenzied, decoration of the interior speaks as much of Arabo-Byzantine sources as of our own chaste Anglo-Norman. Hopper was nothing if not eclectic.

Yet Penrhyn is somehow homogeneous, the creation of a single mind, for Hopper was given a free hand, not only with the building of the castle but with the interior decoration and the design of much of the furniture. Both decoration and furniture are Norman, as Hopper chose to conceive the style. A visitor over a century ago found them 'far from elegant ... yet exceedingly curious'. The visitor today will probably agree.

Penrhyn Castle

Penrhyn Castle; The library, after an engraving by Hawkins

The great hall floored with polished slate – a material much in evidence throughout the interior and one on which the wealth of the owners depended – realizes those effects of space and mass for which Hopper was striving; not surprisingly, seeing that it was modelled on Durham Cathedral. In the library, which recalls, with its deeply recessed windows and ribbed and bossed ceiling, some shadowy Baroque cave, Hopper's carving and plaster decoration are at their most extravagant. But no room in this castle is reticent. Penrhyn is likely to commend itself to those with a robust architectural digestion.

The house contains a selection of paintings from those assembled in the 19th century by the 1st Lord Penrhyn. The Trust has established a collection of some 800 dolls, and in the vast stables, which are a convincing tribute to Hopper's sense of architecture, an important museum of industrial locomotives.

The castle stands, as castles should, on an eminence with splendid views: to the north, Beaumaris Bay and Great Ormes Head; to the north-east, Anglesey; and rising to the south-east, the Snowdon massif. The garden contains a great variety of rare trees and shrubs, and tender species grow well in the mild marine climate.

Petworth House, West Sussex

In Petworth, $5\frac{1}{2}$ miles east of Midhurst, at junction of A272 and A283

As befits so great a house, Petworth has a long history. A connection with the Northumberland Percys begins in 1150, and after 1377 the place is intimately associated with eleven successive earls of Northumberland, powerful, rich, and rarely fortunate. No fewer than six were killed in battle, executed, murdered, or imprisoned, and a seventh, who was unlucky enough to fall in love with Anne Boleyn at the same time as the King, is said to have died of a broken heart.

The 11th Earl left only a daughter, heiress to the vast Percy estates, who married in 1682 the 6th Duke of Somerset, known to history as 'The Proud Duke' on account of his obsessive arrogance. Through his daughter, Petworth passed in the middle of the 18th century to the Wyndham family, whose outstanding representative was George Wyndham, 3rd Earl of Egremont (1751–1837). His beneficent rule at Petworth lasted for sixty-five years. His direct descendant, John Wyndham, formerly Private Secretary to Mr Harold Macmillan as Prime Minister, and created Baron Egremont in 1963, carried on the family tradition at Petworth until his death in 1972.

Of the old manor house, which the Percys obtained leave to crenellate in 1309, little remains except the 13th-century chapel. The Proud Duke, and his wife's fortune, largely rebuilt Petworth between 1688 and 1696. To the Duke we owe such splendid features as the Painted Staircase, the Marble Hall, the Saloon with Grinling Gibbons carvings (in Horace Walpole's opinion Gibbons's finest achievement), and not least the great west front. 'Stately' is the adjective that best describes this façade, 320 feet long, rising from the margin of one of the most beautiful parks in England. 'Capability' Brown's original design exists in the Petworth archives, dated 1752. The stream was dammed to make the serpentine lake, clumps of trees judiciously planted and the 'terrasses reduced to fine undulating steps adorned with Groupes of Cedar, Pines, etc.' to give the incomparable view from the mansion later to inspire some of Turner's most elegiac landscapes.

To the Proud Duke's building, the 18th century contributed the delightful rococo decoration of the White and Gold Drawing Room and the 2nd Lord Egremont's Sculpture Gallery, later enlarged by his son, the 3rd Earl.

Petworth House; The west front from the park

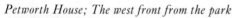

Finally, Salvin in 1870 rebuilt the south front, with marked success, and created a new entrance on the east front.

In spite of its architectural distinction and its superb setting, Petworth is perhaps best known today for its contents, and above all for its great picture collection.

The picture collection, among the most distinguished in England, was formed in three stages: in the 17th century, by the 10th and 11th Earls of Northumberland, who brought together the superb group of Van Dycks and Lelys as well as Northern and Italian paintings; in the 18th century, by the 6th Duke of Somerset and his successor the 2nd Earl of Egremont; and in the 19th century, by the 3rd Earl of Egremont, a renowned patron of British artists. To him we owe one of the chief glories of Petworth, the series of paintings by Turner.

The majority of works by Van Dyck and Lely which are at Petworth today appear in an inventory of 1671. This excludes the colourful early portraits of Sir Robert Shirley, ambassador to Persia, and his wife, which are not recorded at Petworth before 1775, but it includes Van Dyck's moving portrait of Strafford and Lely's large group of the three younger children of Charles I. A number of subject pictures are identified, including the beautiful set of eight little paintings of saints by Elsheimer.

When the 6th Duke of Somerset built this new house at Petworth, he employed Laguerre to decorate the Grand Staircase and Grinling Gibbons to provide the carvings that now adorn the Saloon. He commissioned from Dahl the set of 'Petworth Beauties'. The finest painting known to have been bought by him is Claude's *Jacob and Laban*. His acquisitions are not otherwise documented but it can be assumed that he added further classical works.

Papers have recently come to light which prove that a great many Northern and some Italian paintings, hitherto assumed to have been bought by the Duke of Somerset, were in fact added by the 2nd Earl of Egremont. Among his purchases which can be seen at Petworth today are works by Jacob van Ruisdael, Salomon van Ruysdael, Horst, Bourdon, Millet, Snyders, Van Goyen and Van der Meulen. Important paintings for which there is no evidence of acquisition are a version of the Epiphany by Bosch, two Rogier van der Weyden panels, an early Titian portrait, a Le Nain *Peasant Group*, Bellotto's *Piazza del Campidoglio, Nymwegen* by Cuyp and a *Wooded Landscape* by Hobbema.

Early in life the 3rd Earl said that he would buy nothing but the productions of his own time. He succeeded to Petworth in 1763 at the age of twelve and during his long tenure he offered British artists not only his patronage but also the carefree hospitality of Petworth. Frequent accounts in the memoirs and letters of the period testify to his generosity.

His favourite portrait painter was evidently Thomas Phillips, a predilection borne out by numerous portraits in the house. Reynolds was hardly less favoured, nor were his large subject pictures (e.g. *Macbeth and the Witches*) disdained. There are two landscapes and a dog by Gainsborough, three landscapes by Wilson, evocations of Macbeth and Chaucer

Detail of limewood carving

by Fuseli, a carefully observed interior by Zoffany, Wilkie's sketch for *Knox Preaching*, and paintings by Northcote, Opie, Romney, Allston, Howard, and other contemporary figures. Not only were the popular academicians patronized by Lord Egremont: he also bought three works by Blake and above all he was the patron of Turner.

There are twenty paintings by Turner in the house, the earliest of which is the majestic *Egremont Seapiece* of 1802. The majority were acquired at the artist's exhibitions between 1807 and 1813. The collection culminates in the four famous paintings of the early 1830s: *Brighton Pier, Chichester Harbour*, and two views of Petworth Park. A visitor has but to turn his eyes to the window to see the same scene, unchanged and as beautiful in reality as in Turner's romantic vision.

The 3rd Earl of Egremont also bought contemporary sculpture, among which two pieces by Flaxman, the *St Michael* and the *Apollo*, are notable. The gallery of classical sculpture, formed by the 2nd Earl, is hardly rivalled by any other private collection. It contains for the most part Roman and Hellenistic works, but there is a Greek relief of the 5th century B.C. and there is the great Praxiteles head of Aphrodite.

The furniture in the house, magnificent as some of it is – for example the splendid series of carved giltwood pier glasses – plays a secondary role to the paintings and sculpture.

Philipps House, Dinton, Wiltshire

9 miles west of Salisbury via B3089, north of Dinton

When the house at Dinton was finished in 1817, the architect, plain Jeffry Wyatt, had not been transmogrified into Sir Jeffry Wyatville, for it was not until 1824 that George IV, who was to knight him in 1828, allowed his Windsor architect to distinguish his name from that of his famous uncle, James Wyatt.

Though closely associated with the Gothic revival, Jeffry Wyatt was also, as Dinton proves, an able designer in the neo-classical manner. In its simplicity and lack of ornament, the house is an effective expression of the neo-classical theories which, deriving from France, had by 1800 become widely accepted in England. The well-proportioned south façade is dominated by a graceful Ionic portico. The only other features which relieve the severe design of the house are a simple string course, a shallow bay on the lateral fronts, and an undecorated entablature at roof level.

The interior reflects the same simplicity; 'chaste' is the adjective which inevitably springs to mind. The staircase hall, lit by a circular glazed lantern, is the central and most important feature. It is curious to reflect that the pattern of the staircase which here conveys such an impression of restraint – a central flight to a half landing and returned flights on either side leading to the first floor – originated with the Baroque. The mahogany doors throughout the house, the unassertive cornices, the bookshelves in the library, and much of the early-19th-century furniture, exhibit the same simple and satisfactory treatment.

The Wyndhams, who acquired the property in the late 17th century and

Philipps House; South front

built the present house near the site on which their earlier home then stood, landscaped the park in the style of the late 18th century and planted many of the fine trees, such as the large Spanish chestnut which was already flourishing in 1700. In 1917 the Wyndhams sold the estate to Bertram Philipps, from whom the House now derives its name and who gave the estate to the Trust in 1943.

Plas Newydd, Isle of Anglesey, Gwynedd

1 mile south-west of Llanfairpwll and A5 on A4080

The view of the successive ranges of Snowdonia enjoyed by the statue of Field-Marshal the Marquess of Anglesey from his column at Llanfairpwll is one of the most impressive in Wales. The mountains are seen to no less advantage from his house, Plas Newydd, on the Strait below. There may be more exhausting ways of appreciating the Glyders, the heights of the Trust's Carneddau estate and Snowdon itself, than looking out from the saloon of Plas Newydd across the Menai Strait, but there is none more civilized.

It was this view, brilliantly transmogrified to the sunnier climes of northern Italy, which inspired Rex Whistler's *trompe l'oeil* decoration in the dining room. The shores of the Strait rise in Whistler's painting into precipices throwing waterfalls far out into space; a huddle of granite cottages becomes an architectural fantasy wilder even than Sir Clough Williams-

Plas Newydd; View over the Menai Strait

Ellis could have devised: southern German baroque, Italian Renaissance, English Palladian, medieval Gothic, all mingle happily. Trajan's Column and the spire of St Martin-in-the-Fields are not in the least incongruous. Never was stylistic anarchy more fruitful. Whistler's astonishing technique enables him to carry it off with complete conviction: decorative painting in this country had to wait until the late 1930s before it found a native artist of quite this virtuosity.

The inscription on the triumphal arch and the equestrian statue on the quay commemorates the 'founding of the city' by the 6th Marquess of Anglesey. His son, the 7th Marquess – Whistler depicted his baby cello momentarily disregarded in one of the loggias on the side wall – gave Plas Newydd to the National Trust in 1976. The Paget family's descent from the 15th-century owners of the estate was through the marriage in the 16th century of Sir Nicholas Bagenal into the powerful Griffith dynasty of nearby Penrhyn (see p. 160), one of the first great landowning families of north Wales. The estate passed through the female line to the Bayly family, thence through the marriage in 1737 of Sir Nicholas Bayly to Caroline Paget to the descendants of William, 1st Baron of Beaudesert. The portrait of the 1st Lord Paget in the Gothick entrance hall conveys all the gravity and shrewdness needed for survival as Henry VIII's Secretary of State, Governor of Edward VI and Queen Mary Tudor's Lord Privy Seal. None of his successors in title matched these achievements until Henry William Paget was made 1st Marquess of Anglesey for his role at Waterloo. As Lord Paget, and later better known as the 2nd Earl of Uxbridge (his father having been created 1st Earl after his inheritance of Plas Newydd in 1784) he was the most brilliant cavalry officer of his day. His command of the allied cavalry at Waterloo was as impetuous as it was brilliant and he was also Wellington's second-in-command. It was when the battle was virtually over that his right leg was smashed by grapeshot, supposedly provoking the celebrated exchange with the Duke: 'By God, sir, I've lost my leg'—'By God, so you have.' The 1st Marquess's uniforms and campaign relics, a boot and mutilated trousers worn at the battle, a fine portrait of him by Winterhalter and his articulated wooden leg are shown in the Cavalry Museum at Plas Newydd.

The present house, the last of several on the site, was given its Gothick guise in 1793 by the 1st Earl of Uxbridge. His architect was James Wyatt, assisted by Joseph Potter of Lichfield, who continued working at Plas Newydd until well into the next century. The style would have been deplored by Pugin and his followers as a travesty of true Gothic, but it is in fact imaginative and highly decorative – never more so than in the stables, which are flanked to excellent effect by planting specified in Repton's *Red Book* for Plas Newydd of 1798.

The hall and the music room are the only state rooms in which the Gothick of the exterior is continued with any conviction. The decoration of the other rooms is neo-classical. This lack of consistency is characteristic of Plas Newydd, particularly of its collections. Much of the finest furniture came from other houses; for instance, the pair of Kentian tables in the saloon with bases in the form of lions with scaly serpents' tails are from Ingestre in Staffordshire. Many of the 16th- and 17th-century portraits and the superb 'angel' or flying tester bedstead in painted Chinese silk which is in Lord Anglesey's bedroom, came from Beaudesert in Staffordshire, the Pagets' other home.

The arrangement of the state rooms today remains largely that of the 6th Marquess and his wife, Lady Marjorie Manners. The 1930s were, after all, one of the most significant periods artistically in the history of the house. At that time the north wing was raised and remodelled and Wyatt's Gothick spires replaced with Tudor caps. Half the bedrooms were turned into bathrooms, to make Plas Newydd one of the most comfortable houses in the country. The terrace garden, with its planting of lines of Mediterranean cypresses, was also laid out. Most important of all, and vividly illustrated in the small museum devoted to his work, Rex Whistler was a frequent visitor, amusing the children with a rebus one moment; designing screen walls for the garden the next; and intermittently dashing in another incident to his masterpieces in the dining room.

Polesden Lacey, Surrey

1½ miles south of Great Bookham, off the A246 Leatherhead/Guildford road

Only one slight drawing is known to survive of the Caroline house at Polesden Lacey which Sheridan, the dramatist and politician, bought in 1797 with over 300 acres of farmland. It was evidently attractive, for he wrote jubilantly to his wife, 'I have every hour some new reason to be pleased with our purchase ... we shall have the nicest place, within prudent distance of town, in England.' After Sheridan's death the property was sold and in 1823 a villa to the designs of Thomas Cubitt, and more in accord with Regency taste, rose on the site of the old house.

It was this simple neo-Grecian building which in 1906 became the home of Mrs Ronald Greville. A skilful hostess, she entertained at Polesden Lacey for nearly forty years people of power and fashion. Her guests included King Edward VII, who was an intimate friend, and George VI and Queen Elizabeth, to whom, as Duke and Duchess of York, she lent Polesden for part of their honeymoon. On her death in 1942 she left the house, with the 1,000 acre estate, to the Trust.

The south front of the house with its Ionic colonnade retains an echo of the Regency, but inside everything was remodelled after 1906. The interior survives today as a fascinating expression of sophisticated Edwardian taste, and of the wealth and character of its highly competent owner, who filled it with a large and important collection of works of art.

A 'Jacobean' corridor built in 1910, a hall panelled with the reredos of a demolished Wren church, a drawing room whose gilded carving and painted ceiling were transported from an Italian *palazzo*: such juxtapositions in-

Polesden Lacey; Garden façade

dicate the eclecticism of Mrs Greville's taste. So do the rich and rare objects with which she filled the house. For the amateur of easel paintings and of miniatures, of porcelain and faience, of silver, of English cabinet work and French marquetry furniture, Polesden has much to offer.

The paintings fall into three main types which illustrate movements in artistic fashion from 1890 to 1940. Firstly, a splendid series of Dutch 17th-century works, mainly acquired by Mrs Greville's father in the 1890s, which include pictures by the Ostades, Cuyp, Van der Neer, Van de Velde, de Hoogh, Van Goyen, Jacob van Ruisdael, Salomon van Ruysdael, and Terborch (the last and the elder van Ruisdael represented by particularly fine examples). Secondly, a series of English portraits – Richardson, Reynolds, Lawrence, and four excellent Raeburns – bought for the most part soon after the First World War. Thirdly, a series of earlier paintings, mainly Italian and Flemish of the 14th–16th centuries which reflect the artistic climate of the 1930s and include works by Luca di Tommé, the Master of St Severin, and Bernard van Orley.

Pottery and porcelain wares include rich collections of Italian majolica (mainly 16th-century Urbino ware), K'ang-Hsi 'powder blue', *famille verte* and *famille rose*; and the productions of the Meissen, Fürstenberg, Chelsea, Nyon, and Zurich factories.

The silver collection is notable for the number and quality of 17th-century pieces, several dating from the 1680s with *chinoiserie* decoration. Finally, the French furniture includes a rare Renaissance table and a number of important signed pieces by 18th-century *ébénistes*.

The firm history of the garden begins in 1796, when Sheridan extended and improved the great grass terrace which had been started in 1761. To walk in spring or autumn along this terrace, flanked by the green or rusty brown of beeches and by a dark yew hedge, is one of the delights of Polesden. At the far end is a screen of Doric columns which once formed the portico of the house. The urns, on plinths inscribed with quotations from Pope, must date from the 18th century.

The south front of the house, on which grow successfully two plants of *Clematis armandii*, ceanothus and other shrubs, looks over a great lawn, prefaced by superb 18th-century urns, and so across a valley to woods climbing to Ranmore Common. On the flanks of the lawn rise blue Colorado spruces, cedars, beeches, limes and ilex. Framing the east front a long vista stretches between woods. Many good conifers thrive on the chalky soil, including *Podocarpus andinus*, *Cephalotaxus drupacea* and *Juniperus chinensis*. Even sweet chestnuts, rhododendrons, and *Pinus parviflora*, thrive on patches of soil from which the lime has leached out over the centuries.

At the entrance to the walled garden is the tomb of Mrs Greville. Though guarded by towering yew hedges, it keeps company with the gayest of 18th-century statuary. Much of the garden as we know it was her creation. Her extensive rose garden, dominated by a water tower over which climbs a venerable wistaria, is divided by cross walks under pergolas which carry Edwardian ramblers. *Viburnum foetens* and *Daphne odora* 'Aureomarginata' thrive on a sunny border. Smaller enclosures are devoted to lavenders and irises, and a garden of winter flowers is being developed under large specimens of *Parrotia persica*.

Outside the walled garden stretches a long herbaceous border. On the ample lawn beyond, an ardent Diana, perhaps the most lively of the many works of sculpture which adorn the garden, sets out confidently for the chase.

Powis Castle, Welshpool, Powys

West of the A483 Welshpool/Newtown road

Perched on a knoll that commands the upper reaches of the Severn valley, and encircled by an ancient park set with giant oaks, Powis is among the most romantic of the castles that once guarded the Welsh Marches. It is also one of the most interesting on account of its architectural continuity. The red sandstone walls no doubt once enclosed a typical Edwardian castle but, unlike Caernarvon and Conwy and most of the other great 13th-century fortresses in Wales, Powis never became ruinous but continued to change and develop. Successive generations adapted it to their differing needs, and seven centuries have left upon it their architectural signature. Thus the visitor, entering a gateway of 1668, passes through a 13th-century doorway to enter a house which was first remodelled to suit more peaceable times at the end of the 16th century, and again extensively altered on at least two occasions, in the late 17th and the late 19th centuries.

The interior is thus a rich amalgam of style, period, and association. The 15th-century sword of the Lord of the Marches, Limoges enamel of the 16th century, the silver sconces made out of coffin plates of the 2nd Marquess, the Sèvres service of the formidable Tipu Sahib: such things are the

Powis Castle; Terraces and hanging garden

splendid wrack of time at Powis. So too are a monumental Italian 16th-century marble-inlay table of the greatest rarity, silver toilet sets of 1700, a *View of Verona* by Bellotto, and an array of family portraits which include works by Kneller, Reynolds, Gainsborough and Romney. The long gallery with its painted wainscot and original oak flooring is Elizabethan; the state bedroom with elaborate acanthus mouldings and parcel-gilt decoration is Charles II; the Great Staircase, painted with murals by Lanscroon, is signed and dated 1705; the Blue Drawing Room, with its rich Louis XV furniture, reflects the taste of a Georgian owner; the Oak Drawing Room brings us to G. F. Bodley and the first years of the 20th century.

The interest of the house derives largely from the royalist Herberts who have lived at Powis since 1587 – the 6th Earl of Powis does so today – but for a break when the 1st Marquess went into exile with James II. (His wife was Lady of the Bedchamber to Mary of Modena and witnessed the disputed birth of the young Prince of Wales, whom she helped to smuggle to France.) It was through a Herbert heiress who married Lord Clive, son of Clive of India, that Tipu Sahib's service, and the collection of Indian works of art (now shown in the ballroom) reached the Castle.

While the 1st Marquess was in exile – he returned in 1722 – William III gave Powis to the Earl of Rochford, said to be his illegitimate son. It was the latter who continued work on the justly famous terraces and hanging gardens, which were probably designed by the 1st Marquess's architect, William Winde (see Cliveden, p. 87). With their clipped yews and borders, their statuary, and their ordered architectural character, they are the perfect expression of a formal taste. Unlike most such gardens, they were not swept away by the fashion for 'natural' landscape associated with Capability Brown.

Powis Castle; View from terrace garden

Set on the steep slope below the Castle, there are four terraces, two of them balustraded, and all nearly 200 yards long. The terrace walks are richly planted with shrubs and plants that include *Buddleia colvilei*, *Caesalpinia japonica*, pomegranate, the Chinese Snowball, romneyas, species of roses, eucryphias, embothriums, and several fine specimens of the 'Brilliantissimum' sycamore. Roses and clematis climb up the old pear trees and hang down from the high wall supporting the courtyard.

Across the wide level lawn below, where there was once a water garden, the further hillside is shaded by natural oaks supplemented by fine conifers, rhododendrons, azaleas and other species, a 'handkerchief' tree, rare hollies, Roblé beech, Lucombe oak, narrow-leafed ash, and oxydendrum. The rhododendrons are represented by species and hybrids. Bamboos, dogwoods and gunnera are grouped around a pond and in marshy ground.

Princes Risborough Manor, Buckinghamshire

Near the Parish Church

The house and garden, though a stone's throw from Risborough High Street, are as quiet behind their ancient brick wall as if they were set in the depths of the country. One of the most liveable houses owned by the Trust, the manor is also of more than usual architectural interest.

At first sight the entrance front, with sash windows and pedimented doorway, seems early Georgian. But both the brickwork and the thick pilasters, with attractively moulded capitals, speak of an earlier date. The brickwork is partly English and partly Flemish bond and indicates the

173

Princes Risborough Manor; The staircase

second half of the 17th century, when Flemish bond began to compete with the earlier method of bricklaying. Again, the pilasters which stop short of the eaves and fulfil no structural purpose speak of a date when provincial builders were still uncertain about the use of such classical features. A glance at the garden elevation resolves the matter. Here the survival of two windows with wooden mullions and transoms clearly shows that the house must be Charles II or late Stuart.

The two most attractive features inside the house – the staircase and drawing room – confirm such a date. The oak staircase, a convincing example of local craftsmanship with an openwork balustrade cut out of the solid wood, though Jacobean in type, is just such a country joiner might have produced in the mid-17th century. The panelling of the drawing room is also characteristic of the 17th rather than the 18th century. In particular the heavy mouldings of the elaborate chimneypiece and the motif of a perspective seen through a columned arch indicate an early date.

Elsewhere in the house is a 16th-century fireplace, all that appears to survive of a yet earlier house that was almost wholly transformed soon after the Restoration.

174

Quebec House, Westerham, Kent

In Westerham village, at the foot of the hill

In 1726 the Wolfe family moved to Westerham and there, in what we now know as Quebec House, James Wolfe was born in 1727. Thirty-two years later he died on the heights above Quebec and became part of English military history. His courage, his daring, his ingenuity, and not least his eccentricity, have given him a special place in our national pantheon. 'Oh! he is mad, is he?', George II is said to have remarked, 'Then I wish he would *bite* some other of my generals.' Quick-tempered and, as he himself owned, 'a whimsical sort of person', he was an utterly dedicated soldier. When, mortally wounded at Quebec, he learned that the French were giving way on all sides, he exclaimed, 'Now, God be praised, I will die in peace.'

The gabled house, built of mellowed brick, had been standing some 200 years before the Wolfes came to Westerham in 1726. A single mullioned Tudor window survives, though it was blocked up when the main staircase was inserted in the late 17th century. Several changes were made at that time and more followed at the end of the 18th century, yet Wolfe would recognize the house today, the panelled rooms which he knew until he was eleven, his travelling canteen, his dressing-gown, his parents' portraits, and other relics which relate to himself and his family. He would no doubt be surprised to find the house a place of pilgrimage.

Canada has naturally played a pre-eminent role in the preservation of Quebec House. Mrs J. B. Learmont of Montreal left it to the Trust, and Canadian money has generously contributed to its maintenance and enriched the collection of Wolfeiana.

Quebec House

Saltram House, Devon

South of A38, 2 miles west of Plympton

Fanny Burney, that experienced observer, whose novels gave such pleasure to the late 18th century, wrote of Saltram in 1789: 'the house is one of the most magnificent in the kingdom, its view is noble'. Certainly Saltram is distinguished in at least two particulars. Firstly, it affords the finest example in the south-west of Robert Adam's interior decoration; secondly, it contains a splendid collection of the works of Reynolds, who was born near by and had a long and intimate association with the house. Furthermore, Saltram, which came to the Trust in 1957, remained until 1962 the seat of the Earls of Morley and retains the warmth and atmosphere of a much-loved country house.

Saltram derives its name from the fact that salt was produced in early days from saltpans on the tidal estuary. There was a house on the present site from at least Tudor times. In 1712 the property was bought by George Parker, ancestor of the Earls of Morley, but it was only in 1743 that the family moved into an earlier house and his son John began its transformation into the largest mansion in Devon. It was complete by 1750.

Eighteen years later John Parker II inherited. Created Lord Boringdon in 1788, he was basically a country squire, though he had other interests and was a close friend of Joshua Reynolds. He also bred a Derby winner called Saltram. But in the present context his significance lies in his engaging Robert Adam to decorate his saloon and dining room, and incidentally to design the attractive 'Stag' lodges at the entrance to the park. Apart from the creation of the library, finished in 1819, and the addition of the Doric porch on the entrance front, there were to be no further architectural changes of importance, something for which we may be duly grateful.

Externally Saltram is an awkward house, and the stucco elevation gives little indication of the beauty and interest of the interior. The formal entrance hall proves to be a complete and untouched composition of the reign of George II. The rich stuccowork of the ceiling, supported by a Doric entablature – the Doric order was usually favoured for entrance halls – is attributed to the Italian stuccoer Vassali. The adjoining morning room, also of the time of George II, can have changed little since Dr Johnson saw it in 1762. The delightful ceiling, again Italian work, the carved marble chimneypiece and the carved woodwork are original. The walls are hung with faded Genoa velvet, and the arrangement of the pictures, which include five Reynolds portraits, reflects the fashion of the times when rooms from dado to ceiling were plastered with pictures, set almost as closely as stamps on the pages of an album. The hanging may be contrasted with that of Adam's neo-classical dining room.

The saloon, for which Adam's drawing dated 1768 survives, is a major triumph of late-18th-century interior design. Every detail of the room from the frieze to the gilt-brass door handles was planned, as was Adam's custom, to contribute to the overall effect. Thus the Axminster carpet was specially woven to echo the restrained yet exquisite design of the ceiling. The

Saltram; The morning room, designed by Robert Adam

chimneypiece with Siena marble columns was supplied by Carter of Piccadilly, while the stuccowork and the painted roundels in the ceiling are by Joseph Rose and Antonio Zucchi respectively – both of them talented craftsmen whose contribution Adam frequently enlisted when creating his finished interiors. On the walls, with Adam's four great giltwood mirrors, hang further Reynolds portraits. Adam was responsible also for the superb giltwood stands that support Blue John vase candelabra, with ormolu mounts by Matthew Boulton, yet another outstanding craftsman whose talents Adam engaged.

The dining room which succeeds is no less impressive. Rose and Zucchi were again employed, and the design of the ceiling is again reflected in the pattern of the Axminster carpet. An attractive feature is Adam's curved segmental sideboard, flanked by urn-shaped wine coolers. He also designed the carved mirror and the marble-topped sideboard that stands below it. For Zucchi's decorative paintings on the walls he provided plaster frames, and each canvas was set so as best to fit the space available. There could be no greater contrast to the treatment of the pictures in the morning room, or one that better illustrates Adam's approach to interior decoration.

Among the further delights which the interior of Saltram offers are the Chinese dressing room and Chinese Chippendale bedroom, both papered with the Chinese export papers known to the 18th century as 'India' paper. The bedroom illustrates how happily such exotic *chinoiserie* marries with mid-18th-century mahogany and the four-poster bed which Chippendale supplied in about 1760.

John Parker and his successors provided Saltram with an appropriate setting and carefully planted the park, woods and gardens which surround it. From the front of the house the view stretches uninterrupted above a ha-ha and across the park. To the right a path leads directly into a lime avenue planted about 1820, along whose verges grow narcissus varieties of Victorian times, primroses, and *Cyclamen neapolitanum*, white and pink. Emerging from the avenue, you reach the 'Castle' at the end of the garden. The little octagonal building, in Gothick dress but with a classical interior, was finished in about 1771. The way back to the house by lawn or path, through shade and sunlight, lies among shrubs and trees, where in spring magnolias and cherries vie with camellias and rhododendrons. These with other evergreens, and hoheria and eucryphia, are overshadowed by imposing Monterey and stone pines, old oaks, and an immense plane. The trees alternately mask and reveal the views across the park.

On one of the lawns stands a handsome orangery of 1775, framed by evergreen oaks, and complete with leaden sphinxes and blue African lilies in tubs. It contains orange and lemon trees which are trundled out during the summer to take the air in an oval garden enclosed by tree rhododendrons and palms, magnolias, hydrangeas and a fine specimen black walnut. Near the orangery is a chapel, long ruinous, and an herbaceous border for summer colour. In the woods behind stands Fanny's Bower, a small classical garden house beloved by Fanny Burney.

More good shrubs and trees grow on the east side of the house including pittosporums, eucryphias, *Magnolia delavayi*, *Acer griseum* and an immense lime tree. There is everywhere a feeling of spaciousness to which the generous park contributes with its fine trees planted mostly during the 18th century in the manner and grouping of Capability Brown.

Shaw's Corner, Ayot St Lawrence, Hertfordshire

3 miles north-west of Welwyn, at south-west end of the village green

Shaw was fifty when in 1906 he bought, at Ayot St Lawrence, The Villa which he characteristically re-named Shaw's Corner; he died there in 1950 at the age of ninety-four.

Since the accession of Queen Victoria there has been something of a divorce between taste and genius. Shaw's Corner is an undistinguished, indeed a thoroughly unattractive, house. It is on two counts a most interesting one. Firstly, it is in many respects a faithful reflection of typical middle-class furnishing from Edwardian times to the outbreak of the Second World War. Such unaltered interiors are rare and their survival is exceptional. Secondly, the house is an equally faithful reflection of the habits and interests of someone in many respects untypical of his class. Here in a very ordinary setting is detailed evidence of an extraordinary man and the way he liked to live.

Shaw's Corner is a mine of biographical material. In the hall are the array

Shaw's Corner; GBS on the lawn

of hats which came to form part of Shaw's public image, the basket chair where he put on his shoes every morning, and the bicycling machine on which he used to exercise. Against the wall is his Bechstein piano at which he would sit and sing Italian opera to his own accompaniment while the air raid sirens wailed over Ayot. After drama, music was the branch of the arts that meant most to him and he began his literary career as a brilliant and provocative music critic.

His study is in every sense the heart of the house. His desk with its gear, where he started work daily at 10.15, is precisely as he left it. To hand are his elaborate filing cabinets and his working library, and in the room are the

Shaw's Corner; Interior of the garden study　　　　*The garden study*

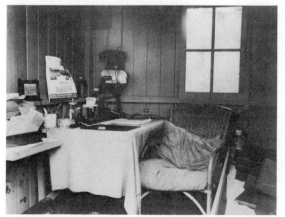

photographs of the friends whom he admired: William Morris, Wickham Steed whose economic theories deeply influenced him, Sean O'Casey, Barrie, Sidney Webb, his compatriots W. B. Yeats and Lady Gregory, and Gene Tunney who, somewhat surprisingly, was a close friend.

The adjoining drawing room was very much Mrs Shaw's province, and after her death in 1943 Shaw used it little except when he had visitors. On the desk, however, is a memorial of the greatest interest: his bust by Rodin, executed at Meudon in the days when Rilke was acting as the sculptor's secretary.

Though a vegetarian, Shaw used the dining room more than might be supposed. His habit of reading over lunch sometimes protracted the meal for two hours. Here hangs Augustus John's splendid portrait, and there are a number of moving personal relics: among them, Shaw's fountain pen and gold pencil, both put to such indefatigable purpose, his steel-rimmed spectacles, and his membership card of the British Museum Reading Room for 1880, when at the age of twenty-four he was embarking with his usual determination on a long literary and dramatic career. In this room he died.

Shugborough, Staffordshire

$5\frac{1}{2}$ miles south-east of Stafford on the A513 Rugeley/Stafford road

Grand but never overweening, the late-18th-century house stands by the junction of the rivers Trent and Sow in a wide shallow valley at the northern edge of Cannock Chase, the medieval hunting forest more usually associated with the Black Country to the south.

Shugborough has belonged to the Anson family since 1624, when it was bought by William Anson, a successful Staffordshire lawyer. His great-grandson Thomas, who succeeded in 1720, was a cultivated and travelled bachelor, a founder member of the Dilettanti Society, and M.P. for Lichfield which was to be represented by an Anson for the next hundred years. Thomas Anson greatly enlarged the late-17th-century house which he inherited, adding the flanking bow-fronted pavilions and linking buildings, and he embellished the park with classical temples and monuments. Such additions and improvements were largely due to financial help from his younger brother George, Admiral Anson the Circumnavigator, who had returned in 1744 from his four-year voyage round the world both famous and rich. His share of the spoils, which included the capture of the annual Spanish trans-Pacific galleon with a cargo worth £400,000, was the basis of the fortune which created Shugborough as it is today.

Admiral Anson and his officers took a great interest in the work at Shugborough: a Captain Brett designed the enchanting Chinese House in the garden, others supplied 'landskip' wallpaper for Lady Anson's bedroom, and when the Admiral died, a childless widower, in 1761, he left his possessions and his fortune to his brother. On the death of Thomas Anson in 1789, his great-nephew, who was to become Viscount Anson in 1806,

Shugborough; The west front and formal garden

inherited the estate. Almost at once he engaged Samuel Wyatt to remodel the house. Between 1794 and 1806 Wyatt built the Ionic portico on the east front, unusual in that it stretches across the whole width of the central block, and on the garden front he created the large projecting three-storeyed feature with verandas on either side. These and other changes – he covered the exterior with slate treated to look like stone – were not altogether fortunate. The slate was partially removed in 1920 when the house was stuccoed and further alterations were made.

The 1st Viscount also extended the park in the grand manner, diverting the main road, removing the remains of a village, and building lodges and a model farm to Wyatt's designs. As befitted a son-in-law of Coke of Holkham, he was keenly interested in agriculture. His son, created Earl of Lichfield in 1831, became Postmaster-General and during his tenure of office Sir Rowland Hill introduced the Penny Post. The Earl was 'liberal, hospitable, frank and gay, quick and intelligent'; but he was also extravagant and imprudent, and his interests in racing, hunting and electioneering were financially disastrous. In 1842 most of the contents of the house, except the family portraits, were sold at an auction lasting a fortnight. Luckily the 2nd Earl, who succeeded ten years later, collected French furniture and it is largely owing to him that the house contains so much of interest. On the death of the 4th Earl in 1960, Shugborough was accepted by the Treasury in lieu of death duties and offered to the National Trust. The County Council leases the estate and administers the house.

The dining room, decorated with large tempera *capricci* by Nicholas Dall, and the library are both Palladian in character and decorated with Vassali's imaginative plasterwork. They date from Thomas Anson's rebuilding in the mid-18th century. The library, with serene classical busts above the bookcases, is unusually small and intimate for such an 18th-century room. Described as 'odd and pretty' when it was finished in 1748, it is in truth one of the most engaging libraries of the period.

The hand of Samuel Wyatt is to be seen notably in the red drawing room and the saloon. The former, with coved ceiling and delicate plaster decoration by Joseph Rose the younger, is a good example of late-18th-century taste, and the suite of gilt chairs and sofas was supplied for the room in 1794. The saloon, with scagliola columns and a great bay window, was contrived a decade later. It attempts, not altogether successfully, a very grand manner.

Shugborough; The saloon   *The library*

The 2nd Earl's furniture includes many magnificent pieces of 18th-century French craftsmanship, among them a Louis XV marquetry commode by Schmitz and a Louis XVI parquetry *jardinière* by Bury. Of the earlier things, acquired by Admiral Anson, perhaps the most notable are a Chinese Chippendale display cabinet, a number of Chinese mirror pictures in elaborate gilt frames, and an armorial china service, decorated with breadfruit and topographical scenes, presented to him by the foreign merchants of Canton in gratitude for his saving the city from a disastrous fire.

Although Thomas Anson's scholarly collection of paintings and classical sculptures was sold, there is a long series of Anson portraits, and much remains to illustrate the interest of the family history. The 19th-century sporting pictures have particular charm, as have the superb animal sketches and portrait drawings by Landseer.

The 18th-century stable block, now a county folk museum, is of almost royal proportions. At Wyatt's Park Farm rare breeds of livestock are once again being reared.

The gardens that lie between the house and the river were laid out about 1855. The earlier monuments in the garden and park are described on pages 281–2.

Sizergh Castle, Cumbria

$3\frac{1}{2}$ miles south of Kendal, north-west of A6/A591 interchange

Until the Union of 1603 the history of the Border country was one of raid and counter-raid. Those who lived in the wide belt within which the Border fluctuated – the Debatable Land, as it was called – had need of security. From the 14th century onward peles, that is to say, towers standing within a protective paling or stockade, were built from coast to coast. Sizergh was originally such a pele tower. But over the centuries it has grown into a fascinating complex of pele tower, great hall, and later enlargements.

The entrance front, flanked by two projecting 16th-century wings, which contained kitchen, offices, and sleeping quarters for the servants, is dominated by the pele tower. Though the Strickland family were possessed of Sizergh in the first half of the 13th century, the present pele dates from about 1350. It is one of the largest to survive and at ground level its limestone rubble walls are over nine feet thick. An unusual feature is the substantial turret rising higher than the tower which originally held the garderobes.

Adjoining the pele tower is a late medieval block which once contained a great hall with open-timbered roof. The elevation, with sash windows, a central window with ogee head, and battlements, now takes its character from changes made in about 1770.

Sizergh Castle; The north front, with the pele tower

The interior of Sizergh is principally distinguished for its panelling and carved woodwork. Possibly no other house has so much early Elizabethan carving of fine quality. Moreover, it shows no trace of that coarseness and grotesqueness so often found in the woodwork of the times. There are no less than five dated chimneypieces of the greatest virtuosity executed before 1580. The panelling ranges from early linenfold to that with lozenges, set in oblong panels, found in the morning room (1563) and the Boynton room (1575). The superb panelling from the inlaid chamber is now in the Victoria and Albert Museum.

Owing to the unbroken association of the Strickland family with the castle, the contents of Sizergh are as interesting as their setting. There is a two-handed sword of *c.* 1340, thus contemporary with the pele tower, and the wide range of early oak furniture includes a set of Elizabethan forms, some of them dated 1562, which may well have been carved by the craftsmen who were executing the chimneypieces in the house at about the same time.

There is plenty of good furniture more familiar in character, both English and Continental, of the 18th century, and a collection of porcelain which includes a silver-mounted Japanese bowl of Kutani ware given by Mary of Modena to the daughter of Sir Richard Strickland. A long series of portraits records likenesses of the Stricklands over many generations. It was their close association with the Stuart cause – for eleven years they were voluntary exiles at the court of St Germain – that brought to Sizergh an unusual assemblage of Stuart relics.

The garden at Sizergh looks across terraces, dating from the second half of the 18th century, to a lake and the park. Though many good shrubs and climbers grow on this front – *Solanum crispum, Escallonia iveyi*, clematis and roses – it is the rock garden, created in the 1920s by Mr and Mrs Hornyold-Strickland, that offers outstanding horticultural interest. Constructed of native limestone, with waterfalls and pools fed by the stream above the castle, it contains a variety of choice plants, including primulas, rodgersias, astilbes and many alpine plants; *Gentiana asclepiadea* grows everywhere from self-sown seedlings. The climate provides conditions suitable for ferns and there is a big collection of species and varieties, some nestling under Japanese maples of good size. *Osmunda gracilis* is one of the least common, noted for its small size compared with the native royal fern and for its coppery tint in spring.

The specimens of dwarf conifers are noteworthy; some now of unusual size were planted in 1926. *Abies procera* 'Glauca Prostrata' is over fifteen feet across, and there is a large *Tsuga canadensis* 'Pendula'. Dwarf forms of *Picea abies* are numerous, and *P.a.* 'Ellwangeriana' measures fourteen feet across and is five feet high. Larger growing conifers are *Pinus parviflora, P. montana uncinata, Juniperus media* 'Plumosa Aurea' and *Taxus baccata* 'Dovastonii Aurea'.

The castle and its contents, and an estate of some 1,500 acres, were given to the Trust by the Hornyold-Strickland family in 1950.

Smallhythe Place, Kent

2 miles south of Tenterden, on east side of the B2082 Tenterden/Rye road

The timbered house, for nearly thirty years the country home of Ellen Terry, was built in about 1840. Though it has been altered from time to time, it retains its essential character and is a testimonial to the sturdy building of the late 15th century. Before the sea receded, it was known as the Port House and served a thriving shipyard. In the garden may still be seen a repair dock that must have been in use until the Smallhythe channel silted up in the 17th century.

Ellen Terry firmly established her reputation between the years 1878 and 1902, when she was acting with Henry Irving. At this period, in 1899, she bought Smallhythe, and it was in this house that she died in 1928. Many actresses have been as widely admired, but very few as universally beloved. The enchanting personality that two generations found irresistible has left its imprint on Smallhythe. It would be difficult to think of a house which more intimately reflects a vanished owner. That the rooms and their contents have been so faithfully preserved is due to Ellen Terry's daughter, Edith Craig, who kept the house as a memorial to her mother and ultimately gave it to the Trust.

The large room on the ground floor is a kind of monument to the theatrical profession, a treasure house filled with possessions and portraits of famous players – from Garrick and Sarah Siddons to Sarah Bernhardt and Duse, the wonderful Italian whom Ellen Terry so deeply admired. Another room is devoted to Ellen Terry's stage costumes which include the famous beetle-wing dress worn by her as Lady Macbeth at the Lyceum Theatre in 1888, and in which she was painted by Sargent.

Smallhythe Place; Ellen Terry's bedroom

The Lyceum room is a record of a professional partnership that is probably unequalled in the annals of the stage. Ellen Terry and Henry Irving acted together for twenty-four years. These years, during which the actress achieved her greatest triumphs, are reflected in this room, which she shares with Irving. Likenesses of the actor show a rather plain youth changing to the dignified man of middle age, with his adored dog, Fussy, and reveal in his death mask an austere, almost Caesarean, countenance.

From Ellen Terry's bedroom the theatre and her public life were excluded. It is touching in its simplicity and in the small intimate objects of sentimental association that it contains. The dressing table is so modest that one can hardly credit that the small mirror reflected year after year the face of a great actress. By the bed lie her crucifix and her well-worn and annotated copy of the Globe *Shakespeare* – the book she prized above all others.

Snowshill Manor, Gloucestershire

3 miles south of Broadway

Snowshill is architecturally a characteristic Cotswold manor. Built of warm local stone, its gables, mullioned windows, chipstone mouldings, and carefully dressed quoins, speak of the sober and dignified local idiom which changed relatively little in 300 years. Though there are clear traces of an older medieval building, the house is substantially of the 17th and early 18th

Snowshill Manor; The entrance front

186

centuries, as is clearly indicated by the attractive entrance front combining mullioned and transomed windows of the 17th century with sashes of later date.

Where Snowshill is decidedly not characteristic of the Cotswolds or indeed of anywhere else, is in its extraordinary contents. The expression of a no less extraordinary personality, the Snowshill collection was the creation, the lifelong accumulation, of Charles Wade (1883–1956). Scholar, architect and artist craftsman, he bought the house, which had once belonged to

Snowshill Manor;
Room of a hundred wheels　　　*Green Room*

Catherine Parr, wife of Henry VIII, in 1919. Having restored it, he lived there in spartan conditions (he would never have electric light), devoting his time, and a fortune derived from family sugar plantations in the West Indies, to accumulating a vast heterogeneous assemblage of objects.

Many people have a bent for collecting, and their approach may be scholarly, dilettante, or aesthetic; but occasionally a real magpie appears. Such was Charles Wade. In his own way and period he may be compared to the classic examples of the species – Beckford at Fonthill, or Horace Walpole at Strawberry Hill. Collecting entered into every corner of his life and living, and Snowshill provides a rare insight into the mind of a passionate collector.

Charles Wade's tastes and interests, if not always marked by discrimination or strong aesthetic judgement, were astonishingly wide and eclectic. The rooms he furnished, and over-furnished, contain an extraordinary variety of unusual, sometimes rare, objects. Jacobean furniture, Spanish *varguenos*, illuminated missals, Japanese armour, camel trappings, and Persian lamps, rub shoulders with an impressive range of craft tools and bygones, the last expressing his evident nostalgia for the ways and things of a fast fading age which he could still remember. One room is devoted to old compasses, telescopes, ship models, and all that speaks of the sea before the age of steam; another to a collection of old musical instruments, others to the crafts of weaving and lacemaking; and the great garret to earlier means of locomotion – hobby horses, sedan chairs, boneshaker bicycles, models of farm wains, and all that once moved on quieter English roads.

Such a collection will not be assembled again. Cost prohibits it, and the things are no longer to be found. Moreover, a Wade occurs perhaps once in a century. The strange accumulation which he gave to the Trust in 1951, therefore, merits careful presentation as he arranged it, exactly and eccentrically. Perhaps no man in our time has left so strongly upon a house the imprint of an idiosyncratic personality.

4, South Quay, Great Yarmouth, Norfolk

The seemly front of the house with its sash windows, ironwork balconies, and trim white portico, proves to be highly deceptive. Added early in the 19th century, it is no more than the refacing of a late Elizabethan house which was probably finished in 1596. Inside much of the early house survives. Both the dining room and north chamber retain their chimneypieces and oak panelling, while the principal chamber, the drawing room, has in addition a fine moulded plaster ceiling. In all these rooms the panelling has been adapted to accommodate the later sash windows on the entrance front.

4, South Quay,
Great Yarmouth

The house was owned in the mid-19th century by Charles John Palmer, a noted antiquary, but his 'restorations' can usually be distinguished easily enough from the genuine earlier work. The old stained glass mounted in the staircase window and in the large kitchen, which retains its mullioned windows intact, was probably collected by Palmer in the course of his Continental travels. The house is now let to the Norfolk Museum Service and displays a collection of decorative art.

Springhill, Moneymore, Co. Londonderry

Just outside Moneymore on the B18 Moneymore/Coagh road

Like so many Scots, the Conynghams came to seek their fortune in Ulster in the reign of James I or soon after. They were to become a notable military family and there were few occasions in the next 300 years when a Conyngham of Springhill was not in command of troops. Staunchly Protestant and anti-Jacobite, they fought for Cromwell and William III; in the 18th century they raised their own regiments of Volunteers; and a Conyngham in the 19th century established a record by commanding the Londonderry Militia for thirty-five years. The tradition continued until the death of Captain William Lenox-Conyngham in 1957, when Springhill passed to the National Trust.

Springhill owes its character to these soldiers and their wives. It is unassuming and straightforward: an agreeable Ulster country house without frills or pretensions. Its atmosphere speaks of the lives of successive generations far removed from the centres of fashion. No echoes here of Palladio or the Grand Tour, of Gothick revival or Grecian taste. Springhill is authentic, and conveys a sense of the life of these vanished soldiers as a more self-conscious and elegant house might fail to do.

The Conynghams acquired the Springhill estate in 1658 for £200. It is on a long wooded ridge about a mile from Moneymore – 'the Great Shrubbery' in Irish – and old yew trees near the house are among the last traces of an ancient forest which once stretched to Lough Neagh. The house itself was not built until the last quarter of the 17th century and like many of the early Ulster houses was originally protected by a defensive barrier and fencework. The great barn still retains its bell tower and the bell that was rung to rouse the martial Conynghams and their dependants in time of danger. The outworks disappeared in the more settled climate of the 18th century, and the white roughcast house, with its curiously narrow and elongated windows and steeply pitched slate roof, is now visible from the drive gates. The lower wings with bays and hipped roofs were extensions added to the main block in 1765. The courtyard in front of the house is flanked by two long ranges which were formerly the servants' quarters.

The outbuildings, which include laundry, brewhouse, slaughterhouse, dovecote, and stables, indicate the self-sufficient economy that characterized such a rural establishment until the beginning of the 20th century. One

Springhill; From the drive

of the outbuildings houses an interesting collection of 18th- and 19th-century costumes. In the simple garden beyond the outbuildings Lord Macartney, envoy to Peking in the late 18th century, planted the first of the roses which still bear his name.

The interior of Springhill contains good 18th-century cornices and panelling, and a staircase of the same period. The early-18th-century wallpaper lately revealed in the Gun Room to the left of the Hall is of particular interest. The contents of the house are such as might be expected where a single family has been in occupation for nearly 300 years: a library of old leather-bound books, including early editions of Gerard's *Herball*, Raleigh's *History of the World*, and Hobbes's *Leviathan*; a series of family portraits; furniture ranging from early oak presses to Victorian chairs with buttoned upholstery, and including, almost inevitably, a set of the 18th-century 'ladder back' chairs so frequently found in Ulster houses. The pleasantly cluttered drawing room has a markedly Victorian flavour.

Standen, West Sussex

2 miles south-west of East Grinstead, on the Saint Hill road off the B2110 to Handcross

Standen is the only house designed by Philip Webb (1831–1915) to have survived without alteration. It was built in 1894 for James Beale, a Birmingham solicitor specializing in work for the railway companies, who had come south to open a London office and settled in South Kensington. In 1891 he decided to build himself a house in the country. It was to be neither a grand mansion nor a cottage, but something quite unpretentious yet big enough for holidays with his large family and suitable in due course for his retirement.

The house stands in open country of small fields and wooded hedgerows with distant Ashdown Forest on the far ridge to the south. When the Beales came to Standen in the last decade of the reign of Queen Victoria, the landscape could scarcely have changed since the days of the Wealden ironmasters in the 17th century. The house is approached along a narrow lane which in due course opens on to Goose Green, a pleasant open space with a timber-clad barn and tile-hung farmhouse. It is characteristic of Webb's sensitivity (he was co-founder of the Society for the Protection of Ancient Buildings and life-long friend of William Morris) that he should have retained this 15th-century farmhouse and its outbuildings as part of his plan for a new house. The link between old and new is formed by an arch through which the forecourt and front door is reached.

Philip Webb's house is a highly idiosyncratic composition dominated by a squat tower rendered in pebble-dash. The building incorporates a multiplicity of techniques and materials drawn largely from local vernacular architecture; brick and sandstone, tile-hanging and weather-boarding, leaded casements as well as sash windows. The effect is restless, but redeemed by the quality of the workmanship, an aspect of building about which the architect was always particular.

Inside, Standen is the antithesis of the conventional idea of a Victorian house. The rooms are large, light and airy, hung with Morris wallpapers and not overcrowded. The furniture is a mixture of antique pieces brought by the Beales from their London home and new furniture supplied by the firm of Morris & Co. The dining room, especially, remains in the memory. It is lined to within two feet of the ceiling with panelling painted the unobtrusive shade of blue-green that Webb favoured for dining rooms. Rows of blue and white plates are ranged above the panelling and on the shelves of two simple

Standen

oak dressers built into a breakfast alcove carefully placed to catch the morning sun. The woven wool window curtains were made by the Morris factory, whilst the needlework chairs were worked by members of the family. The cheeks of the fireplace are of steel chased and burnished to reflect the flames. It is a spacious, simple and restful room, perfectly suited to its purpose. The large drawing room has a superb Morris carpet in a bold design of blue and red. The electric light brackets with backplates of chased copper are the originals designed by Webb.

The 10-acre garden is reached through the conservatory. A sunny terrace beyond is punctuated with large terracotta pots of agapanthus and there are fine flowering shrubs. The garden extends down a south-facing slope with fine views over the Sussex countryside. An old quarry overhung with trees provides the right conditions for ferns and other shade- and moisture-loving plants.

Good design and craftsmanship, simple comfort: it was to promote these principles that Morris, Burne-Jones, Rossetti and Webb banded together to found the firm of Morris & Co. in 1861. Nowhere are they better demonstrated than at Standen where, after her parents' death, their youngest daughter Helen continued to live. Until her death in 1972 she jealously preserved the house as she had known it from her childhood. She bequeathed Standen to the National Trust together with covenants over 169 acres of surrounding farmland.

Stourhead, Wiltshire

At Stourton, west of the B3092 Frome/Mere road

For over 200 years Stourhead has been the home of the Hoare family who still carry on the bank in Fleet Street, founded by Richard Hoare in about 1673. His son, Henry Hoare I (1677–1725), having acquired the manor of Stourton from the Catholic family who had owned it since the Conquest, pulled down their house in 1718, and built a new one facing the western edge of the Wessex chalk uplands.

Stourhead, as he named it, was a squarish building with an engaged portico to the east. Plain and well-proportioned, it was one of the first of those Palladian country houses of which so many were to be built during the course of the 18th century. Colen Campbell was the architect; this was hardly surprising since he was closely associated with Henry Hoare's brother-in-law, William Benson, who succeeded Sir Christopher Wren as Surveyor-General when the Whigs came to power on the accession of George I.

The Palladian style flourished at Stourhead until the 1750s, for at that time Henry's son, Henry Hoare II (1705–85), employed another Palladian architect, Henry Flitcroft, to design temples round the romantic lake that he formed by damming a valley to the west of the house to contain the headwaters of the river Stour.

None of Henry Hoare II's children survived him and Stourhead passed to a nephew, Richard Colt Hoare, who later inherited a baronetcy. Colt Hoare, a distinguished scholar and dilettante, devoted most of his life to travel and antiquities, and is remembered as the historian of Wiltshire. On his return from Italy in 1791, he extended the east front of the house by two wings, one for a library and the other for a picture gallery. In 1841 the 3rd baronet, Colt Hoare's half-brother, added a projecting portico to the house, in accordance with Campbell's original intention. The last owner, Henry Hugh Arthur Hoare, the 6th baronet, made further changes following a fire in 1902, when he altered and rebuilt the west front. Since his only son had died of wounds in 1917, and he had no direct heir, Sir Henry gave Stourhead to the Trust shortly before his death in 1947.

The rooms on the *piano nobile* now serve to display the collections that were mainly accumulated by Henry Hoare II and Richard Colt Hoare. Both of them followed the fashions of their time in purchasing pictures by Continental painters, among which are important works by Carlo Maratta, Cigoli (Lodovico Cardi), Nicolas and Gaspard Poussin. A. R. Mengs's *Octavian and Cleopatra*, commissioned by Henry Hoare in 1759 as a companion to a Maratta, is a landmark in neo-classical taste. Colt Hoare, an early patron of Turner (whose works were unfortunately sold with others in 1883), was particularly interested in topographical and water-colour painting. His collection of pictures by the Swiss artist Louis Ducros is unique in England. British painters are also well represented at Stourhead, especially John Wootton, William Hoare of Bath, Samuel Woodforde and Francis Nicholson. Small-scale sculptures include works by Michael Rysbrack, whose famous statue of *Hercules* may be seen in the Pantheon by the lake.

The furniture includes good examples of all periods from early Georgian to Regency; but the work of the younger Thomas Chippendale from 1797 to 1820 is outstanding. The suites he made in 1802 and 1805 for Colt Hoare's picture gallery and library, two of the least changed and most delightful interiors of their period, are celebrated in the history of British furniture.

Stourhead is pre-eminent among English landscape gardens (see p. 254).

Sudbury Hall, Derbyshire

6 miles east of Uttoxeter on A50

The architecture of Sudbury represents the style of the Restoration at its most individual, and its lavish decoration epitomizes the new extravagance of an age that firmly rejected the austerities of the Cromwellian period. Though Ham (see p. 115) is the most complete house of Charles II's reign, for not only decoration but furniture and fabrics have survived, at Sudbury the richness of the decoration itself has no parallel.

The house was the creation of George Vernon, who inherited in 1659 and was to be squire for forty-three years. For twenty-odd years he was building, and Sudbury dates substantially from the 1660–70s. That the main elevations and the state rooms have survived untouched is something of a miracle, for his successors in the 18th century produced a bizarre scheme to classicize the Caroline house, and in the 19th century they called on both Salvin and Barry to produce designs that would have been disastrous. Fortunately they were not adopted. The 19th century modified only the service end of the old house and added an adjoining east wing, now converted to a Museum of Childhood and administered jointly by the Trust and the local county authority.

Sudbury Hall; The entrance front

Sudbury Hall;
The long gallery

When George Vernon started building, the family had owned the Sudbury estate since 1513. A successor was raised to the peerage in 1762. In 1839 the 5th Lord Vernon, a notable Dante scholar, removed to Italy; though Queen Adelaide leased the house for three years in 1840, it was to remain virtually unoccupied for some twenty years. Towards the end of the century the family again moved out, and the late Lord Vernon did not return until 1922. On his death it was transferred to the Trust by the Treasury, having been accepted in part payment of death duties.

Sudbury has long been known to many people for the impressive view of the house from the main road. The high symmetrically-conceived front has the hipped roof, and cupola above, that are almost hallmarks of Caroline building. But certain features are surprising, and some of them decidedly old-fashioned. There is apparently no domestic precedent for the tracery of the windows, which recall the churches of the Laudian revival, while the diapered brickwork, the oversize windows with nine and twelve lights, and the round and diamond-shaped brooches to the bases of the Doric columns of the frontispiece might well be Jacobean. The explanation may be that George Vernon, like many gentlemen of his time, had some knowledge of building and surveying, and acted as his own architect.

The decoration of the interior is intact and astonishingly rich. Local craftsmen were initially employed, as in the Queen's bedroom with its robust alabaster chimneypiece and ceiling. But for the finest work, carried out in the '70s, Vernon enlisted the most sophisticated London craftsmen: Grinling Gibbons and Edward Pearce for carving and joinery, and Bradbury and Pettifer for stuccowork.

Gibbons's superb carving, executed in 1678 at a cost of £40, is to be seen in the drawing room in conjunction with the most ornate of Bradbury and Pettifer's ceilings. Pearce's masterwork is the staircase. Perhaps the finest of the period to be found in any country house, it has recently been repainted as it was in the 17th century. The most imposing room is the saloon, with stuccowork by Bradbury and Pettifer, wainscot and carving by Pearce, and a series of full-length Vernon portraits, giltwood chandeliers and gilded lead wall brackets, all introduced in the first half of the 18th century. The long gallery at the top of the house, with wainscot walls and a plaster ceiling by Bradbury and Pettifer, is a puzzling feature. The long gallery, so characteristic of large Elizabethan and Jacobean houses, was outmoded before the middle of the 17th century, and this must be one of the few post-Restoration examples. It may express the personal idiosyncrasy of the builder.

Soon after Sudbury was first decorated, murals came into fashion and George Vernon in his old age called in Louis Laguerre, one of the foremost exponents of Baroque mural painting in the country. His contribution to the decoration of the staircase hall and the saloon dates from about 1691. In general the state apartments look today much as they did when he finished with them, a year or two before Vernon died.

The original garden layout at Sudbury disappeared long since. The informal lake and deer park are the creation of the late 18th century, and the terraces on the south of the house, sloping to the lake, were laid out by the 5th Lord Vernon in the 1830s.

Tatton Park, Cheshire

2 miles north of Knutsford, 13 miles south-west of Manchester, off A537

The Egertons had owned Tatton for some 200 years when in the late 18th century Samuel Wyatt was called in to build a new house. Samuel was by no means the most talented of the architects bearing his patronymic, but though his entrance front has suffered from a yellow brick accretion of 1884, the garden front of seven bays with a great Corinthian portico has a certain grandeur. It was almost the last of his buildings, and he died in 1807 before it was finished. His nephew Lewis Wyatt completed work at Tatton and added the triumphal arch at the Knutsford entrance to the park, the orangery, and the conservatories.

The interest of Tatton Park derives largely from its contents and from the fact that the 4th Lord Egerton, in the course of a long life, did so little to alter the interior. Lord Egerton, the last of his line, who bequeathed Tatton to the Trust in 1958, was a remarkable man. An adventurous traveller, who had lived with the tribes in the Gobi desert, and a notable farmer on his great estates in Kenya, he was also concerned with the early development of wireless transmission, and was a pioneer motorist and aviator, owning a

Tatton Park; The garden front

Benz 1900 and gaining his flying certificate in 1910. But it was as a big game hunter that he left his most curious memorial at Tatton. A Nimrod of almost unparalleled effectiveness, he built the vast Tenants' Hall to house his macabre and astonishing trophies. He shot a tiger and tigress while in India at the age of eighty-one. The animal toll of a lifetime might easily be depressing, but the heads that look with glazed stares from the walls of this mausoleum are curiously impressive and beautiful. The thunder of the rhinoceros and the bellow of the bull are silenced, the swift gazelles are motionless; yet the worlds of swamp and sand and steppe are there, so are the long treks, the sweating porters, the moments of danger and nerve, the crack of the rifle that so often *had* to be accurate. In mild Cheshire, the Hall speaks of other places and already of another era. It is one of the most extraordinary rooms in England.

Of the pre-Wyatt house of the Egertons only the dining room survives with its plasterwork of the 1760s by Thomas Pritchard (see Benthall, p. 62). The most successful Wyatt rooms are the entrance hall, with screens of porphyry columns and an elaborately coffered ceiling; the drawing room, where gilded decoration and furniture (supplied, as was so much other furniture in the house, by Gillow's of Lancaster), and walls hung with patterned red silk, convey an impression of relaxed wealth. The library is lined with mahogany bookcases filled with the mahogany-coloured books of an 18th-century dilettante.

Tatton is not to be considered primarily in terms of architecture – indeed such features as the staircase hall have suffered from Edwardian interference – but rather in terms of atmosphere. Few houses, where an owner no longer lives, have so contrived to keep their character. The personality of the late Lord Egerton is relevant here, but so are the varied contents and pictures which achieve a marriage, rarely easy, of the 18th and 19th centuries. The 18th-century contribution owes much to Samuel Egerton who as a young

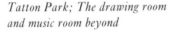

Tatton Park; The drawing room
and music room beyond

The Tenants' Hall; big game trophies
of the 3rd and 4th Lords Egerton

man was apprenticed to Consul Smith of Venice and sent back the Tatton Canalettos before he inherited in 1738. He was the enlightened master of the earlier house at Tatton for over forty years.

The south front of Samuel Wyatt's house is poised above terraces now known to have been designed by Paxton in the mid-19th century. To the west stands Wyatt's orangery of 1811, containing orange trees and exotic plants, while near by is a fern house with New Zealand tree ferns, *Dicksonia antarctica*. Many unusual trees and shrubs grow on the wall, which backs a long L-shaped border, and on the adjacent lawn. At the end of the wall is a small formal garden devoted particularly to fragrant roses, honeysuckles and other climbers. Beyond, the 'sheep-stealers'' tower dominates an enclosed area set with fuchsias.

A long straight walk, leading to a classical building modelled on the Choragic Temple of Lysicrates in Athens, served as the drive to the house until the approach was altered by Humphry Repton. It is now lined with beech and other trees, including *Acanthopanax ricinifolius*, and liberally planted with group after group of rhododendrons and azaleas. There are two small ponds and fountains on the left; on the right a larger lake, called the Golden Brook, culminates in a Japanese garden which incorporates a Shinto temple and an oriental bridge. Its atmosphere must owe much to the importing of Japanese workmen for its construction in 1910. A pinetum to the west, underplanted with rhododendrons and azaleas, boasts many of the choicer conifers.

The garden as a whole may be described as an 18th-century conception, modified and enriched by later buildings and features, and given a new dimension by the introduction, over more than a century, of exotic trees and shrubs.

House and garden lie within one of the most extensive parks in the country to which, when he visited the property in 1791, Repton devoted much thought. We owe to him some of the belts and clumps of trees and the landscaped drive to Knutsford Lodge dated 1811. Tatton Mere was incorporated in his scheme, but the ironically named Melchett Mere, which is due to salt-mining subsidence, did not make its sinister appearance until the 1920s.

It is providential that this sweeping park should, in so populous an area, have survived with so little change into the second half of the 20th century. With its deer and its rare St Kilda and Soay sheep, with its stylized planting, its waters, and its vistas, it evokes an idyllic landscape of the Hanoverian age.

Tintinhull House, Somerset

5 miles north-west of Yeovil, 1 mile east of A303

Tintinhull, which must date from about 1600, was originally an unassuming Somerset farmhouse. It is from the west front, added in about 1700, that it derives its architectural distinction. The front of mellow dressed Ham stone remains substantially unaltered and the windows retain their original mullions and transoms. Four pilasters break up the length of the façade, two of them supporting a central pediment. Further emphasis is given to the centre of the composition by a porch with Tuscan columns. This delightful architectural design is set off by a forecourt which incorporates piers surmounted by eagles, and is also of about 1700. The only decorative features inside the house are a carved staircase, and enriched pine panelling which was formerly painted. Both date from the early 18th century.

The garden, which for many people is the chief attraction of Tintinhull, is

Tintinhull House; The west front from the garden

perfectly in scale with the proportions of the house and has been described as 'a formal garden planted informally'. It grew under the expert hands of Dr Price, a distinguished botanist who bought the property in 1900, and was enlarged by Captain and Mrs F. E. Reiss who acquired Tintinhull in 1933. Mrs Reiss, who gave the property to the Trust in 1954, was largely responsible for the planting and layout as it exists today.

As at Hidcote, the garden comprises a series of separate hedged gardens which, by the clever use of linked steps and a sunken garden, give the impression of being at different levels. The main features of the design are a big lawn on the north side of the house shaded by a single gigantic cedar, a narrow garden leading from the forecourt on the west side, and a smaller lawn with a memorial pavilion at the head of a long rectangular pool.

'Its planting is probably unique,' wrote Sylvia Crowe in *Garden Design*, 'because it combines a use of very varied species grown naturally, and yet used strictly as elements of design.' Most of the borders are mixed, planted with shrubs, small trees, flowering and foliage plants, grasses and bulbs. The two borders flanking the formal pool can be taken as typical. In the spring there are clumps of bulbs, spring flowers and flowering cherries. By midsummer, one border is brilliant with clear colours and the other has a gentler appeal with softer, paler tints. The one is full of verbascums, *Senecio laxifolius*, *Spartium junceum*, red and white roses, dahlias and some copper foliage. In the opposite border, pale lemon roses, pinks and mauves and coppery tones predominate. Yet there is unity, for both borders are backed by yew hedges. Such borders are the outcome of prolonged care and knowledge.

Although the garden is interesting throughout the year, one of the best times to visit Tintinhull is in July, when the Regale lilies are in bloom. Great tubs along the terrace on the west front are full of their tall white flowers whose delicious scent hangs on the summer air.

Townend, Troutbeck, Cumbria

3 miles south-east of Ambleside; at the end of Troutbeck village, west of A592

Townend is probably unique, the only house of the well-to-do yeomanry (small gentry) which has survived unaltered in the Lake District. The Brownes, long settled in the area, built the present house in 1623. For nearly 300 years they were remarkable for their intelligence and range of interest, and as a family they are a useful reminder that even in remote areas there were people of modest position with an alertness and a scale of values that we may envy today. The last of the male line to live at Townend died in 1914. Both an antiquary and a farmer, he represented a type that is now almost unknown.

The house with slate roof and roughcast walls is characteristic of vernacular Westmorland architecture. The interior speaks of the Browne family.

Townend

They lived there for nearly three centuries and almost nothing has been changed. In the library, reflecting the tastes of literate people since the 17th century and the owners' special farming interests, the books that slowly accumulated are huddled on modest shelves. In the hall and throughout the house is the simple yet attractive oak furniture which they acquired or built – for the Brownes, presumably in the long northern winters, were indefatigable makers and carvers of furniture. Nothing here recalls the fashionable

Townend; The living room

and often meretricious haste of the great world. Even some of the fabrics, woven on local Troutbeck looms in the late 18th century, convey a profound impression of the vitality of cottage industry before it was swept away by the Industrial Revolution.

Townend is the record of a yeoman family. The accretion of furniture, obsolete domestic utensils, works by local journeyman painters, and books long ago ordered from the London booksellers, evoke, as few houses can, the life of a class of intelligent and independent yeomen which has almost disappeared.

Treasurer's House, York

At north-east corner of the Minster

The site has been built on for nearly 2,000 years, for in the cellars have come to light the bases of Roman columns which perhaps formed part of a colonnade lining the Via Decumana; but as a house for the Treasurer of York Minster its history goes back only to 1100 when the first treasurer took up residence. His official duties were the care of the treasury and fabric of the Minster, and the control of all persons in the Minster. The choir alone, in the charge of the dean and chapter, was outside his jurisdiction. The office became extinct in the reign of Henry VIII, when the Minster 'being plundered of all its treasures, had no further need of a treasurer'.

Almost nothing remains of the house that the treasurer knew. The

Treasurer's House; The entrance front

attractive entrance front that is first seen across the lawn is mainly of about 1620, though the Dutch gables on the two projecting wings were added towards the end of the century. The fenestration has been extensively altered, but the two Venetian windows on the first floor must date from the early 18th century.

A frontispiece with two superimposed classical orders gives access to the hall. The latter has had a varied history. A 16th-century hall of which the fireplace survives was divided into two floors in the 17th century, which accounts for the upstairs windows. The upper floor was removed in about 1900 when the hall assumed its present appearance. Off the hall to the south lies the dining room with a remarkable plaster ceiling of about 1740, but the main apartments are on the north. The long drawing room was panelled in the early 18th century, and a William and Mary staircase leads to rooms on the first floor that were decorated either in the 17th century – the tapestry room has panelling that dates from the first half of that century – or, like the Queen's room, early in the 18th.

Treasurer's House had come down in the world and was divided into three dwellings, when in 1896 it found a devoted rescuer in the person of Frank Green. He restored the house, and lived there until his death in 1930, when he left it to the Trust.

The importance of his bequest lay largely in the furniture which he collected, much of it of the first quality and rarity. It is the contents which give Treasurer's House so much of its interest and flavour. There are collections of early English china and pottery, and 17th- and 18th-century glass; and there are objects of association like the Indian ivory chairs bought by Warren Hastings and a dressing table on sphinx supports which until 1788 belonged to Louis XVI. The furniture is a cross-section of the craftsmanship of two centuries. The long table in the hall, one of many good oak pieces, dates from about 1600. The late 17th century contributed *verre eglomisé* mirrors, a marquetry longcase clock of 1680, and caned carved-walnut chairs. There are three early 18th-century tester beds, and giltwood mirrors, consoles, tripod tables, and a superb walnut secretaire bookcase all of the same period. French craftsmanship is represented by 17th-century firedogs, Régence parcel-gilt consoles and chest of drawers, Louis XVI *Boulle* cabinets, and a *Boulle* bureau with a Turkish cipher probably made for the palace in Istanbul.

Trerice, Cornwall

3 miles south-east of Newquay via A392, west of A3058

Narrow lanes winding between high Cornish hedges lead to the house, and its grey curving gables appear half hidden by elms. Situated in a quiet valley through which a tributary of the little river Gannel runs down to its sandy estuary by the sea, Trerice has undergone remarkably little alteration since it was built in 1573 by Sir John Arundell, member of a famous Cornish family.

Trerice; The great hall

High walls enclose a turfed forecourt and beyond rises the E-shaped entrance front. Built of silvery grey limestone, the façade is crowned with highly decorative scrolled gables, and in the bay adjoining the entrance porch a vast mullioned and transomed window reveals the position of the great hall. Sir John Arundell may have got the design for his new house when soldiering in the Low Countries, for the curving 'Dutch' gables with their scrolled finials are not found elsewhere in the West Country at this early date.

Inside, the house is arranged on the familiar medieval plan with a screens passage entered from the porch and a great hall beyond. The hall, lit by the vast window of no less than twenty-four lights, has a contemporary plaster ceiling ornamented with medallions, strapwork, and pendants. The fireplace, with a scrolled plaster overmantel supported by caryatids, is dated 1572. Above the screens passage there is a little gallery, whence through a row of recessed arches the musicians could survey the hall.

The solar, reached by a staircase from the hall, must always have been the principal sitting room, and a great semicircular bay window looking south floods the room with light. Here there is a barrel ceiling and frieze with even more elaborate plasterwork than in the hall. Both the frieze and the richly wrought overmantel incorporate the Arundell arms.

The excellence of the plasterwork, so notable a feature of Trerice, is clearly due to a master craftsman. Common features relate the Trerice stuccowork to work of about the same date at Colleton Barton, Collacombe Barton, and Buckland Abbey. It seems probable that the same expert plasterer was employed at all these West Country houses.

Uppark, West Sussex *(See colour plate facing p. 224)*

1 mile south of South Harting on the B2146 Petersfield/Chichester road

In about 1690, Forde, Lord Grey of Werke and Earl of Tankerville, a somewhat dubious character, commissioned William Talman to design a country house for him at Uppark. Talman was of Dutch origin and his building is strongly reminiscent of the Netherlands. Two storeys of mellow brick, a steep hipped roof and pronounced cornice, simple stone architraves, quoins, and stringcourse, give Uppark a seemliness, gravity and order that would not be out of place in Amsterdam. The house, with a simple central pediment on the main front, stands 'like some rose-coloured altar among columned beech trees' on the crest of a steep hill and looks southwards across the rolling Sussex Downs to the gleam of the Solent, the Isle of Wight and the distant channel. The romantic situation of Uppark, one of the most seductive houses in southern England, is matched by the romance of its history. The passage of time seems hardly to have touched this remote and lovely house, and the 18th-century interior looks much as it did when Sir Matthew Fetherstonhaugh returned with his bride from the Grand Tour over two centuries ago.

We owe the unusual situation of the house, on the summit of a steep hill, to Edward Forde. An engineer and a 'considerable mechanist', he gave London its first reliable water supply in the 1650s, and bequeathed to Lord Tankerville, his grandson and successor at Uppark, the wealth and the technique to build perhaps the first large country house in England, without a natural spring, on the top of a hill.

Lord Tankerville's descendants sold Uppark in 1747 to Matthew Fether-

Uppark; South front, overlooking the park

stonhaugh – who had inherited an immense fortune on the agreeable conditions that he acquire a baronetcy and an estate in the south of England. Both these conditions he quickly fulfilled; he also married the charming Sarah Lethieullier, daughter of a rich Middlesex merchant. Together this fortunate pair made extensive alterations to the house and grounds, spending in their first year at Uppark no less than £100,000.

With the exception of the dining room, hall and staircase, which retain their original 17th-century panelling of painted 'fir wood', the young couple redecorated most of the interior in the mid-18th-century taste. They created the white and gold saloon, installed splendidly plastered ceilings, and redecorated the principal rooms, hanging flock and handpainted wallpapers. Curtains, hangings and upholstery date from the 1750s, as does much of the fine English furniture. Early in their married life Sir Matthew and his wife undertook a protracted continental tour. In Rome they bought pictures – often in sets of six or eight – and sat to Batoni for their portraits. Lady Fetherstonhaugh brought to her elegant new home not only a delightful series of family portraits by Devis, but the magnificent doll's house made for her as a child, which is still complete with early Georgian furniture, Waterford glass and silverware.

Fortunately, Sir Matthew kept detailed accounts. In the grand total of £16,615 – laid out in his first ten years on furnishings, books, paintings and travel – we find items such as 1s. for a nosegay; 7s. at Goodwood; £2 14s. on Chocolate; £5 for a china cup; and £1 16s 6d. for a bag-wig. He was a man who took his duties seriously as magistrate, Member of Parliament, and Fellow of the Royal Society. He was involved in various financial schemes, including a project to found a colony, to be called Vandalia, in West Virginia. The only tangible result of this enterprise was the Gothick 'Vandalian' Tower he caused Henry Keen to design and erect at Uppark.

In 1774, Sir Matthew's twenty-year-old son, Harry, succeeded to the estate. This rich and prodigal young man was gay, sociable and deeply extravagant. He hunted, raced, entertained lavishly and became a close friend of the Prince Regent. He also had excellent taste – he added furniture, china and sporting pictures to his parents' collection – and an eye for female beauty. In 1780 he brought a girl of fifteen to live at Uppark who, of all those connected with the house, remains the most alive to us. Emma Hart, later Nelson's Lady Hamilton, stayed a full year, entertaining her host and his friends, and legend says she danced on the dining room table. But 'wild, unthinking Emma' was summarily packed off, six months pregnant, to be rescued and set on her extraordinary career by Charles Greville, who met her at Uppark at a shooting party. Years later, after Nelson's death, Sir Harry lent her money and sent her gifts of game and 'a view of old Uppark dans la belle saison'.

Beautiful Uppark always was, and there Sir Harry retired after falling out with the Prince Regent in 1810. About this time he called in Humphry Repton – at a fee of fifty guineas a visit – to suggest improvements to the house and park. The north portico with its Doric colonnade, the entrance passage, and the remodelling of the dining room, are Repton's work. In spite of these improvements, it appears that Sir Harry considered selling the house which in 1816 was suggested as a suitable mansion for the Duke of Wellington. One sight of the steep approach was enough for the practical soldier. 'I have crossed the Alps once', he is said to have commented. In 1825, in his seventieth year, Sir Harry married his dairymaid, aged twenty. He educated her in France, and adopted her younger sister, and on his death at the age of ninety-two left the dairymaid his entire estate. 'It is a very good thing', she said, 'to be a Downstairs as well as an Upstairs person.' She was clearly a remarkable woman and an excellent manager, and devoted the rest of her life to the conservation of Uppark.

H. G. Wells, whose mother became housekeeper in 1880, spent his childhood at Uppark, and paid his tribute to the dairymaid and the younger sister who succeeded her as châtelaine. It was largely due to their pious concern that everything should continue as it was in Sir Harry's day that Uppark remained miraculously unchanged throughout the 19th century. In the 20th century the work of conservation was carried out with knowledge and taste by the late Lady Meade-Fetherstonhaugh. Her husband, the late Admiral the Hon. Sir Herbert Meade-Fetherstonhaugh, gave Uppark to the Trust in 1954.

Upton House, Warwickshire

7 miles north-west of Banbury, on west side of the A422 Banbury/Stratford-upon-Avon road

Constructed of rich yellow Warwickshire stone, Upton is first seen framed by an avenue of dark Scots pines. The house which creates so immediate an impression of self-assured tranquillity was built in James II's reign by a wealthy London merchant, Sir Rushout Cullen. In 1730 a Mr William Bumstead bought the property and made some alterations, leaving his initials on the lead rainwater heads. By the middle of the century it had been acquired by Francis Child (see p. 156) and passed by inheritance to the Earls of Jersey. In 1927, the 2nd Viscount Bearsted bought Upton and remodelled the house, giving to the exterior and its later additions something of the symmetry and balance of the original 17th-century building.

Inside, the rooms have been almost entirely altered and serve to display the works of art which Lord Bearsted gave to the Trust in 1948. He was one of the most distinguished collectors of his day, and both the paintings and porcelain at Upton are a tribute to his exacting standards.

Flemish and early Netherlands schools are represented in the Upton collection by outstanding works such as Brueghel the Elder's *Dormition of the Virgin*, and portraits by Memling and Rogier van der Weyden. Dutch 17th-century paintings include Metsu's famous *Corsage Bleu*, Steen's *Tired Traveller* and landscapes and seascapes by Jacob van Ruisdael, Jan van der Cappelle and Jan van Goyen. There is a particularly sensitive church interior by Saenredam. Examples of the early French school include a

Upton House; The garden front

miniature by Fouquet, and there are notable Italian works of the Florentine school, and by the Venetians Lotto, Guardi and Canaletto. A beautiful panel by El Greco may be the earliest model for his altarpiece, *El Espolio*, in Toledo Cathedral.

The English 18th-century school is particularly well represented, with fine works by Stubbs and Ben Marshall and by Hogarth's two major scenes of London life, *Morning* and *Night*. There are also portraits by Highmore, Raeburn and Romney, together with the enchanting work of that lesser portraitist, Arthur Devis, whose stiffly poised, yet vivid, little figures inhabit a stylized world.

The collection of 18th-century porcelain is especially strong in the soft-paste porcelains of Sèvres and Chelsea, though it includes pieces from Bow, Derby, Worcester and other English factories, as well as Meissen and other German marks. The few remarkable figures of the rare Chelsea red anchor period of 1753–8, and the unrivalled collection of gold anchor figures dated between 1759 and 1769 are part of a collection which contains more pieces of the highest quality in its chosen field than almost any private collection in England.

The 18th-century furniture includes a mahogany suite of settees and chairs with their original gros and petit point embroidery and there is a magnificent set of Brussels tapestries, *The Hunts of Maximilian*.

The garden at Upton has great character, and its layout and situation are as surprising as they are satisfactory. On one side of a steep-sided valley, long terraced borders, linked by a balustraded stairway, with tumbling roses, clematis and flowering shrubs, drop to a formal lake. Another valley forms a natural amphitheatre fringed by deep woods, and is the setting for a

Upton House; La Nourrice *Chelsea, c.1753 porcelain*

Upton House; The gardener and companion 'Summer' Chelsea, 1757–8 porcelain

water garden. Some way to the east, a classical temple, built by Sanderson Miller (who lived near by at Edgehill) surveys a second larger lake.

The Vyne, Sherborne St John, Hampshire

4 miles north of Basingstoke, off the A340 Reading road

William Sandys, the builder of The Vyne, was both astute and fortunate, for he managed to serve Henry VIII for over thirty years and to retain the King's confidence and his own head; this in spite of his Catholic sympathies and his discreet support of Catherine of Aragon. In 1520 he helped to organize the Field of the Cloth of Gold, the glittering stage-set for the meeting of Henry VIII and Francis I of France, and three years later he was created Lord Sandys of The Vyne, subsequently becoming Lord Chamberlain. He died in 1540.

For a century the Sandys family flourished, only to fall on evil times in the Civil War. In 1653 the 6th Lord Sandys retired to live at Mottisfont Abbey (see p. 345), selling his house and estate to Chaloner Chute, a fearless advocate, who had defended Archbishop Laud in 1643 and who was to end his career as Speaker of the House of Commons under Richard Cromwell. The sale was fortunate in that Chaloner Chute and his descendants were men of taste. Though they altered the original Tudor house, it owes much of its charm and interest to the changes they made. In particular John Chute, the intimate friend of Horace Walpole and the poet Gray, was a man of unusual talent with a decided gift for architecture, and when he inherited in

209

The Vyne; The north front, with the portico designed by John Webb

1754 he set his stamp firmly upon the house. It was to remain in the family until 1956 when Sir Charles Chute, the last of his line, bequeathed The Vyne, its contents and an estate of over a thousand acres to the National Trust.

As you approach The Vyne down the short drive from Sherborne St John, the south front of the long two-storeyed house, with its projecting wings and rose-red brickwork patterned with diapering in purple brick, still recalls an exterior of the time of Henry VIII. The Chute additions, however, are soon apparent. The stone window surrounds and the shallow porch were added in the 17th century, and the original mullions and transoms were replaced by Georgian sash windows.

On the other side of the house, where lawns run down to a lake, an 18th-century landscape feature, the 16th-century front, with Sandys's chapel on the extreme left, has received the addition of a classical portico. Built in 1650 by John Webb, Inigo Jones's son-in-law, it is the earliest example of a portico on an English country house.

Lord Sandys's chapel, in the late Perpendicular style and built before 1528, remains substantially unaltered and is among the finest private chapels in England. The splendour of the curved stalls, canopy and screen is only exceeded by that of the stained-glass windows. The glass, probably of Flemish origin, comparable in importance to that of the chapel of King's College, Cambridge, is exceptional in the brilliance of its colour and its jewel-like clarity. Henry VIII and Catherine of Aragon are among the figures depicted, which must have caused Lord Sandys no small embarrassment when Anne Boleyn, the new queen, came to stay at The Vyne in 1535. In an adjoining tomb chamber lies the recumbent marble effigy of Speaker

Chute; carved more than a century after his death, it is among the most notable sculptured memorials produced in 18th-century England.

The drawing rooms at The Vyne reflect the hand of John Chute, the 18th-century dilettante, being still hung with the damasks he is said to have brought from Italy. So also does the Ante-Chapel, an example of the fanciful 18th–century Gothick, so dear to his friend Horace Walpole. But John Chute's most notable contribution to The Vyne is the Staircase Hall (c. 1765). Executed in a Palladian manner, already at that time somewhat old-fashioned, it is a *tour de force*, and the quality of its detail, in carved wood and moulded plaster, is exceptional.

There was little left for the 19th century to add, though the library is a creation of about 1835, and on the ground floor is one of those rare Print Rooms, decorated with paper-framed prints applied to canvas, which came into fashion in the Regency period and of which all too few have survived.

The contents of The Vyne are the pleasant and haphazard accumulation of three centuries – family portraits, Soho tapestries, Charles I cabinets, Chinese Chippendale side-tables, late-18th-century hall chairs, Meissen and Bow porcelain figures, and a set of rare Venetian painted glass plates which may well have been brought back by John Chute when he visited Venice on the Grand Tour with the poet Gray.

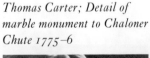

The Vyne; The staircase hall, c.1756

Thomas Carter; Detail of marble monument to Chaloner Chute 1775–6

Waddesdon Manor, Buckinghamshire

6 miles north-west of Aylesbury, on the A41 Aylesbury/Bicester road

The exterior of Waddesdon Manor does not prepare the visitor for what he will see inside. Between 1874 and 1889, Baron Ferdinand de Rothschild employed a French architect, Gabriel-Hippolyte Destailleur, to build a manor house of 16th-century inspiration, composed of ingredients borrowed from the châteaux of the Loire.

Within the house the atmosphere is totally different. Except in the Bachelors' Wing, where the panelling of the rooms and some of their contents are of the French Renaissance period, the accent is emphatically on the French 18th century and its taste. In no other house or museum outside France can one see so complete an assemblage of all the elements which make up an 18th-century French interior: panelling, paintings, sculpture, furniture, porcelain, carpets, books, drawings and gold boxes. This is not to say that the rooms are arranged as if they had been transplanted from an 18th-century French *hôtel*: there is undoubtedly a 19th-century feeling to the house which it had in Baron Ferdinand's day and has since retained. Even so, in the choice of the contents, in the disposition of the rooms, in the association of works of art of differing categories with a common past, the visitor is introduced to a collection which has been formed by collectors with a rare understanding and sympathy for the France of the 18th century.

The links between Waddesdon and 18th-century France are manifold. For example, in the disposition of the rooms a parallel can be drawn with Versailles. The Red Drawing Room, which is formal, royal and grand, recalls the Versailles of Louis XIV both in its scale and in its contents. The Low White Room, with its delicately carved 18th-century panelling and intimate furniture, likewise recalls Versailles, but the Versailles of the low-

Waddesdon Manor; Left: *Writing-table c.1780 by Jean-Henri Riesener*
Right: *Commode by Charles Cressent*

Waddesdon Manor; The Baron's Room

ceilinged private apartments where Louis XV and Louis XVI relaxed and entertained their friends. The combination of 17th-century Dutch painting, of which there is a fine collection at Waddesdon, with lavish 18th-century French furniture, porcelain and sculpture, is also characteristic of French 18th-century taste.

The visitor sees, displayed on Savonnerie carpets made for the French Crown, furniture by the finest Parisian cabinet-makers of the 18th century such as Charles Cressent, furniture-maker to the Duc d'Orléans, Regent of France from 1715 to 1723, as well as Martin Carlin and Jean-Henri Riesener, both extensively patronized by the Crown in the second half of the century. One of the gems of the collection is a small writing-table, made for Marie Antoinette at the Petit Trianon, which Baron Ferdinand acquired in 1882 for the immense sum of £6,000. Another is a large writing-table delivered in 1786 for Louis XVI's study at Versailles. The collection of Sèvres porcelain ranges from a diminutive snuff box painted for Madame de Pompadour, with portraits of her pet dogs, Inès and Mimi, to a turquoise blue service of over one hundred pieces, painted with birds, which had been made for a Russian admiral marshal, probably Cyril Razumovski, the Empress Elizabeth's cousin by marriage.

The presence of 18th-century English portraits by Reynolds, Gainsborough, and Romney is perhaps an indication of the close ties which the three owners who formed the collection increasingly felt for the country of their adoption. Baron Ferdinand was the grandson of the founder of the Austrian branch of the family. On his death in 1898 Waddesdon passed to his sister Miss Alice, who in 1922 left it to their great-nephew Mr James de Rothschild, the grandson of the founder of the French branch. Mr de

Rothschild left the house and its fabulous contents to the Trust in 1957.

The three owners collected paintings and works of art of the finest quality. They admired them, in the words of Baron Ferdinand, not only for their beauty but also 'for the associations, for the memories they evoke ...' The works of art are enhanced by their provenance, a provenance which at Waddesdon is intimately linked with the French royal family, their favourites and friends. It is this sense of history, this feeling for the past, which makes Waddesdon such a complete collection, so doubly rewarding to visit.

The gardens were laid out by the French landscape artist, Lainé. Baron Ferdinand acquired a fine collection of garden sculpture, principally the work of Italian, French and Netherlands sculptors dating from the 17th and 18th centuries. These can be seen in varied settings – against a background of trees and shrubs, as the centrepiece of two important fountains, and beside gravelled walks, some of which lead to a splendid 19th-century aviary containing a wide variety of colourful and rare birds.

Wallington, Cambo, Northumberland

12 miles west of Morpeth, along B6343; 1 mile south from Cambo, off B6342

When in the 16th century relative peace came to the Borders, the Fenwicks, who had long owned Wallington, added a Tudor house to the medieval pele tower which they had inherited. Sir John Fenwick, the last of his line and an ardent supporter of the house of Stuart, was executed in 1697 on a charge of plotting the assassination of William III. Sir John was posthumously avenged, for White Sorrel, his famous horse, confiscated by the Crown, stumbled on a molehill, threw the King and killed him. The manner of his death gave rise to the Jacobite toast 'to the little gentleman in black velvet'.

Thirteen years before his execution Sir John Fenwick had sold Wallington to Sir William Blackett, a rich and influential Newcastle businessman. The new owner proceeded to demolish the old house, and in 1688 began to build the stone mansion which stands today.

In the 18th century Sir Walter Calverley Blackett, a man of considerable taste, altered the entrance front from south to east, changed the windows throughout and rebuilt the north front. He remodelled the interior of the house and laid out the park and garden. When he died childless in 1777, Wallington passed to his nephew, son of his sister, who had married Sir George Trevelyan of Nettlecomb in Somerset. Sir Walter Calverley Trevelyan, who inherited in 1846, and his brilliant wife Pauline made further changes. In their time the house became a focus for men of science, painters and writers, among them Millais, Ruskin and Swinburne. The tradition thus established was continued by Sir George Otto Trevelyan, the eminent historian, and his son Sir Charles Trevelyan who was President of the Board of Education in the first Labour Government. Sir Charles gave Wallington to the Trust in 1941.

The house, in the depths of remote Northumbrian countryside, is ap-

Wallington

proached across James Paine's noble bridge that spans the Wansbeck. Crowning a long slope of parkland, the late-17th-century building of finely jointed ashlar is grave and restrained. A simple cornice, window architraves, and rusticated coigns are the only decorative features, though the design is relieved by the slight projection on the south front of three central bays which carry a pediment, and of two bays at either end of the entrance front. Behind the house lie the stable courtyard, built in 1737, and the coach house and clock tower added in 1754.

The sober elevations give no hint of the elaborate interior decoration of the mid-18th century. Walter Calverley Blackett inherited an imposing but inconvenient house. Though built round a courtyard, it has no corridors and no main staircase. He proceeded to make Wallington liveable by introducing internal corridors around the courtyard and an ample staircase. He then summoned the Francini brothers, in 1740, to decorate his main rooms with plasterwork of unusual elegance and virtuosity. The marriage of rococo designs with the sturdy mouldings of an earlier period gives the interior of Wallington its special architectural flavour.

A century after Walter Blackett's changes there was further innovation. In 1855 Pauline, Lady Trevelyan, employed John Dobson, the Newcastle architect, to roof over the open courtyard and to create the central hall which was then decorated with murals and paintings by the Northumbrian Pre-Raphaelite painter, William Bell Scott.

The architectural framework of three centuries acquires an added dimension from the things that successive generations of Blacketts and Trevelyans have introduced. One room is hung with needlework panels worked by Sir Walter Calverly Blackett's mother in 1717. Another is rich with the pottery and porcelain, the latter traditionally having been brought to Wallington in

1791 as part of her dowry by Maria, Lady Trevelyan. The porcelain formed part of her share of her mother's vast Cabinet of Curiosities. The range of association is rich and wide, passing without discordance from the grand mid-18th-century saloon, with its elaborate Dutch, French and Italian furniture and Reynolds's dominating full-length of Sir Walter Blackett, to Morris wallpapers and the taste of the Pre-Raphaelite period.

The garden, first laid out by Reynolds's Sir Walter, has received the later impress of the Trevelyans. It can be divided into three distinct sections. The lawns around the house contain flower borders, shrubs and trees; a new avenue of limes leads away to woodland walks to the west. In front of the house by the road stand four stone griffins' heads, brought by sea from London in 1760. Beyond the road lies a woodland, and the China Pond (so-called from the rococo China House erected there in 1752) and the Garden Pond, both constructed in 1737. Set in the wall of the old kitchen garden is an 18th-century *plaisance*, prettily reflected in the waters of the pond. Groups of early and late flowering rhododendrons and azaleas provide colour in spring and summer.

Sir Water Blackett, who made the ponds and planted trees, constructed a walled garden (from a hawthorn-filled dell) in the third section of the grounds. Roughly L-shaped, it now contains a conservatory resplendent with ancient fuchsias and heliotrope, a long terrace walk set with leaden figures, opposite a border of cool-coloured flowers and grey foliage shrubs and plants, and sloping lawns which were designed by the late Lady Trevelyan in 1938, with a water garden and a rocky water course. On the lichen-covered walls of the garden there are old and new roses, honeysuckle, clematis, and other climbers; the rocky stream, verges and retaining walls are gay in spring and summer with small plants, and a wide border is designed for the summer and autumn months. *Hydrangea villosa* thrives, also phloxes. An arched way joins upper and lower walks; the arches support yellow roses and the attendant borders are devoted to blue, purple and yellow flowers.

Washington Old Hall, Tyne & Wear

In District 4 Washington, 5 miles west of Sunderland

The Old Hall was the house of George Washington's direct ancestors for five generations, and of Washingtons and their descendants for 430 years. Indeed, it was from this place that the family took its name, for William de Hertburn who came to Washington in 1183 and acquired the manor from the Bishop of Durham in return for, among other things, 'the service of attending the Bishop's hunt with four greyhounds', changed his name to de Wessyngton or Washington.

The de Wessyngtons lived in their manor until the early years of the 15th century, when it passed through the female line. It was finally sold by Washington descendants in 1613 to the Bishop of Durham, to whose

Washington Old Hall; The panelled room

predecessors it had belonged over four centuries earlier. With the coming of the Industrial Revolution, the surroundings of Washington began to lose their charm, and the manor gradually went down in the world. By 1936 it was divided into squalid tenements and was condemned to demolition. At this point a Preservation Committee was set up. With the help of generous support from the United States, the Committee acquired the Old Hall, and restored it over a period of some twenty years. It was handed to the Trust in 1957, who have furnished the lower floor with appropriate pieces paid for by Anglo-American benefactors. It is hoped to do likewise with the upper storey in time.

Whether the first Washington built the original manor house after he bought the property towards the end of the 12th century, or moved into a recently built house of the medieval hall type, is unknown. Features of the 12th-century house subsist in what is now a fairly typical small manor house of the 17th century. Built soon after 1613, when the Washington descendants sold to the Bishop of Durham, it is of the familiar H-plan, having a central hall flanked on either side by a gabled wing.

Before its transfer to the Trust, the house underwent extensive restoration, during which the 12th-century arches which led from a screens passage to the medieval kitchens were exposed. At the same time, the early-17th-century chimneypiece in the great hall was imported to replace a 19th-century kitchen range, and the fine Jacobean panelling was installed in the panelled room. There are two important Washington relics: a bust by Houdon, who stayed with Washington at Mount Vernon in 1785, and the fan given to Martha Washington by Lafayette. The Stars and Stripes are flown from the flagpole at the Old Hall on Washington's birthday, July 4th and Thanksgiving Day.

West Green House, Hartley Wintney, Hampshire

1 mile west of Hartley Wintney, 5 miles south-west of Camberley, 1 mile off A30 between Camberley and Basingstoke

This is the 18th-century house that everyone would like to own. Not too large, virtually unaltered, ravishingly pretty, with an atmosphere that welcomes and a garden that charms, it is one of the most desirable of the Trust's buildings. The atmosphere is perhaps a little surprising, since West Green is associated with General Hawley, 'Hangman Hawley', as he was called on account of his brutalities after the battle of Culloden. Perhaps he was not as bad as he was made out, for in the floor of the garden house he set a memorial stone to his favourite spaniel which reads:

Oh Poor
Monkey
Come all yee shooters come, my losse bewaile
The best black spaniell, that ere wag'd a taile
Of questing kinde, and royall breed shee came
Great was her science, and as great her fame ...

Roughly square in plan, the house, with a hipped roof, pedimented dormers, and a wooden cornice, dates from the first decades of the 18th century. A polygonal bay and battlements on the entrance are later, about the middle of the century. The delight is the garden front, where the first-floor windows are replaced by a row of niches with busts. Bacchus himself, and a tablet with the motto of the Monks of Medmenham, *Fay ce que vouldras*, extend a welcome above the doorway. The latter is boldly treated in the manner of Gibbs.

The interior has kept its early-18th-century panelling and, apart from a pleasant stone staircase with iron balustrade of about 1770, is much as it always was. The best feature of the interior is the panelled saloon, two storeys high, with a coved ceiling, pedimented doorcases, and mantelpiece in a restrained Palladian manner. Its four windows look out on the grass terraces of the garden.

West Wycombe Park, Buckinghamshire

2 miles west of High Wycombe, off the A40 London/Oxford road

The manor of Wycombe, which in medieval times had belonged to the Bishops of Winchester, was acquired at the end of the 17th century by Francis Dashwood, a wealthy London merchant who built the nucleus of the present house. He was created a baronet in 1707, and was succeeded in 1724 by his son, the famous Sir Francis. The latter, possessed of every advantage and a large fortune, was born with a zest for life. Even as a youth

West Wycombe Park; The south front

on the Grand Tour, he earned an equivocal reputation both as a *farceur* and as a man of learning. In 1732 he was instrumental in founding the Dilettanti Society. Formed by a group of young bloods returned from the Grand Tour, the Society, through its patronage of the arts and learning and particularly of the study of classical antiquity, played no small part in formulating and influencing English taste.

It was not until about 1745 that Sir Francis founded another society with which his name is all too readily associated. The Knights of St Francis of Wycombe, or the Monks of Medmenham, held their meetings in a chalk chamber or cave dug out in West Wycombe hill, on the opposite side of the valley from the park.

As joint Postmaster-General, a post he held from 1766 to 1781, Sir Francis proved himself a capable administrator, but as Chancellor of the Exchequer in 1762 he was a disaster. Perhaps his chief interests lay elsewhere. The creation of the landscape garden and park at West Wycombe, and enlargements, improvements and embellishments to the house, can never have been far from his mind. Work, which began possibly as early as 1730, was to continue until his death in 1781. He clearly consulted and employed several architects including John Donowell, Nicholas Revett and Robert Adam, but it is possible that Sir Francis Dashwood was largely his own designer. The result bears the stamp of his personality, a classical house of individual charm and originality, set in grounds which rank among the most successful essays in 18th-century landscape planning.

Porticoes or colonnades adorn all four façades of the rectangular building which conceals an earlier square brick late-17th-century house. The north front is a competent Palladian exercise, its central feature given prominence by the addition of Ionic columns. So too is the great Tuscan or east portico, which was built about 1755 and is decorated with frescoes. The two-storeyed colonnade on the south front, with the Corinthian superimposed on the Tuscan order, is the most striking feature of the exterior, and was designed by Donowell in about 1754. This was the main entrance to the house until the addition in 1771 of Revett's west portico, by which visitors since that date have entered, to re-emerge under the south colonnade and thence gain access to the state rooms. This unusual arrangement was remarked on by Mrs Lybbe Powys in 1775: 'The house is nothing remarkable, tho' very habitably good – you enter it sideways thro' a portico – odd and uncommonly pleasing.' Mrs Powys's easy dismissal of the results of Sir Francis's labours is unlikely to be echoed by the visitors to the splendidly decorated rooms with their series of painted ceilings.

The Hall has a staircase of exceptional elegance, of mahogany inlaid with satinwood. The Ionic columns and Grecian motifs of the dining room suggest that it may have been altered by Revett in 1771. The charming tapestry room, an antechamber to the state bedroom once occupied by George III, is hung with Flemish arras, said to have been given by Marlborough to Sir Francis's uncle, the Earl of Westmorland. Facing the lake, the saloon and red drawing room have elaborate marble fireplaces, painted ceilings, and some of the finest furniture in the house. The most impressive room, however, is the music room, which gives on the tall east portico. The ceiling is decorated with the 'Banquet of the Gods' after Raphael's designs in the Villa Farnesina in Rome.

West Wycombe Park; The hall   *The saloon*

The park and garden, adorned with every variety of temple and architectural fancy, received Sir Francis's attention no less than the house. Its picturesque layout, of about 1739, modified by Thomas Cook – a pupil of Capability Brown – and later by Repton, includes the lake, with an island on which stands the exquisite Temple of Music, designed by Revett. The Temple of the Winds is one of five examples in Britain (see Mount Stewart p. 246, and Shugborough, p. 281), and was built in 1759, about the same time as the Temple of Apollo, which curiously doubled as a pit for cock-fighting. The imaginatively conceived planting is now in its full maturity.

Sir Francis was succeeded by his half-brother, Sir John, 'the best master of harriers England ever saw', a sportsman who bred hounds on an extensive scale. The 8th baronet, who inherited in 1881, was one of the three white men who made the first arduous overland journey in 1830 from Canterbury to Marlborough in New Zealand. In 1943, Sir John Dashwood, the 10th baronet (and premier baronet of Great Britain), gave the house and grounds to the National Trust, and his son, Sir Francis, lives in the house.

Wightwick Manor, West Midlands

3 miles west of Wolverhampton, up Wightwick Bank (A454)

Wightwick Manor, one of the most important Victorian buildings owned by the Trust, is one of the very rare surviving examples of a house built, decorated, and furnished under the influence of the Pre-Raphaelite Movement.

The ideas of William Morris, poet, artist, and craftsman, were the inspiration of Theodore Mander, the enlightened manufacturer who built Wightwick between 1887 and 1893. The many-gabled house, of half-timber construction on a base of red sandstone, was designed by Edward Ould of Liverpool. The elaborate bargeboards carved with a flowing Gothic design are characteristic both of the medievalizing spirit of the Movement and the fine standard of craftsmanship to be expected in an architect who was a disciple of Morris.

The drawing room, which the visitor enters first, is an epitome of Pre-Raphaelite influences. The walls are hung with a Morris silk-and-wool tapestry and the panelling is carved with a motto from Ruskin's *Modern Painters*; the Italian chimneypiece has a surround of de Morgan tiles, the candelabra were designed for Holman Hunt, and the stained-glass windows are by Charles Kempe, most distinguished of the Victorian glaziers. Among the paintings and drawings are a portrait of Effie Gray (Lady Millais) by Watts, an alpine view by Ruskin, a *Mother and Child* by Madox Brown, and a fascinating composite portrait by Rossetti and Madox Brown representing Mrs Morris with the flaming red hair of Elizabeth Siddal.

The centrepiece of the manor is the great parlour, rising two storeys with an open-work timber roof. Kempe was responsible for its decoration; he designed the fireplace and the coloured plaster frieze that portrays the story

Wightwick Manor; The great parlour

of Orpheus. The electric light brackets were designed by the Morris firm, and the walls are hung with Morris's last textile design, the 'Diagonal Trail'. In this room further examples of the extensive Pre-Raphaelite collection of paintings and drawings at Wightwick include works by Holman Hunt, Burne-Jones, Millais, Watts and Elizabeth Siddal.

At Wightwick even the garden reflects Pre-Raphaelite taste. The beds between high yew hedges contain shrubs and plants from Morris's Kelmscott Manor, from 'The Pines' at Putney, and from the gardens that Kempe, Burne-Jones, and Ruskin made nearly a century ago.

Wightwick was given to the Trust by the late Sir Geoffrey Mander, and his widow who lives there has made, and continues to make, important additions to the Pre-Raphaelite contents of the house.

Wilderhope Manor, Salop

7 miles south-west of Much Wenlock, 7 miles east of Church Stretton, $\frac{1}{2}$ mile south of B4371

The Manor, lying east of Wenlock Edge and looking over a wide and mild Shropshire landscape that has altered little since the day the house was built, embodies the essential characteristics of innumerable substantial country houses of the late Elizabethan era. The solid walls of uncoursed rubble, the stone-tiled roof, the busy gabled roof line, the towering chimney shafts, the three-storeyed projecting porch, and the generous mullioned and transomed windows, all these speak convincingly of the fashions of the late 16th century.

Few manor houses are so little altered, and even the treads of the circular staircase, each tread a baulk of solid timber, are original. Internally the plaster ceilings are the special attraction of Wilderhope. Of unusual sensitivity, they embody the symbolism that was significant and dear to the Elizabethans. So distinguished are these ceilings that at one time they were attributed, most improbably, to Italian craftsmen. Almost certainly they were put up by provincial craftsmen for Thomas Smallman who built the house some time before 1590.

The house is leased to the Youth Hostels Association, and the consequently sparse and simple furnishings, the cheerful bustle, evoke the spirit of this remote and untouched house.

The Smallmans owned Wilderhope until 1742, and the house is romantically associated with the exploits of another Thomas Smallman, a major in the Royalist army during the Civil War. On one occasion, when carrying dispatches to Shrewsbury, he was captured by Cromwellian troops and imprisoned in his own house. He escaped, got to horse, and galloped away. With his captors in close pursuit, he rode his mount over Wenlock Edge at the point still known as the Major's Leap. His horse was killed, but his fall was broken by a crab-apple tree and he escaped safely to Shrewsbury.

Wilderhope Manor

Woolsthorpe Manor, Lincolnshire

7 miles south of Grantham on B6403, ½ mile north-west of Colsterworth, ½ mile west of A1

Woolsthorpe Manor is a small, compact, limestone house, such as might have been built by any well-to-do gentleman farmer of James I's reign. Twenty years later, in 1642, Isaac Newton was born there. The house retains many of its simple features, notably, in the large upper room, the wainscot partition which, according to tradition, the scientist erected to form an undisturbed retreat.

To Woolsthorpe, Newton was driven by the plague in 1665 and 1666; at Woolsthorpe he formulated three great discoveries – the differential calculus, the composition of white light and the law of gravitation. 'In the two plague years', he said later, 'I was in the prime of my age for invention, and minded mathematics and philosophy more than at any time since.' At Woolsthorpe Manor he acquired that gift for concentration which led one of his biographers to record that his capacity for meditation, both in intensity and duration, has probably never been equalled, and his own secretary to write that his diligence 'made me think he aimed at something beyond the reach of human art and industry'.

Woolsthorpe Manor

Ashdown House,
Oxfordshire; west front

Uppark, West Sussex; The
red drawing room, decorated
c. 1751

Glendurgan, Devon; The lawn below the house

Killerton, Devon; Hillside arboretum

Hidcote, Gloucestershire; The red borders and gazebos, with pleached limes beyond

In one of the window jambs and upon the plaster walls of the passages and rooms, mathematical diagrams, intersecting circles, and the figures of a bird and a church, may be identified. These may well have been scratched by Newton as a boy; according to Stukeley, his first biographer, he would scratch or carve diagrams upon any surface within reach.

In the apple orchard in the front of the house, Newton is supposed to have watched the fall of the apple which inspired him to formulate the law of gravitation. A legendary descendant of the famous tree is stated by Kew Gardens to belong to a very old species called 'Flower of Kent'.

Woolsthorpe Manor was transferred to the Trust in 1943 by the Royal Society and the Pilgrim Trust, who had purchased it the previous year and provided funds for its repair.

Wordsworth House, Cockermouth, Cumbria

In main street

The substantial but unpretentious house was built in 1745, and some years later John Wordsworth, agent to the Lowther family, came to live there. His second son, the poet William Wordsworth, was born in the house in April 1770, and his daughter Dorothy, William's brilliant and devoted sister, in the following year.

Cockermouth enshrined for Wordsworth all his childhood experience of happy family life and profoundly influenced his later development. He loved the house and the Derwent, fairest of all rivers, which flows past the garden. He wrote in later years how

> ...many a time have I, a five years' child,
> A naked boy, in one delightful Rill,
> A little Mill-race sever'd from his stream,
> Made one long bathing of a summer's day,
> Bask'd in the sun, and plunged, and bask'd again
> Alternate all a summer's day, or cours'd
> Over the sandy fields, leaping through groves
> Of yellow groundsel, or when cragg and hill,
> The woods, and distant Skiddaw's lofty height,
> Were bronz'd with a deep radiance, stood alone
> Beneath the sky.

It was in their favourite playground, the garden beside the river, that Wordsworth first felt the influence of his sister, the constant companion and inspiration of his life. This modest strip of flowered ground thus recalls one of the most creative relationships in literary history.

> She gave me eyes, she gave me ears;
> And humble cares, and delicate fears;
> A heart, the fountain of sweet tears;
> And love, and thought, and joy.

Wordsworth House

For all who owe to Wordsworth's writings pleasure or inspiration, the house and garden at Cockermouth are a place of pilgrimage. They were the home of his first affections, and under the influence of his mother and father, and of his sister, a child's character took the bent which, with time and circumstance, produced the poet of genius.

Wordsworth House is an austere north country version of a simple mid-Georgian design. From the main street the house, with moulded stone architraves to the windows, its entrance sheltered by a porch with Doric columns, looks much as it did when John Wordsworth moved in. Two or three of the rooms retain their mid-18th-century softwood panelling, and there are many original features such as dentilled cornices, fireplaces, brass door furniture, and not least the staircase with its elegant balusters.

Among the Wordsworthiana are pieces of the poet's Crown Derby dinner service, his bureau bookcase with Gothick glazing, an early-19th-century longcase clock, and some of his first editions. There is an excellent set of early Georgian chairs with carved splats and claw-and-ball feet which belonged to Robert Southey, whose engraved portrait hangs in the house with those of many of Wordsworth's friends.

226

II
Gardens and
Landscape Parks

Introduction *by Miles Hadfield*

For long after it was established, the gardens and parks owned by the National Trust were incidental to those 'Places of Historic Interest or Natural Beauty' for whose acquisition it was formed. In 1895 there were still few economic problems in maintaining a fine house and its garden. As time went on, more and more houses became Trust property through the force of economic and other circumstances and often with them came a garden and the surrounding estate. Thus it was that many lovely gardens in our islands passed almost by chance to the Trust.

By 1949 it was realized that many of our finest gardens were associated with houses that lacked qualities to justify their acquisition by the Trust. Consequently, in conjunction with the Royal Horticultural Society the Trust decided to acquire a number of gardens of outstanding merit, un-associated with great houses, which in the course of time – and no long time – would have disappeared. Today, therefore, the history of garden-ing in England, Wales and Northern Ireland (likewise in Scotland through the Scottish National Trust) can be displayed by living gardens in the ownership of the Trust. These now include a majority of the finest gardens representative of our gardening history.

When the Trust acquires a fine house and its garden, two problems are set. The first concerns the house, a comparatively static entity of stone, bricks and timber probably needing repair and redecoration. It may be of one or more periods, each addition being purposefully designed to accord with the original fabric. Architects' drawings, account books and other documents usually make the necessary restoration, repairs and redecorations, compara-tively straightforward.

But what of the setting of the house – the garden? Its substance is a variety of vegetation in a continuous process of change. The most stable element, providing what in 1661 John Evelyn called its 'architectonial qualities', consists of trees, but even these will alter in their height and shape sufficiently to change the whole character and proportions of the environment of a building – even though a thoughtful designer will to some extent have taken this into account and planned for it. The impermanence of vegetation, compared with that of a builder's structure, let alone the changes that will occur after even a year or two's neglect, gives any garden a transient life.

There is, however, another feature of garden history peculiar to England: it is that in the name of fashion the English (more than the Scots or Welsh) have been the most dreadful garden vandals. There is not a Trust house built between late Tudor times (when the coming of Renaissance sentiments and fashions to England from the Continent launched the English garden on its remarkable history) and the early part of the 18th century which stands in its original garden setting. And how important this setting was to house and garden conceived as a single unit can be seen by studying the drawings in, for example, the library of the Royal Institute of British Architects. Again and again it is the architect of the house who designed the garden. It was geometrical in plan, with small buildings such as summer houses and so-called 'banqueting houses' (not indeed intended for grand meals!) designed in the same style as the house. Innumerable clipped evergreens gave perpendicular accents; occasional fountains brought to life the still, flat sheets of water (laid out, like all else, in regular geometrical shapes). The level grass was covered with elaborate patterns first in the simple form of knots, later developed into elaborate parterres: they were outlined usually in box or some other dwarf shrub and filled not only with plants but with coloured gravels, glittering spars, shiny coal dust, and so on.

Practically all this has vanished without trace. Today, we look at the houses as at pictures from which the frame, carefully chosen by the artist, has at a later date been ruthlessly torn and replaced by a new one of a kind not dreamed of by the painter.

The great era of the formal garden was during the decades after the return of Charles II and his court from the Continent in 1660. There they had seen the gardens of Le Nôtre, the greatest of all formalists, and his con-temporaries. Curiously enough, the first Frenchmen working in the formal style in England were employed by Cromwell, and expatriates, such as John Evelyn, who returned before their King, adopted the new manner prior to the Restoration. It should be added that a little later, with the coming of William and Mary, the style was modified, even though perhaps only in detail, by Dutch influence which laid more emphasis on simplicity of design and horticulture, the Dutch then and today being remarkably skilful horti-culturists, with a particular enthusiasm for topiary.

The typical garden of this period is well known in numerous engravings from the drawings begun about 1694 by Leonard Knyff; some were drawn also by his engraver, Johannes Kip. By examining those of houses now in the hands of the Trust, we can see how utterly unlike the present scene was the setting originally envisaged. (Even if the engravings were sometimes ideal-ized, or if they pictured what was never achieved, at least they show the owners' and architects' intentions.)

Perhaps most frequently reproduced is Kip's engraving of the Trust's

Dyrham Park, published in 1712. What William Blathwayt, who commissioned it, and William Talman, his architect, would say if they today saw this glorious house arising nude, as it were, from the hilly ground, and devoid of its clothing of terraces, canals, parterres, fountains, close walks and vistas, is beyond speculation.

A picture at Charlecote shows the original house in the elaborate setting of which only the great avenue from the road remains. Likewise, an early painting of that superb house, Sudbury Hall, shows that the original setting has totally disappeared; typically, what replaces it is an 18th-century lake and an early-19th-century terrace.

Such changes are due to fashion and, it must be admitted, violate the original conceptions of those who built the houses. The first and most destructive violators were the creators of the English landscape garden.

Can the gardens of the Trust show any remains of the earlier formal gardens? The answer is: No more than traces. The great terraces of Powis Castle, its once neatly clipped yews now grown into giants, belong to the late 17th century: the elaborate garden on the level below them has gone. The garden at Montacute is often wrongly said to be contemporary with the house of 1588. The exquisite pavilions are so, but they were part of the original entrance court. The entrance was moved to its present position on the west front in 1787, and surely it was on this front that the original garden with its elaborate knots and fountains would have been situated. Much of the delightful garden we now see, and for which the plans exist, is late Victorian.

There is much more of antiquity in the garden of Packwood House in Warwickshire, notably the yew garden believed to have been laid out about 1655. It incorporates a 'mount', a not unusual feature of early gardens, whose spiralling path the owner would climb to survey his estate. On it stands a great yew, said to represent Christ preaching the Sermon on the Mount to the assembled multitude (represented by smaller yews). Unfortunately, this tradition goes back no further than 1892 when Sir Reginald Blomfield recorded (with some scepticism) that he had been told it by a gardener. On the other hand, an aerial photograph shows that the yews conform to the pattern of a typical mid-17th-century layout. A garden gateway and its adjoining walls, with alcoves for bee skeps, are accepted as belonging to about 1655: they are delightful.

Elsewhere, the Trust owned little more than minor and pleasing relics of pre-18th-century gardens, such as the octagonal garden house at Melford Hall in Suffolk. Then in 1967 it acquired the garden of Westbury Court in Gloucestershire, constructed between 1696 and 1705. Illustrated by Kip in 1712 and with plenty of contemporary documentation, Westbury is a canal garden, more in the Dutch than the French style. So too is Erddig, near Wrexham, which came to the Trust in 1973 and may well be slightly earlier in date. Among some half dozen gardens of the period still in existence, both were, though sadly decayed, capable of reinstatement in a form which their original creators would have accepted and appreciated.

Other relics of 17th- and early-18th-century gardens in the hands of the

Trust include the newly restored Restoration layout of the garden of Ham House, Surrey and the enormous terrace of 1666, 400 feet long and 25 feet wide, which is all that remains of William Winde's great house at Cliveden built for the Duke of Buckingham. Beneath the terrace lay coal cellars, a water tank and an ice-house. The terraces at Clevedon Court in Somerset, and probably the great chestnut avenue at Croft Castle in Herefordshire, must surely also have been part of older designs that have long since vanished, while the sycamore avenue at Lanhydrock in Cornwall, another link with the age of formal gardening, is known to have been planted in 1657.

At Moseley Old Hall in Staffordshire the small garden has been laid out by the Trust as it might well have looked when Charles II took refuge in the house after the battle of Worcester in 1651. It is, however, no more than an imaginative reconstruction.

Most people interested in the history of taste know that the English invented the informal, landscape garden. So far as our islands were concerned, it eclipsed the style of the 'Sun King's' gardener, Le Nôtre, which had long inspired our designers. Later it even crossed the channel to France as the fashionable *jardin anglais.*

The first stirrings of the movement occurred when Joseph Addison, after his visit to Italy from 1701 to 1703, derided the great Italian gardens which were the inspiration of France but praised the view of the Campagna, 'so often worked upon' by painters such as Claude, Poussin and others who furnished the scene with the symbolic relics of ancient times and architecture.

Soon Alexander Pope joined Addison in attacking the old style, and William Kent began to work in the new manner. His conversion of the grounds at Rousham in Oxfordshire remains a tribute to his skill and sensitivity. The new style accorded, and still accords, with the English character. Its main constituents – the free placing and free growth of trees, and the apparently free, uncontrolled use of water – have deep and as yet uncharted associations with the spirit of the English (surely one should not say British) people in all strata of society.

But aspects of the landscape revolution do not stand up well to the scrutiny of the English comic spirit; the recreation of an ancient Roman landscape, appropriate to hot sunlight, in our dark, dank lands is a little absurd. Similarly, to scatter the countryside with exquisitely reconstructed classical temples, suited to the Mediterranean of the ancient gods rather than to the soggy habitat of the Druids, must seem to the unscholarly not without humour.

The prototypes that introduced this remarkable new style to our landscape were perhaps half a dozen. Woburn Farm in the Thames Valley has disappeared and Shenstone's Leasowes in Worcestershire lies under Halesowen's suburbia, but the form of neighbouring Hagley (and some of its original trees and ornaments) can still be studied. Kent's Rousham in Oxfordshire and Stowe in Buckinghamshire remain. The newly restored garden at Claremont, which dates from about 1715, appears today as the combined and successive work of Vanbrugh and Bridgeman, Kent and lastly Capability Brown and thus predates Stourhead by some twenty years. That most wonderful of all these man-made landscapes was created by Henry Hoare and developed by successive generations until it passed to the Trust in 1946.

All these gardens, except Stowe (where several designers were concerned), had very individual qualities emanating from the personality of their owners. Woburn Farm and the Leasowes were essentially idealized, lyrical English scenes; Hagley was somewhat similar but with more substantial buildings in a revived classical manner. Rousham was created by a man so inspired by the Italian scene that he became known as 'the Signor'. At Stourhead the objective was nothing less than an earthly paradise in the classical manner.

All these and the writing and talking about them, different as we now see the individual gardens to have been, began the landscape movement. The straight line gave way to the sinuous curve, the straight canal was sent meandering, and avenues were felled to be replaced by trees in wandering bands and carefully placed clumps. Not only were the time-honoured traditions of garden design abandoned, but the old gardens which reflected these traditions were destroyed.

The first gardens in the new style, each in a different way inspired by such artists as Claude, Poussin, Salvator Rosa, Albani, and others whose works are to be seen in many National Trust houses, were individual, imaginative creations. Soon this individuality disappeared and the famous Lancelot ('Capability') Brown (1715–83), his assistants and imitators, and on Brown's death his successor Humphry Repton (1752–1818), developed a much less imaginative, indeed almost standardized, system of design.

In this the grassy, 'natural' yet carefully contrived, landscape flowed right up to the house, any earlier terraces on which it stood being obliterated and turned into smooth contours. The deer, cattle and sheep, held to be highly appropriate as a rural ornament, were prevented from looking through the windows by a dry ditch, used in the 17th-century French formal gardens, now known as the ha-ha.

The Brown and Repton style of landscape gardening was nearly always formed from, or enclosed to create, a park, and will be mentioned in due course. With its typically English restraint and only very occasional bursts of excitement or drama, it was dominant well into the 19th century (the self-effacing setting of, for example, Jane Austen's *Mansfield Park* of 1814). The imagination of a Kent or Henry Hoare had disappeared.

However, during the same period, another aspect of gardening, that of practical horticulture, was developing at an unprecedented pace. Even though the late 18th century was an era of maritime war, a large number of exotic plants were introduced from overseas. The functional greenhouse, as opposed to the ornamental orangery, was developing. Above all, scientific study was beginning seriously to affect traditional practice. Evidence of this was the founding in 1807 of what is now the Royal Horticultural Society.

These developments were inappropriate to an aesthetic of garden design in which a herd of domestic cattle would emerge from a sylvan scene to gaze languidly into the windows over a ha-ha. Thus it was that the great landowners, often vying one with another to achieve success in growing the new introductions, yet horrified of intruding upon the grassy idylls, built their great walled gardens, often at some distance from the house, in some concealed spot where their exotics could show their gaily painted glories without upsetting the pure, idyllic scene.

One exception was often made to the restriction on the use of exotics outside the walled enclosure. That was the planting of foreign trees. Brown in particular often used the Lebanon cedar, while robinias, oriental planes and tulip trees are among those that were planted alongside our native oaks. The sweet chestnut, which has been with us since Roman times, was also popular.

Here we can notice the great delight the English have always had in the greenness of grass, so preponderant in our landscape gardens. A Frenchman, d'Argenville, advised his countrymen in 1702 to follow our practice of rolling and mowing: 'You can't do better than follow [this] method, where the grass plots are of so exquisite beauty, that in France we can scarce ever hope to come up to it.' In 1771 Horace Walpole when in Paris cried out for a little of our grass as would (he wrote) a seaman after a long voyage. Other visitors from abroad have for centuries praised it. This passion for fresh grass as a major element in our garden existed long before Francis Bacon wrote that 'there was nothing more pleasant to the eye than green grass kept finely shorn', and it persists today. On any summer morning, one can be sure to hear the (now noisy) whirr of a mower and smell the sweet scent of cut grass (today mixed with petrol fumes) in any Trust garden.

As Brown, Repton and their school worked and landscaped in what were at least called parks, even if strictly speaking some of them were not, it is interesting to recall that these were originally enclosures, part of the demesne lands of the lord of the manor, usually of valueless wild land suitable for game and sport. They were carefully fenced in: the ancient type of wooden deer-fencing can still be seen at Charlecote. Other parks such as Berrington in Herefordshire are surrounded by iron deer-fencing of a later period.

Most of the 18th-century landscaped parks still existing are significantly on land that is infertile. Brown and Repton between them landscaped about three hundred and fifty, predominantly in the home counties and Midlands, around the homes of fashionable landowners. It is today largely forgotten that future timber production lay behind the planting of the serpentining belts that marked boundaries and the carefully placed clumps. This was of immense value during two world wars. Our failing has been not to replant and replace when it was needed. And now we are faced with the difficult problem of dealing with the remaining trees which have lived out their lives and become decrepit, and of restoring the landscape – if indeed that is possible.

Among the landscaped parks of this era the Trust owns several. Brown's work includes Berrington in Herefordshire, very little spoiled, Charlecote in Warwickshire where he spared the great avenue, and not least the superb park at Petworth which proved so great an inspiration to Turner.

A very delightful park surrounds George Steuart's Attingham Hall near Shrewsbury, through which the little River Tern meanders just before it reaches the Severn. This is one of Repton's most successful landscapes and perhaps the most sensitive of his designs in the Midlands. It was created in 1798. At Tatton Park also, Repton is the genius of the place. Clumber Park – the house has since been demolished – is a huge landscaped estate created on typical park-like heathland in the late 18th century. There is a three-mile-long double lime avenue which winds across it (the longest avenue in England).

Significance lies in the dates of Attingham and Clumber. In 1794 Richard Payne Knight, an amateur philosopher, published his 'didactic poem' *The Landscape*. It was dedicated to Uvedale Price, who in the same year published *An Essay on the Picturesque*. Both attacked the work of Brown (in particular) and Repton as being dull and unimaginative. Both wanted some return to formality and gaily planted terraces near the house. Price was the first writer to urge the naturalization of rhododendrons and other exotics in the home wood.

These two writers soon influenced Repton, who even went so far in his later designs as to admit avenues so long as they were not straight. Thus by the time the Clumber avenue was planted, fashion had again changed.

When Knight and Price died, in 1824 and 1829 respectively (Repton predeceased them in 1818) their theories had become widely accepted. The days of 'endless serpentines that nothing show' were over. Terraces and formality were now the vogue, with elaborate planting near the house, while immediately beyond exotic trees and shrubs led to the park. Not surprisingly, Sir Walter Scott was an enthusiast for the new theories, writing in their support and putting them into practice at Abbotsford.

When the Queen came to the throne, what was later to be known as the typical Victorian garden had already come into being: its elements, more or less, lay in the Knight-Price picturesque theories. Her reign was a period in which garden design was eclectic and unoriginal, as well as bemused by the wealth of plant introductions from abroad – from Western North America, China and Japan – which occurred on a hitherto unknown scale in a mere quarter-century from, say, 1825 to 1850. Artificial stones, such as those invented by Mrs Eleanor Coade in 1778 and Felix Austin at the turn of the century, enabled both period reproductions and new designs to be manufactured relatively cheaply. Cast-iron seats and garden ornaments also came into fashion.

Knight and Price were for the most part arbiters of taste, not practical designers. The most outstanding of the latter, and a close disciple of Price, was W. S. Gilpin (1761–1843), a very talented man with a large practice.

Few of his gardens remain, for fashion and circumstances unfortunately have resulted in their disappearance. The terraces at Sudbury Hall are his work. But most notable is the garden at Scotney Castle which, though not actually designed by him in detail, is in accordance with his suggestions made to Edwin Hussey in 1836. The picturesque style of this lovely garden has been carried on to the present day.

The Trust has not, I think, any examples of the work of the prolific W. A. Nesfield (1793–1881), soldier turned artist, turned garden designer. However, that other great mid-Victorian architect, Sir Charles Barry, who was, like Nesfield, not concerned with planting but solely with garden architecture, was active at Cliveden.

The Trust has three 19th-century gardens much influenced by the French style. The smallest is the elaborate and delicate parterre garden of about 1830 standing incongruously almost in the shadow of the weighty 15th-century gate-tower at Oxburgh. Some four decades later Baron Ferdinand de Rothschild acquired Waddesdon and built his French 'Renaissance' *château*. The magnificent garden designed by Lainé accords well with the house. Fountains, statuary (including a group by the 17th-century sculptor Girardon), trees, views, are all on the grandest scale and quite un-English.

Ascott, near Wing in Buckinghamshire, is another Rothschild garden which reflects the French taste. It includes an exquisite, very 19th-century little fountain garden and a larger fountain garden framed in topiary from which one looks far away over Bedfordshire. There is a fascinating collection of weeping and other, particularly abnormally and brightly coloured, trees and shrubs. The topiary sundial in different coloured yews and box is delightful.

The early part of the present century was dominated by the noisy William Robinson and the subtle Miss Jekyll with their 'natural gardening' and lovely colour schemes. It was soon greatly affected by the wonderful range of new plants introduced from central and western China as well as from South America, New Zealand, and even Tasmania.

First to be assigned to this period, though with earlier origins, is Nymans in Sussex. Here most styles and types of gardening are carried out with an extraordinarily wide range of plants, magnificently grown, both new and old. It will long be associated with Lt-Col. J. R. Messel and his celebrated gardener, Mr J. Comber, and the latter's plant-collecting son, H. F. Comber. Its magnolias, rhododendrons, camellias, eucryphias, davidias, roses and much else, such as a very early heath garden, fine topiary and a pinetum, make it famous.

Next in point of time comes Rowallane, one of those gardens enjoying the equable climate of the neighbouring Strangford Lough in County Down. It was begun by the late Armytage Moore in 1903. He was primarily concerned with the growing of trees, shrubs, and plants of particular horticultural – even botanical – interest in the natural setting of the undulating countryside, through which paths apparently meander, though in fact they are skilfully placed. To see the sheets of daffodils in spring is to take a lesson in the art of naturalizing, while to walk in the walled garden is to learn something of the art of skilful cultivation of rare and difficult plants.

In 1905 came the beginning of Major Lawrence Johnston's Hidcote Manor garden on the scarp of the Cotswolds overlooking Shakespeare's country. Its combination of formality with informal, natural-style gardening, and its selection of trees, shrubs and all kinds of plants, common as well as rare, to create groups combining form and colour with outstanding artistry, have never been surpassed. Particularly did he, perhaps as one who was not a native, grasp the ever-changing beauty of the English skies, which often terminate his vistas and avenues. Not least his foresight was astonishing, for the original plan and planting, now some sixty years old, progressively reveal their innate and masterly qualities, indeed will continue to unfold them as time goes on.

The year 1921 saw the beginnings of the magnificent new developments by the Marchioness of Londonderry in the gardens of Mount Stewart, another of those gardens in the blessed climate of Strangford Lough. It is probably the last great garden to be made in the grandest style: architecture, formality, and the most lavish natural planting are combined.

Hidcote has been an inspiration to many gardens of the present day, and admittedly so to that gem, the garden created around the derelict castle at Sissinghurst in Kent and particularly associated with the genius of the late Victoria Sackville-West, though in its creation her husband, the late Sir Harold Nicolson, played an important part 'behind the scenes'.

Finally, a garden of an entirely different style from anything hitherto possessed by the Trust came to it in 1966 with the acquisition of Lord Fairhaven's Anglesey Abbey. The garden lies on a flat, even desolate, site in Cambridgeshire on which its many acres are, as it were, picked out and isolated from their bare surroundings by wide plantings of trees and avenues on a scale not practised for very many years, and often with the use of unaccustomed species for the purpose. Within the vast overall plan lie individual small gardens, each with a quality of its own.

The Trust in its gardens must have by far the finest collection of trees in Britain. Stourhead has an amazing variety of splendid specimens that, apart from the original planting, were first established in 1791 when Sir Richard Colt Hoare introduced examples of all that was good and new, a practice continued by his successors down to the present time. The beginning of the remarkable collection on the hillside garden at Killerton in the mild air of South Devon, where planting still continues, dates from a little later. Sheffield Park, an 18th-century landscape, is rather different. It was designed and planted for visual effect, particularly autumn colour, at the beginning of the present century.

In the Cornish properties, as, for example and notably, at Glendurgan on the Helford River, skilful use has been made of the mild climate to grow trees and shrubs unmanageable in most parts of the British Isles. The same applies to Knightshayes Court in Devon, and to Rowallane and Mount Stewart in the soft air of Northern Ireland. Bodnant in the Conwy Valley, surrounded by dramatic Welsh mountain scenery, had its first plantings all but a hundred years ago. They were gradually, and very extensively, added to by the Aberconway family during the present century, when in particular new species from Western China were introduced.

Wakehurst Place in West Sussex, now administered for the Trust by the Royal Botanic Gardens at Kew, has a fine collection. A comparative new-comer, Winkworth Arboretum in Surrey, is already well known for its collection of the recently introduced species of *Acer* and *Sorbus*.

Many of these gardens have exceptional specimens in their collections. There are outstanding trees in other Trust gardens; such as the plane tree (*Platanus hybrida*) at Mottisfont Abbey, the holm oak (*Quercus ilex*) at Westbury Court, and the tallest of all British Douglas firs just outside, but seen from, the Trust property at Powis Castle.

The Trust's gardens are well able to illustrate the history of the use of buildings to protect tender plants. At first these structures were used for the protection and display of ornamental evergreens in the winter, notably oranges. The only evergreen shrubs that are native are holly, juniper and box. Most of the introduced kinds were slightly tender. A collection of 'greens', the leaves kept beautifully clean and glossy, among which the owner and his friends could walk in an elegant building on a winter's day, was desirable. In summer these 'greens' in their tubs were usually stood out of doors. In these buildings were also wintered half-hardy bulbs, often from the Cape, and obtained from the long-famous Dutch nurserymen.

Architectural merit for long took pride of place over horticultural efficiency; the roofs of such buildings were not glazed, and they starved the plants of essential light. While the Trust has nothing to compete with the magnificence of Vanbrugh's orangery at Kensington or Chambers's at Kew, it can show the façade of the little 18th-century gem moved from its original position to one of the terraces at Powis Castle, and the delightful restored orangery at Saltram, having been designed in 1773 by one Stockman in the style of the Adam building at Croome Court. Other elegant examples include the greenhouses at Blickling and Wallington, and a 19th-century Jacobean-style orangery at Montacute.

Two considerable steps forward in functional design are seen at Tatton Park where Lewis Wyatt's splendid orangery (1811–12) has walls that are mostly glass. It was at about this time that the problem of efficient heating was first solved and that the importance of light was understood. Also at Tatton Park is a functional glasshouse of fine mid-Victorian design containing immense New Zealand tree ferns. It marks horticulturally a notable advance over the earlier orangeries and greenhouses in the Trust's owner-ship.

Gardens and Landscape Parks

Those properties in which both house and garden are open to the public are described in Chapter I and will be found on the garden maps.

Bodnant, Gwynedd

8 miles south of Llandudno and Colwyn Bay, on A496

In the history of gardening Bodnant is one of the newer creations, but it is also one of the most renowned, on account of its design, its wonderful collection of plants skilfully used, and its splendid situation above the Conwy Valley with distant views towards Snowdon. The garden, developed since 1875, is a family creation and it is now superintended by the present Lord Aberconway whose father gave it to the Trust in 1949. A series of large terraces, begun in 1905, leads down the hill from the house and gives shape to the garden which elsewhere spreads out with calculated informality. One large terraced lawn holds two great cedars and a formal pool with many-

Bodnant

Bodnant; The Pin Mill

coloured water-lilies. Below is a paved rose walk and below this again a formal canal and the Pin Mill, a garden house built in 1730 and moved to Bodnant some 200 years later. These terraces, connected by pergolas and flights of steps, decorated with balustrading, wall fountains and ornaments, are enriched by a great variety of rare shrubs and plants. Among shrubs against the walls will be found *Hydrangea involucrata* 'Hortensis', *H. quercifolia, Camellia reticulata, Magnolia delavayi*, while the uppermost terrace is overhung by the brown stems of *Arbutus andrachnoides*. In the walls grow lewisias and *Primula forrestii*. Well-kept hedges control the views, and at the end of the canal is a raised theatre in the Italianate 18th-century taste, with wings of clipped yew. These terraced gardens remain immensely attractive throughout the whole spring and summer.

Below the terraces one loses the distant views, but there is compensation in the feeling of being in the depths of a Welsh dell with outcrops of rock and the sound of rushing water. The exotic trees are magnificent and the widespread groupings of camellias, rhododendrons, azaleas and magnolias are among the finest in the country. The largest conifers in the dell were planted from 1876 onwards. *Abies bracteata, A. pinsapo*, wellingtonias and sequoias, *Pinus contorta* and *P. ayacahuite, Juniperus recurva coxii, Picea breweriana* and species from the Southern Hemisphere, rare birches, embothriums, eucryphias, kalmias, davidias, thrive in the dell and in the extensive shrub borders above it. Native ferns, Japanese azaleas and rare shrubs link a flowing and informal composition.

Plant breeding has been carried on at Bodnant for many years, and hybrids have been raised in many genera, *Viburnum bodnantense*, rhododendrons – both hardy and tender – and orchids. In the midst of so much varied horticulture it is delightful to pause on the south lawn on the way out to admire the robust oaks on the knoll in the near landscape. Everyone pauses also to see, when in flower, the borders of gentians and the long pleached walk of laburnum.

Claremont, Surrey

On the south edge of Esher, on the east side of the A307 (no direct access from new A3 Esher by-pass)

The 18th-century landscape garden at Claremont, designed as a pleasure garden to the house, already in 1727 described by Switzer as 'the noblest of any in Europe', is the combined work of Vanbrugh, Bridgeman, Kent and 'Capability' Brown and deserves to be far better known. It is one of the earliest gardens in the 'natural' manner to have survived, preceding the now much more celebrated Stourhead by some twenty years. When Kent succeeded Bridgeman as surveyor in charge in the 1730s, he extended and modified but did not obliterate the more formal work of his predecessor. Similarly Brown was content to leave intact the work of a man he much respected. The result is that Claremont today presents a microcosm of the English landscape garden, *le jardin anglais*, often noted as this country's most original contribution to the culture of northern Europe.

In about 1709 Sir John Vanbrugh built for himself a little villa on a piece of land near Esher, then known as Chargate Farm. It is likely that he chose the site for the picturesque qualities of the adjacent landscape: sharp contours, fine trees, water, dramatic views suddenly revealed across dips and hollows and all within a few acres. In 1711 Vanbrugh sold the property to his friend and patron, Thomas Pelham, Earl of Clare (later created Duke of Newcastle) and from this new owner the estate received the name by which it is known today. Over the next nine years Vanbrugh was employed by Newcastle on the transformation of his small villa into a ducal mansion. At the same time, with the assistance of Charles Bridgeman, he gradually imposed on the tumbled landscape to the north-west a garden that was still formal in design, but which none the less took advantage of the natural beauties of the site. From this period date the Belvedere Tower (not owned by the Trust), built to Vanbrugh's design in about 1715 on the summit of the principal knoll and Bridgeman's great turf amphitheatre, a prodigious earthwork carved out of the hillside in about 1726.

Early in the 1730s William Kent was called upon to extend and informalize the garden in the manner he had recently pioneered at Stowe. He enlarged Bridgeman's round pond into an apparently natural lake with an

Claremont; from an early-18th-century oil painting

island and on it built a rusticated pavilion with a pyramidal roof. He planted trees in groves, laid out serpentine paths and dotted the garden with other small pleasure buildings, of which only the Grotto at the head of the lake survives.

The Duke of Newcastle died in 1768 and in the following year the estate was sold to Lord Clive of India (see p. 171). Clive demolished the Vanbrugh house and replaced it with the present building (not owned by the Trust) on a site on higher ground near by to a design by Brown and Henry Holland. Beyond altering the course of the ha-ha to relate to the position of the new house and that of the Portsmouth road to divert it away from the edge of the lake, there is no evidence that Brown made significant changes to the area of the landscape garden.

In the 19th century Claremont became better known, first as the home of the ill-fated Princess Charlotte of Wales and her husband, Prince Leopold of Saxe-Coburg and later, after the death of the Princess, as the place where Queen Victoria spent the happiest times of her childhood in the company of her favourite uncle. For some years after 1848 it was the refuge of the exiled King Louis Philippe and his family and in 1882 it was given by the Queen to her youngest son, the Duke of Albany, on his marriage. The estate was finally sold and divided on the death of his widow in 1922. In due course the house and park were bought by Claremont School, who own it today, and the landscape garden was given to the National Trust in 1949 for permanent preservation. Since then it has been managed for the Trust by Esher (now Elmbridge) Borough Council.

By 1949 twenty years of neglect had reduced Kent's New House on the island to a ruin; Bridgeman's amphitheatre and many of the 18th-century paths had become totally obscured by great banks of laurel and *Rhododen-*

dron ponticum; in places rhododendrons extended 15 feet beyond the perimeter of the lake. The importance of the garden at Claremont as one of the first man-made landscapes in the 'natural' manner had been forgotten. Thanks to a generous gift from the Slater Foundation, however, a full programme of restoration was undertaken between 1975 and 1977. Today many of the features so laudatorily described in prose and verse by 18th-century visitors can be seen and admired once more. The modern visitor may gaze up at Vanbrugh's Belvedere across the green sward where bowls was once played by men in long-waisted coats and tricorne hats; or peer into the recesses of the Grotto, whose fern-fringed chambers sparkle with felspar and mica; may follow Kent's serpentine paths through groves of beech and yew and sweet chestnut, see his little island pavilion mirrored in the surface of the lake or stand amazed at the sheer size of Bridgeman's turf amphitheatre fashioned out of the hillside by hand. The splendid trees in their maturity, including one of the finest cedars of Lebanon in England, are a pleasure for which the 18th century would envy those who visit Claremont landscape garden today.

Glendurgan, Cornwall *(see colour plate facing p. 225)*

4 miles south-west of Falmouth, ½ mile south-west of Mawnan Smith on the Helford Passage road

Three small valleys converge at Durgan where their attendant streams flow into the tranquil estuary of the Helford River. To one of these delectable valleys, Glendurgan, came in about 1820 a certain Alfred Fox. He built the present house soon after and began the garden which falls away invitingly down the 'glen'. His was the laurel maze, planted in 1833, and he must have been responsible for many of the fine trees and the serpentine paths laid out

Glendurgan; The laurel maze

in the romantic taste. His interests and talents passed to his successors, and three subsequent generations carried on the gardening tradition.

They did so in a propitious setting. Glendurgan is warm and sheltered. Tender exotics thrive, providing infinite variety in shape and colour through the year. Noted specimens in the valley garden are two immense tulip trees, a weeping swamp cypress, a Japanese loquat, cedars, weeping Mexican cypress, pines, firs, and bamboos. In such a setting, specimens, however rare, can but add grace to the natural beauty of the valley. In spring it is scattered with Lent lilies, primroses and bluebells, and glows with the colour of magnolias, cherries, camellias, and rhododendrons. By midsummer Bentham's cornel spreads its pale gold down the slopes and later the hydrangeas and eucryphias take over. There are tree ferns from New Zealand, aloes from Mexico, and mimosa from Australia. A formal garden also contains its specialities, such as ailanthus, and feijoa.

Glendurgan came to the Trust as a gift from Mr and Mrs Cuthbert Fox and their son Mr Philip Fox in 1962.

Hidcote Manor, Gloucestershire *(see colour plate facing p. 225)*

At Hidcote Bartrim, 4 miles north-east of Chipping Campden, 1 mile east of the A46 Stratford-upon-Avon/Cheltenham road

The essence of Hidcote is the combination of formal design with seemingly haphazard or informal planting which is the archetype of a whole style of 20th-century gardens. It is the highly sophisticated creation of an expert plantsman with an architect's ability to create a structure of interesting spaces; likewise, it has been an inspiration to modern gardeners, exerting in our time a profound influence. Hidcote may be said to have been founded on the tenets of Gertrude Jekyll but it is also based on the traditional cottage garden, where plants of interest and beauty have been grown through several centuries little affected by changing fashions in grander places. Apart from the pleasant 17th-century house, a few walls, a cedar and a clump of big beeches, there was nothing at Hidcote when Major Lawrence Johnston acquired it. The garden was created from 1905 onwards. Though covering eleven acres, and high on the Cotswolds, it is sheltered from cold winds. The soil, mainly lime, has acid pockets, as is common in the district, and this acidity was increased by importing suitable soil and rotted sawdust.

Walls or hedges – the latter of many kinds, one being a mixture or 'tapestry' hedge – enclose numerous separate gardens, each one different in design from the next, each planted with a careful selection of shrubs and plants to provide flower from spring to autumn, and each with a distinctive colour scheme. The main vista moves from quiet colours by the house, enters a *rondpoint* of lilacs and hellebores, then passes between borders of reddish-tinted flowers and copper foliage up steps to a pair of gazebos, and on, flanked by hornbeam hedges on stems and by beds of grasses, to the great gates which give a view of the open countryside. A series of such

Hidcote

changes and surprises is provided throughout the garden, not the least being
the change from the formal enclosures near the house to the informal stream
garden, which has its own colour schemes, and so up slopes to the 'Weston-
birt' area, also entirely informal.

Everywhere there are rare and choice plants. An old double tulip, for
instance, not seen elsewhere; peony species, both herbaceous and shrubby;
Houttuynia cordata 'Plena', meconopsis, primulas, kirengeshoma and many
ground-covering plants. Rare trees and shrubs include *Alangium platani-
folium, Pittosporum dallii, Hydrangea aspera* 'Macrophylla', *Acer griseum,
Nothofagus antarctica, Quercus pontica* and *Q. coccifera, Aesculus neglecta*
'Erythroblastos', birches and magnolias. This is the home of 'Hidcote'
hypericum, 'Hidcote' verbena, 'Hidcote' lavender and several more, including the rose 'Lawrence Johnston' which was raised in France.

Besides this lavish display on the south of the main vista, there is the
tranquil greensward of the Theatre Lawn with great beeches beyond, an
immense and ancient wistaria, a davidia, a long walk in the kitchen garden
which contains a big collection of old French roses, an alley of limes, and an
avenue of beeches.

Killerton, Devon *(see colour plate facing p. 225)*

7 miles north-east of Exeter, west of B3185, forking left from the A38 Taunton road

The Aclands have lived since 1778 in the old house they built at Killerton, and Sir Thomas Acland, 10th baronet, laid out the grounds after the Napoleonic Wars. In 1944, as another war drew to its close, his descendant, Sir Richard Acland, gave the property to the National Trust.

The splendid tree-clad hill, which the 10th baronet tamed and planted for the delight of future generations, is volcanic, a lime-free area in a limy countryside. It suits rhododendrons and conifers, and the many species which successive Aclands procured from distant continents and raised from seeds. On this propitious soil, care and climate have, over nearly a century and a half, given us a great arboretum.

Though the shrub borders and plant beds that surround the house – where pomegranate and *Lagerstroemia indica* flourish – and the long herbaceous border might elsewhere call for special comment, the main theme at Killerton is the wooded hillside, an arboretum which is especially attractive in spring and autumn. An ancient avenue of beeches, perhaps 200 years old, bisects the grassy lawns which sweep up the hill, ever more thickly planted with trees and shrubs as the slopes ascend.

Among the rarer conifers are *Fitzroya cupressoides, Saxegothea conspicua, Picea breweriana,* and *Pinus flexilis.* There are gigantic cork oaks, and a wellingtonia said to have been raised from the first packet of seeds to reach this country in 1850. Magnolias are represented by many species; Roblé beech, tulip tree, tree of heaven, limes, maples and oaks abound; among shrubs of note are *Pittosporum dallii,* embothriums, eucryphias, styrax, snowdrop tree, fringe tree and Japanese maples. *Cyclamen purpurescens*

Killerton

(europaeum) carpets the spring grass, with Lent lilies, *Narcissus pallidus*, daffodils and primroses; *Cyclamen hederifolium (neapolitanum)* follows in autumn.

In the chapel grounds near by are further rare specimens, Lucombe oaks, tulip tree, *Ostrya carpinifolia, Quercus acuta* and species of hickory.

Rarely have imagination and the skill of the arboriculturist used natural landscape to more satisfying purpose. From the summit of the hill the wooded slopes of Killerton perhaps create their deepest impression. Beyond huge Chinese and Himalayan rhododendron species and groups of camellias and bamboos, beyond palms, pampas grass and great spreading trees, rise the sombre slopes of Dartmoor.

Mount Stewart, Co. Down

On the east shore of Strangford Lough, 5 miles south-east of Newtownards on A20

Protected by woodlands and with soft damp climate and good soil, it is small wonder that the gardens at Mount Stewart are famous for their plants. But they owe even more to the fact that the complete design from start to finish is the conception of a single talented gardener, the late Marchioness of Londonderry. Beginning in 1921, she developed and improved them for nearly forty years. They were transferred to the Trust in 1955. Her daughter, Lady Mairi Bury, gave Mount Stewart House in 1976 (see p. 149).

The formal parts of the garden lie to the south and west of the house. On the south front is the Italian garden; a long terrace gives onto a sunken lawn with twin parterras, surrounded by walls set with unusual stone ornaments made to Lady Londonderry's design. This leads to the Spanish garden with a sunken pool as its central focus and a garden house roofed with Spanish tiles beyond. Sheltered by high hedges and groups of tender eucalyptus, a variety of trees, shrubs and plants make a splendid showing in spring and summer. The New Zealand kowhai, *Camellia reticulata*, feijoa, cordylines, callistemons, beschorneria and tender rhododendrons grow to perfection; lowly plants include *Iris laevigata* 'Rose Queen' and *Hosta plantaginea*.

The west front looks on to a sunken garden. Shut in by high hedges and surrounded by a raised walk overhung by climbers on a pergola, it is planted with beds of azaleas. *Rosa gigantea*, ceanothus, solanums and delphiniums grow well. The colours here are blue and purple, orange and yellow. Beyond is a paved garden in the shape of a shamrock for winter with early spring shrubs and plants. At the east end of the house lies the Mairi garden, with summer house and dovecote, planted mainly with blue and white flowers, particularly blue African lilies. Leading off in various directions are tunnels of scented rhododendrons, woodland paths for ferns and lilies, and a rock bank for dwarf shrubs and heaths.

The scenic drive that leads to the front of the house and to spacious lawns with specimen trees is flanked with large-leafed rhododendrons and conifers. Here, on the north side of the house, winding ways between rare shrubs arrive at a lake, richly planted with shrubs and trees. A private burial ground, looking down on the lake, is surrounded by olives, *Cupressus cashmiriana* and leptospermums. To the east an informal avenue of red, white and blue, carried out in rhododendrons, eucalyptus, embothriums and hydrangeas, commemorates the jubilee of King George V and Queen Mary. The way to the house leads back through a rhododendron woodland. In all it is a garden of varied design, with a rich collection of plants from all over the world.

Mount Stewart

It remains to describe the Temple of the Winds that for all but the most dedicated plantsman must surely be the outstanding feature of Mount Stewart. Some distance north-west of the house, set on a wooded knoll and looking out across Strangford Lough, stands one of the most elegant of 18th-century landscape buildings. The hexagonal temple, with little porticoes over three of the ground-floor windows, was designed by 'Athenian' Stuart in about 1780. Derived from the Temple of the Winds in Athens, it is a sister building to Stuart's Tower of the Winds at Shugborough (see p. 281), but the Mount Stewart version is constructed of ashlar instead of brick and stucco, and the position is incomparably finer. So too is the upper chamber, with a plasterwork ceiling that is echoed in the design of a superb parquetry floor.

Nymans, West Sussex *(see colour plate facing p. 256)*

At Handcross just east of the M23/A23 London to Brighton road

Nature and a family of talented gardeners have combined to create this masterpiece, one of the great gardens of the Sussex Weald. On rich soil, standing high yet well sheltered, this was a site of infinite possibility and must, one feels, have long awaited a gardener such as Ludwig Messel. He started planting in 1885 and the conception which he initiated was carried on by his son, L. C. R. Messel, who bequeathed Nymans to the Trust in 1954.

Over nearly three-quarters of a century, father and son here assembled a remarkable collection of trees, shrubs and plants from all over the world, yet at the same time they managed to ensure that Nymans remained a garden of intimate charm. It is this combination of the rare and the exotic with the simple and the friendly that is so unusual and so remarkable.

From the car park we enter an area where grow magnolias, deutzias and specialists' shrubs: eucryphias and embothriums, *Lindera megaphylla*, *Tetracenton sinense* and *Meliosma veitchiorum* among them. But before walking down the long path we should look into the pinetum with its sheets of daffodils in spring, its garden temple and remarkable specimen conifers.

Beyond, surrounded by hedges and further shrubs, lies an old rose garden. Crossing the drive and passing groups of *Cardiocrinum giganteum* we enter the walled garden under an Italian archway. This is the heart of Nymans. The old apples are now dwarfed by well-grown exotics such as davidia, *Magnolia campbellii*, *Nothofagus dombeyi* and *Styrax hemsleyana*.

Nymans; The dovecote

Quiet walks – one devoted to spring flowers and another to summer perennials – converge at an Italian fountain set off by topiary. Just outside, *Lilium speciosum* gives a superb annual display.

The house, built in the 1900s, suffered a disastrous fire after the last war, and is in part a picturesque shell, with choice climbers on its walls. It dominates a lawn fringed by Himalayan rhododendrons, hydrangeas and camellias. Other features of this garden, so varied and so appealing, are a sunken garden in front of a classical garden house, a long and close alley of evergreens, a heath garden where grow all manner of dwarf shrubs, and a wistaria-covered pergola that flanks a bowling green decked with blue and violet flowers through the season. There is a vast collection of rhododendron species and hybrids, many rare species and varieties of roses, camellias and magnolias. The original *Camellia* 'Leonard Messel', *Magnolia* 'Leonard Messel', the Nymans forsythia and eucryphia, commemorate one who left his mark unmistakably on British horticulture.

Rowallane, Co. Down

11 miles south-east of Belfast, 1 mile south of Saintfield on west of A7

The wind-swept and undulating countryside of County Down carries a poor soil with frequent whinstone rock outcrops, and particularly is this so where Rowallane lies. The Rev. John Moore planted the belts of trees for shelter, and several of the older conifers; he also built the walls and outbuildings which after his death in 1903 passed to his son, Hugh Armytage Moore, who devoted most of his life to developing the garden with catholic taste and wide knowledge. He improved the drive, where stand his father's stone seats and cairns, with large-leafed rhododendrons, and converted the walled garden, originally intended for vegetables, for growing and housing all manner of bulbs, plants, shrubs and trees. Hostas and meconopsis, primulas

Rowallane

and lilies are the ephemera, but they are complemented by magnolias and shrub roses, desfontainea, acradenia and clematoclethra among others. Here also grow the original chaenomeles, viburnum, hypericum and primula named after Rowallane.

The unique part of the garden, however, is the area situated on rocky pastures that are intersected by drystone walls. Here in a spring garden, rare shrubs and trees blend with the landscape, creating the 20th-century equivalent of effects beloved by the 18th century. The views are controlled by the lie of the land and immense groups of rhododendrons. Maples and dogwoods, birches, nothofagus, sorbus, magnolia, viburnum and hydrangea are a few of the genera well represented. Beyond lies the rock garden, where rocks, worn smooth by glaciers in the Ice Age, have been uncovered to provide a setting for dwarf shrubs and alpines. This whole area, one of immense variety, is most judiciously planted. It is at its best from the early daffodils to the last rhododendron, and once again in autumn when the colour is splendid.

Scotney Castle, Kent

½ mile south-east of Lamberhurst

The charm of the garden at Scotney owes everything to the care and affection lavished upon it by successive generations of the Hussey family over the last hundred and fifty years. Before then, things may be said to have happened: since then, the creation of a series of 'garden pictures' has been the aim. Few gardens are more richly endowed not only with beautiful terrain – a wooded valley with a stream, a lake, and fine trees – but also with the character that ancient buildings contribute to a landscape. The ruins of a moated castle of the 14th century and fragments of a 17th-century house are integral and highly romantic components of the setting.

Scotney Castle

The present house, one of Salvin's most imaginative and successful exercises in the Gothic Revival style, stands high above the picturesque garden valley. In the quarry from which the stone was taken, an iguanodon millions of years ago left its imprint, and the quarry sides are today clad with the flowing shapes of great mounds of rhododendrons. From the terrace in front of the house the eye falls to the 14th-century battlements and the lake.

In the valley there is a rich yet restrained planting of shrubs and old roses, rushes, bamboos and marsh plants, while immense limes, tulip trees, and cut-leaf beech dominate the lesser things. There are some very large clumps of *Kalmia latifolia*.

Sharpitor, Devon

$1\frac{1}{2}$ miles south-west of Salcombe

The most striking features of the garden at Sharpitor are the magnificent views over the sea and up the Kingsbridge estuary and the way in which full advantage has been taken of the steep sunny slopes below the house. Within the six-acre garden an astonishing range of exotic trees, shrubs and plants flourish in the mild climate of south Devon.

The garden was laid out in its present form in the early years of this century. The steepest parts were terraced by masonry and retaining walls and planted between 1901 and 1928 when the late Otto Overbeck bought the property. He continued to nourish Sharpitor until his death in 1937, when he bequeathed it to the National Trust, for use as a park, museum and Youth Hostel. One notable feature of the garden are the numerous palm trees, mainly the Chinese Cu-San *Trachycarpus fortunei*, but also the little *Chamaerops humilis*, the only palm native to Europe.

There are many rare and tender herbaceous plants in the lawn borders and elsewhere, including agapanthus, criniums and watsonias. The most remarkable sight at Sharpitor is the large *Magnolia campbellii*, a splendid sight in March covered with brilliant pink flowers and visible nearly half a mile away.

Sheffield Park, East Sussex *(see colour plate facing p. 256)*

$\frac{1}{2}$ mile from Sheffield Park station, midway between East Grinstead and Lewes, 5 miles north-west of Uckfield on east side of A275

The 1st Lord Sheffield, intimate friend of Edward Gibbon, had the good taste to call in Capability Brown to design his landscape and James Wyatt to design his Gothick house. The latter, which looks so well from the gardens, does not belong to the Trust, nor does the famous cricket ground near by. On this historic turf from 1876 to 1896, the 3rd Lord Sheffield's XI met the visiting Australians for the opening match of successive Test tours.

Sheffield Park; The top lake from the bridge

The splendour of the gardens, which the Trust acquired in 1954, is due to the combination of Lancelot Brown's basic design of 1775 – trees, sward and serpentine waters – with the inspired planting of the late A. G. Soames who acquired Sheffield Park in 1909. For over a quarter of a century he devoted himself to the introduction of all manner of exotic trees and shrubs. Rarely have the conceptions of the 18th and the 20th centuries been more happily married.

Lakes spanned by ornamental bridges, waterfalls and watery vistas recall the spirit of the original layout (though certain of these features are in fact later), while by contrast the cunning planting of the shores speaks convincingly of the eye and the expertise of the 20th-century gardener. The views across the water owe much to the introduction of dark conifers, pampas grasses, and white-stemmed birches, all of which contrast with the autumn colours.

Autumn, and especially the second half of October, is the great moment for Sheffield Park. Hundreds of trees and shrubs planted specially for their autumn colour create an effect unrivalled in these islands. Tupelo trees, azaleas, mespiluses, maples, eucryphias, birches, swamp cypresses and larches contribute, by the dozen, to the magnificent spectacle. Because of the high trees growing to the west, the colour is best seen in the morning or early afternoon. By contrast spring comes almost modestly, yet the greensward is covered with Lent lilies and later types of daffodils, narcissus and bluebells; great belts of rhododendrons, azaleas, and other early-flowering shrubs are followed by *Kalmia latifolia*; and hundreds of water-lilies seem to float their blossoms on the surface of the lakes.

Many rhododendrons of the 'Angelo' class were raised here; also some daffodils and *Kalmia latifolia* 'Clementine Churchill'. There is an avenue of hardy palms, and autumn gentians give a regular display. Among the many noted tree specimens are *Eucalyptus gunnii*, *Abies procera*, *Taxodium distichum* and *T. ascendens*, stewartias, nothofagus, libocedrus, *Juniperus coxii*, wellingtonias and redwoods, cedars, *Pseudolarix amabilis*, *Picea omorika* and *P. orientalis*, *Athrotaxis selaginoides*, *Saxegothea conspicua*, *Pinus montezumae*, *Cornus florida*, *Acer nikoense*, *Stewartia sinensis*, *Parrotia persica* and *Magnolia kobus*.

Sissinghurst Castle, Kent *(see colour plate facing p. 257)*

2 miles east of Sissinghurst village, off the A229 Maidstone/Hawkhurst road

The visitor who climbs the spiral staircase to the top of the Elizabethan tower is rewarded by one of the loveliest views in southern England. The broad valley of the Weald sweeps upwards to the North Downs twelve miles away, and closer at hand the woods, lakes, fields and oast-houses of the Sissinghurst estate illustrate the detail of which that view is so subtly composed. Immediately below the tower is the six-acre garden. Other buildings stand in puzzling isolation in different parts of it, and framing one angle of the orchard are two arms of an older moat.

The explanation is simple. The moat enclosed a medieval house which has totally disappeared. The buildings are the relics of the most splendid Elizabethan house in this part of Kent. Until about 1800 it stood battered but entire, and was then partially demolished, leaving these substantial fragments for use as barns and stables, or as cottages for undemanding labourers. For over a hundred years Sissinghurst slowly degenerated, and today it would probably be a ruin but for its rescue in 1930 by two imaginative people, Victoria Sackville-West and Harold Nicolson. They were husband and wife, both writers, she a poet and novelist, he an historian, biographer and diarist. They repaired the surviving buildings,

Sissinghurst; The castle lawn from the rose garden

and began gradually (he planning, she planting) to create a garden between the old walls and buildings which imposed its basic shape.

Sissinghurst, as Victoria Sackville-West once put it, is a series of 'outdoor rooms' connected by 'corridors' open to the sky. The walls which they found or built, the hedges of yew, rose and hornbeam which they planted, create a succession of enclosures and make the garden seem much larger than it really is. It is easy to get lost in this small space, and even on busy days several hundred people never curdle into a crowd. The garden is still private in feeling and intimate in scale. It combines (to quote Harold Nicolson's definition of the secret of good garden design) 'the element of expectation with the element of surprise'. There are carefully contrived vistas criss-crossing the garden from end to end and terminating in a statue, a poplar, or a distant view of the Weald, and to right and left of them the smaller gardens open unexpectedly. Two long lawns, one above and one below the tower, provide restful centres, the common-rooms, as it were, of this horticultural mansion.

While perfectly tended, Sissinghurst is not too tidy. It is a romantic place. Against the slender brick buildings roses and honeysuckle climb to the eaves, and clematis, vine and magnolia tumble in profusion over the tops of walls. It is, however, a sophisticated garden, in which rare plants find themselves neighbours to traditional cottage-garden flowers. The scale of the planting is deliberately varied from one part to another – from the rough orchard where daffodils are succeeded by fruit blossom and later by roses lacing the upper branches of the apple trees, to the formal herb garden, the paved lime walk bordered by spring flowers, a wide bed confined to purple and dark-blue flowers, and the square garden beneath the Priest's House from which any flower that is not white or the palest grey is eliminated like a gate-crasher.

This White Garden is the most original of all the separate gardens, but Sissinghurst is best known for its old roses, which are found concentrated in the largest garden of all, a great rectangle divided by brick and stone paths and a circular yew hedge. There one can best understand Victoria Sackville-West's attitude to gardening – her abhorrence of regimented rows of flowers, her careful grouping of plants according to mass, colour and season, and her bold experimentation. Since her death in 1962 Sissinghurst has been in the care of people who knew her well and appreciated her originality and taste, while they have not hesitated to experiment with variations on her many themes. Sissinghurst, at all flowering seasons of the year, is a delicate work of art, from which the expert and the amateur will in their different ways derive much pleasure.

Stourhead, Wiltshire *(see colour plate facing p. 257)*

At Stourton, west of the B3092, 3 miles from Mere

The theories behind the development of the 18th-century style of landscape gardening – the *jardin anglais* – are more complex than may at first appear. They are nowhere better exemplified than at the celebrated pleasure grounds of Stourhead, among the earliest and best known of its kind to survive (see also Claremont, p. 239). The formal garden of the 17th century, both in this country and on the continent, culminated in the grandiose creation of Le Nôtre laid out for Louis XIV at Versailles. Enormous gravelled terraces, intricately patterned parterres, broad avenues cut through the surrounding forest and radiating from the *château* served to emphasize the centralized absolute rule of the monarch. The influence of Versailles spread throughout Europe from St Petersburg to Naples. It was, however, alien to the English spirit, whose reaction against 'the formal mockery of princely gardens' began as early as the second decade of the 18th century. The philosophy of the essential goodness of natural man, linked with ideas of the individual freedom from the power of the state as expressed by writers such as Locke, led men like the poet Alexander Pope (who was also a practitioner of garden design as well as a theorist) to give their ideas practical form. This movement away from formality to the 'natural' and picturesque in landscape gardening is commonly held to have originated in Lord Burlington's circle, amongst whom were included William Kent and Colen Campbell, designer of Stourhead House.

Linked with these ideas was the influence of the literature and art of classical antiquity, the latter as then expressed in the work of Claude Lorrain and his school, whose paintings of the Italian countryside around Rome, embellished with temples and figures to illustrate classical themes, were fashionable. Aristocratic travellers who made the Grand Tour returned home to recreate on their own estates the Palladian villas, Roman and Greek temples and other buildings of the classical world and to set them in artfully contrived landscapes.

Stourhead; The Temple of Flora from the Temple of the Sun

Henry Hoare II, whose father had acquired the Stourhead estate in 1717 and built a new house before his death in 1725, inherited the property but did not live at Stourhead until after his mother's death in 1741. Soon after he began the work on his pleasure grounds which was to be perhaps his most absorbing interest for the next forty years. The site was the shallow valley, known as Six Wells Bottom, north-west of the house, which runs from the wedge-shaped plateau beneath the western end of the Wiltshire chalk downs. It is the watershed of three rivers one of which, the Dorset Stour, has its source in the springs of the valley opening out into a triangular area. This was dammed by Henry Hoare to form a lake round which he planned his scene of temples and grottoes, set against a background of trees as carefully placed as in a painting to give effects of contrasting light and shade, Arcadian groves, and pastoral vistas.

Gradually the principal buildings arose, designed by Henry Flitcroft, a protégé of Lord Burlington; first the Temple of Flora (formerly Temple of Ceres), then the Grotto dedicated to the Nymphs of the Grot and containing the baroque statue of a River God by John Cheere. The Pantheon was finished next in 1754 and houses Rysbrack's magnificent marble *Hercules* as well as other plaster and marble busts and statues. Lastly, the Temple of Apollo that stands on higher ground overlooking the lake, was finished by 1765. By this time a taste for medieval architecture had been made fashionable by Horace Walpole. The 14th-century Bristol Cross was transported from that city and re-erected near the village church. Gothick cottages and follies, including a Gothick greenhouse (now demolished) were added. The conspicuous landmark of Alfred's Tower on the plateau demonstrates Hoare's later interest in British antiquities.

Henry Hoare's tree-planting was mostly of firs and beeches. The woodlands with which he enclosed his Arcadia were established, however, on sound economic principles, for timber was then the basic raw material of technology. His successor, Sir Richard Colt Hoare, did not altogether approve his choice of trees and widened the range of species. He also underplanted the woodlands with laurel and, in 1791, introduced the first rhododendron *R. ponticum*. He laid down the gravel paths round the lake, thus altering the character of the gardens so that Stourhead became more of a lakeside garden and arboretum than an idealized classical pastoral landscape.

In the 19th century, successive Hoares added to the collection of trees, introducing ornamental conifers, many new to the British Isles. The 6th baronet, Sir Henry Hoare, who lived at Stourhead from 1894 to 1947 and bequeathed the estate to the National Trust, planted many of the shrubs and trees now in their prime. He and his wife added azaleas together with many new varieties of rhododendron. Though the ideas and work of generations of the Hoare family have overlaid the original conception, Henry Hoare's vision still lends magic to the Stourhead landscape. It is as Horace Walpole wrote in 1762, 'one of the most picturesque scenes in the world'.

Trelissick, Cornwall

4 miles south of Truro on the B3289 Truro/St Mawes road

Early engravings show a modest two-storeyed villa, built about 1750 on the foundations of a yet earlier building, but the columned portico and other additions were made in the second quarter of the 19th century. Trelissick changed hands many times, and it is believed that the Gilbert family who owned it from 1844 to 1913 did much to improve the landscape, planting woods and probably some of the great conifers and holm oaks in the garden. Mrs Copeland inherited the property in 1937 and she and her husband created the garden as we know it today. Though there are splendid views towards the Fal from the house and drive, yet in general, owing to the situation and the prevailing wind, the garden needs protection rather than extensive vistas.

The Copelands planted a great range of rhododendrons, azaleas and choice trees and shrubs. *Rosa bracteata*, *Caesalpinia japonica* and *Solanum*

*Nymans, West Sussex;
Italian fountain and
herbaceous borders in the
wall garden*

*Sheffield Park, East
Sussex; View across the
lake*

Sissinghurst Castle, Kent; The lime walk, or spring garden

Wakehurst Place, West Sussex

Stourhead, Wiltshire; The Temple of Flora

Trelissick; The main lawn

jasminoides – climbing through *Hoheria sexstylosa* – grow on the entrance walls. A fine Japanese 'cedar' stands on a sloping lawn, at the side of which are borders devoted to summer-flowering shrubs and plants. There is a large *Hydrangea villosa* and a *Michelia doltsopa* below the lawn. Spacious lawns give Trelissick its character. Winding walks lead under great beeches and holm oaks, with trees such as magnolias, nothofagus, eucalyptus, oxydendrum, maples and *Picea smithiana* here and there, and everywhere are rhododendrons, early and late. The walks eventually lead to a summer house and a Saxon cross, and so back to a raised drive which crosses the main road – giving a glimpse of a dell with tree ferns and banana – to the Carcadden area. Recently reclaimed, this contains big cedars, cypresses and geans, and on the sloping lawns a collection of over 130 hydrangea species and varieties, a speciality of Trelissick. While many Cornish gardens fade into greenery in summer, Trelissick shows colour until the autumn. Crinums, agapanthus, fuchsias, acanthus, cannas, and other rather tender perennials, together with astilbes and hypericums, grow well, and flower from July onwards.

Trengwainton, Cornwall

2 miles west of Penzance, $\frac{1}{2}$ mile west of Heamoor on the B3312, Penzance/Morvah road, $\frac{1}{2}$ mile off St Just road

The mild climate of south Cornwall, where frosts are rare, favours not only the cultivation of very early crops of flowers and vegetables but also of tender trees, shrubs and plants impossible to grow in the open in other parts of Britain. The garden at Trengwainton, set at the foot of the low range of

Trengwainton; Primulas by the stream

granite hills behind Penzance and facing south on Mount's Bay, is well placed in this respect.

There has been a dwelling here at least since the 16th century, but the present house and garden were established after 1814 by Rose Price, the son of a wealthy Jamaican sugar planter. He set about improving his property, first planting trees (mainly hardwoods) on a considerable scale round the house and sheltering a new drive – the present long walk. At the foot he built a series of brick-walled gardens with raised terrace beds. The present garden design has evolved from these original plantings and now extends for about a quarter of a mile from the entrance lodge to the house.

After Sir Rose Price's death the estate was sold, and in 1867 Trengwainton was acquired by the Bolitho family. It is to Lt-Colonel (later Sir Edward) Bolitho who inherited in 1925 and died in 1969 that the exceptional quality of the garden today is due. Lt-Colonel Bolitho was offered a share in Kingdon Ward's botanical expedition to Assam and Burma in 1927–8; the present outstanding collection of rhododendrons is largely founded upon the seed obtained during the expedition. *Rhododendron macabeanum, R. elliottii, R. taggianum* were flowered here for the first time in this country. The only earlier planting of rhododendrons – apart from *R. ponticum* near the house – were *R. falconensis* and *R. griffithianum*, dating from 1904.

Another major work in the 1920s was the opening up of the stream beside the drive, which previously ran underground through a culvert. This became the setting for primulas and other moisture-loving plants. Perhaps the most striking single feature of Trengwainton is the series of linked walled enclosures, close to the drive entrance, with their raised terrace beds. Each square is planted with a few large specimens of magnolias, rare conifers and evergreens, many from the southern hemisphere, *Athotaxis, Dacrydium* and *Podocarpus salignus*. One area is dominated by a magnificent *Magnolia veitchii*, another is entered under a huge *Styrax japonica* with *Styrax hemsleyana* beyond. These enclosures are underplanted with a wonderful assortment of shrubs and plants normally seen under glass. There are also camellias, fuchsias, tender sweet-smelling rhododendrons and *Pittosporum*. In spring the scent of rhododendrons and azaleas perfumes the whole garden. The woodland areas are a mass of bluebells and later awash with underplanting of pale-blue hydrangeas.

Trengwainton's charms are not confined to the walled gardens or the borders beside the stream. There are fine specimen trees and exotic tree ferns, besides summer-flowering borders and masses of Himalayan poppies. From the upper garden there are splendid views of St Michael's Mount and inland over the surrounding countryside. Near the house is an immense tree of *Magnolia sargentiana* 'Robusta', perhaps Trengwainton's crowning glory.

Wakehurst, West Sussex *(see colour plate facing p. 257)*

$1\frac{1}{2}$ miles north-west of Ardingly on B2028

The Sussex Weald with its retentive acid soil, varied terrain, and wooded slopes and valleys has seen the creation of many famous gardens, but none has so spectacular a setting as Wakehurst, with its rich collection of trees and shrubs. The house, which retains one late-16th-century façade, was bought by Gerald W. E. Loder – one of a famous trio of gardening brothers – in 1903, when the garden as we know it today was started. The property bequeathed to the Trust by the late owner, Sir Henry Price, was leased in 1965 to the Royal Botanic Gardens at Kew.

Wakehurst owes much of its variety and charm to its setting. Near the house are formal lawns, rock and heath gardens, shrub borders and beds, and a pinetum. The recently planted walled garden contains plants of predominantly soft flower colours and silver foliage. Beyond, paths lead steeply downward by pools and rills to a wooded valley that cradles a peaceful lake, and so back through the area known as Bloomer's Valley.

In the rock garden near the house grow *Dicentra macrantha* and *Fascicularia bicolor*, and near by are the silvery rapier-like leaves of astelia. Across the lawns the heath garden contains a fascinating assortment of heaths and close relatives, dwarf rhododendrons and azaleas, and rare dwarf shrubs and conifers. Next come numerous shrub borders and beds where the specimens crowd upon us – *Nothofagus betuloides* and *N. solandri*, two evergreen beeches from the Southern Hemisphere, a superb *Stewartia sinensis*, davidias and magnolias, *Castanopsis chrysophylla*, *Lomatia tinctoria* and *Rhus verniciflua*. In the pinetum rise *Pinus patula*, whose needles are rich green and drooping, *P. attenuata* whose cones stay on the branches for many years, and rare cypresses and larches.

Rhododendrons from the compact *R. yakusimanum* to great species such as *R. calophytum* thrive everywhere and transform the valleys into a fairyland during spring and early summer. In autumn a variety of trees and shrubs, grown for their tinted foliage and berry, come into their own: the rare American beech, *Fagus grandifolia*, which has attained a great size, the golden larch, azaleas and brilliant Japanese maples.

The exotic planting, the great native oaks, wild ferns, streams, and limpid pools, the natural variety of the terrain, all contribute, with the quiet and the birdsong, to the quality of a most unusual garden.

Westbury Court Garden, Gloucestershire

By the church in Westbury-on-Severn, 9 miles south-west of Gloucester on A48

An engraving by Kip, published in 1712, shows a house of some size with its attendant outbuildings, a church with a tall spire, and in the grounds of the house long canals, an elegant pavilion of two storeys, a parterre and hedges, and rows and rows of little formal trees. The church spire still dominates the surroundings, but the house has gone. In fact, not only did it disappear a century or more ago, but two later houses have also come and gone. The parterre has vanished too, but the pavilion is still reflected in the deep clear water of one of the two canals that remain.

A few years ago this historic layout, dating from between 1697 and 1705, and one of the few gardens of Dutch inspiration to survive in England, had all but disappeared. Mud more than two feet deep silted the canals, the formal hedges were dying, smothered in brambles, and the pavilion was ruinous.

When the Trust acquired the garden in 1967, an extensive programme of renovation was launched, financed by grants from the Historic Buildings Council, a most generous anonymous donation and a public appeal. In conformity with the Kip design, the pavilion was restored, the canals dredged and their walls repaired. New hedges of yew and holly were planted and the lawns which had become hayfields were ploughed and resown. The parterre, originally near the house, was re-created on the east side in the pattern of dwarf box, coloured sages, *Festuca glauca* and other plants sprigged with box topiary. The rebuilt west wall was planted with espalier apples, pears and plums of varieties available before 1700. Fortunately the original planting records survive as a guide. Only plants on these lists and others in cultivation at the time have been introduced. They include herbaceous plants such as *Hemerocallis flava*, *Iris pallida*, *Centaurea mon-*

Westbury Court; The pavilion and canal

tana, Salvia pratensis and *Delphinum elatum* and climbers as for example *Clematis flammula, Lonicera periclymenum* and *Vitis labrusca*. Sweetbriars, *Rosa gallica* 'Versicolor', *R. foetida* and *R. centifolia* 'Muscosa' now flourish as they did more than three centuries ago. Crocus, narcissi and scillas have been planted and the charming *Fritillaria meleagris* now so rarely found growing wild. Tree plantings include medlars, quinces and morello cherries. In the garden at Westbury grows one of the largest and most venerable holm oaks (*Quercus ilex*) in the country. It is thought to be between 350 and 400 years old.

Westbury is coming to life again and is assuming its rightful place as one of the finest examples in this country of the early formal layouts which were nearly all swept away by landscape gardeners in the 18th century.

Winkworth, Surrey

3 miles south-east of Godalming, on the east side of B2130

The only true arboretum owned by the National Trust, Winkworth covers ninety-six acres of hillside, sloping down to two lakes, part of a chain of ornamental lakes and fish ponds in the upper valley between Bramley and Horscombe. Sixty acres were presented in 1932 by Dr Wilfrid Fox, who had

Winkworth

devoted himself for many years to the care and extension of the neglected woodlands. Rare trees and shrubs stand out from the native British species, including many whose autumn foliage is a blaze of colour, the reds, oranges and gold rivalling the glory of an American fall. The trees include cherries, maples, oaks and magnolias. The collection of sorbus is extensive, featuring Himalayan, Japanese and North American species; hollies are well represented. In spring the carpet of bluebells and daffodils complements the delicate greens and yellow of the budding trees, reflected in the waters of the lakes.

III
Follies, Monuments, Villages, Dovecotes, Chapels, and Buildings of Useful Intent

Introduction *by Barbara Jones*

The first trade goods from the East reached Europe by the new sea-routes early in the 16th century. Almost 150 years later, the porcelain, silks, lacquers, engravings, paintings, and travellers' tales had begun to leaven the heavy arts of the Renaissance in France, and before the middle of the 18th century they were dictating fashion in the British Isles, the country that received the message last but took it most to heart.

The British turned to *chinoiserie* like ducks to water. It came at the right time. There had been peace at home since the Civil War, and the rich landed classes, in a cultural climate that encouraged curiosity and learning, had leisure to enjoy it. Moreover, the great Elizabethan houses had given full rein to the native love of fantasy and display, whereas the new Palladian style, though grand, was hardly gay. Gothick, the picturesque and *chinoiserie* offered release; especially *chinoiserie*. Here were screens, wallpapers, silks, and porcelain depicting a different, lighter architecture: curved roofs, slanting walls and pavilions fretted and tilted in curious perspective, with palm trees, pines and pineapples to set them off. What a relief after Vanbrugh, whose idea of fantasy was to circle a park with a castellated wall and curtain towers.

Ideas on Chinese architecture and decoration were sketchy, because the traders who brought back information and oriental goods could not penetrate beyond Canton, while the Jesuit missionaries were more interested in converts than in architecture, though they were freer to travel and indeed were sometimes so welcome at court that they were asked to design gardens in the European taste for the Emperor (the ruins of this exotic exchange existed in this century, though nothing seems to have been heard of them recently). In the circumstances, the message that reached Europe from China, though reasonably correct about pagodas and bridges with bells on them, stressed lightness and fantasy, and in any case was stated in that oriental perspective which made even such massive works as the Great Wall look lighter and more elegant than western perspective would have done. It was this new perspective (in fact not so far different from that of medieval tapestries and illuminations) which, I believe, had more influence than Chinese architecture itself on the ornamental buildings of Britain in the 18th century.

The word 'rocaille' neatly links the English and the Chinese picturesque landscapes, for rocks abound in both. We gratefully adopted, from Chinese export trade wares, versions of rocks, geometric fences, contorted pines, pagodas, and men in pagoda hats, and we added them to shells from the Indies, Moorish domes, classical ruins from Greece and Italy, and local ruins from the barons' wars of the 15th century, to furnish our own miraculous contribution to the world's landscaping, the English garden, the desirable *jardin anglais*, a green paradise for dreams of the green lands of the travellers' tales.

Stourhead, visited when the rhododendrons are *not* in flower, is still the prototype of many later English gardens. It was built by Henry Hoare in the 1740s and we are lucky to see it at this moment of time; for we can enjoy the results of the immense effort and imagination that went into the great gardens – the choice of a fine natural site with plenty of water, the daunting earth-moving, the planting of sapling trees, the quarrying of harsh new stone; everything bare and raw, crude and sparse; little for the planter and everything for the future.

The lakes and the landscaping and the now splendid trees enclose, lead up to, and depart from, a series of ornamental buildings. A 14th-century Cross and St Peter's Pump, both brought from Bristol, are medieval work, but a Rustic Cottage, a Rustic Convent far down the park (it must have had a hermit – perhaps a unique female one?), and Alfred's Tower, built for the prospect from the highest point of the park, represent the new taste for Gothick. The Pantheon, the Temple of Flora, and the fine Temple of the Sun are all in the classical style. There is a big rock-pebble-water-and-statuary grotto, and a very Chinese rock and tufa bridge. Alas, we have lost a Gothick greenhouse made of stone and burnt cinders, a Turkish tent, and a Chinese hump-backed bridge spanning ninety-eight feet. The 'Mosque with a Minaret' and other buildings planned for islands in the lake were never built, but Stourhead still shows magnificently most of the standard architectural elements of the mid-18th century, and presents them to us with piled-up compositions in both the Chinese, and the Italian tastes.

'Improvements' on this scale cost enormous sums. Henry Hoare was a banker and could afford such expense. At Shugborough, the money came more dramatically from Admiral George Anson's capture of the Spanish galleon that crossed the Pacific every year from Acapulco to Manila, said to be the richest prize ever taken by a single ship of the British Navy. On the famous four-year voyage which took him round the world, Anson went into Canton for shelter during the monsoon season and also to take on stores, including, of course, works of art. Shugborough belonged to his elder brother Thomas – a foundation member of the Society of Dilettanti, an explorer and industrialist; he was one of those many amused and interested people of the 18th century who are often ridiculously said to be extinct, because most people find it hard to admire the platinum-plated private aircraft and the parallel extravagances of the very rich today.

Admiral Anson's fortune probably paid for the first works at Shugborough, finishing a house started by the brothers' father. By 1750 large paintings of the voyage were on the walls, Lady Anson's dressing-room was decorated with the 'very prettiest Indian paper of the Landskip kind with figures', and one of Anson's officers had designed the Chinese House to take the porcelain treasures from Canton. Many memoirs and letters of the period refer to curiosities, shells, minerals, and of course natives, brought back by naval officers and given to friends or auctioned to eager collectors and grotto-builders.

Admiral Anson died in 1762. Thomas inherited his fortune and continued work at Shugborough. He employed James 'Athenian' Stuart to build a group of Grecian monuments, some of the earliest in the country. In the end, Shugborough had sham ruins, a Gothick pigeon-house, the Chinese House ('true pattern of the Architecture of the Nation'), with a Chinese bridge, a pretty monument to a Persian cat (perhaps the very one which went on Anson's voyage), the Shepherd's Monument, and a Doric temple. Most of them are still there. Away in the park are Stuart's Tower of the Winds, the superb triumphal arch to the memory of Lord and Lady Anson, and the little Lanthorn of Demosthenes. Shugborough is like Stourhead, yet very different; Staffordshire and Wiltshire are different counties, and the admiral and the banker were different men. But both show how effectively the 18th century used ornamental architecture on a big estate.

This happy association of ornamental architecture and landscape is found throughout Britain not only in elaborate parks but also on farmland where changes of ownership and land-use had stranded in the fields monuments that it is difficult to connect with the builders of the great fortunes that sponsored them. They include temples, for example, the two classical temples at Rievaulx, towers, sham ruins, mausoleums, monuments, grottoes, ornamental villages, any one of which may be in the classical, Gothick, Moorish or oriental taste. In the 19th century were added the influences of India, the Druids, and the strict Gothicism of Pugin.

Such occasional architecture, sometimes the accurate copy of a classical model, sometimes the essay of architect or *amateur*, is often on a gigantic scale. Thus the Penshaw Monument is a vast building, a Doric temple built in 1844 to the memory of the 1st Earl of Durham. It is visible for miles, as a temple should be, though now black with soot, and approached not through woods and fields but through a great industrial landscape of collieries, cement works, chimneys, tips and drifting smoke, a surreal and amazing place.

There are, as one would expect, some very elegant things in Ireland. A version of the Temple of the Winds at Mount Stewart, designed like its counterpart at Shugborough by 'Athenian' Stuart, the Mussenden rotunda at Downhill, perched on the cliffs of Antrim, and a mausoleum at Templetown designed by Robert Adam, are examples of the 18th-century taste for classical architecture set in all their 'alien correctness' against the untamed northern landscape.

Smaller monuments and memorials are scattered even more freely all over Britain; to a favourite pet, to a coaching accident, a duel, a racehorse, a nobleman, to the poet Gray at Stoke Poges, or the poet Paul Whitehead at West Wycombe, where his heart was once kept in a marble urn. They may be comical or bizarre or dull; few of them stir the emotions as do the Riley graves at Eyam in Derbyshire where seven members of the Hancock family are buried in a meadow. The plague broke out in the village of Eyam in 1665, and the inhabitants, instead of fleeing their homes, remained and vainly drew a cordon round the village so that the infection might not spread.

Much of our countryside is hilly, some of it mountainous, and many landowners from the 16th century onwards built prospect towers, as well as some remarkable little squatty towers with no purpose at all, no view, nothing to protect, no room to have tea in, no vista, set somewhere on the edge of the park and now lost in brambles. Towers tend to be Gothick in style; elaborate or simple, they generally have castellations and at least make a gesture at medieval ornament. They added to the impression made by a sham ruin that the owner had held the land at least since the Conquest, and that here were some corners he had not bothered to improve. It is curious that some of the dullest little towers have the strangest and most persistent folly stories attached to them. For instance, Box Hill in Surrey has a round flint tower, dateless and doorless. It is said to stand over the grave of Major Peter Labellière, buried one hundred feet down and head first, because he believed that at the Resurrection the world would be turned topsy-turvy, and he alone would land on his feet.

Some monuments are triangular in plan – and there are at least two trefoil-plan houses in existence – joining fantasy in the plan itself to the fantasy of machicolations, arrow-slits, three-centred ogival arches, and a lot of very unorthodox shapes and curves that undoubtedly could have been, but were not, copied correctly from contemporary books on architecture, improvement, and the picturesque. Rushton Triangular Lodge, a more scholarly essay than most, was built in 1593–5 by Sir Thomas Tresham with measurements based on three and multiples of three. The twenty-seven-foot vertical walls (he eschewed the pyramid) are each surmounted by three triangles, and there is great elaboration of triangular pinnacles, rooms, and windows. Two hundred years later, the triangular tower had settled into a pattern well exemplified by Paxton's Tower in Carmarthenshire, high above the Towy valley: three-sided, a turret at each corner, and a central tower in the middle.

Admiration for the Navy is expressed in a number of monuments; there is the Kymin in Monmouthshire where a group of gentlemen built a Round House for dining on the hilltop, and then in 1800 added a Naval Temple near by, to commemorate some later admirals and their voyages and victories.

Shell architecture in the 18th century is something of a British speciality. Sea captains such as Cook brought back exotic specimens, and many towns near a shell beach have a modest shell house, decorated with anything from a simple mussel porch to the most elaborate encrustation. Shellwork came in two styles. The early grotto-rooms do not stray far from conventional modes and emphasize standard architectural forms. The masterpiece of this style is the Shell House at Goodwood built in about 1740 by the 2nd Duchess of Richmond. The other, generally later, style was the true rocaille, the collection of rock, tufa, mineral specimens, coral, stalactites and stalagmites from local caves, and of every possible size and shape of shell, which were assembled to make a simple alcove with a fountain, or a whole series of Neptune caves, with statues of the god, tritons, mermaids, dolphins, fountains, cascades and as much moss as could be encouraged. Bones or pebbles were the smart thing for the floor, and furniture was made cunningly of bones, horns, or contorted branches, or simply in the shape of gilded fish supporting shells.

Early in the 19th century, shellwork, having been first a novel covering for a wall surface, then free-form, tended to revert to surface decoration, but added representational features – shells outlining vases of flowers or animals, or enshrining birds with real feathers. An endearing example is the Trust's little Shell House in Hatfield Forest. Grottoes were sometimes tunnelled into the ground if a suitable hillside did not exist, as at Hawkstone in Shropshire, where a long black labyrinth, cut into the solid rock of an outcrop, leads to a huge half-lit rock hall, and finally emerges through the ruins of a shell room. Here we are a long way from the light picturesque of the prospect tower, and it is clear that such things were built not merely to startle but to terrify. They should be visited alone for maximum sensation. The hermitages, with the live shaggy hermits that some gentlemen provided, must have been equally startling. Several still exist, but many of them were flimsy affairs, and hermits were not infrequently known to desert.

Such buildings of sombre intention have no monopoly of atmosphere. Some of the eye-catchers – arches, ruins, and sham façades on hilltops – even if intended to be trivial or gay, are strangely compelling. One walks round and through them uneasily at the end of the climb. Three particularly fine ones belong to the National Trust.

Mow Cop in Cheshire, a large and elaborate sham castle, was built in 1750 to enhance the rugged view of the hill from Rode Hall in the valley below. Though in 1807 the first Methodist camp meeting was held on the steep hillside here, the ruin does not feel at all like nonconformist England, but more like a small patch of Syria bundled into Cheshire.

At Slindon in West Sussex, Nore Folly, a fine conceit, stands on the edge of a high beechwood. It is constructed of crisp black-and-white knapped flint with arches and a square turret, and is known to have been built in the 18th century by an Earl of Newburgh.

Best of all the National Trust follies, to my mind, is Creech Arch, built in 1746 by Denis Bond of Creech Grange, to improve the view from the house. On a crest of the Purbeck Hills above the Dorset coast its massive pale stone arches handsomely dismiss the tourist charms of Corfe three miles away. Another world. This is what the wilder temples, follies and grottoes, down in the park or on the distant hill, offer to the country house visitor. Different in spirit from the great house itself, they were often built at the same time by the same people; but they are the age of elegance and reason seen through a distorting mirror. Another world.

Few buildings are safe today, but the buildings in greatest danger are those made for use, because utility is the criterion by which they are judged – at least until they are two or three hundred years old. Any public or industrial building that needs reconsideration within 150 years of its erection will be at hazard because most people are able to recognize beauty in a church or house of an earlier generation, but will gaze blankly at a utilitarian building – unless it is old. A medieval packhorse bridge in worn stone is felt to be worth the visit, but cast-iron is holy metal to very few.

The utilitarians find it hard to avoid thinking that if something has been built as a market-house or a school or a pub, then that is the only reason for its existence, and it must therefore be modified with changing needs. Thus, such buildings, especially at risk, are too often either demolished or ruthlessly disembowelled, when some intelligent thinking might have found a new use for them. A good example of preservation by change of use is the Blewcoat School in London. It was built in 1709, a school with master's house and garden, for educating poor children. It became the Infant's Department of a larger school, and later was used by the Services, the Girl Guides, and a Youth Club. In 1954, the National Trust bought it, demolished the accretions and repaired the building. It was restored and set in a little formal enclosure in 1976. The main façade, with Doric columns supporting the entablature, and the painted statue of a Blewcoat Boy in a niche, is a fine early-18th-century composition. Inside is a panelled hall with Corinthian columns, used today for the meetings of the Trust's committee.

Survival is often largely a matter of chance, as with the fine market-house at Winster in Derbyshire. Again, it was surely chance that saved the Jacobean Wool Market Hall in Chipping Campden when the wool trade declined later in the 17th century. Had the trade increased, the little open, arcaded building might have been clumsily enlarged, given another storey or, being on a valuable site, pulled down. Good buildings in cities are subject to greater hazards. Yet sometimes a charming city building gets passed by, like the 17th-century George Inn at Southwark, untouched even by the arrival of the railway at London Bridge and the 19th-century rebuilding on the river front. The George was a coaching inn, and the courtyard is still there, with balustraded galleries leading to the bedrooms. Surviving country pubs include the Castle Inn at Chiddingstone, a big 16th-century place with lattice windows, elaborate gables, and a fine roof. Throughout the country there are happily still many pleasant inns and county-town hotels (the latter often with large and rich ballrooms).

Churches are safer from neglect and vandalism than most buildings; their hazards are heavy-handed restoration and embellishment. A single enthusiastic patron in touch with the wrong architects and stained-glass painters has often done more damage than the passage of seven or eight hundred years. The Trust owns some twenty churches and chapels. The three we shall look at now were all privately built and are post-Reformation, so that they are not typical of medieval village churches; they have escaped every hazard and are representative of three distinct periods of architecture. Staunton Harold in Leicestershire is the earliest; built in 1653, it is one of the few Anglican churches erected during the Commonwealth, and stands at the end of the true Gothic tradition, when Renaissance styles were in vogue. (The first example of 18th-century 'Gothick', Vanbrugh's vast sham fortifications at Castle Howard, was less than seventy years in the future.) Staunton Harold is not only very late Gothic; it is good Gothic, built in the Perpendicular style for a royalist, Sir Robert Shirley, by men who never doubted that this was the right style for a church. It is set among cedars above a lake, with a massive pinnacled tower and elaborate parapets. The Chapel has box-pews, and panelling not only round the walls but also round the pillars of the nave; an early organ exuberantly supported by a Jacobean screen; a very fine early-18th-century grille; and a painted ceiling, the Creation in gaily rolling clouds. The west door is classical and carries a moving inscription:

In the yeare 1653
when all thinges Sacred were throughout ye nation
Either demolisht or profaned
Sir Robert Shirley, Barronet,
Founded this church;
Whose singular praise it is,
to haue done the best things in ye worst times,
and
hoped them in the most callamitous.
The righteous shall be had in everlasting remembrance.

How did he dare? How did the Chapel survive? When he refused to offset the Chapel with a regiment, Cromwell put him in the Tower, for the seventh time, and there he died.

Gibside Chapel in Tyne & Wear was built during the 1760s to designs by James Paine in a robust and perfectly modulated Palladian style, the pediment surely a little sharper, and the richly ornamented urns on the parapet a little bigger, than the drawings in the rule books demand. The interior was not finished until 1812, when plasterwork was added to the pendentives supporting the dome, in very pretty thin Gothick – an elegant surprise to perfect the elaboration of the Corinthian decoration.

Sandham Memorial Chapel in Hampshire was built in 1926–7, by Mr and Mrs Behrend, in memory of a relation killed in the First World War. The walls were painted by Stanley Spencer with superb and unheroic scenes from the Salonika front. Down the east wall is a great tumble of white crosses that overwhelms afresh at every visit. It is Spencer's masterpiece.

The church is the centre of the English village; other important buildings accumulate round it: the rectory or vicarage, the manor, with a grange, dovecote, maltings, the watermill, or the windmill on a near-by hill, the tithe barn, the butter cross, the wool or cattle market, according to the type of farming and the chances of taste. Around these the barns, byres, and cottages that house the produce, livestock, and peasants. Outside, again, the common fields, in strips, some belonging to the peasants, most to the lord of the manor.

One of the most important village buildings was the dovecote. Three hundred years ago there were thousands of them, and judging by those that survive and by old records they were extremely impressive. The pigeons provided eggs, meat, and fertilizer: economical birds, though they ate a lot of the peasants' corn and the landlords got most of the pigeons. Our pigeon-houses are the westernmost towers of a great chain that stretched across the world from China, a line as long as the Silk Road. Probably the most beautiful towers are the ones outside Isfahan, no two alike, and built to house thousands of birds: pigeons to provide eggs and meat in a climate where large carcases would not keep, and dung from the bottoms of the towers for fertilizing the melon fields. Every year a chain of camels carried thirty loads of melons packed in ice to the Emperor of China. Only a few of them arrived in perfect condition, but the melons of Isfahan were the best in the world.

Presumably, in England also the droppings were used to fertilize the fields, but fresh meat for the winter was the main need. Hay was the only winter foodstuff in the days before root crops were developed in the 18th century, and only as many breeding sheep and cattle could be kept as the hay crop could feed. The rest were killed and salted down. Pigeons were thus a welcome and necessary addition to a monotonous salt diet. Even in the castles, where space was at a premium, there was usually a pigeon-house. One may be seen at Tattershall in Lincolnshire where the whole south-west turret on the second floor was lined with a cote. There is another at Rochester in Kent, and small ones may be seen in the gables of many barns and farmhouses. The big free-standing ones, however, are the most impressive. At Willington in Bedfordshire is a particularly large one with stepped gables and elaborate architecture, while Kinwarton in Warwickshire has a circular cote with more than 500 nest-holes in the thick walls. It has an ogival door and a tiled conical roof. Inside, Kinwarton still has its 'potence', a central vertical beam that rotates, and supports ladders for access to the nests.

The Trust has seventeen villages, but three deserve special mention. Lacock, a wool village on an unusually grand scale, has been cherished over the centuries by the local landowners, the Talbots. The range of vernacular architecture, from a cruck-built dwelling to early-19th-century work, from modest cottages to plain 18th-century façades, is perhaps unrivalled. It would be difficult to find a village of comparable size which has suffered less in the last hundred years.

West Wycombe is a simpler village, mostly built along the old road from Oxford to London and now happily by-passed, but like Lacock the fine houses have a wide date-span. The remarkable thing is that the village street is sandwiched between a landscaped park and a hill which share one of the most interesting groups of follies in the country. There is more to see than in any other village I know, although no single building could be called a great work of art.

Blaise Hamlet is a contrast. John Harford wanted new houses for his estate pensioners, and he commissioned John Nash to build the Hamlet in 1811. It must have been a wonderful change from Regent Street and Brighton, to design nine charming cottages round a little green. They are all different, with ingenious variations in their roofs, outsize chimneys, curious windows, gables and porches, thatch and rustic work. They lie round their green in settled assurance, England's answer to the *hameau* at Versailles, the most placid piece of picturesque in the world.

Follies

Creech Grange Arch, Dorset

3 miles west of Corfe Castle, 4 miles east of Worbarrow Bay

The arch was erected in the first half of the 18th century on a ridge of the Purbeck Hills. The builder was Denis Bond, whose descendants still own Creech Grange, the house which sits comfortably in the wooded valley below. He wished from his windows to look up and see some diverting architectural feature on the skyline, so there today stands the arch, or rather arches.

The eye-catcher, built of Portland ashlar, is simply a screen of arches, surmounted by obelisks and with a crenellation over the central opening. The pronounced keystones reflect the influence of Vanbrugh.

From the arches there are immense views, northward over a singularly unspoilt stretch of Dorset countryside, and southward across the Purbeck Hills to the sea.

Creech Grange Arch; View to the north

Mow Cop, Cheshire/Staffordshire

5 miles south of Congleton, 1 mile south-east of Mow Cop station

Mow Cop, crowning a rocky escarpment nearly 1,100 feet above sea-level, is a notable example of the artificial ruin or folly beloved by sophisticated landowners in the 18th century. The squire who in 1750 built this Gothick tower and linked it to a suitably ruinous curtain wall was Randle Wilbraham. His purpose was to create a romantic eye-catcher as seen from his neighbouring estate at Rode Hall. His sham castle silhouetted against the sky is still highly effective.

Mow Cop

But Mow Cop has other than architectural associations. In its modest way it has become a shrine. Some half a century after it was built – at 6 a.m. on Sunday 31 May 1807, to be precise – it witnessed the start of an open-air prayer meeting that was to last twelve hours and was to lead not only to a revival of nonconformist fervour but ultimately to the birth of Primitive Methodism. In 1907, to mark the centenary of this austere discipline, 70,000 people flocked on a single day to worship on 'The Holy Mount' of Mow Cop. The congregation, one must suspect, would have been profoundly uncongenial to the creator of the folly.

274

The Pepperbox, Wiltshire

5 miles south-east of Salisbury, on north side of A36

On the turfy brow of Brickworth Down, half-way between the valleys of the Avon and the Test, stands a curious Jacobean tower, known impartially as The Pepperbox, or as Eyre's Folly. The brick building, erected in 1606, is octagonal with a pyramidal roof, and the lower storey consisted originally of eight open arches which have since been blocked. The tower may have been built as an eye-catcher (though there is no great house in the immediate neighbourhood), or it may have been designed to enable ladies to follow the progress of falconry and the hunt from the room in the upper storey.

The Pepperbox

Monuments

The Kymin, Gwent

1 mile east of Monmouth, south of A4136

Since the Kymin so picturesquely dominates the town, it was natural that a group of 'the first gentlemen in Monmouth' should have wished, in the spirit of the late 18th century, to take their pleasure on the hill, light-heartedly adorning the summit with a bowling green, pavilion and Naval Temple.

The pavilion, or round house, was opened on May Day 1794, and we may imagine the 'first gentlemen' on the roof contemplating the view through the telescope presented by the Member of Parliament for Monmouth. The Duchess of Beaufort soon added a carriage road to make the hilltop more accessible to the ladies, and in 1800 there followed the Naval Temple to commemorate 'the glorious and ever memorable Battle of the Nile'. Dedicated appropriately to the Duchess, who was Admiral Boscawen's daughter, it was opened in the summer of 1801 with a public breakfast and dancing on the sward.

The rustic temple, set within a walled enclosure, is decorated with medallions to fifteen admirals and to the battles with which, in 1800, they were most closely associated. A year after it was opened, Nelson, coming down the Wye by boat from Ross with Emma Hamilton and her husband, visited the temple and congratulated those concerned on 'the only monument of the kind erected to the English Navy in the whole kingdom'.

The Naval Temple

Lyveden New Bield, Northamptonshire

4 miles south-west of Oundle, 3 miles east of Brigstock

Sir Thomas Tresham was knighted by Elizabeth and seemed set for a brilliant career, when in 1580 he was converted to the Roman faith. Soon there was no more intrepid Catholic in England. Convicted as a recusant, he was repeatedly fined and imprisoned. In the circumstances it was only because religion and building were for him complementary passions that he was able to leave so unusual a mark on the architecture of his native country. He made a profession of faith in stone.

Lyveden New Bield

The Market House at Rothwell, a distinguished secular building, ante-dates his conversion; it was followed in 1593–5 by the eccentric and fascinating Triangular Lodge at Rushton which symbolizes the doctrine of the Trinity. But his masterwork was Lyveden. The architect of this enigmatic and strangely compelling building that stands solitary in the Northamptonshire countryside was a certain Robert Stickells, but the inspiration and the guiding hand were, as always, Tresham's.

Lyveden, built as an equal-armed cross with a polygonal bay at the end of each arm, is symbolical of the Passion. It was planned with infinite care and treated with great elaboration. Not only the general plan but the precisely calculated correspondence, the repetitions of certain measurements, and the carved emblems, have a symbolic significance. The love of symbolism that was an essential attribute of the Elizabethan genius finds at Lyveden its most complete expression.

The elevations – two storeys above a basement – have plain mullioned and transomed windows. The sense of richness derives from a frieze of shields at basement level, an entablature above the first floor with a frieze embodying emblems of the Passion, and a further entablature at roof level with a running Latin legend in the frieze, embodying phrases from the Vulgate, again with reference to the Passion.

An elaborate timber lantern was designed to crown this affirmation of the Catholic faith, but Tresham died in 1605 before the building was finished and it was never roofed. It was despoiled of its floors during the Commonwealth.

The Mussenden Temple, Co. Londonderry *(see colour plate facing p. 320)*

1 mile west of Castlerock station on the A2 Coleraine/Limavady road

Something has already been said (see p. 125) of Frederick Hervey, the Earl-Bishop of Derry. Downhill, the great house daringly set on a wild headland facing the North Channel, was probably designed by James Wyatt. It is now in ruin, but there still stands, poised on the edge of the cliffs above a savage sea, the Temple which the Earl-Bishop built in 1785 and dedicated to his cousin, Mrs Mussenden.

This elegant object, built in beautiful ashlar, derives from the Temple of Vesta at Tivoli. It is a rotunda, and twelve engaged and Corinthian columns support the entablature, while the domed roof carries, as a finial, a huge urn. The frieze is inscribed with a quotation from Lucretius, which in Dryden's translation reads:

> 'Tis pleasant, safely to behold from shore
> The rowling Ship; and hear the Tempest roar.

Within the Temple, the Earl-Bishop placed a library, treasured volumes of the classics and scientific treatises (for he was a member of the Royal Society). In the undercroft, Mass was celebrated on Sundays for the local Catholics, a provision which, coming from a Protestant Bishop, was uniquely tolerant in 18th-century Ireland.

In this classical eyrie, surrounded with book-lined shelves, the Earl-Bishop, as he read, will have heard the roar of the waves breaking on the rocks and from the windows will have watched gulls and petrels effortlessly drifting on the dizzy spaces below. It is the most romantically situated Temple in the British Isles, and its creation was an act of imagination as splendid as it was expensive.

Paxton's Tower, Dyfed

1 mile south of Llanarthney, 7 miles east of Carmarthen, south of the B4300 Carmarthen/Llandilo road

No valley more elegantly exemplifies romantic landscape than that of the Towy: lush pastures, ruminating cattle, a meandering river, and eminences crowned with noble trees. Combining the untamed and the pastoral, it is the landscape celebrated in Dyer's *Grongar Hill*, one of the poems that most nearly express the 18th-century attitude to nature.

Opposite:
*Mussenden
Temple*

Paxton's Tower

Surveying this valley, an architectural accent in a purely pastoral scene, stands Paxton's Tower. Sir William Paxton, a wealthy banker, built it in 1811 as a tribute to the memory of Nelson. Triangular in plan, boldly machicolated and turreted, and crowned with a central tower, it is an impressive tribute to Romantic taste and perfectly illustrates that feeling for the marriage of architecture and landscape that was characteristic of the period.

279

Rievaulx Terrace and Temples, North Yorkshire

$2\frac{1}{2}$ miles north-west of Helmsley, off the B1257 Helmsley/Stokesley road

The grass terrace and classical temples poised on the edge of the wooded escarpment above Ryedale, overlooking the ruined medieval abbey of Rievaulx beside the river Rye, are among the most beautiful and imaginative achievements of 18th-century landscaping. Dating from about 1758, the temples were erected by Thomas Duncombe as a pendant to the similarly situated terrace and temples built about 1730 near his house about a mile downstream at Duncombe Park. It was perhaps intended to link the terraces by a scenic drive above the river, but the project was never carried out.

Duncombe Park had belonged to the Earls of Rutland until it passed by inheritance, early in the 17th century, to George Villiers, 1st Duke of Buckingham. Seized by Cromwell and given to General Fairfax, it was recovered by the 2nd Duke through his marriage to Fairfax's daughter. After Buckingham's death the estate was bought by Sir Charles Duncombe, a goldsmith-banker and later Lord Mayor of London, said to be then the richest commoner in England. His nephew succeeded in 1711 and built the present house and laid out the surrounding grounds possibly to Vanbrugh's designs. Thomas Duncombe, the Rievaulx builder, came into the property in 1747. His great-nephew became the 1st Baron Feversham, whose grandson was created Earl of Feversham in 1868. The 3rd and last Earl died in 1963 and in 1972 the Trust bought the terrace and temples at Rievaulx.

The 'noble, winding terrace', as Arthur Young enthusiastically described it after a visit in 1768, follows a gently serpentine course for half a mile; swathes cut through the hanging wood that flanks the terrace reveal at intervals dramatic glimpses of the ruined Cistercian abbey far below. At either end of the terrace rise the temples: at the north-west a rectangular Ionic structure and at the south-east a Doric or Tuscan rotunda. The tessellated pavement floor was brought from the choir of the abbey.

The design of the rotunda, a 'scaled down version of the Mausoleum at Castle Howard' a few miles away, may have been by Sir Thomas Robinson

(see Claydon House, p. 85) who may well have known Thomas Duncombe through his marriage to a Howard of Castle Howard. The temple is built of dressed sandstone and surrounded by a colonnade of unfluted Doric columns. Although it carries a Doric entablature, the columns have no base.

The Ionic temple is built of a similar sandstone and stands on a high podium with a deep portico of six Ionic columns and a pediment. The interior is decorated with ornamental plasterwork above a panelled dado. The room has an elaborate cornice, and a painted ceiling by Giovanni Borgnis. The contents of this elegant room were transferred to the Trust by the Treasury and include William Kent settees, George II console tables, and an imposing Worcester dinner service. Kitchen and living quarters in the basement ensured that visitors could dine in a setting which combined in happy juxtaposition a classical temple with views of authentic medieval ruins.

Shugborough, Staffordshire

5½ miles south-east of Stafford on the A513 Rugeley/Stafford road

Few country houses can offer so fascinating and so historically interesting a collection of park and garden monuments as Shugborough. The three monuments situated in the landscaped park are – with the exception of an Ionic temple at Hagley – the first buildings in this country in the neo-Grecian style that was introduced by their designer 'Athenian' Stuart. Most prominent is the Triumphal Arch, a reproduction of the Arch of Hadrian in Athens. Begun about 1762, it was turned into a memorial with sculptures by Peter Scheemakers to commemorate Admiral Anson and his wife. The Tower of the Winds is modelled on the Tower of Andronicus Cyrrhestes. The original has deep sculptured reliefs of the winds in the frieze, and no windows; at Shugborough the ground-floor windows were possibly put in later when Wyatt converted it into a dairy for Lady Anson. The Lanthorn of

Opposite:
*Rievaulx Terrace; The
Ionic Temple and
The Doric or Tuscan
Temple*

*Shugborough Park; The
Triumphal Arch*

Demosthenes is a copy of the 4th-century Choragic Monument of Lysicrates, but its tripod and bowl are fibreglass substitutes for the original cast iron, made by Matthew Boulton at his Birmingham ironworks.

The garden buildings near the house and river include the Doric Temple, another work attributed to Stuart, since it closely resembles his earliest work, the Ionic temple he designed at Hagley in 1758. The enchanting Chinese House, built in 1747, was designed by one of the officers of Anson's flagship *Centurion*. On an island in the river, the Cat's Monument dating from 1767 possibly commemorates Thomas Anson's Persian cats, or a ship's cat said to have travelled round the world with the Admiral. Half-hidden in shrubberies, the Shepherd's Monument, dating from the mid-18th century, takes its name from its marble relief by Scheemakers after a painting by Poussin.

Stoke Poges, Gray's Monument, Buckinghamshire

East of Stoke Poges Church, west of the village, on the B473 Stoke Poges/Farnham Royal road

On 30 July 1771, Thomas Gray died at Cambridge, from 'severe internal gout'. The poet had left directions that he was to be 'deposited' in the vault, 'made by my late dear mother in the churchyard of Stoke Poges, near Slough'. Accordingly, his remains were removed to Stoke Poges where a week later his instructions were carried out. He lies next to his mother under that east window in the churchyard which he himself had so eloquently celebrated just twenty years earlier in his 'Elegy Written in a Country Churchyard'.

Gray's Monument

Opposite: *Wellington Monument*

In 1799, Mr John Penn, who had built a house near by at Stoke Park, raised a monument to Gray in a field next to the churchyard. He commissioned James Wyatt to design the beautiful classical sarcophagus upon a square plinth that stands today. An inscription records Mr Penn's tribute and Gray's lines:

> I feel the gales that from ye blow
> A momentary bliss bestow.

The field and the monument to the poet were presented to the Trust in 1922.

Wellington Monument, Somerset

2 miles due south of Wellington

On 20 October 1817, following a meeting of local gentry who resolved to perpetuate the memory of the military achievements of His Grace the Duke of Wellington, the foundation stone of this imposing obelisk was laid. The site was well chosen. Standing high on the Blackdown Hills, this polite gesture to the Iron Duke, 175 feet of beautiful ashlar masonry, is visible across half Somerset. It was designed by Thomas Lee, the architect of Arlington Court (see p. 51). A winding staircase of 235 steps leads up to the summit. The views can only be described as breathtaking.

The exposed position – the wind can whistle with extraordinary ferocity through the apertures of the little chamber at the top – makes the obelisk particularly vulnerable to the weather. The cost of repair is a recurring problem.

Villages

Blaise Hamlet, Bristol

4 miles north of central Bristol, west of Henbury village on B4057

These nine gabled cottages, dispersed about a village green, are an eclogue to the rustic virtues and recall much that has vanished from the countryside in the 20th century. They were built by John Harford between 1810 and 1811 for his retired servants. The architect was none other than John Nash, and they are his most deliberate and successful exercise in the 'picturesque'. The repeated yet always varied combination of crazy hips, gables, chimneys, verandas and porches, the gay yet subtle use of projections and recessions, reveal Nash as the master of cottage romanticism. Blaise in its way is no less important than Regent's Park or Carlton House Terrace.

Blaise Hamlet was given to the Trust in 1943.

Blaise Hamlet

Chiddingstone, Kent

4 miles east of Edenbridge, off B2027

Chiddingstone, with its row of little 16th- and 17th-century houses facing the parish church, is one of the most attractive hamlets in a county rich in such modest buildings. The style is characteristically Kentish: brick or half-timbering, tile hangings, wide eaves with steeply-pitched tiled roofs, and a picturesque use of gables.

Most striking is the long 16th-century house in the centre of the row, with three overhanging gables. The middle gable is carried forward on oak posts to form a porch, and the western gable contains an oriel. The vigorous timberwork rising from a brick plinth suggests a date about 1600.

In the adjoining grounds of Chiddingstone Castle, which, like the hamlet, was for centuries the property of the Streatfeild family, stands the 'chiding stone' from which Chiddingstone is said to take its name. It is rashly assumed to have once been a Druidic judgement stone.

Chiddingstone

Lacock, Wiltshire *(see colour plate facing p. 320)*

3 miles south of Chippenham, east of A350

Wool built Lacock. From the 14th to the 18th century the wool trade brought wealth and prosperity. As a result, we owe some of our most agreeable domestic architecture to wool villages, both here in Wiltshire and in East Anglia. It is a vernacular architecture, sober and sensible, that speaks of economic well-being and a wise building tradition. Yet few of these villages have been as fortunate as Lacock or have preserved their character with so little mutilation and addition since, with the coming of the Industrial Revolution, wool, as a cottage industry, ceased to be profitable business.

The unique flavour of Lacock is due to its long association with the adjoining abbey. The last religious house in England to be suppressed at the Dissolution, it was acquired by Sir William Sharington, a Renaissance

Lacock

adventurer of talent, and with the greater part of the village it subsequently passed by descent to the judicious ownership of the Talbot family. They carefully preserved the character of the village and transferred it, with the abbey, into the keeping of the Trust in 1944.

Every century from the 13th to the 19th has contributed to the character of Lacock and this diversity gives the village much of its charm. Half-timbering with 'wattle and daub' or brick infilling, the beautiful local stone from the Corsham quarries in rubble or ashlar, and occasional brick buildings, are juxtaposed in natural and happy fashion. Older gables and mullions co-exist alongside the later formality of cornices and sash windows. The roofs are predominantly of local stone tiles. Traditional methods and materials have adapted slowly to changing taste, so that it is not always easy to date a particular house. For instance, mullions at Lacock persist into the late 18th century. Among the more unusual buildings are a 14th-century house of cruck construction, a technique exceedingly rare in the south of England; the village lock-up, a little domed 18th-century chamber, and one of the few surviving examples of a convenience that was once common; and a great tithe barn with eight massive bays.

The conservation of such a village poses considerable problems for the Trust. Television, giving better reception, has been piped into Lacock from a single aerial, well-recessed on a near-by hillside, thus suppressing wires and a host of aerials; and with the co-operation of the local authorities a suitable type of lighting has been installed. The Trust also sees to it that Lacock is not 'prettified' and so escapes the ignominious fate of many Cotswold villages. Upkeep of these old houses and cottages is expensive, yet the Trust of set, and wisely set, policy does not let them to 'outsiders', the rich retired middle classes. Lacock remains, as it did under the Talbots, a living village for local people. It remains also, for all its delightful diversity, one of the most homogeneous and architecturally distinguished villages in England.

Dovecotes

Amongst the cottages, barns and byres that clustered together to form the medieval village, certain buildings stood out: the church, the vicarage, the large house of the lord of the manor and often a mill operated by wind or water. Besides these there was nearly always another building – the dovecote or pigeon-house. It belonged to the lord of the manor, and the right to keep pigeons was a privilege jealously guarded.

Until the introduction of root crops it was possible to preserve only a few livestock through the winter for breeding purposes. The rest had to be slaughtered and salted down. Not only did this provide a monotonous winter diet, but after a cold and wet summer the supply of salt, obtained by the evaporation of sea water, was often inadequate and much of the meat went bad.

The Romans discovered that fresh meat in any quantity must be provided by birds and that the pigeon was the best source of supply. They also realized that by building convenient pigeon-houses the birds could be to some extent tamed, and their writers on husbandry – Pliny the elder, Varro, Columella – have left accounts of how the Roman *columbaria* were constructed.

The pigeon (not its close relative, the dove) almost always returned to the same place to sleep. It was not difficult, therefore, when facilities for sleeping and nesting were provided, to induce birds to take up residence in a house specially built for them. In the centuries following the Norman Conquest, the use of pigeon-houses became widespread in England. The pigeons found their food in the surrounding country and probably, for the most part, in the acre and half-acre strips in the great common fields surrounding the village. Many of the strips formed part of the demesne and were owned by the lord of the manor, but most of the grain in the birds' crops was provided by the peasantry. The latter were in fact obliged to feed both the birds and their owner.

It was soon realized that the position would become intolerable if there were no limit to the number of pigeon-houses, so it was laid down that only the lord of the manor, clerical or lay, could possess a pigeon-house, and he not more than one. There seems, however, to have been no restriction as to size – some containing between one and two thousand nesting boxes – and there is little doubt that deep resentment at this injustice existed for many centuries. As late as 1659 there were still 26,000 dovecotes in the country.

Some of the keeps in Norman castles – Rochester is one – possess nesting boxes in the walls, but the earliest known example of an isolated pigeon-house is inscribed '1326'.

Bruton, Somerset

½ mile south of Bruton, ½ mile west of B3081

The little village of Bruton, with one of the finest medieval churches in Somerset, was the site of an Augustinian abbey that has vanished almost without trace. Nothing remains but part of the abbey wall and the abbey dovecote.

The latter is set in a meadow on a hillock outside the village. Like so many dovecotes that were once an essential part of the rural economy, it has not known the flurry of wings for centuries. The tower-like structure – stone-built, with mullioned windows and four gables – is unusual, and was probably built early in the 16th century.

Kinwarton, Warwickshire

1½ miles north-east of Alcester on B4089

This is one of the earliest dovecotes that can be approximately dated, as the doorway has an ogee arch, a form that was becoming common by the middle of the 14th century. Probably the dovecote was built just prior to the Black Death. It is a notable example of the most practical form of pigeon-house. Circular in plan, with walls 3 ft 7 in. thick, it contains over 500 rectangular nest-holes. A tiled roof is surmounted by a lantern and has a dormer window. The building contains a good example of a potence, one of the ingenious fittings to be found in these structures. A potence – a French term meaning 'gallows' – consists of a tall beam in the centre of the pigeon-house, pivoted at the top and bottom. From this two or three horizontal members project. At their outer edge they support a ladder which enabled the servant in charge easily to reach the nesting boxes.

Wichenford, Hereford & Worcester

5½ miles north-west of Worcester, north of B4204

A timber-framed dovecote with wattle and daub infilling is a considerable rarity. The example at Wichenford, which stands on a sandstone plinth, is square in plan and the gabled roof carries a small central lantern to admit the birds. There are some 580 nesting boxes.

The timber framing is characteristic of that often found in domestic buildings in Worcestershire, and the dovecote probably dates from the late 17th century, as does the adjoining farmhouse.

Opposite:
Kinwarton and the interior, showing the 'potence'

Wichenford

Willington Dovecote and Stables, Bedfordshire

4 miles east of Bedford, just north of the A603 Bedford/Sandy road

Standing isolated in the flat Bedfordshire landscape, a dovecote and stables are all that remain of a large mansion and dependencies built by Cardinal Wolsey's Master of the Horse. The tall rectangular dovecote, whose serrated roof line is to be seen for miles around, is imposing. The roof has crow-stepped gables and, most curiously, rises in two pitches. These are separated by louvers for the passage of the birds. The crow-stepped gables incorporate some 13th-century corbels. Probably filched from priories in the neighbourhood, they are a reminder that when the dovecote was built Henry VIII was busy suppressing the religious houses.

Willington dovecote

The interior consists of two squares divided by a cross wall. Situated in the walls, three feet thick, are kidney-shaped nesting boxes for 1,500 pigeons. The customary potence for reaching the boxes seems to have been replaced by an alternative wooden structure.

A hundred yards from the dovecote is a barn-like building of the same date and with similar crow-stepped gables, but with well-preserved late Gothic windows, known as Henry VIII's Stables. John Bunyan once stayed in the loft and carved his name and the date '1650' on the stone fireplace.

Chapels

Clumber Chapel, Nottinghamshire

2½ miles south-east of Worksop, 4½ miles south-west of East Retford; approached west of the A614 Bawtry/Ollerton road

This handsome chapel, larger than many parish churches, dedicated to St Mary the Virgin, was built by the 7th Duke of Newcastle for his private worship and for the people of Clumber Park. The architect was G. F. Bodley (1827–1907), one of the most distinguished names in the later history of the Gothic Revival.

In 1886 when the chapel was built, the pioneer days of the Revival, associated with such names as Pugin, Scott, Butterfield and Street, were over. There remained the virtues of refinement, and these, with sensibility, taste, and great ecclesiological knowledge, are the hallmarks of Bodley's 'cathedral in miniature', as Clumber has been aptly termed.

Built of warm red sandstone contrasting with white Streetly stone, Clumber is a cruciform building in the Decorated style of the 14th century. The spire over the central tower rises to 180 feet, and the height of the chapel is consciously accentuated by the narrowness of the nave. The stone-carving inside and out is of the highest quality, as are all the interior details and appointments, such as the elaborate rood-screen, the font cover, the walnut and cedar choir stalls, and the carved limewood statues. Most of the fine stained-glass windows are by C. E. Kempe, the foremost glazier of the 19th century who was largely responsible for the revival of glass-making on medieval lines.

Clumber Chapel

Gibside Chapel, Tyne & Wear

6 miles west of Gateshead, east of Rowland's Gill on A694

Sir George Bowes, who inherited the Gibside estate in 1722, was a Whig Member of Parliament for thirty years, master of hounds, bloodstock breeder, and a powerful figure in County Durham. He was also a man of notable taste. He enlarged and remodelled Gibside Hall, his 17th-century house, and in 1729 embarked on an imaginative scheme of landscape design. In a setting of wooded slopes and radiating avenues he sited a series of buildings, each admirably placed, each part of a harmonious plan: a Gothick banqueting house, an orangery, and a stable block; and, at either end of a great terrace avenue, a statue to British Liberty, on a column rather higher than the Nelson column, and the building known as Gibside Chapel.

The roofless Hall has been deserted for fifty years; mining subsidence has wrecked the banqueting hall; the orangery is in ruins; the stable block was used as a farmhouse until recently. Only British Liberty on its gigantic column and the Chapel survive intact, facing each other down George Bowes's long terrace flanked with oaks.

The Chapel, presented to the Trust by the 16th Earl of Strathmore in 1965, is an imposing exercise in the Palladian style. It was designed by James Paine and, though started in 1760, was not completed until the early years of the 19th century. It remains the family mausoleum, and services are taken regularly by the Earl's private chaplain.

The side and rear elevations are relatively austere. The architectural impact is created by the entrance front. A double staircase rises to a great Ionic portico with pediment, and the composition is surmounted by a parapet, set with classical urns, that screens a central dome. The plan of the

Gibside Chapel and the interior

building is cruciform: the portico constitutes one arm of the cross, the other three being formed by semicircular apses with barrel vaults.

The detail inside and out, notably the plasterwork, is of the finest quality and the furnishings are wonderfully complete. The altar table, surrounded by communion rails, stands under the dome in the centre of the chapel. To the east stands a rare mahogany three-tier pulpit with an oval sounding board supported on a single Ionic column. The box pews are of cherrywood.

Loughwood Meeting House, Devon

4 miles west of Axminster, off the A373 Honiton road, 1 mile south of Dalwood village

A narrow lane leads steeply off the Honiton road, and in four hundred yards the thatched church comes into view, set on the slope above a farmyard.

In 1650 the Baptist congregation at Kilmington near by, harassed by the Puritan administration, abandoned their meeting house and moved to a cottage, then surrounded by dense woodlands, across the county boundary. In 1653 they erected a church in this place which remained in use until 1833, when they returned to Kilmington. Finding it impossible to maintain the two churches, the Kilmington congregation conveyed Loughwood to the Trust in 1969.

Loughwood Meeting House and the interior

The plain rectangular building, with simple round-headed windows, stands within a small burial ground. Made of the local sandstone with a steeply thatched roof, the exterior is unremarkable. In the pantiled stable beside it the minister stalled his horse.

Within is a feeling of peace and simplicity, of scrubbed boards and fresh air, where men might worship God according to the dictates of their conscience. The original plastered barrel ceiling has survived, but the fittings are of the 18th century. A tall pulpit dominates the south end;

beneath it the baptismal tank under the floor is covered by stout boards. Pews of unpainted pine, complete with entrance doors, fill the body of the church. At the north end, below a gallery, are two retiring rooms, one for each sex, each with a small fireplace. Here the worshippers spent the time between morning and evening service, in talk and the instruction of their children.

Sandham Memorial Chapel, Burghclere, Hampshire

4 miles south of Newbury, north of Highclere station

The Oratory of All Souls was erected as a memorial to H. W. Sandham, killed in the First World War. A brick building of simple proportions with stone dressings, it is connected to flanking wings designed as almshouses.

Sandham Memorial Chapel; Stanley Spencer mural

The oratory was intended as a 'canvas' for Stanley Spencer's ambitious murals. He took six years to execute them, and they are the most important series of decorative paintings produced in England in this century. In the First World War, Spencer served in the R.A.M.C. on the Salonika front and the murals were inspired by the experiences and incidents of his daily duties. They reflect the life of the ordinary British soldier, set either against the dour Macedonian landscape or within the walls of a field hospital. The large painting behind the altar depicting the Resurrection on the Salonika front is arguably Spencer's greatest work.

Staunton Harold Chapel, Leicestershire

5 miles north-east of Ashby-de-la-Zouch, just west of the B587 Melbourne road

Few churches have been built with greater courage or in more moving circumstances. The inscription over the west door of Staunton Harold records that 'when all thinges Sacred were throughout ye nation Either demolisht or profaned Sir Robert Shirley, Barronet, Founded this church'. Sir Robert's faith and his audacity incensed Cromwell, who announced that if a man could afford to build so splendid a church he could provide the money to raise a regiment. Sir Robert, a staunch Royalist, refused and was sent to the Tower, where he died at the age of twenty-seven.

He left in the chapel of the Holy Trinity at Staunton Harold a worthy memorial. Seen across the parkland that slopes to the lake and guarded by giant cedars, the chapel-church conveys at first sight, with its decorated east windows and its low-pitched roofs and embattled parapets of late Perpendicular character, the impression of a medieval building. But the classical west doorway with its sculptures, its flamboyant coat of arms and noble inscription, betrays the true date. Built in 1653, it is one of the few churches to be erected between the outbreak of the Civil War and the Restoration. Its plan and general appearance are striking proof of the continuity of the Gothic building tradition in the middle of the 17th century.

The interior of the chapel has seen little change since Sir Robert's time. A screen of purely Jacobean character supports the loft, with an English-built organ that is probably one of the earliest examples to have survived. Above the organ, an elaborately carved wooden tympanum, also of Jacobean character, displays the Shirley arms. The nave with its clerestory is separated from the aisles by arcades of three bays and carries a wooden painted ceiling representing the Creation and dated 1655. In the aisles hang hatchments of the Shirley family.

Staunton Harold; The Church and Hall, and Church interior

The box pews have simple oak panelling and contemporary ironwork. Similar panelling is carried up to the capitals of the columns in the nave and provides a dado around the walls. During the 17th century, the separation of the sexes was observed during church services, and at Staunton Harold this custom has been preserved, men sitting in the pews on the south of the aisle and women in the pews on the north.

The chancel is separated from the nave by a splendid wrought-iron grille that is probably by Robert Bakewell of Derby.

Buildings of Useful Intent

Assembly Rooms, Bath

From medieval times the waters of Bath, first discovered by the Romans, had attracted the sick. By the middle of the 18th century, the town had also become a centre of fashionable life. Its architectural development by John Wood and his son and successor produced a highly original form of urban composition which had a marked influence on British architecture; the Royal Crescent, built by John Wood the younger, was widely imitated. His other major work, the Assembly Rooms, stands near to his father's monumental conception, the Circus.

Opened in 1771 and built of smooth Bath stone, the Assembly Rooms are approached across a wide pavement and dominate the surrounding houses. The somewhat sombre air of the exterior belies the splendid suite of rooms within. The ballroom with a musicians' gallery, the octagonal cardroom and tea-room all run the full height of the building. Plasterwork decoration is concentrated on the high coved ceilings, the cornices and around the tall windows. Decoration below this level would have been lost in crowded rooms.

The Assembly Rooms admirably fulfilled their role and for fifty years were at the centre of Bath's social life. George IV, when Prince of Wales, came here to a ball in 1796 and with these Rooms many famous names are associated – Jane Austen (and her characters), Franz Liszt, Johann Strauss the elder and Sir Arthur Sullivan. Dickens gave readings here in 1867 and again in 1869; when the immortal Mr Pickwick visited Bath in 1836 he found the Rooms as gay and lively as ever and 'the hum of many voices, the sound of many feet perfectly bewildering. Dresses rustled, feathers waved, lights shone and jewels sparkled.'

Bath Assembly Rooms; The tearoom

Tastes changed, and by 1931 the Assembly Rooms had long been used for more mundane purposes and had sadly deteriorated. The late Ernest E. Cook bought the building and presented it to the Trust, who leased it to the City of Bath. It was restored and opened in 1938, but in 1942 was completely burnt out in an air raid. Not until 1963 was the Trust able to restore the Rooms for the second time to their former beauty.

Blewcoat School, Westminster, London

Caxton Street, SW1

The Blewcoat school, founded in 1688, moved to Caxton Street in 1709, when the present building was put up by a prominent local brewer for the education of poor children. It was still in use as a school after the First World War. In 1954 it was acquired by the Trust, restored, and opened in the following year as the Trust's Membership Department. Twenty years later it was further restored and set in a small paved enclosure and is now used for the Trust's central committee meetings.

There is no record of the architect who built the school. It consists of a single lofty panelled room over a semi-basement; on each brick elevation, Doric pilasters rising from a plinth support an entablature with a continuous cornice and divide the façades into bays. The entrance front, above a wooden doorcase with fluted Doric pilasters, incorporates a niche with stone dressings in which stands the painted statue of a Bluecoat Boy.

The attractively proportioned hall is entered through a vestibule formed by a screen of Corinthian columns. The walls panelled in painted pine rise to a dentilled and modillioned cornice which in turn supports a coved ceiling.

Blewcoat School

Chipping Campden Market Hall, Gloucestershire

From the 13th to the 17th century Chipping Campden was a great wool centre, and sheep provided the money to raise the buildings which lend the little town such architectural distinction. It is a distinction to which both the beautiful natural setting of Chipping Campden and the uniformity of the building materials, a fine Cotswold stone, make an important contribution.

Chipping Campden; Market Hall

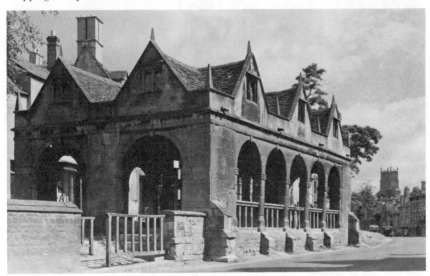

The Market Hall, standing detached in the High Street, was not, it seems, connected with the wool trade, but was reserved for the sale of cheese, butter and poultry. The little gabled building has a cobbled floor, and at ground level an open arcade with semicircular arches, the five bays on each side of the building having stone balustrades. The market was erected in 1627 by Sir Baptist Hicks, who ensured that his arms appeared on the building (at one end under an ogee gable).

George Inn, Southwark, London

On east side of Borough High Street, close to London Bridge

The George Inn, now tucked away behind London Bridge station, is the last galleried inn left in London. It stands on the site of a much older building of the same name, which until the late 19th century enclosed a yard where Shakespeare is said to have acted.

The present inn was built in 1677 and in the late 18th and early 19th centuries was an important coaching post, a terminus for traffic to the south-east. Dickens almost certainly visited the George, for he mentions it in *Little Dorrit*.

George Inn, Southwark

Opposite:
Newtown; Old Town Hall

The long wooden galleries with their heavy balustrades form the only passageway from one room to another on the first and second floors. Downstairs, the coffee room retains its Victorian box-pew compartments, and the bar is warmed by an open fire. Upstairs, there is a large panelled dining room.

Newtown: The Old Town Hall, Isle of Wight

1 mile north of A3054, 5 miles from Newport

This building, which now comes as an agreeable surprise in an entirely rural setting, was the town hall of the most ancient borough in the Isle of Wight. A surviving Charter dates from 1356, and the Corporation, consisting of a number of landowning burgesses, controlled the most important town on the island. Its prosperity was derived from its harbour, saltpans and oyster beds. Newtown suffered seriously from a French raid in 1377 from which it never altogether recovered, and by the middle of the 16th century it had lost much of its importance and was being superseded by Newport.

Strangely enough at this time, the shrinking borough received its parliamentary franchise in 1584, returning two members until the Reform Act of 1832. Among the distinguished men who sat for Newtown were Robert Cotton, the noted antiquary; John Churchill, later Duke of Marlborough; Richard Jones, 1st Earl of Ranelagh, Chancellor of the Exchequer from 1668 to 1674; Henry Dundas, later 1st Viscount Melville; and George Canning,

later Foreign Secretary and Prime Minister. The list indicates the valuable parliamentary role sometimes played by rotten boroughs.

Little remains of the town but the alignment of its ghostly streets. Of the few modest houses that survive, most appear on a map dated 1724, but the town hall, the scene of so many parliamentary elections, is the only monument that bears witness to the past eminence of the borough. Built of brick with stone dressings, it was put up by public subscription, probably in 1699. Architectural features, such as the round-headed windows with bold keystones, the stone dressings, and the interior panelling, are characteristic of such a date. The Gothick fenestration and the columned Tuscan portico on the north front are an addition probably dating from the late 18th century.

The town hall had been derelict for many years, when in 1933 it was acquired and repaired by Ferguson's Gang (see p. 376), and presented to the Trust.

Old Post Office, Tintagel, Cornwall

This building, which derives its name from the fact that it was used as the village post office in Victorian times, is in fact a very small manor-house, dating from the 14th century. As such it is something of a rarity, particularly in the extreme south-west of England where few domestic dwellings of the Middle Ages survive.

The local stone has weathered to every shade of grey and the building

Tintagel; The Old Post Office

seems almost to have grown out of the spare Cornish soil. There is a delightful sense of idiosyncrasy about the unexpected gables and the wavy roof tiles, the massive slates having long since warped the supporting rafters. A notable and picturesque feature are the stout chimneystacks, built in two or three stages. Provided with slate drips and flashings, and capped with a chimneypot of four slates set on edge, such stacks were once common in north Cornwall but are fast disappearing.

In spite of its modest scale, the interior is surprisingly roomy. Over the centuries it has inevitably seen changes, but the hall is still open to the roof and has a primitive screen in the shape of a low wall dividing the hall from the kitchen.

Theatre Royal, Bury St Edmunds, Suffolk

Surrounded by vast brewery buildings on the edge of the town is the delightful early 19th century Playhouse, the Theatre Royal, Bury St Edmunds. This little theatre survives almost unaltered from pre-Victorian days and still has regular productions. It was built in 1819 by William Wilkins, the architect of the National Gallery and Downing College, as the crowning point of his circuit of East Anglian theatres. Complete with its boxes and gallery, painted friezes and proscenium arch, the theatre is unrivalled in scale and proportion anywhere in the kingdom.

The Georgian public playhouse, in this case, originally seating 780, was a theatre for all, whether in the pit, boxes or gallery, and was in marked contrast to the theatres of the metropolis like Drury Lane where the emphasis was on spectacle, as opposed to acting.

Theatre Royal, Bury St Edmunds; The auditorium

The Bury St Edmunds theatre has been visited by many famous actors, including Macready in 1828. It was also, surprisingly, the theatre chosen for the world première of *Charlie's Aunt* in 1892. Rescued from the ignominy of being a barrel store, the theatre has been restored over the last decade and the spectator can now discover anew the delights and peculiar pleasures of the Georgian playhouse.

IV
Medieval Buildings

Introduction *by John Harvey*

Buildings of the Middle Ages are important for two main reasons. Firstly, they are the earliest we have that are still in use for living purposes identical with or closely analogous to those for which they were made. While we view the archaeological remains of early times with detachment, as simple onlookers, we are ourselves subjectively concerned with the structural continuity of English buildings since, roughly, the reign of Edward the Confessor. Although there are considerably earlier fragments of Anglo-Saxon churches, no substantially complete structures survive from before the 11th century. The start of what we must consider medieval is then to be set about nine hundred years ago; its end came with the coincidence of the Renaissance in art, the Reformation in religion, and the Dissolution of the monasteries, by the middle of the 16th century.

In the second place, medieval building is more intimately national, regional and local than work of more recent times. In spite of the foreign sources of Romanesque and Gothic architecture, the development of style and the forming of tradition both in design and structure took place in this country. Explicitly alien motives and importations were far less frequent than they were to become in the mercantile and industrial epochs. The difficulties and expense of transport ensured that most buildings were constructed of local materials, so that there was usually a particular consonance between the church, castle or house and the natural surroundings in which it was set. Stone walls had been quarried out of near-by pits, and timber framing felled in the neighbouring woods. Bricks and tiles were made on the spot or not far away, of whatever clay happened to be furnished by the geology of the region, resulting in infinite variety of colour and texture.

English buildings of the five centuries from the Confessor to Henry VIII thus possess in the highest degree that first quality – Historic Interest – which the National Trust was founded to preserve. They have also in special measure a close relationship to the second quality of Natural Beauty. This affinity with the scenery is heightened by the placing of a large proportion of our medieval buildings: monasteries in remote or sheltered nooks and close to running water, castles set on inaccessible crags to add the defences of nature to those of art, houses with their gardens and orchards laid out to give visual pleasure and quiet recreation as well as fresh food and home-grown medicines. For it is an error to suppose that English landscape gardening first began in the 18th century: as far back as the opening of the 12th century Henry I had, at the highest social level, set a fashion by forming his park at Woodstock, the nine acres of his royal garden at Dunstable, and the bower at Havering in Essex, where the king's gardener Salomon was the first of a hereditary line paid three-halfpence a day for the next hundred years. By the first half of the 13th century a newly rich layman, Paulin Peyvre, was satirized by Matthew Paris for his lavish expenditure on manor-house, orchards and pools, emulating the wealth and luxury of earls. In less than 150 years, then, the garden as a setting for the luxurious dwelling had descended from the court to the burgess; and a century later still Chaucer's many references to trees, exotic as well as 'hoomly', demonstrate a high degree of sophistication in the times of Edward III and Richard II.

In the nature of things little can now remain of the gardens of from four to nine hundred years ago, apart from some pools and watercourses which may have escaped change. It is worth noting in this context that the great lake at Kenilworth Castle, which washed the walls beneath the state apartments of John of Gaunt, was for amusement as well as defence: a survey of the reign of Henry VIII remarked that the large windows of the chambers in the Strong Tower were placed 'opening towards the park and the great mere . . . very commodiously to see the deer coursed and the fish taken'. On a humble scale many of the arrangements made by Henry de Bray at Harlestone in Northamptonshire at the end of the 13th century survived into the 20th: an instance probably unique because the survival of his private estate book tells us exactly how a small medieval estate was improved in the twenty years from 1289 to 1309. De Bray built a hall and chamber in 1289 and eight years later a new herb garden; in 1303 a dovecote at the corner of this garden and in 1305 another, next a garden called the Newyard, which was walled about in 1307 with a wall 24 perches long (indicating a garden equivalent to 99 feet square). All the other buildings, and their cost, are described, including walls and gates, a pound, a pigsty, a fowl-house, a barn, a bakehouse, a new kitchen, fountains, a sheepfold, a carthouse; besides levelling the courtyard and planting oaks, forming ponds, a millpond and a watermill. In imagination we must transfer these particulars from a single instance to the many houses, larger and smaller than de Bray's, up and down the countryside.

It is remarkable that, in the course of over three-quarters of a century, the properties acquired by the National Trust should include a selection, so well spread in period and in function, of the main classes of domestic architecture. It would be possible to illustrate most of the trends of medieval development by means of representative properties, subject to the express reservation that this would exclude much of the specifically religious life, including the social life, of the period. To the nevertheless substantial minority of buildings of religious origin we shall return. At the start of our period in the 11th century, most laymen dwelt in houses of timber and mud; stone masonry was little used except for churches and monastic buildings and, after the Norman Conquest of 1066, to a slowly increasing extent for the main towers of castles. Even in fortified buildings, however, stonework was the exception until well into the 12th century. The dangers of the age had to be repelled by the defences of religion – and strong walls – for those who retired from the world to monasteries; and in civilian life by living in, or closely under the protection of, palisaded castles and walled towns.

The story of the English castle as a private dwelling may well begin with Rayleigh Mount, formed soon after the Conquest by Suen the son of Robert FitzWimarc, who had been one of the principal Norman courtiers of Edward the Confessor. Suen, sheriff of Essex and Hertfordshire, was expected to control the Saxon population from his home on top of the high mound, guarded by outer and inner baileys surrounded with palisades. Stone walls later took the place of palisades, but after a life of less than two centuries the site was let for grazing; by 1394 the villagers had the king's permission to repair their chapel with stones from the 'foundations of a certain old castle which used to be there'.

The earliest stone castles included, as well as Colchester and the White Tower of London, the keep of Bramber in Sussex in a vital strategic position warding off any repetition of the Conqueror's invasion from the continent. Whether or not the keep was yet built, the castle was one of those few mentioned in Domesday Book. A hundred years later a much larger stone keep was added to the early Norman castle of Duffield in Derbyshire. Except for the Tower of London, Colchester Castle, and the keep at Dover, the Duffield donjon was the largest in England, 99 feet long by 93 feet wide; and its walls were the thickest except for those at Dover, probably rather later in date. A new era in castle building, within a few years after 1200, was marked at Skenfrith, where the keep was a circular tower and the bailey a quadrilateral with round corner towers. The remarkable fact, noted by the late Sidney Toy, that the upper floors of the towers are all at exactly the same level, indicates the work of a skilled engineer, perhaps the Master Fortin who was in charge of repairs to Colchester Castle for the same patron, Hubert de Burgh.

The next stage in the development of fortifications, exemplified at Cilgerran Castle, dispensed with the keep altogether and made the curtain wall and its towers the essential features of design. There the residential aspect was minimized; but at Powis, which by historical accident has remained continuously inhabited, the 13th-century castle has become primarily a great mansion, though originally contemporary with the flourishing of concentric fortifications, built curtain within curtain, designed for the pacification of Wales under Edward I. Another phase supervened early in the 14th century with the exaltation of the great gatehouse into a new form of keep, and of such castles the noblest survivor is Dunstanburgh on the Northumbrian coast, where the main work was done in 1313–16 for Thomas, Earl of Lancaster, and extensions were carried out in 1380 for John of Gaunt by the great mason-architect John Lewyn.

At Dunstanburgh the interweaving of architecture and landscape is forcibly brought home to us. We now sense a magnificence in the defiance of the elements by the great buildings planted along the coasts of Northumbria, from Scarborough to Berwick. It comes as something of a shock to read the letter, probably of the end of the 12th century, sent back to St Albans by one of the monks dispatched to colonize Tynemouth Priory.

> Our house is confined to the top of a high rock, and is surrounded by the sea on every side but one. ... Day and night the waves break and roar and undermine the cliff. Thick sea-frets roll in, wrapping everything in gloom. Dim eyes, hoarse voices, sore throats are the consequence. Spring and summer never come here. The north wind is always blowing and brings with it cold and snow; or storms in which the wind tosses the salt sea foam in masses over our buildings and rains it down within the castle. ... In the spring the sea-air blights the blossoms of the stunted fruit trees, so that you will think yourself lucky to find a wizened apple, though it will set your teeth on edge should you try to eat it. See to it, dear brother, that you do not come to so comfortless a place.

Though applauding the magnificent jewelled shrine of St Oswin and the beauty of the priory church, the unhappy monk ended by revealing his mixed feelings in regard to the local diet: 'We are well off for food, thanks to the abundant supply of fish, of which we tire.' No appreciation of the picturesque, nor apparently any satisfaction over religious duty fulfilled, could soften the impact of the North upon this inveterate southerner.

Despite these natural drawbacks and the continuing risks of savage raids from across the Border, the northern counties supported a considerable population in the Middle Ages. It was, however, necessary for anybody with property, and especially cattle, worth stealing to live in a defensible house. Consequently a wide area is studded with massive pele towers, commonly with a vaulted chamber on the ground floor into which cattle might be driven at the first warning of raiders, and upper storeys arranged for human occupation. A particularly fine example, datable by heraldry to about 1340, forms part of the oldest buildings at Sizergh Castle. Another pele tower is at Dalton, the former capital of Furness, and is of much the same period; it was probably built by the monks of Furness Abbey. An even later instance of the special need for protective works is the real Lindisfarne Castle which underlies the modern house on the peak of Holy Island.

Across southern England the last of the castles merge into the earliest of the unfortified mansions as the civil discord of earlier times was subdued by the law and order imposed by Edward I. No precise chronological order can be maintained, for such a manor-house as Old Soar in Kent, completely unfortified, was built a generation earlier than Boarstall Tower, where a licence to crenellate was obtained in 1312. Compton Castle in Devon and Croft Castle near Leominster, later still, must have owed their fortification to their remote positions. At much the same date, and not so far away, important houses were being built virtually without defences: Clevedon Court, the timber-framed Lower Brockhampton, Shute Barton in eastern Devon and Lytes Cary in the south of Somerset. Also to the 14th century belong the earliest parts of the noble Cornish mansion of Cotehele and of Grey's Court. Though begun only in 1419, Bradley Manor close to Newton Abbot may be regarded as part of the same phase of social life.

In the meantime there had been fresh alarms: of foreign invasion and of internal strife. Fear of the French along the south-eastern coasts was responsible for the building of a new wave of castles in the reign of Richard II. The finest of these, and the most perfectly preserved, is Bodiam, a little masterpiece of sophisticated architecture. The century of dynastic struggle started by the usurpation of Henry IV in 1399 caused a further recrudescence of fortification. Noblemen hired armies of mercenaries, who commonly got out of hand and from whom their masters needed protection. The castle 'of livery and maintenance' was the result, and of it Tattershall is the most distinguished example. The immense brick keep, at least in part due to German brickmen, was the private mansion of the lord and his family, and fitted out with a luxury unknown to the true keeps of the early Norman castles. Throughout the Wars of the Roses the anxieties of life made themselves apparent in similar and other devices, the digging of moats, the building of gatehouses. Only three years before Bosworth Field the Bedingfelds of Oxburgh obtained licence from Edward IV to crenellate their Norfolk mansion – again of brick – and the magnificent gatehouse has survived.

As the turbulent 15th century wore away towards its close, private houses became more palatial in all parts of the country: Great Chalfield in the south-west, Smallhythe Place, of timber, in Kent; and Speke Hall and Rufford Old Hall, also framed, in Lancashire – all tell the tale of increasing comfort and, for the times, luxury. Even at the middle of the century, in a period of the greatest political uncertainty, an Archbishop of Canterbury began in 1456 to build Knole, which ever since has remained one of the greatest private houses of England. Social emulation was soon to bring the new luxurious style to smaller homes. Towards the end of the 15th century there was a substantial middle class, comprising on the one hand the lesser gentry and upper yeomen, for whom houses such as Stoneacre in Kent were built, and on the other merchants who had made their way by business acumen. The opulent display of the timber-framed Paycocke's at Coggeshall is the type of this category, while the more functional counterpart at Tenby is perhaps more representative of the mercantile dwelling. Uncertain both in date and in precise status, but possibly to be grouped with these buildings, is the 'Old Post Office' at Tintagel.

In spite of the disappearance of most of the medieval cottages of England, the homes of the great mass of the population, we can form some impression of their character in a few small towns and large villages that have been left on one side by the tide of industrial progress. In their historical grouping such collections of houses, built for owners and occupiers of varying status within the same community, have still greater value as evidence of past life than the larger manor-houses and mansions cherished for their individuality. The great houses of the countryside are jewels; but they would be deprived of much of their significance if the setting did not, at least in some representative instances, survive as well. Outstanding examples of the medieval urban scene are Lacock, formerly a market town, with a wide variety of houses, some of stone, others framed of timber; and, nearer to London, West Wycombe and Chiddingstone. West Wycombe, a village rather than a town, but formerly a centre of home industries, is perhaps the most important of the three, particularly as a permanent memorial to the national interest aroused on its behalf in 1929 by the Royal Society of Arts – one of the historic landmarks in British conservation.

Important for a proper understanding of an earlier way of life are buildings of certain special types. The hostelry is represented by the King's Head Inn at Aylesbury, of the mid-15th century. Social life in fraternities, part religious, part benevolent (in the sense of social security), part concerned with trade and industry, is exemplified by the guildhalls: the splendid St George's Hall at Lynn, built about 1420; and the Lavenham Guildhall of 1525. Likewise used for the holding of local and manorial courts were the court houses at Long Crendon (originally perhaps a warehouse), and at Hawkshead in the Lake District. Among minor monuments the great class of crosses is represented by two which served very different purposes: the Colston Bassett Market Cross; and at Sharow near Ripon the last remains of one of the series of sanctuary crosses which offered the shelter of a religious taboo to the refugee in fear of his life. The dietary problems of the Middle Ages are brought to mind by the dovecotes which were put up by every lord of a manor (see p. 287).

So much for the daily life of the medieval world. What of its spiritual side: the emphasis upon religion and the existence of a transcendent other world beyond? For obvious reasons the great majority of churches remain fabrics still in active use for the same fundamental purposes for which they were erected. Just a scattering of chapels, mostly in ruin, hint at aspects of the devotional life of the ordinary men and women of the time. The chapels of ease at West Humble in Surrey and at Keld in Cumbria catered for those who dwelt too far from the parish church, or on the opposite bank of a river seasonally in flood. The Chantry Chapel at Buckingham is one of the earliest examples of the typically medieval cult of soul-masses, abolished as superstitious at the Reformation; the Perpendicular tower of St Michael's Chapel on Glastonbury Tor stands as a mark, seen from afar, of the cradle of Christianity in Britain. A different sort of mark is the minuscule lighthouse of St Catherine's Oratory in the Isle of Wight, built about 1314 as a sign of contrition by a repentant wrecker.

Transitional in character between the secular and the ecclesiastical are the priests' houses, ranging from the noble example built by the Treasurers of Wells Cathedral at Martock in the 13th and 14th centuries to the little lodge of Easton-on-the-Hill, Northamptonshire. Especially fine examples of the 14th century are those at Alfriston in East Sussex, of timber framing, and of Muchelney in Somerset, built of stone. Showing the higher standards of luxury that were invading the priestly life towards the close of the Middle Ages, the Priest's House at Smallhythe in Kent, with lavish use of large timbers in close studding, might stand as the perfected small house of Tudor times. The rectors for whom these houses were put up were often in fact the lords of small manors, and lay administrators and farmers as well as clergymen. For the storage of the tithes that formed their main support they, and the monastic houses who were rectors elsewhere, built tithe barns, a notable category of medieval buildings, often of beauty and always of structural interest (see p. 326).

Finally we reach the remains of houses of religion: the institutional buildings designed for the communities of monks and nuns who followed one of the recognized monastic Rules of the Catholic Church. Since the Reformation the survival of parts of such buildings has been largely a matter of chance. Some of those to whom Henry VIII made grants of the dissolved monasteries took their profit by the demolition and sale of materials; others, to whom we may feel a qualified gratitude, thought it better to convert the fabric into a domestic dwelling. Such conversion is part of a later story, but has preserved for us important architectural remains. The most ancient rule, that of St Benedict, was followed by the Saxon monasteries founded at Westbury-on-Trym near Bristol in 961 and at Ramsey in Cambridgeshire in 974. The surviving fragments are much later in date: at Westbury the gatehouse of a College of secular priests to which, by a reversal of episcopal policy, the older monastic foundation was converted; and at Ramsey too a part of the great gatehouse; both of them works of the 15th century. Smaller Benedictine priories, subject to abbeys in France and thus known as 'alien priories', were those founded on the peak of St Michael's Mount near Penzance, and the little grange at Steventon in Oxfordshire. This latter was in fact simply a house of the period, interesting because an inventory of 1324 survives to tell us that there were then a chamber, hall, pantry and buttery, larder, kitchen, brew-house and dairy. The two monks who lived there must have employed a good number of lay servants, for the kitchen had not only the usual pots and pans but also twenty plates, twenty dishes, and twenty saucers of wood.

Less strictly monastic than the Rule of St Benedict was that of St Augustine. The canons who followed the Augustinian rule were all in holy orders – in the earlier Middle Ages very many monks were not – and undertook parochial duties and mixed in worldly affairs. Hence a few of their houses had national significance, notably Merton Abbey, a fragment of whose precinct wall survives, along with magnificently carved stones re-discovered in excavating Nonsuch Palace, where they had been used as building stone by Henry VIII. Great mansions formed out of houses of Austin Canons are Anglesey and Mottisfont Abbeys; and the gatehouse, of *c.* 1330–40, of the house at Cartmel still stands. Lacock Abbey was a convent of nuns. The Crusading Orders, which built preceptories and com-manderies, mostly of relatively small size, were none the less employers of distinguished architects. The little chapel of the Hospitaller commandery of St John's Jerusalem at Sutton-at-Hone, dated by Henry III's gift of oaks for the roof in 1234, is a gem of the Early English style. It is not unlikely that the architect was the Cistercian lay-brother John of Waverley, who (in spite of the rule of his order to the contrary) was busy about the king's works.

The Cistercians following the Rule of St Bernard were a strict and reformed order, setting their houses in remote sites where they would be undisturbed by the worldly life, and avoiding ostentatious carving and colour decoration in their buildings. An interesting result was their early adoption of the pointed arch and other marks of Gothic style, which gave interest to the fabric without the use of enrichment. Hailes Abbey was founded by Richard, Earl of Cornwall, Henry III's brother, and its plan closely follows that of Waverley in Surrey, though after 1271 an unusual polygonal chevet was substituted for the east end, as a shrine for the famous relic of the Holy Blood. From that amiable oddity of the 15th century, Margery Kempe, we get a glimpse of Cistercian life at Hailes in 1417. She went forth from Bristol

> to the Blood of Hayles, and there she was shriven and had loud cries and boisterous weepings. Then the religious men had her in amongst them, and made her good cheer, save they swore many great oaths and horrible. And she rebuked them therefor, after the Gospel, and thereof had they great wonder. Nevertheless some were right well pleased, thanked be God for His goodness.

Possibly more typical of the remote Cistercian norm was Buckland Abbey in Devon, where the church, unusually, was turned into the post-Reformation house.

The best, it may be said, was kept till last. Unlike the communal orders of the Western Church, the Carthusian Rule of St Bruno represented a break-away, or in some sense a reversion to the individual lives of the early hermits. Reflecting this exceptional rule, the buildings of the order are quite unlike other monasteries. The church was always small, the cloister very large; but instead of common dormitory and refectory and other buildings for general use, the cloister had grouped around it a series of individual walled plots, each containing a cell for a single inhabitant, who would pray, read, write, and cultivate his garden plot. Devised for men of highly individual devotion and dedication, the Charterhouses attracted remarkable personalities; and though the order never became popular it expanded notably towards the end of the Middle Ages. Of all its remains in this country, by far the most perfect are those of Mount Grace Priory in North Yorkshire. There, in an exquisite countryside, enough is left of the ruins to enable a complete picture to be formed of the life of the house in the 15th and early 16th centuries. Though scattered in many libraries, a remarkable number of devotional books, once the property of Mount Grace Priory, have survived, including works by the prior, Nicholas Love, of the early 15th century and the later monk, Richard Methley; as well as that unique autobiography already quoted, the *Book of Margery Kempe*.

Castles

Bodiam Castle, East Sussex

3 miles from Hawkhurst, via A229

Against a background of green slopes and ageing trees, the grey walls of Bodiam Castle rise sheer from its lake-like moat. In summer the moat is carpeted with water-lilies. Swans and the furtive dabchick as they paddle the waters break the reflection of towers and machicolated gates. Lord Curzon, who restored this romantic ruin and gave it to the National Trust, thought it 'the most fairy of English castles'. Such indeed it is.

Yet this incomparable ruin of the 14th century – it was built in 1385 by Sir Edward Dalyngrigge, a veteran of Edward III's continental wars – never withstood a serious siege and could hardly have hoped to do so. In terms of late medieval defence it is unimposing and incorporates neither the concentric principle of fortification brought back by the Crusaders from Syria nor a massive strongwork such as often replaced the earlier keeps. In the age of gunpowder it was an anachronism almost before it was built.

The castle was desperately called into being in the early years of the reign of Richard II. The French were in control of the Channel, Rye had been sacked a few years earlier, and a defensive bastion on the river Rother, which in those days was navigable for large vessels as far as Bodiam, seemed essential. An English victory off Margate, two years after the foundations of the castle were laid, happily ensured that the defences of Bodiam were not put to the test.

Bodiam Castle; The barbican

Outside, the 'fairy castle' looks much as it might have appeared to the French sailing up the Rother in the late 14th century. Rectangular in plan, with four round corner towers and two machicolated gate towers, it surveys the Sussex marshes perhaps with greater confidence than it did nearly 600 years ago. Time, and careful restoration, have treated Sir Edward Dalyngrigge's creation gently and the setting remains superb. For the historian of military architecture the castle is interesting in two respects. Firstly, access was devised with cunning. Opposite the main gate the existing octagonal stone-cased island was originally approached by a bridge at right angles from the west. This meant that the troops of a besieging force must expose their right flank, the flank unprotected by a shield, in any attempt to cross the lake moat.

Secondly, elaborate measures were taken inside the castle to isolate the garrison from Sir Edward and his household, and to ensure that the latter, in case of disaffection in the garrison, would retain control of key points such as the water supply and the strongest of the curtain towers. These measures reflect the fact that Bodiam was not defended, as early castles had usually been, by faithful feudal retainers, but by a less dependable mercenary garrison, no doubt composed largely of foot-loose soldiers who had fought in the continental wars.

But today it seems irrelevant to speak of Bodiam in terms of mercenaries and foreign invasion, of portcullises and machicolated gateways, of flanking fire and the salient of curtain towers. The centuries have transformed it effortlessly into the symbol of a distant and chivalrous age. The silent towers will epitomize at one moment the authentic rust of the Barons' Wars and at another the idyll of the courtly life of the Middle Ages. Reflections in the lake-like moat seem to have become more real than the mortared masonry.

Bramber Castle, West Sussex

South-east of Steyning on A283

Bramber, situated where the Adur river slips through a gap in the Sussex Downs, was strategically important and an early centre of Norman administration. Until the river silted up, it was also a sizeable port.

Bramber Castle; Remains of the keep

Opposite:
Cilgerran Castle

Little survives of the great castle which the Normans built on a natural mound except the deep fosse which surrounded the bailey, remnants of the bailey wall, and a fragment of the keep. The latter, built soon after the Conquest, still towers seventy-six feet above the bailey, and must have been comparable to Rochester and the largest keeps of the period. In the centre of the bailey rises an artificial mound or motte, the strongpoint of pre-Conquest date.

The site is romantic and the Trust of set purpose keeps it so. The unshorn sward is grazed by sheep, and the trees long since rooted in the banks of the fosse remain undisturbed.

Cilgerran Castle, Dyfed

On a rock above the left bank of the river Teifi, 3 miles south of Cardigan

Though chance or caprice may situate a country house, the site of a castle, as Cilgerran well illustrates, must be determined by considerations of defence. Superbly couched on a rocky promontory above the gorge of the Teifi river, the castle is almost unassailable on two sides. The picturesque ruin, familiar from the paintings of Wilson, de Wint and Turner, consists of a triangular promontory (the inner ward) defended by a curtain wall set with two great circular towers and a gatehouse. Beyond lies a rock-cut ditch, and an outer ward originally protected by a further wall and ditch.

The castle was built, as part of the Norman penetration of south Wales, in about 1225, though minor features probably date from 1372 when Edward III ordered the repair of the castle owing to the imminent threat of a French landing in Pembrokeshire. The castle fell to the Welsh in 1405 at the height of Owain Glyndwr's revolt. Possibly it was not repaired subsequently. At all events it played no role in the Civil War and by that time was probably already ruinous.

When built early in the 13th century, Cilgerran embodied the newest military conceptions. The two great towers which dominate the inner ward are circular, and thus more efficient than the old rectangular type of tower. They also have a deep salient: more than half of the east tower stands outside the curtain wall, enabling the defenders' fire effectively to rake the curtain.

Finally there is no keep. Instead, the towers constitute a linked strongwork at the point of greatest danger. This facilitated a less passive type of defence, and foreshadows the imposing keepless castles that were to be evolved before the end of the 13th century.

Dalton Castle, Lancashire

On A590, in the centre of Dalton-in-Furness

Dalton was once the capital town of Furness, but this fortified tower is all that survives of its former state. The castle is a good example of the pele towers erected in the north as a defence against Scottish raids, and was probably built by the monks of Furness Abbey in the 14th century. After the Dissolution, 'the tower was in great ruin and decay'. It later became the courthouse of the lords of the manor, the Dukes of Buccleuch, and was in use as such until the 20th century. The present Duke gave the castle to the Trust in 1965.

Dalton Castle

An unbroken rectangle, with rubble walls five feet thick surmounted by a defensive parapet, the tower must have been a useful strongpoint in the late Middle Ages. The upper floors are reached by a spiral staircase in the thickness of the wall. One or two of the Gothic two-light windows in the uppermost storey are original. The rest are 19th-century replacements.

Skenfrith Castle, Gwent

6 miles north-west of Monmouth, 12 miles north-east of Abergavenny, on north side of the B4521 Abergavenny/Ross-on-Wye road

The Normans reached the pastoral valley of the Monnow above Monmouth soon after the Conquest, and for protection against the raiding Welsh threw up a motte and fortified it with bank and ditch. Early in the 13th century Hubert de Burgh, Chief Justiciar to King John and Henry III, built the existing castle. As there were no earlier stone defences, the military engineer had free play, and the result is a perfect example of the type of small castle evolved in the early 13th century.

The castle consists of a circular central keep which was placed on the summit of the old motte and set within a quadrangular curtain wall defended by a circular tower at each corner. The keep was of sufficient height to enable the garrison to sweep the ground beyond the curtain and to provide covering fire for the men on the wall walks. Against the south curtain stood the great hall, which has long since disappeared, though a scar in the curtain wall marks the position of the fireplace. A moat some forty-five feet wide surrounded the castle on three sides, and on the fourth the river Monnow washed the walls.

Providentially for us, Skenfrith had little later history, and no work seems to have been carried out after the middle of the 13th century. The original plan is thus unobscured and Hubert de Burgh's feudal stronghold, now on the edge of a quiet Gwent village, cannot have been very different when he built it, probably in about 1201-5.

Skenfrith Castle; The keep

Tattershall Castle, Lincolnshire

3½ miles south-east of Woodhall Spa, on south side of the A153 Sleaford/Louth road

Visible for miles across the Lincolnshire levels, the great keep at Tattershall, over a hundred feet high, is almost all that remains of the elaborate castle built in 1434–45 by Ralph Cromwell, Lord Treasurer to Henry VI. Though the double moat which protected them is still there, the walls have gone, and the keep which once looked on the enclosed inner ward of the castle now stands in isolation.

At the date when Tattershall was built, square keeps had long been out of fashion, and there is much here – for instance, the large two-light windows on all sides of the keep – to indicate that the Lord Treasurer's Castle was for show and comfort rather than security. The keep was in effect a splendid country mansion dressed to resemble the great defensive keeps or donjons of the 12th century.

One of the finest and earliest examples of East Anglian brickwork, Tattershall keep is a most unusual building. With four hexagonal corner towers, it rises through four storeys to a roof-gallery built out on corbels and said to be unique. The brickwork of the exterior is remarkable enough, but perhaps the skill of the bricklayers is best seen in such interior features as the moulded brick vaulting of passages, window recesses, turret rooms, and not least in the twisting brick staircase.

The carved stone chimneypieces, fine examples of late Gothic work, are pleasantly associated with the man who saved Tattershall in the 20th century. The Castle, unoccupied since 1693, was ruinous when Lord Curzon of Kedleston bought it in 1911. The fireplaces had actually been removed and had reached London on their way to America; Lord Curzon was able to recover them, and they were replaced at Tattershall when he repaired, and saved, the castle. He bequeathed it to the Trust in 1926. A small museum has been established to illustrate the history of the castle.

Tattershall Castle

Opposite:
Alfriston Clergy House

Ecclesiastical Buildings

Alfriston Clergy House, East Sussex

4 miles north-east of Seaford on B2108

> A good man was ther of religioun,
> And was a povre Persoun of a toun;
> But riche he was in holy thoght and werk.

Chaucer's poor parson, the only type of cleric for which the poet felt affection and respect, lived in just such a modest dwelling as the Alfriston Clergy House. Designed for a small community of parish priests, it was built in about 1350, in the appalling aftermath of the Black Death which in 1348–9 reduced the population of England from perhaps four million to two and a half, and left half the land untilled, and thus villages and manors ruined or abandoned.

The setting of the clergy house is delightful. It lies near the Saxon church and on the edge of the village green, close to the river Cuckmere running through its downland valley. Built of oak framing, with wattle and daub walls and a thatched roof, the building contained separate apartments, and a common hall for dining and recreation open to the roof with large tie-beams and moulded kingposts. By the 19th century, the house had been converted into labourers' cottages and altered almost beyond recognition. In 1896 it was bought for £10 by the National Trust, the second property and the first building to be acquired, and carefully restored. It is one of very few clergy houses to have survived.

Buckingham Chantry Chapel, Buckinghamshire

On Market Hill

Chantry chapels were buildings endowed for the singing of Mass in perpetuity, usually for the soul of the founder. The Chantry Chapel of St John, the oldest building in Buckingham, was established in 1260. It was largely rebuilt in 1475 and at the Reformation became a school. It continued as such until 1907.

The most interesting feature of the little rubble-built chapel is the Norman doorway, which probably is earlier than the building itself and is believed to have been brought from elsewhere. The semicircular outer arch is enriched with characteristic chevron moulding and the inner arch carries a curious design resembling linked pointed arches. There are a piscina and a two-light window that date from the 15th-century rebuilding, and the west gallery incorporates some elaborate 17th-century poppyhead bench-ends. The chantry was much restored by Gilbert Scott in 1875.

Buckingham Chantry Chapel; The Norman doorway

Cartmel Priory Gatehouse, Cumbria

2 miles west of Grange-over-Sands via B5277; 4 miles west of Lindale, turning off A590 at Cartmel signpost

The grounds of the Augustinian priory of Cartmel, founded in the 12th century, were in due course separated from the profane world by a curtain wall and gatehouse. The gatehouse built about 1330–40 has the character of a fortified tower, and resembles many such towers erected when the Lake District was subject to Border warfare.

Mussenden Temple, Co. Londonderry

Lacock village, Wiltshire

Clevedon Court, Avon; c. 1320; Entrance front, with the chapel window on the first floor to the right of the porch

Houghton Mill, Cambridgeshire

Cartmel Priory
Gatehouse

At the Dissolution the fine monastery church happily survived, but with the exception of the gatehouse the domestic buildings were demolished. The gatehouse was probably spared because it was also the court house of the manor and an obviously useful building. In the early 17th century it was converted into a 'Publicke Schoolhouse' and such it remained until 1790. The conversion was probably responsible for the removal of a turret and battlements and the insertion of the later windows. The school's most eminent alumnus was Edmund Law, later Master of St John's College, Cambridge, and Bishop of Carlisle.

By the 1920s the gatehouse had seriously deteriorated. It was repaired and restored by a local enthusiast who recognized its importance as a pre-Reformation building. In 1946 it was made over to the Trust.

Hailes Abbey, Gloucestershire

1 mile east of the A46 Stratford-upon-Avon/Cheltenham road; 2 miles north-east of Winchcomb

Hailes, one of the last Cistercian houses to be founded in England, dates from about a century after the order was first established in this country. The Cistercians, deriving their name from the Abbey of Cîteaux in Burgundy, sought a return to the more austere monastic life of the late 11th and early 12th centuries. Combining their liturgical duties with manual labour,

Hailes Abbey; Cloister ruins

they were notable farmers and their abbeys were, like Hailes, usually situated in remote and secluded country.

Hailes was founded by Richard, Earl of Cornwall, the brother of Henry III, in fulfilment of a vow made on escaping shipwreck in the Isles of Scilly in 1242. The Abbey church was dedicated in 1251, five years after building began, and in 1270 Earl Richard's son presented the Abbey with the 'Blood of Hailes'. This phial of the Redeemer's blood, authenticated by Pope Urban IV, made the Abbey a centre of pilgrimage. Even so its fortune did not always prosper. By 1412 there were only two monks, no lay brothers, and income had fallen to £100. Fortunes revived in the last decades before the Dissolution, but in 1542 the estate and buildings were sold and the church demolished. Though parts of the complex were transformed, as often happened, into a gentleman's country house, and were so used until the 18th century, by 1800 practically everything had been demolished and the stone used for building elsewhere. Today only rudimentary walls, parts of the chapter house, one or two gateways, and three sides of the cloisters remain above ground, but excavation has revealed the impressive plan of the church and monastic buildings.

The plan, with one exception to be mentioned below, reveals the characteristic Cistercian pattern. The cloister, to enjoy the sun, lies to the south of the Abbey nave, and the refectory extends further southward from the cloister, thus removing the effluvia of kitchen and dining room as far as possible from the church. On the east side of the cloister, abutting on the south transept of the church, are situated successively the chapter house and the dormitory. The cellarium, the lay-brothers' quarters, lies in the usual position to the west of the cloister.

The cruciform Abbey church must have been imposing in the severe Cistercian fashion and is over 340 feet long. But it departed in one graceful particular from the Cistercian pattern. A relic as distinguished as the 'Blood of Hailes' demanded a special setting, and after 1271 a chevet or curved apse with a coronet of five polygonal chapels was added to the square east end.

Here a splendid ark-like shrine contained and exhibited the precious phial. Such chevets, associated with French Gothic, are distinctly rare in England.

Some impression of the splendour of the monastery in the late Middle Ages, and of the workmanship which went to its building and decoration, is to be obtained in the adjoining museum, which like the ruins of the Abbey is now under the care of the Department of the Environment. It contains, with much else of interest, some of the wonderful carved bosses which adorned the 13th-century ceiling of the chapter house, and a collection of rare armorial tiles found in the ruins.

Keld Chapel, Cumbria

At Shap, south-west of A6

The small and appealing hamlet of Keld, on the banks of the river Lowther, was perhaps built by Shap Abbey, which is a mile or so distant, to house tenants of the monastery employed in milling.

'Keld' is from a Norse word meaning a spring, and the village may derive its name from a well, no doubt once a holy well, close to Keld Chapel. Whether the latter was a chantry like the Trust's chapel at Buckingham (see p. 320), or was erected by the Abbot of Shap for the convenience of the Keld tenantry, is in dispute. Among the most modest of ecclesiastical buildings, it is low, rubble-built, and slate-roofed. The date, as the uncusped lights of the east window suggest, is early 16th century.

Keld Chapel from the south-east

Mount Grace Priory, North Yorkshire

6 miles north-east of Northallerton, $\frac{1}{2}$ mile east of A19 and $\frac{1}{2}$ mile south of its junction with A172

With a steep wooded hill rising behind its grey walls, Mount Grace has a tranquillity and a beauty, particularly in spring when the cloisters are scattered with daffodils, that seems to reflect the lives of the good Carthusian monks who worked and prayed in this pleasant place for nearly a century and a half.

Stemming from the mother-house of the Grande Chartreuse, the Carthusian Order reached England late in the 12th century. The strict and solitary rule, however, made little headway until the middle of the 14th century, and Mount Grace, licensed in 1398 by Richard II, was only the eighth foundation in this country. The founder was the Duke of Surrey, grandson of the Fair Maid of Kent. Beheaded two years later for rebellion against the new King, Henry IV, the Duke's body was in due course brought to Mount Grace for burial.

The history of the Monastery was comparatively uneventful, and on its dissolution in 1539 the prior and convent surrendered quietly to Henry VIII and were pensioned off. Though it passed at once into lay hands, the priory strangely enough seems to have undergone no major alteration until 1654, when the range of buildings adjoining the entrance-gate was converted into a small country house. The property came to the Trust through the Treasury in 1953 and, apart from the house, was placed in the care of what is now the Department of the Environment.

Reflecting the special nature of the Carthusian rule, Carthusian monasteries differ from all others. The monks were in some degree hermits and lived in seclusion not only from the world but from their fellows. They met for the office in the convent church, but there was no common dormitory and meals were taken in the refectory only on special occasions. This dictated a different layout for Carthusian buildings. Each monk had his separate cell, with a garden attached, situated round the cloisters, and this in turn meant that Carthusian cloisters were larger than others. At Mount Grace the longest side of the cloister, an irregular quadrangle, measures 272 feet.

Nowhere in this country is the Carthusian plan better seen than at Mount

Mount Grace Priory

Grace, where some cells are relatively well preserved. They were of two storeys, with a workshop on the upper floor, and at ground level a lobby, a living room, and a bedroom which also served as an oratory. For each cell there was piped water to a tap – Charterhouses were notable for their efficient water supply – and a garderobe projecting over the precinct well above a drain. Beside the cell doorway giving on the cloister, there was a service hatch for food brought from the kitchens. The hatch has a right-angled bend so that server and served could not see each other.

The long narrow priory church also survives. Originally a plain aisleless rectangle, it acquired, probably in the 14th century, a tower and lateral chapels. The nave, as might be expected in a monastic church, is much shorter than the choir and presbytery designed for the use of the monks.

Ramsey Abbey Gatehouse, Cambridgeshire

On outskirts of Ramsey, 10 miles south-east of Peterborough on B1096

The Abbey was dedicated in 974, and like the older foundation of Ely stood originally on an island in the fens. It developed into one of the most important monastic houses in East Anglia. Little remains of the Abbey except the Lady Chapel and the gatehouse.

The latter is incomplete, for half the building was carried off to Hinching-brooke after the Dissolution. It dates from about 1500. In the ornate late Gothic style, it has panelled buttresses, and fleuron and quatrefoil friezes both round the doorway and the oriel window above.

Ealdorman Eolwin, half-king of East Anglia and foster brother of the Saxon King Eadgar, collaborated with St Oswald, then Archbishop of York, in founding the monastery. Eolwin's remains lie in a marble tomb of about 1230.

Ramsey Abbey Gatehouse

Tithe Barns

Tithe barns, for storing the tithes, received from the tenants of church lands and payable in kind, are usually associated with wealthy monastic foundations. As such foundations held large estates in different parts of the country, tithe barns are not necessarily situated near the abbey or priory to which they belonged.

Exemplifying the beauty of good functional buildings, tithe barns were usually built of random stone with ashlar dressings, and roofed with stone tiles. There was an open timber roof, much of the weight often being carried on two rows of oak posts resting on stone bases, which give to the interiors something of the effect of long church naves. A gabled porch to admit carts was sometimes a feature of each side of the building, and in one of these porches a small upper chamber or tallat loft was often inserted to accommodate the *grangerius*, the monk or bailiff in charge of the barn and responsible for receiving and checking the tithes.

Among the largest structures of the Middle Ages, the barns were vast. The largest recorded was that at Cholsey in Berkshire, now demolished, 303 feet long. It was rivalled by that at Abbotsbury in Dorset, 282 feet long, and now only partially roofed. The largest extant barn still wholly roofed is apparently that at Frindsbury in Kent (219 ft).

Among the larger medieval barns owned by the Trust are those at East Riddlesden Hall, Great Coxwell, Buckland Abbey and Middle Littleton. The Court Barn at West Pennard in Somerset, though on a smaller scale, is beautifully conceived and was once combined, most unusually, with a dovecote, the nesting boxes being situated in the thickness of an external wall.

Ashleworth, Gloucestershire

6 miles north of Gloucester, $1\frac{1}{2}$ miles east of Hartpury on A417

Much of the charm of the barn derives from its position between the Court, a little-changed house of the mid-15th century, and the tidal Severn with the remains of an old wharf and a riverside inn.

The magnificent barn, rather later than the Court, was built about 1500. Ten bays long, of limestone with ashlar dressings, it is still in active use. The timbering of queenpost construction carried an immense stone slate roof. The usual gabled porches on the flanks have curved wooden lintels. A hundred and twenty-five feet long, it is comparable to the famous barn at Great Coxwell.

Ashleworth; Tithe barn

Bredon, Hereford & Worcester

3 miles north-east of Tewkesbury, just east of M5 on B4080

Built, and beautifully built, of local limestone, with dressed quoins, plinths, and buttresses, the barn belonged to the see of Worcester until it passed to the Crown in the 16th century. The stone-shingled roof is of exceptional pitch: thus the gabled end walls rise forty-two feet, while the side walls are only about twelve and a half feet high. The walls are pierced with narrow eyelets to provide light, and with numerous square six-inch holes for ventilation. A feature of special interest is the tallat loft surviving above one of the two gabled cart-porches on the east side of the building. The porch was heightened in the 15th century to accommodate it, and the tallat is reached by a small external staircase. Its fireplace, which must have been very necessary, is provided with an octagonal stone chimney.

Bredon

Great Coxwell, Oxfordshire

West of Faringdon, off the B4019 Faringdon/Highworth road

Built in the middle of the 13th century, the barn belonged to the Cistercians of Beaulieu Abbey in Hampshire, to whom King John granted the lands round about 1204. The barn is 152 feet long; its scale is conveyed by the fact that the 'nave' of oak posts which supports the original timber roof rests on stone bases seven feet high. The original doorways are those to the porches on the sides of the barn. There was formerly a tallat above the west porch. The doorways in the ends of the building are 18th-century introductions, and were perhaps necessary to accommodate the larger wagons of the period.

*Great Coxwell;
Interior*

Middle Littleton, Hereford & Worcester

3 miles north-east of Evesham, east of B4085

Once standing among orchards, now in the heart of market-garden land, Middle Littleton village still preserves a fine group of church, 17th-century manor and tithe barn, one of the biggest of its kind. According to documentary evidence it was built by Abbot Ombersley of the Benedictine foundation at Evesham between 1367 and 1379 but carbon-14 analysis suggests that it could be about a hundred years older and the building style supports this theory. Stone built and buttressed, with ten bays and two wagon porches of which one survives, externally it is 140 feet long and 32 feet wide. Internally the framing consists of an angled bay at either end and eight base-cruck tresses dividing the bays. There are windbraces throughout the length of the roof, which is covered with stone tiles.

Houses

Anglesey Abbey, Cambridgeshire

In Lode village, 6 miles north-east of Cambridge on the B1102 Cambridge/Mildenhall road

An Augustinian priory (never an abbey), Anglesey was founded in 1135. Almost exactly 400 years later the priory was dissolved and the small community of black-robed canons was dispersed. The many owners over the next 400 years included two persons of note: Thomas Hobson, the Cambridge carrier to whom we owe the phrase 'Hobson's choice', and Sir George Downing, the eponymous founder of Downing College. Today these owners seem almost as insubstantial as the vanished friars. They belong to a shadowy ruined house that was transformed as decisively as the surrounding landscape when in 1926 Anglesey was bought by Huttleston Broughton, later 1st Lord Fairhaven. The existing house and garden were his remarkable creation over the forty years that followed.

Lord Fairhaven was a dedicated and immensely wealthy patron of the arts, and to contain the extraordinary collections which make Anglesey so interesting and so unusual a house he transformed the old priory. But his most remarkable achievement was to evoke from the unpromising fen landscape a garden unique in the 20th century, a garden that challenges in conception and scale the masterpieces of the Georgian era. This garden, the house and its contents were left to the Trust on his death in 1966.

Of the original priory little remains but the chapter house and the vaulted Canons' Parlour, the latter now the dining room. Some time about 1600, when most of the ecclesiastical buildings had been demolished, the chapter house was provided with mullioned and transomed windows and a typical Jacobean porch. It became a country house, and on the garden front looks like any manor-house of the period.

The real interest of Anglesey lies not in its architecture but in its contents. The interior bears little resemblance to an English country mansion; with its sumptuous furnishings and assemblage of rare continental works of art, it recalls rather one of the palaces of Long Island. There was in fact a strong American connection, for Lord Fairhaven's father made a fortune in the United States and his mother was an heiress from New York. The muted lighting, the silver gilt, the jewelled crucifixes, the oriental hardstone, the Italian mosaics, the bronzes, the medieval figure sculpture, and the tapestries, contribute to a richly exotic atmosphere that it would be difficult to parallel in this country.

The visitor passes bemused from the red lacquer furniture of the Ming dynasty to Renaissance cabinets, Louis XV commodes and Sir Robert Walpole's superb writing desk, from Ch'ien Lung vases to Blue John cassolettes, from an Egyptian bronze cat 2,500 years old to a life-size

Anglesey Abbey; The Canons' Parlour

terracotta goat by Rysbrack, from the earliest known Garter, bestowed by Henry VIII on the Emperor Maximilian, to the rapier which belonged to Prince Rupert and to Gainsborough's elegant paint box. The variety of impact is astonishing. Among the pictures are two of Claude's noblest works, Constable's great view of Waterloo Bridge, and paintings by Cuyp, Oudry, Wootton, Gainsborough, and Bonington.

While not everyone will respond with the same enthusiasm to the rich eclecticism of the interior, it is impossible to be in two minds about the garden. An imaginative and successful combination of formal and landscape gardening, it is conceived with a liberality and expresses a sense of scale that this country has hardly known since the Georgian era. The contrasts between controlled geometrical design and free landscaping are beautifully calculated, and the eye is constantly surprised and satisfied. The grasp of scale is apparent in the splendid urns and statuary, placed with an assurance worthy of the *grand siècle*. With less than half a century behind them, the Anglesey gardens already speak with an authority far beyond their years. By A.D. 2050 they will probably be the only major layout in England that is not past maturity.

The features of the garden which best emphasize its quality and proportion are the majestic semicircular herbaceous garden framed by beech hedges, the Emperor's Walk over a quarter of a mile long and set with Imperial busts, the Daffodil Walk, and the hurriedly conceived Great Avenue. The garden has also much to offer the specialist. The herbaceous borders feature *Crambe cordifolia, Aruncus sylvester*, thalictrums, verbascums, lactucas, scented peonies, salvias (*S. turkestanica, haematodes, virgata*), white flowered *Argentia, Dictamnus albus*, and a variety of delphiniums. Among the specimen trees on the Arboretum Lawn are fastigiate Dawyck beech, Algerian oak (*Quercus mirbeckii*), a great sycamore (*Acer pseudoplatanus* 'Worleii'), a Japanese hop hornbeam (*Ostrya japonica*), the maidenhair tree (*Ginkgo biloba*), and such flowering trees as Indian chestnut (*Aesculus indica*) and Indian bean (*Catalpa bignonioides*); the tulip tree, Judas tree (*Cercis siliquastrum*) and magnolias (*M. denudata, M. soulangiana* and its varieties 'Alba Superba' and 'Rustica Rubra') are all to be found.

Barrington Court, Somerset

At the east end of Barrington village, $\frac{1}{2}$ mile east of B3168, 3 miles north-east of Ilminster

The 'wet end of Somerset', the low-lying fertile countryside south of Taunton, still seems remote, untouched by changes in taste and fashion. Yet here, in the mid-16th century, arose a country house whose traditional medieval architecture is spiced with Renaissance features. For example, the south (originally the entrance) front is symmetric, designed on the E-plan which is often regarded as an Elizabethan innovation. The simple vertical lines of the house, built of honey-coloured Ham Hill stone, lead the eye upward past dormer windows to the many-gabled roof, where twisted spiral chimneystacks and finials, topped with scalework caps, are set along the skyline like giant chessmen.

For many years Henry Daubeney has been named as the builder of Barrington Court. The property had belonged to his family from the 13th century and when he inherited it in 1508 there was probably an old house on the site of the present buildings. Henry gravitated to the court of Henry VIII, financing his extravagant way of life by disposing of his country properties; in 1543 he sold Barrington to his cousin, Sir Thomas Arundell, retaining only a life interest. Soon after his death in 1547 the property was purchased by William Clifton, a wealthy Norfolk merchant who lived there from 1559 until 1564. It is now suggested that he may have built Barrington Court, because a mid-16th-century date accords better with its architecture and there is no documentary evidence to suggest it was built by the Daubeneys. Subsequently the property was acquired by the Strode family, who built the brick stable block adjoining the house about 1670 and lived at Barrington for a hundred and fifty years.

During the 19th century, the property was repeatedly sold and gradually fell into disrepair. In 1907 it was bought by the National Trust, the first sizeable country house to come into its possession and still the only one with a garden designed by Gertrude Jekyll. Not until the 1920s was restoration possible, when the late Col. A. A. Lyle completely restored and refurbished it. Thus Barrington, a house which curiously blends elements of the Middle Ages and the Renaissance, again became habitable.

Barrington Court;
The south front,
originally the
entrance front

Bradley Manor, Devon

At west edge of Newton Abbot, off the A381 Newton Abbot/Totnes road

The manor lies low in the Lemon valley and on three sides rise steep wooded slopes. Though there had been a house on the site at least since the 13th century, it is the surviving 15th-century east wing that makes Bradley Manor one of the best examples of domestic Gothic in the West Country.

Bradley Manor; East front, with the chapel on the right

The remarkable east elevation, roughcast and limewashed as it has always been, with its picturesque oriels and gables, represents three stages of 15th-century building. Initially, there was a great hall of the usual medieval type with a service block at one end and a private block with parlour and solar at the other. An external porch gave access to the screens passage of the hall (the present screens are a Jacobean replacement). This great hall of 1420, with a collar-beam roof, is now concealed by the gabled east façade, behind which lie an ante-chapel and oriel chamber added in 1495. The additions took in the original porch of 1420, and the round-headed entrance on the east front is none other than the old porch doorway. Meanwhile, in 1427, a chapel had been added to the parlour and solar blocks at the north end of the great hall. Its splendid Perpendicular window is one of the features of a later Gothic composition that is delightfully varied and informal.

In the south wing there survives the undercroft of the earlier great hall of the mid-13th century. This wing has been considerably altered, but contains an elegant panelled room of about 1695 with a contemporary plaster cornice.

In 1909 Cecil Firth, an archaeologist, bought Bradley Manor, and restored it with much thought and care. His daughter presented the house to the Trust in 1938.

Buckland Abbey, Devon

6 miles south of Tavistock, 11 miles north of Plymouth, 1 mile south of Buckland Monachorum, west of the A386 Plymouth/Tavistock road

A Cistercian abbey was founded at Buckland in 1278. The remote, withdrawn site was just such as the white-robed monks favoured, and their large estates, which are said to have amounted to 20,000 acres, must have profited from their customary agricultural expertise. The parts of the 13th-century abbey which still stand indicate that here, as elsewhere, the style of their building was massive, simple, and without ostentation; though it seems that the nature of the terrain compelled them to place their cloister and domestic buildings north of the church rather than south, as was the usual monastic practice. In 1539 the last abbot surrendered Buckland to the Crown and the monks – only twelve by that date – departed after a tenure of 260 years.

Within two years the abbey was sold by the Crown for £233 to Sir Richard Grenville. He apparently did little to convert the monastic buildings, and it was his grandson, Sir Richard of the *Revenge*, the most famous of the Grenvilles, who re-modelled Buckland as a country house, albeit of unusual character. Most people possessed of monastic property after the Dissolution demolished the church and adapted the domestic buildings (see p. 28). Not so Richard Grenville. He reserved for his house the nave, the crossing, and the chancel. He retained the square tower over the crossing, which is so prominent a feature of Buckland, and between the soaring walls of the church he inserted three floors and created his living rooms, including a one-storeyed great hall, with a fireplace dated 1576 and with contemporary plaster ceiling and frieze portraying scenes of the chase. The ancient church remained, and remains, visible in innumerable details – in blocked and unblocked windows, in vaults, arches, and mouldings – and gives the house its curious, slightly uncomfortable, atmosphere. The conversion throws an interesting light on the attitude of the hero of the *Revenge* towards the Church.

Buckland Abbey

In 1581 the abbey-house was bought by Sir Francis Drake, lately returned from his circumnavigation of the world. The tang of the sea was to be long associated with this bit of green Devon countryside, for as late as the second half of the 18th century the Drake family produced two vice-admirals. Sir Francis left little trace of his occupation, and Buckland remained largely unaltered until about 1770, when a Georgian chamber and the main staircase with its dog-gates were added.

In 1813 the property passed to remote collaterals, and in 1948 was acquired by the Trust. It is managed by the Plymouth Corporation, who have established a naval museum with Grenville and Drake relics, not least Drake's immortal drum, and a local folk museum. Behind the house is a buttressed medieval tithe barn, 180 feet long (see p. 326).

Clevedon Court, Somerset *(see colour plate facing p. 321)*

$1\frac{1}{2}$ miles east of Clevedon on the B3130 Bristol road

Though there remains an earlier tower of the 13th century, the manor house was built by Sir John de Clevedon in about 1320, and is one of the few houses of the period to have survived. Its most striking and unusual feature is the large window with reticulated tracery that lights the chapel on the entrance front. In plan Clevedon Court is, for the most part, typical of its age. A projecting two-storey porch gives access to a screens passage. This forms the spine of the building, dividing, in customary fashion, buttery and kitchens from the great hall and the living quarters of the lord of the manor.

On one side, three linked 14th-century arches lead to the service quarters and to what later became the Justice Room, so called because the Lord of the Manor as Justice of the Peace there dealt summarily with local misdemeanours. On the other side of the screens passage lies the great hall, with Sir John's 14th-century pointed windows and octagonal chimney shafts. The 16th century added the fireplace and the north and south windows, while the coved plaster ceiling was an 18th-century introduction. At the dais end of the hall is a deep projection entered through a fine 14th-century arch. Such a recess or alcove, unusual at the period, anticipates both the oriels and little hall chambers of Tudor times.

Clevedon Court was acquired in 1709 by Abraham Elton, a wealthy Bristol merchant. His descendants, dedicated and intelligent, were to be useful Members of Parliament, inventors, writers, patrons of the arts.

Lamb, Landor, Tennyson and Thackeray were among the men of letters who knew Clevedon more or less intimately in the time of Sir Charles Elton (1778–1853). His grandson in about 1880 created the 'Elton Ware', which enjoyed an international reputation, and of which a representative collection is now shown in the 13th-century kitchen. Sir Arthur Elton, 10th baronet, ensured the transfer of the house to the Trust in 1961.

The garden that lies below a south-facing and splendidly wooded hillside is of considerable interest. Its terraces, which probably follow the lines of

334

Clevedon Court

earlier defence fosses, may be of 18th-century construction. The Esmond or Pretty Terrace, so called from its encrustation of small beds in Victorian times, terminates at one end in an 18th-century octagonal garden house and at the other in a Gothick niche of perhaps later design.

Compton Castle, Devon

4 miles west of Torquay off B3203, 1 mile north of Marldon; off the A381 Newton Abbot/Totnes road

For 600 years, since shortly before the battle of Crécy and the Black Death of 1348, Compton has been, with a single break, the home of the Gilbert family. The castle dates mainly from the 14th–16th centuries and is among the few fortified houses to survive without later alterations and additions. But the paramount interest of Compton is historical. In the 16th century, the Gilbert brothers, John, Humphrey and Adrian, were part of the closely related group of West Country gentlemen who formed the core of Elizabethan naval defence and enterprise and led the movement of colonial expansion in America.

After the death of Otto Gilbert in 1547, his widow married Walter Raleigh of Fardell and became the mother of Sir Walter Raleigh, who was in part brought up with his three Gilbert half-brothers at Compton. One of them, John Gilbert, inherited Compton and played a considerable part in the defence of the country at the time of the Armada, and in the last decades of Elizabeth's reign, when we were more or less continuously at war with Spain. He became Sheriff and Deputy Lieutenant of Devon and Vice-Admiral of the Western Coast. His brother, Humphrey Gilbert, was 'at all

Compton Castle

times ready to take anything in hand for the service of Her Majesty and Country'. He served in the defence of Le Havre in 1562–3 and later in Ireland, where he was knighted by Sir Henry Sidney. In 1566, he wrote *A Discourse of a Discoverie for a new Passage to Cataia*, which may have inspired Frobisher's voyages. In 1573 he drafted a plan for a University of London, 'Queen Elizabeth's Academy', to train 'Her Majesty's Wards and others . . . of the nobility and gentry' for the Navy and Army; and in 1577 he presented the Queen with a treatise on '*How Her Majesty may annoy the King of Spain*'.

Sir Humphrey's claim to immortality rests, however, on the decisive part he played in the early colonization of America. In 1578, at the age of forty, he received the first Letters Patent granted by the Crown for the 'planting' of an English colony. His first expedition set sail from Plymouth later in the same year.

This first enterprise came to nothing, but in June 1583 Gilbert led a further expedition from Plymouth of five ships and 260 men, which included the *Golden Hinde*. They reached Newfoundland on 3 August and Gilbert 'entered here in the right of the Crowne of England'. Later with three ships he explored the coast southward as far as Cape Breton. After his flagship went ashore in a gale, and was lost with almost a hundred men, he decided to return to England. On 9 September 1583, in bad weather near the Azores, the *Squirrel* with the commander on board was 'in a moment devoured and swallowed up in the sea'. Gilbert was last seen 'sitting abaft with a book in his hand giving forth signs of joy'. The only known portrait of this man, who represents the quintessence of the Elizabethan spirit, hangs at Compton.

The movement across the Atlantic continued. Adrian Gilbert and his associates, who included Walsingham, Drake, the Raleighs, Hawkins and Franklin, obtained fresh Letters Patent for exploration of the north-west passage to China. In 1584 and 1586 Sir Walter Raleigh established a short-lived plantation on Roanoke Island in Virginia. In 1606 Letters Patent were granted by James I for the planting of two colonies. An expedition sailing from London in 1607 established the first permanent English settlement in America at Jamestown, Virginia. The second settlement, the Plymouth colony, was established by Raleigh Gilbert, Sir Humphrey's younger son, on what is now the coast of Maine. A year later, in 1608, when news reached the colony that Raleigh Gilbert had inherited the family estates at Compton, the colonists returned home.

The estates which Raleigh Gilbert had inherited were sold in 1800. Happily Compton Castle was bought back in 1930 by Commander Walter Raleigh Gilbert, eighteenth in line of descent from Sir Humphrey. He restored the house and rebuilt the great hall which had become ruinous in the 18th century. The late Commander and Mrs Gilbert gave the property to the Trust in 1951 and Mrs Gilbert continues to live in the castle.

When its medieval defences were complete with towers, gun-ports, loopholes, lookouts, a crenellated portcullis, and a curtain wall twenty feet high, Compton Castle, though far from impregnable, must have been strong enough to protect the manor against the French raids which were so regular a feature of the first half of the 16th century. Tucked in a steeply-sided coomb and invisible from a distance, its position, secure as a rabbit burrow, was an added safeguard against surprise attack.

The great hall, buttery, pantry and solar were built about 1350; the house was enlarged about 1370 with the addition of a larger solar, the chapel, watch tower, and kitchen. Its unaltered medieval layout does little to recall the architecture of Queen Elizabeth's dazzling court, but when the great Tudor mansions were going up all over England the Gilberts tended to be otherwise engaged.

Cotehele, Cornwall

On west bank of the Tamar, 2 miles west of Calstock by footpath (6 miles by road), 8 miles south-west of Tavistock, 14 miles from Plymouth via Saltash Bridge

Sheltered by woods and above the steep banks of the Tamar, which here loops to the west before emerging into Plymouth Sound, rise the grey granite walls of Cotehele. This highly romantic house is among the most authentic surviving examples of a knightly dwelling built in the late medieval tradition.

William Edgcumbe, who married the Cotehele heiress, took possession of this delectable place in 1353. His descendant, Sir Richard Edgcumbe, among the most colourful figures in Cornish history, confirmed the family fortunes. Having revolted against Richard III, he was forced to fly to Brittany, where he joined Henry Tudor. He returned to fight at Bosworth in 1485 and to enjoy the favour and friendship of the new king. He and his son, Sir Piers, were chiefly responsible for remodelling the old fortified manor which stood on the site of the present house. The Edgcumbes continued to prosper, acquiring in the 18th century a barony, a viscountcy and an earldom. On the succession of the 6th Earl in 1944, Cotehele was offered to the government in satisfaction of estate duty and in due course was transferred to the Trust.

Before the end of the 17th century the Edgcumbes moved to a grander

Cotehele; The courtyard

mansion, Mount Edgcumbe near Plymouth. The remote house above the Tamar was left much to itself. This was providential, for the Tudor buildings thus remained remarkably unaltered and Cotehele acquired the tranquil atmosphere, the sense of time distilled, that is so striking.

Beside the short approach to the house lies Sir Richard Edgcumbe's barn, built soon after his return from Bosworth Field, and dominating the entrance front rises his gatehouse. Entering the courtyard round which Cotehele is built, we find him again in the Perpendicular east window of his chapel, and facing us across the courtyard lawn is the great hall added by his son, Sir Piers, in about 1520. Nothing seems to have changed, and even the east side of the courtyard, an alteration of much later date, tactfully preserves the architectural uniformity.

The great hall, one of the most impressive in the West Country, is unusual in that it seems never to have had screens; the entrance gives straight into the room and not into a screens passage in the normal medieval fashion. The fine open roof is decorated with moulded wind-braces, and the hall is furnished with armour, pewter and furniture, of the 16th and 17th centuries. The note of tradition and authenticity is immediate, and the same note is struck in the other Tudor rooms and in the chapel, where Cotehele time is still measured by the massive iron clock which Sir Richard installed before 1489. Most of the rooms are hung from floor to ceiling with 17th-century tapestries, a notable feature of Cotehele, and contain a rare collection of Jacobean and Stuart furniture. In such a house even the few fine early Georgian pieces seem almost an intrusion.

Whoever created the garden at Cotehele did it with a sure hand, for its conception suits the medieval house, and the stonework of terraces, pools and walls is firmly in the vernacular. Ancient sycamores flank the approach, and above a bowling green rises a large *Podocarpus salignus*, a native of Chile. Beyond the Retainer's Court to the west lies the orchard, which is strewn with daffodils in spring, and whence a gate in a low wall leads to the Upper Garden, with a formal pool containing an island and fed by a stream, and there are several good trees, including a yellow-twigged ash and a tulip tree. Fuchsias and blue African lilies grow in the raised border.

The upper walk in the orchard leads to a little dell filled with Japanese

Cotehele; The kitchen   *Cotehele; The great hall*

maples. Here, under a white wistaria, a door in a wall opens, with an element of surprise characteristic of the garden, on grass terraces below the east front of the house. On the house itself the Passion flower ripens its orange fruits, *Rosa bracteata* and other roses thrive, while the terraces overlook two big magnolias (*M. soulangiana*, and *M. s.* 'Rustica Rubra') guarding the view to the valley. Rosebeds, set with flowers for spring display, stretch along the length of the terraces.

Below, the sloping ground opens out into a deep valley. The overflow from a spring-filled pond cascades downward among primulas, irises, a fine specimen of *Davidia involucrata*, the 'ghost' or 'handkerchief' tree, ferns, and gunneras with their immense leaves. On one side rises an ancient dovecote, and along the banks in every direction grow rhododendrons, azaleas, hydrangeas, eucryphias, and hoherias. This planting gradually mingles with the native woodland that climbs from the depths of the valley. Here paths thread their way down towards the glint of the Tamar.

Great Chalfield Manor, Wiltshire

$1\frac{1}{2}$ miles from Holt, off the B3053 Bradford-on-Avon/Melksham road

Rebuilt about 1480 on the site of an earlier fortified manor-house, Great Chalfield is among the few surviving houses of the period in this country. The property forms a neat complex, comprising dwelling house, farm buildings and parish church, enclosed by a narrow moat. Set close to the river Avon in placid open countryside, the house is the centre of a medium-sized agricultural estate worked today as it has been for 900 years.

The builder of the house was Thomas Tropnell, a wealthy Wiltshire landowner and businessman, who made a fortune during the Wars of the Roses when a new middle class became prosperous on the ruins of the old feudal nobility. The older house was fortified. The foundations of the walls and bastions survive, and the moat has still to be crossed to reach the outer courtyard, from which an archway leads to the forecourt and the house. Architecturally Tropnell achieved a composition that was extraordinarily

Great Chalfield Manor

balanced for the 15th century: a great hall of conventional medieval type, two storeys high and lit from both sides, is flanked by gabled wings, with highly enriched oriel windows. The exterior is remarkable for the fine detail of the fenestration, arches and buttresses, and for the intricately carved stone figures on the gable ends. Modest in scale but perfectly proportioned, the house owes much to the yellowish-grey Corsham stone of which it is built.

The north or main front is, by some miracle, much as Tropnell left it in 1480. The south front was sympathetically restored and the south wing added about 1910.

The projecting west wing, built in the 18th century, was originally a farm building and faces the tiny 14th- or 15th-century church across the court-yard. Tropnell rebuilt the south chapel of the church and added the little projecting bellcote with crocketed octagonal spire. The moat forms the fourth side of the rectangle.

The plan of the interior follows the late medieval pattern. The great hall, entered directly from the porch, is screened at one end from the pantry and kitchen beyond and from the bedchamber that lies above; at the other end a spiral staircase leads to the solar or day chamber. Squints, in the unusual form of hollow masks, enable one to look down upon the hall. A rare feature for the period is the separate dining room beyond the screens between the hall and the kitchen. It contains a mural portrait of the builder, who resembles a Chinese mandarin as he sits grasping the arms of his chair.

The history of Chalfield Manor is well recorded. The Domesday Book mentions it as the property of Ernulf de Hesding, first Earl of Percy. It belonged to various branches of the Percy family until the 15th century. In the Civil War Chalfield was garrisoned by Parliamentary forces during 1644–6 and withstood a short siege. The 1st Duke of Kingston married the heiress to the estate, which his son sold in 1770. It remained in the hands of the Neale family until 1878 when it was acquired by the family who presented it to the Trust in 1943 and live there today.

Grey's Court, Oxfordshire

3 miles west of Henley, on right of road to Rotherfield Greys

The house derives its name from Lord de Grey who fought at Crécy, became one of the original Knights of the Garter, and was granted a licence to crenellate Grey's Court in 1347. Towards the end of the 15th century the de Grey line died out, and in 1538 Henry VIII secured the property to Francis Knollys, who was to be for many years Lord Treasurer of the Household to Queen Elizabeth. His son, an unattractive man who was probably the model for Shakespeare's Malvolio, succeeded in 1596. During his lifetime Grey's became associated with one of the most notorious murders of the 17th century. In 1613, in mysterious circumstances, Sir Thomas Overbury, the poet, died in the Tower of London. Within two years, Robert Carr, Earl of Somerset, the favourite of James I, and his wife Frances Howard, the reigning Jacobean beauty, were found guilty of his murder by poisoning. They were reprieved, but confined at Grey's Court during His Majesty's pleasure.

Today little remains of the de Greys' medieval courtyard house except the crenellated Great Tower of the 14th century and three smaller medieval towers. The present house, though its kitchen incorporates medieval features, is basically a gabled 16th-century building erected by the Knollys family, in an agreeable mixture of brick and stone, on the west side of the medieval courtyard. But constant occupation over the centuries has brought changes reflecting changing taste, which contribute a good deal to the charm of the house. The 17th century grafted an attractive oriel window on the south front, and the early 18th century added a small wing, while about 1760 the house acquired the splendid plasterwork which is to be seen at its best in the drawing room. It has been attributed to Roberts of Oxford, and the masterly decoration, with festoons of fruit and flowers and floral cornucopias, recalls his work in Christ Church library.

Grey's Court   Right: *The Great Tower*

The brick 16th-century outbuildings, such as the Old Stables, the Bachelor's Hall, and the Wellhouse, are part of the Knollys contribution. The well is 200 feet deep, and until the advent of mains water in 1914 supplied the house. The water was raised by a great wheel, turned by a donkey, which appears to be the largest surviving English example of a donkey wheel.

These outbuildings, the old walls, the ancient trees, and the green lawns are half the flavour of Grey's Court. The walls of the tithe barn enclose a garden of Japanese cherries; a medieval archway leads into a rose garden which in turn opens into a circular walled area planted long ago with old wistarias; the white flowers of the Tower Garden are reflected in a lily pond. More than many houses of greater architectural distinction Grey's Court is a place of atmosphere, a place where time has accumulated graciously.

Lacock Abbey, Wiltshire

3 miles south of Chippenham, east of A350

Lacock Abbey has been lived in continuously since Ela, Countess of Salisbury, founded the house for Augustinian nuns in 1232 in memory of her husband William de Longespée, and became the first Abbess. Her husband had witnessed Henry III's confirmation of Magna Carta in 1225 and the Lacock copy was treasured here until presented to the British Museum by Miss Matilda Talbot, who gave Lacock to the National Trust in 1944.

Lacock Abbey was not suppressed until 1539. The Commissioners found all in good order, and the nuns, 'of vertuous lyving', were given pensions. The estate was bought by Sir William Sharington, a Tudor profiteer of doubtful reputation but excellent architectural taste, who preserved most of the medieval building except the church and converted the Abbey into his dwelling house, employing a craftsman with a serious knowledge of Italian Renaissance detail. His niece married a Talbot in which family the Abbey descended, though often through the female line.

The sacristy, the chapter house and the warming room are Ela's work but her church has disappeared. The beautiful cloisters were rebuilt in the 15th century, and the refectory and dormitory above were transformed in the 1540s by Sharington, who introduced his characteristic console windows

and splendid Tudor chimneys. The finest Renaissance work is in the octagonal tower which he added at the south-east corner. His mason was John Chapman, who worked for Henry VIII and was conversant with Continental practice. He vaulted the tower chamber in a most original manner with pendant scorpions and the Sharington crest. The latter appears again on the stone table in the centre of the chamber upheld by four magnificently carved satyrs.

In the middle of the 18th century John Ivory Talbot again introduced the newest architectural fashions to Lacock when between 1753 and 1755 Sanderson Miller designed a new Hall for him in the Gothick style and decorated it with terracotta figures in niches by the little-known Austrian sculptor Sederbach. The ceiling is emblazoned with the coats of arms of Ivory Talbot's friends, the local landowners, for whom he gave 'a grand sacrifice to Bacchus' when it was finished.

In the first half of the 19th century, William Henry Fox Talbot remodelled the South Gallery and planted many rare trees in the Abbey grounds. He gained an international reputation as a pioneer of photography, conducting many of his early experiments at Lacock. In 1835 he produced the first photographic negative, a representation of the small oriel window in the South Gallery. The achievements of this versatile Victorian are now commemorated in the Fox Talbot Museum in Lacock village.

Lower Brockhampton, Hereford & Worcester

1 mile east of Bromyard, north of the A44 Leominster/Worcester road

Lower Brockhampton is remote even today, and it is not difficult to envisage its isolation, or the need for a defensive moat (of which three sides survive), when it was built in about 1400. With its exposed timber framing, partly in close-set upright studs and partly in square panels, with its elaborately carved bargeboards, and its leaded windows, the house is one of the most attractive of the 'black and white' manors of the Welsh Marches.

The building, originally H-shaped in plan, has been much reduced in size, but the great hall survives. It has an interesting openwork timber roof and a timbered screens passage.

The most unusual, and certainly the most picturesque, feature of Lower

Opposite:
Lacock Abbey

*Lower Brockhampton;
Manor-house and
gate-house*

Brockhampton is the detached gatehouse on the edge of the moat. This, and the well-known example at Stokesay Castle, are among the few timber gatehouses to have survived. The Brockhampton building, which dates from the late 15th century, has an upper storey which projects charmingly from curved brackets springing from the angle posts, and the gables have bargeboards carved with a running design of foliage. The close-set upright studding is exposed both inside and out, and the archways which lead through the gatehouse have four central heads. As a structure it looks delightfully improbable and seems to totter, yet it has stood for nearly 500 years.

Lytes Cary, Somerset

$2\frac{1}{2}$ miles north-east of Ilchester, north-west of the Fosse Way

No Trust house stands in quieter farming country or in a setting that seems to speak less of the 20th century than the medieval manor of Lytes Cary. From the 13th century to the 18th it was the home of the Lyte family and they left their architectural memorial in a 14th-century chapel, a 15th-century hall, and in the 16th-century additions which we owe to John Lyte. His son Henry was a distinguished botanist; in 1578 he published the *Niewe Herbale*, his translation of a Dutch work, dedicating it to Queen Elizabeth 'from my poore house at Lytescarie'.

The Lytes and their memory are rightly associated with the house they built, to which their successors added only an 18th-century farmhouse and a 20th-century wing. But Sir Walter Jenner, son of the eminent Victorian physician, deserves a place in the story, for in 1907 he rescued the ruined manor and restored it, bequeathing it to the Trust in 1948.

The architectural quality of Lytes Cary is at once apparent when seen from the east front where a stone-paved path between cushions of clipped yew leads to John Lyte's 16th-century porch with its charming oriel above. To the left lies the great hall with chapel beyond, and to the right the staid but cumbersome 18th-century addition which no doubt replaces an earlier gabled extension. The great hall of the 15th century, with an arch-braced roof typical of the West Country, an elaborately carved timber cornice bearing the Lyte arms, and its original fireplace, acquired its triple-light windows, added by John Lyte, in the 16th century. The screen is Sir Walter Jenner's replacement. The so-called oriel room, a little adjunct to the hall, foreshadows the evolution of the dining room and shows that by about 1530 a separate eating apartment was already considered desirable. The adjoining great parlour was used as a farm store in 1907, but providentially the early-17th-century panelling incorporating Ionic pilasters was found intact under layers of paint. The 'great chamber' above, reached by a stone staircase from the hall, is remarkable for its plasterwork ceiling of about 1533. One of the earliest examples of a coved and ribbed plaster ceiling, and displaying the arms of Henry VIII, it shows none of the Renaissance influence to be found

Lytes Cary; The east front

at Hampton Court and elsewhere, yet already anticipates the spidery technique of the Elizabethan plasterers. These rooms are mainly furnished with suitable oak and walnut pieces of the 17th century collected by Sir Walter Jenner.

Nothing remains of the botanic garden laid out by John Lyte, except possibly some ancient walls; the present garden is the creation of Sir Walter Jenner. South of the lawn in front of the house lies a summer border. Buttressed clipped hedges and stone urns lead to a small 'white' garden and this in turn to a raised walk and a yew alley. A formal pool, a pleached hornbeam alley, and further hedged lawns, lead back to the house.

Mottisfont Abbey, Hampshire

$4\frac{1}{2}$ miles north-west of Romsey, $\frac{3}{4}$ mile west of A3057

There are those who hold that no house in England is more peaceably and harmoniously set than Mottisfont. Yet the setting is simple: cool green lawns, shadowed by enormous planes, cedars, oak and beech trees and bordered by the loveliest of chalk streams, the Test. So true is the scale, so right the balance of this landscape that a flower would seem a superfluity. The collection of species, shrub and old-fashioned roses planted by the Trust in the old walled kitchen garden in 1972–3 is an addition which does not destroy this picture.

Here early in the 13th century was established the priory of the Holy Trinity. It was not a large foundation, for its full complement of Austin canons never exceeded eleven, but it boasted a special treasure, the forefinger of St John the Baptist with which he had once indicated the Saviour. The Black Death seriously impoverished Mottisfont, and it seems not to have recovered, for towards the end of the 15th century its revenues could support only three canons. Suppression came in 1536, and the priory and

345

lands were conveyed, in exchange for no less than the villages of Chelsea and Paddington, to Henry VIII's Lord Chamberlain, William, Lord Sandys of The Vyne (see p. 209).

Lord Sandys at once began the transformation of the priory into a Tudor mansion. His operations, however, were most unusual: instead of carving his house from the residential parts of the priory, he demolished them and chose to use the nave of the church itself (cf. Buckland Abbey, p. 333). Thus the north front still represents the full length of the north wall of the nave up to the crossing.

Sir Richard Mill, who lived at Mottisfont throughout the reigns of the first two Georges, was responsible for a further transformation, and changed the Tudor seat of his Sandys ancestors into the pleasant mid-18th-century house that stands today.

It remained for the 20th century to make a final and striking contribution to the much-altered priory of the Austin canons. Mr and Mrs Gilbert Russell, who had acquired Mottisfont a few years earlier, in 1938 commissioned Rex Whistler to decorate the saloon. In 1957 Mrs Russell gave Mottisfont and the estate of over 2,000 acres to the Trust.

Though varied and informal, the façade of Mottisfont, in weathered brick with stone quoins, announces the 18th century, as does in general the agreeable and unremarkable interior. But this house, in its idyllic framework of trees, lawns and river, has surprises. Though set with Tudor and Georgian windows, the north front, as already noted, is the nave wall of the priory church. On the east front survives a great pointed arch with foliated capitals that once led from a vanished chapel into the south transept, and on the south is the undercroft of the monks' cellarium. Its sturdy 13th-century columns support a stone-groined roof as perfect today as when the priory was built over seven and a half centuries ago.

But the outstanding feature of the interior of Mottisfont is the decoration of the saloon. This Gothick fantasy in *trompe-l'oeil* is executed in grisaille; the simulated stuccowork of the coved ceiling, the slender colonnettes painted against pale pink walls, and the trophy panels of ecclesiastical, military, musical, and sporting subjects, are of an astonishing virtuosity. An alcove with a smoking urn, draped with an ermine stole, has a base heaped with books; a lute is propped on one side, and upon the feigned cornice the artist left with studied carelessness the simulacrum of a small paintbox and brush. Given the idiom that Whistler chose, the room is faultless.

Mottisfont Abbey; Detail of Rex Whistler trompe-l'œil decorations

Oxburgh Hall, Norfolk

7 miles south-west of Swaffham, on south side of Stoke Ferry road

The history of Oxburgh relates to a single family. In 1482 a patent granting licence to build Oxburgh was issued to Sir Edmund Bedingfeld. His descendants still live there.

In the second half of the 15th century not only was Oxburgh less of a backwater than it now seems, but some sort of fortification was more than necessary as protection against the widespread unrest resulting from a decline in agricultural prosperity and from the return of the soldiery from the Hundred Years War.

Rising sheer from its formal moat, the gatehouse is the glory of Oxburgh. Unlike the rest of the house it was spared from Victorian restoration by its 'very perfect state', as Pugin put it. The remainder of Oxburgh, built round a courtyard, is as medieval as Pugin could make it, with battlements, decorated chimneys, oriels and elaborately cusped windows.

Oxburgh Hall   Right: *The gatehouse*

The great hall, opposite the entrance gate, was demolished in 1775 and the saloon was built in a simple neo-classical style. Fifty years later, in the 1830s, began the restoration and re-modelling of the interior which produced the present dining room, library and drawing room. These are dark, richly patterned rooms with views over the moat whose limpid reflections enliven their decorated ceilings.

These Victorian rooms are in marked contrast to the lofty King's and Queen's Rooms in the gatehouse. These chambers and the roof above are reached by the rubbed cut-brick spiral staircase which is the most interesting architectural feature of Oxburgh. From the roof on a clear day the octagon of Ely Cathedral can be seen eighteen miles away. The King's

Room, where Henry VII was lodged in 1487, is furnished with a bed dated 1687. Upstairs the Queen's Room is hung with two rare Sheldon tapestries. One, dated 1595, depicts the story of Judah, the other a map of Oxfordshire and Buckinghamshire. In another room are displayed the celebrated hangings with panels worked by Mary Queen of Scots and by Elizabeth, Countess of Shrewsbury, better known as Bess of Hardwick (see p. 118).

In the grounds beside the moat is the 19th-century French Knot Garden laid out after designs by Alexandre Le Blond.

Paycocke's, Coggeshall, Essex

On south side of West Street

There are four Paycocke tombs in the parish church of Coggeshall, and the family, probably starting as sheep graziers, made a fortune as clothiers when the cloth-making industry came to the area in the late Middle Ages.

Though Paycocke's House, built in about 1500 by Thomas Paycocke, has been much restored, it remains one of the most attractive half-timbered houses in East Anglia. For all its elaboration, it stands modestly on the village street. The narrow studding characteristic of early half-timbering must once have been infilled with wattle and daub, now replaced by brick. Many of the timbers bear the original carpenter's marks. The upper storey of jetty construction has a richly carved bressummer, bearing the initials and trade sign of Thomas Paycocke, and five evenly spaced oriel windows.

Inside the house several rooms have moulded and carved timberwork and original fireplaces. There is some interesting early oak furniture.

Paycocke's

Opposite:
Rufford Old Hall

348

Rufford Old Hall, Ormskirk, Lancashire

5 miles north of Ormskirk at north end of Rufford, on east side of A59

Rufford, the home of the Hesketh family, is essentially of three periods. Facing the drive, as you come in, is the late-15th-century great hall. With upright timber studding, quatrefoil decoration, and windows with moulded timber mullions, this is the central and sole surviving portion of a 'black and white' house, which according to medieval pattern would have had a cross wing at each end: to the west the family apartments and to the east the domestic offices.

The architectural effect of the interior of the great hall is largely due to the fact that the richness of the decoration is concentrated above window level – in the splendid hammerbeam roof, with quatrefoil motifs, that rests on an embattled and moulded wall plate. At the west end of the hall stood the high table, where blocked doors still lead to the vanished parlour and solar in the demolished west wing. Two features at the east end of the hall call for particular mention. The room is framed by two spheres, gigantic oak trees of slightly differing girth, carved with moulding and panelling, where embattled tops support a cambered tie-beam that is hardly less massive. Between the spheres, in place of the usual fixed screens that commonly divided the hall from the kitchen, is a huge movable screen. This rare feature, seven feet wide and richly worked, is surmounted by three immense carved finials. It is a fascinating survival.

At right angles to the 15th-century hall, and making a strong contrast in texture, is the Caroline wing constructed in brick in 1661. Though the mullioned windows have unusual brick labels over them, the general effect is one of simplicity. Internally the wing exhibits the same simple character.

Rufford Old Hall; movable screen   Right: *Detail of movable screen*

Further building took place at Rufford early in the 19th century, and on the site of the 15th-century domestic offices rose a block which links the great hall with the Caroline wing. It contains the main staircase and the drawing room.

When transferring Rufford Old Hall to the Trust in 1936 Lord Hesketh included in his gift much 17th-century oak furniture and a collection of arms and armour. The hall now also houses the Philip Ashcroft Folk Museum, a collection which reflects life and work in this part of Lancashire since the days when Rufford was first built.

St John's Jerusalem, Kent

3 miles south of Dartford at Sutton-at-Hone

The curious name derives from the fact that at the end of the 12th century the manor was given, no doubt as a pious contribution towards the crusading enterprise, to the Knights Hospitallers, the military order whose headquarters was in Jerusalem.

Of the original Commandery of the Knights, whose order was dissolved at the Reformation, only the chapel survives with three tall lancet windows. The moated house, first seen across the water between a vast Lebanon cedar and a copper beech, is substantially the creation of Abraham Hill, one of the founders of the Royal Society, who acquired St John's in 1665 and lived there until his death in 1721. The brickwork, the pitch of the roof, the dormer windows and the wide staircase indicate a house of the late 17th century.

Edward Hasted, the historian of Kent, lived at St John's from 1755 to

St John's Jerusalem

1776, and his improvements, which include the south door and the sash windows, contributed to his financial ruin. We can still be grateful to him for much of the interior decoration, including the rich plasterwork and rococo chimneypiece in the room that was once Mrs Hasted's boudoir.

St Michael's Mount, Cornwall

$\frac{1}{2}$ mile south of Marazion (A394) whence there is access on foot over the causeway at low tide or by ferry at high tide

The view of St Michael's Mount rising from the sea – 'the great vision of the guarded mount' as Milton called it – is one of the most dramatic and moving things on our coast. From the causeway, revealed at low tide, and the little harbour lined with fishermen's cottages, to the airy summit of the castle tower, the Mount presents a unique blend of nature, romance and architecture. In summer, set in a halcyon sea, with the steep slopes that climb to the castle walls carpeted with bracken and bright with mesembryanthemum and the long spikes of *furcraea* that grow so splendidly there, the Mount is all smiling welcome; yet its face can change in autumn or winter, when its shore is lashed by angry waves and the full force of a sou'wester screams round the battlements. At such times it has something of sublimity.

Perhaps the Saint chose one of the calm, scented summer nights of Cornwall for his dramatic appearance on the Mount one evening after dark in the year 495. Thenceforth at any rate the Mount was sacred, and in due course Edward the Confessor, for 'the redemption of his soul', established a foundation there dependent on the great Benedictine Abbey of Mont-Saint-Michel in Normandy. As an alien priory it was suppressed in 1425, and the

St Michael's Mount

Mount for over 200 years became a garrisoned fortress. One of its strangest inmates was Perkin Warbeck who, claiming to be the elder of the Princes murdered in the Tower by Richard Crouchback, landed at Mount's Bay and established his base at the castle. After playing a considerable role in the Civil War, the Mount passed in 1660 into the private ownership of the St Aubyns. From the entrance to the castle, which bears the arms carved in granite of the first St Aubyn owner, to the extensive new buildings put up just over a century ago, the family has impressed its personality on one of the most unusual sites in England. Lord St Levan, the present head of the family, transferred it to the Trust in 1954.

Though the Mount must have been inhabited from time immemorial, the oldest surviving buildings appear to date from the 12th century, but the chief impression is of a castlehouse that has grown and changed with the centuries and represents an amalgam of architectural styles. The church with its 15th-century rose windows is austere and impressive, whereas the Lady Chapel of 1463 was converted into drawing rooms in the 18th century and decorated with Gothick plasterwork of the gayest and most light-hearted sort. Similar changes are reflected in the charming Chevy Chase room, originally the refectory and then the great hall of the medieval house. Its walls are 12th-century, its open timber ceiling is 15th-century, and the delightful plaster frieze was added in the 17th century by the St Aubyns who later also contributed the Georgian Gothick doorways.

St Michael's Mount; Gothick decoration

The Cloud, Congleton, Cheshire;
View from the Macclesfield
Canal

Coast near Tintagel, Cornwall

Mam Tor and the Hope Valley, Derbyshire   *Woods on Ashridge Estate, Hertfordshire*

Malvern Hills, Hereford & Worcester; Midsummer Hill

Speke Hall, Merseyside

On north bank of the Mersey, 8 miles south-east of the centre of Liverpool, on east side of the airport

The Domesday survey refers, not very helpfully, to the Manor of 'Spec'. It was just over 400 years later, in 1490, that Sir William Norreys started the building of Speke Hall. During the 16th century it assumed its present quadrangular form, surrounding an enclosed courtyard. Though the moat has disappeared, the building looks outside as it did towards the end of the reign of Queen Elizabeth and is one of the most richly timbered houses in existence.

Sir William's son and grandson, to whom we owe the essential character of the house, were traditionalist in outlook. The fascinating variety of pattern in the timberwork, the pitch of the roofs, the continuous cove under the eaves, and the fenestration, show no concession to Renaissance taste. A late Elizabethan stone bridge leads to this 'black and white' house and its cobbled central courtyard. Two ancient yews, over 400 years old, contribute to the romantic gloom of the enclosure. The great hall is one of the most architecturally astonishing rooms imaginable. To the hall of 1490 was added in about 1560 an elaborate western bay and a vast and extraordinary chimneypiece, an incongruous Elizabethan attempt at heavy baronial Gothic, which must be one of the earliest examples of archaistic taste in the country. The wainscoting, of Flemish origin, was imported about thirty years earlier. The great chamber has a ceiling of superlative quality. Its date, of about 1560, and its character indicate the intermediate period between the simplicity of early English Renaissance and the fussiness of much later Jacobean.

Basically the interior of Speke reflects the tastes and planning of the Norris family in the 16th century, but it was acquired in 1797 by Richard Watt, a wealthy West Indian merchant, and it has a special interest today – an interest not generally apparent in 1942 when the house came to the Trust – on account of the 17th-century furnishings introduced by the Watt family in the mid-19th century. They are a revealing expression of the romantic nostalgia of the time.

Throughout the house these two complementary influences, of the 16th and the 19th centuries, are juxtaposed, and contribute to the richness of cultural texture. Few Tudor houses are structurally so little altered, yet few so convincingly exemplify the affinity which 1850 felt for 1550. The 17th and 18th centuries left little imprint on Speke. Probably at the time its casual half-timbering was regarded as wholly unsuitable for a large country seat.

Stoneacre, Otham, Kent

3 miles south-east of Maidstone, 1 mile south of A20

Built about 1480, a modest gentleman's house of the conventional hall and screens type, Stoneacre had become derelict by the end of the First World War. It was carefully but extensively restored in the 1920s, and is therefore a scholarly recreation of a timber-framed house of the early Tudor period, rather than a dwelling that has survived in its original condition.

The main part, with its reconstructed twelve-light window and the timber-framing exposed by the restoration, is picturesque. The rear elevation contains another twelve-light window, original to the 15th century, and also uncovered at the same time. The north-west wing is modern but incorporates 16th- and early-17th-century timber-framing from North Bere Place.

Stoneacre

On the main front, the door with its 16th-century Flemish knocker and Elizabethan lock gives on the great hall. The oak screens are original and the hall, since its restoration, presents much the same appearance as it did in 1480, though the central hearth, from which smoke escaped through a louver in the ceiling, has been replaced by a 15th-century chimney. The timbered roof and the deeply moulded, projecting wall plate are unusual, but the most remarkable feature of the house is the rare and beautiful kingpost formed of a cluster of four engaged shafts.

The Treasurer's House, Martock, Somerset

In Martock village on B3165, 2 miles north of A303

In the 12th century the church at Martock belonged to the Monastery of Mont-Saint-Michel, but in 1227–8 the church and advowson were acquired by the Treasurer of Wells Cathedral, who became both the rector and patron of Martock, an arrangement which continued until 1840.

Treasurer's House; Collar-braced roof

Built of Ham stone, the Treasurer's House is the country house which the Treasurer began at Martock in the 13th century; it later became the vicarage and so remained until the middle of the 19th century, when it passed into private hands. The earliest part of the house is the solar or great chamber of the 13th century, but its most impressive feature is the later 14th-century hall with a timber roof of collar-braced type and five windows of about 1330. The following century saw the addition of the kitchen and the parlour, a private sitting room, the latter with two mullioned Perpendicular windows, and an impressive fireplace that may be rather later. Few small houses have retained so much original medieval work, or have been so sensitively restored.

Tudor Merchant's House, Tenby, Dyfed

Quay Hill, opposite Bridge Street

Tenby was a trading post of some consequence in late medieval and Tudor times, and the old house, whose precise history is unknown, is said to have belonged to a wealthy merchant adventurer. It dates from about 1500 and once formed part of a larger building, parts of which survive in the houses adjacent on either side.

The Merchant's House has interesting architectural features, notably original fireplaces and garderobe flue, a circular chimneystack of a type once characteristic of the region, and projecting windows on the first and second floors supported by corbels. When the building was restored, the late medieval painted floral decoration in red, black and yellow, on the only original interior partition that survives, emerged from beneath no fewer than twenty-three coats of whitewash.

Tudor Merchant's House

Public Buildings

The King's Head, Aylesbury, Buckinghamshire

The market square at Aylesbury lies at the heart of a bustling county town. Set back from a corner of the square, and reached through a narrow passage, the King's Head is a typical coaching inn with a large stable yard and an archway wide enough to admit carriages. It boasts a most unusual feature. The original 'hall', now the bar, has a large wooden-framed window of twenty lights with mullions and transome. This window contains 15th-century glass, notably figures of angels bearing shields on which appear the arms of Henry VI and his Queen, Margaret of Anjou. The symbol of the Evangelist St Mark also appears, with a scroll on which the name 'Marcus' is inscribed. This rare glass, and parts of the building, date from about 1450. An exposed section of old wattle-and-daub construction may be seen.

Hawkshead Courthouse, Cumbria

½ mile north of Hawkshead, at junction of the Ambleside and Coniston roads

Secular buildings of the medieval period are rare in the Lake District. The Courthouse, so called because the manorial courts are traditionally said to have been held there, consists of little more than a single upper chamber constructed, like most buildings in the area, of rubble and masonry. It is substantially 15th-century, and a traceried window and smaller trefoil-headed windows of this date survive. A fireplace with a dog-tooth moulding of the 13th century is something of a puzzle, but it was probably brought from Furness Abbey after the Dissolution. The abbots of Furness were for long lords of the manor of Hawkshead.

Hawkshead Courthouse

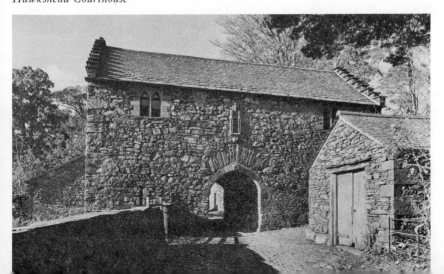

The Guildhall, Lavenham, Suffolk

At junction of B1070 and B1071

When Edward III encouraged Flemish weavers to settle in England, the woollen industry was already well established in East Anglia. Lavenham was one of its centres, and the wealth derived from the wool trade, particularly from the 14th to the 16th centuries, is reflected in its splendid church and its medieval buildings, of which the Guildhall is the most impressive.

Built by the guild of Corpus Christi, one of three guilds founded to regulate the wool trade, its purpose was primarily economic, but religious feasts and festivals, often held in the hall itself, played a large part in the affairs of the guild, which was dissolved not long after Henry VIII's suppression of the monasteries. The hall was later put to many strange uses. During the Marian persecution the Rector of Hadleigh was confined in the hall before he was burnt at the stake on Aldham Common; later it served as the town hall for nearly eighty years; before 1689 it became a prison where malefactors were committed from all over Suffolk (the pillory, whipping post and stocks being set up in the Market Square outside); nearly a century later it served as workhouse and almshouse; finally during the Second World War it housed evacuees and was at different times a 'British Restaurant' and a nursery school. It was vested in the Trust in 1951.

A picturesque half-timbered building, it was built in the 1520s. Though much restored, it retains interesting features, such as the carved overhang of the first floor, a carved corner post with an effigy said to represent the 15th Earl of Oxford, and an original oriel window. The interior contains moulded beams and joists, doorways with carved spandrels, and some linenfold panelling and fireplaces – all of conventional Tudor pattern. The rooms now house an interesting collection of material relating to the history of Lavenham and the wool trade.

The Courthouse, Long Crendon, Buckinghamshire

2 miles north of Thame, via B4011

This long jettied timber-framed building with infilling of brick, wattle and daub, dates at least from the beginning of the 15th century. Though the old rectangular chimneystack is a Tudor addition, and features such as doors and windows have been altered, the open timber roof is unchanged and retains its original queenpost, trusses and braced collar beams.

The building was probably put up as a wool store or staple hall in the days when sheep accounted for much of the wealth of the surrounding country-side. So large and substantial a building was a convenient venue for the manorial court. It was used as a courthouse as early as the reign of Henry V (1413–22), and successive lords of the manor held courts there until the late 19th century. Bought in 1900, the Courthouse was one of the first buildings to be acquired by the Trust.

V
Industrial Monuments

Introduction *by J. M. Richards*

'Monument' is perhaps a misnomer. The buildings and artefacts which this essay introduces were constructed for essentially practical purposes, with no thought of creating works of architecture to be admired as such. And yet, as we see them now, these buildings have become monuments. They are, collectively, the best possible memorial to an age – the age of the Industrial Revolution and of the multiple activities that derived from it – when Britain led the world into a new era dominated by manufactures and communications. They therefore stand as monuments to the heroic age of engineering and technology and to the men who pioneered it; not only the famous men like Arkwright and Abraham Darby and Telford, the Stephensons and the Brunels, but the hundreds who built on their foundations and elaborated the impressive array of functionally based, dignified and highly satisfying buildings (the warehouses, dockyards, textile mills and railway sheds) that are still so sparsely recorded as to make travel around Britain full of agreeable surprises, especially travel in industrial areas and mean localities not otherwise distinguished architecturally.

The qualities possessed by such buildings are, however, ones that we are increasingly coming to appreciate, if only because they have so much in common with the qualities we seek in modern architecture: a forthrightness derived from immediate response to the purpose the building has to serve; avoidance of irrelevant ornament; the use of building materials so as to create the effects natural to them. Structures like the Quarry Bank cotton-mill at Styal, Cheshire, are straightforward geometrical statements which nevertheless display considerable subtlety of form and detail. This mill and the houses grouped round it are typical of the hundreds of buildings, in which Britain is richer than any other country, stemming from the Industrial Revolution and the new demands it created.

Industry and the buildings serving it did not, of course, begin as a revolution. The episode we call the Industrial Revolution was only a sudden intensification, arising from the practical application to daily needs of lately understood scientific principles, of a process that had been mounting through the ages. In particular it brought about the congregation in new centres of population of the manufacturing activities that had previously been cottage industries, country crafts or small-scale service industries in towns; so that the development of the new categories of architecture with which I am here concerned – the new types of warehouse, factory and mill –

coincides with, and is part of, that urbanization of English life which began nearly two hundred years ago.

But before this sudden acceleration of the process of urbanization, there were industrial buildings associated with the life of the countryside which already showed the characteristics just described as being typical of those created by the Industrial Revolution. These earlier buildings are perhaps best exemplified by windmills and watermills, those first examples of the harnessing of natural forces for human benefit, which can truly be called the predecessors of the great power-driven mills and factories of the 19th century.

The National Trust owns some splendid specimens of both, including windmills at Bembridge in the Isle of Wight (the last one left on the island), at Ivinghoe, Buckinghamshire, at Horsey, Norfolk, and at Wicken Fen, Cambridge – the two last being more strictly wind-*pumps*, since their function was to raise water as part of the drainage system of meres and fens – and watermills at Alderley Edge, Cheshire, at Houghton, Cambridgeshire, at Burnham Overy, Norfolk, and at Shalford, Surrey.

Windmills in full running order are rarities now, but at one time they were part of the essential economy of the countryside, in the cornlands of England crowning every hill. They are nevertheless far less ancient than watermills; the earliest references to windmills occur late in the 12th century, when they still seem to have been something of a curiosity, though a hundred years later they were plentiful. Earlier written references to mills mean watermills or cattle-mills.

For some reason, windmills were the first to be rediscovered as things of beauty as well as utility, and to benefit from their admirers' efforts to preserve them. The Society for the Protection of Ancient Buildings formed a Windmill Section as long ago as 1931. Perhaps this was due to the windmill and its function being comprehensible at a glance. It is not just another building, but a machine that can be seen at work and, like all the best machines, can be admired for its combination of elegance and economy. Like the ocean-going sailing ship, the windmill was superseded at the moment when it had achieved the height of aesthetic and mechanical refinement – there was no period of decline to blur its gracious image.

The popularity of the windmill long before other early industrial buildings were similarly valued, let alone admired, may also be to some extent due to its place in English landscape paintings. From Constable to Crome and Morland and the 19th-century watercolourists, painters gave windmills a prominent place in their pictures and they became associated in the public mind with idyllic rural scenes and the beauties of the English countryside.

Watermills attract the eye less obviously – they stand in river valleys instead of on hilltops – and have fewer romantic associations, yet the groups of vernacular buildings by which the mill-wheel is enclosed, or often totally concealed, are likewise characteristic elements in the rural English landscape; related architecturally to farm buildings and others in the vernacular tradition, of brick and white-painted weatherboarding in the home counties, of stone in the north and west. They are still domestic in scale, and are therefore a bridge between the industrial buildings of the handicraft age and those which followed the Industrial Revolution. Besides showing that the tradition of bold functional building, though given a new impetus and power by the Industrial Revolution, has its roots many centuries before, they illustrate the overlapping and continuity of cultures; for although they perpetuate an ancient tradition, most of the watermills that survive today – and they are many, though fewer every year earn their living in the old way – were built in the late 18th or early 19th century, after the Industrial Revolution was well under way.

Although the Industrial Revolution was the cause of that rapid urbanization of English life that took place in the 19th century, the first of the notable buildings arising from it were located deep in the countryside. These were the early textile mills which, like the corn-mills just described, were dependent on water-power. They followed the inventions of Arkwright and Crompton which mechanized the cotton-spinning process. Vast cotton-mills were established in the valleys of Derbyshire and Lancashire where the damp air suited the spinning process and the fall of the land made water-power easy to harness.

Soon afterwards came the mechanization of the woollen industry and the establishment of similar mills in places like the Stroud valley in Gloucestershire, near to the sheep-farms of the Cotswolds. These cotton-mills and woollen-mills are, incidentally, curiously misnamed; they were not mills (Latin: *molere*, to grind), but factories run at first by water-power, like the corn-mills from which their power machinery was derived and whose name they also borrowed.

They did not survive for long; steam-power superseded water-power and the textile industries moved to the big centres of population and nearer to the coalfields and the ports where their raw material was brought in; cotton remaining in Lancashire, wool moving largely to Yorkshire after raw wool imported from Australia and New Zealand had taken over from the home-grown product. At the same time the textile factories became bigger still, because weaving, which had remained a cottage industry long after the mechanization of spinning, became in its turn a factory process, when the power-loom came into use after about 1830. But the first textile mills, deep in the countryside where water-power was cheapest, are big enough, and to come upon them in their remote valleys is to be confronted by a grandeur of scale that must have appeared astonishing indeed when it was matched only by cathedrals and castles.

These multi-storey structures, standing massive and four-square above the huddle of lesser buildings around them, are not only aesthetically delightful as examples of the functional tradition I have already described, but are important as representing some of architecture's most significant advances in construction. Within their orthodox-looking stone outer walls – sometimes brick, though most of the textile mills were within the limestone belt that crosses England from south-west to north-east – were concealed the earliest experiments in iron construction, which led eventually to the modern steel frame. The first multi-storey building with both beams and columns of iron was a flax-mill at Shrewsbury designed by Charles Bage in 1796, though iron columns had been used in his mill at Derby by Strutt, one of the pioneers of mechanized cotton-spinning, as early as 1792. The weight of machinery the floors had to carry made this an essential step forward; no less essential as manufactures of all other kinds developed and factory building changed the whole character of large tracts of England. These early industrial buildings are thus at the same time memorials to an enduring quality in English architecture and memorials to a key moment in the evolution of English technology. It is time that more active steps were taken to ensure that the best examples are preserved.

One branch of manufacture that produced an especially interesting range of building was brewing. The brewing of beer was one of the first industries to be transferred from the home to the factory. This occurred as early as the 14th century, though it was not until well into the 19th that brewing became fully industrialized. Until then, in rural England, the wealthier classes brewed their own beer, farmers brewed beer for their workers and many publicans for their customers. The process of industrialization was completed as the tied-house system spread throughout the country.

Handsome brewery buildings, dating from the 18th and early 19th centuries, are to be found all over England, at their most striking in country towns where the brewery is often, after the church and perhaps the market hall or corn exchange, the dominating building and architecturally the most satisfying. The qualities that make it so are not very different from those I have already defined as characteristic of early industrial buildings generally – geometrical simplicity and an assurance in the handling of form and materials that comes from meeting new challenges boldly but unselfconsciously; but the loss when such a building is done away with – being perhaps no longer needed and not valued, or occupying a site from which profit can be made – is often disastrous, not only for its own sake, but because of the prominence of its site. A recent instance was the dominant and very distinguished Simpson's Brewery in the High Street of Baldock, which a philistine local council acquired and demolished, thereby sadly impoverishing the look of the town centre.

But if breweries themselves, their situation apart, can be classed with factory buildings, the brewing industry produced two other kinds of building, unique to it and deserving a word to themselves: maltings and oast-houses. In my own book* on early industrial buildings I wrote:

> In the whole wide range of anonymous industrial architecture, maltings are probably the buildings whose beauties have been least noticed. They have neither the rural charms of water- and windmills nor the romantic associations of the pioneer textile mills. They are mostly nineteenth century, yet they have the same vigour as the earlier buildings . . . Architectural ingredients common to nearly all maltings are the high pyramid-roofed kilns, or groups of kilns, breaking into

* *The Functional Tradition in Early Industrial Buildings* (Architectural Press, 1958).

the skyline and the long lines of the flooring blocks with their rows of louvred windows. Often these emerge from a jumble of other buildings. When they stand free they sometimes have a spectacular scale . . .

This undervaluation of the architecture of maltings is nearly as true today, though the possibility of converting them to new uses when no longer needed for their original purpose has been shown by the highly successful transformation of a range of maltings at Snape in Suffolk into a concert-hall for the Aldeburgh Festival. The National Trust owns a more modest specimen at Burnham Overy in Norfolk, adjoining the watermill already referred to.

The charm of oast-houses, on the other hand, is more easily appreciated. Like windmills, they have an agreeable rural character; their plain geometry sits snugly in the wooded Kentish countryside. Like maltings, many oast-houses have become redundant through changes in the brewing industry, but their rural surroundings and domestic scale suggest their conversion into houses – not, however, always as sensitively done as it should be. There is a particularly fine and well-preserved group of oast-houses, which only went out of use a few years ago, attached to the National Trust's property of Sissinghurst Castle.

The other principal factor, besides the growth of industry, responsible for the Industrial Revolution, was the growth of communications, and the monuments that celebrate this are widespread. First there was the age of canal-building, that brought with it not only the canals themselves with their locks and aqueducts and bridges, possessing their own economical but sturdy vernacular, but also the warehouses and dockside buildings constructed where the canal system passed through manufacturing towns or debouched into navigable rivers which it connected one with another. Many of these handsome canal and canal-side buildings are being allowed to become derelict, though the National Trust has rescued and is safeguarding a $13\frac{1}{2}$-mile stretch of the Stratford-upon-Avon Canal. The Trust also owns five miles of the beautiful tree-lined Royal Military Canal in Kent that bounds Romney Marsh. This, however, must not be classed as an industrial monument, since it was built as a defence against invasion during the Napoleonic wars.

Then there was the age of the oceanic carrying trade, first in sailing vessels and soon in steam, on which the growth of manufacturing industry depended. It necessitated the building of great harbour basins – in London, Liverpool, Bristol and elsewhere – surrounded by ranges of tall warehouses of a scale and impressiveness that rivalled those of the northern textile factories. These splendid buildings are also now mostly obsolete; many have already become derelict or been demolished, and some of the very best – like the Albert Dock at Liverpool – are threatened; but so substantially are they built and so vast are the internal spaces they provide that they could surely be put to some other productive use.

Such docks and warehouses of course only continue an earlier tradition, now best exemplified in the Royal Naval dockyards. Here – at Portsmouth, Devonport, Chatham and Sheerness – some splendid ranges of buildings survive, hardly known to the public because never seen by them. But it is the even grander warehouses of the industrial age that present the dramatic challenge to the imagination, sited as they are just where civic improvement could exploit them.

Parallel with the age of canals was the age of road building, stimulated by John Macadam's inventions and at last allowing wheeled transport to move freely in all weathers, making it no longer more economical, for example, to bring building stone to Kent and Sussex from across the Channel by ship than in wagons along rutted and waterlogged roads. These were the great days of the stage-coach, but they were also the great days of that new professional man the civil engineer – of men like Telford, who carried the new arterial roads over obstacles that proved such a challenge to their skill as to advance technology further in one decade than in the whole preceding century. Telford's suspension bridge that carried the Holyhead Road over the Menai Straits to Anglesey was a unique achievement when it was completed in 1826, and it is still one of the great monuments of the Industrial Revolution.

The civil engineer came even more into his own in the subsequent age of railway building, which transformed the landscape, and stimulated the economy, of Britain to an even greater degree; and the monuments with which he endowed the proliferating railway system are too numerous to recount: stations and bridges, great arched train-sheds in iron and glass spanning distances never achieved before and noble viaducts of brick or stone crossing mile-wide valleys.

This was the age of some of the most courageous and self-confident characters of the 19th century, men such as the younger Brunel and Robert Stephenson, whose creative energies were stimulated by the sense they had of being instruments of destiny. They were so intent not only on exploiting the new technologies but on asserting the significance of the new epoch they were creating that they regarded all past cultures as equally at their disposal. Witness the Egyptian sphinxes that embellish the pylons of Robert Stephenson's Britannia tubular bridge over the Menai Straits, and the crenellated Gothic turrets that Telford gave to his suspension bridge at Conwy (in this case a road-bridge) now in the care of the National Trust.

So the railways have not only given us powerfully functional monuments like the roof of York station or the Wharncliffe viaduct or the Roundhouse at Chalk Farm; they have endowed us with more strictly architectural monuments such as the Doric portico at Euston, London's gateway to the north (alas, no longer surviving), Temple Meads station at Bristol and the stations at Newcastle and Monkwearmouth. Here, for once, engineers and architects shared the same objectives, and buildings like these are among the glories of English 19th-century architecture.

Industrial monuments, nevertheless, are not limited to buildings; the age is to be remembered by the machines that brought it greatness as well as by the buildings that served them. The blast-furnace site carefully preserved at

Coalbrookdale in Shropshire constitutes an instructive memorial to Abraham Darby and his successors, showing the new technology confidently feeling its way towards the limitless developments ahead; while a notable item among the National Trust's possessions is the collection of beam-engines, some still in working order, at various mines in Cornwall, presented in 1967 by the Cornish Engines Preservation Society. These are a memorial to one of the earliest applications of steam to industry. The growing interest in artefacts such as these is indicated by the welcome given to Brunel's great iron ship, the *Great Britain*, when she docked at Bristol in 1970 after being towed back to her first home from the Falkland Islands.

The preservation of things like ships and machines and blast-furnaces is not easy. They are more vulnerable than buildings to damage and decay and retain less of their meaning when they cannot be seen in operation. Moreover, both they and the buildings that house them exist for the most part in localities which, because of their industrial nature, require continuous renewal and modernization. We cannot treat the industrial heart of England, where much of the country's living is still earned, as though it was an archaeological site.

The price Britain pays for having been the first industrial nation, for having pioneered construction in iron, the harnessing of steam and the building of railways, is that the buildings and equipment we possess, the factories and harbour installations and railway stations – indeed, the entire railway systems – are more obsolete than anyone else's, simply because they are older. The problem we are faced with, therefore, is how to renew them without sweeping away all evidence of the heroic age they commemorate and all the best examples of the monuments it bequeathed to us. To resolve this problem needs a conservation policy of the subtlest kind. It must begin with greater appreciation of what we have; the railway authorities, for example, must themselves understand the value of the monuments in their possession, rather than let amateurs of architecture and transport enthusiasts remain the only people who mind about them. The monuments must be listed, surveyed and recorded, so that any necessary replanning or rebuilding can be based on conservation as well as on demolition; and what is to be conserved must be determined by national architectural and historical value, not by the short-term economics of railway management. Furthermore, the same careful integration of old and new must be sought not only on the railways but elsewhere; otherwise, we shall find ourselves, at the very time that we are learning to appreciate this episode in our history, destroying the very monuments on which that appreciation is founded – and for that posterity will not thank us.

Windmills

Though watermills have been known from the earliest times, it is curious that the windmill was apparently only developed from the 7th century, in Persia or thereabouts, and did not reach Western Europe until the end of the 12th century. The first reference to an English windmill dates from about 1190. By the end of the following century they were common throughout south-east England. Yet windmills for a number of reasons are vulnerable and no medieval windmill seems to have survived. The oldest windmill in this country that can be dated with any certainty is the Trust's Pitstone windmill of 1627 (see p. 370). It may be noted in passing that windmills provide useful observation points in time of war: Edward III is said to have watched the Battle of Crécy from a post-mill and Charles I certainly watched Edgehill from one.

Millers were persons of importance, and in the Middle Ages were privileged members of manorial economy. The toll they took of the grain they milled varied within wide limits, but could be as much as a twelfth part. It was also a dangerous calling, and incautious millers from time to time were killed by their sails.

Windmills fall into two clearly defined types. The earliest type is the post-mill and those built at the end of the 12th century differed little from those built in the 19th. A wooden box-like structure contains the grinding machinery. It is carried on an upright post, and this in turn is supported by sloping struts which transfer the weight to crosstrees resting on supporting piers enclosed in a round-house. The working part of the mill can be rotated round the central post, so that the sails face into the wind, by means of a long pole, called the tailpole, which sticks out behind.

Rotating a whole mill was a cumbersome process, and the 16th century saw the invention of the tower-mill. The body of such mills is a fixed structure and only the cap of the mill, with the sails and their gearing, rotates. The cap was originally turned by means of a chain wheel, as at Bembridge Mill (see p. 368), but in the middle of the 18th century the inventor of the threshing machine devised the fantail. The fan remained stationary as long as the sails faced into the wind, but if the wind veered it caught the fans which revolved and in turn caused the cap to revolve until the sails once more faced into the wind. If built in wood, rather than in brick or stone – the most usual wooden form is octagonal – such mills are known as smock-mills. They usually stand on a brick base.

Internally all mills worked roughly in the same way. The wind, through the sails, transmitted the power to the windshaft, which in turn was geared to the millstones. Corn was fed to the stones through the hopper, and a series of complex mechanisms controlled the speeds of the sails, the supply of grain, the rate of rotation of the millstone, and the fineness of the milling.

Bembridge, Isle of Wight

½ mile south of Bembridge

The Bembridge windmill, so familiar a landmark to local yachtsmen, dates from the first half of the 18th century and is the last surviving mill on the Island. For some two hundred years, until it ceased work after the harvest of 1913, the last harvest before the outbreak of the First World War, the mill ground flour and meal, and latterly bran and cattle feed, to meet the needs of the village and the surrounding countryside. By the 1950s it had become derelict; it was then restored by public subscription and presented to the Trust by Mrs E. Smith in 1952. It is of particular interest as it retains so much of its original 18th-century machinery.

Four storeys high and built of random local stone, Bembridge mill is a tower-mill. The turning gear can be seen on the outside of the cap, and the miller could turn cap and sails to the required position by walking round the base of the mill and hauling on an endless chain attached to the turning gear.

The vast sails which converted wind to power are sixty feet long, and the power was transmitted by gearing through the oak shaft which ran down through three floors and provided the main drive. A great brake wheel, eight feet in diameter, controlled the speed of the mechanism.

Bembridge windmill

High Ham, Somerset

2 miles north of Langport via A372, ½ mile east of High Ham

The mill, a fine landmark, is the last survivor of several windmills that once existed in the neighbourhood. A substantial stone-built tower-mill, it dates from about 1820, and went out of use by wind early in the present century. Though the sail blocks survive, the original sails have gone, and so has most of the milling machinery. An unusual feature is the thatched cap (which is said to be of reeds from Abbotsbury in Dorset).

High Ham windmill

Pitstone, Buckinghamshire

½ mile south of Ivinghoe, 3 miles north-east of Tring, just west of the B488 Tring/Leighton Buzzard road

One of the timbers bears the date '1627', which makes Pitstone the earliest dated windmill in England. Like all early windmills, it is of post-mill type, and since it antedates the invention of the fantail, it is luffed to face the wind by means of the traditional tailpole.

The mill was working until 1902. In that year a sudden freak storm struck the mill from behind, before the superstructure could be turned into the wind. Blowing the sails forward, it unshipped the windshaft and severely damaged the mill, which subsequently went out of use. When it came to the Trust in 1937 it had sadly deteriorated, and first aid repairs were undertaken.

Not until the 1960s was the mill completely overhauled, and a major work of restoration carried out, with voluntary labour, by the Pitstone Windmill Restoration Committee. Though the surviving machinery is mainly 19th-century, the mill, with its two pairs of grindstones, is now complete. The speed of the sails, it is interesting to learn, was approximately fifteen revolutions per minute, and that of the grindstones a hundred and twenty.

Pitstone windmill

Watermills

Bourne Mill, Colchester, Essex

1 mile south of Colchester, just east of the B1025 Mersea road

The curved and stepped gables of Bourne Mill speak of Holland, and Sir Thomas Lucas who built it in 1591 may well have employed some of the Dutch Protestant refugees who had settled in Colchester. If, as seems probable, Sir Thomas originally intended it as a fishing lodge, he took unusual pains with the little building, furnishing his gables with elegant finials, his chimneys with octagonal shafts, and his windows with stone mullions and moulded labels, and finally setting the Lucas arms above the double-chamfered arch of his lower doorway.

A mill had probably stood on the site since the 12th century and Sir Thomas's father had bought the property with the ruined Abbey of St John soon after the dissolution of the monasteries. The association of Bourne Mill with the vanished Abbey probably indicates that the pond was at one time also a stewpond for the monks. It certainly held large fish in the 19th century, for on one occasion a monster pike was dispatched to the Queen at Buckingham Palace. Strangely enough, these tranquil waters were at the same period a favoured resort for suicides; the last miller's daughter, who attained the age of ninety-two and lived well into the 20th century, could recall helping her father to remove two bodies in one night. For the famous herbalist, John Gerard (1545–1612), the pond had happier associations, and he noted in his *Herball* 'Marsh Cinkfoile groweth in a marsh ground adjoyning to the land called Bourne ponds from whence I brought some plants for my garden, where they flourish and prosper well'.

Bourne Mill; Front and rear elevations

The Lucas family suffered for their Royalist sympathies in the Cromwellian period, and Bourne Mill passed to Dutch refugees who turned it into a cloth-mill for weaving and bleaching. By 1800 the wool trade in Colchester had declined, and some time after 1823 the building suffered a further change and was converted to a flour-mill. Operations ceased some years before the First World War and in 1936 the mill was presented anonymously to the Trust.

Much of the mill machinery is still in place. The huge overshot water-wheel, twenty-six feet in diameter, is, unusually, situated within the building. The wheel has recently been restored and can now, together with the gears and shaft, be turned again by water-power.

Burnham Overy Mill, Burnham Market, Norfolk

$\frac{1}{2}$ mile north-west of Burnham Overy Staithe, on south-east side of the A149 New Hunstanton/Wells road

Burnham Overy mill is set astride the river Burn, which reaches the sea a mile northwards at Holkham Bay. It forms part of a complex – with maltings, barn, miller's house, and cottages for the mill hands – such as once was familiar enough in Norfolk. All too few survive unchanged today. The picturesque group of red-brick buildings dates from the end of the 18th century.

The mill itself is a substantial building rising to three storeys, and its white painted woodwork contrasts boldly with the rich red-brick façade. Weather-boarded cantilevered structures, called 'lucams', project on either side of the roof. They house the hoisting gear which raised the grain to the

Burnham Overy Mill; Maltings louvers to the right of the illustration

storage loft on the top floor, whence it passed by gravitation to the grinding floor below. The mill was also a malting, where barley was converted into malt by first encouraging and then arresting the process of germination. This was achieved by storing the barley in cisterns in low-ceilinged chambers and then drying and curing it in kilns. Air admitted through smallish square windows with louvers (which give maltings their characteristic appearance) circulated through the chambers. A row of these louvered windows can be seen beneath the roof on the upstream side of the mill, and on the ground floor on the downstream side.

A wooden tower-windmill, which formed part of the milling business, was erected in 1816 and stands on the brow of the hill a few hundred yards to the east.

Houghton Mill, Cambridgeshire *(see colour plate facing p. 321)*

Just south of A1123, 2½ miles from St Ives

Running slowly through a wide shallow valley, the Ouse divides into numerous interconnecting channels in the water meadows between Brampton and St Ives. Here Houghton, one of the oldest and last surviving watermills on the river, stands on an artificial island in a quiet backwater.

A mill has existed on or near this site for at least a thousand years. Its history is unusually well documented. In 964 Ealdorman Eolwin (or Aylwin) founded Ramsey Abbey some ten miles away and soon after presented the mill and a meadow at Houghton to the Abbey. Tenants of the Abbey had to have their corn ground at the mill on pain of a heavy fine. From time to time there were disputes between the local inhabitants and the abbot or

Houghton Mill

the miller about tolls or water rights; the abbot or the miller usually won.

After the dissolution of Ramsey Abbey in 1539, Houghton mill became Crown property. In 1625 it was sold by Charles I, and after passing through various hands it came, early in the 19th century, to the Lady Olivia Bernard Sparrow, an intractable high church Anglican. Her tenant Potto Brown, a Quaker merchant, was an equally intractable nonconformist. Despite theological dissent between landlady and tenant, Potto Brown and his partner Joseph Goodman flourished. In East Anglia nonconformity and business went well together. In 1852 the rent was £352, a very considerable sum at that time. Potto's sons carried on the business until 1876. The mill ceased working in 1930, and is now a youth hostel.

Nothing remains of the medieval mill, and the present large rectangular building, four storeys high, dates from the mid-17th century to the 19th century. It is of brick and timber construction, with tarred weather-boarding. Unfortunately its thatched roof has been replaced by slates.

Watermills work on the same principle as windmills, but the grinding stones are naturally above rather than below the source of power, to which they are similarly geared by a vertical driving shaft. There were once three waterwheels at Houghton, each wheel driving a pair of stones (the largest pair is $4\frac{1}{2}$ feet in diameter). Though the wheels have been replaced by sluices, which control the water passing through the old wheel-channels, much of the machinery survives. It includes a pair of governors which controlled the speed and pressure of the stones and which are inscribed 'B' and 'G', for Potto Brown and his partner Joseph Goodman.

Nether Alderley Mill, Cheshire

$1\frac{1}{2}$ miles south of Alderley Edge, on the west side of A34

Nether Alderley corn-mill is situated on the flat and fertile Cheshire plain, about a mile from Alderley Edge. The stream that drives the mill-wheels is small and inadequate to power the machinery effectively. This difficulty was overcome by the Elizabethan millwrights who built the present mill by constructing two reservoirs or lakes above it. Radnor Mere stored the winter floods and replenished the lower reservoir, whose waters were used to drive the mill-wheels. The mill itself was built right up against the dam across the valley, the back wall forming part of the bank. Hence the unusual appearance of Nether Alderley Mill, with its long sweep of stone-flagged roof. The walls are of a warm red local sandstone that is soft, evenly textured and easily dressed. Yet it weathers so well that after 400 years, the surface is quite undamaged.

Inside, the original Elizabethan woodwork survives. The oak trusses, windbraces and rafters are secured by wooden pins or 'trenails'. The present machinery dates from the 1870s. There are two waterwheels driven by water running through a culvert from the lake above, which runs away down the tailrace to a deep culvert that rejoins the brook below. There are two pairs of

Nether Alderley Mill

French grinding-stones, although in about 1900 there were two more sets at a lower level. About 150 years ago there was also a perforated tiled floor heated by a fire below for drying grain, but this operation was not found to be economic and the kiln was abandoned many years ago.

The earliest mention of a mill at Nether Alderley is 1290, and in 1591 an 'Inquisition Post Mortem' on the property and effects of Thomas Stanley of Nether Alderley was held, at which both the Hall and the watermill were recorded. It was worked as a corn-mill by a long line of country millers until 1939 when the machinery had become derelict and the mill was closed. In 1950 the owners, Mr and Mrs Shelmerdine, presented Nether Alderley Mill to the National Trust, who repaired the fabric of the building. It was not until 1967 that a start was made on repairing the machinery when Dr Cyril Boucher, assisted by his two sons and other helpers, undertook the monumental task of restoring the mill to working order. This was completed in 1976 and once again water flowed down the culverts, the wheels and grindstones turned and fine meal poured out of the chutes into the waiting flour sacks.

Shalford Mill, Surrey

$1\frac{1}{2}$ miles south of Guildford, on east side of the A281 Guildford/Horsham road

This picturesque watermill, astride the River Tillingbourne, probably dates from the first half of the 18th century. The ground floor is made of brick, but the walls of the two upper storeys are of oak and chestnut framing, filled with brick nogging and tile-hung. The larger of the mill-wheels, which remains almost intact, is geared to a twelve-sided vertical shaft made from a

Shalford Mill

single pine trunk. This shaft drove the grinding stones and the winnowing and grading machinery, and operated a sack hoist to the top floor.

The mill is closely associated with a mysterious fraternity, known as 'Ferguson's Gang'. Elected by secret ballot and bearing such colourful pseudonyms as 'Sister Agatha', 'the Nark', 'Bill Stickers', and 'the Bloody Bishop', its members were dedicated to the preservation of the English countryside. Since 1930 they have conferred great benefits on the Trust in cash and kind. In 1931 the Gang repaired and endowed Shalford mill, where subsequently their secret meetings were often held. Its members preserved a strict anonymity.

Wellbrook Beetling Mill, Kildress, Co. Tyrone

$2\frac{1}{2}$ miles west of Cookstown, just north of the B159 Cookstown/Omagh road

Wellbrook is the last water-powered 'beetling' mill in the British Isles in working order. Beetling is the final process in linen manufacture in which the cloth is pounded for up to three or four days by heavy timbers to give the finished cloth a sheen. For centuries Ireland had been noted for the quality of its linen goods, and by the 18th century the growing of flax and the manufacture of linen had become the most important manufacture in Ulster. The introduction of beetling machines as early as 1725 – beetling had previously been carried on in the home by women using a heavy wooden mallet – contributed greatly to the reputation of Irish linen goods.

Wellbrook was built in 1765, modified in the 19th century, and did not

Wellbrook Beetling Mill and beetling machinery

cease working until 1965, three years before it came to the Trust. Serious and functional as befits an industrial building, the mill is a two-storeyed rectangular structure of whitewashed masonry and stands at right angles to the Wellbrook, a small trout stream tumbling over a rocky bed, from which it derives its power. Water is carried from a weir above the mill down a race and along an elevated trough or 'flume' to the exterior mill-wheel.

Inside, the lower floor of the mill houses seven beetling machines drawn up in close formation and powered by a main driving shaft meshed to a gear on the shaft of the mill-wheel. A wooden lever controls the water supply and sets the machines in motion. Each consists of two heavy timber beams over which the dampened cloth is wound. These beams, as they slowly rotate, are flailed by a set of beetles or wooden rams on a second rotating beam. The noise is appalling, and those who worked in beetling mills often went deaf.

On the upper floor are situated the airing racks on which the pounded cloth was hung to dry. Louvers instead of windows allow a free circulation of air and exclude direct sunlight.

Winchester City Mill, Hampshire

In the centre of Winchester at the foot of High Street

Winchester Mill has a long history and has stood firmly athwart the river Itchen in the middle of the town since the reign of Richard Coeur-de-Lion. The survival of a mill in such a position is most unusual. At the Dissolution it was monastic property, and was presented to the City by the Crown 'for

Winchester City Mill; The mill race

the relief of the poor'. In 1553 it was let by the corporation for a rent of 6s. 8d. annually. It passed into private ownership in 1820 and ceased working some time in the present century.

The City mill as we see it today, with its charming south-facing gable, dates substantially from 1744. At that time the tenant rebuilt the old mill, re-using some of the materials of the previous 14th-century structure.

Styal Village and Quarry Bank Mill, Cheshire

11 miles south-east of Manchester on B5166

The village, mill and associated buildings, dating mainly from the end of the 18th century, are an early and fascinating example of architectural planning for industrial purposes. The transition from rural cottage production to the factory system took place first in the cotton industry, and the mill at Styal was established by Samuel Greg in 1784. Styal was exceptional in that a self-contained community was carefully planned and was of set purpose provided with a rural framework. Industry in Arcady. The wooded banks of the Bollin are still unspoilt though only eleven miles from the centre of Manchester.

Constructed of local brick, the buildings – mill, manager's house, Apprentice House and the cottages for the workers – are simple functional architecture, yet express an 18th-century feeling for proportion and design. They are self-confident, yet seemly.

378

Samuel Greg's enterprise prospered. The initial community of a hundred and fifty had trebled by 1820. A hundred youths were lodged in the Apprentice House. Though the apprentices had a long day even by the standards of the time (5.30 a.m. to 8 p.m.) they were well fed, went to school in the afternoon – such education was highly unusual – and to the interest of posterity were subjected to regular medical inspection and treatment. Their medical records survive and indicate the nature of the first industrial medical service.

Though the mill-wheel disappeared with the coming of steam-power, and none of the machinery was surviving when Samuel Greg's great-great-grandson gave Styal to the Trust in 1939, the great millhouse remains an impressive example of industrial architecture. It is hoped that it may become a permanent museum for the cotton industry.

Styal village; The apprentices' house and rear of the mill

Canals and Bridges

The River Wey and Godalming Navigation, Surrey

Extends for $19\frac{1}{2}$ miles from Godalming to the Thames

Rising in the Hampshire and Surrey uplands, the river Wey flows north-east and north through Godalming and Guildford to join the Thames at Weybridge. It has always been a spirited stream, and the volume of water coming down from the hills made it necessary to bridge the river as early as the 13th century (a bridge of that date survives at Eashing). The steady flow of water also provided through the centuries the power for numbers of watermills. It seems that at one time there were as many as fifty strung along the course of the river from the hills to the Thames. Most have now disappeared, but a few fine examples happily survive, such as the town mill at Guildford, built in 1766.

The taming of the Wey, its change from a river to a navigation, was the work of a remarkable man, Sir Richard Weston (1591–1652), the owner and builder of Sutton Place. This distinguished agriculturist, who pioneered in this country the rotation of crops and irrigation to increase yields, also adapted the principle of the canal-lock. From 1635 onwards he supervised the canalization of the Wey. His 15-mile navigation from the Thames to Guildford, which included twelve locks and called for the digging of some ten miles of artificial channel, was completed in 1653. The undertaking cost £15,000, then a considerable sum. In 1760 an Act of Parliament extended the navigation a further four miles upstream to Godalming.

The traffic on the navigation was chiefly timber, corn and other agricultural produce, and its commercial hey-day came after 1796, when the Basingstoke Canal was linked to the Wey. With the opening of a railway from London to Guildford in 1845 decline set in. Though the navigation has long ceased to play an economic role, it fulfils a social one. The laden barge

Wey Navigation; Lock-keeper's cottage

has been succeeded by pleasure craft and the Wey has become a cruising playground.

These nineteen miles of water, though so close to London and to suburban sprawl, are for the most part strangely unspoilt. Beyond the alder-fringed banks are lush meadows, church towers, and Surrey hills. Boats move past Wisley's Norman church and the ruins of Newark Priory, past Sutton Place, where the late Mr Paul Getty succeeded Sir Richard Weston, and St Catherine's 14th-century chapel where those on the Pilgrims' Way from the west to Canterbury once crossed the river.

The Navigation Office is situated at Dapdune Wharf Road, Guildford.

The Navigation was presented to the Trust in the 1960s by Mr H. W. Stevens and the Commissioners of the Godalming Navigation.

The Royal Military Canal, Kent and East Sussex

Some 3½ miles of canal bank between Appledore and Warehorne and a stretch of some 1½ miles between Winchelsea and Pett

Unique among British waterways, the Royal Military Canal was not incorporated by Act of Parliament, but was constructed for military purposes in 1805 during the Napoleonic Wars. It was intended for use both as a canal and as a defensive line to close the gap between the cliff defences across Romney Marsh, which lay open as an obvious landing place for the vast invasion forces which the French massed across the Channel after the Treaty of Amiens was broken in 1803.

The canal was the idea of a Lt-Col. Brown and it was speedily taken up by the War Office. A survey was made in early September 1805, the report submitted on 18 September to the Commander-in-Chief, who gave orders next day for its immediate execution, so pressing was the danger felt to be. Work started by the end of October with John Rennie as consultant engineer, and a firm responsible for the building of some of London's docks was given the contract. A canal 60 feet wide and 30 feet deep was planned, to run from Hythe Sluice near Shorncliff for 28 miles (incorporating the river Rother for some stretches) to Cliff End beyond Winchelsea, where the Pett Cliffs began the long line of defended cliffs extending to Hastings. It was designed as a means of moving troops rapidly into place and also as a defence line with gun positions linked to the chain of Martello towers near the coast. The work proceeded with almost incredible speed and was finished within a twelvemonth and within the estimated cost of £200,000, which included the price of land. William Pitt, then in his last year of office as Prime Minister, supervised the operations from time to time, staying at Walmer Castle near by. The French invasion never came. After 1807 the canal was made suitable for commercial traffic and continued to be administered by the Ordnance Department of the War Office.

In 1877 the canal was leased by the Secretary of State for War to the Lords Bailiff and Jurats of the Level of Romney Marsh for one shilling per

Royal Military Canal, Appledore

annum for 999 years. By that time revenue from the sale of grass and hay from the canal banks was almost as much as from tolls and dues; by the end of 1909 commercial traffic had ceased. The canal fell into disuse, although in the 1914–18 and 1939–45 wars it was refortified as the first natural line to hold against any force put ashore by the Germans.

The Royal Military Canal is today not only a historic and industrial monument but a place of great natural beauty. It runs along the ancient shoreline skirting the edge of Romney Marsh, whose rich pastures were originally won from the sea by the Romans, who built the first seawall. This was later extended and strengthened in the Middle Ages. There are glorious views from the towpath upland to the Isle of Oxney with the medieval village of Appledore at its foot and seawards across the wide panorama of the Marsh with its lonely windswept churches. The fine avenue of trees planted along the bank by the War Office is now sadly decimated by Dutch elm disease.

Stratford-upon-Avon Canal, Southern Section, Warwickshire

13½ miles of the canal, south from the Kingswood junction to the Memorial Theatre garden basin in Stratford

In the 1760s, Stratford was a decaying town in an agricultural area some thirty miles from the newly established mines and factories of the Midlands. Proposals were made to link the two areas by canal and thus facilitate the exchange of corn for coal, an exchange that was hardly possible on the

Stratford-upon-Avon Canal; The Wilmcote Flight   Right: *Working a lock*

turnpike roads. Nothing came of the proposal until 1793, when the Grand Union Canal was launched to link Birmingham and London. In that year £100,000 was raised in Stratford by local subscription, and a company formed to build and operate a canal from Stratford both to the Worcester–Birmingham canal at King's Norton, nineteen and a half miles to the north, and also, by a branch, to the Grand Union. Work began at the northern end, but stopped in 1802 and was not resumed until 1812. By the time the southern section was finished in 1816 the cost had risen to half a million.

Canals did not prosper for long. With the rapid growth of the railways from 1845 onwards, they gradually decayed and fell into disuse. Many canal companies were bought by railway companies, others went bankrupt. The Stratford canal was no exception. Commercial traffic had ceased by about 1934, and the southern section, which had long been unnavigable, was in 1958 about to be abandoned. It was saved by the National Trust, which acquired the freehold and, after an intensive programme of restoration largely carried out by voluntary labour, opened this section of the canal to river craft in 1964.

The thirteen-and-a-half-mile length of canal rescued by the Trust has thirty-six locks, and twenty-six cast-iron bridges in which towlines for barges could be passed through slots in the centre of the bridge. Three interesting iron 'trough' aqueducts carry the canal and towpath across valleys. There are pleasant single-storey lockhouses with barrel-shaped roofs which contrast with plainer building of an earlier northern section.

The canal passes through a peaceful and rural landscape and today conveys the spirit of Shakespeare's country as no road can do.

Conwy Suspension Bridge, Gwynedd

On A55

The Conwy river constituted for centuries one of the natural defences of the Welsh. Its gorges and its strongly flowing current, with the mountains lying to the west, were a formidable barrier. Not until 1636 was the river bridged – at Llanrwst, eight miles upstream of the town of Conwy; the beautiful stone-arched structure still stands and carries traffic as effectively as it did 300 years ago. But communication between Shrewsbury and Anglesey remained difficult and by the early 19th century the growth of traffic to Ireland through Holyhead made improvements essential. Something had to be done, and Thomas Telford was called in.

Telford (1757–1834) was one of the most eminent of the small band of engineers of the late 18th and 19th centuries whose prodigious energy and achievements transformed communications in this country. He built bridges, canals, docks and roads, and he was also, as St Mary's at Bridgnorth testifies, an accomplished ecclesiastical architect. Furthermore, he was a sensitive and delightful man, and Robert Southey, the poet, wrote of him: 'A man more heartily to be liked, more worthy to be esteemed and admired I have never fallen in with.'

In 1811 Telford was commissioned to survey a road westward from Shrewsbury. He chose and created the route now known as the A5. Though climbing above Capel Curig, it never exceeded a gradient of 1 in 10, which enabled a stagecoach to maintain a steady ten miles an hour. At Betws-y-Coed his road crossed the Conwy on the Waterloo Bridge. It still carries the full summer traffic and is perhaps the most elegant of his bridges.

A few years later Telford was presented with the more formidable challenge of spanning the river where it reaches Conwy on the coast. He originally had in mind – for cast-iron was his speciality – a single 200-foot iron span with smaller flanking arches, but he eventually decided in favour of a suspension bridge. Though suspension bridges employing iron chains were in use in China in the 3rd century, the first such bridge in Britain, with a span of seventy feet, was thrown across the Tees only as recently as 1741. Telford's Conwy Bridge required a span of 327 feet. This may seem modest compared with such contemporary giants as the Severn suspension bridge (3,240 ft), but a century and a half ago its construction was a major achievement.

Work started in 1822 and was completed four years later. The situation of the bridge, immediately below the rocky eminence on which Edward I had placed his imposing concentric castle in 1283, posed a problem of style for the engineer. While using the materials of the new Iron Age, he decided – he was after all the contemporary of Sir Walter Scott – to give his bridge a medieval dress, and on towers and outworks he introduced features, such as crenellation and machicolation, appropriate to the military architecture of the late 13th century. The result was a blend of the picturesque and the utilitarian to which the structure owes much of its charm.

Conwy is probably the only old suspension bridge which has kept its

Conwy Bridge and Conwy Castle

original chains. This is partly due to the fact that, like all the metal-work, the links, nine feet long, were hot-dipped in linseed oil, which has preserved them even in the salty marine atmosphere of the Conwy estuary. The chain supports at each end consist of a pair of massive stone turrets in closely-jointed ashlar. The wall linking the turrets is pierced by an arched opening ten feet wide to provide entrance to the bridge. The carriageway is slung from vertical rods which descend at five-foot intervals from the chains above. The original wooden decking of the carriageway was replaced in 1896.

In 1958, with the completion of a new bridge to meet the needs of a rapidly increasing coastal traffic, the old suspension bridge became re-dundant and its demolition was proposed. The National Trust took action. With the help of a generous gift from the Conwy Council and funds raised by public appeal, the bridge was saved and in 1966 was transferred to the Trust.

Presses and Beam-Engines

Gray's Printing Press, Strabane, Co. Tyrone

Gray's printing works and shop are the survival of a time when Strabane, today a small town on the border of Eire and Northern Ireland, was an important publishing centre. In the late 18th century there were ten printing concerns in operation, and several citizens emigrated to carry on successful businesses as printers and publishers in America and the Colonies. Between 1779 and 1840, many books and pamphlets were printed in the town, which by 1780 had two newspapers, one founded in 1771.

The special interest of Gray's printing works lies in its historical associations. John Dunlap, printer of the American Declaration of Independence in 1776, came from a Strabane family and is traditionally supposed to have served his apprenticeship in Gray's 'Printery' before emigrating at the age of ten to America, where he joined his uncle, an established printer and bookseller in Philadelphia. He took over his uncle's business in 1768 and developed it, launching in 1771 what became the first daily newspaper in the United States; he was shortly after appointed printer to the 'Continental Congress' whose members drafted the Declaration.

The printing works are housed in the upper storey of a long whitewashed building approached by an external stairway. They give on a paved yard, behind a shop which still carries on business as 'Gray, Printer', its early 19th-century bow-fronted façade little changed. The works are arranged as a printing museum and contain three 19th-century presses, illustrating the development of technique over some sixty years. The earliest press, the Columbia, invented in Philadelphia about 1813, was brought to England in 1817. This decorative machine, topped with a distinctive cast-iron eagle

Gray's Printing Press; Gray's shop and 19th-century printing presses

which acted as a counterweight, became the best-known press in England and on the Continent. The Albion, also an American invention, came into use after 1822, and both machines were used commercially well into the 20th century.

Cornish Beam-Engines

East Pool Mine, Camborne; Holman's Museum, Camborne; South Crofty Mine, Camborne; Levant Mine, St Just.

The Cornish beam-engine represented the ultimate refinement of the engine first introduced by Newcomen in 1712 and subsequently improved by Watt. Developed by Richard Trevithick and other Cornish engineers in the late 18th and early 19th centuries and built by such famous local firms as Harvey's of Hayle, it was renowned throughout the world for its reliability, longevity and economy. The classic Cornish type was single-acting and non-rotative, and it was widely used for mine and waterworks pumping.

Cornish beam-engine

After a century or more of service, the Cornish engine began to disappear rapidly from its native county in the 1930s as a result of the closure of mines and the introduction of electric pumps. It was at this time that the Cornish Engines Preservation Society was formed with the object of saving a representative selection of surviving engines. In this it was successful and in 1967 gave these engines to the National Trust.

An outstanding example is the Harvey water-pumping engine of 1892 at Taylor's Shaft, East Pool mine, which has a cylinder 90 inches in diameter and a 52-ton beam. Altogether the engine weighs 684 tons and – to give car owners an idea of its scale – its cylinder capacity totals 12,500 litres.

Also at East Pool mine, its exposed flywheel and connecting rod a prominent landmark beside the A30 road to Penzance, is a smaller engine with a 30-inch cylinder built in 1887 by Holman Bros, of Camborne. This is an excellent example of the type of double-acting rotative Cornish engine, and was used for winding both men and tin ore from a depth of 1,490 feet.

Last of this group of preserved engines to continue in operation is Robinson's Shaft engine, with an 80-inch cylinder, to be seen at the South Crofty mine near Camborne. This was built for £2,700 in 1854 at the Copperhouse Foundry, Hayle, and shut down only in 1955 after pumping continuously night and day for fifty years. It pumped water from over 2,000 feet.

Oldest of these engines and in an exposed position high on the cliff between Pendeen and St Just is the 24-inch Levant Mine rotative beam winding engine which dates from 1840 and is at present in poor condition.

Finally the Restowrack engine, which works under compressed air at Holman's Engineering Museum, can be seen during museum opening hours.

VI
Archaeological Sites

Introduction *by Jacquetta Hawkes*

In the Britain of the 1970s our deepest anxieties come from the threat of too many people. One of the great responsibilities of the National Trust is to save some stretches of wild or at least open country for the enjoyment of all those trampling, motoring, house-building millions of us who otherwise would kill the thing we love. It is almost as difficult for us to imagine the wild, sparsely populated islands of five thousand years ago as it would have been for those first little communities of farmers to picture our teeming cities or the endless rush of our traffic. How could a man laying his stone axe to yet another tree of the seemingly limitless forests conceive of a day when there would be too little 'nature' instead of too much, too many human beings instead of so few?

Almost as difficult for us; but of course not quite, for those prehistoric inhabitants of our country have left some traces of their lives and deaths, so that archaeologists, working together with those who study the natural setting of climate and soil, plants and animals, are able to offer a sound outline picture on which our imaginations can work. Today, unhappily, the pressures of too many people are causing the irrevocable destruction of many of these ancient heirlooms. Faster and faster, despite all our efforts, earthenworks are ploughed away, countless ancestral sites of every kind are covered by buildings, roads, airports, reservoirs. With sites such as these, most of them not very striking or attractive to the eye, the very best that can be hoped is that they can be carefully excavated before they disappear. Yet the picture is not altogether black. Many of our ancient monuments, including most that are imposing, beautiful or historically famous, have come into safe keeping. Here is another of the responsibilities of the National Trust. Although the number of prehistoric and Roman monuments in the keeping of the Trust is small compared with those maintained by the Department of the Environment, it is still very considerable and includes some that are of outstanding interest.

In trying to picture the world of all those inhabitants of these islands who lived and died before any written records were being kept, it must be recognized that no 'stills' are acceptable. We have to attempt the motion pictures of continuous process and change. In the earlier days our famous British climate fluctuated enough to make tremendous changes in the scenery and wild life. The human societies and their ways of making and doing things were affected by these changes and also by immigrations, trade and the more gradual internal evolution brought about both by social enterprise and the genius of individuals. Of course the rate of change was very slow: in the Stone Ages at least many generations could pass without any noticeable development. All was held fast by the bonds of tradition. Yet looking back over the millennia, it is easy to see cultural evolution accelerating until we reach the terrifying rate of today, when those of us over sixty have survived into a technological world completely different from that into which we were born. Already by the end of prehistoric times, in the Britain of the days immediately before the Roman conquest, it is possible to study cultural evolution in terms of half- or even quarter-centuries, rather than in the hundreds of years needed for the age of the early farmers, or the thousands for that of the hunting peoples of the Old Stone Age.

This is in fact a difficult time to present an introduction to prehistoric Britain; like everything else, archaeological thinking has been changing at high speed, and interpretations are in a state of flux. This is particularly true of chronology where sudden shifts brought about by a proposed modification of the dates given by radio-carbon analysis have not as yet been digested. There has also been a strong tendency to reduce the role of invasions as the agencies of cultural change and instead to attach more importance to internal evolution. This is all very well up to a point – 'waves' of invaders were already being made fun of in *1066 and All That*. Yet it is only necessary to recall the millennium and a bit more before 1066 to see that fairly frequent immigrations into these islands were an historical fact. Caesar recorded that Belgic tribes had crossed to Britain not very long before his own expeditions. The Roman conquest itself was to be followed by the attacks of Picts and Scots, the settlement of the mixed groups of Anglo-Saxons, of Danes and Norwegians. These folk movements and settlements were to be crowned by the typical dynastic, ruling-class conquest of the Normans. When all this is historical fact, why should we doubt that fairly frequent invasions of various types were equally prehistorical fact?

Evidence shows that British prehistory, like British history at least until the 17th century, was usually dominated by immigrations, conquests, cultural influences reaching our islands from the continent. Occasionally, of course, there was a rebound, and British or English invaded or strongly influenced western Europe. But this was the exception. It is important, however, to remember two things. First, that when new settlers or conquerors did arrive they always mingled to some extent with the existing population, while at the same time being cut off from their own roots. This is one of the chief reasons why distinctive insular cultures were invariably and as a rule quite rapidly evolved. Second, that even in prehistoric times very considerable cultural changes could be brought about by trade, or by the employment of foreign craftsmen, without any large-scale invasion or conquest. It is therefore right to concede that every archaeological claim for an invasion should be carefully weighed.

Men of a kind had been hunting the land that was to become the British Isles for an immensely long time before they were numerous or socially organized enough to leave any monuments worth conserving. The scientifically precious fragments of the thick skull of Swanscombe Man, who died there in the Thames Valley some quarter of a million years ago, can be seen in the Natural History Museum, South Kensington. The shapely flint tools made by his contemporaries and those who lived before and after him have come to light in some numbers, usually in river gravels, and are on display in many of our museums – but that is all. Even when we come to the last phase of this Palaeolithic or Old Stone Age, there is nothing in Britain to set beside the famous painted or sculptured caves of France and Spain. There are, it is true, a number of caves in England and Wales which were occupied intermittently by small groups of hunters. Protected against the intense cold of the final ice age by stitched fur clothes, they hunted reindeer, horse and bison on the open tundra. Although already they liked to deck themselves with shell and ivory beads and buried their dead with ceremony, so far as we know they achieved no more as artists than some poor animal engravings on bone.

At this time our land was still a part of the continent, a mere promontory of the North European Plain. As the icesheets and glaciers retreated, forests spread in their wake, first mostly of pine and birch, but then, as the climate grew warmer and wetter, of oak, elm, lime and alder. Meanwhile the melting of the ice released huge volumes of water and the ocean began to encroach on the swampy, low-lying country now covered by the North Sea. One of the most stirring of our Stone Age antiquities is a barbed antler spear trawled up by fishermen from the sea-bed. Since it was lost by its owner some eight thousand years ago, it lay buried in peat while the sea rose to cover it.

Britain was probably in fact cut off from Europe between 5000 and 6000 B.C. Its people were still hunters and food gatherers, having adjusted their way of life to forest conditions. There was plenty of venison to be had, and the men had become skilful in the use of bow and arrows to bring down birds. Fishing with nets, traps, and hook and line had also become an important part of the economy.

To fish for a living demanded boats: dugout canoes and solid wooden paddles were shaped with axe and adze. Here we first encounter an activity that was to continue far into historic times. These hunters, of what is usually known as the Mesolithic age, did not yet need corn plot or pasture, but they did make a very small beginning in the clearance of the forests that grew in green luxuriance over so much of Britain. With characteristic human ingenuity they responded to the challenge of the trees by developing effective implements for felling them.

Yet the Mesolithic communities were still too few and too much pre-occupied with wresting a livelihood in difficult conditions to undertake large-scale building for either the quick or the dead. The hollowed-out floors of simple huts that were once roofed with skins, sods or thatch can be seen here and there, and in Yorkshire a platform of birch branches thrown down to make a dry platform for the support of shelters of some kind. As for their dead, these people had some method of disposing of them that we have so far failed to trace. The great change was to be brought about by the arrival from abroad of the first farmers, an event which was unquestionably one of the turning-points in our history. From that time onwards until quite recently the economic foundations on which most communities in Britain depended was to be one of mixed farming with cereal crops, mainly wheat and barley, and the breeding of cattle, sheep, goats and pigs.

Even the strongest anti-invasionists concede that the farming economy was introduced into Britain by newcomers from overseas. This is inescapable since the domesticated breeds of livestock and seed for cultivated cereals could not be other than foreign introductions. Mixed farming had begun in the Near and Middle East as long ago as the 7th millennium B.C. or even before, but it is at present difficult to say with any precision where immediately the British settlers came from. On the whole their crafts, customs and buildings suggest southern Germany, Switzerland, Belgium and northern France.

As well as the farming skills, they brought with them the art of potting. They also came with, or soon developed, the will and social capacity to undertake quite considerable building works in earth, timber and stone. These early farmers were in fact the creators of the first considerable field monuments that have come down to us – and the oldest to have come into the care of the National Trust.

What was the date of these fundamental changes, for this turning-point in British history? Radio-carbon dating has pushed it farther back than was previously thought. It looks as though the pioneers could have been arriving by about 3400 B.C. (or even earlier if certain new adjustments prove correct) and as if within a few hundred years they had settled widely and were changing the face of the land. This was a time when a civilized kingdom was being established in Egypt, but several centuries before the building of the first great pyramids.

There is no need to suppose that the Mesolithic hunters would have made much resistance to the new arrivals – there was plenty of room for all. Rather they gradually adapted the new way of life to their own needs. The farming communities themselves seem first to have occupied the great stretches of chalk downland and the limestone and other uplands of southern and eastern England, but also to have spread on to the gravel terraces of some of our river valleys. In all these areas the growth of trees would have been lighter and less tangled by undergrowth than on the heavy lowland soils. For tree-felling, the Neolithic farmers soon began to acquire good polished stone axes made from the tough rocks of western and northern Britain. They may also have used fire for clearing field and pasture.

A modest part of the building activity undertaken by these people was in the service of the living. On a number of hilltops on the downs of Sussex and Wessex, with outliers in Devon and on the Bedfordshire chalk, they built earthworks of a type known to archaeologists as causewayed camps. The latest view is that they probably served as tribal meeting places where folk gathered together for social, trading, cattle-dealing and other purposes – which certainly included eating quantities of meat. It so happens that the causewayed camp held by the Trust, Windmill Hill (see p. 408), has given its archaeological name to the entire culture.

The Neolithic communities put their greatest efforts in the service of their dead. Throughout approximately the same range of upland country as that of the camps, they carried out elaborate rituals for the bodies or dried bones of their dead, often placing them, many together, in houses built of logs, turf or stones. As a final act, they piled over them the banks of chalk and earth that we know as long barrows. They were often contained by a trapezoidal palisade of split logs, with a loftier façade across the wider end where the burials were placed.

As these monuments could be over 300 feet in length, they represent a big expenditure of effort, and must have been by far the most conspicuous man-made features in their landscapes. More striking still, however, was another form of funerary architecture also characteristic of Neolithic times. This was the building of massive tomb chambers from large, sometimes enormous, blocks of stones or 'megaliths'. Most are in areas accessible from our western coasts all the way from Cornwall to the Orkneys. Although it is too soon to be sure, it seems that these impressive and enduring megalithic tombs were introduced into Britain rather later than the long barrows, and the fact that they are concentrated near the coast, and find their nearest parallels in Spain, Portugal and Brittany, suggests that those responsible for their building, possibly a small élite, must have come by sea routes from these countries.

There is a little, isolated group of megalithic tombs centred on the Medway valley in Kent. These, including the Trust's Coldrum monument (see p. 402) with its neat chambers and rectangular stone-kerbed mounds, look more like tombs in Holland and Germany, and their builders may well have had connections in that direction.

The Coldrum chamber, as we shall see, had received no fewer than twenty-two bodies, and it has been claimed that they show some degree of family likeness. It may be that not only megalithic chamber tombs but also earthen long barrows were used for burials over many generations, not by the entire community but by ruling families who alone were considered worthy of the privilege.

During the second half of the 3rd millennium B.C. the Neolithic peoples, who of course included the descendants of the hunters, developed regional cultures and, while long barrows and megalithic tombs remained in use, they seem also to have developed new forms of building intended for religious rites. The earliest of the circles of standing stones (see p. 400), so striking a feature among the moors and mountains of western and northern Britain, may have been set up at this time. A distinctive form was the very long, narrow embanked enclosure, of which the best known is the Cursus near Stonehenge. We have no idea of their purpose. Another, with a great future before it, was a circular area bounded by a ditch with a bank on the outer edge; it could be entered by a causeway and an opening in the bank. There seems no doubt that these were sanctuaries, the ditch delimiting the sacred area. Cremated human remains were sometimes placed inside them, perhaps as ordinary burials, perhaps as some form of sacrifice.

A sanctuary of this simple kind was the first to be constructed at Stonehenge, and they have been dubbed 'henges' after this famous temple. Soon they were to be greatly enlarged and elaborated, often by the addition of rings of standing stones or tree trunks, the noblest examples being Stonehenge itself, and the Trust's great monument at Avebury (see p. 399). These sanctuaries are unique to Britain and must owe their origin to our late Neolithic peoples, yet their amazing aggrandizement may have owed something to new invaders who indubitably were reaching Britain soon after 2000 B.C.

These were the people long known as 'Beaker folk', the favourite butt of those who, understandably, liked to make fun of primitive archaeology. The big drinking pots (occasionally true mugs) from which they got their name are very widespread in Europe and must represent vast movements of people and spreads of culture very hard to explain in historical terms. The main invasions of Britain seem to have come immediately from the Low Countries, and they brought about a revolutionary effect so far as the field monuments of Britain are concerned. The Beaker people still wished to bury their dead, at least their chiefly leaders, with ceremony, still ended by piling a mound over the grave, but now instead of the burying of many together in a communal rite, each dead man or woman was laid in a solitary grave, and the barrow raised over each was perfectly circular. These were in fact the first of the round barrows, or in stony country round cairns, that remained in fashion throughout the Bronze Age and are by far the most numerous of all our prehistoric monuments. Some 20,000 are still recognizable throughout the country, often in clusters so sited on the brow of a hill that they stand out commandingly against the sky.

The skeletons of the Beaker invaders prove them generally to have been taller, more round-headed and with stronger facial features than the small, slender 'Mediterranean' type most characteristic of the Neolithic population. The men were often buried with the equipment of bowmen, with flint, copper or bronze daggers and stone battle-axes. It seems, then, that this was primarily a warrior people, and they may, until they became merged with islanders, have formed an élite and had an influence out of proportion to their numbers.

In some such way as this, the Beaker folk had a role in the development of the native henges. They were certainly involved in the second building phase at Stonehenge, when the bluestone circles were set up, and also in the main constructional period at Avebury where Beaker burials had been made at the foot of several of the standing stones. Though such speculations are rash, there is at least some tangible evidence to suggest that while Neolithic religious ideas had been mainly concerned with fertility and the earth, the Beaker folk were more concerned with celestial divinities, and in particular with the cult of the sun.

Stonehenge and Avebury stand in the heart of the Wessex chalk uplands, and it was in this then prosperous region that a ruling class, by now made up of the descendants of both Beaker folk and the earlier population, were able to develop the first societies in which bronze was of real economic significance. The Beaker invaders had made use of a little copper and bronze, and it was probably they who gave the lead in exploiting Cornish tin and Irish copper. By about 1600 B.C., while their main wealth was probably in cattle, the Wessex chiefs were involved in a trade that carried these metals and also Irish gold to the continent. The great sanctuaries were still holy places and many of the Wessex chieftains and their womenfolk, with their finest ornaments and weapons, were buried in their neighbourhood, particularly under the round barrows that stud the downs round Stonehenge – many of them on National Trust land. The simple pudding-shaped 'bowl' barrow favoured by the original Beaker invaders remained the commonest form, but the Wessex rulers also developed the bell and disc varieties (see p. 410), the latter apparently normally reserved for women. The symmetry and perfect finish of these barrows are remarkable. However, by far the greatest achievement of this age was the addition of the gigantic sarsen circle and trilithons to Stonehenge, a pious act that has given us the finest prehistoric monument in all Europe.

The succeeding centuries of the Bronze Age saw a steady increase in population and advances in metallurgy, in agriculture and in the management of large flocks and herds. There is not, however, very much to be added in an account of field monuments. Throughout Britain the Bronze Age communities continued to build round barrows and cairns, and perhaps also to put up circles of standing stones. Their other activities have left no very conspicuous marks on our countryside. One inconspicuous change was that the barrows now usually covered mortuary urns, for cremation almost entirely displaced inhumation – with what religious implications we do not know.

By the beginning of the last millennium B.C. bronze was in free supply, much of it going into spears, swords and other weapons, as well as into craftsmen's tools. Continental types of swords began to reach the hands of British warriors, sometimes through trade, sometimes perhaps by an exchange of princely gifts. The whole appearance of many parts of the countryside also was being changed by the spread of more settled villages with small but regular fields which now might be cultivated with simple ploughs in place of the hoes and digging sticks of the past.

Europe was entering one of its recurrent periods of disturbance and folk movement, and Britain was a natural haven for migrating peoples and scattered refugees. Some may have helped to bring about the changes of the late Bronze Age, others certainly came to various parts of Britain at the time when iron was beginning to displace bronze. These invasions probably began on a considerable scale in the 6th century B.C. and they continued through the remaining pre-Roman centuries.

We are now in fact on the very verge of history, for we know that these invaders can properly be called Celts. As the Romans were to record, the Celts loved fighting and their influence on Britain was to change completely the nature of field monuments surviving from their era. One can tell where a people's heart lies by the purposes for which they will move the greatest quantities of earth, wood and stone. Hitherto in prehistoric Britain this kind of labour had been lavished on religious buildings, on tombs and sanctuaries. Now the Celtic tribesmen turned their greatest efforts to the building of forts, usually encircling the crowns of hills or defending promontories. The earliest forms, built only to withstand the attacks of men armed with swords and spears, usually consisted of no more than a single rampart, originally faced with wood or stone, and an outer ditch. The Trust has a good example of this simple type of hillfort in Cissbury (see p. 401). Later, when attackers might be armed with powerful slings and other siege weapons the ramparts were multiplied and the entrances more strongly fortified. The most extravagant example of this kind of military architecture is to be seen at Maiden Castle, but there are scores of others.

Many hillforts were probably built as places of refuge during inter-tribal wars, but some may have been strongholds of single chieftains, others thrown up against new invaders. The Celtic aristocracy's love of warfare is further proved by the splendour of their arms and armour – their decorated swords, shields and helmets, and their war chariots drawn by richly harnessed horses. Before the Roman conquest these people had created a true Heroic society of the kind brought alive for us in Celtic literature.

Caesar wrote that some time before his British expeditions of 55 and 54 B.C. tribes of the Belgae, of mixed Celtic and German ancestry, had invaded Britain. Archaeology suggests that the first of them arrived in southwestern England well back in the 2nd century B.C. More followed at intervals, some indeed driven across by Caesar's own Gallic campaigns, and they were soon able to conquer much of southern England. Now we begin to meet individuals: the Cassivellaunus who opposed Caesar, the Cunobelin (Cymbeline) who established his capital at Colchester and traded much with Rome.

Belgic princes, indeed, began the Romanization of Britain, issuing their own coinage and having many contacts with the empire. They might refurbish existing hillforts to hold down a subject tribe, but their own centres of rule were often on low-lying riverside sites which they defended with lines of massive dykes such as can still be seen at Colchester, Verulamium, near Chichester and elsewhere. They in fact began to shift the balance of settlement from the uplands, clearing woodland from fertile valleys and the good loams of East Anglia.

There is no need to tell the familiar story of the Roman conquest of Britain launched by Claudius in A.D. 43. The lowlands were taken in three years: the Britons defended some of their hillforts, but they all fell after the kind of hopeless struggle represented by the war cemetery at Maiden Castle. It took until A.D. 78 to quell Wales, and even thereafter it had to be controlled by forts such as the Trust's Segontium (see p. 416). The even tougher resistance put up by the Brigantes and other northern tribes was brought to an end a few years later when Agricola conquered to the edge of the Highlands.

Under his governorship, the Romanizing of the Celtic tribes went on apace, and the pattern of the Province was established. The lowlands were turned over to civilian life. Forts like that at Letocetum, Wall (see p. 414), built during the conquest, were abandoned and towns were founded where the Britons could be introduced to all the amenities of Roman civilization. Many of them served as capitals for the tribal areas. In the vicinity of towns, too, the Celtic aristocracy gave up the old, rough life of their farmsteads to become villa-dwellers, able to read some Latin and enjoy central heating. Chedworth (see p. 412) is an excellent example of the larger and grander of these country houses, set in their great estates.

Meanwhile the west and north remained military areas held against the untamed barbarians beyond the frontiers. Defence was based on the three legionary fortresses of Caerleon, Chester and York. In spite of periodic attempts to hold a line on the Forth–Clyde isthmus, from its ambitious beginning in A.D. 122 Hadrian's Wall from Tyne to Solway was made one of the strongest and most complete of all the imperial frontiers of Rome. And of all the forts which, on second thoughts, the military decided to build along the line of the Wall, Housesteads (see p. 414), on its lofty perch of Whin Sill, is the finest and most interesting.

The change that the Roman conquest made in the nature of the British scene was, of course, complete. In the prehistoric past human endeavour had been allied to nature, most building softly rounded, of local stuff and intuitively fitted into its setting. Trackways followed the contours of the hills. Now intellectual planning from a distance was the rule; there was town-planning, road-planning, and everywhere red brick and tile, masoned stone, right angles and dead straight lines. There was, in fact, to be nothing like it again until the approach of modern times.

Prehistoric Sites

Avebury, Wiltshire

1 mile north of A4 between Marlborough and Calne, on the A361 Swindon/
Devizes road

The religious architecture of the Beaker and Bronze Age people is our most
spectacular legacy from prehistoric times. Avebury is certainly the largest of
the 'henge' monuments in Britain (see p. 394) and is perhaps the most
important Early Bronze Age monument in Europe. It dates from about 1800
B.C. and is therefore roughly contemporary with parts of Stonehenge, some
eighteen miles away to the south. Though the stones themselves are smaller,
the complex at Avebury is much larger than at Stonehenge.

   The monument consists of a circular area about 360 yards in diameter,
surrounded by a vast ditch now about 13 feet deep only as it contains some
17 feet of silting; this is in turn surrounded by a massive outer bank of chalk.
It is unique among henges in having four entrances, the bank being
interrupted and the ditch not cut. Close to the inner lip of the ditch was a
great outer circle of nearly one hundred standing stones, enclosing two
smaller circles; it is estimated that the southern comprised twenty-nine
stones and the slightly smaller northern two fewer. Both contained interior
settings. The stones were of sarsen, the hard sandstone still found lying as
slabs and boulders in the locality; they were not dressed but chosen for their
natural pillar or diamond shapes. Starting from the causeway of the south
entrance, an Avenue fifty feet wide, bounded by paired stones, led for a mile
and a half to The Sanctuary, on Overton Hill.

   Avebury is a magnificent monument even in its sadly reduced state. Its
excavation, and the judicious restoration of about one half of it to its present

Avebury; Aerial view from the west

Avebury; Upright stones of the outer circle

Opposite:
Castlerigg stone circle

appearance, were achieved by Alexander Keiller in the 1930s. (*See also* Windmill Hill, p. 408.) During the Middle Ages, as heathen rituals persisted, a number of the stones were felled: some were carefully buried, others left on the surface. From the latter half of the 17th century until 1925, stones were deliberately broken up for use as building material and road metal.

Avebury has fascinated scholars and antiquarians since John Aubrey persuaded Charles II to visit it; the plans and drawings of William Stukeley and Sir Richard Colt Hoare are invaluable for our knowledge of its condition in 1724 and 1812 respectively. A succession of other workers followed. Dean Merewether excavated many of the barrows on the surrounding land in the 1840s, but his finds are lost. The finds of work during the present century are in the Museum, near the parish church.

Castlerigg Stone Circle, Cumbria

2 miles east of Keswick, just south of the old Penrith road

On the high land between Keswick and Thirlmere stands in a windy field a circle of upright unhewn stones. This is a well-known example of the stone circles, probably religious in purpose, which are quite numerous in the highland zone of Britain. Probably nearly all were set up from late Neolithic to Middle Bronze Age times. Some can certainly be attributed to the Beaker people. There are thirty-eight stones in this circle, of which five have fallen. Eight stones exceed five feet in height. Inside the circle, which averages 102 feet in diameter, there is an interior rectangle of ten stones (eight still standing).

Castlerigg, also known as the Carles or the Druids' Circle, was visited by William Stukeley (1687–1765), and early antiquarians popularized the anachronistic Druid association. The site is perhaps at its most impressive in stormy weather, with curtains of rain falling across the fells. Keats saw it thus in 1818 and described the experience in *Hyperion*.

Cissbury Ring, West Sussex

$1\frac{1}{2}$ miles east of Findon, 3 miles north of Worthing, off A24

Cissbury has been the scene of human activity since the Neolithic period in about 2500 B.C. Intensive flint mining was carried on, second only in importance to the mines at Grimes Graves in Norfolk. The mineshafts were about forty feet deep and radiating galleries followed the flint seams. Lamps were used in these dark passages and one was found at Cissbury, a shallow chalk cup with blackened edges.

The flint nodules were worked loose by using red deer antler picks. Antlers were also used as rakes, and the shoulder-blades of oxen as shovels, to clear the rubble, which was carried away in baskets and dumped in worked-out shafts. Such bone tools have been found in other excavated mines.

Set in a commanding position 600 feet above the sea with wide views over the Channel from Beachy Head to the Isle of Wight, Cissbury is well suited to defensive purposes. It is indeed one of the largest Iron Age fort-sites in the country, erected in about 250 B.C. Nearly eighteen acres of defences enclose an area of some sixty-five acres. An inner and an outer bank are in all probability the remains of a solid backing of chalk rubble packed behind a high protecting timber palisade. A hoard of smooth beach pebbles found within the banks were in all likelihood part of a slinger's arsenal.

The fort was abandoned some time before the Roman invasion of A.D. 43, and in the interior can be seen traces of cultivated Celtic fields. Soil has piled up against the inner face of the ramparts, and ploughing outside the banks has gradually pushed soil down the hillside to form earthbanks, known as lynchets. These are also to be found inside the ramparts.

Cissbury Ring

Roman pottery has been picked up from the surface. At the end of the Roman occupation Cissbury was again fortified, perhaps against Saxon raids along the Sussex coast. A defensive turf bank was added to the top of the existing rampart, and at the two entrances the main bank was strengthened and widened.

Coldrum Long Barrow, Kent

1 mile east of Trottiscliffe, between the Pilgrims Way and the A20 London/Folkestone road

The small isolated Medway group of megalithic chambered long barrow tombs dates from the Neolithic period, perhaps from the second half of the 3rd millennium B.C. In general form Coldrum resembles the *dysser* tombs of Denmark, which belong to the earliest Neolithic culture of northern Europe, established by 3000 B.C.

Of this group, Kit's Coty is probably the best known, but Coldrum is the most complete survival. The rectangular barrow, once enclosed by standing stones, is unusually short for its width, about seventy feet by sixty. It is orientated east and west, with the burial chamber at the east end. The barrow mound has almost disappeared, and the enclosing stones are now prostrate. The last few at the east end of the south side have gone, and those on the east side have slipped down the steep slope, leaving the rectangular stone burial chamber poised, empty and unroofed, at the edge of the terrace.

Coldrum was spasmodically excavated by 19th-century antiquarians. In 1910, the bones of at least twenty-two people were discovered. Sir Arthur Keith, the anatomist, identified them as probably having been all of one family, of both sexes and all ages. They were short, delicately boned, and long-headed – all Mediterranean characteristics. One skull had been placed separately on a carefully made stone shelf.

Figsbury Ring, Wiltshire

4 miles north-east of Salisbury, $\frac{1}{2}$ mile north of A30

The immigrant farmers of the northern European seaboard, whose culture was derived from the earliest iron-using culture of Europe, that known as Hallstatt, began to settle in Britain in the 6th century B.C. Though they lived mostly in undefended farms or hilltop villages, a few sites of the period are defended by earth ramparts following the contours of the hilltops. Figsbury is a conspicuous example, sited on a promontory of the Wiltshire Downs. A single bank and outer ditch, roughly circular in shape, with two entrances of the simplest gap type, enclose an area of some fifteen acres. An interesting feature is the internal quarry ditch, about forty-five feet wide and about thirty yards inside the bank. This doubtless provided the chalk from which the outer rampart was raised in height.

Excavations carried out in 1924 revealed few signs of occupation. However, the area of excavation was small and no firm conclusions can be drawn. Pottery found suggests that there was activity on the site in the late Neolithic and Bronze Ages. A fine Bronze Age leaf-shaped sword was found. It has been suggested that Figsbury served more as a refuge in times of trouble for farmers living in neighbouring villages than as a continuously occupied township.

Figsbury Ring

Highdown Hill, West Sussex

1 mile north of Ferring off A2032, 3 miles north-west of Worthing

Lying between the South Downs and the sea, the most prominent feature of Highdown Hill today is the early Iron Age fort dating from 550–300 B.C. Excavations, however, have revealed traces of earlier Late Bronze Age occupation of 650–500 B.C. A metal hoard discovered in the 19th century possibly belonged to a Deverel-Rimbury tribe, Bronze Age people from northern France, who employed the ard, a light plough which could be drawn by oxen. The use of this plough determined farming methods for centuries and led to the formation of the so-called Iron Age 'Celtic' fields, whose worn-down earth boundaries may still be traced all along the chalk hills of Wessex and the south coast of England.

Highdown Hill

The Iron Age defences of the Highdown hillfort, built over existing earthworks, comprised a wide steep-sided ditch some six feet deep and a rampart. The post-holes of rectangular Iron Age huts have been discovered inside the perimeter.

Highdown was occupied again some time in the 3rd century A.D., as evidenced by large quantities of Romano-British pottery found within hut remains of the period. After these successive occupations, Highdown finally became a Saxon burial ground. In 1892 a rich, pagan cemetery, dating from not earlier than the late 5th century A.D., was uncovered.

Lanyon Quoit, Cornwall

2 miles south-east of Morvah, 4 miles north-west of Penzance, by the roadside

Lanyon Quoit is one of a small series of megalithic tombs in Cornwall, Devon and Dorset, usually known as the Penwith group from the name of the Cornish peninsula. Like several of the others, this great stone burial chamber was once covered by a long mound. Here at Lanyon the mound ran north and south with the main chamber at the northern end. There are some traces of what may have been a smaller lateral chamber toward the south.

Very little is known of the date of the Penwith group, but it may well be relatively late in the history of megalithic architecture, perhaps towards the end of the 3rd millennium. Some authorities would derive the type from Brittany, while others seek a link with south-eastern Ireland.

Lanyon Quoit is the best known and most visited of all Cornish megaliths. The group of four huge stones, which may be best described as a gigantic three-legged table, is all that remains of a chamber tomb which was originally rectangular. It stands at the end of a long barrow, of which scant traces remain. Before 1815, when Lanyon Quoit was blown down in a gale, it stood so high off the ground that 'a man could ride a horse under the capstone'. It was re-erected in its present position nine years later.

Lanyon Quoit

Midsummer Hill, Hereford & Worcester

3 miles east of Ledbury, north of the A438 Tewkesbury/Ledbury road

The property consists of the entire irregularly-shaped hillfort, with the exception of the southern tip, which has been destroyed by quarrying. The ramparts are of great strength, consisting of a bank and outer ditch, with a counterscarp, or smaller bank, on its downhill lip. They enclose Midsummer Hill, which rises to 937 feet, and the lower Hollybush Hill (795 ft) at the southern tip of the Malvern Hills (see p. 490).

There are two entrances: the southern had guardrooms, and the gateway had been reconstructed many times. The interior had been permanently occupied over a long period from the beginning of the 3rd century B.C., and huts built on the terraced slope. A large pillow mound lies between the two hills.

Midsummer Hill; View to the south from the hill fort

Oldbury Hill, Kent

3 miles south-west of Wrotham, on north side of the A256 Sevenoaks/ Wrotham road

Two overhanging ledges on the east side of Oldbury Hill seem to have been occupied by Middle Palaeolithic hunters during the last Ice Age. The flint implements found there in the excavations of 1890 included small hand-axes and other implements of a kind usually associated with Neanderthal Man. Shelters of this age are very uncommon in Britain, rarer still in south-east England. The Oldbury discoveries are therefore of exceptional interest. The larger shelter (where most of the implements were found) is in the hard green stone of the Folkestone Beds; the smaller is in a kind of sandstone.

This greensand hill is scarped on all sides except to the north, and commands a Medway crossing and entrance to the Weald. As an ideal natural defensive site, it is not surprising to find that it was fortified by the Iron Age Britons. The first hillfort was built in about 100 B.C. by people of the so-called Wealden culture. This had no more than a modest rampart and ditch with simple entrances to north and south, but it was unusually large, covering no less than 123 acres. Later it was considerably strengthened, the rampart being enlarged, the ditch made wider, and the entrances protected with inturned banks. Excavation of the northern entrance revealed the post-holes of a heavy timber gate. According to one opinion, these additional defences were thrown up against the Roman invaders of A.D. 43; according to another, against the western expansion of the Belgae. Whatever the occasion, Oldbury seems to have been attacked and to have fallen: many sling-stones were found on the outer slopes of the rampart and the north gate had been burnt.

The northern half of Oldbury Hill Fort is a covenanted property. The southern half belongs to the Trust.

Trencrom Hill, Cornwall

3 miles south of St Ives, 2 miles west of junction of A3074 and A30

This Early Iron Age fort, overlooking a wide stretch of country, is situated on a natural rampart or outpost of the Land's End peninsula.

Excavation on any scale has never taken place on Trencrom; its archaeological history is therefore conjectural. It is possible to trace the line of a single drystone rampart, which follows the outline of the hill and enclosed the twin granite outcrops and the saddle between, a rectangular area of about an acre. Huge granite boulders have been pushed into place, with rubble and smaller stones filling the space between to form a wall. Inside the fort, traces of circular huts are visible, rather like rough saucers outlined by walls of granite blocks. Contemporary pottery of about the 2nd century B.C. has been picked up in the huts and inside the wall.

Shards of later 'grassmarked' pottery, a type peculiar to Cornwall, have been found, and suggest that Trencrom was re-occupied during the period of the Saxon advance into Cornwall, in the 8th and 9th centuries, and used as a refuge by the local people.

Treryn Dinas (Treen Castle), Cornwall

4 miles south-east of Land's End, via B3315

Treen is an example of the sea-girt cliff castles or defended headlands found around the Cornish coast and in Wales. The Rumps, the Dodman, and Maen Castle are other examples which belong to the Trust in Cornwall, as does part of Dinas Gwynfor in Anglesey. Such castles were evidently

407

Treryn Dinas; Cliff fort, from Treen Cliff

erected throughout the Celtic Iron Age, sometimes by immigrant groups, sometimes by peoples already in possession.

Treen is hard to date. The defences were probably built at different times, the earliest probably during the 3rd–2nd centuries B.C., and the latest probably in the 1st century.

The headland is cut off by a series of earthbanks, the first being a bank and ditch of immense proportions. Some distance behind it are three much less massive banks and ditches. The middle earthwork not only spans the headland but also curves south at each end, following the sides of the promontory.

The extreme tip of the headland carried an interesting fortification: a bank faced with heavy masonry spanning the waist of the headland at the narrowest part. A ditch with a central causeway was dug immediately outside this bank. It lies to the north of the famous Logan rock or Rocking Stone – a great boulder weighing some sixty-six tons.

Windmill Hill, Wiltshire

$1\frac{1}{2}$ miles north-west of Avebury, 1 mile north of A4, 6 miles west of Marlborough

The causewayed camp on Windmill Hill has become the type-site for early Neolithic causewayed enclosures and has given its name to the culture of the Stone Age farmers who arrived in southern England from France towards the end of the 4th millennium B.C.

Windmill Hill camp has been radio-carbon-dated as about 2570 B.C., already some five hundred years later than the first settlement of the primitive farmers. The gentle summit of the low hill, which drops steeply to

Windmill Hill

the plain at one point only, is crowned by three irregular and roughly concentric circles, which altogether enclose about twenty acres of downland. What remains of the earthworks stands about three feet high and is broken at intervals by numerous causeways or bridges of untouched chalk.

The camp cannot have been used as a fort or as a permanent settlement. It may have been the appointed place where scattered tribal groups came together at certain times for social or religious ceremonies.

Much domestic equipment has been discovered on the site: flint axes, knives, scrapers, saws, stone querns with rubbers, and pottery of the characteristic simple deep round-bottomed shape called Windmill Hill pottery. This is the earliest type found in Britain.

The skeleton of a young child was discovered crouched at the bottom of one section of the outer ditch, while a baby had been buried in another.

The excavations at Windmill Hill, as at Avebury, owe much to the work of Alexander Keiller between 1925 and 1939. Avebury and Windmill Hill were bought in 1943, with the aid of the Pilgrim Trust and Mr I. D. Margary, and given to the National Trust.

Winterbourne Stoke Barrow Group, Stonehenge Down, Wiltshire

$1\frac{1}{2}$ miles south-west of Stonehenge, just north-east of the roundabout at junction of A360 with the A303 Andover/Exeter road

The region around Stonehenge contains a greater concentration of prehistoric earthworks than any other area in Britain. Many are Beaker and Bronze Age burial barrows, grouped in cemeteries which are often strung out in a line. One of the most important of these is the Winterbourne Stoke Group (about half of it on National Trust land), which contains round

Winterbourne Stoke Barrows, from the north-east

barrows of all types, the rarer pond, saucer and disc barrows in addition to the bowls and bell-barrows (see p. 395). Bell-barrows have large mounds, separated from the surrounding ditch by a platform, and there is commonly a bank outside the ditch. These were usually raised over the burials of men, some of whom, to judge by their possessions, were warrior chieftains. Disc barrows are almost exclusively women's graves, and consist of a flat circular area defined by a ditch and an outside bank, with a small tump in the centre over the burial.

Most of the barrows on Stonehenge Down were opened by Sir Richard Colt Hoare (see p. 192) and published by him in *Ancient Wiltshire,* and many of his finds are to be seen in Devizes Museum.

Closest to the roundabout, just off National Trust land, stands a particularly fine long barrow, antedating the Group by about a millennium. On the property, north of the Clump, is a good specimen of a pond barrow, then two large bell-barrows, both over ten feet high. In the first Hoare found the remains of an elm and oak box with bronze fittings containing, with the cremation, two daggers, a bronze pin and tweezers. In the second, which he called the King Barrow, there was an elm-trunk coffin with a skeleton, a bronze awl with bone handle, two grooved daggers (of which one still retained the remains of a wooden sheath ornamented with gilt) and a rounded box-wood handle.

Next comes a line of bowl barrows; one yielded a grape-cup, an incense cup, bone beads and whetstones, and another contained a boat-shaped wooden coffin in which was a skeleton with a necklace of shale and amber beads, a bronze dagger and awl. Another bowl barrow contained two skeletons which were accompanied by a long-necked beaker, and a further sequence of burials in this grave was carefully observed and recorded by Hoare.

410

Roman and Romano-British Sites

Cerne Giant, Dorset

On Giant Hill, north of Cerne Abbas, 8 miles north of Dorchester on A352

Huge figures cut in chalk or limestone hills and downs in conspicuous places are a well-known type of monument in southern England. The earliest examples may date from the Iron Age, although few authentic figures survive. Their original purpose is unknown, but they may well have been religious symbols possibly associated with fertility or of tribal significance.

The Cerne Giant is an unmistakable fertility figure, with many of the attributes of Hercules. It has been suggested that he may date from A.D. 191, when the Emperor Commodus declared himself the reincarnation of Hercules. A traditional name for the Giant is Helio or Helith. The Giant is 180 feet high, and brandishes a club well over a hundred feet long. He is a folklore character and, until recent years, was the centre of midsummer rites.

Above the Giant is the Trendle, a rectangular earthenwork with two banks and raised ground in the middle, until recently the site of a maypole. Both lie close to the well-preserved remains of a settlement with outlying fields, probably dating from the Iron Age.

The Trendle does not belong to the Trust.

Cerne Giant

Chedworth Villa, Gloucestershire

3 miles north-west of Fossebridge on the A429 Cirencester/Northleach road. Approach by the Yanworth/Withington road

In Roman times a villa meant a farm and its outbuildings, but the term has now come to cover all Roman country houses from smallholdings to large establishments. Of these there are more in Gloucestershire and west Wiltshire than in any comparable area in Britain and over a dozen exist within a ten-mile radius of Cirencester. Chedworth, whose buildings date from about A.D. 180–350, is the finest and the most fully excavated.

Chedworth Roman villa;
Mosaic floor in the bath-house

Below:
'Winter', detail of mosaic floor

    The Villa, situated in a beautiful and lonely site in the wooded valley of the Coln, was a large mansion belonging to a wealthy landowner, most probably a Romanized Briton, who lived a quiet civilized existence on his estate. He had an excellent supply of spring water – his *Nymphaeum*, dedicated to the water nymphs, still runs cold and limpid – and he was within easy reach of the Fosse Way, the Roman road from Exeter to Lincoln. When and how Chedworth met its end is not known. Following the breakdown of the Empire in the 5th century, many such estates were simply abandoned and others destroyed. The Villa was rediscovered, dramatically enough, in 1864 when Lord Eldon's gamekeeper, digging for a lost ferret, found instead a mosaic pavement.

    The buildings occupy three sides of a rectangle facing east across the valley. Living rooms, dining room, and bedrooms can be traced, all with underfloor hot-air heating. The most prominent feature of the house are the baths, so important in Roman life. There are both steam baths of Turkish type and a *laconicum* or Spartan dry hot bath, the equivalent of the modern sauna. Mosaic floors have survived in the *tepidarium* and *frigidarium* (the moderately warm and the cold rooms) and in the *triclinium* or dining room. Mosaic work, based often on standard patterns, was common throughout the Roman world. Generally speaking, the farther from Rome and the later in date, the cruder the design and workmanship. Chedworth mosaics are mostly of the Cirencester school, whose reputation is high.

Excavation began in 1868. The walls above ground were capped by little slated and gabled roofs which give a bizarre appearance to the site, as does the incongruous half-timbered hunting lodge, now a museum, erected in the Villa courtyard at about the same time.

Hadrian's Wall, Northumberland

4 miles north-east of Haltwhistle. Best point of access at Housesteads fort, north of B6318

Stationed on these wild Northumbrian moors Roman soldiers kept watch on the Wall for over two and a half centuries. Begun by the Emperor Hadrian in A.D. 122, strengthened with forts and milecastles, and flanked with ditch and vallum, this defensive work that linked two seas remains Rome's most impressive monument in Britain.

But the Wall is more, far more, than an object of interest to archaeologists and historians. It marches, our own Great Wall of China, over the hills with nobility and confidence. Dramatic, solemn, or elegantly sinuous, the Wall has many qualities – sometimes it has been levelled for miles at a stretch – but it is, above all, an object of beauty. It offers an aesthetic experience to the tens of thousands who in the course of a year walk the airy wall top, and look northward, no doubt with greater pleasure than did legionaries and aux-iliaries far from home, at the incomparable yet sombre landscape that stretches to the distant Cheviots.

The Trust owns the most spectacular section of Hadrian's Wall: some three and a half miles where the wall runs mainly on the top of a steep

Hadrian's Wall

escarpment and crosses Cuddy Crags whose perpendicular walls fall to a remote and reed-fringed lough. The Trust's fort at Housesteads, one of the best preserved, is (with its associated museum) under the guardianship of the Department of the Environment.

The ever-increasing number of summer visitors poses problems, particularly where the mortared Roman Wall was rebuilt as a drystone wall in the 18th and 19th centuries. Throughout the year two full-time masons are employed by the Trust on maintenance.

Letocetum, Wall, Staffordshire

2 miles south-west of Lichfield, on north side of A5

The small Romano-British town at Wall on Watling Street was of sufficient consequence to be included in a list of twenty-eight British cities drawn up by Nennius in the 8th century. It appears as *Cair Luitocoyt*, 'the fortified place in the grey wood', and the Romans called it *Etocetum*, a Romanized version of the Celtic name. To the Romanized Britons it was Letocetum.

Watling Street, one of the most important Roman roads, ran from London north-west through St Albans to Chester and north Wales. Imperial post routes were furnished at intervals with posting stations for changing horses (*mutationes*) and hostels or lodgings for the night (*mansiones*). Letocetum grew up round such a posting station. Coins have been found which cover the whole period of Roman occupation, from the reign of Tiberius to that of Valens who died in A.D. 378.

The bath-house, which together with another neighbouring building was bought by the Trust in 1924, is the most complete surviving example of a Romano-British town bath-house. The series of chambers, whose temperature and humidity were controlled by a sophisticated method of underfloor hot-air and water heating, ranged from the cold room, the *frigidarium*, through the warm room, the *tepidarium*, to the hot dry chamber, the *laconicum*, and the wet steam chamber, the *caldarium*. A cold plunge, and then massage and unction with aromatic oils, would follow. An exercise courtyard, resting rooms, and public meeting places, were also essential adjuncts to the bath-house, used by travellers on the road and by the citizens of the town.

Ribchester, Lancashire

10 miles north-east of Preston, off B6245, close to the church

Agricola, the Roman governor who by A.D. 83 had extended the frontiers of the Empire to the Forth and the Clyde, on his way north established a legionary fortress at Chester. He then penetrated the western side of the Pennines, setting up a chain of roads and garrisoned forts as he advanced.

Replica of parade helmet and mask found at Ribchester in 1795. British Museum

The Roman fort at Ribchester, situated in the Ribble valley running up to Bowland Forest and to the Yorkshire moorlands beyond, formed part of this system. It has been identified as the Roman Bremetennacum from an inscribed votive stone dedicated to the 'god Apollo Maponus by the Sarmatian horsemen of Bremetennacum'. The name occurs in three Roman documents and in the Ravenna *Cosmography*, a list of the countries, towns and rivers of the known world compiled in the 7th century.

The remains at Ribchester have long been known, and Camden visited 'Ribblechester' in 1582. Many finds described in the 17th and 18th centuries have been lost, but a collection of antiques, which includes a tombstone sculpture of a cavalry trooper of the 1st century, inscribed stones, pottery, jewellery, metal-work and glass, are housed in a museum on the site. A fine parade helmet and mask, discovered in 1795, is in the British Museum.

The earliest fort at Ribchester was timber, covering some five-and-a-half acres and defended by a puddled clay rampart. This military establishment, large enough to house an auxiliary cavalry regiment, can be dated from the Flavian period, A.D. 69–80.

The only part of the fort uncovered today is a section of two large granaries, which would have held a year's supply of grain for the garrison. Handfuls of barley, burnt black but still clearly recognizable, are in the museum.

In the 3rd century, the fort was garrisoned by Sarmatian horsemen, part of a contingent of 5000 picked men recruited from Sarmatia on the Danube. These auxiliaries, having served their time, settled in Britain as farmers and horsebreeders. Ribchester became a centre for these retired veterans, although the area remained a military zone different in character from the civilian south.

By the end of the 3rd century, the frontiers of the Roman Empire were crumbling fast. When coastal raids led to the establishment of a sea-fort at Lancaster, Ribchester became redundant. It seems to have been abandoned during Gratian's reign (367–83).

415

Segontium, Gwynedd

On south-east outskirts of Caernarvon, on east side of the A487
Caernarvon/Beddgelert road

After the Claudian invasion of A.D. 43, the lowland area south of a line
between the Severn and the Trent, formally delimited by the Fosse Way,
came to form the civilian heart of the Roman province. Successive governors
gradually extended the frontiers and pushed the military zones farther north
and west, where Wales was the centre of stubborn resistance and the wild
Silures, led by Caractacus, raided across the border. In A.D. 60, the Romans
advanced as far as Anglesey, the headquarters of the Druids, but they hastily
retreated to deal with Queen Boudicca's revolt. It was not until A.D. 74–8
that Julius Frontinus defeated the Silures, and established garrisons in the
centre and north of Wales among the Ordovices.

The fort at Segontium was probably built as part of Frontinus' chain
of fortified bases for auxiliary troops, established on or near navigable
estuaries. It corresponded with Carmarthen in the south. Strategically
Segontium is excellently placed, commanding the Lleyn peninsula, the
Menai Straits, and the Snowdon massif.

Within its four-and-a-half acre site, Segontium probably housed an
auxiliary cohort of 500–1,000 men with accompanying service units, their
families and the core of a civilian settlement. In Britain about the year
A.D. 100, auxiliaries were mostly drawn from north-east Gaul, the Low
Countries, the Balkans, and Spain. After twenty-five years of military
service auxiliaries were rewarded with Roman citizenship, and by the end
of the 1st century there may have been 200,000 in the army.

The fort at Segontium, originally defended by a broad earth rampart and
ditch, was of the invariable rectangular shape with four gateways. The
troops were probably first housed in tents. The later stone defences, comprising walls, gateways, and associated buildings, date from about A.D. 150.
The structures within the perimeter were mostly rebuilt during the 4th
century.

The plan of the fort, based on the Roman town-concept of a grid centred
on a basilica and forum, is common to almost all legionary establishments.
It is possible to trace the arrangement of the commander's house (the
praetorium), the basilica, offices, and colonnaded court. An apsidal chamber behind the basilica and the remains of a bath-house have the only
hypocausts in the fort and some attempt at wall decoration. Two large
granaries give some indication of the strength of the garrison.

A series of coin-finds indicates that the fort was probably held until
A.D. 383. Nothing is known of Segontium's later fate. Silver pennies dating
from Edward I's conquest of Wales nine hundred years later show that the
dressed stone of the ruined fort was used in the building of his great
medieval castle at Caernarvon.

VII
Coast and Country

Introduction *by C. H. D. Acland*

Never before has such a wealth of beautiful country been gathered into the hands of a single owner for the purpose of preserving it for the public benefit. There is no evidence that the civilizations of the past had either the need or the desire to care for natural beauty, and in historic times the great and the wealthy owned and preserved their 'forests' for the purpose of the chase rather than of tranquillity, and the beneficiaries were certainly not the common people.

What has made the scenery of this country worth preserving? What has inspired the Nation's undoubted and increasing will to preserve it? What has the National Trust achieved, and what may be expected from it in the future?

In North America one may travel by fast train for half a day over flat country where the geological upheavals of the past have done nothing to distinguish one mile from another. These islands of ours are so full of variety that the geologist can often attribute a landscape picture to within a mile or two of its place of origin, and even the casual observer unconsciously links the scenery to its underlying rock formations. A chalk down such as Culver in the Isle of Wight proclaims its similarity to other chalk downs such as Ashridge and Coombe Hill along the great scarpland stretching from Dorset to Lincolnshire. The glacial valleys of north Wales and the Lake District not only resemble each other with their flat fields between steep sides, but are obviously different from the water-worn coombs of Exmoor, where rounded hills fall ever more steeply to the wooded cleft and the hidden stream. They in their turn differ from the precipitous flanks of the valley cut by the River Dove into the limestone of the Peak District. The basalt cliffs of Antrim produce a different type of coastal scenery from the contorted shales and limestones of north Devon and Cornwall, which again change dramatically as one reaches the granite of Land's End. In south-west Wales the characteristic evenness of the cliff tops was worn by Pliocene seas which were then several hundred feet higher in relation to the land. In East Anglia the changing face of the fenlands and the formation of new coastal spits of gravel are geological changes happening before our very eyes.

This rich and varied heritage from the past is still further diversified by our climate. The traveller who has flown over Egypt has seen, hour after hour, a lifeless landscape in the grip of a monotonous and extreme climate. We have the good fortune to live in the temperate zone, where some life, both animal and vegetable, can survive even our harshest climate and where, only a hundred miles away, cattle wade belly-deep in rich grass for six months out of the twelve. Since the retreat of the last Ice Age our climate has fostered a gradual progression from tundra through birch and pine forest. Then came the oak and the hazel, the grasses and smaller plants, each to leave its tell-tale pollen stratified in the mud and peat of our lakes and fens.

Our present climate supports a wide variety of habitats occupied by countless plants and creatures. The vegetation of our highest mountains verges on the Alpine, and in some of our western valleys plants survive which are otherwise known only from Europe's south-western extension. Moist winds from the Atlantic dictate that our western agriculture shall present a grassy face to the eye, while the drier lands of the east continue to grow corn.

Our climate, and our position on the edge of the continent, add variety to our bird population. We have one population which is wholly resident, another which breeds here but winters elsewhere, either at sea or in the south, and a third population which passes us twice each year on its journeys between northern breeding grounds and southern winter haunts.

If our scenery had been influenced only by the geology and climate of these islands it would certainly have displayed wide variety, but it would have been very different from that which we know today. It may be that our mountains, above the natural tree line, would have looked much as they do now even if man had never progressed beyond the stage of the nomadic herdsman. Nor has man much altered the appearance of some parts of our coasts. Overlook oil-soaked seabirds and plastic bottles along the tide line, and some of our cliffs and beaches look today much as they did when the Britons first saw Caesar's fleet or when St Cuthbert was a hermit on the Inner Farne, where it is said that he tamed the eider ducks, which today will still sit tight on their eggs to be stroked by visitors. But apart from our mountains, coasts and cliffs there is scarcely a yard of these islands still in its 'natural' condition.

Man, the grazier, cleared scrub for his flocks; man, the agriculturist, ploughed the common field. Between the Dark Ages and the Reformation the feudal system had delineated the boundaries of the manors which today correspond with most of our parishes, and the great monastic establishments had become the equivalent of any latter-day landed estate. Although the churches and the ruins of the monasteries have come down to us as the tangible relics of medieval society, it had as great an effect upon our open country as upon our buildings. Wild Britain had begun to be tamed. It is not easy to understand the present importance of our commons and open spaces without appreciating the changes which have taken place in British agriculture since those days.

At the heart of each manor the virgin forest had been cleared for the common fields where the lord of the manor and the villeins each had his strip or strips of ploughed land. Each of these great fields, usually only three to a manor, grew but one crop at a time. The low balks which separated the strips would not have interrupted what must have been the monotonous appearance of several hundred acres of corn or of bare fallow. But the country which surrounded the common fields was still wooded, the cattle, sheep and pigs being driven each day to graze among the trees.

Far the greatest cause of change in our rural scene was the age of enclosures. Already at the end of Tudor times, and despite protests about depopulation, most of the common ploughfields of Kent, Essex and Sussex had been divided up into individual holdings. But it was during the reigns of the Georges that enclosure of the open fields was most rapid, reaching its greatest rate at about the end of the 18th century. When Victoria came to the throne virtually all the strip system of agriculture had gone and the emphasis had shifted to the enclosure of the common grazings, at first by private Acts of Parliament, but later under the General Enclosure Act of 1845. By 1865 most of this country had been taken into the ownership of the great landlords, who often paid inadequate compensation to the manorial tenants and parcelled the land out amongst their new rent-paying tenant farmers. Only in the north, the south-west and Wales was the land so poor or the terrain so rugged as to escape the improving hand of the great agriculturists such as Coke and Townshend and those who learned from them.

Great improvers they certainly were, introducing new crops such as turnips and new methods such as the marling of light soils. But they changed the face of Britain. It was they who gave us the pattern of field and hedgerow still to be enjoyed at its best from the Malvern Hills or from the summit of Bradnor Hill on the Welsh Marches. The hedgerow trees, whose disappearance is now so much regretted, were a feature of this new system. Let there be no doubt that the new agriculture which they introduced was far more productive than the old manorial system. For the first time there was sufficient fodder to bring store cattle through the winter: the great autumn slaughter was a thing of the past. The urban population was growing: the increased production went to feed it.

The Industrial Revolution did not so much alter the scenery as destroy those parts of it which fell beneath its onslaught, and little of what was affected has later been thought worthy of preservation by the Trust. Perhaps there is some justice in the fact that it was the descendants of the dispossessed peasants who, as the landless labourers of the Industrial Revolution, took their revenge upon the countryside and later upon agriculture itself. The fall of agriculture which set in about 1875 has continued ever since. Not even the near-starvation brought about by two world wars has made this country wake up to the importance of home production. It may not be long before mountain sheep are valued as park-keepers rather than as producers of mutton and wool!

It is worth considering how the Englishman's appreciation of the countryside has altered over the centuries and whether it will change in the future. Understandably the earlier references to beautiful scenery are related to productivity. Bunyan viewed the Chilterns as 'a most pleasant Mountainous Country, beautiful with woods, vineyards, fruits of all sorts; Flowers also, with Springs of Fountains, very delectable to behold'; and Evelyn 'passed over a goodly plaine, or rather sea of carpet, which I think for evenness, extent, verdure and innumerable flocks to be one of the most delightful prospects in nature'. Conversely Defoe described the Surrey heathlands, including 'some hills call'd the Hind Head' as 'a foil to the beauty of the rest of England: or a mark of the just resentment shew'd by Heaven upon the Englishman's pride'.

The Romantic school of poets undoubtedly influenced the appreciation of wild nature but they were in part the effect of a continuing process, rather than the cause of a sudden change of outlook. Wordsworth's *Guide to the Lakes*, written when he was forty, is more famous than its predecessor published by West while the poet was still but a lad at Hawkshead Grammar School. Perhaps the changing attitude was a reaction to the gradual taming of so much of the lowlands. In the same way the earliest gardens were formal areas tamed out of wilderness and later gardens have developed along romantic 'natural' lines as a relief to a universally conquered landscape. Words such as 'awful', 'horrible' and 'dreadful' lost their literal meanings, and the torrent no longer plunged in a fearful cataract into a chasm or abyss of unimaginable depth where no sunbeam ever gleamed! We had come to terms with waterfalls and cliffs.

If the quality of our appreciation of open country has altered comparatively little, the intensity with which we value it has increased enormously. Ironically, the end of enclosure was brought about, not on a plea for the dispossessed landless peasantry whose opposition had been loud in previous centuries, but by the objection of the urban population, who now outnumbered the countrymen, to being excluded from their holiday playgrounds. The battle to keep Berkhamsted Common as an open space was fought and won in 1865, the same year which saw the foundation of the Commons Preservation Society. This was the germination of a seed which was to grow, a generation later, into the National Trust, now, appropriately, the owner of Berkhamsted Common. The effect of the Industrial Revolution was to shift the emphasis from rural productivity towards access. City populations, living in crowded noisy conditions, increasingly felt the need for solitude and tranquillity. Overworked factory hands demanded recreation. The Bank Holiday Act of 1875, coupled with improved means of transport, gave them their chance to get into the country or to the seaside.

Yet even this need for relief from city life was no new conception. Thus Milton, the Cockney:

> As one who long in populous City pent,
> Where Houses thick and Sewers annoy the Aire,
> Forth issuing on a Summers Morn to breathe . . .
> The smell of Grain, or tedded Grass, or Kine.

Our love of open spaces includes a purely aesthetic element. Trees and flowers, birds' flight, reflections in still water, the sinuous flow of the river, the movement of wind over corn, cloud shadows over hillsides – these are absolutely beautiful.

There is also an intellectual satisfaction to be had from the preservation of a rare species, or from the combat of pollution whether by toxic pesticides or noise of traffic. Just as we judge our forebears by the scars or beauty they bequeathed to us, so shall we in our turn be judged by posterity. We wish to be well remembered.

It is, however, a psychological pleasure which extends the joy of a day or a week in the country beyond the actual duration of the visit. Which of us has not planned, with map and guide-book, just where he will go and how he will reach his goal? Which of us, buying boots or binoculars, tents or waterproof clothing, has not savoured the joys to come? Which of us, returned from the country, has not relived and recounted his experiences? Which of us could endure the long sojourn in urban filth and noise, but for the knowledge that the surf still pounds on Polzeath beach, the curlew calls on Howden Moor, the wind blows clean over Braich-y-Pwll and Great Gable still looks down on Wasdale Head?

Yet it is too facile to attribute our present love of the open air purely to a reaction from city life. Many of the most devoted and knowledgeable countrymen have never suffered the claustrophobia of the town. To analyse our feelings when we come into contact with wild nature – the sense of greatness we experience when we survey broad counties from a hilltop, the littleness we feel as we watch waves thunder against a towering cliff, the intensity of our interest in the minute delicacy of a flower or the perfection of an insect's wing, the almost primeval thrill we derive from each manifestation of each succeeding spring – to analyse these feelings is to cross the boundary between reason and mysticism. It would have been easier before Darwin destroyed our belief in the literal truth of the first chapter of Genesis. Easier – yes; but different? – no. Our great-grandfathers knew that the worship of God was something which extended beyond the church walls. Today the exodus from the towns is still an act of worship.

Perhaps in the ultimate it is superfluous even to try to analyse what we feel. To find it remarkable that man still loves the country after a mere half-dozen generations of city life is to forget the countless aeons of his earlier rural life. Suffice it to say that the love of nature is natural to him.

It has become fashionable during the last decade to denigrate the concept of preservation and to substitute the word 'conservation'. There is nothing wrong with either word. Both mean that something is being looked after with love and care. What are the threats from which our scenery should be preserved? What must be done to care for it properly?

The mere fact of ownership by the Trust is a form of preservation in itself. Incredible as it now seems, on the north Cornish coast Pentire Head, in Surrey the Devil's Punch Bowl, in Gloucestershire Haresfield Beacon, and in the Lake District Manesty and Glencoyne Woods were lotted up as building sites when the public appeals were launched to save them. In those days there was no effective planning law. If the Farne Islands had not come to the Trust, most of them would have fallen into the hands of a shooting syndicate. In those days laws for the protection of wild birds were quite inadequate. The dark patches on the Long Mynd will, for evermore, be racing cloud shadows, not slab-sided softwood plantations. There is still no law to control such forestry. Constantly the Trust has had to ask itself what will befall a piece of land if it takes no action. Constantly the answer has justified a new acquisition.

Time and again land which has come to the Trust was marred by some ugly feature. How quickly one forgets the hutments and wire fences on the headland at Kete in Dyfed, the fifty-four Nissen huts inhabited by squatters near Blickling Hall, the four hundred concrete posts removed by volunteers from Cemlyn in Anglesey, the cars on the beaches at Formby and Brancaster, the military camps now gone from Clumber Park and from the cliff tops at Killigerran Head and Mawnan Glebe in Cornwall, the hideous caravan site removed from Porth Farm. What a triumph it is that a whole generation has savoured Stonehenge, blissfully unaware that the surrounding downland, now in the care of the Trust, used to be defiled by a clutter of shacks.

As a great national institution the Trust accepts its duty to behave in a responsible way. Part of its greatness and its power in the land stems from the fact that it has considered other national needs besides pure preservation. For example, during the emergency of the war years Ludshott Common in Hampshire was used as a tank training ground, yet it has recovered. How often the Trust's reaction to a major threat has been to consider firstly whether the national need is imperative, secondly whether alternatives exist, and thirdly, where there is no other place in which an essential requirement can be met, how it can be met with least damage to the beauty and atmosphere of scenery and open spaces. Sometimes this kind of preservation takes place as a discussion on the ground with a local road surveyor who is trying to eliminate a danger spot or with a telephone engineer seeking the right route for a new line. Sometimes battle must be joined, and untold time and money spent, in exploring and demonstrating alternatives and in presenting the case for preservation at public inquiries, or even before Parliament itself. It is regrettable that on these occasions it may be necessary to oppose some development or industry in itself desirable. It is, however, often comforting to the Trust to find allies amongst other public bodies such as planning authorities, the Countryside Commission or the Councils for the Protection of Rural England and Wales, with whom it has so often co-operated.

Apart from countering threats and removing eyesores, the Trust, just like other rural landowners, must enter into the industries of the countryside. In the country one expects to see fields and woods, livestock and trees. It is not surprising that so much of the Trust's time, thought and money is devoted to good estate management. It is the policy to let agricultural land to farm tenants. In areas of rugged beauty, where public access is most desirable, it is inevitable that the quality of the land, from the point of view of food production, will be low. Except where farm land is owned as a buffer to protect some great country house from the outside world, land of really good quality has seldom come to the Trust. In the mountains, along the cliff tops and among the heathlands where the scenery is best, farming is often marginal. This is fortunate from the point of view of access because in these places the feet of the masses do less harm. But this low productivity of so many of its acres has deprived the Trust of agricultural rents which other landlords enjoy. It is not easy to pay for the maintenance and improvement of farmhouses and buildings when rents are low. Yet if they are not maintained, if succeeding generations of farm tenants are not forthcoming, then dereliction is the inevitable result. Those who are familiar with some of the water-gathering grounds, where agriculture has been deliberately extinguished for the sake of pure water, will know the repulsive aspect of the derelict scenery. Conversely, it is recognized how great a contribution thriving farming makes to scenery, provided that it really is agricultural farming and not factory farming. Schemes to retain hedgerow trees, a relationship with farm tenants which will discourage (sometimes by means of a rent abatement) the proliferation of the little aluminium huts known as 'pigloos' or the vast slab-roofed milksheds called 'mootels', the provision of well-designed new buildings in the right position when they are genuinely needed, the deliberate reintroduction of sheep on to chalk downs such as Coombe Hill to prevent its reversion to scrub, these are some of the methods which are used to foster the kind of farming which has contributed so much to our countryside.

It is the Trust's general policy to keep the management of its trees in its own hands. As with agriculture, so with forestry the extremes of commercialism and neglect are equally unacceptable. Although these islands boast of three indigenous conifers – the yew, the juniper and the Scots pine – our natural woods were deciduous. The birch, oak, ash, lime and elm are amongst our earliest trees, and although the sycamore and the chestnuts (and some say the beech) are of later introduction, they did not fundamentally change the general aspect of our forests. It was the coming of the conifers, first the larch and Norway spruce introduced into our woods from Europe two or three centuries ago, and then the Douglas fir and Sitka spruce from the New World after the Napoleonic wars, which altered the woodland scene. Moreover from about that time iron began to replace timber for our ships and there was no longer the great need for the branches of open-grown oaks to provide the curved ribs of wooden hulls. Since then the economic climate, and latterly the fiscal policy, has continued to favour strictly commercial planting.

This commercial attitude to forestry – the large plantation of a single species, the straight fence line – has had more effect on our landscape than the alien tree species. It is this appearance of commercial forestry which the Trust seeks to avoid. Some evergreens in a deciduous wood add to its beauty and to its shelter in winter.

Wordsworth detested the larch, not only when planted commercially in a 'vegetable manufactury', but even individually because 'its green is so peculiar and vivid, that wherever it comes forth a disagreeable speck is produced'; yet there can be few country-lovers today who do not look with eager anticipation for the first spring green of the larch.

If no timber is produced from a wood there will be no revenue to pay the woodmen, and without them dereliction will result. It is a regrettable fact that a tree or a wood felled at its economic peak will not have yielded a tithe of its beauty in the landscape or of its value as a place in which to walk and appreciate the majesty of great trees. It is also true that a great tree, left to die and to fall, may destroy the saplings which have been encouraged to take its place and, lying neglected, may choke the woodland floor and prevent public access.

Even the most beautiful woods are more than adornments to the scenery. Much of our wildlife depends on them for shelter and for food. Many beasts and birds, shade-loving plants, including mosses, lichens and fungi, but most of all, a host of insect species, require woodland conditions to survive. The perpetuation of woodlands, especially the oak woods which support such an army of dependent creatures, is an important part of the Trust's work, yielding dividends, not in cash, but in beauty, access and natural history.

The woods are but one example of preservation for more than a single purpose. It is surprising how often natural history combines with other interests. Some visitors to the Farne Islands pay more attention to their association with the first introduction of Christianity than to the birds. At Wicken Fen, Cambridgeshire, the water is maintained at the right level for the wildlife by a windpump which is a facsimile of an old wooden windmill. The Strangford Lough Wildlife Scheme in County Down started imaginatively enough as a plan to bring naturalists and sportsmen into common cause for the sake of the birds, but its scope has enlarged until the Trust is now involved in planning matters, access, the siting of yacht clubs, the character of the scenery and the surrounding villages, the removal of litter and the eradication of an invasive alien grass, *Spartina angelica*. This is conservation in the round.

Although the Trust has often kept in its own hands, or in the hands of its dedicated local committees, the management of its older nature reserves such as Blakeney Point, Wicken Fen and the Farnes, all acquired during the first quarter of the century, nevertheless it has been quick to co-operate with the younger and more specialized bodies which have come into prominence since the war. There could be no happier example of this than Leigh Woods near Bristol, where the Trust and the Nature Conservancy have demonstrated how effectively they can work together so that public access and natural history can be maintained in harmony. Or again, the purchase of Whitford Burrows, the north-western point of Gower, with Neptune funds, has secured not only a national nature reserve, but a coastland delightful in its own right.

There can scarcely be one of the county naturalists' trusts which is not in league with the National Trust. The Dorset Trust runs the nature reserve on Brownsea Island; the Glamorgan Trust made possible the purchase of Port-Eynon Point; and Salthouse Broad is managed by the Norfolk Trust. The Field Studies Council is thrice the tenant of the Trust. It runs its educational courses at Flatford in the old water mill, at Juniper Hall, nestling under Box Hill, and at Malham Tarn House, high among the Yorkshire moors. Finally it is fitting that at Selborne, the home of Gilbert

White, that first field naturalist, so much of the country upon which he based his studies is now preserved for ever.

The management of farms and woods, or even the preservation of nature and landscape, would be more straightforward were it not for the duty imposed by the National Trust Act of 1907 to preserve these 'for the benefit of the Nation'. What is the value of pure preservation without enjoyment? What is the value of unlimited public access if it destroys what it has come to enjoy? The management of the public is an art so subtle and at the same time a science so intricate that it is difficult to distil a coherent account from the broad complex of experience gained by the Trust over more than three-quarters of a century.

The first essential is to study the character of an open space and to assess its capacity to absorb public access without destroying its soul. Clumber Park and Ashridge are green lungs for heavy populations. Formby is the nearest seashore to Liverpool, a place for the masses. Runnymede, Dunkery Beacon, Tarn Hows are famous names and must live with their fame. But in other places it has been proved over and over again that reasonable public access is perfectly compatible with the preservation of the intrinsic qualities of open spaces. In the Dove and Manifold valleys there is the greatest freedom of access coupled with real preservation of the natural features of the landscape. Before it came to the Trust Brownsea Island was utterly neglected, inhabited by three people; visitors were forbidden. Now it receives well over 120,000 visitors each year and supports a nature reserve, a restaurant, a shop, an information office, a holiday centre let to the John Lewis Partnership, who have given the Trust generous support, a camping area for Scouts and Guides, an adventure centre and a church which is used. Yet, save for peak pressures at Bank Holidays, it retains tranquillity.

A word should be said about solitude, an essential ingredient of true recreation. It is fashionable in some quarters to cry woe from the rooftops, to point to Land's End in August or to Box Hill or Tarn Hows on a fine Sunday afternoon. Of course these places are crowded at such times. The visitor who finds these honeypots distasteful has only himself to blame for having become one of the herd which he seeks to avoid, for having yielded to the hypnotism of the masses from which he would escape. If he comes at the right time of day or at the right season of the year he may have these places to himself. Even at crowded times he has only to deviate from the trodden path, to scramble a little down the cliff, to wander away into thicket or woodland, and there he will find himself alone. There are of course many properties which are preserved expressly for their solitude, but it cannot be expected that the Trust should advertise this!

Whereas the Trust quite rightly charges for admission to its houses and gardens it has steadfastly insisted that access to open country shall be free. This is as it should be, for one visits the countryside in search of freedom. But it does make it more difficult to control or to limit the numbers of the public who come. Other means must be found.

Foremost amongst these in this age of motors is the car park. A large car park will concentrate the crowds; scattered or small parks will disperse or limit them. Large or small they should be informal and screened. The footpath too plays its part. It can lead people towards places where their numbers will do no harm, or away from the most sensitive areas, for example, sand dunes often rich in natural interest and always in danger of erosion by wind or sea. The notice board, always to be kept to a minimum, and the leaflet for a self-guided walk, the information centre or the guide map can all be used with the same object. But it remains, and will always remain, a matter of nice judgement as to where and how these devices are to be used.

Similarly the Trust has had to give careful thought to the question how far it should go towards providing facilities for the enjoyment of country holidays. The fact that Borrowdale is not ruined by caravans, nor Wastwater by tents, is largely due to the well-equipped alternative sites made by the Trust. The provision of these is an act of pure preservation. Again it is a matter of judgement, and pressure from minority groups such as water skiers, motor cycle scramblers or even horseriders, should be firmly resisted wherever their activities would conflict with the Trust's basic task of preservation.

Perhaps the Trust is at its most successful when it is strong-minded enough to do nothing. The non-event can be a splendid act of preservation, whether it is the absence of a seat from a wild lake shore, of an ice cream kiosk from the Inner Farne, of a car park from a pristine beach, or of a mountain railway from the top of Glyder Fawr just across Llanberis Pass from poor ravished Snowdon.

Perhaps this ability to do the minimum coupled with a real goodwill towards the public distinguishes the Trust from other organizations and landowners. Perhaps also the character of the Trust as a Charity, established indeed by Act of Parliament, but dependent upon public support, gives it advantages from two directions. Inevitably an open space owned by a local authority will sometimes be subjected to the whims imposed by party politics and so-called democratic control. On the other hand, places in private ownership are often, though not always, managed to the deliberate exclusion of the public, or on purely commercial lines. Compare the upper (the Trust's) part of Cheddar Gorge with the lower length where the money is made.

What of the future? What may society, which has created the National Trust and seen such a collection of landscape, open spaces and natural country pass into its keeping, expect of it over the next decades? There will be increases in its possessions. At places such as Golden Cap in Dorset, all round the Cornish coast and in the Lake District, where its holdings have been built up by many separate acquisitions, there will be further pieces of the jigsaw puzzle to be fitted in. Whole new areas will come into Trust hands. There will be other opportunities for great campaigns such as Enterprise Neptune which not only secured so many miles of shoreline but woke the nation's conscience to the need to preserve what is left of the fast vanishing beauty of its coasts.

Pressures will increase, not least because the intensification of industrial society will produce a greater need for country recreation and at the same time more leisure with still faster means of escape to the open air.

Because of man's gregarious nature the pressure will be most marked at those properties which are already approaching the limit of their capacity to accept the public. It is less likely that the remote and solitary areas will be affected. But at the pressure points, especially along some of our coasts, the mild and persuasive methods evolved by the Trust and hitherto used with fair success to marry access and preservation may prove inadequate. New and more positive forms of management may have to be developed, and if necessary imposed on the public, if it is not to destroy what it has come to enjoy.

The Trust will bring a balanced judgement to these problems, examining each on its merits, distinguishing between more clamorous demand and genuine need, seeking a solution which will recognize that good taste is more to be valued than much that is advocated in the name of so-called progress, and holding a balance at each property between public access with all that it entails, and the preservation of beauty, peace and quiet.

The traveller in this country cannot fail to see much which has been spoiled without justification, overrun by industry and urban sprawl, places where public access has been allowed to cross the line which divides freedom from licence, places where man's instincts have prostituted nature's beauty to commercial ends. As the traveller passes by in sadness or in horror he may console himself by saying, 'There, but for the National Trust, goes Great Langdale' – Great Langdale, or any other of the properties listed in the pages which follow.

Properties

ENGLAND

Avon

Leigh Woods, Bristol

$1\frac{1}{2}$ miles west of the centre of Bristol, east of B3124

No city in England, except perhaps Durham, has as dramatic an approach as Bristol from the west. From fertile, wooded Somerset, a peaceful, undramatic country of remote villages and tall church towers, the road suddenly turns a corner to reveal Brunel's great masterpiece, the Clifton Suspension Bridge, poised 250 feet above the Avon Gorge. To the left of the Bridge on this Somerset side are Leigh Woods, like a green landslide tumbling down towards the river. Originally they belonged to Aston Court, the chaste neo-classical house just the other side of the village of Abbotsleigh; the grand gateway, with its giant Ionic columns and one-storeyed lodges, which now leads into the wood was built by Thomas Hopper at the same time, in 1814. Nightingale Valley, also at this end of the woods, a dip in the plateau that lies back from the Gorge, is dark and romantic. Above it is Stokeleigh Camp, the

Leigh Woods; View up the Avon Gorge with Leigh Woods to the right of Clifton Suspension Bridge

remains of a triangular Iron Age earthwork covering seven acres, difficult to find now in the undergrowth but an example of the superb siting of these primitive forts. Nearer our own times it was at a house in these woods, now disappeared, that Sir George Norton sheltered Charles II after his flight from the Battle of Worcester.

However, it is the view from the ridge overlooking the Avon Gorge that most will remember: from here the bridge looks at its finest, a miracle of engineering beauty with the river sparkling far below and shipping ploughing its way up from Avonmouth on the high tide. The rise and fall of the tide here is one of the greatest in the world. On the other side, directly opposite Leigh Woods are St Vincent's Rocks and Hotwells, the Regency spa that first made Clifton fashionable.

Leigh Woods, where 110 kinds of mosses and liverwort are recorded and two species of whitebeam (sorbus) found nowhere else, have become a national nature reserve through an agreement reached between the Trust and the Nature Conservancy who share the costs of administration. This co-operation will ensure the future of these oak woods both for the ordinary visitor and for the natural historian.

Buckinghamshire

Coombe Hill

South of B4010, 1½ miles west of Wendover, 3½ miles north-east of Princes Risborough

The hill, 852 feet above sea-level, is one of the highest points in the Chilterns, which form part of the long chalk ridges stretching from Dorset to the Wash. From the summit one looks across the clay Vale of Aylesbury to the low hills of Portland limestone on which Waddesdon (see p. 212) stands. On the skyline rise the Berkshire Downs to the south-west, and the Cotswolds to the north-west. A monument on the hilltop is dedicated to the men of Buckinghamshire who fell in the South African War.

Coombe Hill; The Monument

Although Coombe Hill is substantially chalk, its flat top is an acid clay with flints. The alkaline chalk slopes and the acid plateau above create an interesting variety of vegetation. The Trust has re-introduced sheep-grazing to keep down the scrub. Among the trees and shrubs found on the chalk slopes are junipers, privets, elders and whitebeams. Plants include thyme, harebell, marsh thistle, wild strawberry, bird's-foot, trefoil, mullein, wall speedwell and dog violet. The acid clay plateau supports heather, honeysuckle, broom, gorse, sheep's sorrel, lords and ladies, foxglove, blue-bell, St John's wort, ragwort and chickweed.

Cambridgeshire

Wicken Fen

Access south of A1123 at the village of Wicken, 3 miles west of Soham, on A142; 17 miles north-east of Cambridge, via Stretham on A10

Scientifically one of the most important 'wetland' nature reserves in western Europe, Wicken Fen is a remnant of the Great Fen of East Anglia which once covered 2,500 square miles from Lincoln to Suffolk. While most of the fens have been drained, Wicken remains substantially as it has been for centuries. When fenland is drained, the peat soil contracts; today, Wicken Sedge Fen stands as an isolated 'island' several feet above the surrounding countryside.

The property, acquired piecemeal by the Trust since 1899, comprises a 730-acre reed and sedge fen, an open mere, and areas of dense alder and buckthorn scrub or 'carr'. No habitat requires more careful management than fenland. If left to itself, Wicken Fen would dry out. The rotting remains of aquatic and marsh plants would build up in the open water, and this would eventually be invaded, first by reeds and then by sedge; in time the uncut sedge would be colonized by buckthorn, alder, and guelder-rose, and finally the mature carr would give way to forest trees and a climax vegetation of oak and ash woodland. The Trust's policy is to maintain a balance between the carr, the reed and sedge beds, and the open water. Only vigilant control ensures the continuing existence of the Fen's several distinct wildlife habitats.

Wicken Fen is rich in insect, plant and bird life. The British subspecies of the swallowtail butterfly has been re-introduced and is closely watched. But it is only one of at least 5,000 insect species to be found at Wicken. These include over 700 kinds of butterflies and moths, and nearly 200 spiders, of which six are unrecorded elsewhere. There are over 300 species of flowering plants. The birds visiting the Fen include bittern and heron, marsh and Montagu harriers, shoveller, mallard, great crested grebe, wigeon, teal, black tern, bearded tit, owls, and many waders and smaller marshland species.

Wicken Fen

Compared with many nature reserves, Wicken Fen is well documented and is visited by ecologists from all over the world. Laboratory facilities are available. Collecting specimens is not allowed, except by permit. A tower bird-observation hide overlooks the main area of open water as well as other areas of the Fen.

Cheshire

Alderley Edge

$4\frac{1}{2}$ miles north-west of Macclesfield on B5087

In a countryside fast becoming a dormitory for Manchester and Stockport, this unspoilt stretch of wooded sandstone escarpment has become a refuge from the world of pavements and street lights. On the south the hill slopes gently upwards with magnificent beech woods to the ridge road between Alderley and Macclesfield, but on the other side a sheer escarpment, 600 feet above sea-level, looks north over Wilmslow and the whole south Lancashire plain. Here the pink sandstone rocks have been worn into smooth ribs by the weather. The Edge was the site of a considerable Neolithic settlement; the slopes are scarred with primitive copper, lead and cobalt workings, and mining tools have been found, showing that the ore was smelted in open-air hearths close to the mines. Stone circles, tools, weapons, and Bronze Age pottery have also been unearthed. On the highest point is a heap of stones marking the site of a beacon, used since medieval times to broadcast news of threatened invasions, victories or defeats.

View from Alderley Edge

The Cloud *(see colour plate facing p. 352)*

3 miles east of Congleton

In a country not on the whole famous for dramatic natural scenery, this huge hill, rising suddenly out of the flat Cheshire plain, comes as a surprise, its dark heather and screes of huge granite boulders making a sombre contrast with the green squares of the fields and hedgerows below. From the 1,000-foot summit of this far-flung outcrop of the Pennines, the views extend for hundreds of square miles. To the north-west can be seen on a clear day the chimneys and furnaces of south Lancashire, to the west the fertile plain around Crewe and Nantwich, to the south the Potteries, and eastwards, up the Dane Valley, the main range of the Pennines. A large square earthwork, probably Roman, can be seen half-hidden amongst the bracken at the southern end of its ridge.

Cornwall

In terms of coastal walking, there is something over 300 miles of coast between Morwenstow, on the Devon border, and Rame Head, at the entrance to Plymouth Sound. Rather more than a quarter of this length belongs to the National Trust.

With trifling exceptions there is now a right of way on foot along the whole length of the Cornish coast but the standard of upkeep of this path varies enormously. The County Council, which takes the credit for the establishment of the path, is responsible in law for its upkeep and has failed in its duty. It has delegated the work to parish councils, some of whom do an excellent job, while others follow the County Council's example and do little or nothing. So the walker should beware. Only by trespassing can he negotiate some sections.

The Trust tries to keep all the paths on its coastal properties to a good standard. This work, with much else, is done by a small team of wardens, directed from the county office in Bodmin.

THE NORTH COAST

The coast from Morwenstow to Bude is for the man on his feet. It is remote from any town, wild, often grim and inhospitable. In the days of sail the traditional couplet ran:

> From Padstow Bar to Lundy Light
> Is a sailor's grave, by day or night.

Except where the cliffs descend to the low ground north of Bude they are uniformly high, formed of limestone and shale, their strata tortured into fantastic shapes. Reefs run out into the sea at right angles to the cliffs, and inland they are cut by deep narrow valleys or by clefts formed by streams which tumble over the cliff edge to the sea below.

Except in the valleys the country is austere, windswept and treeless, but grandly beautiful. There are no great houses; the manor houses are small, ancient and hidden away – Tonacombe at Morwenstow is the best – and the farms hug the soil, barely sheltered by a handful of wind-strained trees.

The Trust owns two blocks of land between the Devon border and the large holiday village of Bude.

Morwenstow

At Morwenstow 136 acres of the former glebe land between the church and the sea form a memorial to the Rev. Stephen Hawker (1835–74), the eccentric parson-poet who was the subject of Baring-Gould's *The Vicar of Morwenstow* (1876). Rectory Farm beside the church was added in 1976. Its name derives from its ownership before the dissolution by a monastic house which allotted to itself the 'great' tithes and appointed a vicar who was allotted the 'small' tithes. On the very lip of the 450-foot Vicarage Cliff is perched Hawker's Hut, made of driftwood dragged up from the rocks below. Here, clad in the fisherman's jersey he habitually wore, he wrote 'The Quest of the Sangraal' and 'The Song of the Western Men', ballads forgotten today but much admired by his contemporaries.

The approach to the cliff is past the beautiful Norman church, surrounded by the graves of drowned sailors. In the valley beside it is the comfortable vicarage which Hawker built, its chimneys modelled on the towers of the several churches in which he had served. Over the door is Hawker's inscription in Old English lettering:

A House, A Glebe, a Pound a Day,
A pleasant Place to watch and pray;
Be true to Church, Be kind to Poor,
O Minister, for evermore.

Apart from Baring-Gould's book, Hawker's entrancing character is best realized in *Footprints of Former Men in Far Cornwall*, a collection of his prose writings which gives a fascinating picture of life in this remote spot, many miles from the nearest railway, just a century ago.

In the face of the cliff is the traditional holy well of Morwenna, virgin and saint, with a tiny well-house built by Hawker. It is a prickly scramble to reach it and needs a sure foot and a steady head.

The church, the vicarage and a few cottages, the wild cliff, the memories of 'Passon' Hawker, the sea boiling on the rocks below, make this one of those atmospheric places best appreciated by the traveller on his own.

Two miles to the south of Morwenstow is the parish of Kilkhampton, with another splendid church. The Norman motte and bailey of Kilkhampton, in the valley below, belong to the Trust. The parish, and much of the surrounding country, belonged to the Grenvilles of Stowe, one of the great families of the West Country. Old Stowe House, described in Charles Kingsley's *Westward Ho!* lay half a mile back from the cliffs, where is now Stowe Barton.

It was from here that Sir Richard Grenville set out in 1591 to perform his last service for his Queen and win imperishable fame 'at Flores in the Azores'. A. L. Rowse's *Sir Richard Grenville of the Revenge* in its early chapters describes the Grenville country, much of which the Trust now protects. The large farm of Stowe Barton belongs to the Trust as part of the endowment for St Michael's Mount. Adjoining land has been bought or given, a thousand acres in all. The best approach is by the steep lane leading west from Kilkhampton Church and thence via Lee Farm.

Duckpool

Above Duckpool, a good surfing beach once the tide ebbs clear of the reefs, is Steeple Point (300 ft) with wide views inland and along the coast south to Bude. To the north of it rise two immense space-age saucer aerials which are part of the intercontinental communications system completed in 1970, beaming wireless messages via an orbiting satellite all over the world. Although massive, they are not eyesores, rather the reverse, and their attendant buildings are low and well designed.

Coombe

Behind Duckpool is the sequestered Coombe valley, a happy example of co-operation between the imaginatively conceived Landmark Trust, which owns the several cottages and the little watermill (which form the hamlet of

435

Coombe), and the National Trust which owns the farmland and woods for a mile inland from the sea. To the south is a fine walk for two miles along the cliffs, on Trust land all the way, to Menachurch Point to the north of Bude.

Sandymouth

At Sandymouth, where a valley opens on to an immense beach of yellow sand, the surrounding land belongs to the Trust. The farming here is large-scale arable cultivation. Behind the big cliff-fields are scrub-covered clefts and gullies: a good country for the bird-watcher. At low tide one can walk for miles along the beach. This is the best way to see the tormented strata of the carboniferous sandstone and shale which form the cliffs towards Bude. This coast is one of the few remaining stations of the Large Blue Butterfly whose complicated life-cycle requires special conditions which the Trust seeks to maintain.

At Northcott Mouth the Trust's ownership starts again and continues along Maer Cliff all the way to Bude. For several miles to the south of the town the coast is undistinguished. Widemouth Bay is a particularly un-attractive scattered development of the inter-war period, but from Wanson Mouth the picture changes. The coast road plunges up and down the steep valleys leading to the sea and rises to nearly 500 feet at Dizzard Farm. Here the Trust's territory begins again and, with two small gaps, the whole of the coast is owned by the Trust for the next seven miles. It is rough country, not for those in flimsy beach clothes.

The Dizzard

The Dizzard is the wildest of cliffs and runs from Dizzard Point for a mile west to Chipman Point. Its 130 acres were the generous gift of the Duchy of Cornwall, as its contribution to the Trust's Enterprise Neptune campaign to preserve the coast. Cleave Cliff, adjoining to the west, is privately owned.

Crackington

At Pencannow Point the Trust's major Crackington property begins. Here is some of the most splendid cliff-walking in England. Most of the 500 acres of land, stretching unbroken for three miles, were given by a local man in memory of his brother, killed in the Battle of Britain in 1940, and of the aircrews who gave their lives with him. Pencannow Point, bought at the same time, shelters the inlet of Crackington Haven from the north. Its extraordinary folded rock strata are best seen from the beach below. Half a mile inland and surrounded by Trust land is the parish church of St Gennys. Like the majority of Cornish churches it is well away from the hamlets which provide its congregation.

The houses of Crackington Haven are not beautiful, but are mercifully hidden in a cleft, and thence the path leads via Tremoutha Haven to the remarkably shaped headland of Cambeak, a rocky proboscis stretching into the Atlantic. From it, and even more from the cliffs to the south of it, are dramatic views away to the south-west, headland after headland diminishing into the distance. As the sun goes down into the sea on a summer's evening, and the haze thickens, it is easy to see how this coast attracted the Victorian romantics, led by Tennyson who 'discovered' Tintagel for them.

To the south of Cambeak is a fine rock arch and beyond this the fearsome Strangles, a wicked beach backed by the screes leading up to High Cliff which rises to 731 feet and is the highest in Cornwall. It is the scene of a dramatic episode in Thomas Hardy's early novel *A Pair of Blue Eyes*. Hardy, as a young architect, came to Cornwall in 1870 to restore the church of St Juliot, in the adjoining parish. He fell in love with the rector's daughter, Emma Gifford, courted and eventually married her.

At the south end of Strangles the broken cliff of Voter Run projects seawards. In certain conditions of wind and tide it gives off weird noises. Local men say:

> When you hear the Voter roar,
> But one fine day and nothing more.

The gated road behind the cliffs runs through the fields and homestead of Trevigne, which with a handsome Tudor farmhouse belongs to the Trust. The high broken cliffs continue southwards past Rusey Beach to enter privately owned land for a mile.

Boscastle

At Penally Point the Trust's territory begins again. It is topped by a pole surmounted by a large fish which acts as a weathervane for fishermen cut off from the winds in the sheltered cleft of Boscastle, which suddenly and dramatically comes into view below. This most curious of English harbours is the only natural haven in the forty miles of iron-bound coast from Hartland to Padstow. It is a terrifying place to enter in anything but the calmest seas, but many sailors have sought it thankfully with this cruel coast on their lee. Penally Point to the north, and Willapark (317 ft) to the south, guard a gorge-like entrance which turns through two right angles before funnelling into the mouth of the harbour. The slightest swell builds up at this point and from early times there has been a breakwater. The present curving jetty was rebuilt by Sir Richard Grenville in 1584. It is deliberately built hollow to absorb the force of the seas, the slate stones set upright in courses. Without major reconstruction it is as good nearly 400 years later as when Sir Richard built it.

During the hey-day of the harbour, when slate was exported in large quantities in the early 19th century, an outer breakwater was built. This was blown up by a drifting sea-mine in 1941, and one of the Trust's tasks on acquiring the harbour after the war was to rebuild it. No contractor could be found willing to do the job and the work was done by the Trust's own masons backed up by a team of gardeners and woodmen brought from

Boscastle Harbour

Cotehele, who between the tides worked in icy weather, often soaked to the skin, for a whole winter, and completed the job to the consternation of the local wiseacres who had said "twasn't possible".

Beyond the outer breakwater is a good specimen of a 'blowing hole'. At the right combination of sea and tide the thump of the swell entering the hole, the snort as the compressed air forces it back, and the sudden spurt of spume it throws over the harbour entrance, is an enthralling sight.

The Palace Stables at the head of the harbour belong to the Trust. They housed the carthorses which worked the capstans and hauled the slate when the harbour was busy, and have now been converted into a youth hostel. The former blacksmith's forge is now the Trust's forge and information centre. The harbour is still used by fishermen bound for the valuable shell-fishing grounds south of Hartland.

Surrounding the harbour are 300 acres of land, running up the beautiful Valency Valley behind the village and including Forrabury Common to the south, where the Celtic tenure of 'stitchmeal' precariously survives. The land is individually cropped in stitches (long rectangular plots) in the summer and grazed in common in the winter. Comfrey flourishes near Forrabury Church at the side of the common.

Tintagel *(see colour plate facing p. 352)*

There is a beautiful coast between Boscastle and Tintagel but it is privately owned and the Trust's land starts again at Willapark, a dramatic headland above Bosinney Cove (not to be confused with Willapark at Boscastle). Then there is a short gap before Barras Nose to the north of Tintagel Castle. This is one of the Trust's early acquisitions, bought after a local appeal in 1897, two years after the Trust was founded. At the time of this appeal there was widespread concern at the number of houses and hotels engendered by the growing popularity of Tintagel. Even the connoisseur of Victoriana can scarcely be asked to admire the King Arthur Castle Hotel, perched above

Beach at Tintagel

Barras Nose, an elephantine monument to the directors of the London and South Western Railway. South of Tintagel the Trust's cliffs stretch away for two miles, past the old slate quarries in the cliff face at Dunderhole, to Trebarwith Strand near the fine early Norman parish church of St Materiana. The quarry buildings, perched on a ledge, now house a youth hostel. It is difficult to believe that in the hey-day of the quarries thousands of tons of slates were winched down the cliff face into the holds of sailing ships anchored at the foot of these beetling cliffs. From here the views south and west across the bay to Pentire and the Rumps are splendid. The distant headlands seem to float on the sea like great Leviathans.

Trebarwith Strand, Tregardock

Two miles to the south of Trebarwith lies a sombre and menacing place, Tregardock. It is close to Delabole, where the vast slate quarries have been worked since Norman times, and there is an abandoned quarry in the cliff face. The approach is down a track from the farm which curls round The Mountain to enter the beach under the crumbling cliffs. The Trust owns some sixty acres stretching for over a mile. The place has its devotees but calls for an acquired taste.

To lovers of Cornwall the seven miles of coast from Port Isaac to Polzeath are holy ground. The cliffs, which have been wild and often grim all the way from the Devon border, suddenly become kinder. They are still high, but the country begins to smile. The parishes of St Endellion, with its light airy church above the sea, and St Minver contain some of the best coastal farms in Cornwall. They are occupied by families who have farmed the land for generations. The country has a settled look about it. The hedges, made of small stones laid dry in a herringbone pattern with earth filling, are covered with flowers in spring and summer. May and early June are the best months. On the cliffs the vernal squill is overtaken by violets, sea-pinks, thyme, bladder campion, kidney vetch, and stonecrop. In the lanes primroses are followed by a glorious mixture of bluebells, pink campion and stitchwort. Later, miles of hedges are smothered in valerian in its three colours of white, pink and purple. Poppies have not been sprayed out of existence. The land has a bloom.

Portquin

The coast for two miles westward from Port Isaac is privately owned, and the Trust's ownership starts again at Portquin. This can be a frightening place in a north-west gale in March, great rollers sweeping in and breaking over the road and the buildings at the head of the inlet. But most people see it in its smiling summer dress, children playing in pools and caves on the beach, and the little stone cottages sleeping in the sun. Its *aficionados* will go nowhere else. The Trust has deliberately not opened fields up the valley for car parking. The approach lanes are narrow and these are its best defence. There is no factual evidence for the legend, so often attached to Portquin, of the lost fishing fleet, the men of the village drowned, and the cottages abandoned.

Doyden

At Doyden to the west the little cliff-edge folly, an elongated octagon in plan, takes the shape of a minuscule castle complete with battlements. It was built about 1820 by a Wadebridge merchant as a summerhouse where he gave parties to his friends. The wine-bins in the cellar remain.

Except for two cliff fields the Trust now owns the coast (and much of the hinterland) all the way to New Polzeath, 700 acres stretching for five miles. The square shaft on the cliff edge west of Doyden, fenced with slate posts, connects to a sea-cave below. It forms part of the workings of a 19th-century antimony mine, the adit of which drains into another cave at Portquin.

The cliff paths here are in an excellent state, the walking is easy, the bathing in the coves (Epphaven, Lundy) is good. This was a coast where smuggled goods were landed and there is a hidden way up from the sea, now wholly overgrown. The path leads on from Lundy Bay via Carnweather Point on Pentireglaze Farm. Above the farm are the remains of a silver lead mine worked in the 18th and 19th centuries. Pentireglaze is the scene of Baring-Gould's thriller *In the Roar of the Sea*, and his picture of the Cornish countryside of the early 19th century rings true.

Beyond Pentireglaze the coast sweeps on to Pentire Farm, 360 acres, bought by public appeal in 1936 when the whole farm, incredible as it may now seem, was divided up into desirable building plots. This was the Trust's major acquisition in Cornwall before the 1939 war, and the walk round the headland from New Polzeath, and back via the lane from the farmyard, is one of the best introductions to the Cornish coast.

On the Rumps the defences of the Iron Age cliff castle, which cross the neck of the little peninsula, are clearly visible. These fortified headlands are common in Cornwall and seem to have been used by the pastoral tribesmen of the time as retreats when trouble was brewing. The amateur geologist will have noted that the limestone and shale give way, on approaching Pentire Point, to the distinctive pillow lava, it surface pricked by tiny holes. The Mouls, a small rocky inlet off the Rumps, rises to 165 feet.

To the south of the farm is Polzeath beach, one of the best surfing beaches at any time of the tide or of the year. There is a fine view up the Camel estuary to Padstow. At low water the sea breaks on the dreaded Doom Bar at the entrance to the channel.

The Trust has so far been little involved in the Camel estuary which owes its beauty to its lack of roads, and partly to landowners who have resisted development in the recent past. To the west, Padstow and its environs, the property of St Petrock's Priory at Bodmin until the Dissolution, still belong to the Prideaux, now Prideaux-Brune, family, who live in the beautiful house of Place close above the town as their ancestors have done for centuries.

Beyond Padstow the coast is beautiful but scarred by development between the wars and to some extent since. Trevone, Harlyn, Constantine, Treyarnon Bay and Porthcothan are full of holiday houses, hotels and smartened pubs. Away from the houses there are still fine cliff walks, but the sense of peace has been lost. At Porthcothan, indeed, the Trust owns the north side of the inlet, and there is a good cliff walk for a mile to the north.

Park Head

At Park Head, a mile to the south, the scene changes. Here we are back on the best of the north coast of Cornwall, breezy open country, farmed nearly to the cliff edge with corn and sheep. Pentire Farm of 220 acres, with more than a mile of coast, is approached by a narrow lane from the coast road; thence a path leads down the valley to the sea at Porth Mear. From here is a walk west and south with eight tiny coves, some of which can be reached with a scramble, and on the headland itself a fine rock arch where the sea has gouged out a vein of softer rock.

As the headland is reached there opens a view to the south across Bedruthan Steps in the foreground – the rocky islets in front of the cliffs are the Steps – for six miles to the headlands of Newquay and beyond this on clear days for twenty-five miles to St Ives. Although the principal holiday town of Cornwall is close, and the crowds must often be near, they do not penetrate here, for it is necessary to walk at least a mile and the Englishman's legs have long been atrophied.

Bedruthan

At Bedruthan itself the Trust had owned Pendarves Point, overlooking the beach, since 1930. The celebrated cliff staircase, cut obliquely into the cliff face, had to be closed because the shattered and riven nature of the rock here, which is always on the move, made conventional safety measures impossible. In 1974, however, acquisition of further land including the main car park, the former Mine Court House, led to a re-appraisal. New techniques of rock bolting were used and the dramatic staircase down the cliff face was re-opened.

On a sunny day the prospect is superb: a sparkling blue sea, yellow sands, cotton wool clouds, and rocks of every colour adorned by lichens and great drifts of sea-pinks. But in winter it can be very different, for there are no harbours in case of storm. In 1850 the *Good Samaritan*, richly laden with silks and cottons from Liverpool, came ashore at the north end of the beach. It was not an unmixed disaster. A locally printed broadsheet celebrated the event:

> The Good Samaritan came ashore
> To feed the hungry and clothe the poor,
> Barrels of beef and bales of linen,
> No poor man shall want a shillin.

From Bedruthan south to Newquay there is good cliff walking, and the magnificent sandy beaches provide the best surfing in Europe. But one is never far from the holiday trade at its most strident. Newquay is, however, a blessing to those who love Cornwall. It provides the happiest of holidays for the gregarious and, most efficiently, anchors them firmly to its beaches, greatly to the benefit of the undeveloped coast.

Immediately south of Newquay the estuary of the River Gannel cuts off the town from the villages of Crantock and Cubert. The Trust owns 700 acres of the coast there, from Penpol, half-way up the Gannel estuary, along the broad Crantock beach, round West Pentire Point to the delightful cove of Porth Joke, thence across the bold Kelsey Head to the great beach at Holywell. There and back makes a good day's walk.

Cubert and The Gannel

The Cubert and Gannel properties provide the best sort of bathing, on the big beaches of Crantock and Holywell or in the coves on either side of West Pentire Point. Porth Joke at the foot of the wild marshy valley leading to the sea from Cubert Common is the perfect sandy cove of tradition and the bathing is safe. In the valley and on the slopes above is a variety of flora, from the marsh and bog plants beside the stream to the lime-loving plants on the cliffs, which have flourished here (on what is an acid soil) because of the strong calcareous content of the wind-blown 'sand'. This sand is really composed of the broken remains of sea-shells deposited on the beaches thousands of years ago. It has been used for centuries by Cornish farmers to sweeten their soils and an Act of James II gives the inhabitants the valuable right to take sand for this purpose, regardless of private ownership, from 'below the sea mark'.

Seals breed in the waters round The Chick, the little island off the Kelsey

Head. To the south, what was formerly farmland has been covered within living memory by the high sand dunes behind Holywell Beach. These great dunes build up and change their shape rapidly. At times the sand is blown away to disclose the stones of long-buried walls and farm buildings.

The so-called Holy Well consists of a spring issuing from the rock in a cave near the north end of the beach. There is no doubt that it has long been venerated, but the true Holy Well of the place, with a medieval well-house, lies neglected in the valley to the north of Trevornick Farm, at the back of the hideous modern village of Holywell. This farm, until recently a seemly place with pleasant stone house in a fine landscape, has been mercilessly developed in the last fifteen years.

Between Holywell and Perranporth is the 3,000-acre military establishment of Penhale, set up in 1940 to house troops snatched from Dunkirk. This large area of cliffs and high dunes, if much disfigured by hutments, is nevertheless a peaceful place for much of the year. The trespasser will have no difficulty in evading the eye of the caretaker, and the dunes which rise a hundred feet or more are full of flowers found in few other places in Cornwall.

The Trust has no land here or at Perranporth.

The character of the coast changes markedly around St Agnes and Chapel Porth. Although every parish in Cornwall has been worked over for its minerals in the past, it is here that we first meet the relics of mining on a large scale.

The cliffs are still high, between three and four hundred feet. From the village of St Agnes, above Trevaunance Cove, for two and a half miles to Porthtowan the landscape is scored by old workings for copper and tin. St Agnes was one of the great mining parishes of the 18th and 19th centuries and Seal Hole, a mine close to the village, is said to have paid vast dividends to 'Guinea-a-Minute Gilbert', who from his princely mineral income re-built Trelissick House overlooking Falmouth Harbour (see p. 256) and planted the park and woods there. The scarred landscape, the burrows (heaps of waste rock) and the ruined engine houses with their attendant stacks have a melancholy beauty in their decay.

St Agnes Beacon

The Trust owns over 400 acres here, dominated by St Agnes Beacon, rising to 629 feet near St Agnes Head. From the top are splendid views across the country to the south coast on a clear day and up and down the north coast. From Carn Naun, near St Ives in the west, to Trevose Head in the east there is a prospect of twenty-six miles of coast, much of it seen obliquely to show the sandy beaches, or the breakers crashing beneath the cliffs. The Beacon is covered with heather, ling, and a particularly prickly dwarfed furze, so it is wise to keep to the paths. When these plants flower together in August, the hill is a sheet of purple and gold.

Below the Beacon the Trust's cliffs start at Tubby's Head just south of St

Agnes Head. The mines here were worked until the steady fall in the price of tin forced their closure in the 1920s. On a ledge below the top of the cliff is the spectacularly sited Towanroath Shaft, its roofless engine house and circular stack still remarkably sound. The miners' track continues at this level to enter the narrow cleft of Chapel Porth.

Chapel Porth

On the left as the path drops into the valley is a small subsidiary valley. Here is the site of the chapel, possibly of the 10th century, which gives the place its name.

At high tide the sea thunders to the base of the cliff but retreats at half-tide to open up a flat sandy beach two miles long. There is good surf, but this is not a safe beach and only the foolhardy will ignore the warning signs. All the way up to Chapel Coombe behind the beach the land is scarred by mine workings. The cliff path edges steeply up towards Wheal Charlotte high above the sea, now crumbling into decay, and continues to the seedy holiday village of Porthtowan where developers have recently been active.

Chapel Porth; Towanroath Shaft, Wheal Cote Mine

Beyond Porthtowan the coast has hitherto been virtually closed by the military establishment of Nancekuke which is being given up. In 1977 its future was still uncertain. Beyond, things change for the better. The little harbour of Portreath, once busy importing coal and timber for the mines of Camborne and Redruth (the greatest mining area in Cornwall), is no longer in use. The place has become a holiday resort. From here the Trust owns the coast, with one small gap, for six miles to Godrevy on the east side of St Ives Bay.

For miles the flat-topped cliffs, high and often sheer, are tidily farmed almost to their edge by the Trust's tenants at Carvannel Farm to the east and Godrevy to the west. All this coast was part of the great Tehidy estate of the Basset family, who prospered mightily on their mineral dues in the 18th and 19th centuries and became Lords de Dunstanville.

Much of the coast was given to the Trust by the Thomas family of Camborne and the visitor who falls in love with it is urged to repair to the local library and ask for the *Journal of the Royal Institution of Cornwall*, Part I (1966) and Part III (1967).

Tregea Hill

From Portreath the path ascends steeply to Tregea Hill and thence continues along the cliff top to the narrow and precipitous cleft known as Ralph's Cupboard. The sun never reaches the base of the cliffs here. Further on is Samphire Island, a high detached piece of cliff where samphire (*Crithmum maritimum*) grows profusely.

At Porthcadjack Cove, at the foot of a narrow valley below Carvannel Farm, there is good bathing off the rocks. The next place where the beach can be easily reached, down a steep path through former mine workings, is at Basset's Cove. Above it lie the remains of the earthwork known as Crane Castle.

Hell's Mouth

From here the path follows the cliff edge, nearly sheer and of a uniform height of 250 feet. The walk is exhilarating, the views magnificent. In two miles the coast road and the cliff converge at a yawning chasm known as Hell's Mouth.

Godrevy Point

From here round Navax and Godrevy Points the walk is even finer. This is a splendid coast for flowers and, in the shady places, ferns. The royal fern (*Osmunda regalis*) and the sea-spleenwort (*Asplenium marinum*) can both be found.

Seals breed in the caverns on the east side of Navax Point and can often be seen, particularly at Fishing Cove where the headland turns boldly northward from the line of the cliffs. These caves can be entered only from the water, though formerly one of them was connected to the North Cliff Mine, the workings of which honeycomb this area.

Strong currents swirl around Godrevy Point. On the day of King Charles's execution a ship containing his wardrobe and household possessions was sunk here. Its dangers are now advertised by the little lighthouse, offshore on Godrevy Island. Virginia Woolf entitled her novel *To the Lighthouse* in affectionate memory of childhood days spent here. Lovers of that best of diaries kept by a Victorian clergyman, *Kilvert's Diary*, will remember his description of the fight here between a seal and a conger-eel.

St Ives Bay is beautiful but close inspection of its hinterland is not advised. Caravans and chalets abound and, although Hayle's celebrated 'Five Miles of Golden Sands' are indeed lovely, they have been prostituted. St Ives itself has suffered severely, but beyond it is the splendid rocky coast of West Penwith, the Land's End peninsula.

From St Ives to Land's End is one of the sections of the coast where the coastal path is almost non-existent. There is much furze and blackthorn, and, until the County Council cuts it out, the best method is to make forays from the beautiful coast road, B3206, which runs below the uplands forming the core of the peninsula.

The visitor will notice a change in the scenery. The limestones and shales which run from the Devon border down to Hayle have stopped and we are now in a granite country. Haunted by the ghosts of early man, grey and lonely, sparsely populated except in the mining villages near St Just, this is in many ways the most fascinating of all the coasts of Cornwall.

Granite is everywhere, protruding on the skyline, great blocks tumbled about the little farms, gathered into the great stone hedges of the tiny fields, and yet always outcropping wherever cultivation is attempted. The farms are very productive, dairy holdings with Channel Island cattle, and where the land is ploughed it turns up almost black in colour.

This is the coast in which to see the phenomenon known as the 'green flash'. As the sun sinks into the sea on a summer's evening, a green light will suddenly suffuse the western sky. It is not always seen and has to be looked for, and one of the best places to do this is from the Trust's Zennor Head.

Zennor Head

The approach is via the track from the churchtown, past Treveglos Farm – the homestead (*tre*) beside the church (*eglos*). Some years ago the headland caught fire and the fire burned in the peat below the surface for weeks. It will take years for the flora, which was exceptionally rich, to re-establish in this windswept spot, as a walk to the Trust's Tregerthen Cliff, to the east, will show. Below the headland is Pendour Cove, whence the celebrated Mermaid of Zennor lured the squire's son to her watery home. This is depicted on a bench-end, now made into a seat, in the little granite church.

The light in West Penwith has special qualities which have attracted artists for more than a century. It is constantly changing and seems to be alive. Celtic magic is real here and the most insensitive visitor cannot but feel that this is a different world to his own. The Trust owns little of this coast, which is in the hands of small farmers, many of whom have lived in the homes of their ancestors over many centuries. Beyond Zennor this matchless coast marches on to reach its noblest expression in the mighty cliffs of Bosigran below the granite massif of Carn Galver. Here mountaineers come for some of the best rock-climbing in Britain.

Zennor Head

Rosemergy Cliff

West of Bosigran, beyond Porthmoina Cove, the Trust owns Rosemergy Cliff, fifty acres of boulder-strewn, bracken-covered land, stretching for a mile between the road and the sea. There are old mineshafts here and the visitor should beware.

The three Brandys rocks awash in the sea below the cliffs are so called because, seen from above, they form the triangular shape of a *brandis*, the Cornish word for a three-legged trivet, the iron stand on which cooking pots stood in farmhouses and cottages when food was cooked on an open hearth.

From Morvah, whose church is in view, past St Just, where tin mining has never stopped and is increasingly active today, the coast sweeps round Cape Cornwall and the curving sweep of Whitesand Bay to reach Land's End itself. Though vulgarized with every device to part the visitor from his money, it is impossible to advise visitors to keep away. The islands of Scilly, seeming to swim on the Atlantic horizon, and the Longships lighthouse at one's feet, are worth seeing. The water is gin-clear beneath the 200-foot cliffs. On a hot day one can look down and see the great basking sharks, twelve feet long and more, sinuously edging their way round the weathered granite rocks which lie tumbled at the cliff foot.

Mayon and Trevescan

The Trust has owned the mile of unspoilt cliff at Mayon and Trevescan, to the north, for many years. Beneath them is the Irish Lady rock, presiding queenly over the far end of England. The cliffs immediately to the south, and for many miles thence, are beautiful.

447

THE SOUTH COAST

The five-mile walk from Land's End to St Levan is peaceful and unspoilt. The granite cliffs are most impressive, and at any time of year there is much to see. Big ships come close to the shore at this point, making their landfall at the Bishop Lighthouse off Scilly, and many coasters and fishing vessels skirt the cliffs. The only settlement is at Porthgwarra, a tiny hamlet in a cleft in the cliffs. The farms lie well back from the sea and every prospect pleases.

Pedn-mên-an-mere

The Trust owns the headland of Pedn-mên-an-mere south-east of St Levan. The lovely church, with a Norman font, the vicarage and church-town farm, lie a little back from the sea in a sheltered valley. Houses have been allowed to scatter upward out of the next valley in which sits the modern village of Porthcurno. This owes its being to the fact that the first Atlantic cable was brought ashore here and ever since it has been connected with telecommunications. Cable and Wireless have a training school here and most of the cottage parlours can show a polished section of the many-cored undersea cables.

On the cliffs to the west is the Minack Theatre, the remarkable creation of Miss Rowena Cade, who conceived the idea of adapting the stepped granite cliff at the bottom of her garden to make an auditorium of great beauty. Wherever the natural granite could be put to use or shaped, she adapted it to her design. The tiered seats face south and east, the stage below hangs over the sea. The theatre has an active summer season and an evening at the Minack lives in the memory. The superb backdrop formed by the headland of Treryn Dinas across the bay sparkles in the moonlight.

Treen Cliff and Penberth

Immediately west of Porthcurno lies Treen Cliff and Penberth, 200 acres of one of the best of the Trust's coastal properties, already glimpsed from the Minack. It runs for two miles round the headland to Penberth Cove.

Soon after gaining the cliff top from Porthcurno beach, which has truly golden sand, a whitewashed granite pyramid appears. The fishermen from Penberth use it as a sighting mark, together with the Runnel Stone rock, two miles to the south-west, to lead them to a particularly rich fishing ground. Pedn-vounder beach (pronounced Pednefounder) beneath the cliffs, with a steep access path, is a curving strand of the finest sand. The bathing is good if the sea is calm, but care should be taken of the sand bar which builds up offshore in some seasons and can cause currents.

The walk continues on to Treen Cliff and out to the headland. Here, as in many places, the Trust acts as landlord to H.M. Coastguard Service, by whose co-operation the ugly line of telephone wires leading to the lookout has been buried – no small undertaking on a granite cliff. The granite on

Derwentwater,
Cumbria

Clumber Park,
Nottinghamshire;
View across the lake
to the chapel

Holnicote Estate, Somerset; View westward over Porlock Vale

Malham Tarn, North Yorkshire

these western cliffs assumes a characteristic block structure, cube piled on cube, for all the world like a child's bricks.

Treryn Dinas is a good example of a cliff castle (see p. 407) of the Iron Age, with a complex of defensive ditches, the principal one deep and well-defined.

Arrows painted on the rocks lead the way to the Logan Rock. (The Cornish verb, *log*, means 'to heave', 'to move'. The word is pronounced 'loggan'.) This example of a moving rock – there were formerly many such in the county – has long been celebrated and visited by tourists since the 18th century. It is said to weigh sixty-six tons and to have rocked easily before 1824, when Lieutenant Goldsmith, nephew of the poet, landed with a party of sailors and with a good deal of effort and ingenuity succeeded in dislodging it. A fine old row ensued. Petitions were soon on their way to the Admiralty, and the Lords Commissioners sent a peremptory order to Goldsmith to replace the Rock. This needed much greater effort, and spars, cables and sheaves sent from Devonport Dockyard at Goldsmith's expense. At last all was ready and with a long heave and a strong heave the Rock was reset. Half the county attended and the near-ruined Goldsmith became a hero.

Beyond Treryn the path leads across Cribba Head and then steeply down to Penberth Cove, the most perfect of Cornish fishing coves. The Trust owns most of the valley behind the cove and its policy is to let the little granite cottages to those who earn their living here, fishing and growing violets and narcissi for the early markets. The fishermen have formed a co-operative and fishing flourishes, whereas in so many former fishing coves it is virtually dead. Crab and lobster pots are still made here from withies grown at the head of the valley, and the sturdy open motor boats are drawn up in ranks on the slip beneath the enormous wooden capstan winch. Many of the small stone buildings are the fishermen's 'cellars', the local word for

The Logan Rock, Treen Cliff

stores, containing their pots, lines, buoys, anchors, fuel. The Penberth valley, with its little flower gardens and cottages, is both beautiful and scruffy, in a lively pleasant way. It is living and not decaying.

Veronica and fuchsia hedges surround the flower gardens, seals wallow about the rocks. There is usually a sea running and it takes skill to motor in or out from the cove into the chop. When a gale is forecast the boats run for home and all hands turn to, to winch them clear of high-water mark. The cottages by the water's edge are covered with spray as the rollers crash on the rocks. It is then, perhaps, that Penberth is at its finest.

The coast from here round to Mousehole (pronounced 'muzzle') and Newlyn is remarkably peaceful. All is in private ownership. The path is rough and ill-defined, and beyond Lamorna the granite stops and the coast reverts to limestone.

The Trust's next property is St Michael's Mount, dominating the great sweep of Mount's Bay. The Mount never looks the same and yet always looks perfect. It changes in colour, or in the play of light and shade on its superb silhouette, within minutes. Rain or shine, calm or storm, by day or night, it rises majestically and unforgettably from the water. It is further described on page 351.

Rinsey Cliff

The Trust's next property lies five miles to the east, on either side of the privately-owned Rinsey Head. Lesceave Cliff, to the east of the headland, seals off the scattered development of Praa Sands, a wilderness of caravans, chalets and bungalows which disfigures the coast for a mile. To the west is Rinsey Cliff surrounding a delightful cove and dramatically set off by the roofless engine-house and stack of Wheal Prosper, a copper-mining venture of the last century. Beyond Rinsey lies the bold Trewavas Head, with a mineshaft perilously dug on its summit, and then the coast turns southward to Porthleven, once busy with fishing and shipbuilding, dying since the last war and now reactivated by a purchaser of the harbour and shipyard who has injected not only new capital but fresh ideas.

The Loe

Immediately beyond Porthleven starts the 1,600 acre Penrose estate, the largest gift ever made to the Trust in Cornwall by an owner whose family had cherished it for two centuries. The freshwater lake of The Loe runs inland for over a mile from the great shingle beach of Loe Bar. Carminowe Creek forms a branch of the lake to the east. The wooded banks are utterly peaceful and the Trust owns the whole of the surrounding landscape. It was a farsighted condition of this princely gift that cars should be kept well away and the lake remain free of boats and water-skiers. So the Trust has made a number of small car parks set back from the water, linked by a network of footpaths which provide some of the most beautiful walks in the country.

The Loe Pool and Bar

Cliffs, shingle beach, sea and freshwater, with woodland, marsh and farmland beyond, make up an unforgettable whole.

Gunwalloe Church Cove

Adjoining the Penrose estate Gunwalloe Church Cove has a curving beach
where the 14th-century church of St Winwalloe nestles under a rock. This
church, satisfying inside as out, is in constant danger of being engulfed,
since a hundred yards to the north the sea has almost broken through a soft
patch in the cliffs. If this should happen, the church will be perched on an
islet, approachable only at low tide.

The cliffs, here of 'killas', a mixture of slate and clay, run round to Poldhu
Cove, dominated by the large Poldhu Hotel, just beyond which is the
Marconi Memorial. It was from here that on 12 December 1901 the first
transatlantic wireless message was sent to Marconi in Newfoundland. Here
also, twenty-two years later, the short-wave beam system which rev-
olutionized long-distance communication was successfully tested. Seventy
years ago most of the fifty-five acres owned by the Trust was covered in
lattice masts, cables, guy ropes, aerials and sheds, all now vanished. A stone
memorial recalls the story of the Italian inventor who so greatly changed our
environment.

Mullion Cove

The Trust owns the harbour of the picture-postcard Mullion Cove – the
quays are constantly damaged by storm and are a heavy liability – and
Mullion Island offshore.

At Mullion there is a sudden change in the rock, from the shales of
Gunwalloe to greenstone, a basaltic rock of fine granular structure. It is very
hard and strikes fire with steel. The breakwaters of the harbour are built of
this intractable stone. South of Mullion Cove the rock changes to the
serpentine formations which have long made the Lizard a pilgrimage for
geologists. Serpentine is found in many colours, grey, green, blue and
reddish-brown, with veins of brighter colour where washed by the waves.

451

Predannack

At Predannack the Trust owns a great tract of the true Lizard scenery: a 600-acre wilderness of heath, bog, rock and stream sweeping down to the cliffs and coves below. Many rare plants grow here. The soils are so mixed, and so weatherworn, that the flora is unique and much of the area is leased by the National Trust to the Cornwall Naturalists' Trust. The botanist will have his specialist books at the ready, but the layman would do well to beg or borrow a copy of that delightful, and remarkably readable, book, *A Week at the Lizard*, by the Rev. Charles Alexander Johns, better known for his bestseller *Flowers of the Field* and *British Birds in their Haunts*. Johns was headmaster of the Grammar School at Helston, and his little book, first published in 1848, is still by far the best introduction to the Lizard peninsula and succeeds wonderfully in evoking its character.

Beyond Predannack is a walk along the most unspoilt of coasts, past the lonely Kynance Farm, for some two miles before Kynance Cove is reached. Though a place of pilgrimage since the late 18th century, visited today by hundreds of thousands every year, the cove itself has obstinately refused to lose its character.

Above and to the east of Kynance Cove the Trust owns eighty acres of the Lizard Downs. Bleak, pitted with holes made by diggers of serpentine, the land runs as far as Pentreath Beach. From here to the Lizard Point, the southern-most piece of English soil, is a good mile of cliff walking. The headland is a disappointment, but the views from it, particularly the immense view up the whole length of the Cornish Coast to Rame Head, and beyond to Bolt Tail in Devon, are memorable.

Kynance Cove, Lizard peninsula

Once round the Point the bleakness softens, the coast is sheltered from the south-west wind and although it can be wild, and the cliffs and head-lands are still noble, it is a softer coast. In the valleys there is lush vegetation. Honeysuckle thrives, cottage gardens bloom. The next Trust properties are Bass Point, a mile east of the Lizard, and the fine cliff on the north side of Landewedock Church cove. A mile further on is the extraordinary Devil's Frying Pan. The sea has eaten away a softer vein of rock to form a cave, the roof of which has fallen in, leaving a spectacular rock arch. Behind the arch is a steep cauldron (the pit formed by the collapse), nearly 200 feet deep, in which jackdaws swoop and the water boils eerily.

From Cadgwith there is a good cliff path to Caerleon Cove and the beautiful Poltesco valley which runs inland from it, now all the Trust's property. The ruins in the valley bottom mark the site of the factory built by the Lizard Serpentine Company here about 1850. From it chimney pieces, tables, urns and ornaments were exported all over the world. The leat which powered its waterwheel runs through the garden of the attractive house built for the company's manager.

Beagles Point

It is some four miles of roughish walking before the Trust's next property at Beagles Point, just inside Black Head, is reached. Here there is a farm at the end of a network of lanes south of the village of Coverack. This little place, formerly a fishing hamlet, now almost entirely given over to holidays, has a lifeboat still devotedly manned by local men which has seen more service

Beagles Point and Treleaver Farm

than most others. Three miles away to the north-east are the dreaded Manacles Rocks on which so many fine ships have come to grief. An almost impassable path leads from Coverack to the Trust's Lowland Point just south of the Manacles. This curious headland, jutting out into the sea only a few feet above the surface of the water, is a relic of the Ice Age, one of the many raised beaches which have survived from that era. The cliffs of the former coast rise to 250 feet in the escarpment half-a-mile inland.

Trewarnevas Cliff

Northwards again, the Nare Point, privately owned, marks the opening of the Helford River, one of the most lovely of the several wooded estuaries of the south-west of Cornwall. Before the start of the estuary proper the little Gillan Creek winds its way for a mile to the hamlet of Carne, where the Trust owns two cottages and a few acres. On the south bank is Trewarnevas Cliff and Coneys Burrow Cove, acquired before the last war, when houses were beginning to spot the shores of the creek. The three-mile walk to Helford, past the beautifully sited church of St Anthony-in-Meneage (as lovely within as without) is strongly to be recommended. It is in a single private ownership.

Penarvon Cove and Frenchman's Creek

Just beyond Helford is the sheltered Penarvon Cove, surrounded by low wooded cliffs, almost like a scene from Treasure Island. Here the Trust owns forty acres and the cottages in the valley and on the bluff opposite Helford Passage. The only way to explore the estuary properly is by water, and boats may be hired at the boatyard between Penarvon and Helford village. A mile upstream from Penarvon is the entrance to Frenchman's Creek; the narrow wooded banks wind south, ever narrowing until the branches meet over the water at high tide.

Situated on the north bank of the estuary is the little hamlet of Durgan, where the Trust owns half of the cottages and the valley behind with the beautiful garden of Glendurgan (see p. 241). There is still some fishing from Durgan, whose history goes back before Roman times to the days of the early traders from the Mediterranean. But its chief function today is to provide a sheltered anchorage for a fleet of small boats which, riding at their brightly coloured buoys, the pine-clad cliffs rising behind them, are a brilliant sight. The visitor seeking to reach Durgan by car will find he has to park half-a-mile before reaching the village and walk down to it; the proper approach is by water.

At the mouth of the estuary rises the headland of Mawnan Shear which, with Parson's Beach beneath, formed the glebe of the Vicar of Mawnan whose church tower peers out of the trees at the top of the cliff. The forty acres of glebe were bought and given to the Trust by donors in memory of their son.

Frenchman's Creek, Helford River

Rosemullion Head

The main coast path now resumes, and a mile to the north is Rosemullion Head, fifty acres of one of the countless smaller headlands on this soft, kindly coast overlooking Falmouth Bay. No longer is the scenery wild or grim; the rocks are clothed with vegetation almost to the water's edge. Bathing is easy and safe from innumerable coves, or indeed off the rocks of Rosemullion. A mile north is the busy beach of Maen Porth, its surroundings now much developed, and there soon appear the outskirts of Falmouth. This is a town of character.

To the east, and guarding the entrance to the harbour, is Pendennis Castle, built by Henry VIII, and the last fortress, but for Raglan, to hold out for King Charles in the Civil War. Beyond the Castle the coast turns sharply west again and within the sheltered waters of the harbour is the old town, largely dating from the 1660s, with its fine church dedicated to King Charles the Martyr. As well as the old quays and warehouses there is now a large modern ship repair yard, with an immense dry dock built to take the super tankers of the 1970s. These three disparate parts of the town, the family resort, the old port, and the ship repair yard, hang together and make a walk through the streets and alleys in the higher parts of the old town an exciting experience, with views of all these activities over the chimney pots, and with the broad sweep of the Carrick Roads, the estuary of the River Fal, beyond.

Trelissick

At the head of the Carrick Roads, where the estuary narrows before running for five miles through wooded banks to Truro, lies Trelissick, a grey porticoed house looking down the full length of the harbour, with its gentle sweep of parkland looking across to Turnaware Point on the opposite bank. The Trelissick gardens are described on page 256.

Turnaware Point

Turnaware can be reached by car via Camerance Farm or, better, by boat. It is a good place for picnics and for blackberrying, with a beach that is gentle and safe. Past the headland goes the busy traffic of the river, small cargo boats bound for Truro, river trips to and from Falmouth, fishermen and dinghy sailors or, from October to March, the stoutly built oyster boats which here continue the only fishery where no boats with engines are allowed. The oyster beds belong to Truro City Council which years ago wisely enacted, in the interests of equal opportunity for each fisherman, that only sailing boats could be used. Whenever the weather is favourable, the winter through, they can be seen beating up and down the estuary trawling the oysters from the bottom. On the east shore of the harbour the Trust owns useful farmland at St Just-in-Roseland and at Newton Cliff to the north of St Mawes Castle, all traversed by footpath. At the very mouth of the estuary, where St Mawes Harbour opens opposite Pendennis, lies the beautiful peninsula of St Anthony-in-Roseland.

Porth Farm, St Anthony-in-Roseland

St Anthony-in-Roseland

This was a monastic estate owned by Plympton Priory in Devon. Since the Dissolution it has remained a peculiar, only owing such allegiance as it thinks fit to the parish of Gerrans to the north where its pastoral care is officially placed.

The Trust owns St Anthony Head of thirty-five acres, and 450 acres of farmland to the east, joining the sea coast to the estuary coast opposite St Mawes.

At the foot of the headland, just above the water, is the little St Anthony Light, shining out a white beam to mark the entrance to Falmouth Harbour which flashes through a red segment to warn of the Manacles Rocks across the bay.

From Place the Trust has made a circular walk of $3\frac{1}{2}$ miles round the northern half of the parish. It runs close above the water's edge through a wood of Scots pine opposite St Mawes, and thence to North Point at the mouth of the sequestered Froe Creek.

From the Point the view up the estuary is to the modern houses at Percuil now beginning to be merged into the countryside by the plantations which the Trust has made on Tregassick Farm, where there is another recently made footpath along the shores of this lovely estuary. In the big Trewince wood on the north bank of Froe Creek there is a heronry in the beeches and the herons have the unusual habit of repairing to the meadow beside it and holding what appears to be a heron conclave, standing solemnly in groups of half-a-dozen in the long grass.

At the head of the creek is a dam which impounds several acres of water. There was formerly a tide-mill here. The rising tide filled the pool and as soon as it began to ebb a sluice gate in the dam swung shut. The water was then drawn off after half-tide through a spillway where it drove the water-wheel which worked the mill. The walk continues over a footbridge at the head of the mill-pond and thence through a pasture to Towan Beach, a gently curving strand formerly much disfigured by a large caravan site which the Trust removed ten years ago.

The walk now runs south and west along the sea-coast past Killigerran Head and Porthmellin Head, back to Place. West of the latter headland is the delightful Porthbeor Beach (locally Polbeer) with a steep path cut down to it through the blackthorn. North of St Anthony the cliff walking is good as far as the picturesque village of Porthscatho which, although much of it faces north, always seems to be sleeping in the sun.

Pendower Beach and Carne Beacon

Development, much of it recent, then intervenes and the coast is cut up and difficult of access as far as Pendower Beach, at Gerrans Bay. This, though overlooked by hotels and a few houses, is beautiful except in high summer when the approaches are jammed with cars. From Pendower the road rises to the hamlet of Carne where the Trust owns over 600 acres of the surrounding land, including the prominent Carne Beacon, a round barrow which makes a fine viewpoint.

Nare Head

The coastal path crosses a roughish patch under an old quarry and then re-enters Trust property at Polcreek Cliff before plunging down the little beach at Paradise Cove beside the ruins of an old cottage, to start the climb to Nare Head. Here the contrast with the north coast is most apparent. From the headland the coast and the country appear prosperous and smiling. The approach from landward is through the Trust's substantial Penare Farm. The road is deliberately kept rough to discourage the motor car.

Nare Head and Veryan Bay

Kiberick Cove

Half-a-mile to the north of the Nare is Kiberick Cove. Beyond, the walk continues, still over the Trust's land, to Camels Cove below the house of Broom Parc in its little pine plantation. This was a favourite place of Cosmo Gordon Lang, Archbishop of Canterbury, who used in the 1930s to sit for hours looking over the little cove.

Beyond Portloe, a tiny and still active fishing hamlet, is a difficult stretch of coast with few paths, mostly owned by the Caerhays Estate with a picturesque castle built by Nash in 1808.

Lambsowden Cove and The Dodman

The second headland past Porthluney is the Greeb Point and just to the west of this is Lambsowden Cove, very difficult of access, with seventy acres of surrounding land. The Greeb is privately owned, but soon afterwards the path enters the western boundary of the Trust's Dodman property which has been built up by numerous acquisitions since 1919. To the north-west of Dodman Point is the sheltered Hemmick Beach and, with access through a rock arch, the smaller Percunning Cove. The beach here is a good place for pebbles of many colours, worn smooth by the action of the waves. The rocks are full of narrow veins of other minerals, white, pink, green and brown, and it is these veins which give such a variety of colours. The little cottage beside the beach has not met the fate of so many in Cornwall. It is still occupied by a family of small farmers, the midden still steams below the front door.

The Trust has in recent years cut a new path from Hemmick right round the Dodman Point, the route to which had been impassable. It makes a fine walk and the return journey can be made by the lanes across the neck of the headland. The Point itself is a cliff castle cut off by a very deep ditch known as the Balk. On the summit is a high granite cross erected in 1896 by a Rector of Caerhays to act as a mark for fishermen and a reminder of the all-seeing eye of Providence. When the work was finished the Rector consecrated it and slept the night at its foot. Back from the cross, on the spine of the headland, is a tiny watch-house for the coastguard, apparently the only survivor of this early 19th-century pattern built in the great days of sail, when every yard of the coast was patrolled twice daily, originally as a precaution against smuggling and later on as a safety measure, for scarcely a mile of these coasts but has had its wreck. There have been many wrecks on the Dodman itself. The currents offshore are notorious, and vessels which overran Falmouth at night or in dirty weather often ended their days here. In 1897 the destroyers, *Thrasher* and *Lynx*, went ashore in thick fog, and in July 1966 the pleasure boat *Darlwin*, returning from Fowey to Falmouth with a full load of holiday visitors, sank with all on board.

In a hollow on the headland is the hamlet of Penare, humble grey cottages and buildings from which the little Dodman holdings were once farmed. The land is now served by two large modern barns which the Trust prides itself on having successfully hidden in the landscape.

Eastwards there is a short stretch of privately owned land and the Trust's property starts again at Lamledra above the gently curving sweep of Vault Beach. This is one of the few big beaches which is not crowded in high summer. The path down from the farm is an easy one and the fine gravel of which the beach is composed is as pleasant as sand. The path follows the cliffs round Maenease Point and then down to the pretty village of Gorran Haven clustered round its little harbour under the cliffs.

Hemmick Beach and the Dodman

Bodrugan's Leap

The coast to the east is now privately owned for many miles. Much of it is fine but the coastal path has been particularly neglected despite the proximity of the busy town of St Austell, the centre of Cornwall's china clay industry. Mevagissey is still the picturesque fishing harbour of tradition, though many of its boats switch to the carriage of visitors during the summer months. Apart from three acres at Bodrugan's Leap, near Chapel Point, the Trust owns nothing until the great headland of The Gribbin is reached. This is the start of a nearly continuous ownership by the Trust for ten miles to Polperro.

The Gribbin

The Gribbin closes the bay to the east and in misty weather its 260-foot snout can be confused with the Dodman nine miles to the south-west. For this reason it carries a 'day-mark', a slender 80-foot tower erected by Trinity House in 1832. The three seaward faces of the tower are painted in broad red and white stripes. The effect is more handsome than bizarre.

On either side crouch plantations hugging the slopes, wind-pruned, of sycamore, ilex, beech and *Rhododendron ponticum*. They survive tenaciously in the teeth of the winter gales. On the western cliff is one of the few stations in Cornwall of the sea buckthorn, *Hippophaë rhamnoides*, a grey-leaved, prickly shrub with bright orange berries in autumn. Below the cliffs on the western side are several small sandy coves among the rocks, the preserve of those prepared to scramble across the rocks or down the broken cliffs.

More easily accessible is Polridmouth (called Pridmouth), a beautiful beach surrounded by the woods of Menabilly, the seat since the 16th century of the Rashleigh family, who still live there. Pridmouth is reached by a half-mile walk from Lankelly to the east, or Menabilly Barton to the west. Menabilly appears as Manderley in Daphne du Maurier's *Rebecca* (1938) which begins 'Last night I dreamt I went to Manderley again', and in which the woods, the beach and the coast are faithfully described.

St Catherine's Point

The coastal path leads up through the wood to the east of Pridmouth and thence across Southground Point and over Lankelly Cliffs. Coombe Farm is privately owned and the Trust's land is entered again at St Catherine's Point at the entrance to Fowey Harbour. There are splendid views up the harbour, always busy with small boats, and out to sea. The curious object surrounded by iron railings on top of the Point is the mausoleum erected in 1867 in honour of himself and his family by William Rashleigh of Menabilly.

Fowey

Above the harbour mouth is the little St Catherine's Castle, one of the many coastal forts built by Henry VIII to protect the rapidly growing shipping trade at the dawning of the Elizabethan age. Fowey has a long and exciting history as a seaport. In the French wars of the 14th and 15th centuries its ships were in the forefront of the English fleet. The town is closely associated with 'Q' (Sir Arthur Quiller-Couch), who died in 1944 and is commemorated by a great monolith of granite at Penleath Point where the beautiful creek of Pont Pill branches east off the main estuary. Most of this side of the harbour is owned by the Trust. Hall Walk, below the ancient ferry at Bodinnick, is celebrated for an incident in the Civil War when Charles I narrowly missed decapitation by a Parliamentary cannon ball lobbed across the water from Fowey. Hall Walk was the promenade of the ancient house of Hall, behind the cliffs, seat of the Mohun family who owned the parish of Lanteglos. The Walk, held by the Trust in memory of the men of the parish and of Fowey who gave their lives in the Second World War, is entered at the top of the nearly vertical village street at Bodinnick and continues past the 'Q' Memorial up the unspoiled north bank of Pont Pill. At the head of the creek the path descends through a wood to the delightful hamlet of Pont, much of which is owned by the Trust, which has rebuilt the quays and restored the footbridge connecting them. The Walk continues along the south bank of the creek, with views over the harbour, to reach the second ferry at Polruan which takes the pedestrian back to Fowey.

From Polruan eastwards to Polperro lie eight miles of quiet and peaceful coast, not rugged or wild, though the cliffs are high and the spray flies in a winter's gale, but a smiling land of good farms, many of them occupied by the ubiquitous clan of Talling, and centred on the two beautiful churches of Lanteglos and Lansallos. Except for a short stretch near Polruan, and the farms of Raphael and Lizzen a mile west of Polperro, all now belongs to the Trust.

Pont Pill Creek, near Polruan

Churchtown, Lanteglos-by-Fowey

A path leads from Pont up a bosky valley to Lanteglos church, mainly of the late 14th century and dedicated to St Wyllow. The church lies in a hollow behind Pencarrow Head, two steep miles away from its village of Polruan inside the mouth of Fowey Harbour. As with so many Cornish churches the 'churchtown' is in the middle of the parish whereas the population lives elsewhere. The Trust owns Churchtown Farm beside the church, which has been well restored and is flooded with light from windows of clear glass. At the east end of the south aisle is a beautiful brass to Thomas de Mohun of the first decade of the 15th century.

Lantic Bay

From the church a lane leads upwards to the coast road and thence a footpath runs out to Lantic Bay, the sheltered cove east of Pencarrow Head. A precipitous path descends to the long curving beach. There is excellent bathing here and in the small coves further east. At the back of the beach grow several plants at home in the shingle – sea holly (*Eryngium maritimum*), sea kale (*Crambe maritima*), and the beautiful pink sea bindweed (*Calystegia soldanella*), an exotic cousin of the common bindweed of gardens and hedges.

Pencarrow Head

Pencarrow Head is on two levels. From the Ordnance Datum pillar at the top (447 ft) there are immense views. To the east, Rame Head marks the end of Cornwall, and beyond it Bolt Tail in south Devon reaches out into the Channel. Westwards the noble Roman profile of the Dodman on the far side of St Austell Bay is backed by the Lizard peninsula, curving away to the south, a panorama of some seventy miles. Beneath are Lantic and Lantivet Bays with many tiny beaches, all reached from the cliff path which follows round the lower level of the headland to the most beautiful of coves, Lansallos Beach at the foot of West Coombe below Lansallos church. A perfect semicircle surrounded by rocks, approached through a narrow entrance, it is the epitome of a smugglers' cove and it is not so long ago that contraband was landed here. A track cut deeply through the rock, just wide enough for a two-wheeled cart, runs steeply up to the 15th-century church of St Ildierna, one of those shadowy female saints with whom Cornwall is so richly endowed. The church has a fine wagon roof, many of its original pews, simple slate floors, and an atmosphere of peace. Its tower alone is visible from the cliffs and seems to ride in the sky as it appears and disappears from view.

From West Coombe the path is cut half-way up the cliff, with rocky crags jutting out above. Ravens and kestrels wheel and float above these cliffs, which run unbroken to Polperro with only a single house in sight. At all times of the year there are interesting flowers. Centaury, both in its common form and the rarer *Centaurium pulchellum*, can be recognized by its bright pink flowers from June to September. Great mats of thyme abound in the cliff turf. Mallow grows tall near the base of the cliffs and, hugging the ground closely, the inconspicuous but beautifully named orchid, Lady's Tresses (*Spiranthes spiralis*), flowers in August and September.

Polperro

As the path approaches Polperro little cliff gardens appear in the Chapel Cliff. So closely are the cottages packed into the steep valley in which the village lies that there is no room for gardens and in the past some fifty little plots were dug in the cliffs, closely hedged with veronica and escallonia. Some are still cultivated, growing early potatoes and carnations for market. The harbour and the huddle of cottages are picturesque, but the village has been much prostituted and is best avoided. Beyond Polperro lies The Warren, a mile of cliff bequeathed to the Trust by the novelist Angela Brazil. The Trust's land ends at Talland, with another fine church standing high over the sea.

The coast hereafter, through Looe, Downderry and Portwrinkle, to Rame Head and Plymouth Sound, is less beautiful, and spoilt in places by development and the army firing range of Tregantle. It improves immediately beyond this with the fine sweep of Whitesand Bay running out to Rame Head and here the Trust owns Higher Tregantle Cliff and Sharrow Point. At the foot of the point, just above the sea, is the artificial cave of Sharrow Grot, a folly of peculiarly unpatrician type. During the War of American Independence a naval lieutenant, Lugger by name, stationed near by and troubled with gout, decided to cure his affliction by hard work. He hacked out a circular grotto, fifteen feet long by seven high, with a seat cut in the rock. In the centre he placed an oak table and on the rock walls carved sixty-six lines of abominable poetry of his own composition, most of which survives. The result is not a notable monument, but it worked: Lugger's gout was cured. Sadly the entrance to the grotto has had to be sealed off, as repairs were difficult and the grotto might have collapsed.

The nasty chalet village of Freathy now intervenes but beyond it there is a splendid coastal walk over the Mount Edgcumbe estate. For six miles the cliff path sweeps round the barren Rame Head to Penlee Point, and thence past the villages of Cawsand and Kingsand, to Plymouth Sound and the beautiful wooded park of Mount Edgcumbe. It is the end of three hundred miles of coast in the county of Cornwall.

Derbyshire/Yorkshire

The Derwent Estates and Hope Woodlands

13 miles west and north-west of the centre of Sheffield

The 24,450 acres of the Derwent and Hope Woodlands estates constitute one of the biggest single properties owned by the National Trust, straddling the boundary between Yorkshire and Derbyshire and stretching from Kinder Scout in the south-west corner to Alport and Howden Moors in the north. Much of its spectacular scenery is less than eighty years old, for three enormous reservoirs have been built to serve Sheffield, Nottingham, Leicester and Derby, filling what were wide dales and drowning whole villages. The resulting scenery is, however, no less dramatic for that. Above all, this is hikers' country: the views from the ridges of Howden Moors across the chain of lakes to Hope Woodlands, the high moorland without house or tree above Alport Dale, the cairns, Pike Low above Derwent Dam, or Bone Low with its three barrows, lonely reminders of another civilization – all these are unforgettable.

To the west of the reservoirs, the Hope Woodlands estate includes Ashop and Blackden Moors, the Edge, the precipitous north face of Kinder Scout, and the land either side of the Snake Road – the highest part of the whole Peak District rising at one point to 2,070 feet. The twisting Snake Road following a Roman course climbs the valley of the Lady Clough far above the tree-line, until suddenly at the top of the pass a magnificent view unfolds over Glossop towards Manchester.

To the left a footpath, the Pennine Way, crosses the High Peak and the peat plateau of Crowden Head before descending again to the heather and woodlands of Edale Moor. Grouse and curlews are common here, and golden plovers, redshanks and dunlins can also be seen.

Derbyshire

The Dove Valley

4–9 miles north-west of Ashbourne, south-east of Buxton

The 'silver shining Dove' has been a place of pilgrimage for anglers and sightseers since the end of the 17th century, when Charles Cotton, intimate friend of Izaak Walton and part author of the *Compleat Angler*, eulogized it in his poetry. Set in the gentle rolling foothills of the Peak District –

Dovedale; Ravens Tor and Nabs Hill

rounded green knobs divided into jigsaw patterns by a thousand stone walls – the steep gorge of Dovedale comes with unexpected drama. Approached from the south, two hills, Bunster Hill and Thorpe Cloud, guard the entrance to the valley. From there a footpath winds up the valley along the river and past a series of spectacular limestone rocks weathered into strange shapes. Most of these in true Derbyshire fashion have had names and legends attached to them: the Twelve Apostles, Lover's Leap, Jacob's Ladder, Tissington Spires, and the Lion Face Rock. Huge natural caves open high in the rock. Reynard's Cavern has a height of thirty feet inside and the Dove Holes slightly farther up are equally impressive. The river itself, with the occasional weir and stepping-stone, its deep clear pools overhung with alder and blackthorn, seems strangely docile compared to the precipices above, once cut by its torrent.

Part of the joy of the Dove Valley is that it is virtually inaccessible by car. Footpaths from Ilam and Thorpe in the south follow its course as far as the hamlet of Milldale, with its medieval packhorse bridge, a two-mile stretch which covers the most celebrated part of the river. The upper reaches, however, from the road at Lode Mill up towards Hartington, are almost deserted by comparison, though they offer scenery quite as beautiful. The Dove here passes close under Wolfscote Hill (1,270 ft) and opposite Beresford Hall, Charles Cotton's home. The Hall itself has been in ruins since the 19th century, but the famous Fishing Temple, built in 1674 and dedicated to Walton, can be seen across the river above Pike Pool, where a tall and narrow grey rock like a giant fish rises from the river.

Longshaw

1–3 miles south-east of Hathersage, via A625

'Strange, mountainous, misty, moorish, rocky, wild country . . .' a 17th-century traveller found this part of the Derwent valley, and even today it is hard to remember that the centre of Sheffield is only eight miles away. The Longshaw estate comprises over a thousand acres of rocky moorland and woods on either side of the Burbage Brook, dry for some of the year but at other times a torrent rushing down its ever-steeper valley. From the ridge above Sheffield Plantations on the eastern boundary, and from Millstone Edge overlooking Hathersage, there are magnificent views of the Derwent to Bamford Edge, Crook Hill, and in the distance Mam Tor and the High Peak.

The outcrops of rock so characteristic of the Derbyshire landscape are often strangely shaped and weathered on these bleak hillsides, like the huge smooth boulder called the Rocking Stone, precariously balanced on a pile of large rocks in Lawrence Field, or Toad's Mouth to the north of Owler Tor. Almost the best time to see this dramatic landscape is in stormy weather, with the shadows of the clouds moving swiftly over the hills and the sheep huddled under the grey stone walls. It comes as no surprise to know that the inn at the top of Longshaw Wood was Charlotte Brontë's Whitcross, where Jane Eyre was set down from the coach during her flight.

Farther down the valley, under Froggatt Edge with its jagged crest of rock looking like a walled hill-town, the Trust also owns Froggatt Wood and the pastures sloping steeply down to the Derwent.

Mam Tor and the Winnats *(see colour plate facing p. 353)*

1 mile west of Castleton on A625

Mam Tor, or the shivering mountain, earned its name from the layers of grit and shale apt to slide down its sides in exceptionally wet or frosty conditions. A guide-book of 1700 claimed that it was 'perpetually shivering down earth and stones in such abundance and with such a noise (even in calm weather) as to frighten the neighbouring inhabitants', while Celia Fiennes wrote that it was 'very dangerous to ascend and none does attempt it'. Owing to this natural slipping process the western face of Mam Tor looks like a giant quarry, but today the climb seems safe enough and the 'Fifth Wonder of the Peak' is appreciated more for other attributes. From its 1,700-foot summit there are superb views towards Kinder Scout and the High Peak, and west over Castleton, with the remains of the castle of the Peverils, towards the Derwent Valley. The Iron Age camp at the northern end of its ridge covering sixteen acres is the largest in Derbyshire. Its giant ramparts with two inturned entrances, combined with its position on one of the steepest headlands in the Peak District, must have made it virtually impregnable.

Less than a mile to the south of Mam Tor is the Winnats Pass, the original course of the main road from Castleton to Chapel-en-le-Frith which now

466

follows an easier gradient up the side of Treak Cliff. Winnats is a corruption of 'wind-gates', and the howling gale which blows down this narrow limestone gorge again confirms the aptness of Derbyshire placenames. High up in the cliffs which tower above this steep road are the openings to caves, the remains of lead mines (some of them Saxon in origin) and Blue John mines. This famous crystal spar with its amethyst colour, found only in this neighbourhood, became fashionable in the 18th century for ornaments, urns, vases and candelabra, though its seams are now almost exhausted.

West of Mam Tor the Trust's land dips to the saddle of Mam Nick and climbs the steep razor back of Rushup Edge, far along which is Lord's Seat, a seven-foot barrow which is the burial place of some tribal chieftain.

The Trust's Hardenclough Farm drops north through a tumbled landslip of humps and hollows to the green level pastures on the floor of Edale, where at the head of the dale and farther down almost to the village of Hope the ownership of Lee, Orchard, Edale End, Fullwood Holmes and Harrap farms helps to protect its pastoral charm.

Mam Tor and Hope Valley

Devon

Branscombe

5 miles east of Sidmouth, south of the A3052 Exeter/Lyme Regis road

Less a village than a collection of stone and cob cottages straggling to the sea down a long, lush green valley, a natural break in the high cliff-wall of this coastline, Branscombe is one of the most peaceful and attractive places in south Devon. Since 1964 a series of gifts, and acquisitions purchased with Enterprise Neptune funds, have secured much of the valley itself as well as part of the cliffs towards Beer Head on the east and to Weston and Dunscombe on the west, 560 acres in all. Among the buildings are a number of rose-covered thatched cottages, three farmhouses, the village forge, and the bakery, still producing crusty loaves from its faggot-fire ovens. H. J. Massingham and W. H. Hudson have both written lovingly of the backwater life of this little community.

At the bottom of the valley, overlooked by a row of coastguard cottages (now a private house) perched on the hillside, the river finally reaches the sea across a beach of grey and pure white pebbles, worn smooth by the continual pounding of Atlantic rollers. Pebbles are collected each year from this beach for use in the paint grinding industry. From here, amongst upturned fishing boats and stranded jellyfish, the vast expanse of Lyme Bay can be seen on a clear evening, with Torbay and Berry Head far to the right, the Chesil Bank and Portland Bill even farther to the left. In the foreground on this side, half-way to Beer Head, is the dramatic silhouette of Hooken Cliff, the first of the great landslips of the Devon and Dorset coasts. One night in March 1790, about ten acres of land suddenly dropped 250 feet vertically and moved 200 yards out to sea, breaking up into extraordinary columns and pinnacles of white chalk. From Branscombe beach the huge square rock at its summit looks like a man-made fortress, but viewed from the cliff walk that runs behind on the 500-foot ridge to Beer, the sweep of this astonishing landslide can be seen at its most impressive – as if a giant foot had trodden too near the edge. The cliffs along this stretch and at Duncombe are riddled with caves, many of them used by smugglers in the 18th century. Small plots on the cliffs were cultivated until recently, donkeys being used to carry the produce to the village.

Goodameavy, Dartmoor

Properties near Shaugh Prior, 6 miles north-east of Plymouth

Even before the 12th century, when the richest source of tin in Europe was discovered there, Dartmoor was one of the most densely populated areas in England. Willings Walls Warren and Hen Tor in the south-west corner, where the river Plym rises, are now some of the wildest, remotest parts of Devon, but the amazing number of Bronze Age hut circles are reminders that in the pre-Christian era, when the lowlands were disease-ridden

Goodameavy; The river Meavy

swamps, this treeless expanse was a centre of civilization. Here where wild ponies graze against vast skies, with tor-outcrops on the horizon the only features of an unvarying grey-green landscape, are the eerie remains of once flourishing settlements. In some 3,700 acres of this bleak country, accessible only by foot or on horseback, and no longer even thronged with rabbits as it used to be, there are today no houses save the lonely farm at Trowlesworthy Warren. 'A holy peace pervades this moorland solitude', wrote the poet Carrington who lived near by.

To the west, past Cadover Bridge, the Trust also owns Goodameavy, where the twin gorges of the Plym and the Meavy descend to meet at Shaugh Bridge under a thick canopy of oak woods. Between the two rivers is the towering mass of Dewerstone Rock with sheer sides gradually eaten away by foaming winter spates. Here small boys clambering up with ropes are given their first taste of mountaineering, while lower down by still, dark pools fishermen cast deftly over round granite boulders covered in lichens and ferns.

Three miles south at Plym Bridge the Trust owns 111 acres of oak woodland beside the river Plym. The woods are rich in industrial archaeological remains such as a slate quarry and granite railway.

Heddon's Mouth

9 miles east of Ilfracombe, 4 miles west of Lynton

Difficult to find, down lanes like green tunnels, with foxgloves growing at the roadside and honeysuckle straggling wild over the hedgerows, this is one of the least known and most rewarding of all the Trust's Devon properties. The steep, wooded valley of the river Heddon, in a great cleft between

Heddon Valley

rounded hills of patchwork fields, becomes more dramatic as it approaches the sea, finally emerging in a rocky cove surrounded by high cliffs on which once stood a Roman signal station. A path leads down this valley from the Wagnerian-looking Hunter's Inn to the sharp rocks on the shore by the remains of an 18th-century lime kiln, where there is good sea-fishing.

For those who prefer walking, so long as they haven't a bad head for heights, there is the precipitous path along the hog-backed cliffs to Trentishoe Down. Almost nowhere in England are there more exhilarating views than these, down the coast to Widmouth Head and across the Bristol Channel to Wales. On a bright spring day with cloud shadows moving swiftly across the downs, with the blue sea breaking white and noiselessly on the rocks 500 feet below, and seagulls wheeling over shoals of mackerel far out in Elwill Bay, it is a lonely, unforgettable place.

East of the Heddon, over the top of Martinhoe hill, is Woody Bay, bought in 1965 from Enterprise Neptune funds, and so called because of the magnificent oak woods typical of the Devon landscape which here sweep down to the sea. West of Haddon the Trust owns Trentishoe Common, part of Holdstone Down divided into small plots and the Great Hangman rising to 1,046 feet above Combe Martin. The old coast road – now the only coast path – links these two properties.

Lundy

11 miles north of Hartland Point, 30 miles south of St Gowan's Head, Pembrokeshire

The final upthrust of a submarine mountain, Lundy, a small island about three and a quarter miles long and a quarter of a mile wide, lies in the middle of the Bristol Channel. Often out of sight of land, isolated by storm for days or weeks, it conveys the sense of an independent kingdom. Indeed the overlord of the island once owed allegiance to the Crown alone, otherwise claiming sovereign rights over land and sea around his domain. Even today there are no rates, licensing laws, customs dues, or income tax on money earned on the island. The island once issued its coinage and still issues its own unofficial stamps with, appropriately, puffins on them, for in Norse 'Lund-ey' means the 'puffin isle'.

The land slopes down from the towering cliffs on the west, 400 feet high, to the gentler eastern shore, where little coombs, some wooded, others filled with deep bracken, rhododendrons and occasional fuchsias and hydrangeas, run down to the sea. There is no harbour and landing is possible only in good weather in a cove on the south-east. The ruins of the medieval Marisco castle stand on the edge of a great precipice overlooking the 'High Street'. The latter consists of a straggle of cottages, a farm, a 19th-century church, a shop, and an inn which opens and shuts when the landlord pleases. In a wooded coomb close by stands Millcombe House, a pleasant house of 1840, once the home of the lord of the manor.

A path leads north from the village, crossing three drystone dikes which run right across Lundy, to open moorland and to a lighthouse at the north end of the island, where puffins nest in deep burrows on the steep grassy slopes. Thence the path winds back along the west coast above the formidable cliffs, rock chimneys, and screes which a multitude of seabirds have made their own. Lying on a migratory north-south route, Lundy is an important bird sanctuary. Kittiwakes, fulmars, Manx shearwaters are among the species which breed on the island, and peregrines have nested in the same eyrie for hundreds of years.

Lundy's isolation has produced an interesting fauna and flora. The rabbit population is notable for the number of black and brown specimens, the result of inbreeding, and there is a type of rat and pygmy shrew found only here. The Atlantic seal breeds and favours particularly a cove near the landing place. Lundy ponies, originally brought over from the New Forest thirty years ago, and crossed with Welsh mountain mares, are now also recognized as a distinctive breed. The island boasts one unique botanical specimen, *Brassicella wrightii*, an ancient member of the cabbage family.

The history of Lundy is long and varied. There are written references to it in Icelandic sagas and Welsh chronicles, but firm history begins with a charter granted to the De Marisco family in 1153. After a century of piracy and lawlessness the Crown garrisoned the island and gave control to the Knights Templar. The isolated situation of Lundy always exposed it to attack. It was raided by the French during the Hundred Years War and later by Barbary pirates, and it may even have been abandoned for short periods. At the same time it was an ideal base from which to harry shipping in the Bristol Channel, so much so that it became known as the 'tollgate of the Channel'. Spanish, French and English privateers at one time or another established themselves on Lundy.

About 1750, Thomas Benson, M.P. for Barnstaple, leased Lundy and used it as a base for smuggling and other shady enterprises. One of his schemes was to ship convicts for transport to America and divert them to the

Lundy; The south lighthouse

island where he employed them as slave labour. They built the walls quartering the island. When accused of breach of contract, his ingenious defence was that he had only engaged to ship them out of the country. He overreached himself at last by filling a ship with a valuable cargo of pewter, salt and linen, insuring it heavily and then quietly unloading it on Lundy. He then scuttled the ship, claimed the insurance money and sold the cargo. The business came to light and the captain of the vessel was hanged, but Benson disappeared.

In the 1830s, with the advent and ownership of the Rev. Hudson Heaven, Lundy acquired respectability. Inevitably it became known as the Kingdom of Heaven. He built the early Victorian mansion and developed the farm, and another member of the family later erected the church. In 1925 the island passed to the Harman family. After the death of Albion Harman, it was bought by the Trust in 1969 with a generous gift from Jack Hayward, an Englishman living in the Bahamas. The island is now administered by the Landmark Trust.

Lydford Gorge

7 miles north of Tavistock, west of A386

The village of Lydford lies on the edge of Dartmoor at the point where the river Lyd plunges from the high plateau, cutting a deep wooded gorge through the dark rock and peaty soil of this fertile rolling country. Once it was an important town, headquarters of the tin-miners who built a castle here in 1195 on a spur above the ravine as a prison for those who disobeyed the mining regulations. As the industry declined so did the town, until by the 17th century it was no more than a remote moorland village, while the gorge was inhabited by a fearsome and 'lewd' family of outlaws called Gubbins, described by Kingsley in *Westward Ho!* But the 18th century saw a return to safety and moderate prosperity as the gorge, and the square keep of the Norman castle in a loop of the river, became places of pilgrimage for the sightseer. Today the enchanting walk through the gorge along both sides of the river is extremely popular. It is best approached from the car park beside the bridge below the village.

The most famous single feature of this walk is the waterfall known as the White Lady, described by a visitor in 1788 as 'neither too perpendicular to be one confused heap, nor too much divided to be ungraceful; but one continued silvery chain of two hundred feet'. Between the trees the river rushes down a great curving groove in the rock with a roar that drowns the birdsong. On either side huge oaks almost roof the gorge, their trunks covered with lichens, moss and ferns which flourish in this humid atmosphere and give an almost tropical air to these most English woodlands. The ground is carpeted with wild garlic stretching down to the dark pools, smooth black boulders, cascades and rapids, of the river below.

Lynmouth

Almost within sight of the sea two Exmoor rivers, East Lyn and Hoaroak Water, cascading through ravines and crags, join in a beautiful gorge at Watersmeet near Lynmouth, 'discovered' by Shelley in 1812 when he brought his sixteen-year-old wife to a cottage here to escape the wrath of her parents. Southey, and a host of Romantic tourists, were quick to follow and establish this as one of the most popular parts of Devon. Murray's handbook of 1879 described the walk along the riverside, with wooden bridges and stepping-stones, as a succession of Ruysdael pictures, and a hundred years have brought little change to its quiet beauty. Mature oak woods, mixed with holly, yew and the rare whitebeam, clothe banks that seem too steep for any vegetation, hanging above waterfalls, rapids and pools of clear, reflecting water far beneath.

Watersmeet, Lynmouth

The wide downs above these wooded valleys are a spectacular contrast: from the paths that cross Myrtleberry Cleave and South Hill Common there are magnificent views inland to Exmoor and north to the sea, a blue rim on the horizon. Only recently an anonymous donation has given the Trust the whole of Foreland Point and Town Farm, Countisbury, between Watersmeet and the coast. The cliffs at Foreland, rising 900 feet sheer from the sea and reputedly the highest in England, give amazing views across the Bristol Channel to the Welsh hills and down the coast in both directions. For the sure-footed, a path leads virtually down the precipice to Sillery Sands and the pleasure-boats of Lynmouth Bay.

Morte Bay

5 miles south-west of Ilfracombe

'Morte is the place which Heaven made last and the Devil will take first.' The point of this Delphic Devonshire proverb depends on the weather: in the thick fogs of autumn with visibility down to a few yards, and with gale-force winds lashing this coast from the Atlantic, its rocks have claimed many ships and more lives, especially before the days of radar; yet in sunny weather, across the pale yellow sands of Woolacombe, few places are more immediately appealing. The beach, protected by the two rocky promontories of Morte Point and Baggy Point, can claim to be the finest in north Devon, a huge sweep of sand pounded by white-crested waves almost ideal for surfing. Behind on the Down with its wild flowers and butterflies, or in the Warren sand dunes, are idyllic picnic places. Barracane Beach just to the north of the village of Woolacombe is famous for the shells which drift ashore here in greater numbers than anywhere else on this coast.

The walk round Morte Point itself is particularly worth while, where the rollers crash on jagged reefs, and stacks of razor-edged slate glisten under the spray. In one winter, that of 1852, five ships went down on the Morte Stone, the farthest of this treacherous line of black rocks. Baggy Point at the southern end of the bay is geologically different, composed of hard, flaggy sandstones and grits with softer olive-coloured shales embedded with fossils. The variety of its colours and its vegetation, the views to Lundy and out across the entrance to the Bristol Channel, with tankers plying their way up to the Avonmouth ports, make this one of the most beautiful headlands in Devon. Baggy Hole, a huge cave near the point, can only be reached by boat at low tide.

Bull Point to the north of Mortehoe, with its patchwork of arable and grass farming mixed with bracken-covered screes, was acquired in 1973. Following the acquisition of the old golf links at Damage Barton, this makes the Trust's ownership virtually complete between Croyde and Lee, east of which the Trust owns Flat Point and the Torrs, Ilfracombe. The seven hills of the Torrs make a magnificent backdrop to Ilfracombe.

Salcombe

4 miles south of Kingsbridge, via A381

Salcombe has an almost Mediterranean air about it. Looking up the estuary from Sharpitor Gardens, between pines and cypresses, banana palms and sweet-smelling syringa bushes, one could be in the south of France. The wet, warm climate of this southernmost tip of Devon encourages the growth of exotic flowers and shrubs, in particular different species of magnolia, and of fuchsia which grows almost wild in the hedgerows. Sharpitor House is

Opposite:
Morte Point and the race at Mortehoe

Soar Mill Cove, near Salcombe

now used partly as a youth hostel and partly to house the Overbeck Museum of ship-models, and other relics of the days when Salcombe was famous for building schooners. The garden is described on page 250.

From Sharpitor a footpath runs along the coast to Bolt Head cliffs at the mouth of the Kingsbridge estuary. A six-mile stretch of coastline to the west, as far as Bolt Tail, now belongs to the Trust, providing one of the most beautiful walks in south Devon. Far from any road, with the wind rippling through the long grass, the marram and sea-pinks, with the roar of waves on rocks far below and the pungent smell of seaweed, this is the English seaside at its loneliest and best. Soar Mill Cove half-way along has a sheltered rocky bay good for bathing, dominated by the high, pointed Lantern Rock to the west used as a beacon in the days before lighthouses. Bolt Tail, guarding the semicircle of Bigbury Bay, has the remains of an Iron Age promontory fort at its tip looking right across to the mouth of Plymouth Sound, while the coastguard cottages of Hope Cove, doorsteps piled high with lobster pots, lie behind to the east.

Another cliff walk, almost as long and certainly as beautiful, begins from the other side of the Kingsbridge estuary accessible from East Portlemouth. It stretches from Rickham Common to Gammon Head and Prawle Point, against a panorama of dark cliffs and weird-shaped lichened rocks – the Bull, Pig's Nose, Ball Rock – pushing out towards the breakers.

Yealm Estuary

6 miles south-east of Plymouth

The Yealm is one of the less-well-known rivers of south Devon, although the estuary is a favourite amongst yachtsmen. The Trust has long owned

Yealm Estuary

land on the north side, including 1½ miles of the coast from Wembury by the disused mill near St Werburgh's church to Warren Point, one of the fine headlands on either side of the estuary mouth. In recent years the Trust has acquired, partly through Enterprise Neptune funds matched by public subscription and partly from generous gifts, almost the whole of the south side, including Passage Wood to the west of the Ferry landing, 27 acres of beautiful hanging woods immediately west of Noss Mayo and the sea coast from Mouthstone Point past the old coastguard lookout and Gara Point to Blackstone Point beyond The Warren cliffs. The old coast path runs round the whole property passing Warren Cottage on its way.

Dorset

Ballard Down

North of Swanage

Magnificent Ballard Down is the easternmost tip of the chalk ridge of south Dorset that continues in the Purbeck Hills to terminate in the 500-feet-high vertical cliffs at the north end of Swanage Bay with the remains of the Old Harry group of rocks below, marking the natural division between the Isle of Purbeck and the waters of Poole Harbour and the undisturbed heathland that fringes its southern shore.

From the top of the headland with its Bronze Age barrows there are noble views eastward to the Isle of Wight, where the line of chalk downs begins again at The Needles Point, north over the harbour to the uplands of central Dorset, and to the south and west over the intimate landscape of the Isle of Purbeck, with its grim grey cliffs, to the distant Isle of Portland.

Ballard Down from the east

Brownsea Island

In Poole Harbour, near Sandbanks

Though this 500-acre island is visited by almost 100,000 people a year, it remains strangely unspoilt and offers a striking contrast to Poole, which lies not far away across the water. Landing by the old cottages on the quayside, the visitor enters a seemingly timeless world – a world of wild heathland and woodland, of quiet beaches, and of reed-fringed marsh frequented by innumerable wildfowl.

In about the 6th century the monks of Cerne Abbey built a chapel dedicated to St Andrew, the patron saint of fishermen; the island's name, however, probably a corruption of *Brunci Insula* ('Bruno's Isle'), seems to commemorate an owner later in its history.

In the 16th century, when Henry VIII built, on the site of the existing castle, a blockhouse, or 'gun castle' as part of a chain of defences against the French, the island acquired a certain importance. The castle was maintained and garrisoned by the citizens of Poole and during the Civil War was strongly fortified in the Parliamentarian interest. By the reign of Charles II, however, it had become ruinous, and its military functions were at an end.

Brownsea has had a number of unusual and eccentric owners. Early in the 18th century, it was acquired for £300 by the notorious William Benson. An active Whig, he persuaded the Government in 1718 to dismiss the octogenarian, Christopher Wren, from the Surveyorship of the Works, and got himself appointed in his place. It was not a happy choice and a year later he was obliged to resign, having, it was said, 'got more in one year (for confusing the King's Works) than Sir Chris. Wren did in 40 years for his honest endeavours'. This terminated his official architectural career, but it was he who converted Brownsea Castle into a dwelling house and added the Great Hall. He was also an amateur botanist and the first owner to examine,

Brownsea Island

record and preserve the unusual flora of the Island, cultivating the 'untended chaos of foliage which flourished in wild profusion'.

The Castle was further enlarged, and the landscape gardens and the Pheasantry laid out, in the second half of the 18th and the first half of the 19th century. It must have been a desirable estate when acquired by a certain Colonel William Waugh in 1852. On the slenderest of evidence, he was convinced that there was a valuable bed of china clay on the shore. He spent the fortune that he anticipated from the clay pits on building a village for the workers, a pier, a school, a public house and the present church. He reclaimed St Andrew's Bay by building a sea-wall and refaced the Castle. When the clay proved to be suitable only for making drainpipes, the Colonel was ruined and fled to Spain.

At the beginning of the 20th century the island was acquired by Charles van Raalte, a man of taste and immense wealth, who maintained a staff of thirty in the castle, ten gardeners, and a silver band of twenty players. It was in the time of van Raalte and his wife that General Baden-Powell, a family friend, persuaded them to allow him to hold a summer camp on the island for twenty boys from mixed backgrounds. Thus, in 1907, the Scout Association was born on Brownsea Island.

The last owner of the island, Mrs Mary Christie, was in many respects the most unusual. During her ownership from 1927 to 1961, Brownsea acquired an aura of mystery. Except for a gamekeeper and a blonde and powerful female Scandinavian 'P.T.' instructor, employed to keep out intruders, Mrs Christie lived in solitude, caring little for human beings, but greatly for birds and beasts. Gradually the undergrowth took control, and when the Island came to the National Trust after Mrs Christie's death (having been accepted by the Treasury in lieu of death duties), the jungle was dense and the ecological balance had suffered. None the less, we owe to her the inviolate character of Brownsea. During critical years, she kept the Island as a clandestine garden, natural and overgrown, a paradise for her peacocks and for herons, seabirds, red squirrels and a variety of wildlife.

The Dorset Naturalists' Trust now manages a 200-acre Nature Reserve, to which there is controlled public access. Volunteers have cleared rides, built hides, and established a laboratory. Magnificent views of the mainland, miles of woodland paths, and a splendid bathing beach, are enjoyed both by visitors and by Scouts and Guides, who alone are permitted to camp on the island. The castle has been leased to the John Lewis Partnership as a holiday centre for their staff.

Golden Cap Estate

4 miles east of Lyme Regis, 3 miles west of Bridport

From the sea a band of bright orange sandstone stands out above the grey rock cliffs on the shoreline of Lyme Bay. It is the unmistakable shape of Golden Cap hill, centre of a complex of Trust properties, farmland, woodland, gorse-covered common, undercliff and beach, with about seven miles of coast extending from the rock formation known as the Spittles just east of Lyme Regis to Eype Mouth south-west of Bridport, with only one break near Charmouth. Nearly 2,000 acres owned here, between crowded main road and lonely sea, have been bought with Enterprise Neptune funds and constitute one of the triumphs of this campaign.

The two most westerly properties are now leased to the Dorset Naturalists' Trust which runs them as a nature reserve: Black Venn with its precipitous cliffs appropriately called the Canary Ledges, and Newlands Batch. On Black Venn a twelve-year-old girl found in 1811 the famous fossilized *Ichthyosaurus* now in the South Kensington Natural History Museum. Westhay, Upcot, and St Gabriel's farms stretch from here to Seatown beach, one of the only two points on this coastline accessible by car. There are marvellous walks from the village of Morecombelake along the cliffs and over the rolling hills of the hinterland, and holiday cottages shelter in gentle coombs. There are sandstone farm buildings, and the remains of a 13th-century chapel can be seen at St Gabriel's. To the east of Seatown are more high cliffs at Doghouse Hill and Thorncombe Beacon. Many of the little beaches and rocky coves below, accessible only at low tide, were used by brandy smugglers in the 18th century, and the lonely clumps of trees planted on the horizon are supposed to have been landmarks for their boats.

Golden Cap Hill

Behind Golden Cap itself (over which covenants are held), lies Filcombe farm, and then comes Hardown Hill above Morecombelake on the other side of the main road. The views from here are magnificent, both towards the sea and inland over Marshwood Vale a good five miles to Coney Castle and Lambert's Castle, both high wooded hills with the remains of Iron Age forts which belong to the Trust. The character of this scene, with perhaps a kestrel hovering high over the hillside or the smoke of a distant bonfire rising straight to the sky, reminds one that this is the edge of Hardy country.

Carneddau area, Ysbyty Estate, Gwynedd; The Glyders and Llyn Ogwen

Carneddau area, Ysbyty Estate, Gwynedd; Head of Nant Ffrancon Pass, Mynedd Perfedd and Foel Goech

Carrick-a-rede, Co. Antrim; View along the coast

Giant's Causeway, Co. Antrim; View west across the bay

Golden Cap Estate: Black Venn, view to the east towards Golden Cap Hill. Portland Bill in the distance

Fontmell Down

3 miles south of Shaftesbury, east of A350, between Compton Abbas and Fontmell Magna

It is fitting that Fontmell Down near Shaftesbury was bought by public subscription in 1976 as a memorial to Thomas Hardy. No English writer was more steeped in the history and traditions of his native country than he, and the 'manor of Funtamell' has the distinction of having been mentioned in the oldest West Saxon charter of which a good text survives, recording a grant of land in 704 by Coinred, father of King Ine of Wessex (who also granted the land on which Glastonbury Abbey stood). 150 acres of this immaculate grassy down which now belong to the National Trust, were part of Funtamell Manor.

Fontmell Down looking west

481

From the crest there are magnificent views; to the north over the ancient hunting forest of Cranborne Chase, to the south-west over the fertile Blackmoor Vale and south towards Blandford Forum and the coast. There are two Iron Age defensive dykes across the down where today Dorset Long Horn sheep and cattle graze on the short grass starred with spring and summer flowers, part of the Trust's management plan for controlled and selective clearance. Buzzards and kestrels wheel overhead, while below in the valley part is managed as a nature reserve.

Southdown Farm

About 7 miles north-east of Weymouth, off A353

The downlands of Dorset have an atmosphere that is almost magical where they end suddenly in the vertical cliffs of Weymouth Bay. Constable captured this in some of the pictures painted during his honeymoon at Osmington, barely a mile down the coast to the west of Southdown, and the artist and his young wife must often have walked the length of the cliffs from Ringstead to White Nothe which Enterprise Neptune has now secured for the National Trust. Both Ringstead, almost on the edge of the cliff, and Holworth, a mile inland at the northern end of the farm, are deserted villages of grass-covered banks and ditches where there were once streets, houses and paddocks. Their population disappeared during the 15th century, though whether as a consequence of plague, the enclosure of strip fields for sheep-farming, or a general economic decline, no one knows. An air of melancholy haunts them now as the sea breeze whistles through the rye grass and round the corners of tumbledown barns.

Burning Cliff in the centre of Ringstead Bay earned its name from peat fires said to have smouldered on it in the 18th century for six years. Here and as far as White Nothe landslips have caused cliffs to form in many places facing inland, perfect sheltered spots for nesting seabirds. The path round White Nothe Cliff has been gradually eroded by the battering of many storms but is still used by walkers; it was once the legendary smugglers' escape route described in *Moonfleet* by J. W. Falkner. From this coast the views to Portland Bill over the blue expanse of Weymouth Bay, flecked with white sails on a summer afternoon, are exhilarating.

Southdown Farm

Essex

Danbury and Lingwood Commons

5 miles east of Chelmsford, astride A414

Little remains of the huge royal Forest of Essex that once covered virtually the whole county, but these two commons, together over 200 acres of heath and woodland, are a survival from the time of the medieval manors. Situated on a gravel ridge between Chelmsford and Maldon, high for this low-lying country, these areas where the commoners from all the settlements around could graze their beasts must have remained basically unchanged since the 10th century.

Danbury has the more characteristic open common landscape with colonies of low scrub, heather, bracken, broom, gorse, brambles and sloe, although silver birch and oak have seeded in places on the sandy soil. In summer the clearings are full of bees and butterflies; one in particular is the only known breeding ground in England for the Rosy Marbled Moth. Lingwood Common has the feeling rather of a forest with open glades, more isolated than its neighbour and in many ways more attractive. Neolithic flints have been found on Beacon Hill, its highest point, looking over Danbury village and the Chelmer Valley.

Because of its height and its nearness to the sea, Danbury was an important army camp from 1780 to 1815, and during the Napoleonic invasion scares over fourteen regiments were stationed there. The redoubt built in those years can be seen on the Sandon road, at the west end of the Common, its parapet still discernible among the bracken and gorse. Smugglers too found it an ideal centre, being so near the estuaries of the Crouch and the Blackwater. Their ponies grazed innocently on the common during daytime, and at night were rounded up and taken away to haul illicit cargoes to hiding places amongst the bracken.

Two miles north-west of Danbury, near Little Baddow, Blake's Wood is also looked after by the Trust. It consists of over eighty acres of hornbeam and chestnut coppice, with a wide variety of wild flowers.

Hatfield Forest

3 miles east of Bishop's Stortford, on south side of the A120 Bishop's Stortford/Colchester road

Originally an outlying part of the extensive Forest of Essex, Hatfield was a royal hunting demesne even before the Conquest. Administered by Crown officials, its usages were established, and its boundaries protected, by special laws. A map of 1594 indicates that the forest was then much the size it is today. It was acquired in 1729 by the Houblon family, who drained and replanted much of the woodland, created the ornamental lake, and in 1759 built the attractive little Shell House upon its banks.

The Forest covers some thousand acres of woodland, laced with wide

Hatfield Forest

grassy rides that are known as 'chases'. It is famous for its large hornbeams, many of which were pollarded for firewood in the distant past, and for its monumental oaks. The Old Doodle Oak, which last showed green over a century ago, and measured sixty feet in circumference, is 700–800 years old and was once thought to be the very oak shown on the site of the Domesday Survey.

The soil is largely heavy London clay overlying chalk, with small areas of sand and gravel. The undergrowth is typical of Essex woodland, with primroses, anemones, and occasionally wild thyme, herb Paris, and the small flowered buttercup. Sheets of oxlip bloom in the spring, and on the marshy ground occur the lesser spearwort, water plantain, and many species of orchid.

The last descendants of the red deer pursued by medieval kings were killed off in the First World War, but there are still fallow deer, foxes, and a well-established badgers' set. Among the more interesting birds that frequent the forest are greater and lesser spotted woodpeckers, redstarts, hawfinches, and grasshopper warblers. The lake and adjoining marsh harbour mallard, teal, grebe, water-hen and snipe.

Greater Manchester

Medlock Vale

$1\frac{1}{2}$ miles north-east of Ashton-under-Lyne

In the centre of a triangle between Manchester, Oldham and Ashton is a tiny corner of countryside by the banks of the river Medlock which has miraculously kept its rural, Pennine character in an advancing tide of suburbia.

Medlock Vale

The motorist hurrying through Failsworth, neither town nor country but a depressing continuation of Manchester's Oldham Road, could hardly guess that less than a mile to the right a suddenly winding lane leaves the rows of terrace houses and plunges through trees down to the river. Here Daisy Nook bridge, among timber-framed cottages, might be the subject of a Morland picture with a flock of sheep being driven across it. Fifteen acres of pasture on both sides of the river belong to the Trust, popular for walks on a summer's evening, and also Hen Cote Cottage, as pretty as its name.

Hampshire

New Forest Commons

The Trust owns three groups of commons on the periphery of the New Forest. The main group, centred round Bramshaw to the north of the Forest and covering 930 acres, consists of Cadnam and Stocks Cross Greens, and Bramshaw, Cadnam, Furzley, Penn and Plaitford Commons; next in importance comes Hale Purlieu, 410 acres in extent, north-east of Fordingbridge; and finally there is Hightown Common, of 30 acres, east of Ringwood. These commons are subject to ancient common rights, the most important being that of pasture. Other rights include pannage (the right to turn pigs out to common), estovers (the taking of firewood) and turbary (the right to take turf).

   The commons are contiguous to the New Forest, so that animals put to pasture on them can stray onto the Forest and vice versa. Under the New Forest Act of 1964 the adjacent commons were included in the perambulation of the Forest so that the common rights now apply to the whole

New Forest Commons

open Forest and the verderers' by-laws controlling stock operate on the commons.

The commons mainly consist of open heathland, a gravel and peat soil covered with heather, bracken, and seeded birch. In the wetter parts bog plants thrive and there are several stands of alder. The only true woodland is on an area of heavier clay on Plaitford Common, where there are woods of oak and beech, a favourite haunt in autumn for the pigs.

Apart from the woodland the vegetation is entirely natural, controlled only by haphazard grazing of the commoners' beasts, and therefore interesting to botanists and lepidopterists.

Selborne Hill

4 miles south of Alton, between Selborne and Newton Valence, west of B3006

Selborne is sacred to naturalists as the birthplace and lifelong home of Gilbert White, the father of field studies and author of the enchanting *Natural History and Antiquities of Selborne*. The Trust's holdings here, though not as yet extensive, are among its most precious possessions.

Selborne's two main features, which contrast yet complement each other, are firstly the great hill, 700 feet above sea-level, beech-covered along its steep northern flank which is still climbed by the paths which White knew well, and secondly the lovely vale of the Lyth and Dorton (the last not yet the Trust's) that is intimate and retired below the hill and village and runs gently down to Oakhanger and the rough belt of Woolmer Forest. On either side of the hill a small stream flows, to unite at the head of this vale in Dorton, and together they eventually reach the river Wey. It is these streams and their vales which contribute to the 'green retreats' so beloved by White and his companions.

The Trust's holding amounts only to some 257 acres, with thirty acres under covenant, yet, including the hill and hanger and the Lyth's long beech-clad slopes and rough pastures, the area is the mecca of naturalists and nature-lovers, the living green outdoor laboratory of Gilbert White. Over every inch his quick and eager ghost presides.

It was the contrast in soils, its wooded character and consequent humidity and the abundance of plants of all kinds, that made Selborne so perfect for a field naturalist. The hill is of chalk (the soil in general Upper Greensand) but beneath it stretches a belt of stiff clay, and then, on the other side of the village, is that extraordinary 'black malm' which White the gardener writes of with envy and does not succeed in explaining. On all the high fields which the vale and its small subsidiary valleys cut into there is, in the main, only the common grey malm, which is freestone broken down by frosts into a soil good for corn arable and pasture, and superb for hops. As White said, 'it grows the brightest hops'. It is equally good for vines too, as Cobbett discovered. But the rare patches of black malm are of an incomparable richness.

Not far beneath the surface on the valley sides lie hard freestone strata which make good building stone. Selborne's church of St Mary and many of its attractive houses and cottages are built of this hard stone, which has turned a creamy white with time.

View from Selborne Hill

Stockbridge

At junction of A30, A272 and A3057

The Trust became lord of the manor of Stockbridge in 1946 and with the lordship came the Down, the Common Marsh, and a small strip of ancient Manorial Waste on either side of Stockbridge High Street.

The Down, a mile to the east of the little town, is a prominent chalk hill of 150 acres capped in places with clay. It has probably not been cultivated since ancient times and is thus rich in chalkland plants and shrubs. Yew trees and stands of juniper are prominent, and on the clay caps there is blackthorn and hawthorn scrub.

Archaeological remains include Bronze Age barrows, and the north-east corner extends to the fortifications of the Iron Age camp of Woolbury Ring dating from about 300 B.C.

On the fifty-five acres of Common Marsh, just south of the town itself, the burgesses still exercise their ancient rights of pasture. The date for the opening of the Marsh is decided at the annual Courts Leet and Baron over which Miss Hill, the donor of the property, presides on behalf of the Trust as lady of the manor. These proceedings are opened by the crier, and the officers for the ensuing year are appointed and take their oaths, the hayward responsible for supervision of the marsh-grazing receiving his staff, and the bailiff taking custody of the mace presented to the borough in 1685 by its Member of Parliament, Essex Strode. The lady of the manor addresses the burgesses and the jury, who after deliberation make presentations on the affairs of the borough.

Hereford & Worcester

Bradnor Hill

$\frac{1}{2}$ mile north-west of Kington, north of A44

The Welsh Marches provide some of the least known but most beautiful open country in Britain. This borderland, constantly fought over during the Middle Ages, seems since to have been forgotten, an area of lost, sleepy agricultural communities set amongst smooth hills where the red-brown cattle match the colour of the rich soil. Bradnor Hill above Kington has perhaps the finest views in a county famous for them: to the east stretches England, woods, meadows and winding streams criss-crossed with hedges and walls; to the west, Radnor Forest and the dark mountains of Wales, brown and purple with bracken and heather. Far to the south is Hereford and the valley of the Wye, mile upon mile of the plain which was once the ancient kingdom of Mercia. Bradnor Hill used to be common land belonging to Kington, but since the enclosures of the 16th century it has been used for sheep-grazing. The golf course which now covers much of it, including the summit, 1,284 feet above sea-level, claims to be the highest in England.

Bradnor Hill, looking south-east

From the northern slopes, away from fairways and bunkers, can be seen the line of Offa's Dyke crossing Rushock Hill from Kennel Wood: this is one of its best-preserved stretches, though it has puzzled archaeologists because part of it has a ditch on the north side and part on the south. Perhaps two different gangs were employed here in the construction of this great earthwork.

Clent Hills

3 miles south of Stourbridge

Climbing the Clent Hills is a breathtaking experience in every sense. From the top of these steep but smooth green hills, where the breeze is always strong, stretch the finest views in the Midlands. A vast chequerboard of green fields and hedgerows extends south towards the Cotswolds, and further west to the Malvern Hills. On the north-west Hagley Park lies in the

Clent Hills; The summit

lee of the hill, the house and church far beneath looking like toys and the parkland dotted with obelisks, temples and sham ruins. Beyond it is Kinver Edge and beyond that again loom Wenlock Edge and the Shropshire Hills on the horizon. North and east is the smoke of the Black Country and Birmingham, mile upon mile of towerblocks and chimneys. In that direction also, but tucked just under the fold of the hill, is a tiny 13th-century chapel marking the supposed site of the martyrdom of St Kenelm, the Mercian prince killed by the order of his ambitious sister while hunting over Clent Hills.

The four great stones on the summit, over 1,000 feet above sea-level, have fooled many. They are not the remains of a megalithic cromlech but the 18th-century Gothick fantasy of the poet-cum-landscape-gardener William Shenstone who lived at The Leasowes near Halesowen, two miles away. Walton Hill to the south-east, the only other peak as high as this, also belongs to the Trust, and some of the farmland and woods between in the Clatterbach valley. This great expanse of open country ideal for hiking or for pony-trekking is justly one of the Trust's most popular properties.

Malvern Hills *(see colour plate facing p. 353)*

4–8 miles south of Great Malvern, along A449

There is no landscape more quintessentially English than the view from the Malvern Hills over the Worcestershire plain, a vast jigsaw puzzle of bright-green fields and hedgerows with the occasional splash of yellow from a mustard crop, and the weathered brown farmhouses like toys far beneath. On these hills too events important in English history and culture have taken place. The summit of the Herefordshire Beacon still carries the remains of an Iron Age camp, once an almost impregnable citadel with a thick stone

Malvern Hills; View to the north

wall fifty yards in circumference at its centre and an intricate network of ditches and earthworks covering forty-four acres. The Normans later used the fort against the Welsh, and Owain Glyndwr stormed it as late as 1405. Just south of Midsummer Hill can still be seen also part of the Red Earl's Dyke built by Gilbert de Clare, Earl of Gloucester, about 1287, to mark the boundary between his land and the Bishop of Hereford's. In the more peaceful years of the 14th century it was at a spring somewhere on the Malvern Hills that the poet William Langland 'slombred in a slepyng' and dreamt the Vision of Piers Plowman, one of the first great works of English literature.

Its springs were to bring Malvern fame and prosperity in the 18th and 19th centuries, when the polite world discovered that the waters had health-giving properties, but older springs like Walm's Well under the shadow of Hangman's Hill indicate that the waters were valued far earlier. Today the southern hills are the least spoilt in the range. Quarries have not been allowed to encroach too far on the wooded slopes, and new building is forbidden. The sleepy villages are tucked in the shadow of the hills and the only sign of human life is the proud 18th-century obelisk in Eastnor Park. Chase End Hill, the southernmost point on the ridge, is also the quietest and the greenest. Cuckoos call in the woods below and there are grasshoppers on the gentle slopes that lead to the summit, where suddenly the wind takes away the breath and a panorama of fields and villages stretches to the horizon. Elgar drew his inspiration from this landscape; his oratorio *Caractacus* was directly based on these hills where the British chieftain is supposed to have lived, while the romance of the Enigma Variations and passages in some of his symphonic works seem even more to be musical descriptions of this unparalleled scenery.

While the greater part of the Malvern Hills is controlled by the Malvern Hills Conservators, the Trust owns 36¾ acres, including 26 acres of Midsummer Hill (see p. 406). Some 1,207 acres of the Southern Hills are covenanted to the Trust.

Hertfordshire

Ashridge Estate *(see colour plate facing p. 353)*

3 miles north of Berkhamsted, north of A41, astride B4506

The estate of nearly 4,000 acres lies on the main ridge of the Chilterns, and divides conveniently into four roughly equal areas of downland, common land, woodland and farmland. The downland is chalk, but on most of the lower ground the chalk was overlaid during the Ice Age by clay and sand which contain large numbers of flints.

The Ivinghoe Beacon, which is part of the turf downland on the north of the property, is laced with prehistoric tracks and earthworks typical of the English chalk downs. Excavations on the Beacon have helped to date the opening phases of the Iron Age in Britain to the 6th and 7th Centuries B.C.

Ashridge Estate; Frithsden Beeches   *Bridgewater Monument*

In the woodland area, forestry is a major activity and a large acreage has been planted in the last thirty years. The plantations, initially a mixture of hard and soft woods, are designed eventually to produce a characteristic English hardwood forest, primarily of beech and oak. The woodlands are attractive to birds and there are as many as fifty-one breeding species, which include redstarts, wood warblers, nightingales, and sometimes the lesser redpoll.

Besides fallow deer, the rarer muntjak deer and Chinese water deer have established themselves on the estate. Smaller mammals include the water shrew and the greater horseshoe and long-eared bats.

The Ashridge estate is of considerable interest to the botanist as it covers several differing types of habitat. The chalk gives fine stretches of downland at Ivinghoe Beacon and isolated slopes elsewhere; among the most attractive plants to be seen are burnet, saxifrage, cowslip, clustered bellflower, hare-bell, dropwort, horseshoe vetch, kidney vetch, felwort, restharrow, and rock rose with various species of orchid such as the spotted, pyramidal, fragrant, bee and frog. The beech woodlands produce fly and bird's nest orchids, helleborines and a ground flora of wood sorrel, woodruff and sanicle.

At the centre of the estate is the Bridgewater Monument, a landmark erected in 1832 to the memory of the celebrated Duke of Bridgewater, the father of inland navigation; 172 steps lead to the top.

Isle of Wight

Bembridge and Culver Downs

These downs, the most easterly point of the Isle of Wight, form part of the great chalk feature which runs right across the island. The vegetation is typical of chalk downland, much of it close-cropped by sheep, the traditional downland grazers which have now sadly become all too rare on the island. Culver Cliffs, which drop sheer to the sea, are a nesting site for many types of gull and other seabirds.

The property includes Bembridge Fort, one of Lord Palmerston's chain of south-coast fortifications built in the 1860s and still in the last war occupied by the army. Apparently it was long regarded as a secret defence, as it does not appear on any but the most recent editions of the Ordnance maps. Though substantially built of brick and flint, it is cut deep into the down and appears from a distance to be little more than a large earthwork.

When the Trust bought the property the fort had been badly damaged by vandals, and to prevent further damage, the bridge across the moat was removed and the entrance sealed. But with an ingenuity worthy of earlier siege experts the defences were scaled and looting continued until an island company took a lease, repaired much of the interior, and began to manufacture precision sprays there. Geese live in the moat and guard the defences as they did the Capitol in ancient Rome.

Culver Down itself was also heavily fortified to protect the entrance to Spithead. The Trust has removed all the fortifications and has demolished the gun positions with the exception of two late-19th-century emplacements; but some scars still remain and will take time to heal.

Knowles Farm, St Catherine's Hill and St Catherine's Down

Knowles Farm, on the extreme southerly tip of the Isle of Wight, stretches from the cliffs down to the foreshore and surrounds St Catherine's Lighthouse. This land between the cliffs and the sea consists of the blue lias clay, known locally as Blue Slipper, which is so unstable that over the centuries landslides have created a strange and beautiful pattern of undulating hills and valleys. The western part, overwhelmed by a major landslide in 1928, is wild and rugged but full of sheltered hollows with a wide variety of flora. It

St Catherine's Point

also forms ideal cover for birds. St Catherine's Point is a major assembly area for migratory birds, and their numbers and species are recorded by the Hampshire and Isle of Wight Naturalists' Trust.

Above St Catherine's Point, 780 feet up, lies St Catherine's Hill. At the southern end stands a much earlier lighthouse. St Catherine's Oratory, built in the early 14th century, is said to have been erected by the local inhabitants in expiation of their indulgence in an outbreak of ship wrecking. The building is enchanting, shaped like a pepper-pot and thirty-eight feet high.

At the other end of the Down on the Trust's land, though not itself owned by the Trust, stands the Hoy monument built in 1815 to commemorate a visit by the Tsar. On the opposite side of the monument there is a later inscription in memory of British troops who died fighting against the Russians in the Crimea.

From the bracken-clad ridge linking these two features which slopes steeply on either side, it is possible to see both the eastern and western extremities of the island.

Newtown

Midway between Newport and Yarmouth, 1 mile north of A3054

The Borough of Newtown was formed in 1256 by the Bishop of Winchester. In 1584 it received the right to elect two Members of Parliament and this continued until the Reform Act of 1832, though from the 17th century onwards the number of dwellings probably never rose above twenty. It seems, indeed, that the town did not recover its economic prosperity after its sacking by the French in 1377. Much of the layout of the original town can still be seen. The house plots are now small fields bounded by hedges, and parts of the High Street and Gold Street are grassy lanes where cattle graze.

The Trust's ownership at Newtown which began with the Town Hall (see p. 300) is varied and extensive. It also controls the river, the quays, and four miles of Solent foreshore, and its harbourmaster supervises the moorings of visiting yachtsmen for whom Newtown provides a remote and beautiful anchorage.

Near Newtown quay the remains of old saltpans survive, though this industry died out over a hundred years ago. By contrast the ancient oyster fishery has recently taken on new life and a clam industry has been established. Clams, no doubt originally thrown overboard from Atlantic liners, have established themselves in Southampton Water where the discharge from Fawley refinery has raised the water temperature by the critical margin necessary to enable them to breed. They are collected and taken to Newtown where they can grow to maturity in the clean water.

The Isle of Wight Natural History and Archaeological Society has established a Nature Reserve over an area of 300 acres including much of the Trust's land. As many as 4,000 waders and 2,000 wildfowl have been recorded at one time, and 170 species of birds have been listed.

The Needles Point

The prominent chalk downs that stretch from the Trust's Culver property on the east to the western tip of the island terminate dramatically in one of the most famous landmarks on the English coast, the serrated white pinnacles known as The Needles. There are now only three of these eroded tottering giants, for the most imposing, rising a hundred and twenty feet from the water and known to sailors as 'Lot's Wife' (for it was said to be white as salt) crashed into the sea in 1764. The erosion continues. In the days of sail the entrance to the Solent Channel, north of The Needles, was a dreaded passage and at certain times a violent tide still runs here.

The Needles Point and The Needles

An interesting Palmerstonian fort with circular gun emplacements, built in 1863, is situated on the turf down behind The Needles. It is still partly occupied by the Coastguard Service, but the Trust, which acquired the property in 1975 with the generous help of an anonymous donor, is undertaking its gradual restoration and the demolition of later accretions. A row of outlying coastguard cottages have been converted for holiday visitors.

West Wight

The Trust owns about seven miles of coast in West Wight, stretching from Freshwater Cliffs eastwards to Chilton Chine. Most of this land is chalk down, unploughed and covered with short downland grass and flowers, interspersed with clumps of gorse and hawthorn. The many different types of chalk grasses are of particular interest to botanists and there is a rich and varied flora and insect life. Seabirds nest on the cliffs, and the downland species include meadow pipits, wheatears, and ring ouzels. The main group of downs running east from Freshwater Bay consists of Afton (on which there is a golf course), Compton, Brook, and Mottistone. Perhaps the last has the most breathtaking views of all, not only over the English Channel, but also over the beautiful cultivated and wooded valley immediately beneath it, running east from the prehistoric Longstone to the aptly named Strawberry Lane.

Compton Beaches are a popular family bathing place and the surfing here is the best on the island; Malibu boards are allowed on part of the beach. At Mottistone the estate includes the greater part of the village, one of particular charm nestling round the manor and the church. The bluebell woods behind the manor, reached from the footpath to the Longstone, are worth a special visit in May.

The ancient ridgeway from Freshwater Bay to Brook Shute is now wholly on Trust land and the downs are sprinkled with Bronze Age barrows and tumuli.

On the chalk cliffs of Tennyson Down, rising steeply from the sea, the Poet Laureate took his daily walk when in the 1870s he lived at Farringford near by.

Kent

Bockhill Farm, Dover

3½ miles north-east of Dover; access north of St Margaret's-at-Cliffe from cliff path to Kingsdown

The point where the North Downs meet the Straits of Dover is arguably the most evocative in England, for this is where the white cliffs of Dover stretch eastwards from the harbour beyond St Margaret's Bay. On the clifftops lies Bockhill Farm, bought by the National Trust in 1974 as part of the Enterprise Neptune campaign to save the coast. The 270-acre farm is the first extensive tract of land to be acquired by the Trust in this area and forms a continuation of St Margaret's Leas, which came to the Trust in 1968.

The coastline is renowned for its bird life which includes fulmars and kittiwakes and till recently peregrine falcons which bred there regularly. As Dover is the busiest of the Channel ports for human passengers, so the clifftops are a landfall and takeoff point for migrant species crossing the Straits of Dover.

The flora too is of special interest, for this part of the country is thought to have been one of the very few regions not to have been covered by the great forests that spread over Britain after the last Ice Age. Consequently the area was a refuge for grassland plants most of which spread to other areas as the forests were gradually cleared by man. Some species, however, have remained local and peculiar to this part of Kent.

Bockhill Farm and Dover Cliffs

On a less peaceful note, the Dover Patrol Memorial on Leathercoat Point bears witness to the more recent occasions when the cliffs formed Britain's front line of defence. Most of the paraphernalia of war has been cleared away, but the remains of gun emplacements can still be seen in the valley below the farm, where the heavy guns 'Winnie' and 'Pooh' fired across the Channel. At low tide and out to sea, wrecks of ships emerge, some casualties of war, others victims of the waters round the Goodwin Sands.

Toys Hill

$2\frac{1}{2}$ miles south of Brasted, 1 mile west of Ide Hill

These ninety-three acres of woodland rise to a height of over 800 feet and include the highest point in Kent.

From early times until the mid-19th century Toys Hill was part of the commons of Brasted Chart, where local people kept pigs and cattle, gathered peat and firewood, and quarried churtstone for their roads and buildings. The beech-woods were cut in rotation to provide, among other things, charcoal for the wealden iron trade while it flourished and for drying hops in the local oasts. The pollarded beeches which survive date from the days of grazing, for pollarding kept the young shoots out of the reach of cattle.

If the pigs and cattle had not gone by the time of the enclosure they went with it, and the last charcoal-burners and woodcutters have been gone with the local hop yards half a century or more. People no longer have to gather firewood; and churtstone, in so far as it is quarried at all, is won more easily elsewhere: and so the woods are silent except for the sounds of nature, while the slowly dying pollards grow ever more grotesque and the churt pits gather moss.

Those who now come to Toys Hill do so for their pleasure, to enjoy the woods and views and their ever-changing aspects: a film of green in spring, cool shade in summer, rich colours in autumn.

In 1906 a house called Weardale Manor was built with a terrace and landscaped grounds, and man-made order reigned. Its demolition in 1939 left only the terrace and vanishing traces of gardens and grounds. Nature has largely reclaimed her own, and only the tougher exotic plants and shrubs remain as witness, with crumbling stonework, to the hill's brief taste of opulence.

The well, near the cottages to the south of the hill, was sunk for the benefit of local people by Octavia Hill, whose sister Frances owned the house above, now called Chart Brow, where Octavia was a frequent visitor. From the seat beside it one of the finest views in Kent can be had over the Weald. This part of Toys Hill, which was given in 1898, is one of the National Trust's earliest acquisitions.

Lake District (Cumbria)

Buttermere Valley

Along B5289

Nowhere but in the Lake District could so extraordinary a variety of scenery lie within a single valley. From the wilderness of Honister Pass, littered with huge boulders, it is only ten miles to the rich green meadows of the Vale of Lorton. Gatesgarth, half-way down the pass coming from Borrowdale, is the classic viewpoint looking down on Buttermere itself with a line of summits behind it – Hay Stacks, High Crag, High Stile, Red Pike – and Burtness Wood fringing the shore, part of it given by the historian G. M. Trevelyan. Waterfalls high on the mountainside show white against the dark slate screes and heather. Farther down the valley, through the pastures of

Buttermere

grazing cattle that gave Buttermere its name, is Crummock Water, dominated by Grasmoor on the north. Apart from Lanthwaite Wood at the foot of the lake, this is almost treeless country; its beauty is in the contrast between flowing grassy slopes and the knobbly crags and precipices that suddenly emerge above and below them. There are geological reasons for. this: one is the juxtaposition of Skiddaw slate formation and Borrowdale volcanic rock.

Lowest of the three lakes is Loweswater set in a more pastoral landscape than its neighbours. Holme Wood stretches almost the length of the south side, conifers and deciduous trees climbing the slopes of Carling Knott. As on Buttermere and Crummock Water, boats are let out by the Trust, mainly for fishing, and the tranquillity of the place is not spoilt by pleasure steamers or water-skiers.

Coniston Water

Of all the Lakes, Coniston has perhaps the gentlest, most cultivated aspect. 18th-century travellers compared it to the pictures of Claude, as opposed to the Salvator Rosa crags of Derwentwater. Instead of rock and scrubland, fields full of buttercups and deciduous woods slope gently down to its shores; yet the landscape, especially from the south-east end, is both impressive and beautiful. Here the Trust owns Park-a-Moor fell and Nibthwaite Woods on the edge of the water with superb views across to the Old Man of Coniston, most southerly of the great Lake District peaks. Peel Island, just off this shore, and Fir Island farther up the lake on this side, also belong.

But the best vantage points near Coniston Water are undoubtedly at its head, the fells surrounding Tarn Hows, most of which fall within the Monk Coniston estate. This property was partly bequeathed to the Trust by Beatrix Potter (Mrs William Heelis). The word 'tarn' came originally from the Norse word meaning 'tear-drop', and looking down from the high ground above Tarn Hows over its mirror reflection in the hollow beneath, one can see why. Beyond and far below is the thin ribbon of Coniston Water

Coniston Water

stretching out towards the sea, while on the right is the summit of Wetherlam, again Trust-owned, and the silhouettes of Bow Fell, the Langdale Pikes and Helvellyn. The trees are almost all evergreens planted at the beginning of this century, although larches have also seeded here and there. The tarn itself contains pike, perch, roach and rudd; its shallowness makes it especially warm in summer and cold in winter. It is as memorable glistening with ice and overhung by snow-covered trees as it is on a hot summer's evening with a gentle breeze rippling the surface. Wetherlam too is worth exploring. The smooth whale-like outline of this great hill is deceptive, for it is in fact pierced and pitted with caves, tunnels, shafts and excavations, mostly the workings of a long-dead copper-mining industry.

Derwentwater and Borrowdale *(see colour plate facing p. 448)*

For many people Derwentwater represents the essence of the Lake District. It was the main place of pilgrimage for 18th- and early 19th-century tourists led by Gray, Coleridge and Wordsworth, and it was also the scene of the Trust's first activities in this part of the world. Since 1902, when Brandelhow on the west side of the lake was bought, a series of acquisitions has preserved a total of almost 6,000 acres here and in Borrowdale, including all the best-known viewpoints and natural features: Ashness Woods and Reecastle Crag with their unforgettable views over Derwentwater to Bassenthwaite Lake and the slopes of Skiddaw; the hamlet of Watendlath high up in the fells, whitewashed farmhouses shaded by dark yews round a peaceful tarn; the Bowder Stone, a huge up-ended rock weighing around 2,000 tons poised above the Jaws of Borrowdale; Castle Crag, an ancient fort facing it across the gorge; and Manesty, once a lead mine, now green fingers

Derwentwater

of conifers stretching out into the lake. The credit for this formidable list must go largely to the pioneering work of Canon Rawnsley, co-founder of the Trust and vicar of Crosthwaite near Keswick. In 1922 Calf Close Bay and Friar's Crag at the Keswick end of the lake were bought by subscription as a memorial to him. A nature walk here is open for people in wheelchairs. The view from the rocky headland of Friar's Crag is one of the most famous in the Lake District, and it was here that another apostle of conservation, John Ruskin, awoke to aesthetic experience. 'The first thing I remember, as an event in life,' he wrote, 'was being taken by my nurse to the brow of Friar's Crag on Derwent Water; the intense joy, mingled with awe, that I had in looking through the mossy roots, over the crag, into the dark lake.' Today this whole stretch of wooded shore together with the four islands off it – Lords Island, St Herbert's Island, Rampsholme and Derwent Isle – survive little changed in the hands of the Trust. St Herbert's, sanctuary of a hermit in the 7th century, was Beatrix Potter's 'Owl Island' in *The Tale of Squirrel Nutkin.*

The 'beauty, horror and immensity' which overwhelmed the 18th-century tourist at the Jaws of Borrowdale rarely induced him to go farther up the valley, but it is here that the best walks and the most dramatic landscapes in the Trust's protection can be found. One path leads from Stonethwaite between the two sentinels of Bull's Crag and Sergeant's Crag up the long narrow valley of the Langstrath, until eventually the Stake Pass leads through into Great Langdale under the shadow of the Langdale Pikes. Another path, laid out as a Nature Trail in collaboration with the Cumbria Naturalists' Trust, climbs High Doat from Seatoller, pauses to take in the view back to Keswick and Skiddaw eight miles away in the blue and hazy distance, and then descends through Johnny's Wood.

The Langdales

The unmistakable silhouette of the Langdale Pikes, subject of a thousand picture postcards, is never hackneyed. Set between Scafell and Helvellyn in the central mountain range of the Lake District, and overlooking the steep, narrow valleys of Great and Little Langdale, it is magnificent from every angle. The twin summits are part of a vast stretch of high land, from Stone Arthur above Grasmere and Seat Sandal on the slopes of Helvellyn to Bow Fell (the peak between the head of Great Langdale and Scafell), all of which the Trust holds on long lease and at a peppercorn rent from the Earl of Lonsdale. Altogether 16,842 acres, it provides walkers with some of the most exhilarating and challenging routes in the Lakes. Ropes and rucksacks may be more popular now than the sketchbooks and 'Claude glasses' of the 18th century, but the appreciation of this huge unchanged expanse of mountain, tarn and fell is as great as ever.

Immediately to the south of the Pikes is Great Langdale, whose splendid scenery is typically glacial; the crags poised on the heights above it are hardened tuffs, and the flat valley floor was left by the retreating ice. Here in the Neolithic Age was an important axe factory on the slopes where an

Langdale Pikes

outcrop of workable rock was exposed. Weapons produced here have been found by archaeologists as far away as Hampshire. But today the distinctive twisting valley, dotted with whitewashed farmhouses and barns, sheltered by ancient yews, is protected from the disfigurement of modern industry. At the foot of the valley are two small but attractive lakes, Elterwater and Loughrigg Tarn, the latter and all the land between it and Grasmere now owned by the Trust.

One of the most persistently generous benefactors in this area was, again, Beatrix Potter, who devoted most of the royalties from her books to the purchase of sheep farms, woods and fells which she wished to see preserved. Busk and Dale End farms, together with Fletcher Wood and land overlooking Elterwater, were all acquired through her unselfish efforts. These and later purchases by the Trust, particularly of Fell Foot, the sheep farm at the head of the valley, have ensured the future of Little Langdale, no less beautiful than its neighbour to the north. In spring the stone-walled fields running down to the river Brathay are filled with lambs, new additions to the 18,000 sheep owned by the Trust at the last count.

Ullswater

Ullswater is unique among the Lakes for the twisting outline which adds an element of surprise to its varied landscape. From Patterdale it looks small enough, contained by the steep flanks of Place Fell and the Brown Hills, then suddenly from Stybarrow Crag on the road by Glencoyne Wood appears a vast expanse of water, three or four times as big again, stretching eastwards towards Skelly Nab. With the trees a blaze of colour in the autumn there are few more beautiful spots. The creation of estates round the

Ullswater

lake in the 18th and 19th centuries led to the planting of exotic trees, copper beeches, wellingtonias and variegated oak, which are now mature and add diversity to the lower slopes. Glencoyne and Gowbarrow, which together form a three-mile stretch on the north and west shore, are both estates of this order, though they originated as medieval deer parks. Down on the shore here, near Lyulph's Tower, a pretty Gothick folly of 1780, Wordsworth saw the daffodils which were to inspire his famous poem; while in the background is the distant roar of Aira Force, the biggest waterfall in the Lake District, with its 65-foot drop into a gorge.

South of Ullswater and at the foot of the pass to Windermere and Ambleside is Brotherswater. The Hartsop Hall estate which surrounds it, from Hart Crag and Dovedale to the Kirkstone Pass, was given in 1947 by the Treasury who had accepted it in lieu of death duties, the first property ever to be acquired by the Trust in this way. Today Hartsop Hall is actively maintained as a farm, and the cold tidiness of non-productive conservation has been avoided in these sheep-filled valleys.

Wasdale and Scafell

As Wordsworth pointed out, it is not the size of the Lakes which impresses so much as their rightness of scale. Wastwater is considerably smaller than its more famous neighbours, yet seen from the wooded shore of Wasdale Hall, with the scree slopes of Illgill Head on the right and Scafell towering behind, its perfect proportions are unforgettable. The fact that there is no linking road between Wasdale Head and Eskdale or Langdale has also meant that this valley has preserved its quiet and air of mystery, almost as inaccessible now as it was in the 18th century. Its dark, still waters, so deep that in parts they lie below sea-level, are free of boats and reflect only the dark conifer woods of Bowderdale and the vast smooth fells behind. The Trust now has a long lease on Wastwater. The last dalehead in England was linked to mains electricity in 1977, the cables being laid beneath the lake or underground, thus leaving untouched the beauty of the dale. The road ends at Wasdale Head, a scattered hamlet amongst a patchwork of bright green fields, a rare example of 16th-century enclosure in the Lakes, where the common land system usually survived. In dramatic contrast the grey crags of Great Gable rear up directly behind.

Great Gable from Scafell

To the hardy climber who reaches the summit of Scafell Pike, highest point in England, the mountain reveals itself as a great knot at the centre of a series of radiating valleys. From here the becks and dales extend in every direction like the points of a star, and lakes and tarns glimmer like rock pools far below. The formations of this volcanic scenery – Great End, Lord's Rake and Mickledore, the nick between the two summits – provide the wildest and most rugged of all Lake scenery. All of it above the 2,000-foot contour, up to the 3,210-foot summit, is now in the Trust's care and has remained substantially the same since Wordsworth climbed it for the first time in 1818. 'The stillness seemed to be not of this world,' he wrote; 'we paused and kept silence to listen, and no sound could be heard. The Scafell cataracts were voiceless to us, and there was not an insect to hum in the air.'

504

Windermere and Ambleside

Characteristic of Windermere are the thick woods which have always clothed its shores. From the early Middle Ages its coppice woodlands of oak, ash, hazel and alder were especially cultivated for charcoal-burning by the monks of Furness Abbey. The charcoal was used for iron-smelting, and the local industry reached a climax in the 17th–18th centuries. The least altered of all these woods are on the Lancashire side of the lake, a continuous stretch over three miles from Ferry Nab to Wray Castle. The commercializing of so much of Windermere makes all the more valuable the quiet walks along this shoreline, where the trees sweep down to the water. The grounds of Wray Castle itself are by contrast typical of the 19th century, terraces and rhododendrons round a neo-Tudor pile (now used as a training school for merchant navy radio officers) with magnificent views over the head of the lake and Ambleside. Opposite Wray across the lake, however, there are even finer views from Jenkyns Crag on Wansfell, looking down almost the length of Windermere, a strip of blue lined with dark trees and dappled fells. From here too, and from High Skelgill farm which adjoins it, can be seen the Langdale Pikes and Scafell in a splendid vista across the core of Lakeland.

In 1900 a proposal for a tramway along the shores of Windermere from Bowness to Ambleside was successfully resisted by Canon Rawnsley, and soon afterwards followed the acquisition of Queen Adelaide's Hill on this same shore, west of Windermere station. From its pretty *cottage orné* and

Low Wray, Windermere

landing stage can be seen the lonely island of Lady Holme farther down the lake, site of a pre-Reformation chantry chapel. Cockshot Point on the edge of Bowness, and Fell Foot under the shadow of Gummer's How at the southern end of the lake, are also small but important properties sandwiched between the main road and the water.

Not on Windermere itself, but very close, are two other properties of great importance. At Near Sawrey first of all, between the lake and Esthwaite Water, is Hill Top, the small 17th-century farmhouse owned by Beatrix Potter (see p. 123). Secondly, overlooking Rydal Water north-west of Ambleside, is Dora's Field, a one-and-a-half-acre plot of sloping land bought by Wordsworth in 1826 and virtually an extension of his garden at Rydal Mount. After planning to build a house on it, he finally gave the field to his daughter, Dora, but she died before her father. It was ultimately inherited by the poet's grandson, Gordon Wordsworth, who gave it to the Trust in 1935. In spring, Dora's Field is a mass of daffodils.

Leicestershire

Charnwood Forest

6 miles south-west of Loughborough, via B5350

Ulverscroft Nature Reserve, only two miles from the M1 junction at Markfield, is part of 200 acres of wood and moorland preserved out of the 15,000 acres that once comprised Charnwood Forest. In a valley not far away are the ruins of Ulverscroft Priory, an Augustinian monastery founded in 1134. Under a stand of hardwood, mainly oak and beech, is a particularly varied range of undergrowth, including broad fern, furze, crowberry and whortleberry, which has encouraged wildlife of all sorts. Pheasants, curlews, and rarer birds such as redstarts and tree pipits, can be found as well as many species of lepidoptera. Ulverscroft is administered by the Leicestershire Trust for Nature Conservation and access is by permission of the secretary.

Merseyside

Formby

6 miles south-west of Southport, via A565

To most people the Lancashire coast means piers and promenades, candyfloss and illuminations, but Formby Point, midway between Liverpool and Southport, is a decided contrast. Bought by public subscription in 1967 as part of Enterprise Neptune, these 400 acres of sand dunes dotted with rye grass and sea-pinks are inhabited for much of the year by shelduck, waders and oyster-catchers.

Formby was once a fishing village on the edge of the shore but here, as elsewhere on this coast, the channel silted up and the sea receded. Now the roar of the waves can just be heard in the distance, two miles away across the pinewoods and sands.

As well as a sanctuary for birds, Formby is a place where the red squirrel has found a home. It is notable too for wild flowers, and amongst the brushwood and pines, inshore from the dunes of Mud Wharf, can be discovered many rare specimens. Some of them are thought to have come from the sweepings of grain ships berthing in Liverpool, and later washed up here by the tide.

The nearness of Liverpool is above all what gives Formby its unique value. The closest stretch of unspoilt coastline to the Mersey, looking out to sea over lines of channel buoys to the blue hills of north Wales, it seems extraordinary that its remoteness and quiet should have survived.

The Wirral

9–18 miles north-west of Chester

On the west side of the Wirral peninsula, a group of four National Trust properties has helped to preserve the character of this once remote country which has suffered more than any other part of Cheshire from building development.

Caldy Hill, just to the south of West Kirby, has views over the mouth of the Dee to the Point of Air lighthouse five miles away on the other side. At low tide, islands, bars and spits of wet sand stretch out on either side up the main channel, and the gulls wheel screaming above them. Another mile farther south-west is Thurstaston Common with pink sandstone hills and gorse looking out again over the estuary to the Welsh hills, and with clearings for picnic places. In the middle of the common is a huge rock known as Thor's Stone, supposed to have been used by the Vikings for pagan sacrifices. Harrock Wood is slightly inland, near Irby, a plantation of oak, beech and pine overlooking water meadows, while Burton Wood, above one of the prettiest Wirral villages, is at the base of the peninsula where much of the estuary marshland has been reclaimed. Burton Point, where Richard II's archers embarked for Ireland in 1399, is now inland and the still marvellous views from the wood are no longer over the sands of the Dee, where Mary called the cattle home, but over the vast cooling towers of Shotton steelworks, the silver ribbon of the river beyond, and the dark Welsh mountains in the background.

Norfolk

Blakeney Point

8 miles east of Wells-next-the-Sea

The sand dunes and mud flats of Blakeney have been a paradise for bird-watchers and botanists for many years. It is known that there has been a ternery here since at least 1839, and by 1912, when the Point was acquired by the Trust, it was already famous for its spring and summer migrants. From Blakeney itself, one of the most beautiful villages in Norfolk, one can either walk via Cley to the narrow shingle beach and thence westwards to the Point, or more easily go by boat at high tide with one of the local boatmen who operate from here and Morston. The geographical formation of the Point made it a natural bird sanctuary. The long shingle beach on the seaward side acts as a barrier behind which are high sand dunes, beyond the reach of normal tides, and then saltings, mud flats and creeks. Breeding birds include common and little terns, oyster-catchers and other waders. Altogether 256 different species of bird have been sighted here. Scarce varieties, such as long-tailed duck, wryneck, bluethroat and Lapland bunting are seen each year. The list of flowering plants and ferns at Blakeney is impressive, for the huge depth of the shingle is able to support a wide variety of vegetation: 190 species of flowering plants have been recorded, among them the shrub *Suaeda fruticosa* and *Limonium bellidifolium*, a kind of sea lavender, which are primarily Mediterranean and flourish here because of the unusual conditions.

But Blakeney is not merely interesting to the scientist; it has a magic that draws people back again and again to its wild, sandy landscape, with the

Blakeney Point

sound of the sea hammering on one side and the cries of gulls over lost salt marshes and inlets on the other. Sunk among the dunes is an old lifeboat house which is now used as accommodation for student parties from London University.

An important addition to the Trust's property at Blakeney was made in 1950 when twenty-nine acres of marsh and shingle at Salthouse Broad, a mile down the road towards Sheringham, were bequeathed by Mr E. C. Arnold. The salt lagoons of Arnold's Marsh, as it is known locally, attract large numbers of immigrant waders in spring and autumn passage; birds observed here annually include avocet, black-tailed godwit, ruff, bearded tit and bittern. Arnold's Marsh is let to and administered by the Norfolk Naturalists' Trust, and adjoins their Cley nature reserve.

Scolt Head

3 miles north of Burnham Market

Scolt Head, the most northerly point of the Norfolk coast, is an island unlike its sister nature reserve at Blakeney Point. The marshes that separate it from the mainland are treacherous even at low tide and the only way to get there is by boat from Brancaster Staithe and Burnham Overy Staithe. The voyage is well worth while. This wild and lonely stretch of sand dunes and shingle ridge, rich in marine flora, is the home of large nesting colonies of seabirds. Sandwich tern in particular breed regularly at the western end of the island in larger numbers than anywhere else in England. Redshanks and green-shanks, oyster-catchers, gannets, kittiwakes and Arctic skuas are only a few of the other birds to be seen here, while plant and insect life rival them in interest. Thrift, sea lavender, sea aster and glassworts thrive together with marram grass and mosses on the dunes and foreshore.

Scolt Head was bought by the Trust in 1923, with funds raised by the Norfolk and Norwich Naturalists' Society. In 1937 the foreshore was purchased. In 1953 it was leased to the Nature Conservancy, and since then has been looked after, as a national nature reserve, by a joint committee of representatives of the three organizations and local residents. The eastern tip of the island is owned by the Norfolk Naturalists' Trust, which was founded in 1926, and is also leased to the Nature Conservancy.

Scolt Head is perhaps the least frequented and the most attractive of all nature reserves on the north Norfolk coast.

Northumberland

Allen Banks

These mature deciduous woods cling to the steep banks of the river Allen whose peaty waters, draining from the high moorlands, have cut a deep ravine above the point where the Allen joins the river Tyne. At a time when the planting of hardwoods is giving way to more economic coniferous forestry, the Allen Banks woodlands maintain the variety and grandeur associated with mature stands of beech and oak. They harbour roe deer, and more especially the red squirrel which sadly has deserted so many parts of the country.

There are pleasant walks along the river, where a small suspension bridge spans the waters, or for the adventurous there are steeper paths, originally carved by the Bowes-Lyon family from the precipitous banks. Ascending the eastern bank, and passing small depressions where long ago exposed seams of coal were worked, one may come to a small tarn which is a favourite haunt for several species of duck and the solitary heron. From the top of this eastern bank, a marvellous view stretches northwards through the trees and across the Tyne valley to Hadrian's Wall.

Dunstanburgh Castle

9 miles north-east of Alnwick, on the coast, approached from Embleton on B1339

Dunstanburgh Castle and the adjoining Newton Links and duneland can fortunately be approached only on foot. The Castle, begun in 1316 by Thomas Earl of Lancaster and enlarged later in the 14th century by John of Gaunt, was built on top of one of the most easterly outcrops of the Great Whin Sill. Now a spectacular ruin, it dominates the coastline for many miles north and south. A wild landscape of sea and undulating links induces the feeling that life in the Castle must have been a lonely and sometimes bleak experience. The fortress is protected for at least half of its periphery by the sea; on the north, steep crags form a natural barrier forbidding enough to deter the boldest assailant. They provide nesting sites for a variety of seabirds including kittiwakes, guillemots and fulmar petrels.

The Castle itself is under the guardianship of the Department of the Environment, but the dunelands for about a mile north – where with the increasing number of visitors the problem of duneland erosion is beginning to cause concern – are managed by the Trust.

Dunstanburgh Castle

The Farne Islands

2–5 miles off the coast, opposite Bamburgh, reached by motor boat from Seahouses

Sometimes in spring and summer the Farnes – the group of small islands and rocky islets lying a mile or two off the Northumbrian coast – will seem to float on a halcyon sea, their fretted shores barely rippled by the tide. Yet for weeks on end they are wave-lashed, their rocks fiercely creamed with foam,

Staple Island, Farne Islands

and for centuries they were recognized as a hazard to vessels beating up the north coast. A first lighthouse was established in the reign of Charles II, and its successor, the Longstone Lighthouse, will always recall Grace Darling, the lighthouse-keeper's daughter, who in September 1838 in a fierce northerly gale rowed out to the wreck of the *Forfarshire* and brought back nine survivors.

But the history of the Farnes is more than a long perspective of rock and restless water. In the 7th century St Cuthbert came to live, and die, as a hermit on the Inner Farne. The saint's prestige attracted, over five centuries, a succession of anchorites and prompted in the 13th century the foundation of a Benedictine house which survived until the Dissolution. Of this religious activity a 14th-century chapel is now the sole memorial. It stands on the Inner Farne near a pele tower which is the cell of the modern anchorites – ornithologists, botanists, and wardens – who watch over the islands.

Today the Farnes have a different fame as the summer home of one of the largest and most varied colonies of seabirds on the coasts of Britain. Among the nesting species that the visitor to the islands may hope to see are puffins, guillemots, razorbills, shags, cormorants, oyster-catchers, fulmar petrels, ringed plovers, terns (four species), eider duck, kittiwake, and other more familiar gulls. The Farnes are also the home of a colony of Atlantic grey seals, and of interesting plants, notably *Amsinckia intermedia*, a native of Southern California and rarely found elsewhere in the British Isles.

Young grey seal (halichoerus grypus)   *Kittiwake* (rissa tridactyla)

The Farnes were acquired for the National Trust by public subscription in 1925. They can be visited by fishing boat from the near-by harbour at Seahouses.

North of Seahouses the Trust owns St Aidan's Dunes. The dune hills and foreshore, which are much visited in the summer, offer views of the Farne Islands, and of Bamburgh Castle two miles up the coast.

Ros Castle

12 miles north-west of Alnwick, south-east of Chillingham

Near the eastern boundary of Chillingham Park, famous for its herd of white cattle, a steep conical hill rises from the Northumberland moors. Though there are vague traces of earthwork ramparts which formed the eastern half of an Iron-Age hillfort, this remote eminence is not, as its name would suggest, the site of a ruined castle. Its special attraction is the vast view which seems to comprise the whole county. Although it is quite a climb to the summit, and it may be a little bracing on top, the prospect – across the Cheviot Hills into Scotland, towards the coast and the castles of Lindisfarne, Bamburgh and Dunstanburgh, and down to the Northumbrian lowlands, with Alnwick and Newcastle beyond – makes the ascent well worth while. Lord Grey of Fallodon certainly though it so, and used often to climb to Ros Castle for the views. It was as a memorial to him that the property was vested in the Trust in 1936.

Nottinghamshire

Clumber Park *(see colour plate facing p. 448)*

5 miles south-east of Worksop, east of the A6009/A616 road to Ollerton; $4\frac{1}{2}$ miles south-west of East Retford, west of the A614 Bawtry/Ollerton road

Clumber Park; Lime avenue in autumn

One of the great estates forming part of the Dukeries in and around what was once the Royal Forest of Sherwood, Clumber covers nearly 4,000 acres. Though the princely mansion of the Dukes of Newcastle was demolished in the 1930s, the landscaped park and the long serpentine lake that lay in front of the house splendidly demonstrate how much Lancelot Brown could achieve with a flat unpromising terrain. Other features dating from the second half of the 18th century, when the 2nd Duke of Newcastle tamed a wild waste, are the lodges and gate-piers at the entrances to the park, two garden temples, a solid Palladian bridge, and the red brick stables that stood behind the vanished mansion.

Flanked by magnificent cedars, beyond which rises the tall spire of Bodley's chapel (see p. 291), a long formal walk on the north side of the lake gives views across the water to ornamentally planted clumps and woodlands and to a little temple set among densely grouped rhododendrons. The planting, as so often in our 18th-century parks, is now approaching its term and much replanting is being undertaken by the Trust. Happily the most unusual feature of Clumber – the double lime avenue, three miles long – was not planted until shortly before the middle of the 19th century and has a long life still before it.

Oxfordshire

Buscot and Coleshill Estates

On A417 (Faringdon/Lechlade) and B4019 (Faringdon/Highworth) respectively

The Trust inherited the Buscot and Coleshill estates of 7,500 acres from Mr Ernest Cook in 1956. The gift included the attractive villages of Coleshill and Buscot Park (see p. 69) and the hamlet of Eaton Hastings.

The land for the most part is heavy clay with some areas of sand on the higher ground. Though less sought after since the advent of fertilizers has

Buscot Weir, on the river Thames

made poor land fertile, the rich but intractable clay has been for centuries prosperous farmland. This is evident from the large comfortable-looking farmhouses, many of them dating from the 18th century. The lush grass supports large dairy herds, almost all now Friesian, and the main arable crop is wheat. Though most of the 800-acre woods is let to the Forestry Commission and largely planted with conifers, oak woods survive. The main feature in the landscape is the hedgerow elms, magnificent trees which are as fine as any in Berkshire and are carefully preserved by the Trust.

On a primarily agricultural estate, the farmland and the woods cannot be open for unrestricted access, but there are numerous footpaths and several view points; picnic spots have been formed, the two principal being Badbury Hill and Buscot Weir. Badbury Hill, an Iron Age hillfort, lies just off the Faringdon–Coleshill road. Strategically sited on the highest ground in the area, it has superb views northwards over the gentle landscape of the upper Thames Valley and southwards towards White Horse Hill and the Berkshire Downs.

The village of Coleshill will always be associated with the great 17th-century house, one of the most perfect houses in England, destroyed by fire in the 1950s; nothing remains but the imposing gate-piers. The attractive village houses are of Cotswold stone and many have stone-tiled roofs. The gardens are hedged with box, and clumps of aubrieta grow in the drystone walls fronting the road.

Watlington Hill

1 mile south-east of Watlington, on an escarpment of the Chilterns, east of B480

Watlington Hill, 108 acres of chalk down and copse on the north escarpment of the Chilterns, climbs to just over 700 feet. Half Oxfordshire seems spread out below.

Watlington Hill

The soil is chalk with flints, and at the top of the hill there is an overlay of clay with flints. Thus plants characteristic of both types of soil occur. The chalk-loving plants include a number of rare species. There is also a fine natural yew forest, and whitebeam, wayfaring tree, dogwood and hawthorn are common.

The hill is an ideal spot on which to walk, to picnic, or simply to sit and enjoy the view. The Upper Icknield Way, a prehistoric trade route, passes along its foot, and on its lower slopes the shape of a church steeple is to be seen carved in the chalk. This curiosity is thought to be the work of an 18th- or early-19th-century eccentric.

Salop

The Long Mynd

Above Church Stretton on A49, 15 miles south of Shrewsbury

Impressive in almost any weather, the Long Mynd is perhaps best suited to those changeable days when the shadows of the clouds race across black, heathery moorland, and patches of sun suddenly light up distant valleys. From the Shropshire plain below, the great ridge towering above little pink brick villages is a constant dramatic backdrop – the boundary wall of civilization, or so it seemed for centuries to English eyes before the conquest of Wales. Its name, long anglicized, is in origin Welsh, from the word 'mynydd' (mountain), and it was from its heights that raiders swept down into the peaceful valleys in reprisal for the determined invasions of the Marcher barons. In all, the ridge is about ten miles long and from two to four across. About half of the high land now belongs to the Trust, preserved from the disastrous softwood plantations that have robbed so many hills on the Welsh border of their character and beauty.

The Long Mynd

From Church Stretton a steep and narrow lane leads to a high plateau in the very centre of the Long Mynd, then down, even more steeply, to the villages of Ratlinghope and Asterton on the other side, remote hamlets barely visible in the panorama of green hillocks and moors stretching into Wales. But the full atmosphere of the Long Mynd can only be felt by leaving the road and walking along its endless ridges of springy heather, putting up the occasional whirring grouse, or watching snipe and curlew high over Bodbury Ring, the remains of an Iron Age hillfort on the promontory above Church Stretton. One of the straightest of the tracks which cross the moor is Portway, a Roman road still clearly visible walking across Wentnor to Linley Hill. The gliders which occasionally swoop over these smooth slopes or spiral upwards over the wide valleys like great birds of prey do not disturb their silence and their solitude.

Somerset

Ebbor Gorge

2½ miles north-west of Wells, east of A371

Ebbor is the loveliest and most unspoilt ravine in the Mendips. Smaller perhaps than its famous neighbour Cheddar Gorge, of which the Trust also owns a part, and less spectacular than the extraordinary caverns and grottoes of Wookey Hole to the south, it will always appeal more than either to true lovers of landscape. No road leads up the valley, only a path snaking up the narrow, secret gorge, mysterious under a ceiling of green branches. A mile's scramble up this rocky cleft brings the persevering walker to the top of the lonely Mendip plateau by Higher Pitts farm, where all around break magnificent views of Somerset and the distant hills of Dorset. The very old

Ebbor Gorge

and the very new mingle here: an enormous television mast now stands on Pen Hill among rings and tumuli of prehistoric rites and burials, dominating the view to the east. This area was thickly populated in the first eras of human civilization, and its inhabitants were particularly advanced. In Bridged Pot Shelter at the head of the Gorge was found a superb axe, of highly polished green stone, which is now in the Wells Museum, and other caverns have yielded remains of the early Stone Age huntsmen who once lived in them.

In 1967, the 116 acres of woodland, including the Gorge itself, were leased to the Nature Conservancy and declared a national nature reserve. To protect the interest of the woodland, visitors are asked to keep to footpaths.

Exmoor (Holnicote Estate) *(see colour plate facing p. 449)*

East and south of Porlock, south of A39

Less wild but perhaps even more beautiful than Dartmoor, Exmoor has a unique atmosphere that was wonderfully conveyed by R. D. Blackmore in *Lorna Doone*. Its loneliness is exhilarating rather than depressing, and its history is always alive in the cairns and barrows on its heights, and the weathered stone farmhouses and packhorse bridges in the folds of its valleys. Almost 7,000 acres of it are preserved by the Trust from the cultivation which at one time threatened to destroy its character. First, just to the east of Porlock come Selworthy Beacon and Bossington Hill jutting out into the Bristol Channel, over four miles of cliff coastline looking one way over the crescent shingle beach of Porlock Bay, the other way towards Minehead and the fertile marshes round Dunster. Across the Channel itself, ploughed by the white wakes of tramp steamers, can be seen St Donat's and the Glamorgan coast. Above the village of Selworthy is Bury Castle, the remains of a large Iron Age hillfort. Both at Selworthy, and at Bossington, Allerford and

Dunkery Beacon from Selworthy Beacon

Luccombe, most of the thatched cottages – porches covered in roses in the summer, gardens crowded with sweet william, hollyhocks and delphiniums – also belong to the Trust through the gift of the Acland family.

The Holnicote Estate and Dunkery Hill to the south of Porlock can properly be called the heart of Exmoor. Here wild ponies graze the moorland, and sometimes a red deer can be seen silhouetted against the horizon, or skirting the edge of Horner Wood. The hunting of the deer was until 1818 a Royal privilege, and today this medieval sport of kings is still pursued over Exmoor by the Devon and Somerset Staghounds based near by at Exford.

One of the best walks is from Dunkery Gate, over the summit of the Beacon, 1,705 feet above sea-level, the highest point on Exmoor, and then

Holnicote Estate; Selworthy

down to the wooded valley below Cloutsham. Still further inland, Winsford Hill between Exford and Dulverton has a group of Bronze Age barrows, known as the Wambarrows, and a 5th–7th-century Celtic stone about five foot high called the Caratacus Stone. Miles from the road and with hardly a track leading to them are isolated sheepfarms where the distinctive Exmoor Horns and Closewools are bred. A little to the south-west crossing the Barle are the Tarr Steps, an ancient packhorse bridge made of gigantic stone slabs of a composition unknown in this part of the world. Periodically floods have swept them downstream and they have been recovered and replaced, but their origins and their age are a mystery.

Staffordshire

Downs Banks

1 mile south-east of Barlaston, $1\frac{1}{2}$ miles north of Stone, west of A520

Downs Banks is like the setting for a Sunday walk in an Arnold Bennett or a D. H. Lawrence novel. Only a mile from the vast Wedgwood works at Barlaston, and only six from the centre of Stoke, it is a peaty valley with rolling moorland on either side covered in bracken, gorse and broom. Coming from Stone, the road crosses railway and canal with the chimneys of a power station behind, a typical industrial landscape of the north Midlands; then suddenly the road becomes narrower, the hedges taller, over the hill a ford is crossed and the gate to Downs Banks appears. Sheep runs and pony tracks, curlews and snipe, and wild flowers in the marsh along the edge of the stream, all give the illusion of complete rurality to this small oasis in a desert of built-up areas.

Downs Banks was given to the Trust in 1950 by the brewing family of Joules and endowed by public subscription as a war memorial, an example of a locality acting on its own initiative to preserve its fast vanishing countryside.

Hawksmoor

$1\frac{1}{2}$ miles north-east of Cheadle on B5417

This combined nature reserve and bird sanctuary was founded and largely given to the Trust by the naturalist, Mr J. R. B. Masefield, in 1926; more land was subsequently acquired. The gates at the entrance were put up six years later and opened by his cousin, the poet John Masefield. Comprising some 300 acres of undulating woodland sloping down to the river Churnet, it has unusual trees such as the lodgepole pine and red oak, and a wide variety of wildlife, pheasants, curlews and peewits, as well as rarer birds, redstarts, nightjars and warblers. Rhododendrons grow well on the sandy soil, and have seeded throughout the woods. Hawksmoor has seen one of the

Trust's most successful experiments with nature trails, set paths through the Reserve with observation points which are aimed particularly at arousing the interest of young people.

Kinver Edge

4 miles west of Stourbridge, 4 miles north of Kidderminster, west of A449

The high heath and woodland just west of the village of Kinver is a surviving remnant of a huge Mercian forest which once covered this area. But the Edge was inhabited long before the Anglo-Saxons. At its summit, with wonderful views of the Clent Hills to the east and Wenlock Edge to the west, are the outlines of an Iron Age promontory fort covering seven acres among the gorse, broom and silver birches. But more impressive still is the group of huge rocks on the north face of the hill with complete houses burrowed out of the soft, bright-pink sandstone. Probably also Iron Age in origin, some of these were lived in until less than twenty years ago, the last troglodyte dwellings known in this country. One of the rocks known as 'Holy Austin' was a hermitage until the Reformation; another, called 'Nanny's', has the most elaborate windows and even chimneys cut into it, with the remains of plaster on the walls. This weird setting for children's games, perched precariously on the beech-covered slopes above Kinver and looking towards the chimneys of Wolverhampton in the far distance, has an air of unreality about it that is haunting.

Kinver Edge; Holy Austin Rock

Opposite:
River Manifold

The Manifold and Hamps Valleys

5–8 miles north-west of Ashbourne, north of A523, south of Buxton

These two little rivers, tributaries of the Dove, pass through gorges as beautiful, if not as well known, as their near neighbour's. The Manifold, as its name suggests, winds in tight bends far below the heights of Ossum's Hill, Wetton Hill and Grindon Moor. Precipices and rock faces like Ape's Tor and Beeston Tor appear on the sides of the valley, with their caves where Roman pottery and Anglo-Saxon coins have been found. But the green fields filled with wild flowers and the narrow roads lined with cow parsley give it a peaceful, fertile atmosphere. The meaning of 'hamps' is 'summer-dry' and in the heat of July and August, both the Hamps and the Manifold are no more than rocky beds, though their upper reaches, above Wetton Mill and Waterhouses, remain full. The reason is that both disappear underground in a stretch of porous limestone, only to re-emerge near Ilam Hall. Dr Johnson, pragmatical as ever, refused to believe this remarkable phenomenon till he had satisfied himself with the help of marked corks.

The village of Ilam, in the gentle undulating country near the junction of the Manifold and the Dove, was used by Johnson as a model for the Happy Valley in *Rasselas*. In the 19th century it was rebuilt as a model village by Jesse Watts-Russell, with pretty estate cottages grouped round a tall Gothic cross. Ilam Hall, which is a youth hostel, and its park, are set in a loop of the Manifold. North of the Hall the park still reveals the steep ridges and furrows formed when it was cultivated in strips as the village open field.

Surrey

Box Hill

1 mile north of Dorking, $2\frac{1}{2}$ miles south of Leatherhead, east of A24

'We are going to Box Hill tomorrow: you will join us. It is not Swisserland, but it will be something for a young man so much in want of a change.' Thus Jane Austen's heroine Emma addressed Frank Churchill, and 150 years later the very English charms of this place still attract lovers of nature in abundance.

The hill rises dramatically on the edge of the North Downs 400 feet above the River Mole which over the centuries has cut a deep gap in this ridge on its northward course to the Thames. But it is the gentle rounded contours of its great chalk escarpment, crowned with beechwoods, which give Box Hill its character. The name seems to have originated from the plantations of box which both John Evelyn and Celia Fiennes noted in the 17th century. 'I went . . . to see those natural bowers, cabinets and shady walks in the box coppses', wrote Evelyn in 1655. Yew and box can still be seen on various parts of the cliff-face, especially on the western slopes known as the 'Whites' where the bare chalk shows through between the bushes, and they are regaining ground after a virtual disappearance in the 19th century.

From the road at the foot of the hill, which follows the course of the Roman Stane Street, a narrow lane zigzags up to the summit past Flint Cottage, where George Meredith once lived. Amongst the woods at the top can be seen the remains of a large fort, built during an invasion scare at the end of the last century. From the open hilltop, with its springy turf, stretch incomparable views over the Weald. Immediately below are the roofs of Dorking and beyond them the greensand hills to the south-west. Due south

Box Hill; The southern slopes seen from Ranmore Common

and over twenty miles away is the line of the South Downs with Chancton-bury Ring prominent, a clump of trees on the skyline.

Plant and animal life on the hill and in the gentler valleys to the north is exceptionally rich for this county, where nature often seems to be losing the battle against cars and houses. Juniper Hall in one of these northern valleys, a centre for French *émigrés* including Talleyrand and Madame de Staël at the time of the Revolution, is now let by the Trust to the Field Studies Council who use the whole area as an 'outdoor laboratory'.

Hindhead Commons

12 miles south-west of Guildford, on both sides of A3

This beautiful holding of the National Trust, covering nearly 1,400 acres which are mainly heathland, can be easily explored on foot from Hindhead.

A special feature is the Devil's Punch Bowl, just north-east of Hindhead. A clear stream, the Smallbrook, rises in this great arena to run through a wooded valley where four species of deer have been recorded and ancient badger sets flourish. Plant life ranges through typical dry heathland species to the many interesting mosses and liverworts in the bottom of the Bowl. As recently as 1918, squatters who had settled in the Bowl were making birch-brooms for a living. They were known as Broom Squires, the term deriving from 'broom squarers'.

To the south, with spectacular views as far as the South Downs, Gibbet Hill rises on sandstone to 894 feet. Here, in 1786, were hanged three footpads who had waylaid and murdered a sailor walking from London to Portsmouth. A memorial stone complete with curse records the events.

From Hurt Hill, to the south-east, there is a view over the surrounding Weald. In Golden Valley and Woodcock Bottom, west of the Churt road, the strange display of the woodcock may still be seen at nightfall.

Devil's Punch Bowl

Leith Hill

3 miles due west of junction of A29 and A24, north of B2126

Rising to 967 feet, Leith Hill is the highest point in south-east England. The Tower on its summit was built by Richard Hull of Leith Hill so that he and others, as a tablet records in Latin above the door, might enjoy the immense view southward. He was buried beneath the Tower in 1772.

Leith Hill was the scene of a furious battle in 851, when the Danes had sailed up the Thames, sacked London and Canterbury and, advancing on Winchester, encountered the Saxon army under King Ethelwulf, father of Alfred the Great. The Danes camped at Anstiebury, the hill on the opposite side of Coldharbour, but Ethelwulf secured the greater heights of Leith Hill under cover of night. When battle was joined the next day, Ethelwulf was victorious. In 1882 bones were found in a field between Leith Hill and Ockley that was perhaps the burial ground of those who died in the battle over a thousand years ago.

Leith Hill Place at the foot of the hill is an attractive example of a small rural estate of rolling farmland managed on traditional lines and with woodland of varied character, including a rhododendron wood, fine old oak and beech woodland, sunlit glades carpeted with bluebells in the spring, and young plantations in which conifers are used to nurse future crops of native hardwoods.

Mosses Wood slightly to the east of Leith Hill extends from the crest of the greensand hills almost down to the rolling Weald. At the top is a breathtaking view to the South Downs; then comes a precipitous landslip, still prone to movement after a wet season, causing great trees to lean drunkenly. Splendid conifers tower above the road as if above some miniature American west-coast highway. Below the road are bluebells and rhododendrons and paths among the steep and ever-changing woods.

Leith Hill; The Tower

Opposite:
Runnymede and
Cooper's Hill

On the north side of the hill lies the Duke's Warren with views the other way to the North Downs. This is mainly bracken-covered and derives its name from the fact that it was once part of the Duke of Norfolk's estates, enclosed against the common land that surrounds it and used as a rabbit warren. Rabbits were kept extensively in this way for food and sporting purposes until comparatively recent times.

Altogether the National Trust's Leith Hill estate, although fragmented, forms with the surrounding commons of Wootton and Abinger a stretch of country of almost unparalleled variety and beauty within forty miles of central London.

Runnymede

South of the Thames, $\frac{1}{2}$ mile between Windsor and Staines, south of A308

These water meadows beside the Thames – and how delightful they must have looked in the 13th century, though now surviving on the fringes of suburbia – are part of our history. Magna Carta, as issued over King John's seal, reads, in translation from the Latin: 'Given by our hand in the meadow that is called Runnymeade, between Windsor and Staines, on the fifteenth day of June in the seventeenth year of our reign [1215].' It was from Windsor that the king and his entourage came daily to Runnymede for the negotiations, as did the disaffected barons from Staines. It was a convenient meeting place. Whether the famous Charter was the progressive document which Whig historians later represented it to be, or whether it prolonged the power of a feudal nobility and retarded the centralized administration of the kingdom, is still a matter for debate. More relevant is the fact that Magna Carta has become a part of our liberal mythology, and as such in later centuries contributed to the freedom of the individual.

In the late 18th century Runnymede became a racecourse, conveniently close to Windsor, and George IV and William IV attended race meetings held on the level meadows. In 1886 the races were cancelled and have not been revived. In 1931 Runnymede was given to the Trust in memory of the father of the 1st Lord Fairhaven, and Lutyens was commissioned to build the kiosks and lodges which at either end mark the limits of the historic ground. Later the wooded slopes of Cooper's Hill behind the meads were given by Egham Council.

The associations of the site have led to the erection of three memorials on the slopes of Cooper's Hill. The first, the Air Forces Memorial (1953) records 'the names of 20,456 airmen who have no known grave. They died for freedom in raid and sortie over the British Isles and the land and seas of Northern and Western Europe'. The second, built by the contributions of 9,000 members of the American Bar Association (1957), is a tribute to Magna Carta and 'Freedom under Law'. The last (1965) is to the memory of John Kennedy, and the inscription records that 'this acre of English ground was given to the United States by the people of Britain in memory of John F. Kennedy, born 19th May, 1917: President of the United States 1961–63: died by an assassin's hand 22nd November, 1963.'

Surrey/Sussex

Black Down

1 mile south-east of Haslemere, between A286 and B2131

Black Down, in the north-west corner of Sussex, stands like a headland jutting into the Weald, and is the highest point in the county (918 ft). The name comes from the Anglo-Saxon 'dun' (a hill) and 'black', which no doubt refers to its dark cloak of pine and heather. Long ago, about 6000 B.C., men of the Middle Stone Age lived here, on the high ground above the impenetrable forest, and left their worked flints. Since then the Down has been uninhabited, though in Elizabethan days it was a beacon and men came to light the beacon fire, and in later times to extract building stone.

Black Down is a high sandstone ridge, geologically part of the Hythe Beds of lower greensand, giving rise to a dry acid soil with a typical moorland vegetation: birch, Scots pine, and heather, with sphagnum moss and other bog plants round a few small pools. There are some fine beeches on the eastern slopes.

This 600-acre stretch of wood and heathland is a place in which to ride, to walk, and to enjoy the wide views across the Weald, from Leith Hill to the South Downs, and the seasonal changes from scented gorse, through heather and bilberry, to autumn's rowan berries and the turning of the bracken. Linnets, yellowhammers, meadow and tree pipits frequent the heath, as do lizards and the occasional adder; roe deer, which live in the surrounding woods, sometimes come as visitors.

Sussex

Crowlink, Michel Dene and Went Hill

East Sussex. South of Friston on A259, 5 miles west of Eastbourne

After Beachy Head the most famous stretch of white chalk cliffs on the south coast is the Seven Sisters, three or four miles to the west, whose regular rolling outline is a familiar landmark from the sea. From the Sussex hinterland, however, the effect is different: through villages of thatch and whitewash sheltering in the lea of the Downs the road twists and turns between ever-higher smooth green hills, their turf so short that it looks almost clipped. Then suddenly comes a surprise glimpse of blue sea through Birling Gap, a depression in the cliff-wall. There, amongst buoys and fishing boats drawn up on the tiny beach, are views to the right along the whole line of the Seven Sisters, and to the left towards the even steeper approaches to Beachy Head. In the 18th century, Parson Darby of East Dean hollowed out a cave high in these cliffs and hung lamps in it to warn ships of the particularly dangerous rocks along this shore.

Lookout Hill, to the east of Birling Gap, bought partly with Enterprise Neptune funds in 1967, is the latest addition to the Trust's Crowlink properties which have grown since 1928 to include over 600 acres of downland stretching from Friston church towards the sea, and from Went Hill and Baily's Hill (the first two of the Seven Sisters) to Flagstaff Point. On Michel Dene, which lies behind them, Neolithic flint implements have been found. The walk along the cliff-edge is not for those subject to vertigo, but it provides some of the most spectacular scenery on the south coast: gulls wheeling far below where the waves crash on the rocks, fishing boats and tankers out in the Channel and, behind, the rolling green turf dotted with sheep.

Seven Sisters and Cuckmere Haven

Slindon Estate

West Sussex. 6 miles north of Bognor Regis, between A285 and A29

Slindon is for many the epitome of unspoilt Sussex countryside, a quiet village of 17th-century flint and brick cottages, a manor house now a school, a park containing magnificent beechwoods. Behind it, cornfields and remote farms lead up to the ridge of the South Downs, where a Roman road traverses the downland.

Altogether about 3,500 acres are in the care of the Trust. The estate once belonged to the Archbishops of Canterbury, and it was here that Stephen Langton died in 1228. Few traces of its medieval importance remain, and primarily it is as landscape composition that Slindon makes its appeal today. It is also famous for an extraordinary geological phenomenon: in Palaeolithic times the sea came up to this point of the South Downs, the shoreline stretching roughly from Arundel to Goodwood, and in Slindon Park can still be seen, 130 feet above sea-level, a beach of shingle and rounded pebbles which somehow escaped being covered, as elsewhere, with a chalk deposit.

To the north of the park the ground rises past Nore Folly, a ruined arch set against the trees on the skyline, to Coldharbour Hill and Glatting Beacon, two miles distant upon the ridge of the Downs, from which there are prodigious views both seaward and inland over the Weald. The Roman road up here is Stane Street, route of the legions marching from London to Regnum (Chichester), and the three-and-a-half miles of it which lie within the Slindon estate, crossing Bignor Hill near the famous Roman villa with its mosaic pavements, are the most complete stretch to survive. Now a bridle-path, the road consists of a narrow causeway or *agger* of several layers of rammed chalk and flintstones, flanked by ditches.

Slindon; Beeches

Yorkshire

Bridestones Moor

North Yorkshire. 12 miles south of Whitby, 7 miles north-east of Pickering, east of A169

A new Forestry Commission road through Dalby Forest and Staindale has made more accessible the wild and dramatic part of the north Yorkshire Moors, only ten miles inland from Scarborough as the crow flies. A steep climb from the Staindale Beck up Dovedale Griff, one of its feeders, through dogwood and Douglas firs, brings one out on high rolling moorland with wide views over the forest to the south and towards Cockton Moor on the north. On the heights to the right of the Griff are the Bride Stones, a curious formation of Jurassic rocks wider at the top than at the bottom. The two largest are known as the Pepperpot and the Saltcellar; the lower strata are of

The Bride Stones

softer rock than the upper and have gradually been worn by the wind and rain to achieve this odd result. On Grime Moor to the left of the Griff three groups of barrows were excavated in the 19th century but they are hardly visible now amongst the purple heather where the grouse nest, sheltered from the strong east wind. The moor is now kept as a nature reserve with the assistance of the Yorkshire Naturalists' Trust.

Malham Tarn *(see colour plate facing p. 449)*

West Yorkshire. 6 miles north-east of Settle

The pretty village of Malham with its group of 18th-century farmhouses, cottages and old schoolhouse is no preparation for the grandeur of the Pennine landscape that lies behind it, what the Romantics called 'sublime' with its combination of beauty, immensity and horror. At Gordale Scar, less than a mile to the north-east, James Ward painted his famous cattle dwarfed by the vast rock-face down which a tiny stream falls like a white ribbon. Just as spectacular is Malham Cove immediately north of the village, a sheer white limestone cliff 240 feet high curving round almost in a semicircle. The river Aire now trickles out from its base, though before the Ice Age it filled the wide valley above and plunged over the Cove in a great waterfall. The two-mile walk up this valley, now dry, to Malham Tarn is through an almost 'science fiction' landscape, a treeless expanse of humps and craters, with brilliant white limestone outcrops and huge boulders, dotted about the green moorland.

The Tarn itself is a natural lake covering about 150 acres, formed by a dam of glacial moraine. Only on its north side does the land rise, and here amongst oak woods looking out over lake and plateau is a 19th-century house, now let to the Field Studies Council. Charles Kingsley used to stay here, and, asked on one of his visits the reason for the black streaks down the white cliff of Malham Cove, he answered jokingly that a chimney-sweep must have fallen over the edge – and thus was born the idea for *The Water Babies*, much of which takes place here. The Gothick boat-house on the water's edge below the house must have been one of his haunts.

Behind the Tarn stretches Malham Moor, higher and wilder country with views towards Ribblesdale. Fountains Fell lies still farther, a reminder that all this land belonged in the Middle Ages to the monks of Fountains Abbey.

Marsden Moor

North Yorkshire. 7–8 miles south-west of Huddersfield, astride A62

Midway between the grimy giants of Lancashire and Yorkshire – Oldham and Rochdale, Halifax and Huddersfield – Marsden Moor is still as lonely and uninhabited as if the Industrial Revolution had never happened. This is the bleak dramatic country which recalls *Wuthering Heights*, where a single, gaunt stone farmhouse may occasionally be seen with smoke wreathing from its chimney down in the shelter of the ridge, but more often the empty treeless moorland stretches in every direction to the sky. The main road crosses the centre of Standedge, rising to almost 1,300 feet before the steep descent to Saddleworth on the west. From here one can walk northwards past the air-shafts of railway and canal tunnels along the top of Close Moss to March Hill, with views over the head of the Colne Valley, or southwards to Wessenden Moor looking down on Marsden itself. Middle Stone Age weapons and implements have been found up here in great quantities. Today they are the only, remote, reminder of human life in this wild Pennine landscape.

Scarth Wood Moor

North Yorkshire. 8 miles north-east of Northallerton, between Osmotherley and Whorlton, south of A172

On the edge of the Cleveland Hills this solitary place, yellow with gorse in summer and purple with heather in the autumn, has finer views than almost any Yorkshire moor, northwards over Stockton and Tees-side, west across the Swale valley and Wensleydale to the Pennines, and south over the vast plain of the Vale of York. The steep valley, known as Scarth Nick, which separates it from Whorlton Moor on the east, came into being as the overflow from a glacial lake in the Ice Age. The reservoir built above the village of Osmotherley has thus partly restored a primeval situation, and at the same time provided a dramatic new landscape from the heights of Scarth Wood Moor.

Scarth Wood Moor itself is a centre for walkers: it is the starting-point for the Lyke Wake Walk, a forty-mile trek across the top of the moors to Ravenscar on the coast without touching civilization; and it is also a stage in the Cleveland Way, a footpath round the perimeter of the National Park from Helmsley to Saltburn, Whitby and Scarborough.

In the Middle Ages, a beacon stood on the highest point overlooking Arncliffe Wood to the south-west. From its site can be seen, far below in the valley, the remains of Mount Grace Priory, which also belongs to the Trust (see p. 324).

Scarth Wood Moor

WALES

Dyfed

Kete

South-west of Dale on B4327

From these 168 acres and a mile of beautiful coastline with views to the islands of Skomer and Skokholm, the Trust has removed all trace of what was once a Royal Naval radar station. The coast has been opened to the public and the land has been restored to its former agricultural use.

Llanborth Farm

North-west of the hamlet of Penbryn

Llanborth Farm, south-west of Lochtyn, safeguards the approaches to the mile-long Penbryn Beach which occupies the seaward end of a pleasantly wooded valley. The sand was rapidly disappearing from the beach, owing to commercial exploitation, before the Trust took over. Today it is a quiet and delightful strand, an ideal place, as many families know, for a tranquil day by the sea.

Lochtyn

Lochtyn, Llangranog

Immediately north-east of the village of Llangranog, at junction of B4321 and B4334

Lochtyn, with its magnificently bold coastline and island, came to the Trust in 1965. There are three sandy beaches accessible to those prepared to walk and negotiate steep paths. The climb to the dominating hill feature of Pen-y-Badell brings the reward of a view to Snowdonia and the Trust's properties in the Lleyn Peninsula, and southward to Cardigan Island. An abundance of seals and bird life adds to the sense of remoteness.

Mwnt

On the coast, about 4 miles north of Cardigan

A charming 14th-century whitewashed church (one of the oldest in Wales) stands at the foot of a curious conical hill from which Mwnt takes its name. A steep path leads to a delightful sandy beach, facing west. Beyond lies Clos-y-Graig farm which was covered with an ugly rash of caravans, chalets and tents, before their removal by the Trust in 1970. To the east, caravan sites still mar the view and are a constant reminder of the treatment to which even the most beautiful coastland may be subjected when not in the Trust's ownership.

St David's Head

Penwaen Dewi or St David's Head is at the western tip of South Wales. It was probably the landfall for the Phoenician and Iberian sailors who came to Britain from the first century A.D. onwards in search of copper, lead and gold and was known to Ptolemy, the geographer, as *Octapitarium* – the Eight Perils – from the group of dangerous rocks offshore to the south-west which were later christened the 'Bishop and Clerks'. Of these it was ironically noted in the 16th century by George Owen that 'they preach a deadly doctrine'. In this remote corner of what is still thought of as Pembrokeshire the past is still very much alive. The headland is rich in prehistoric remains, with a rampart, hut circles and rock shelters. Close to St David's Head are the birthplaces of the patron saints of Ireland and Wales, St Patrick and St David. The fierce Celtic Deisi tribe came from Ireland to convert the Welsh to Christianity across these waters and later the Viking longships were a familiar and dreaded sight. Three centuries later the Normans colonized the fertile south Pembroke region which is still known as 'The Englisherie'.

From the prominent headland of St David's the Wicklow Hills of Ireland can clearly be seen on a fine day across St George's Channel. To the south-west beyond St Bride's Bay lies Ramsey – Isle of Seals – still a large breeding colony of Atlantic seals. The 520 acres of St David's Head overlook the Trust's properties on St Bride's Bay and Whitesands Bay, which range

St David's Head

from land near St Elvis and Solva as far as West Hook, Trehil and Runwayskiln Farms on the southern arm of St Bride's Bay: a fitting climax to the landscape of this wonderful coast.

Stackpole

4 miles south of Pembroke off B4319, beyond Stackpole village

Acquired through the Treasury in 1976, Stackpole is one of the largest and most fascinating of the Trust's coastal properties. Its two thousand acres are remarkable for their diversity, comprising landscape that is both unusual and beautiful, together with areas of great ecological importance.

There are no less than eight miles of coast, mainly cliffland but with two sandy bays, Barafundle and Broad Haven, with safe bathing. Much of this area is traversed by the Pembrokeshire Coastal Path, and the cliffland supports rare plants. Inland, set among woods, are tranquil freshwater lakes with good coarse fishing and a fauna of the first biological interest. Between the cliffland and the lakes lies Stackpole Warren, a solitary and haunting area that was once naked sand dune, but is now grazed by wandering cattle. It supports a varied flora and in summer is blue with immense sheets of viper's bugloss.

Paths give access not only to the coast, but to the woods and lakes; in accordance with the Trust's policy visitors are welcome wherever the interests of good farming permit. Stackpole Court, the 18th-century mansion of the Earls of Cawdor, was demolished some fifteen years ago, but the Trust hopes to establish a tearoom and information centre in the dairy and brewery near by and possibly at a later date holiday cottages in the buildings of the old Home Farm.

534

Saddle Point from Stackpole Head   *Stackpole Quay*

Gwent

The Sugar Loaf

3 miles north-west of Abergavenny, north of A40

This conspicuous landmark rises to 1,950 feet and dominates the Usk valley and the countryside for miles around. Over 2,000 acres in extent, the Sugar Loaf is an extinct volcano. A track up the west side to the summit, and many miles of footpath, give access to open and unfenced land and to the contrasting beechwoods of St Mary's Vale.

The Sugar Loaf

Gwynedd

Braich-y-Pwll

Near Aberdaron on B4413

The westernmost point of north Wales, Braich-y-Pwll, lies at the end of a winding road from Aberdaron through Uwchmynydd. It is open cliffland with fine views of Cardigan Bay and of Bardsey Island (Ynys Enlli), the 'island of the twenty thousand saints' where a monastery flourished from pre-Conquest days to the Dissolution. It was a renowned place of pilgrimage in medieval times and pilgrims would worship at St Mary's Chapel which stood on Trust land below Mynydd Mawr, embark at the inlet below the chapel and perhaps drink from the freshwater 'well', a bowl in the rock above the south side of the inlet. It is filled by a freshwater spring from the rock face behind, but care should be taken approaching it as the sea at high tide laps the rocks and the way can be treacherous.

On Mynydd Mawr, the summit at the north end of the area, was a radar station in the Second World War; it has been demolished, and as far as possible buried or dispersed by the Trust, although scars remain which will take many years to heal.

Dwarf gorse, bracken and close-cropped grass cover most of the hills, which are let for sheep-grazing. Plants and birds are typical of the wild coastlands of North Wales.

A beautiful spot; and on a clear day there is the chance of sighting the Wicklow Hills in Ireland, St David's Head in Dyfed, as well as the mountains of Snowdonia.

Carneddau Area (Ysbyty Estate) *(see colour plates facing p. 480)*

This is mountain country between Aber Falls near the north coast and Llyn Ogwen, and Y Glyder, and Capel Curig, on the London–Holyhead road. It contains some 14,000 acres of the more remote hill country of North Wales. Ten of the thirteen peaks of Snowdonia over 3,000 feet lie within its boundaries: Tryfan, Glyder Fach, Glyder Fawr, Y Garn, Foel Goech, Pen-yr-ole-wen, Carnedd Dafydd, Ys Elen, Foel Grach, Foel Fras. Carnedd Llywelyn, just outside the boundary, is probably named after Llywelyn Fawr, the last Prince of all Wales.

No road runs into the northern area, and here heights are left to climbers and walkers, for whom there is access on foot from Ogwen Cottage, Bethesda, Aber, and over the hills from the Conwy Valley. Access is of set purpose difficult, so that those who like solitude and are prepared to walk may continue to find it. The contours of the hills are more rounded than in central Snowdonia, but from the high land, views of sea, valley and mountain open up as one travels just off the Trust land. The old Roman track from Deva (Chester) to Segontium (Caernarvon) crosses from east to west

Llyn Ogwen looking towards the Glyders

on the foothills above the sea, and in the Aber area, just outside Trust land, is the site of a palace and homestead of the Princes of Gwynedd and ancient Wales.

On the south side of the London–Holyhead road lies Tryfan, one of the most climbed mountains in Britain, a nursery for the fledgeling and a proving ground for equipment and training for the members of the successful Everest expedition. In Cwm Idwal to the west are a nature reserve, where rare plants grow in a superb setting, and the famed Llyn Idwal where a Welsh prince murdered his brother and where it is said no bird will fly across the lake.

The old coach road which followed the line of the farmsteads on the south side of Thomas Telford's present road is said to have been constructed by the 1st Lord Penrhyn in the late 18th century. There are the remains of a very much earlier bridge beneath the arch of the modern bridge over the Afon Ogwen at the top of the long valley of Nant Ffrancon. This valley, gouged by glaciers, has a series of small 'cwms' on its southern slopes with moraines clearly to be seen at their mouths. There are also a number of rocks visible from the main road, smoothed and grooved thousands of years ago by the grinding ice of moving glaciers.

Cemlyn

2 miles west of Cemaes Bay on north coast of Anglesey

On this typical stretch of north Anglesey coast are some of the oldest geological rock formations in the world. They occur in conjunction with low cliffs formed by the great glacial drift down the Irish Sea during the Ice Age. Much of the area is low-lying and carries two lagoons. The brackish outer lagoon is protected from the sea by a long shingle bank and maintained at a

Cemlyn

constant level by a small dam and sluice. The lagoons and adjoining land form a sanctuary in winter for great flocks of wildfowl that find in the area both good feeding and a ready refuge at sea when disturbed. Part of the property, including the lagoons, has been let to the North Wales Naturalists' Trust as a nature reserve. Visitors are asked to avoid disturbing the birds, and during the nesting season to keep off the shingle bank. At the north end of the property, the wild open headland of Trwyn Cemlyn and the cliff path is always accessible.

Cregennan

1 mile east of Arthog (A493)

In the foothills of the Cader Idris range, a thousand feet above the village of Arthog, lie two lakes and 700 acres of rough grazing. It is wild and characteristic lake and mountain scenery, with views to Barmouth and the Mawddach estuary to the west, and to Cader Idris and the far Merioneth mountains to the east. It is also in the centre of an area of great archaeological interest. Neolithic remains have been found round the shores of Mawddach estuary, and Bronze and Iron Age artefacts in the vicinity of Cregennan. Stone hut circles and cairns abound on the surrounding hills, though there is no extensive grouping on the Trust's land.

The large bungalow on the property does not belong to the Trust, but it has a certain historic interest. Erected in 1897, it is one of the earliest prefabricated buildings. Imported from Canada, it was transported in sections by horse and wagon from Dolgellau by the Wynne-Jones family who gave Cregennan to the Trust in memory of their two sons killed in the Second World War.

Dolymelynllyn

5 miles by road north of Dolgellau, on west side of A487

From the Afon Mawddach the Dolymelynllyn estate climbs from riverside meadow to rock- and bracken-covered mountain on the slopes of Y Garn 1,500 feet above.

The main attraction of the property is the Rhaiadr Ddu or Black Water-falls which can be reached on foot through the gate by the village hall. The approach to the falls is through a carefully maintained area of oak woodland, a feature of Dolymelynllyn that contrasts with the conifer plantations of the Forestry Commission in the neighbourhood. The moist conditions under the trees near the falls are particularly favourable to rare ferns and mosses, and an area here is leased to the Nature Conservancy as a nature reserve.

The estate and Dolymelynllyn Hall, now a hotel, were once owned by William Alexander Madocks (1774–1828), the remarkable man who built Tremadoc and the sea-wall, known as the Cob, which seals the estuary of the Afon Glaslyn at Portmadoc. He made Dolymelynllyn in the late 18th century something of an intellectual centre, not unlike Hafod in Dyfed, and established in this valley, which must then have seemed very remote, a distinguished coterie of his young contemporaries. There is a newly restored inscription on a rock face above the lower pool of the falls, on the east bank. It is from a poem in Latin by Thomas Gray written in 1741 and was inscribed on the rock during Madocks's time.

Dolymelynllyn; Y Llethr and Rhinog Fach from Y Garn   *The Rhaiadr Ddu*

Lleyn properties

On west side of Porth Neigwl

Mynydd-y-Graig, a wild bracken-covered rock, and heather moor above the sea, the gift of the Misses Keating of Plas-yn-Rhiw, is approachable only on foot. The moor climbs from the cliff tops to a magnificent pile of ancient dolomite rocks where Iron Age men built a defensive camp of which the traces can still be seen.

Lleyn properties; Looking west towards Bardsey Island from Penarlynydd, Rhiw

There is a splendid view eastwards over the trees of Plas-yn-Rhiw, to the curving shore of Porth Neigwl, known as Hell's Mouth Bay to ships' crews in the days of sail. Once a sailing ship had been driven by a south-westerly gale into the jaws of this bay, there was little chance of escape. In past times there were wreckers too in Lleyn, to finish the job on dark nights by luring ships to disaster with misleading lights.

Beyond Cilan, the peninsula on the other side of Porth Neigwl, can be seen in the far distance the shores of Merioneth, the outline of the Rhinogydd, Cader Idris farther south, and on clear days Aberystwyth and Cardiganshire.

The delightful little bay of Porth Ysgo between Rhiw and Aberdaron is reached from Ysgo farm where there is a car park. The approach, of some 400 yards on foot, is down a small sheltered valley with a stream at the bottom which ends in a high narrow waterfall to the beach. The valley has botanical interest, and provides shelter for birds. The beach is small, but out of season it is a perfect place for a family picnic.

Powys

Brecon Beacons

5 miles south of Brecon, east of A470

Nearly 10,000 acres in the centre of this sombre and dramatic mountain massif are in the ownership of the Trust, and many marked footpaths give access to its wild moorland slopes. The two sandstone summits of the

Brecon Beacons from near Cantref

Beacons, facing precipitously north, slope more gently southwards, and Pen-y-fan, the highest point, rises to just over 2,900 feet. There are immense views, extending south to the Bristol Channel, and northwards on a clear day as far as Cader Idris sixty miles distant. Eastwards rises the isolated mass of The Sugar Loaf (see p. 535).

West Glamorgan

Gower Peninsula

Considering its close proximity to Swansea and the industry of South Wales, the Gower Peninsula is remarkable for its unspoilt character and the absence of commercial exploitation. The limestone cliffs in the south of the Peninsula are among the finest in Britain and the magnificent sweep of Rhossili Beach to Worms Head is unrivalled, while the north coast offers a different landscape of wild salt marshes. Inland, the peninsula is characterized by wide commons, and by small well-wooded valleys of great charm which provide a striking contrast.

Whitford Burrows, the little peninsula (some 670 acres) which juts out northwards at the western end of the Gower Peninsula, is largely sand burrows and salt marsh. Its plant and bird life is of great interest and much of this area is leased to the Nature Conservancy.

Bishopston Valley, a narrow, steep-sided and wooded limestone ravine with a distinguished limestone flora, leads to the sea and to remote Pwlldu Bay. The eccentric river which disappears below ground, but can be

Gower Peninsula; Three Cliffs Bay

explored through the so-called Guzzle Holes, emerges in the lower reaches of the ravine. Half-way down the valley is an Iron Age fort which dominates the eastern sky line.

Gower Peninsula; Cliff path, Rhossili

NORTHERN IRELAND

Co. Antrim

Carrick-a-rede *(see colour plate facing p. 481)*

On the B15 Ballycastle/Portrush road, ½ mile east of Ballintoy

The property consists of the island of Carrick-a-rede, Sheep Island and a number of smaller islands, two salmon fisheries, and a stretch of beach.

Ireland's ancient Celtic tongue lends itself to precise and melodious description. Although the language is no longer in common use in Northern Ireland, the old placenames have survived. Carrick-a-rede means the 'rock on the road'. The road is the path of the salmon on their way to the northern rivers, and the rock is a small island separated from the mainland by a sixty-foot-wide chasm with a drop of eighty feet. During the fishing season, from May to September, the chasm is spanned by a swinging rope-bridge. The bridge is a great tourist attraction, but that is not its purpose; it is a working bridge erected by the fishermen to carry them to and from the island for the fishing. It consists of planks lashed together by stout ropes and fastened to strong supports at either end. There are two rope handrails. This the older people regard as a sign of decadence; there used to be only one. The secret of easy passage is, of course, to go with the swing, and the fishermen cross with the utmost nonchalance, carrying large baskets of fish or nets.

There are magnificent views from both island and mainland: the whole sweep of the north Irish coast from Inishowen in the west to Fair Head in

Antrim coast from Carrick-a-rede

the east, with the great headlands between. To the north is the island of Rathlin, an ornithologist's paradise with great bird stacks and cliffs with tens of thousands of seabirds. Farther north lies Islay and on clear days you can see the Paps of Jura beyond. The stretch of sea between Ireland and Scotland was known to the ancient chroniclers as the Sea of Moyle. It was the great highway along which early man travelled to make his home among the caves and sand dunes of Antrim. In later days the McDonnell clansmen from the western isles crossed the same stretch of water to establish themselves in the Glens of Antrim.

Cushendun

23 miles north-east of Ballymena on the east Antrim coast, on B92

The village is picturesquely situated at the foot of Glendun, one of the loveliest of the Nine Glens of Antrim. The name means 'the foot of the Dun', the river which runs through the village under a graceful old stone bridge to the sea. Cushendun is surrounded by some of Ireland's finest scenery: mountain, glen, moorland and majestic headlands. Each season has its own special charm and beauty: golden whin, purple orchids, and white bog-cotton in spring; a glorious sea of purple heather and hedges hung with fuchsia in late summer and autumn; and in winter the glossy leaves and red berries of the holly everywhere.

As always in Ireland, there is legend and history. Just over three miles from the village there is a passage-grave of 2000–2500 B.C. which is claimed to be the burial place of Oisin, poet son of Finn McCool. The long memories of the villagers stray back over the centuries to Shane O'Neill, 'Shane the Proud', who in 1567 witlessly trusted his ancient enemies the McDonnells so far as to accept their invitation to a feast at Castle Carra, during which he was deprived of his head. The ruins of Castle Carra are close to Rockport, the pleasant Georgian house where Moira O'Neill, the poet of the Glens,

Cushendun

The Dun at Cushendun

was born. Farther along the Torr Head road a cairn surmounted by a cross marks the spot where Shane's headless body was buried.

In the main street of the village and along the sea front there are a number of singularly 'foreign'-looking cottages. They were built in Cornish style as a memorial to Maud, first wife of Lord Cushendun, who was a Cornish-woman. They were designed by Clough Williams-Ellis.

A fine beach follows the curve of the bay and the National Trust has been at considerable pains to prevent its disappearance by erosion.

Dunseverick Castle

On the north Antrim coast, 3 miles east of the Giant's Causeway

According to the ancient annalists, Dunseverick was at once the oldest and most strongly fortified place in Ireland. The dun or fortress of Sobhairce, from which the name of Dunseverick comes, was probably built during the early Celtic period about 2,000 years ago. One of the five roads from Tara, the palace of the *Ard Rí* or High King, ended here, and here the *Ard Rí* held his hostages.

Legend links many famous names with Dunseverick. Deirdre of the Sorrows, Ireland's Helen of Troy, landed here on her ill-fated return from exile in Scotland 2,000 years ago. Conal Cearnach, leader of the Red Branch Knights, Ulster's ancient order of chivalry, lived in the castle. He is said to have witnessed the Crucifixion. In the 5th century St Patrick consecrated the first Irish bishop, Olcan, at the well still known as St Patrick's Well. From Dunseverick, it is said, Fergus the Great and his brothers sailed to western Scotland in the 6th century to found a kingdom and give the name 'Scotland' to Alba.

In 870 and 924 Dunseverick was stormed by the Vikings and after 924 was held by them for a brief period. From the 14th to the 17th century it was held in turn by the Norman MacQuillans, the Scottish McDonnells and the Irish O'Cahans. The last owner was Giladuff O'Cahan who fought with the Great O'Neill in the 1641 rebellion and lost both his head and his lands. The present castle, probably of 16th-century date, was razed by Cromwellian forces in 1642. Only part of the watch tower and curtain wall was left standing.

Dunseverick is peaceful enough today. Wild flowers grow in profusion on its summit and seabirds nest in the cliffs. Cattle graze quietly in the fields where trials of strength took place at the Celtic games, and the warriors of ancient days are only memories stirring in the minds of old people reminiscing by turf fires on long winter nights.

The Giant's Causeway *(see colour plate facing p. 481)*

2 miles from Bushmills

This geological wonderland is the result of extensive volcanic activity which occurred in an area stretching from Greenland to north-east Ireland in the Tertiary era, some sixty million years ago. On the Antrim plateau, of which the Causeway is the most spectacular feature, the lava poured out from fissures and vents in the earth's surface and flowed slowly over the white chalk, eventually solidifying into basalt, often of solumnar structure. Most of the columns are hexagonal, but there are also many pentagons and a number of four-, seven- and ten-sided columns.

Giant's Causeway and cliffs

Dr Johnson once commented that although the Causeway might be worth seeing, it was not worth going to see. Given modern transport, he might have changed his mind. Apart from its geological interest, there is a stretch of some ten miles of beautiful bays backed by the rugged grandeur of towering headlands. The visitor can choose to walk on a low path which runs along the foot of the headlands or he can take the high path along the top. Either way there are fine views. From the headlands there is the wide sweep of the north coast and the Hebridean islands. For the ornithologist there is plenty of interest. All the common seabirds are represented as well as fulmar petrel, eider duck and gannet. There is plenty to interest the botanist too: sea-spleenwort, vernal squill, sea-fescue and frog orchids.

While the evidence of Stone Age man is plentiful in the area, he does not appear to have lived on the headlands, very sensibly preferring the more sheltered valleys and beaches. During the Celtic period most of the bays and headlands were given the names by which they are still known; beautiful names like Port-na-callian, the port of girls, Port-na-boe, the cows' port. Port-na-Spaniagh received its Celtic name after 1588 when the Spanish Armada galleass, the *Gerona*, was wrecked here on a wild November night. Many families in the area claim descent from sailors who survived. In the old graveyard of St Cuthbert's, Dunluce, the bodies of ten drowned Spaniards are said to be buried along the south wall. For almost four centuries scholars speculated on where the great ship had perished; Bush Bay was the most favoured spot. Local knowledge was discounted, and the name Port-na-Spaniagh thought to be fanciful. Then in 1969 Robert Stennuit, a Belgian marine archaeologist, and a team of divers explored the bay. They found the wreck where the local people had always sited it, and a great quantity of treasure: coins, jewellery, and weapons.

The Causeway was commercialized during the 19th century. A house was built close to the Grand Causeway, a toll gate and iron railings were erected, and little trading shacks were set up along the path. These have now been removed by the National Trust and the Causeway has been restored to its natural state. The Trust has also made a ten-mile walk along the top of the headlands from Runkerry to White Park Bay.

White Park Bay

On the north Antrim coast, $1\frac{1}{2}$ miles west of Ballintoy

This beautiful beach, a mile of fine white sand, lies between Port Braddon and Ballintoy. It is flanked on both east and west by headlands of limestone and basalt, and fringed by grassy slopes on which masses of primroses and wild violets grow in spring. Some of Ireland's first inhabitants made their homes here five or six thousand years ago. Their kitchen middens have yielded large quantities of Neolithic flints and pottery. During archaeological excavations in the Potter's Cave in the 1930s a clay figurine four inches high was found. Although it was crudely made it was a find of great

White Park Bay; Looking east towards Rathlin Island

importance, since it is the only 'Mother Goddess' type figure ever to be found in Ireland.

On the grassy slopes the floors of Neolithic round huts may be traced and there is a burial cairn almost immediately below the viewpoint on the main road.

Round the eastern corner of the bay is Ballintoy harbour with its attractive 18th-century church.

Co. Armagh

Coney Island

In Lough Neagh close to the southern (Armagh) shore

This thickly wooded island is about a mile from Maghery, from which it can be easily reached by boat. It was once joined to the mainland by a causeway, parts of which may still be seen, and was inhabited in very early times.

Recent excavations have revealed traces of Neolithic settlements. St Patrick is believed to have used it as a retreat, and the stump of an ancient round tower still stands. It was used as a stronghold by the O'Neills of Tyrone during the 16th century and possibly earlier.

The thick belt of reeds which surrounds the island provides an ideal nesting place for large numbers of waterfowl.

Co. Down

Murlough Nature Reserve, Dundrum

2 miles north of Newcastle, on the T2 Dundrum road

This, Ulster's first nature reserve, consists of 475 acres of sand dunes and heathland, and is of scientific importance, particularly in the fields of zoology, botany and archaeology. For this reason the public can be admitted only to certain areas by permit. There is, however, access by well-defined paths to a wide beach. The Reserve is administered with assistance from Queen's University, Belfast.

Strangford Lough

Stretches from Strangford inland to Newtownards

This great island-studded inlet of the sea cuts into the heart of County Down for upwards of twenty miles, through a countryside dominated by gently rolling hills, the drumlins of the last Ice Age. Many of the islands are 'drowned' drumlins, and geologists describe the lough as 'a shallow depression in the old Palaeozoic rocks'.

Besides being an area of great natural beauty, the lough and the surrounding countryside are of interest to geologists, archaeologists, marine biologists, botanists and ornithologists.

From earliest times man has lived on the lough shore. Burial cairns, hearth sites and stone circles indicate a wide distribution of population which continued from the Neolithic period, through the Celtic, and into historical times.

Patrick, Ireland's patron saint, began his mission in this region and his first church was built at Saul on a site overlooking the lough. Great monasteries, and schools like Nendrum and Movilla, sprang up during the early Christian period and it was the wealth of these establishments which during the 9th century attracted the Norse raiders, whose large fleet was based on the Quoile estuary. These raiders gave the lough the name 'Strangfiord' because of the strong currents. The Normans came in the 13th century and built the tall keep-castles which are still a feature of the landscape. In the 16th and 17th centuries the area was 'planted' with

English and Lowland Scottish farmers whose descendants form the bulk of the present population.

Through the centuries the wildlife of the lough remained largely undisturbed, but with the rapid growth of industry in the area, and the greater mobility of town dwellers over the last twenty years, it was becoming seriously threatened. The Trust's establishment of a Wildlife Scheme in 1966 has ensured that the wildlife is now safe. Many species of wildfowl frequent the lough: tern, duck, geese, swan, and large numbers of waders.

Although the wildfowl attract most popular attention, the lough is of importance in the study of marine biology. It stands at the confluence of two tidal streams, and harbours two distinct elements of marine life, those from both warm waters and cold. Queen's University, Belfast, maintains a Marine Biology station at Portaferry.

Maps

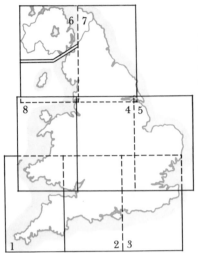

MAPS TO CHAPTERS I—VI

Houses
Gardens and Landscape Parks —
Follies and Monuments; Villages
Chapels, and buildings of
Useful Intent — Medieval Buildings —
Industrial Monuments —
Archaeological Sites

⊙ House
❋ House with Garden
▲ House with Collection
★ House with Garden and Collection
❋ Gardens and Landscape Parks
F Follies and Monuments
● Villages
C Chapels
U Buildings of Useful Intent
○ Dovecotes
M Medieval Buildings
I Industrial Monuments
∴ Archaeological Sites

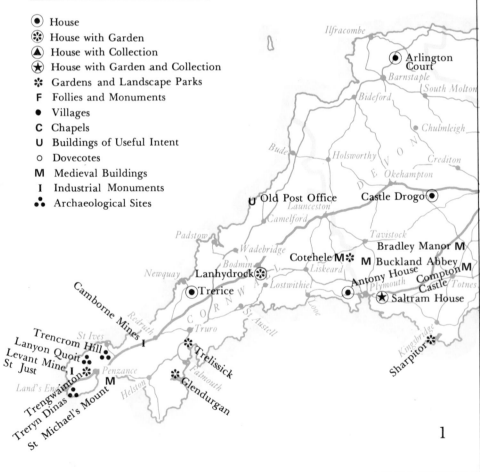

Ilfracombe

⊙ Arlington Court

Barnstaple

South Molton

Bideford

Chulmleigh

Bude

Holsworthy

Crediton

D E V O N

Okehampton

U Old Post Office   Castle Drogo⊙

Launceston

Camelford

Tavistock

Padstow

Wadebridge

Bradley Manor **M**

Bodmin

Cotehele **M**❋ **M** Buckland Abbey

Newquay   Lanhydrock⊙❋

Liskeard

Compton**M**

Antony House

Plymouth   Castle Totnes

Lostwithiel

Trerice⊙

C O R N W

★ Saltram House

Looe

Camborne Mines

Redruth

Truro

St Austell

St Ives

Trencrom Hill ∴

Kingsbridge

Lanyon Quoit ∴

Sharpitor❋

Levant Mine ❋

St Just **I**

Penzance

Trelissick ❋

Land's End

Helston

Falmouth

Trengwainton ❋

M

Glendurgan ❋

Treryn Dinas ∴

St Michael's Mount

1

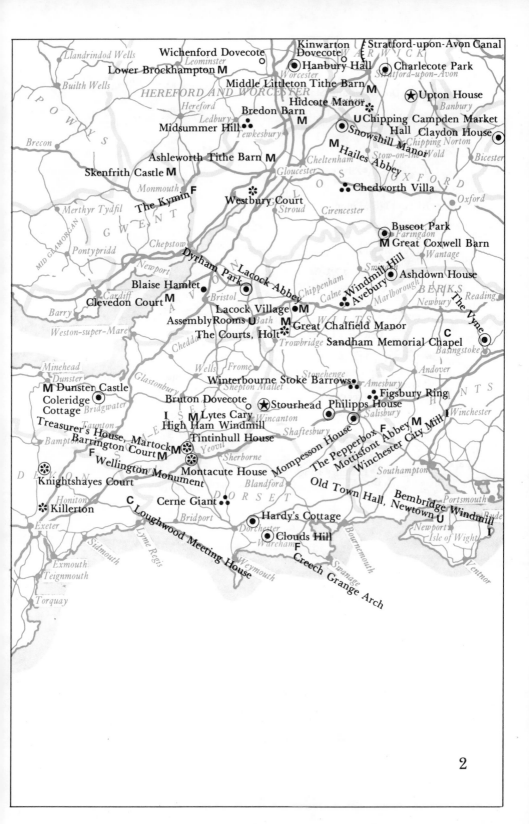

Llandrindod Wells

Wichenford Dovecote

Kinwarton Dovecote

Stratford-upon-Avon Canal

Leominster

M Lower Brockhampton

WARWICK

Hanbury Hall

Charlecote Park

Builth Wells

Stratford-upon-Avon

Middle Littleton Tithe Barn **M**

Upton House ★

Brecon

HEREFORD AND WORCESTER

Worcester

Hidcote Manor ✳

POWYS

Hereford

Bredon Barn

U Chipping Campden Market

Banbury

Ledbury

Midsummer Hill

M

Hall Claydon House

Tewkesbury

Snowshill Manor **U**

Chipping Norton

Ashleworth Tithe Barn **M**

Hailes Abbey **M**

Stow-on-the-Wold

Bicester

Skenfrith Castle **M**

Gloucester

Cheltenham

OXFORD

Monmouth

The Kymin **F**

Westbury Court

Chedworth Villa ••

Merthyr Tydfil

Stroud

Cirencester

Oxford

GWENT

Chepstow

Buscot Park ●

Farringdon

Pontypridd

Newport

Dyrham Park

Lacock Abbey

Windmill Hill

M Great Coxwell Barn

Wantage

MID GLAMORGAN

Blaise Hamlet

Chippenham

Calne

Avebury ●

Ashdown House ●

BERKS

Cardiff

Clevedon Court **M**

Bristol

Marlborough

Newbury

Reading

Barry

Lacock Village **M** ●

WILTS

The Vyne

Weston-super-Mare

Assembly Rooms **U** Bath

Great Chalfield Manor **M**

The Courts, Holt ✳

Sandham Memorial Chapel

Cheddar

Trowbridge

Basingstoke ●

Minehead

Wells

Frome

Andover

Dunster

M Dunster Castle

Glastonbury

Shepton Mallet

Winterbourne Stoke Barrows ••

Stonehenge

Amesbury

HANTS

Coleridge Cottage ●

Bridgwater

Bruton Dovecote

Figsbury Ring •

Treasurer's House, Martock **I**

Lytes Cary **M**

Stourhead ★

Philipps House

Salisbury

Winchester ●

Taunton

High Ham Windmill **I**

Mompesson House

The Pepperbox **I**

Bampton

Barrington Court **M**

Tintinhull House

Wincanton

Mottisfont Abbey **M**

Winchester City Mill **I**

Knightshayes Court ✳

Wellington Monument **F**

Montacute House **M** ✳

Shaftesbury

Sherborne

Old Town Hall, Newtown **U**

Bembridge Windmill

Southampton

Portsmouth

Killerton ✳

Honiton

Cerne Giant ••

DORSET

Blandford

Bournemouth

Newport

Ryde

Exeter

C Loughwood Meeting House

Bridport

Hardy's Cottage ●

Dorchester

Isle of Wight

Ventnor

Sidmouth

Lyme Regis

Clouds Hill ●

Wareham

Creech Grange Arch **F**

Exmouth

Teignmouth

Weymouth

Swanage

Torquay

2

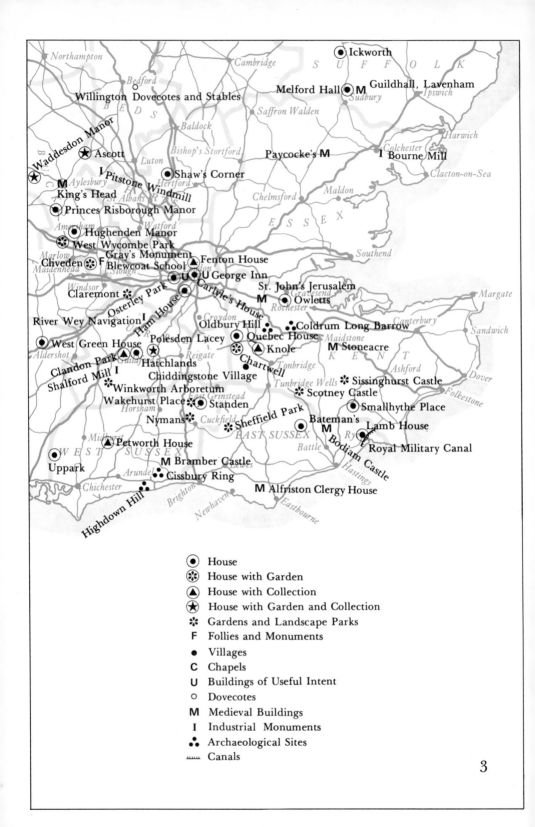

Ickworth

Willington Dovecotes and Stables

Melford Hall M Guildhall, Lavenham

Waddesdon Manor

Ascott

Paycocke's M

Bourne Mill

Shaw's Corner

Pitstone Windmill

King's Head

M

Princes Risborough Manor

Hughenden Manor

West Wycombe Park

Gray's Monument

Cliveden F Blewcoat School

Fenton House

U U George Inn

St. John's Jerusalem

Claremont

Osterley Park

Ham House

Carlyle's House

M

Owletts

River Wey Navigation

Oldbury Hill

Coldrum Long Barrow

West Green House

Polesden Lacey

Quebec House

Stoneacre M

Clandon Park

Hatchlands

Knole

Shalford Mill

Chiddingstone Village

Chartwell

Sissinghurst Castle

Winkworth Arboretum

Scotney Castle

Wakehurst Place Standen

Nymans

Sheffield Park

Smallhythe Place

Bateman's

Lamb House

M

Petworth House

Royal Military Canal

Uppark

M Bramber Castle

Bodiam Castle

Cissbury Ring

M Alfriston Clergy House

Highdown Hill

- ⊙ House
- ✸ House with Garden
- ▲ House with Collection
- ✦ House with Garden and Collection
- ✳ Gardens and Landscape Parks
- F Follies and Monuments
- ● Villages
- C Chapels
- U Buildings of Useful Intent
- ○ Dovecotes
- M Medieval Buildings
- I Industrial Monuments
- ⸪ Archaeological Sites
- ⏝ Canals

3

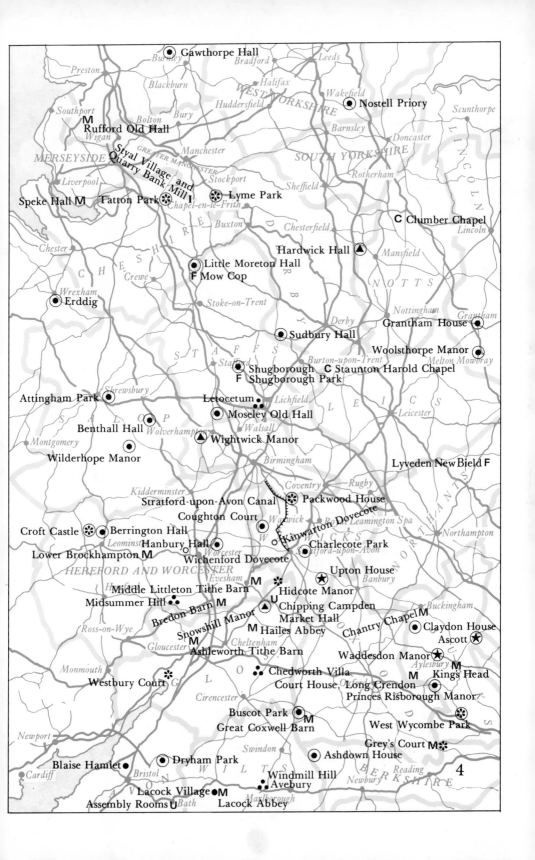

Gawthorpe Hall

Nostell Priory

Rufford Old Hall

Styal Village and
Quarry Bank Mill

Speke Hall Tatton Park Lyme Park

Clumber Chapel

Hardwick Hall

Little Moreton Hall
Mow Cop

Erddig

Grantham House

Sudbury Hall

Woolsthorpe Manor

Shugborough Staunton Harold Chapel
Shugborough Park

Attingham Park

Letocetum
Moseley Old Hall

Benthall Hall

Wightwick Manor

Wilderhope Manor

Lyveden New Bield

Stratford-upon-Avon Canal Packwood House

Coughton Court

Croft Castle Berrington Hall

Kinwarton Dovecote

Hanbury Hall

Charlecote Park

Lower Brockhampton

Wichenford Dovecote

Upton House

Middle Littleton Tithe Barn

Hidcote Manor

Midsummer Hill

Chipping Campden
Market Hall

Claydon House
Ascott

Bredon Barn

Snowshill Manor

Chantry Chapel

Hailes Abbey

Ashleworth Tithe Barn

Waddesdon Manor

King's Head

Westbury Court

Chedworth Villa
Court House, Long Crendon
Princes Risborough Manor

Buscot Park

West Wycombe Park

Great Coxwell Barn

Grey's Court

Blaise Hamlet Dryham Park

Ashdown House

Windmill Hill
Avebury

Lacock Village

Assembly Rooms Lacock Abbey

4

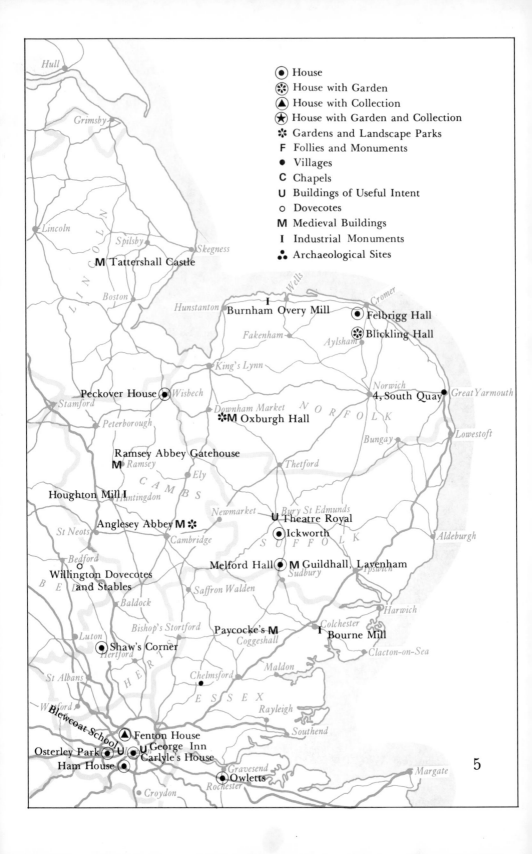

House
⊛ **House with Garden**
▲ **House with Collection**
★ **House with Garden and Collection**
❊ **Gardens and Landscape Parks**
F **Follies and Monuments**
• **Villages**
C **Chapels**
U **Buildings of Useful Intent**
○ **Dovecotes**
M **Medieval Buildings**
I **Industrial Monuments**
❖ **Archaeological Sites**

Hull

Grimsby

Lincoln

Spilsby

Skegness

Boston

M Tattershall Castle

Hunstanton

Wells

Cromer

I Burnham Overy Mill

Felbrigg Hall

Fakenham

Aylsham

⊛ Blickling Hall

King's Lynn

Norwich

Great Yarmouth

Peckover House ⊙ *Wisbech*

4, South Quay

Stamford

Downham Market

N O R F O L K

Peterborough

❊**M** Oxburgh Hall

Lowestoft

Bungay

Ramsey Abbey Gatehouse

M *Ramsey*

Ely

Thetford

C A M B S

Houghton Mill**I** *Huntingdon*

Newmarket

Bury St Edmunds

St Neots

U Theatre Royal

Anglesey Abbey **M** ❊

⊙ Ickworth

Cambridge

S U F F O L K

Aldeburgh

Bedford

Melford Hall⊙ **M** Guildhall, Lavenham

Willington Dovecotes

Sudbury

Ipswich

○

and Stables

B E D

Saffron Walden

Baldock

Harwich

Paycocke's **M**

I Bourne Mill

Bishop's Stortford

Colchester

Coggeshall

Luton

● Shaw's Corner

Clacton-on-Sea

Hertford

H E R T S

Maldon

St Albans

Chelmsford

●

W

E S S E X

Rayleigh

Blewcoat School

▲ Fenton House

Southend

Osterley Park ⊙ **U**

U George Inn

Ham House ⊙

⊙ Carlyle's House

Gravesend

⊙ Owletts

Margate

Croydon

Rochester

5

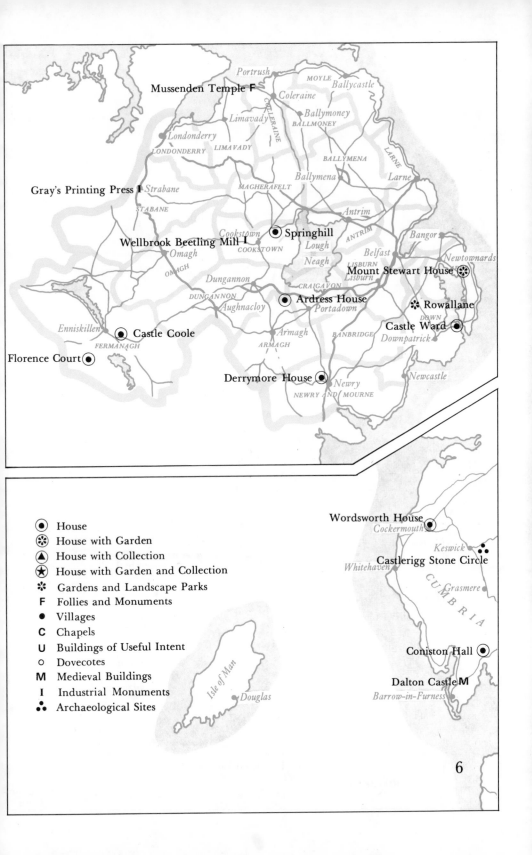

Mussenden Temple **F**

Gray's Printing Press **I** *Strabane*

Wellbrook Beetling Mill **I**

Florence Court ⦿

Castle Coole ⦿

Derrymore House ⦿

Springhill ⦿

Ardress House ⦿

Mount Stewart House ✳

Rowallane ✳

Castle Ward ⦿

Portrush
MOYLE *Ballycastle*
Coleraine
Ballymoney
BALLMONEY
Limavady
Londonderry
LONDONDERRY *LIMAVADY*
BALLYMENA
LARNE
Ballymena
MAGHERAFELT
Larne
STABANE
Omagh
Cookstown
COOKSTOWN
Lough
Neagh
Antrim
ANTRIM
Bangor
Belfast
LISBURN
Lisburn
Newtownards
Dungannon
OMAGH
DUNGANNON
CRAIGAVON
Aughnacloy
Portadown
Enniskillen
FERMANAGH
Armagh
ARMAGH
BANBRIDGE
DOWN
Downpatrick
Newcastle
Newry
NEWRY AND MOURNE
CATTERAINE

⦿ House
✳ House with Garden
▲ House with Collection
★ House with Garden and Collection
✱ Gardens and Landscape Parks
F Follies and Monuments
● Villages
C Chapels
U Buildings of Useful Intent
○ Dovecotes
M Medieval Buildings
I Industrial Monuments
⁖ Archaeological Sites

Wordsworth House ⦿
Cockermouth
Keswick ⁖
Castlerigg Stone Circle
Whitehaven
Grasmere
C U M B R I A
Coniston Hall ⦿
Dalton Castle **M**
Barrow-in-Furness

Isle of Man
Douglas

6

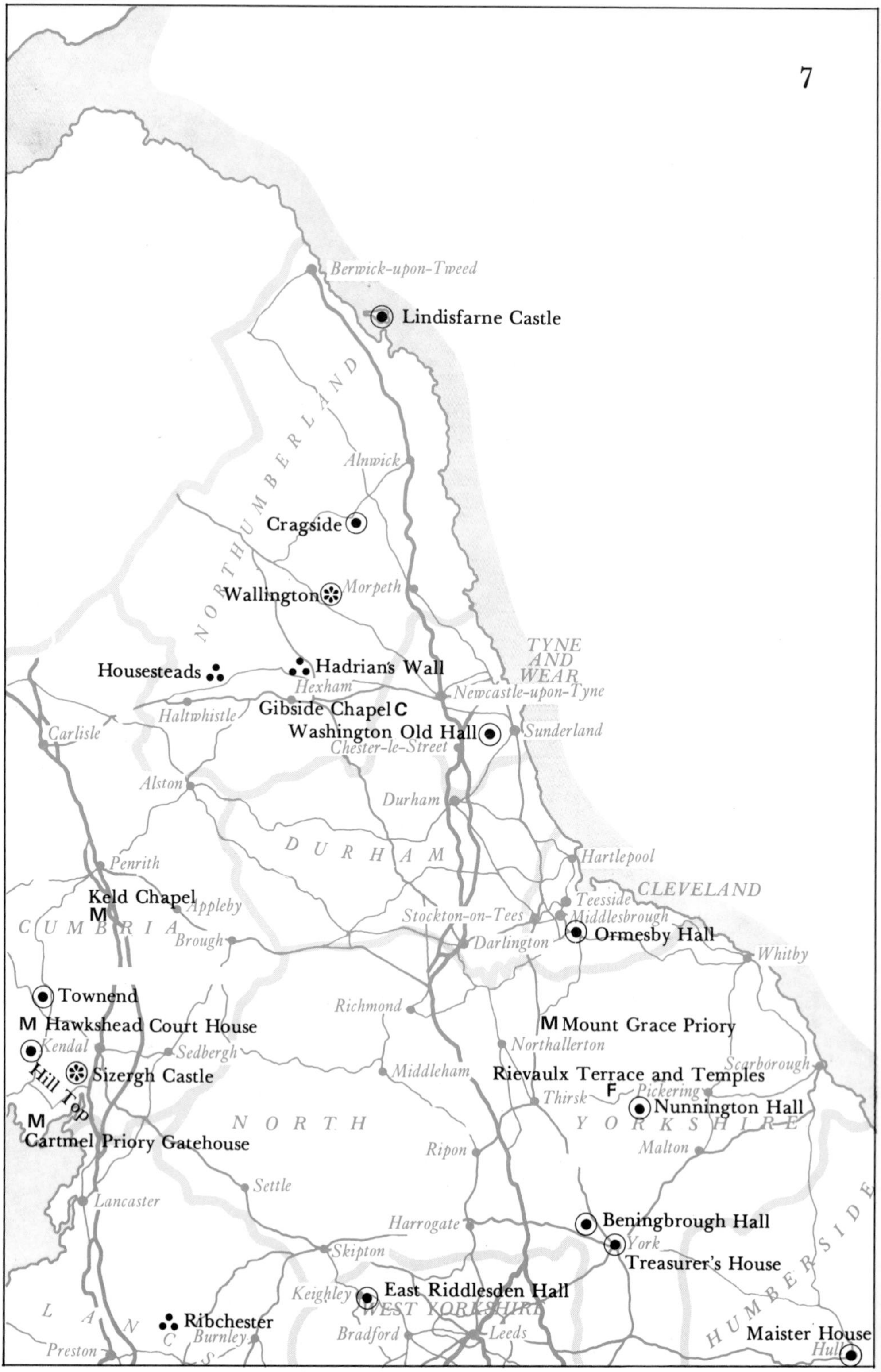

7

Berwick-upon-Tweed

● Lindisfarne Castle

NORTHUMBERLAND

Alnwick

Cragside ●

Wallington ✳ Morpeth

Housesteads ⋰ ⋰ Hadrian's Wall
Hexham

TYNE
AND
WEAR

Gibside Chapel C
Washington Old Hall ● Sunderland
Newcastle-upon-Tyne

Carlisle

Haltwhistle

Chester-le-Street

Alston

Durham

DURHAM

Penrith

Hartlepool

Keld Chapel
M Appleby

CLEVELAND

Teesside
Middlesbrough

CUMBRIA

Brough

Stockton-on-Tees

Darlington

● Ormesby Hall

Whitby

Townend ●
M Hawkshead Court House
● Kendal
✳ Sizergh Castle
Hill Top

Richmond

M Mount Grace Priory
Northallerton

M
Cartmel Priory Gatehouse

Sedbergh

Middleham

Rievaulx Terrace and Temples
F Pickering
Thirsk
● Nunnington Hall

NORTH

Ripon

YORKSHIRE

Malton

Lancaster

Settle

HUMBERSIDE

Harrogate

● Beningbrough Hall
● York
Treasurer's House

Skipton

Keighley ● East Riddlesden Hall
WEST YORKSHIRE

⋰ Ribchester
LANCS
Burnley
Preston Bradford Leeds

Maister House
Hull ●

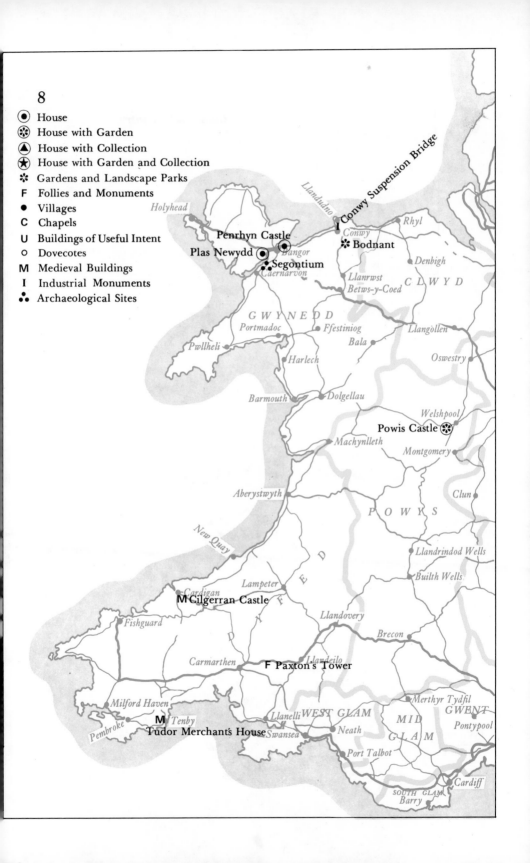

8

- ◉ House
- ✳ House with Garden
- ▲ House with Collection
- ★ House with Garden and Collection
- ✽ Gardens and Landscape Parks
- F Follies and Monuments
- • Villages
- C Chapels
- U Buildings of Useful Intent
- o Dovecotes
- M Medieval Buildings
- I Industrial Monuments
- ⁘ Archaeological Sites

Holyhead

Llandudno

Conwy Suspension Bridge

I Conwy

Rhyl

Penrhyn Castle

✳ Bodnant

Plas Newydd ◉ Bangor

Denbigh

Segontium

Caernarvon

C L W Y D

Llanrwst

Betws-y-Coed

G W Y N E D D

Portmadoc

Ffestiniog

Llangollen

Pwllheli

Bala

Harlech

Oswestry

Barmouth

Dolgellau

Welshpool

Powis Castle ✳

Machynlleth

Montgomery

Aberystwyth

P O W Y S

Clun

New Quay

Llandrindod Wells

Builth Wells

Lampeter

D

M Cilgerran Castle

F

Cardigan

Llandovery

Fishguard

Brecon

Carmarthen

Llandeilo

F Paxton's Tower

Milford Haven

Merthyr Tydfil

GWENT

M Tenby

Llanelli WEST GLAM

MID

Pontypool

Tudor Merchant's House Swansea

Neath

GLAM

Pembroke

Port Talbot

Cardiff

SOUTH GLAM

Barry

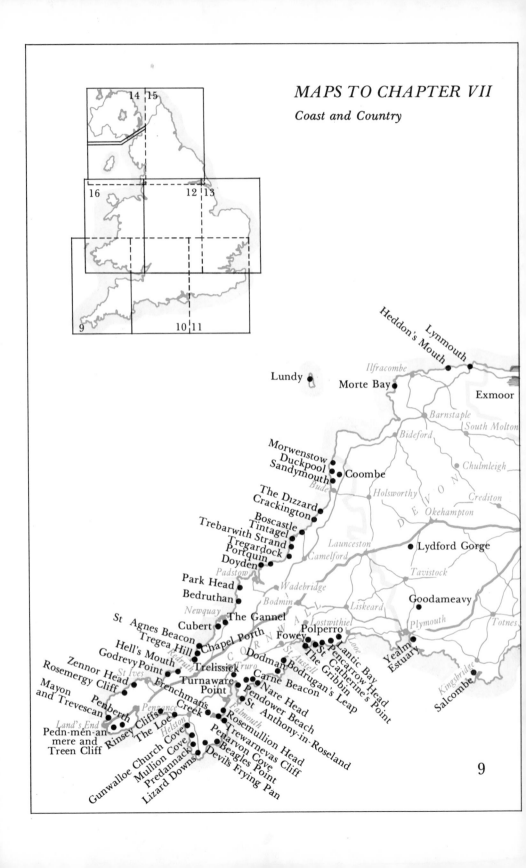

MAPS TO CHAPTER VII

Coast and Country

14 15
16 12 13
9 10 11

Lynmouth
Heddon's Mouth
Ilfracombe
Lundy
Morte Bay
Exmoor
Barnstaple
South Molton
Bideford
Morwenstow
Duckpool
Sandymouth
Coombe
Chulmleigh
The Dizzard
Crackington
Bude
Holsworthy
Crediton
D E V O N
Okehampton
Boscastle
Tintagel
Trebarwith Strand
Tregardock
Portquin
Doyden
Launceston
Camelford
Lydford Gorge
Tavistock
Park Head
Bedruthan
Padstow
Wadebridge
Goodameavy
Bodmin
Liskeard
Newquay
The Gannel
St Agnes Beacon
Cubert
Tregea Hill
Chapel Porth
Fowey
Polperro
Lostwithiel
Plymouth
Totnes
Hell's Mouth
Godrevy Point
Redruth
C O R N W A L L
Dodman
St Austell
Lantic Bay
Looe
The Gribbin
Pencarrow Head
St Catherine's Point
Yealm Estuary
Zennor Head
Rosemergy Cliff
St Ives
Trelissick
Truro
Carne Beacon
Kingsbridge
Mayon
and Trevescan
Penberth
Frenchman's
Creek
Turnaware
Point
Pendower Beach
Nare Head
St Anthony-in-Roseland
Salcombe
Land's End
Penzance
Falmouth
Pedn-mên-an-
mere and
Treen Cliff
Rinsey Cliffs
The Loe
Helston
Rosemullion Head
Gunwalloe Church Cove
Mullion Cove
Predannack
Lizard Downs
Penarvon Cove
Trewarnevas Cliff
Beagles Point
Devils Frying Pan

9

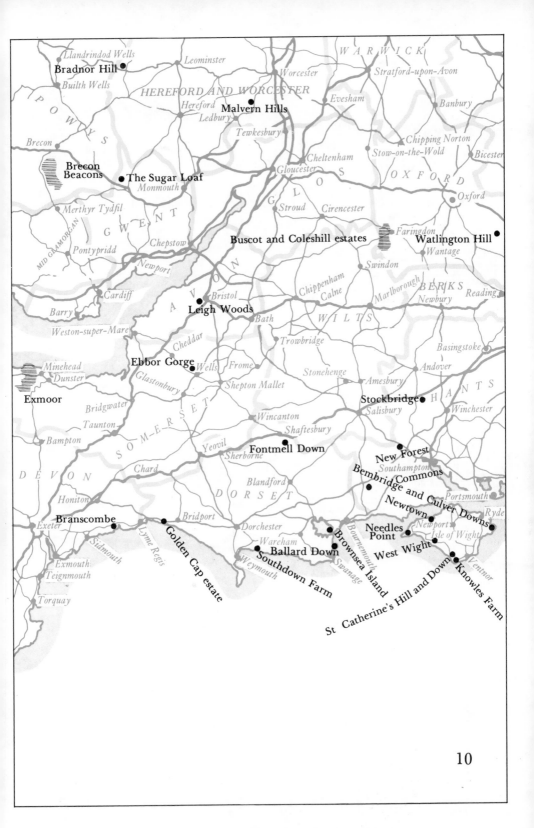

10

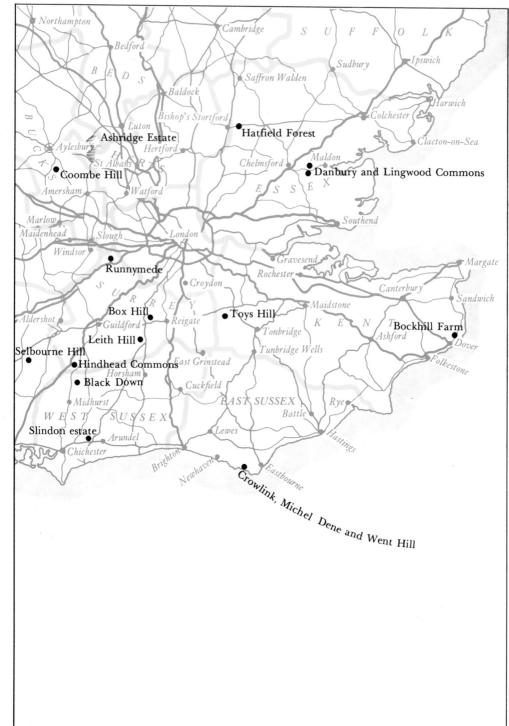

Northampton

Cambridge

S U F F O L K

Bedford

B E D S

Sudbury

Ipswich

Baldock

Saffron Walden

Harwich

Bishop's Stortford

Colchester

Luton

● Hatfield Forest

Clacton-on-Sea

Aylesbury

Ashridge Estate

Hertford

Maldon

● Coombe Hill

St Albans

Chelmsford

● Danbury and Lingwood Commons

Amersham

Watford

E S S E X

Marlow

Slough

London

Southend

Maidenhead

Windsor

Gravesend

Margate

Runnymede

Rochester

Canterbury

S U R R E Y

Croydon

Sandwich

Aldershot

Box Hill

Reigate

● Toys Hill

Maidstone

K E N T

Bockhill Farm

Guildford

Ashford

Dover

Leith Hill ●

Tonbridge

Selbourne Hill

Tunbridge Wells

Folkestone

● Hindhead Commons

East Grinstead

Horsham

● Black Down

Cuckfield

EAST SUSSEX

Midhurst

Battle

Rye

W E S T   S U S S E X

Lewes

Slindon estate ●

Arundel

Hastings

Chichester

Brighton

Newhaven

Eastbourne

Crowlink, Michel Dene and Went Hill

11

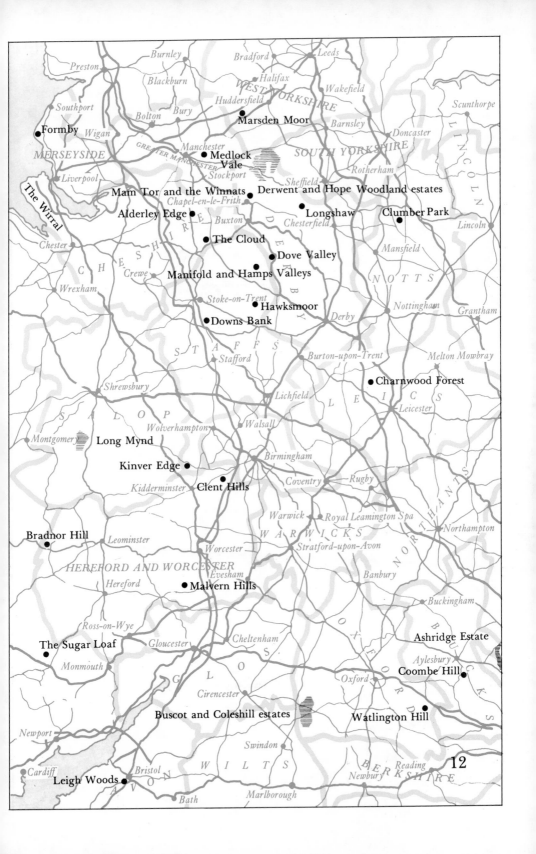

Formby

MERSEYSIDE

The Wirral

Liverpool

Chester

CHESHIRE

Wrexham

Crewe

Alderley Edge

Mam Tor and the Winnats

Chapel-en-le-Frith

Buxton

The Cloud

Dove Valley

Manifold and Hamps Valleys

Stoke-on-Trent

Hawksmoor

Downs Bank

STAFFS

Stafford

Shrewsbury

SALOP

Montgomery

Long Mynd

Kinver Edge

Kidderminster

Clent Hills

Bradnor Hill

Leominster

HEREFORD AND WORCESTER

Hereford

Malvern Hills

Ross-on-Wye

The Sugar Loaf

Monmouth

Newport

Cardiff

Leigh Woods

Bristol

AVON

Bath

Marlborough

Preston

Southport

Wigan

Bolton

Bury

GREATER MANCHESTER

Manchester

Medlock Vale

Stockport

Burnley

Blackburn

Huddersfield

Marsden Moor

WEST YORKSHIRE

Bradford

Halifax

Wakefield

Leeds

Barnsley

SOUTH YORKSHIRE

Doncaster

Scunthorpe

LINCOLN

Sheffield

Rotherham

Derwent and Hope Woodland estates

Longshaw

Chesterfield

Clumber Park

Lincoln

Mansfield

NOTTS

DERBY

Nottingham

Grantham

Derby

Burton-upon-Trent

Melton Mowbray

Charnwood Forest

Lichfield

LEICS

Leicester

Wolverhampton

Walsall

Birmingham

Coventry

Rugby

Warwick

Royal Leamington Spa

Northampton

WARWICKS

NORTHANTS

Worcester

Stratford-upon-Avon

Evesham

Banbury

Buckingham

BUCKS

Ashridge Estate

Cheltenham

Gloucester

GLOS

Cirencester

Oxford

OXFORDS

Aylesbury

Coombe Hill

Buscot and Coleshill estates

Watlington Hill

Swindon

WILTS

BERKSHIRE

Reading

Newbury

12

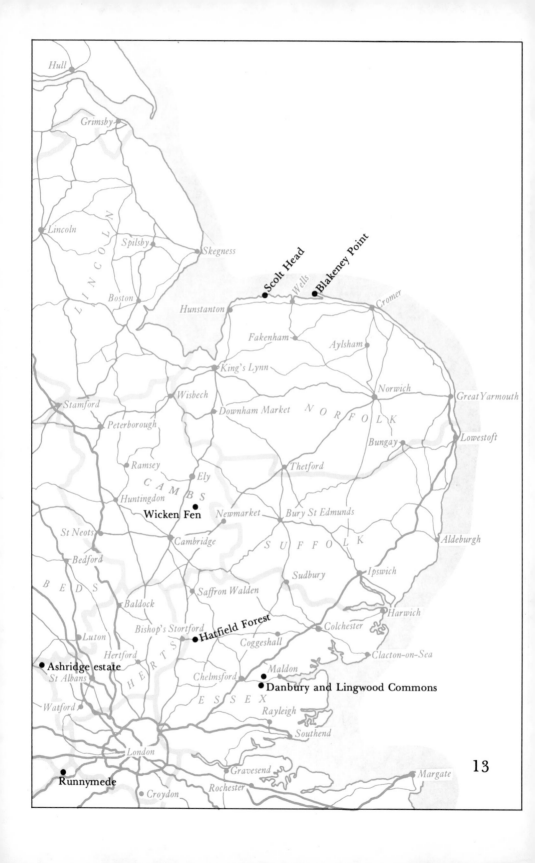

Hull

Grimsby

Lincoln

LINCOLN

Spilsby

Skegness

Boston

Hunstanton

Scolt Head

Wells

Blakeney Point

Cromer

Fakenham

Aylsham

King's Lynn

Wisbech

Stamford

Downham Market

NORFOLK

Norwich

Great Yarmouth

Peterborough

Lowestoft

Bungay

Ramsey

CAMBS

Ely

Thetford

Huntingdon

Wicken Fen

Newmarket

Bury St Edmunds

St Neots

Cambridge

SUFFOLK

Aldeburgh

Bedford

BEDS

Ipswich

Sudbury

Baldock

Saffron Walden

Harwich

Luton

Bishop's Stortford

Hatfield Forest

Colchester

Hertford

Coggeshall

Clacton-on-Sea

HERTS

Ashridge estate

St Albans

Chelmsford

Maldon

Danbury and Lingwood Commons

Watford

ESSEX

Rayleigh

London

Southend

Runnymede

Gravesend

Margate

Croydon

Rochester

13

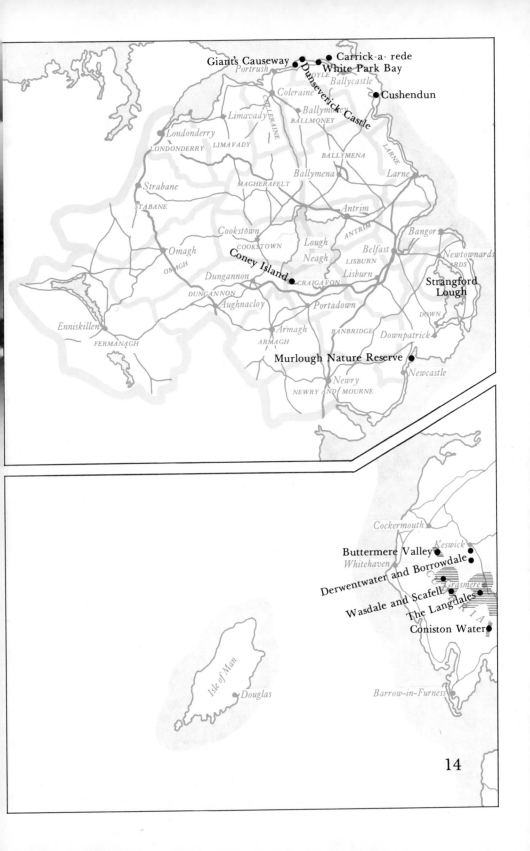

Giant's Causeway
Carrick-a- rede
White Park Bay
Portrush
Ballycastle
Cushendun
Coleraine
Dunseverick Castle
Limavady
Ballymoney
Londonderry
LIMAVADY
BALLMONEY
LONDONDERRY
BALLYMENA
Ballymena
MAGHERAFELT
Strabane
Larne
STABANE
Larne
Antrim
ANTRIM
Cookstown
Bangor
COOKSTOWN
Lough
Belfast
Newtownards
Omagh
Neagh
LISBURN
ARDS
Coney Island
Lisburn
OMAGH
Dungannon
CRAIGAVON
Strangford
Lough
DUNGANNON
Aughnacloy
Portadown
DOWN
Enniskillen
BANBRIDGE
Downpatrick
FERMANAGH
Armagh
ARMAGH
Murlough Nature Reserve
Newcastle
Newry
NEWRY AND MOURNE

Cockermouth
Keswick
Buttermere Valley
Whitehaven
Derwentwater and Borrowdale
Grasmere
Wasdale and Scafell
The Langdales
Coniston Water
Isle of Man
Douglas
Barrow-in-Furness

14

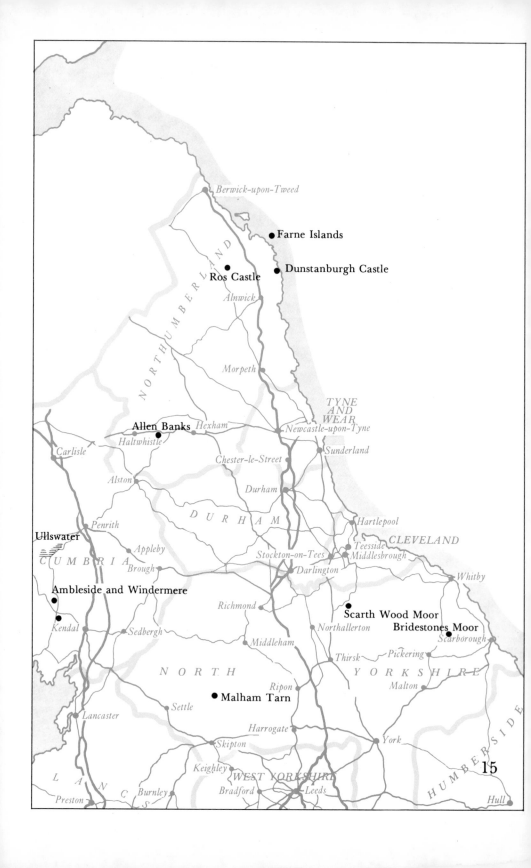

Berwick-upon-Tweed

● Farne Islands

● Ros Castle   ● Dunstanburgh Castle

NORTHUMBERLAND

Alnwick

Morpeth

TYNE
AND
WEAR

Allen Banks● Hexham   Newcastle-upon-Tyne

Carlisle   Haltwhistle

Alston   Chester-le-Street

Sunderland

DURHAM

Durham

Penrith   Hartlepool

Ullswater   CLEVELAND

Appleby   Teesside
CUMBRIA   Middlesbrough
Brough   Stockton-on-Tees

Darlington   Whitby

Ambleside and Windermere

Richmond   Scarth Wood Moor
                      Bridestones Moor
Kendal   Sedbergh   Northallerton   Scarborough

Middleham   Thirsk   Pickering

NORTH   Ripon   Malton

● Malham Tarn   YORKSHIRE

Lancaster   Settle

Harrogate

Skipton   York

Keighley WEST YORKSHIRE   **15**

L A N C S   Burnley Bradford   Leeds   HUMBERSIDE

Preston   Hull

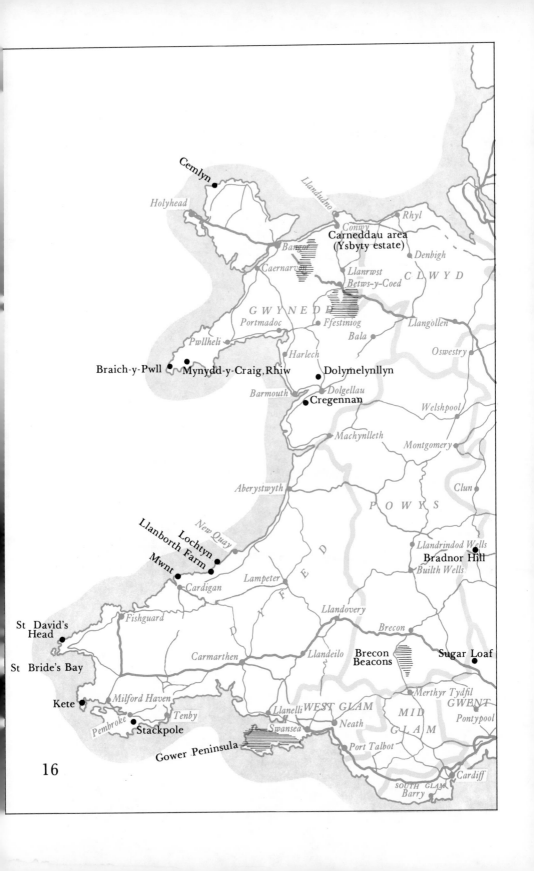

Cemlyn

Holyhead

Llandudno

Rhyl

Conwy

Carneddau area
(Ysbyty estate)

Denbigh

Bangor

C L W Y D

Caernarvon

Llanrwst

Betws-y-Coed

G W Y N E D D

Portmadoc

Ffestiniog

Llangollen

Pwllheli

Bala

Oswestry

Harlech

Braich-y-Pwll

Mynydd-y-Craig, Rhiw

Dolymelynllyn

Barmouth

Dolgellau

Cregennan

Welshpool

Machynlleth

Montgomery

Aberystwyth

Clun

P O W Y S

New Quay

Lochtyn

Llanborth Farm

Llandrindod Wells

Bradnor Hill

Mwnt

Builth Wells

Cardigan

Lampeter

D

Y

F

E

D

Fishguard

Llandovery

Llandeilo

Brecon

St David's
Head

Carmarthen

Brecon
Beacons

Sugar Loaf

St Bride's Bay

Merthyr Tydfil

GWENT

Kete

Milford Haven

Llanelli

WEST GLAM

MID

Tenby

Pontypool

Pembroke

Neath

GLAM

Stackpole

Swansea

Gower Peninsula

Port Talbot

Cardiff

SOUTH GLAM

Barry

16

Glossary

acanthus   Formalized leaves of the acanthus plant, used in classical architecture to ornament the capitals of columns.

arch-braced   *See* braces.

architrave   In classical architecture the lowest of the three main parts which make up an entablature (q.v.). Also the moulded frame surrounding a door or window.

ashlar   Stone walling, with evenly dressed surface.

bargeboards   Projecting boards on the sloping sides of a gable set over the ends of the horizontal roof timbers. Often decorated.

Baroque   Florid and exuberant style in art and architecture distinguished by flowing lines and curves, originating in Italy about 1600.

barrel vault   The simplest form of vault, also called tunnel or wagon vault. A continuous plain arch, semicircular or pointed; barrel vaulting may also be divided into bays by transverse arches.

battlement   Also called crenellation. A parapet with alternating indentations, or embrasures, and raised portions.

Boulle   A style of fine inlay-work used in cabinet-making, with complicated designs of brass, gold or bronze combined with ivory, ebony or tortoiseshell. French, 17th and 18th centuries.

braces   Diagonal subsidiary timbers strengthening the frame of a roof and connecting either a tie-beam (q.v.) with the wall below, or a collar-beam (q.v.) with the rafters below. Braces can be straight or arched, the latter being a refinement of the cruck.

bressummer   A massive horizontal beam spanning a wide opening. Also the principal horizontal beam in a timber-framed building.

camber   To curve a timber beam, either by sawing or bending it.

cantilever   A beam, girder or projection supported at one end only. A cantilever bridge has a central portion suspended between two cantilever arms.

caryatid   A sculptured female figure used as a supporting column. Also used to apply to a column or pilaster (q.v.) wholly or partly carved as a human figure.

castellated   Surmounted with battlements or turrets.

cellarium   Medieval Latin for a cellar or storeroom.

chamfer   The surface made when the sharp right-angled edge of a stone block or piece of wood or metal is cut away, usually at an angle of $45°$ to the other two surfaces.

569

chevron   A deeply cut zigzag-shaped moulding.

chimneypiece   Frame surrounding a fireplace. Often includes an over-mantel – ornamental woodwork – or mirror above.

chinoiserie   European imitations or evocations of Chinese art, in build-ings, follies, interior decoration, furniture, etc. First appeared late in the 17th century, and became very popular in the 18th century.

classicism   Style of architecture imitating or inspired by that of ancient Greece or Rome, or by the Italian Renaissance. *See* Palladianism, neo-classicism.

clerestory   Upper part of the walls of a church nave, with windows above the roofs of the aisles. There is often a narrow wall-passage on the inside of early clerestories.

coffering   Decoration of a ceiling or vault, or the underside of an arch, with a pattern of sunken squares or polygonal panels.

collar-beam   A horizontal beam placed across the inside of a roof con-necting the rafters and set higher up the slope of the roof than a tie-beam (q.v.).

console   An ornamental bracket, usually greater in height than depth and with a compound curving outline.

corbel   A projecting block supporting a beam or other horizontal member and usually of stone.

cornice   The top, projecting part of an entablature (q.v.) in classical architecture. Also any projecting ornamental moulding on the top of a building or wall of a room.

cottage orné   A deliberately rustic or romantic cottage often thatched and asymmetrical in plan.

coursed rubble   A term in masonry, meaning walling of roughly dressed stone or flints set in horizontal rows or courses. Uncoursed rubble denotes unhewn stones or flints straight from the quarry not laid in regular courses.

coving   Large concave moulding made by the sloped or arched junction of a wall and ceiling.

crocket   Carved leaf-like decorative feature projecting from spires, pin-nacles or gables at regular intervals in Gothic architecture.

crow steps   Steps on the coping of a gable, common in the Netherlands, Flanders and Germany and in 16th- and 17th-century Scotland. In England, rare except in East Anglia.

cupola   A small dome, crowning a roof or turret.

curtain wall   In medieval architecture, the sheer outer wall of a castle, usually punctuated by towers or bastions.

cusp   A projecting point at the intersection of circles or arches in Gothic tracery. Such curves are called foils (q.v.).

dentil Small square blocks used in series in classical cornices, mostly in Ionic and Corinthian orders, and more rarely in Doric.

diaperwork Surface decoration of diamond-shaped patterns. In brickwork this may also mean bricks of different colour or shape set at intervals in a wall to make up a diamond pattern.

dog-tooth Ornament consisting of a series of four-cornered stars diagonally placed and raised, or like four-pointed teeth with their sharp ends at the corners.

doorcase The case lining a doorway on which the door is hung.

dressings Stones worked to a smooth or moulded edge and set round an angle, window or any feature of a building.

dripstone Also called hoodmould or label. A projecting mould on the face of a wall above an arch, doorway or window to throw off the rain.

dummy board Life-size or almost life-size figure cut out of board and used as a firescreen. Popular in the late 17th and early 18th centuries.

entablature In classical architecture the horizontal top part of an order (q.v.). An entablature consists of an architrave, frieze and cornice, and is sometimes supported by columns.

fan vault A fan vault consists of solid concave-sided semi-cones which meet or almost meet at the apex of the vault. The cones and centres are decorated with panelling and ribs.

fenestration The arrangement of windows on a building.

fielded panel A door or wall panel, in which the centre square or rectangular section is separated from the border by a broad groove with sloping side or sides. The centre may be raised above the border.

finial A formal ornament at the top of a pinnacle, gable or spire. Often a foliated fleur-de-lis.

flashings Strips of metal or other material used on roofs to protect joints against damp.

flemish bond A method of laying bricks so that alternate headers and stretchers appear in each row on the face of a wall. A header is a brick laid so that the end shows; a stretcher is a brick laid lengthways so that the side appears.

fleuron A formal flower-shaped ornament.

foil A lobe or leaf-shaped curve formed by the cusping of a circle or an arch. A prefix indicates the number of foils, e.g. trefoil, quatrefoil, cinquefoil or multifoil. Used in Gothic tracery.

frieze The middle division of an entablature (q.v.) in classical architecture. Also the decorated band along the upper part of an internal wall immediately below the ceiling or cornice.

gable · The triangular upper portion of a wall supporting a pitched roof.

garderobe A wardrobe; also medieval name for a lavatory.

gazebo   A small summerhouse or lookout tower with a view, usually in a garden or park.

Gothic Revival   The style, based on the growth of archaeological knowledge of medieval architecture, which followed on the Gothick of the 18th century.

Gothic Survival   Refers to the unquestioning continuation of the Gothic style in the 16th and 17th centuries, mainly in churches and in the finishing of Gothic buildings in conformity with their original style.

Gothick, neo-Gothick   The conscious choice of what was thought to be medieval Gothic style, which developed and became fashionable after 1750 and continued into the first quarter of the 19th century in England.

grisaille   Monochrome painting in shades of grey.

ha-ha   A sunken fence or ditch commonly set at the end of a lawn or garden, so as not to interrupt the view.

hammer-beam   A horizontal roof bracket, which usually projects at the level of the base of the rafters to carry arched braces and struts and is itself supported by braces.

hip   The external angle made by the meeting of two sloping roof surfaces.

hipped roof   A roof with sloped instead of gabled ends.

husk chain   A form of plaster, wood or stone decoration consisting of looped chains made up of a formalized pattern of barley or corn husks.

kingpost   The central upright post in a roof truss set on the collar or tie-beam and reaching to the ridge, in contrast to the two queenposts (q.v.).

label   *See* dripstone.

linenfold   Panelling of early to late 16th century decorated with conventional representation of linen in vertical folds. One piece of 'cloth' fills each panel.

louver   Opening in the roof of a medieval hall to let the smoke escape from the central hearth. Also windows or wall-openings filled by a series of overlapping boards or slips of glass which admit air and exclude rain and/or light.

lunette   A semicircular opening; can be filled with a painting or sculpture.

machicolation   A gallery or parapet built on the outside of castle towers or walls, with apertures in the floor to enable the defenders to drop missiles on attackers.

modillion   Small bracket or console; a series of brackets, arranged in pairs, is frequently used to support a Corinthian or Composite cornice.

mullion   A vertical division of a window or other opening.

neo-classicism   Style which developed after 1750 based upon the direct study of Greek and Roman buildings, as opposed to Palladianism (q.v.). The Greek revival at the end of the 18th century was the final development of neo-classicism.

newel-post The principal post at the end of a flight of stairs or on a landing. A newel staircase is a spiral staircase with a continuous post supporting the narrow inner ends of the treads.

nogging Brick infilling, often between the timbers of a half-timbered building.

order In classical architecture an order comprises a column, with or without a base, a shaft, capital and entablature, decorated and proportioned in one of the accepted modes: Doric, Tuscan, Ionic, Corinthian or Composite.

oriel A bay window on an upper storey or storeys.

ormolu Bright gold-coloured alloy of copper, zinc and tin. Gilded bronze or lacquered brass. Furniture ornaments made or applied with ormolu were widely used in French cabinet-making in the 17th and 18th centuries.

overdoor A painting above a door, usually framed to form a decorative feature in harmony with the doorcase.

Palladianism Architectural style derived from the publications and buildings of Andrea Palladio, the 16th-century Italian architect. Introduced into England by Inigo Jones in the early 17th century, Palladianism was revived in the early 18th century.

pantile A curved S-shaped roofing tile.

parcel-gilt A form of decoration in which only selected parts of a frame or carving are gilded. Popular in the late 17th and early 18th centuries, especially for mirror frames.

pediment In classical architecture usually a low-pitched triangular gable above a portico, formed by running the top of an entablature along the sides of the gable. Also a similar feature above doors or windows. A broken pediment has a gap in the upper moulding.

pele, pele tower A small or moderate-sized tower or keep which is easily defended. Peculiar to houses or castles on both sides of the Scottish border. Generally built between the 13th and 15th centuries.

pendentive A concave spandrel (q.v.) leading from the angle of two walls to the base of a dome.

peristyle A range of columns surrounding a building or an open court in classical architecture.

piano nobile The principal floor of a house containing the reception or state rooms, placed above the basement or ground floor. The ceilings are usually higher than those of the other floors.

pier A solid masonry support, usually rectangular, as distinct from a circular column.

pilaster A shallow pier or engaged column projecting from a wall.

portico A roofed space, open or partly enclosed, often forming the entrance and centrepiece of the façade of a temple, church or house.

573

quatrefoil *See* foil.

queenpost One of a pair of vertical posts placed symmetrically close to the ends of a tie- or collar-beam connecting it with the rafters above, as distinct from a central kingpost which serves the same purpose.

quincunx Five objects arranged in a square, with one in the centre and one at each corner. In horticulture, this may also refer to the planting of trees or plants in double rows alternately.

quoins Dressed stones at the angle of a building, usually laid so that the exposed faces are alternatively large and small.

rainwater head Box-shaped structure of metal, usually lead or cast-iron, sometimes elaborately decorated, in which water from a gutter is collected and discharged into a down pipe.

reeding Decoration consisting of parallel convex mouldings touching one another.

rocaille Rococo decoration of any sort. An artificial grotto decorated with stones or shells.

rococo A form of decoration developed from the late Baroque, but lighter and more elegant. Fashionable in England in the mid-18th century.

rondel, roundel A round moulding or aperture, usually in a wall surface.

rotunda A circular room or building usually domed.

rustication Masonry (usually dressed) cut in large blocks, with recessed joints, normally used on the lower part of a wall. Also applied to columns.

scagliola Imitation marble, composed of cement or plaster and marble chips or colouring matter, often used for columns and in interior decoration in 18th-century classical architecture.

screens passage The space or corridor at the service end of a medieval hall, dividing it from the buttery, pantry and kitchen.

shingles Wooden tiles used for covering roofs, spires and sometimes parts of walls of houses. Also used to describe stone roofing tiles.

soffit The underside of any architectural feature.

solar Living room in an upper storey of a medieval house or castle.

spandrel The space between the side of an arch and the vertical of its springing. Also applied to the surface between two arches in an arcade.

squint Obliquely cut opening in a wall to allow a view of the main altar of a church. Also sometimes built in 14th- and 15th-century houses to allow a view of the great hall from the chamber or chambers above it.

strapwork Decoration originating in the Netherlands about 1540 and common in Elizabethan and Jacobean England, consisting of interlaced bands similar to fretwork or cut leather. In buildings, generally executed in plaster or stone on ceilings, screens or parapets.

stringcourse A continuous projecting band or moulding in the surface of a wall.

stylobate   The substructure on which a colonnade stands; more correctly, the top step of the stepped base of a Greek temple.

tempera   Mixture of egg-yolk and water to bind powdered paints, especially used for plaster mural paintings or frescoes.

tie-beam   The horizontal transverse roof beam connecting the feet of the rafters.

transom   A horizontal bar of stone or wood across the opening of a window or across a panel.

trefoil   *See* foil.

triglyph   Blocks with vertical grooves separated by plain square surfaces forming a Doric frieze.

truss   A number of timbers framed together to bridge a space or form a bracket. The trusses of a roof are usually named after the principal feature of their construction.

tufa   Calcareous rock deposited from springs. Also a type of porous volcanic rock.

undercroft   A vaulted chamber, usually but not invariably underground, often below a church or chapel.

volute   Spiral scroll on an Ionic capital.

wallplate   A beam laid along the top of a wall to receive the ends of the rafters.

wattle-and-daub   A method of simple wall construction in which branches or thin wooden lathes (wattle) are roughly plastered over with mud or clay (daub) used as a filling between the uprights of timber-framed buildings.

wind-braces   Short braces, usually arched and laid flat along the rafters, some way up the slope of a roof, which strengthen the wind resistance of a roof area.

National Trust Properties
not Described in the Text

AVON

Bristol Properties *Frenchay Moor:* 8 acres. *Shirehampton Park:* 99 acres overlooking the Avon, part used as a golf course. *Westbury College:* 15th-century gatehouse of the College of Priests, founded in the 13th century, of which John Wycliffe was a prebend.

Cadbury Camp 2½m E of Clevedon. 39½ acres on which there is an Iron Age hillfort.

Failand 4m W of central Bristol on S side of B3124. 363 acres, including several farms and woodlands.

Horton Court 3m NE of Chipping Sodbury, ¾m N of Horton, 1m W of the A46. 146 acres of farmland including a Cotswold manor house, restored and somewhat altered in the 19th century but with a 12th-century Norman hall and unusual late Perpendicular ambulatory detached from the house.

Middle Hope (Woodspring) 5m N of Weston-super-Mare. 158 acres stretching over 2m of coast.

Monk's Steps, Kewstoke On N edge of Weston-super-Mare. 2½ acres and the Steps.

Redcliffe Bay Coastal belt of 2 acres crossed by the mariners' footpath from Clevedon to Portishead.

Sand Point, Kewstoke 5m N of Weston-super-Mare. 32 acres of coastal headland, adjoining Middle Hope Priory.

BEDFORDSHIRE

Dunstable Downs, Whipsnade 2m S of Dunstable, 4m N of Ashridge. 285 acres on the Chilterns.

Sharpenhoe: The Clappers and Roberts Farm On the Chilterns, 1½m SW of Barton-in-the-Clay, 6m N of Luton. 136 acres, crowned by the Clappers Wood.

BERKSHIRE

Ambarrow Hill ½m S of Crowthorne station. 11 acres of pine-clad hill.

Bucklebury 8m E of Newbury. 102 acres of agricultural land adjacent to Bucklebury Common.

Falkland Memorial 1m SW of Newbury, on the Andover road. 19th-century memorial to Lucius Cary, 2nd Viscount Falkland, killed in the first battle of Newbury in 1643.

Finchampstead Ridges ¾m W of Crowthorne station, on the S side of B3348. 60 acres of woodland and a heather ridge. *Heath Pool:* 12 acres of woodland. *Simons Wood:* 35 acres of woodland, with access from Heath Pool.

Lardon Chase Just N of Streatley, on the W side of A417. 38 acres of down. *Lough Down:* 28½ acres, adjoining Lardon Chase.

Manor of Cookham and Maidenhead *Cock Marsh:* 132 acres on which is a group of bowl barrows. *Cookham Dean Common:* 78 acres, including Cookham Dean village green, Bigfrith and Tugwood Commons. *Cookham Moor:* 9 acres W of Cookham. *Maidenhead Thicket:* 368 acres, including Robin Hood's Arbour. *North Town Moor:* 8 acres. *Pinkney's Green:* 167 acres, continuation of Maidenhead Thicket. *Widbrook (Whitebrook) Common:* 65 acres. *Winter Hill:* 16 acres.

Pangbourne Meadow Just below Pangbourne Bridge, E of B471. 7 acres on the S bank of the Thames.

Windsor: The Goswells Between Thames Street and the river Thames. 3 acres.

BUCKINGHAMSHIRE

Boarstall Tower   Midway between Bicester and Thame, 2m W of Brill. The stone gatehouse of a long-since-demolished fortified house, dating from the 14th century and altered in the 16th and 17th centuries.

Bradenham   4m NW of High Wycombe, 4½m S of Princes Risborough. 1,111 acres. Almost the whole of the village, the Manor House, 5 farms and 380 acres of woods. At one time the home of Disraeli's father.

Dorneywood   SW of Burnham Beeches, 1m E of Cliveden. The house, contents and 215 acres given as an official residence for a Secretary of State or a Minister of the Crown.

Hogback Wood   1m W of Beaconsfield station. 23 acres of woodland.

Medmenham: Lodge Farm   3m SW of Marlow, on the N side of A4155. 75 acres. A 17th-century farmhouse and three modern cottages.

West Wycombe Village   W of High Wycombe. 59 acres, including Church Hill and most of the village, which has some houses of the 15th and 16th centuries and many dating from the 17th century.

Whiteleaf Fields   ¾m NE of Princes Risborough. 3 acres opposite the Nag's Head Inn at Monks Risborough and 2 acres extending for about ¼m on either side of the Icknield Way.

CAMBRIDGESHIRE

Wisbech: 14 and 19 North Brink   On N brink of the river Nene. Early 18th-century houses flanking Peckover House.

Wimpole Hall   Near Wisbech. 18th-century house and 2,400 acres. Not open.

CHESHIRE

Eddisbury Park Field   1m E of Macclesfield on the Buxton road. 16 acres of park-like meadow.

Helsby Hill   ½m S of Helsby, just E of A56. 39 acres of the summit, on which is part of an Iron Age promontory fort and lower slopes.

Maggoty's Wood   ½m NW of Gawsworth, 3m SW of Macclesfield. 2½ acres of wood, in which is the grave of Maggoty Johnson, an eccentric 18th-century dramatist and dancing master.

Mobberley   3m NE of Knutsford. 20 acres given to protect the church.

CORNWALL

Bedruthan Steps   6m SW of Padstow. 60 acres of cliffland with views across Bedruthan Steps.

Bodigga Cliff   1m E of Looe. 43 acres: 30 acres of rough cliffland above Millendreath Beach, 13 acres of foreshore.

Cadsonbury   Near New Bridge, 2m SW of Callington. An important univallate hillfort.

Camel Estuary: Trebetherick, Fishing Cove Field   6½ acres.

Chapel Carn Brea   3m NE of Land's End. 53 acres. The first and last hill in England.

Fal Estuary: Ardevora   On S Bank of the river Fal. 32 acres of foreshore. *Trelonk:* 22 acres of foreshore on the E bank.

Hor Point and Hellesveor Cliff   1½m W of St Ives. 24½ acres of rocky coast.

Lanhydrock   299 acres of woodland, river meadows and fishing in the river Fowey for 1½m.

Lansallos: Highertown Farm   125 acres of farmland to the W and N of the village overlooking Lantivet Bay.

Launceston: Lawrence House, Castle Street   A typical country-town house, now a local museum.

Lerryn Creek   On the E bank of the Fowey estuary. 377-acre estate, including Ethy House.

Maer Cliff, Bude   115 acres of clifftop pasture and foreshore, adjoining the town, crossed by the coastal footpath.

Port Gaverne ¼m E of Port Isaac. 16 acres, including the beach, foreshore and fish cellars.

Porthcothan 5m SW of Padstow. 17 acres forming the N side of the inlet.

Porthminster Point On the S edge of St Ives. 12 acres of cliffs and small fields.

Rough Tor 3m SE of Camelford. 174 acres of moorland, rising to nearly 1,300 ft, the second highest point in Cornwall. A Bronze Age settlement.

St Mawes 40 acres of Newton Cliff running for ½m N of the town on E side of Falmouth Harbour.

Tregardock Beach 3m S of Tintagel. 66 acres of the cliffs from Tregonnick Tail.

Whitesand Bay 5m W of Torpoint, 3m NW of Rame Head. 69 acres of cliffs overlooking the Bay. *Trethill Cliffs:* 69 acres.

CUMBRIA

Acorn Bank Garden Just N of Temple Sowerby. Spring bulbs, walled and herb garden. Mainly 18th-century house, not open. 186 acres along the Crowdundle Beck.

Arnside: The Knott 1m S of Arnside. 106½ acres overlooking Morecambe Bay.

Buttermere Valley: Ghyll Wood: 5 acres of woodland running alongside Sail Beck.

Cautley: Cross Keys Inn 5m NE of Sedbergh on B6258. An unlicensed inn, built about 1600 and altered in the 18th and early 19th centuries.

Derwentwater and Borrowdale: Yew Tree and Longthwaite Farms 582 acres of fields and fell pasture around Rosthwaite with various grazing rights and 914 sheep.

Duddon Valley *Baskell Farm:* 216-acre farm. *Blackhall Farm:* 2,700 acres at the head of the valley opposite Cockley Beck stretching from Three Shires Stone to the top of Pike of Blisco, enclosing the whole of Moasdale and reaching the top of Hardknott Pass. *Brighouse and Hazel Head Farms:* 242 acres at Ulpha on the Cumberland side. *Browside and Thrang Farms:* 170 acres with rights over fenced pastures to just below Walna Scar. *Cockley Beck and Dale Head Farms:* 1,215 acres running the whole length of Wrynose Bottom to the Three Shires Stone and rising to Grey Friar and the Carrs, where the property joins the Monk Coniston estate. *High Wallowbarrow Farm:* 381 acres, with land at Low Wallowbarrow and Pannelholme. *Low Hollin House:* not open. *Pikeside Farm and Beckstones:* 255-acre fell farm. *Troutal Farm:* 145 acres with rights over fenced pastures beside the river Duddon. *Wallowbarrow Crag:* 84 acres of rough fell.

Dunthwaite 2m W of N end of Bassenthwaite. 427 acres of farm and woodlands, bordering the Derwent for 1½m, including Dunthwaite House, dating from 1785, and Kirkhouse Farm.

Easedale *Brimmer Head Farm:* 200 acres of farmland. *Kitty Crag Wood:* 1½-acre wood.

Ennerdale *Beckfoot Farm:* On N shore of Ennerdale Water, 48 acres. *Crag Fell:* 294 acres of open fell. *Forestry Commission Land:* 3,624 acres of fell on both sides of the river Liza, held on 500-year lease. *How Hall Farm:* 772 acres with farmhouse rebuilt in the early 19th century on the site of a much earlier house. *Howside Farm:* 50 acres adjoining Trust property. *Mireside Farm:* 447 acres of farmland on the N shore of Ennerdale, including 368 acres of rough grazing and landlord's flock of 203 sheep. *The Side:* 874 acres at the W end of the Forestry Commission land.

Eskdale *Boot:* 5 acres near the church and 15 acres near by. *Burnmoor Tarn:* 57½ acres beside the path from Eskdale to Wasdale. *Butterilket Farm:* 3,328 acres running down the left bank of the river Esk from its source at Eskhause to Wha House Bridge. *Field Head Farm:* 119 acres at the foot of Eskdale under Birker Fell. *Gill Bank Farm:* 87 acres with rights on Eskdale Common and 229 sheep. *Penny Hill:* 156 acres on the left bank of the river. *Taw House Farm:* 223 acres on the right bank near the head of the valley. *Wha House Farm:* 189 acres adjoining Taw House Farm.

Grasmere *Alcock Tarn, Brackenfell and Chapel Green:* 97 acres of the hillside behind Dove Cottage, up to and including Alcock Tarn. *Allan Bank:* 94 acres, including house and garden in Grasmere village, the home of Wordsworth from 1800 to 1811. *Broadgate Field:* 1½ acres in Grasmere village. *Butterlip Howe:* 6 acres arising out of the village of Grasmere. *Church Stile:* 16th-century cottage. *Easedale:* 15 acres. *Grandy Close:* 6 modern cottages with 3 acres. *Lakeside Land:* 20 acres SW shore of Grasmere. *Low Fold:* 4½ acres. *Moss Parrock:* ½ acre in Grasmere village. *Nicholas Wood:* 10½ acres of woodland.

St Oswalds: 3 acres and a house. *Stubdale Cottage:* 2½ acres of land and cottage. *Underhelm Farm:* 80 acres with landlord's flock of 220 sheep. *White Moss Intake:* 6½ acres of rough pasture. *The Wray:* 15 acres of meadow and rough pastureland.

Hawkshead   *Blelham Tarn:* 26 acres. *Dan Becks:* 154½ acres. *Green End:* 177 acres with a house near Colthouse and Latterbarrow. *Hawkshead Village:* 73½ acres and cottages, houses and other buildings, 4 cottages at Hawkshead Field and 68 acres on the W side of Esthwaite. *High and Low Loanthwaite Farms:* 163 acres. *High Wray and Tock How Farms:* 263 acres. *Low Wray Farm:* 385 acres. *North Fen:* 17 acres at NE edge of Esthwaite Water. *Round Parrock Wood:* 1 acre.

Hobcarton Crag   27½ acres on the face of the Crag.

Langdales   *Robinson Place Farm, Great Langdale:* 110 acres of farmland.

Lord Lonsdale's Commons   16,842 acres: all the high land from Seat Sandal to the Head of Great Langdale. The bed of Grasmere Lake and part of Rydal Water, White Moss and Elterwater Common. Leased from the 7th Earl of Lonsdale, the largest acquisition ever made in the Lake District.

Newlands Valley: High Snab Farm   4m SW of Keswick. 93 acres.

Sawrey   201 acres, including about half the village of Near Sawrey, 9 cottages, the Tower Bank estate, and a 1½-acre field. *Tower Bank Arms:* An inn adjacent to Hill Top.

Scafell Group   2,534 acres of the main range, including Scafell Pike, the highest mountain in England.

Silverdale   4m NW of Carnforth. *Castlebarrow:* 21 acres. *Eaves and Waterslack Woods:* 96 acres of wooded hill and 1 acre of Waterslack Quarry.

Silverthwaite, Loughrigg   Nr Ambleside. A house and 8 acres.

Solway Commons   On the S side of the Firth, 1,806 acres of common land, including 12m of coastline held on long lease.

Stockdale Moor   2,507½ acres, on which are enclosures and cairns.

Troutbeck   *Troutbeck Park Farm:* 1,968 acres, one of the most famous sheep farms of the Lake District.

Ullswater Valley   *Glencoyne Wood and Stybarrow Crag:* 4 acres of woodland and lakeshore. *Howe Green Farm:* 509 acres including 428 of fell grazing with 220 sheep.

Wasdale   *Burnthwaite Farm:* 632 acres with mineral and grazing rights over a large area already owned by the Trust. *Gill, Broadgap and Buckbarrow Farms:* 255 acres with flock of 507 sheep. *Harrowhead Farm:* 86 acres with 200 landlord's sheep and grazing rights on Nether Wasdale Common. *Land near Wastwater Hotel:* 11½ acres of grazing land. *Nether Wasdale:* 14 acres of farmland.

Wetheral Woods   On the left bank of the river Eden, 5m E of Carlisle. 6½ acres.

Windermere   *Ash Landing, Far Sawrey:* 2 fields of 6½ acres. *Moorhow:* 43 acres overlooking the lake.

DERBYSHIRE

Alport Height   4m NW of Belper, 2m SE of Wirksworth. 9 acres of hilltop, including a rock known as the Alport Stone.

Curbar Gap   ½m E of Curbar village, 2½m S of Padley. 8½ acres with fine view of the Derwent valley.

Duffield Castle   ½m N of Duffield station, on the W side of A6. 2½ acres. Foundations of the Norman keep, razed in 1266.

Eccles Pike   1½m W of Chapel-le-Frith. 6 acres on the summit.

Eyam: Riley Graves   ½m E of the village. Seven members of the Hancock family who died of the Plague in one week in August 1665 are buried on a steep hillside.

Longshaw Haywood   171 acres of pasture, moor and woodland linking Longshaw with Froggatt Wood. *White Edge Moor:* 124 acres of moorland on E of Sheffield Plantation.

Miller's Dale and Ravenstor   2m S of Tideswell, astride the river Wye. 64 acres.

Oatseats   1½m N of Hathersage. 116 acres of traditional farmland.

Shining Cliff Wood   Alderwasley, 4m N of Belper. 200 acres of woodland on the W bank of the Derwent.

Stanton Moor Edge 2m N of Winster, 4m SE of Bakewell. 32 acres, extending over $\frac{3}{4}$m and rising to over 900 ft.

Taddington Wood $1\frac{1}{2}$m E of Taddington. 49 acres of wooded slopes.

Winster: Market House 4m W of Matlock. Stone market house, late 17th or early 18th century.

DEVON

Bigbury-on-Sea: Clematon Hill On S side of B3992. 7 acres, views over the Avon to Bolt Tail.

Boringdon Gate Piers $\frac{1}{2}$m E Plym Bridge. 2 late-17th-century piers, once entrance to Boringdon House.

Burrough Farm, Northam E of Northam. 45 acres.

Clovelly *Beckland Cliffs:* 140 acres of cliff and farmland, including Windbury Point. *The Brownshams:* 4m E of Hartland. 297 acres of farmland and woods with 2 Tudor farmhouses. *Fatacott Cliff:* 153 acres, 4m W of Clovelly. *Mount Pleasant:* 1 acre, with a view over Bideford Bay.

Combe Park, Lynton $1\frac{1}{2}$m SE of Lynton, on W bank of the river Lynton. 45 acres of woodland.

Compton Castle: *Castle Barton:* 51 acres, immediately opposite the Castle. *Old Forge House:* Early 19th-century house with former smithy adjoining.

Damage Cliffs 3m W of Ilfracombe. 113 acres of hillocky cliffs.

Dunsland $4\frac{1}{2}$m E of Holsworthy, 9m W of Hatherleigh. 92 acres. The house, of Tudor origin and 17th-century alteration, was burnt down in 1967.

East Titchberry Farm 1m E of Hartland Point. 120 acres, including 1m of cliff, with ancient farmhouse.

Golden Cove, Berry Narbor W of Combe Martin. $10\frac{1}{2}$ acres of wooded cliff.

Hembury 2m N of Buckfastleigh, 1m S of A384. 374 acres on W side of the Dart valley. On top of the hill is Hembury Castle, an Iron Age hillfort. *Burchetts Wood and Beechwood Copse:* 25 acres of woodland.

Hentor, Willings Walls and Trowlesworthy Warren On the SW flank of Dartmoor. 3,333 acres of moor rising to 1,600 ft, with many prehistoric remains and an ancient farm.

Holne Woods On W bank of river Dart, 10m W of Newton Abbot. 165 acres, mainly of natural oak woods, along nearly $2\frac{1}{2}$m of the river.

Ilfracombe 262 acres of most of the coastal land from the outskirts of the town westward to the village of Lee.

Little Haldon 3m NW of Teignmouth. 43 acres of heathland.

Lydford Gorge: Bridge House Acquired with 12 acres to complete the Trust's holdings in the Gorge.

Lympstone 7m SE of Exeter. $6\frac{1}{2}$ acres on the E side of the river Exe.

Moretonhampstead Almshouses At E edge of the town. 17th-century granite buildings over an open colonnade.

Old Blundell's School, Tiverton Famous grammar school built in 1604. Moved in 1882 and the Old School converted into dwelling houses.

Orcombe and Prattshayes $2\frac{1}{2}$m ESE of Exmouth. 126 acres, comprising 1m of cliff, the foreshore E from the end of Exmouth parade, and the ancient house of Prattshayes in the valley behind.

Parke, Bovey Tracey 5m NW of Newton Abbot just outside Bovey Tracey. 205 acres of wooded valley of the river Bovey. 34 acres of woodland at Bearacleave. 6-acre Kathleen Wood.

Plym Bridge Woods 5m NE of Plymouth. 111 acres of the wooded valley of the river Plym.

Rockbeare Hill (Prickly Pear Blossoms Park) 3m W of Ottery St Mary. 22 acres of heath and woodland at the top of the hill.

Shute Barton 3m SW of Axminster, 2m N of Colyton. $15\frac{1}{2}$ acres. The remains of a manor house, partly 16th and partly 17th century. The gatehouse dates from about 1570, but was altered in about 1830.

Sidmouth 9½-acre field near the top of Peak Hill. 18½ acres of meadow.

Teign Valley Woods *Bridford Wood:* 3m NE of Moretonhampstead. 84 acres of oak-covered hillside above the right bank of the river Teign.

Westward Ho: Kipling Tors W of the town. 18 acres of gorse-covered hill, the scene of much of Kipling's *Stalky & Co.*

Wheal Betsy 5m N of Tavistock, just E of A386. Roofless engine house and chimneystack of an abandoned tin mine on Black Down.

Widecombe-in-the-Moor: Church House 6m NW of Ashburton. 15th-century granite building near the church, part used as village hall.

Withleigh 3m W of Tiverton. 139 acres in the valley of the river Dart.

DORSET

Bellevue Farm, Isle of Purbeck 2m W of Swanage. 51 acres of rough grazing above the cliffs.

Burton Cliff, Burton Bradstock 83½ acres of cliff and coastal land.

Coney's Castle 86 acres of hilltop with remains of an Iron Age hillfort.

Crook Hill, Beaminster 1m NE of Winyards Gap, 3m SE of Crewkerne. 6 acres.

Hardy Monument 6m SW of Dorchester. Erected in 1846 to Vice-Admiral Hardy, flag-captain of the *Victory* at Trafalgar.

Lambert's Castle Hill 4½m E of Axminster, on S side of B3165. 167 acres of hill and surrounding land, adjacent to Coney's Castle (q.v.).

Lewesdon Hill 3m W of Beaminster, ¼m W of B3162. 27 acres of the wooded summit.

Tolpuddle: Martyrs' Memorial A seat and green commemorating the labourers condemned to transportation in 1834.

West Bexington, Lime Kiln Hill 17 acres of former stone workings and rough grazing.

Winyard's Gap Above Chedington, 4m SE of Crewkerne. 16 acres of woodland.

DURHAM

Ebchester On R bank of the river Derwent, 12m SE of Newcastle. 10 acres of woodland.

Moorhouse Woods 3m NE of Durham. 59 acres of woodland beside the river Wear.

ESSEX

Blakes Wood 5m E of Chelmsford, just SW of Little Baddow. 83½ acres of woodland, mainly hornbeams and chestnut coppice.

Dedham: Bridges Farm Just W of the village. 79 acres.

Ray Island W of Mersea Island, off B1025, by Strood Channel. Salting and tidal creek, comprising 2½m of coastline.

Rayleigh Mount 6m NW of Southend. 4 acres. Mound the site of a Norman castle, abandoned in the 13th century.

Saffron Walden: Sun Inn Gabled building, the earliest part a hall-house, with 17th-century pargework. No longer an inn.

GLOUCESTERSHIRE

Bibury On the S side of A433. *Arlington Row:* A row of early-17th-century stone cottages. *Rack Isle:* A 4-acre field on the road opposite to the Row, bounded by water on three sides, where wool was hung on racks to dry.

Campden Properties *The Coneygree:* 13½ acres of meadow preserving the surroundings of the church. *Dover's Hill:* 181½ acres of a natural amphitheatre. Games were held on it from about 1612 until 1852.

Eden's Hill, Upleadon 2½m E of Newent, at S end of the village. 1½ acres.

Frocester Hill and Coaley Peak Near Nympsfield between Stroud and Dursley. 13 acres on the Cotswolds escarpment, of unusual botanical interest.

May Hill 9m W of Gloucester. 131½ acres with views over ten counties.

Newark Park 1½m E of Wotton-under-Edge. 643 acres of wooded and agricultural land.

Painswick: Little Fleece   A former public house, now a shop.

Stroud Properties   *Besbury Common:* 8 acres above Golden Valley. *Haresfield Beacon and Standish Wood:* 348 acres, including part of Randwick Wood, Ring Hill and Haresfield Beacon, possibly the site of Iron Age promontory fort. *Hyde Common:* 11 acres. *Minchinhampton Common:* adjoining Hyde Common, 580 acres of fine turf. *Rodborough Common:* 242 acres, including part of the site of a 1st-century enclosure. *Stockend and Maitland Woods:* 87½ acres. *Watledge Hill:* 4½ acres of common.

Wotton-under-Edge Properties   12½ acres of pastureland on the northern outskirts of Wotton-under-Edge. *Westridge Woods:* 43 acres of woodland.

GREATER MANCHESTER

Dunham Massey Park   3m W of Altrincham, S of B5160. Mainly 18th-century house with fine state rooms and original contents, and estate of 3,274 acres including a fine deer park. Bequeathed in 1977. Restoration work precludes opening the house until 1979–80.

HAMPSHIRE

Hamble River   1m below Botley at Curbridge. 74 acres of wood and agricultural land, including Harmsworth Row and Eyersdown Copse. A nature reserve.

Ludshott (Hampshire and Surrey)   *Bramshott Chase:* 60½ acres SE of Waggoners' Wells. *Ludshott Common and Waggoners' Wells:* 645 acres, including Kingswood Firs, Croaker's Patch and a string of hammerponds. *Passfield Common and Conford Moor:* 231 acres of common and woods.

Sparsholt: Vaine Cottages   3m W of Winchester. 2 thatched cottages.

Woolton Hill: The Chase   3m SW of Newbury. 131 acres of woodland threaded by a chalk stream; a nature reserve and a small farm.

HEREFORD & WORCESTER

Birmingham Properties   *Chadwich Manor Estate:* 432 acres, mainly agricultural and woodland on SW edge of Birmingham, including the manor house. *Cofton Hackett:* 44 acres of farmland, part of Birmingham's green belt. *Frankley Beeches:* 24½ acres, hilltop with a conspicuous group of beech trees. *Groveley Dingle:* 180 acres of wooded and agricultural land, mainly a bird sanctuary. *Sling Pool:* 4 acres in a small valley running down from the Clent Hills and a 1½-acre pool.

Breinton Springs   On left bank of river Wye. 14 acres of farm and woodland.

Brilley: Cwmma and Fernhall Farms   358 acres of farmland and woods, including 2 interesting timber-framed farmhouses and a small motte.

Clump Farm, Broadway   To S of A44, ½m SE of Broadway. 85 acres of farmland on the Cotswolds escarpment.

Hawford Dovecote, Hawford Grange   1m S of Ombersley. 16th-century timber-framed dovecote.

Knowles Mill   1½m NW of Bewdley, on S side of Dowles Brook. Set in 4 acres of orchard.

Pengethly Park   4m W of Ross on N side of A49. 118 acres of farm and woodlands.

Poor's Acre   1½m W of Woolhope, 6m SE of Hereford. 17½ acres of roadside land in the middle of Haugh Wood.

The Weir, Swainshill   5m W of Hereford, on A338. 254 acres, 18th-century house. Steep river-bank garden.

Worcester Greyfriars   Mainly late-15th-century, timber-framed and tiled house with early-17th- and 18th-century additions.

HERTFORDSHIRE

Barkway: Berg Cottage   At S end of the village, 4m S of Royston. A small thatched house, bearing the date 1687, also 2 modern cottages.

Morven Park   ½m N of Potters Bar on E side of A1000. A Victorian house and 36 acres.

ISLE OF WIGHT

Borthwood Copse 2m W of Sandown, ½m N of A3056. 57 acres of wood and field on Pheasants Hill.

St Helen's *St Helen's Common:* 9½ acres and a cottage, 1m NW of Bembridge. *St Helen's Duver:* 30 acres consisting of a side spit of sand and shingle.

Ventnor *Littleton and Luccombe Downs:* 12½ acres of the crest of the ridge, and 92 acres of the crest of the high down behind the town. *St Boniface Down:* 221 acres of downland rising to the highest point on the island.

KENT

Appledore: Hallhouse Farm 8½m NW of New Romney. Late 15th-century yeoman farmer's house with 6½ acres of pasture.

Crockham Hill *Grange Farm:* 2m S of Westerham, on NE side of B2069. 296 acres. *Close Farm:* Stone and tile-hung farmhouse, ½m E of Crockham Hill.

Emmetts 1½m S of A25 on Sundridge road. 104 acres. A house, 60 acres of farmland, woodland and a 4-acre shrub garden.

Gover Hill 1m W of W Peckham, 3m SE of Ightham. Hilltop of 1½ acres.

Harbledown: Golden Hill 1m W of Canterbury, just off A2. 2½ acres. Children's playground.

Ide Hill 2½m S of Brasted, 1m E of Toys Hill. 32 acres of wooded hillside overlooking the Weald.

Loose: Wool House 3m S of Maidstone, ¼m W of the Cranbrook road. A 15th-century half-timbered house, formerly used for the cleaning of wool.

Mariner's Hill 1½m S of Westerham. 26½ acres with views across the Weald.

Old Soar Manor 2m S of Borough Green. The solar block of a late-13th-century knight's dwelling.

One Tree Hill 2m SE of Sevenoaks, on E side of Knole Park. 34 acres containing a Roman cemetery on the summit of the hill.

Parson's Marsh 1½m S of Brasted. 18½ acres of woodland.

Scord's Wood 2m S of Brasted, W of Ide Hill. 61 acres.

Sole Street: Tudor Yeoman's House 1m SW of Cobham, on W side of B2009. A 16th-century house of timber construction.

Sprivers 3m N of Lamberhurst, just off B2162. 108 acres of parkland, orchard and woods with 18th–century house.

Wrotham Water 1½m E of Wrotham, on S side of the Pilgrims' Way. 260 acres of mainly arable land at the foot of the Downs. *Great and Little Spratts:* 11½ acres on N boundary of the above property. *Hognore Farm:* 64 acres on the lower slopes of the Downs.

LANCASHIRE

Stubbins W of Stubbins, 5m N of Bury, 1m N of Ramsbottom. 436 acres, including 8 farms and 6 cottages.

Calf of Man SW of the Isle of Man. 616 acres, an important nature reserve with seals and large breeding colonies of seabirds. Farm buildings, 2 ruined lighthouses.

LEICESTERSHIRE

Balston: The Thomas Balston Collection of Victorian Staffordshire Figures On show at Stapleford Park, not a Trust property.

LINCOLNSHIRE

Gunby Hall 1,400 acres, including 15 farms. House built in 1700. Associations with the poet, Tennyson.

LONDON

97–100 Cheyne Walk, Chelsea Most of Lindsey House, one of the finest 17th–century exteriors in London, built in 1674 on the site of Sir Thomas More's garden.

Chislehurst *Camden Court Land:* A strip of land by the roadside with row of lime trees, part of a scheme to preserve Chislehurst Common, together with a strip at the top of Station Hill.

Eastbury House, Barking In Eastbury Square, off Tudor Road. Red-brick, H-plan manor house, dating from 1572, in centre of a modern housing estate.

East Sheen Common Adjoining Richmond Park on the N, just S of A305. 53 acres.

Hawkwood Between Chislehurst and Orpington. 245 acres of farmland and woods adjoining the Petts Wood property.

33 Kensington Square On W side. Built 1695. Mrs Patrick Campbell lived here.

Petts Wood Between Chislehurst and Orpington, on W side of A208. 88 acres of wood and heath.

40, 42 and 44 Queen Anne's Gate, Westminster Part of a street of early-18th-century houses. The headquarters of the National Trust.

Rainham Hall Just S of the church, 5m E of Barking. 2 acres. Built about 1729 in red brick with stone dressing. Contemporary wrought iron gates and panelling.

'Roman' Bath, 5 Strand Lane The remains of a bath, restored in the 17th century. Its origin is disputed by experts.

Selsdon Wood 3m SE of Croydon, ½m SE of Selsdon (B268). 198½ acres.

Squire's Mount, Hampstead On SW side of the Heath. A group of late-18th-century buildings and 1½ acres of land.

Sutton House, Hackney 2 and 4 Homerton High Street. The house dates from early in the 16th century and contains panelling of various periods.

Wandle Properties *Happy Valley:* 2 acres on W bank of the river Wandle known as Happy Valley. *Merton Abbey Wall:* Running from Colliers Wood. *Morden Hall:* 124 acres, including the hall, cottage and 17 houses. The park is intersected by the river. *Wandle Park:* 2 acres, known as Millpond Gardens behind the Royal Six Bells Inn near the Abbey Wall. *Watermeads Nature Reserve:* 12 acres on the W bank of the Wandle with secluded walks.

NORFOLK

Bale Oaks In the village, 8m NE of Fakenham, 5m S of Blakeney. A group of ilexes, close to the village church.

Bullfer Grove 4½m SW of Holt. 8½ acres of woodland.

Cawston The duelling stone, and the plot on which it stands, close to the old Woodrow Inn on the Norwich–Holt road, set up near the spot where Sir Henry Hobart of Blickling Hall received fatal injuries in a duel in 1698.

Horsey 2½m NE of Potter Heigham, 11m N of Yarmouth. 1,734 acres including Horsey Mere, marshes and marrams (a further 600 acres), Horsey Hall and farmland. A breeding ground for marsh birds, insects and plants. Drainage wind-pump built in 1912 on the foundations of an older mill.

King's Lynn: St George's Guildhall Built early in the 15th century for the Guild of St George, it was long put to theatrical use, to which it has now been restored.

Salthouse Broad 1½m NE of Cley. 29 acres of marsh and shingle known as Arnold's Marsh. Nature reserve adjunct to Blakeney Point.

West Runton ¾m S of West Runton station, between Sheringham and Cromer. 71 acres, known locally as the Roman Camp, the highest point in Norfolk. The site of iron-working in Saxo-medieval times. *Beeston Regis Heath:* 37 acres of heath.

NORTHAMPTONSHIRE

Brackley Park 3 acres of open space on E side of High Street, Brackley.

Easton-on-the-Hill: Priest's House Pre-Reformation priest's lodge.

NORTHUMBERLAND

Beadnell Lime Kilns   ½m SE of Beadnell, 2½m S of Seahouses. A group of 18th-century lime kilns by the sea.

Bellister, Haltwhistle   1,122 acres, including Bellister Castle and pele tower, cottages in Park village, three farms and portions of the South Tyne river.

Druridge Bay   2m N of Cresswell village, 1½m E of A1068. A mile of coastline, consisting of 99 acres of sand dunes and grass hinterland.

Lady's Well   At Holystone, 7m W of Rothbury. Traditionally associated with St Ninian.

Newton Links   S of Long Nanny in Beadnell Bay. 55 acres of dunes and rough grazing.

St Aidan's and Shoreston Dunes   2m SE of Bamburgh, E of B1340. 60 acres of sand dunes, with views of the Farne Islands.

Wylam-on-Tyne: George Stephenson's Cottage   8m W of Newcastle. The 18th-century birthplace of the inventor.

NOTTINGHAMSHIRE

Colston Bassett: Market Cross   10m SE of Nottingham, 5m S of Bingham. 18th-century square head, surmounted by a ball, with Doric shaft on medieval base.

OXFORDSHIRE

Aston Wood   1½m NW of Stokenchurch, astride A40. 104 acres of beechwood on an escarpment of the Chilterns.

Buscot: The Old Parsonage   In Buscot village. Early-18th-century house and 10 acres.

Coombe End Farm   On W side of B471, 2½m N of Pangbourne. 213 acres of agricultural land and a partly 17th-century house.

Kencot Manor Farm   5m S of Burford, 1½m E of A361. Small early 17th-century house with 2½ acres.

Ruskin Reserve, Cothill   3m NW of Abingdon. 4½ acres of marshy woodland.

South Leigh: Little Bartletts   2½m E of Witney. 2 17th-century cottages with 1 acre.

Steventon: Priory Cottages   4m S of Abingdon, ¼m W of A34. Part of former monastic buildings, converted into two houses.

Trip-the-Daisy, Idstone   1m S of Ashbury. Small 17th-century house, formerly a public house, named after a successful greyhound.

SALOP

Dudmaston Hall   3m SE of Bridgnorth, off A442. Early 18th-century house, with some later Georgian decoration. Landscaped park with 2,000 acres of farmland and woods.

Hopesay Hill   3m W of Craven Arms. 131 acres.

Morville Hall   3¼m W of Bridgnorth on A458, 5½m SE of Much Wenlock. 134 acres and an Elizabethan house converted in the 18th century, when the projecting wings were added.

Shrewsbury: Town Walls Tower   The last remaining watch-tower, overlooking the Severn on S side of the town.

SOMERSET

Blackdown Hills   2m S of Wellington. 61 acres with views over the Vale of Taunton to Exmoor and the Quantocks.

Brean Down   2m SW of Weston-super-Mare. A bold headland 159 acres in extent, the S arm of Weston Bay.

Cheddar Cliffs   8m NW of Wells. 318 acres, including the Lion and Monkey Rocks.

Glastonbury Tor   E of Glastonbury on N side of A361. 62½ acres. Conical hill surmounted by a 15th-century tower, all that remains of two superimposed churches.

King John's Hunting Lodge, Axbridge   A merchant's house, built about 1500 in the middle of the town.

Muchelney: Priest's House $1\frac{1}{2}$m S of Langport. Late medieval house with large Gothic hall window.

The Quantocks *Holford Fields:* $22\frac{1}{2}$ acres of pasture and orchard, 3m W of Nether Stowey. *Longstone Hill:* 61 acres of open moorland adjoining Willoughby Cleeve. *Shervage Wood:* 136 acres of oak coppice and wood and moorland. *Willoughby Cleeve:* $77\frac{1}{2}$ acres of woodland, agricultural land and moorland.

Sedgemoor and Athelney *Burrow Mump:* $9\frac{1}{2}$ acres of isolated hill, crowned by an unfinished 18th-century chapel joined to a ruined medieval one. *Cock Hill:* $\frac{3}{4}$ acre on crest of Polden Hills. *Ivythorn and Walton Hills:* $88\frac{1}{2}$ acres of highland and wood. *Red Hill:* $2\frac{1}{2}$ acres of hilltop. *Turn Hill:* $1\frac{1}{4}$ acres looking across the battlefield of Sedgemoor.

Stoke-sub-Hamdon Priory N of A3088, 2m W of Montacute. 2 acres. 14th- and 15th-century building, once the residence of the chantry priests of St Nicholas in the vanished manor-house near by.

Wells: Tor Hill E of the city, on E side of A371. $19\frac{1}{2}$ acres.

West Pennard Court Barn 3m E of Glastonbury, 7m S of Wells. 15th-century barn of 5 bays with roof of interesting construction.

STAFFORDSHIRE

Hawksmoor: Gibridding Wood 39 acres.

SUFFOLK

Bury St Edmunds: *Angel Corner* Queen Anne house on Angel Hill. Gershom–Parkington collection of clocks and watches.

Dunwich Heath 214 acres of sandy cliffs and heathland with a mile of beach, including a row of coastguard cottages and foreshore below high-water mark.

Flatford Mill and Willy Lott's Cottage On N bank of the Stour, 1m S of East Bergholt. 16 acres including the mill, one of the watermills belonged to John Constable's father and dates from the 15th century. Subject of some of his most famous paintings. *Judas Gap Marsh:* $5\frac{1}{2}$ acres. *Valley Farm:* 17 acres and a half-timbered 15th-century building.

Kyson Hill $\frac{3}{4}$m S of Woodbridge, 1m E of junction of A12 and B1438. 4 acres of parkland overlooking the river Deben.

Outney Common, Bungay 6 'goings', or rights of pasturage, over 495 acres of common.

Thorington Hall 2m SE of Stoke-by-Nayland on N side of B1068. Oak-framed, plastered, gabled house, dating from 1600, extended in 1700 and repaired in 1937.

SURREY

Abinger Roughs Just N of Abinger Hammer, $4\frac{1}{2}$m W of Dorking. 267 acres. A wooded ridge with the adjoining Hackhurst Farm. *Piney Copse:* $4\frac{1}{2}$-acre wood.

Blackheath $\frac{1}{2}$m S of Chilworth and Albury station. $19\frac{1}{2}$ acres of heather and pine-clad land.

Bletchingley: Sandhills Estate 3m E of Reigate. 430 acres of agricultural land and woods.

Bookham and Banks Commons $2\frac{1}{2}$m W of Leatherhead, just N of Bookham station. 447 acres of richly wooded common, with a cottage and roadside verges in Little Bookham. Manorial rights in Great Bookham Common. Handley Cottage and 2 acres.

Brockham: The Big Field An open field of 48 acres.

Cobham: Cedar House On N side of A245. 15th-century building, altered and enlarged in the 17th and 18th centuries.

Eashing Bridge and Cottages $\frac{1}{2}$m W of Godalming, just E of Guildford bypass. A double bridge over the river Wey and a tributary, said to be 13th-century. 2 cottages.

Ewell: Hatch Furlong $1\frac{1}{2}$m NE of Epsom station, $\frac{1}{2}$m SW of Nonesuch Park. 6 acres of field in a built-up area.

Frensham Common Astride A287. 958 acres of heathland, including most of Frensham Great Pond and the Little Pond. On the crest of the common is a line of large bowl barrows.

Gatton 1½m NE of Reigate, just N of A242. 212½ acres on the N slopes of the North Downs.

Godalming: 116-122 Ockford Road Old cottages, now modernized.

Guildford: Weir House 18th-century building, with additions in the 19th century, overlooking the river Wey at Millmead.

Hackhurst Down ½m NE of Gomshall and Shere station. 13 acres, part of a local nature reserve, on the S slope of the North Downs.

Hambledon 2½ acres near the church. *Glebe House:* with 7 cottages and 24 acres.

Harewoods At Outwood, 3m SE of Redhill, 2m E of Salfords. 2,048 acres. Farms, woods and cottages and including Outwood Common.

Headley Heath 4m S of Epsom, 3½m SE of Leatherhead on W side of B2033. 482 acres of open space, including the lordship of Headley Manor.

Holmwood Common 1m S of Dorking on both sides of A24. 632 acres of common land.

Hydon's Ball and Hydon Heath 3m S of Godalming, 1½m W of B2130. 125 acres of heath and woodland.

Limpsfield Common 350 acres including West Heath, The Chart, Little Heath and Moorhouse Bank Common.

Little King's Wood 60 acres of mixed woodland.

Netley Park At E end of Shere, on both sides of A25. 211 acres including a house, farm, cottages and woodlands.

Park Downs 1m SE of Banstead, overlooking the Chipstead valley. Common rights over an open space of 74 acres.

Ranmore Common 2m NW of Dorking, adjoining the S boundary of the Polesden Lacey estate. 472 acres of wooded common. *Denbies, Hillside:* 245 acres on S slopes of N Downs.

Reigate Between Reigate and Banstead Heath. 149½ acres of down, copse and beechwood on the summit and escarpment of the North Downs.

Sandhills Common ½m W of Witley station, W of A283. 11½ acres.

Six Brothers' Field ½m S of Chaldon, midway between Caterham and Merstham. 7 acres used as a sports ground.

Stony Jump 1m E of Churt, 3m NW of Hindhead. Heather hill of 37 acres.

Swan Barn Farm On E edge of Haslemere, N of B2131. 38 acres of farmland and 28 acres of woodland.

Thursley: John Freeman Memorial 8 acres protecting the church, a memorial to the poet buried in the churchyard.

Witley and Milford Commons Between A3 and A286, ½m SW of Milford. 377 acres of common with a warden's cottage.

Woldingham: South Hawke 4½ acres of down and woodland. *Hanging Wood:* 4½ acres on S slope of North Downs.

SUSSEX

East Sussex

Battle: Lake Meadow Opposite the Chequers Hotel. 4½ acres.

Ditchling Beacon 6m N of Brighton, the NE slope. 4 acres with wide views and traces of the rampart and ditch of a hillfort.

Exceat Saltings S of Exceat Bridge, on W bank of the Cuckmere river. 4½ acres.

Fairlight 4½m E of Hastings. 228 acres, including Old Marsham Farm and 58 acres of cliffland.

Nap Wood 4m S of Tunbridge Wells on A267. 107 acres, predominantly oak woods, a nature reserve.

Telscombe 3m NW of Newhaven, 1½m N of Peacehaven. The manor-house with garden in the village and 10 acres protecting the skyline.

Wych Cross: The Warren 2½m S of Forest Row, just E of A22. 15 acres of woodland.

Bosham: Quay Meadow   4m W of Chichester, 1m S of A27. 1 acre between the church and the creek.

Drovers Estate   Astride A286, N of the Goodwood estate. 1,058 acres of farms, woods and agricultural land and including 9 acres of disused railway line.

Durford Heath   2½m NE of Petersfield, on S side of A3. 62 acres.

Lavington Common   1m W of Petworth. 77 acres of heather and pine-covered land, with 4 round barrows.

Marley (Sussex and Surrey)   *Kingsley Green Common:* 7 acres. *Marley Common and Wood:* 132 acres of high common and steep woodland. *Marley Coombe:* 19 acres. *Marley Heights:* 1½ acres of a viewpoint known as the Terraces. *Shottermill Ponds:* 13 acres, including 2 hammer ponds.

Newtimber Hill   Between Pyecombe and Poynings, 5m NW of Brighton. 238 acres of down and woodland.

Selsfield Common   4m SW of East Grinstead on E side of B2028. 7 acres.

Shoreham Gap   2m NE of Shoreham. 596 acres of down, with the remains of an extensive Iron Age/Romano-British field system.

Sullington Warren   ½m E of Storrington, 8m N of Worthing. 28 acres with views of North and South Downs, straddled by two lines of bowl barrows.

Terwick: Church Field   ¾m E of Rogate. 10 acres, adjoining the church.

Warren Hill   8m N of Worthing, astride A283. 243 acres, including Washington Common, a farm, a house and 8 cottages.

West Wittering: East Head   On E side of Chichester Harbour entrance. 76 acres, comprising 53 acres of dunes and saltings and 23 acres of beach.

Woolbeding   2m NW of Midhurst. 1,102 acres. An agricultural estate with 400 acres of common.

TYNE & WEAR

Penshaw Monument   Halfway between Sunderland and Chester-le-Street, E of A138. A Doric temple built in 1844, commemorating the 1st Earl of Durham.

WARWICKSHIRE

Earlswood Moat House   On S edge of Birmingham, 1m E of Eastwood Lakes station. Small, timber-framed house, mainly of the late 15th century, with 65 acres.

Farnborough Hall   6m N of Banbury, W of A423. 389 acres, 18th-century house and grounds, with terrace, temples and an obelisk.

WEST MIDLANDS

Knowle: Children's Field   9m SE of Birmingham, between Kixley Lane and Knowle church. 3-acre field for games.

WILTSHIRE

Cley Hill   3m W of Warminster on N side of A362. 66 acres. A chalk hill 800 ft high, on which is an Iron Age hillfort, within it 2 bowl barrows.

Holt: The Courts   3m E of Bradford-on-Avon. The house has a façade dating from 1700 and an attractive garden.

Lockeridge Dene   3m W of Marlborough, 1m S of A4. *Lockeridge Dene:* 12 acres of agricultural land, on which are examples of sarsen stones, known as the Grey Wethers. *Piggle Dene:* 9 acres, with more Grey Wethers.

Salisbury   *Joiners Hall:* Timber façade of former hall of a livery company.

Stonehenge Down   1–3m W of Amesbury, at junction of A303 and A360. 1,438 acres of farmland, but including the Cursus and half the Avenue, around – but not including – Stonehenge itself.

Warminster: Boreham Field   6 acres.

Westwood Manor 1½m SW of Bradford-on-Avon. 59½ acres. A stone, late-15th-century manor house, altered in 1610.

White Barrow ¾m S of Tilshead, 7m NW of Stonehenge. 3 acres, with a Neolithic long barrow.

Win Green Hill 5m SE of Shaftesbury, ½m NE of B3081. 38 acres, the highest point in Cranbourne Chase.

YORKSHIRE

North Yorkshire

Braithwaite Hall 1½m SW of Middleham, 2m E of A169. 748 acres of moor and farmland. The house, now a farmhouse, dates from the 17th century.

Bransdale 8m N of Helmsley, S of Bransdale Moor. 1,900 acres, comprising 12 small farms in a remote dale between the moors.

Brimham Moor and Rocks 8m SW of Ripon, approached from B6265. 362 acres of moorland.

East Scar Top Farm In Wensleydale, 1m SE of Bainbridge. 288 acres, from the valley to the top of Addleborough.

Hudswell *Calfhall, Round Howe and Billybank Woods:* 94 acres on the S bank of the Swale, between Richmond and Hudswell. *Hag Wood:* 40 acres west of Richmond.

Moulton Hall 5m E of Richmond. 25 acres. The house was rebuilt about 1650 with fine carved staircase.

Ripon: Sanctuary Cross At Sharow, ½m E of Ripon station. The stump of the only surviving cross marking the limits of sanctuary attached to St Wilfrid's Abbey.

Robin Hood's Bay: Rocket Post Field 12 acres of coastal land and cliff purchased for Enterprise Neptune in 1976.

Saltwick Nab 1m E of Whitby. 7½ acres of cliffland, including a low rocky headland.

Stainforth Bridge 2½m N of Settle, just W of B6479. 17th-century, single-span bridge over the river Ribble.

West Yorkshire

Hebden Dale *Gibson Wood:* 44 acres of woodland along the W bank of Hebden Water. *Hardcastle Crags:* 214 acres of woods along the N bank of Hebden Water with the famous Crags and woods in the Crimsworth Dean valley. *High Greenwood Wood and Black Dean:* 112 acres, with 3 small farms and fine woods.

Wales

CLWYD

Glyn Ceiriog 8m NW of Oswestry. 5 acres of meadow and 5 acres of the Glyn Valley tramway, now a public walk.

Graig Fawr, Dyserth 61½ acres, including a limestone hill, a smallholding and a site of special scientific interest.

Llangollen: Velvet Hill 76 acres above the road from Llangollen to the Horseshoe Pass.

DYFED

Caerllan Farm, Cwmtydi 73-acre farm with 880 yds of coastline on the E side of Cwmtydi Inlet.

Dolaucothi At Pumpsaint between Llanwrda and Lampeter. 2,577 acres of farm and woodland, with an ancient gold mine, the Dolaucothi Arms and several cottages in Pumpsaint.

Lawrenny A 71-acre hanging wood on E side of Castle Reach of the river Claddau.

Little Milford   On Western Cleddau, 3m S of Haverfordwest. 72 acres of woodland with three houses.
Lydstep Headland   4m SW of Tenby, 1½m E of Manorbier. 54 acres of headland.
Manorbier Bay: Manorbier Cliff   48 acres.
Ponterwyd: Bryn Bras   12m E of Aberystwyth, just S of A44. 234 acres. A typical Cardiganshire sheep farm, above the magnificent gorge of the Rheidol.
Tregoning Hill   On E headland of Towy estuary, 1m S of Ferryside. 20 acres of cliffland.

GWENT

Betws Newydd   4m N of Usk, 4m W of Raglan. *Coed-y-Bwynydd:* 25-acre hilltop with views of the Usk valley.
Skirrid Fawr   3m NE of Abergavenny, 1½m E of A465. 205 acres of the summit.

GWYNEDD

Aberglaslyn Pass   Extending S for 1½m from Beddgelert on both sides of the pass. 517 acres.
Cadair Ifan Goch   On E side of the Conwy valley, 3m N of Llanrwst. A rocky promontory of 1½ acres.
Cae Glan-y-Mor   On the Menai Strait between road and railway bridges. 7 acres.
Cemaes   On E side of Cemaes Bay. 51 acres of agricultural and cliffland.
Coedydd Maentwrog   203 acres. A steep wooded valleyside in the Vale of Ffestiniog.
Conwy: Aberconwy   At the junction of Castle Street and High Street. A survivor of one of the late medieval houses with which Conwy once abounded.
Derlwyn   2m NW of Ganllwyd, 6m NW of Dolgellau. 114½ acres of rough heather moorland with half a small lake.
Dinas Gynfor   2m NE of Cemaes, 5m W of Amlwch. The northernmost point of Wales: 4½ acres of cliffland, part of the site of an Iron Age fort.
Dinas Oleu   Above Barmouth at its S end. 4½ acres of cliffland, the first property acquired by the Trust, given in 1895.
Dolobran and Braich-Melyn   1m NW of Dinas Mawddwy, just N of A458. 2 Welsh mountain farms, good examples of traditional architecture, with 120 acres and rights of pasturage over a further 121 acres.
Gamallt   3m NE of Ffestiniog. 300 acres of moorland with half of 2 lakes.
Harlech: Allt-y-Mor   1m S of Harlech on A496. 1½ acres with footpaths to the sea. *Coed Llechwedd:* 11 acres with view over the bay.
Llanrwst: Tu Hwnt i'r Bont   At W end of the old bridge over the Conwy, on A496. 15th-century building once used as a courthouse.
Lledr Valley: Rhiw Goch   On road between Betws-y-Coed and Dolwyddelan. 163 acres with view over the valley.
Morfa Bychan   1¼m SW of Portmadoc. 85 acres. Golf course and sand dunes with about ½m of seashore.
Penartynydd, Rhiw   245 acres of agricultural land and rough clifftop grazing, with magnificent views of Lleyn coast.
Plas-yn-Rhiw Estate   On S coast of Lleyn in parishes of Rhiw, Llanfaelrhys, Aberdaron, Llanengan and Llanbedrog. *Manor House:* Part-medieval house with late Tudor and Georgian features. Garden and woodland extending to the shore. *Tan-Yr-Ardd with Penmynydd:* Small traditional cottage with 19½ acres of moorland. *Aberdaron:* 9 acres of cliffland W of Porth Orion. *Llanengan:* Mynydd Cilan, 67 acres of cliff. *Foel Felin Wynt:* 6 acres NW of Mynytho. *Mynydd-y-Graig:* 188 acres on W side of Porth Neigwl. *Penrallt Neigwl:* 17th-century farmhouse with 9 acres. *Llain-y-Morfa:* 1 acre adjoining the sandhills. *Mynydd Bach:* 12 acres, part of the W headland of Porth Neigwl. *Penarfynydd:* 244 acres of agricultural land and rough hilltop grazing.
Rhyd   3m NW of Maentwrog. 114 acres of enclosed mountain with fine views over Tremadog Bay.
Tywyn-y-Fach, Abersoch   On NE outskirts of Abersoch, 6m SW of Pwllheli. 19 acres of sandhills covered with scrub and bracken.

Ynysgain 1m W of Criccieth. 198 acres comprising about 1m of coastland and foreshore including the mouth of the Afon Dwyfor.

Ynys Towyn On SE side of Portmadoc. 2 acres. A small rocky knoll with fine views.

Ysbyty Estate 41,727 acres in 3 different areas (for Penrhyn Castle see p. 160, and for the Carneddau area – 15,860 acres – see p. 536). *Ty Mawr:* The birthplace of Bishop William Morgan, the first translator of the Bible into Welsh. *Ysbyty Ifan:* 25,820 acres of beautiful hills and valleys chiefly W of Ysbyty village, marginal farms and moorland, with Llyn Conwy.

POWYS

Brecon Beacons *Cwmoergwn* 3m S of Llanfrynach. 93 acres of farmland at head of mountain valley. *Cwm sere:* 42 acres.

Henrhyd Falls and Graigllech Woods 11m NE of Neath, just N of Coelbren. 26 acres of deep wooded ravine and the famous waterfalls.

Northern Ireland

CO. ANTRIM

Collin Glen 39 acres on the western outskirts of Belfast.

Fair Head and Murlough Bay 3m E of Ballycastle. 764 acres. One of the most beautiful coastal areas in Northern Ireland.

Layde Cushendun–Cushendall coastal path leading from car park to small beach.

North Antrim Cliff Path 10m right of way from the Giant's Causeway to Ballintoy. 104 acres, including Dunseverick harbour.

Templetown Mausoleum, Templepatrick Designed by Robert Adam and built in 1783.

CO. ARMAGH

Ballymoyer 4m NE of Newtown Hamilton, 8m W of Newry. 49 acres of wooded glen.

CO. DOWN

Ballymacormick Point 1–3m NE of Bangor. 40 acres of rough land on the shore of Belfast Lough.

Blockhouse Island and Green Island 2 islands lying off Cranfield and Greencastle at the mouth of Carlingford Lough, important nesting site for terns.

Cockle Island About ½ acre. Restricted access during nesting season from May to July.

Kearney and Knockinelder 3m E of Portaferry. 31 acres of foreshore and 4 acres of village land with 13 houses at Kearney. 8 acres of beach at Knockinelder adjoining, making 2m of accessible coastline.

Killynether 1m SW of Newtownards. 43 acres, mostly woodland.

Lighthouse Island, Copeland Islands 3m off the mouth of Belfast Lough. 43-acre island with a bird observatory.

Lisnabreeny 2m S of Belfast. 156 acres of farmland, including a glen and waterfall.

Minnowburn Beeches 3½m S of central Belfast. 128 acres on the banks of the Lagan and Minnowburn rivers.

Mourne Coastal Path 58½ acres along the sea from Bloody Bridge.

CO. LONDONDERRY

Rough Fort 1m W of Limavady, on A2. An unexcavated rath or ring fort of 1 acre, surrounded by trees.

Picture Credits

The letters (a) and (b) after the page numbers represent, respectively, illustrations on the left and right of a page.

The National Trust and the publishers are grateful to those agencies, institutions and photographers holding copyright who gave permission to reproduce items in their collections.

Picture research by Rosemary Joekes and Quenelda Avery.

A & C Photography, Belfast   51, 74, 77, 78, 112, 151(a), 151(b), 190, 386(a), 386(b)
Aerofilms Ltd   66, 126, 140, 158, 324, 347, 352, 399, 403, 477, 498, 499
Paddy Aiken   382
W. K. Andrew   387
Archway Publicity   535(a), 535(b)
Associated Press   179

Barnaby's Library   484
R. Belton   **Col.** Nymans garden
Benham & Co.   371(a), 371(b)
Tony Bentley   540
Geoffrey Berry   503
John Bethell   49, 53, 54, 64, 71, 88, 107(a), 107(b), 113, 116, 125, 128, 141, 155, 156, 167, 172, 193, 208, 209(a), 209(b), 219, 220(a), 220(b), 240, 292, 298, 339(a), 342, 345, 350(a), 350(b), 352, 406, 487, 489, 490.   **Col.** Ashdown, Erddig Montacute, Saltram, Malvern Hills
Raymond Blain   485
G. Douglas Bourlton   511
J. Brightmore   **Col.** Clumber Park
British Tourist Authority   277, 315, 333, 510
Alec Brooke   447
Stewart Burness   455
T. P. Burr   117, 276, 314, 333
Peter Burton   54, 135, 249, 341, 359, 529, 531

J. Allan Cash   400, 431, 486, 545
Central Office of Information   541
Robert Chapman   4, 327
Dr Chard   148
Cheshire Life   198
A. C. Cooper   110
Country Life   58, 153, 155, 174, 330
Courtauld Institute   44, 45(b), 47(a), 47(b)
John Cranham   512(a), 512(b)
Marcus Crouch   186, 383

W. F. Davidson   **Col.** Lacock village
Jerome Dessain & Co.   24
J. Arthur Dixon   244

J. Dixon-Scott   322
J. E. Downward   243

Eastern County Newspapers   372

J. Farrow   **Col.** Little Moreton Hall
Forestry Commission   528

Leonard and Marjorie Gayton   251, 299, 354, 401, 475, 518, 538, 539
John Gibbons   514
Gibson & Sons   448

Christopher Hanson   91, 183, 316.   **Col.** Derwentwater
Hawkley Studio Associates   132(a), 132(b), 144, 185.   **Col.** Smallhythe
R. E. Hillgrove   **Col.** Glendurgan
Wendell Holmes   465, 521
G. Leslie Horn   376
Angelo Hornak   101, 191
Nicholas Horne   470
Cyril Howe   102

O. G. Jarman   303
W. T. Jones   288

M. W. Keen Ltd   515
P. J. Kenworthy   116, 378, 380
A. F. Kersting   55, 59, 69, 82, 110, 136, 161, 163, 170, 175, 181, 182(a), 182(b), 187(b), 258, 262, 281, 288(b), 290, 302, 332, 339(b), 341(b), 349, 351, 375, 458, 461, 462, 469, 502, 504, 522, 524, 525
Olive Kitson   370, 491, 492(a), 492(b)

Leith-Air Ltd   45(a)

Eric de Maré   194, 211(a), 211(b), 284
Jeremy McCabe   157
Elsa Megson   **Col.** Wakehurst Place

National Monuments Record   43, 105, 295, 317, 323, 327
National Trust   70, 90, 93, 105, 121, 142, 144, 162, 179(a), 179(b), 187(a), 199, 201, 202, 203, 210, 246, 247, 261, 274, 283(b), 285, 289, 300, 313, 320, 321, 327, 331, 351, 355, 368, 379, 385, 411, 412, 413, 456, 472, 478, 480, 493, 497, 500, 516, 534, 542, 542(a), 548.   **Col.** Plas Newydd (jacket), Cliveden, Houghton
National Trust, Waddesdon Manor   212(a), 212(b)
Nature Conservancy   517
S. W. Newbury   43
Iver Nicholas   226
Doris Nicholson   **Col.** Hidcote
D. Nobbs & Son   188
Alan North   518   **Col.** Castle Coole, Mussenden Temple, Holnicote Estate, Malham Tarn, Carrick-a-rede, Giant's Causeway
Northern Ireland Tourist Board   541
Nottingham County Surveyor's Department   291

Sheila Orme   319

Park Pictures   415
A. E. McR. Pearse   319
Kinney Watters Perry   377(a), 377(b)
Philipson Studio   202
Photo Precision Ltd   77, 325
Paul Popper   489

Derek Powell   279
Peter Pritchard   343
C. M. Radcliffe   Col. Killerton, Carneddau the Glyders, Carneddau Nant Ffran-
   con Pass
John Rea   62
George Roper   412
Royal Academy   46

Salisbury Journal   275
Sanderson & Dixon Ltd   505
Jack Scheerboom   282
Kenneth Scowen   438
Vernon D. Shaw   197, 433.   Col. The Cloud Congleton, Mam Tor
The late Edwin Smith   51, 57, 73, 85(a), 85(b), 98, 99, 103, 120, 131, 160, 165,
   165(b), 166, 224, 237, 238, 253, 255, 318, 328, 347(b), 348, 379, 405
J. Spouge   115
Studio Jon   532
W. Suschitzki   335

Graham S. Thomas   258
Leslie F. Thomas   241
The Times   60
Tourist Information Centre, Northern Ireland   544
Nicholas Toyne Ltd   293(a), 293(b), 336
Turners Ltd (Newcastle)   137, 215

University of Cambridge, Committee Aerial Photography   402, 404, 410, 508

Joy Warren   301
Sean Watters   248
West Advertising Ltd   297
Western Morning News   408
Jeremy Whitaker   41(a), 41(b), 84(a), 84(b), 108, 119, 120, 173, 194, 195, 198, 222,
   280(a), 280(b), 294(a), 294(b), 346.   Col. Charlecote, Sissinghurst, Stour-
   head garden, Clevedon Court
Andy Williams   269.   Col. Blickling, Ashridge estate, Sheffield Park
Reece Winstone   223, 283(a), 429, 527
J. Duckworth Wood   520
Charles Woolf   444, 451, 453, 459
G. Woollat   89(a), 89(b)
John Woolverton   Col. Coast near Tintagel

595

Index

Abbotsbury, Dorset, 369: tithe barn, 326
Abbotsford House, 233
Aberconway, Lord, 236, 237
Acland family, 244, 518
Acland, Sir Thomas, 244
Adam, Robert, and Adam style, 35–6,
  51, 65, 69, 71, 86, 98, 122, 151–2, 155,
  156–7, 176–7, 219, 236, 265, 591
Addison, Joseph, 230
Adelaide, Queen, 195
Adur, river, 314
Afton, Isle of Wight, 496
Agricola, 396, 414
Aidan, St, 137
Air Forces Memorial, Cooper's Hill, 526
Aira Force, 503
Aire, river, 105
Albani, Francesco, 231
Albany, Duke of, 240
Albert, Prince (Prince Consort), 47
Aldeburgh Festival, 363
Alderley Edge, Cheshire, 374, 432;
  watermill, 360
Alfred's Tower, Stourhead, 256, 264
Alfriston, East Sussex, Clergy House,
  310, 319
Allen Banks, Northumberland, 509–10
Allerton, Somerset, 517
Allston, W, 165
Alport Dale, 464
Althorp, 38,40
Aluric the Saxon, 100
Ambleside, Cumbria, 505–6
American Bar Association, 526
Anglesey Abbey, Cambridgeshire, 29,
  235, 311, 329–30
Anglesey, Marquess of, 167–9
Anglo-Saxons, 390
Anne, Queen, 118; see also 'Queen Anne'
  style
Anson family, 37, 180–2, 264, 281
Anson, Admiral George, 180, 264, 265,
  281
Anson, Thomas, 180, 181, 182, 264, 265,
  282
Anson, William, 184
Antony House, Cornwall, 25, 32, 49–50
Antrim, Co., NT land in, 543–8
Ape's Tor, Staffordshire, 521
Archer, Thomas, 61, 87
Arden, Forest of, 92
Ardress House, Co. Armagh, 34, 38,
  50–1
Arkwright, Sir Richard, 359, 361
Arlington Court, Devon, 51–2, 283
Armagh, Co. NT land in, 548–9
Armstrong, Lord, 94–7
Arnold, William, 27, 101
Arnold's Marsh, Norfolk, 509
Artari, G., 84
Arundel Society, 47
Arundel, Thomas, 2nd Earl of, 39, 40
Arundell, Sir John, 203, 204
Arundell, Sir Thomas, 331
Ascot, Buckinghamshire, 36, 53–4, 234

Ash, Baron, 159
Ashdown House, Oxfordshire, 31, 38,
  55–6
Ashleworth tithe barn, Gloucestershire,
  326
Ashop Moor, Derbyshire, 464
Ashridge estate, Hertfordshire, 417, 425,
  491–2
Asterton, Salop, 516
Aston Court, Somerset, 429
Astor family, 36, 87
Astor, Viscountess, 87, 90
Attingham Park, Salop, 25, 34, 56–8,
  233
Aubrey, John, 400
Augustinian houses, 311, 320, 329, 342,
  345
Austen, Jane, 231, 297, 522
Austin, Felix, 233
Avebury, Wiltshire, 394, 399–400, 409
Avill, river, Somerset, 100
Avon Gorge, 429–430
Avon, NT land in, 429–430, 576
Avon, river, Warwickshire, 80
Aylesbury, King's Head Inn, 310, 357
Aylesbury, Vale of, 54
Ayot St Lawrence, Hertfordshire,
  Shaw's Corner, 36, 178–80

Babington plot, 93
Bacon, Sir Francis, 25, 120, 232
Badbury Hill, Berkshire, 514
Baden-Powell, Lord, 479
Bagatelle, Ch. de, 137
Bage, Charles, 362
Bagenal, Sir Nicholas, 168
Baggy Point and Baggy Hole, Devon,
  474, 475
Bagutti, 84
Baker, Sir Herbert, 158
Bakewell, Robert, 143, 296
Baldock, Simpson's Brewery, 362
Ballard Down, Dorset, 477
Ballin (goldsmith), 137
Ballintoy, Co. Antrim, 547, 548
Ballyscullion, 126
Bangor, Viscounts, 35, 77–9
Bank Holiday Act (1875), 420
Baring-Gould, Sabine, 434, 435, 440
Barlow, Francis, 84
Barracane Beach, Morte Bay, Devon,
  474
Barrie, J M, 180
Barrington Court, Somerset, 26, 331
Barry, Sir Charles, 36, 87, 88, 113, 114,
  194, 234
Barry, James, 42
Basingstoke Canal, 380
Bass Point, Cornwall, 453
Basset family, 445
Bateman's, East Sussex, 27, 58–60
Bath: Assembly Rooms, 297–8; Circus,
  297; Royal Crescent, 297
Batoni, Pompeo, 47, 47, 206
Bayly family, 168

Beachy Head, 527
Beagles Point, Cornwall, 453–4
Beaker folk, 394, 399, 400, 409
Beale, James, 190
Beam-engines, Cornish, 387–8
Bearsted, 2nd Viscount, 207
Beaudesert, 1st Baron, 168
Beaudesert, Staffordshire, 169
Beaufort, Duchess of, 276
Beaulieu Abbey, 328
Beckford, William, 187
Bedingfeld, Sir Edmund, 347
Bedingfeld family, 309
Bedruthan, Cornwall, 441–2
Beerbohm, Sir Max, 134
Beeston Tor, Staffordshire, 521
Behrend, Mr & Mrs, 269
Belgae, 390, 396, 407
Belle Isle, Windermere, 126
Belloc, Hilaire, 134
Bellotto, 164, 172
Belmore, Earls of, 73, 75
Belvedere Tower, Claremont, 239, 241
Bembridge, Isle of Wight: Down, 493;
  Fort, 493; windmill, 360, 367, 368
Benedictine houses, 311, 328, 351, 511
Beningbrough Hall, North Yorkshire,
  37, 61–2
Benson, Thomas, 471
Benson, William, 192, 478
Benthall family, 62–3
Benthall Hall, Salop, 27, 30, 38, 62–3,
  197
Benton Fletcher musical instrument
  collection, 109–10, 111
Berchem, Nicholas, 44, 53
Beresford Hall, Derbyshire, 465
Berkhamsted Common, 420
Berkshire, NT land in, 575
Berners, Lord, 61
Bernhardt, Sarah, 185
Bernini, Giovanni Lorenzo, 61, 126
Berrington Hall, Hereford & Worcester,
  34, 36, 63, 232, 233
Berwick, Lords, 56–8
Bess of Hardwick: see Shrewsbury,
  Elizabeth, Countess of
Betws-y-Coed, Waterloo Bridge, 384
Bignor, West Sussex, Roman villa, 528
Bilston enamels, 52
Binning, Lady, 109
Birling Gap, East Sussex, 527
Bishopston valley, West Glamorgan, 541
Black Down, Surrey and Sussex, 526
Black Mountains, 63
Black Venn, Dorset, 480
Blackden Moor, Derbyshire, 464
Blackdown Hills, Somerset, 283, 585
Blackett, Sir Walter Calverley, 214, 215,
  216
Blackett, Sir William, 214
Blackmore, R. D., 517
Blaise Hamlet, Avon, 271, 284
Blake, Admiral, 101
Blake, William, 52, 165

Blakeney Point, Norfolk, 424, **508–9**
Blake's Wood, Essex, 483, 581
Blathwayt, William, 103–4, 229
Blenheim, Oxfordshire, 38, 40, 83
Blewcoat School, Westminster, 268, **298**
Blickling Hall, Norfolk, 13, 25, 30, 31, **65–8**, 108, 236, 422
Blomfield, Sir Reginald, 229
Blue John mines and ware, 71, 177, 329, 467
Blue Slipper clay, 493
Boarstall Tower, 308, 577
Bockhill Farm, Dover, Kent, **496–7**
Bodbury Ring, Salop, 516
Bodiam Castle, East Sussex, 309, **313–14**
Bodinnick, Fowey, Cornwall, 461
Bodley, G. F., 172, 291, 513
Bodmin, St Petrock's Priory, 441
Bodnant, Gwynedd, 235, **237–9**
Bodrugan's Leap, Cornwall, **460**
Boleyn, Anne, 163, 210
Bolitho, Lt-Col. Sir Edward, 258
Bollin, river, 378
Bolt Head, Devon, 476
Bolt Tail, Devon, 452, 462, 476
Bone Low, Derbyshire, 464
Bond, Denis, 267, 273
Bonington, Richard Parkes, 330
Bonomi, Joseph (Giuseppe), 66, 122
Book of John Thorpe, 143
Borghese Gardens, Rome, 88
Borgnis, Giovanni, 281
Boringdon, Lord, 176
Borrowdale, Cumbria, 426, **500–1**
Boscastle, Cornwall, **437–8**
Boscawen, Admiral, 122, 276
Bosch, Hieronymus, 164
Boscobel, 63
Bossington, Somerset, 517
Both, Jan, 44
Boucher, Dr Cyril, 375
Boucher, François, 157
Boudicca, Queen, 416
Boulle furniture, 136, 203
Boulton, Matthew, 177, 282
Bourchier family, 61–2
Bourchier, Archbishop Thomas, 129, 131, 309
Bourdon, S., 164
Bourne Mill, Colchester, **371–2**
Bow porcelain, 110, 208, 211
Bowder Stone, Cumbria, 501
Bower, Edward, 50
Bowes, Sir George, 292
Bowes-Lyon family, 510
Box Hill, Surrey, 266, 424, 425, **522–3**; Flint Cottage, 522; Juniper Hall, 424, 523
Bradbury (plasterer), 195, 196
Bradley Manor, Devon, 309, **332**
Bradnor Hill, Hereford & Worcester, 419, **488–9**
Braich-y-Pwll, Gwynedd, 421, **536**
Braithwaite family, 68
Bramber Castle, East Sussex, 307, **314–15**
Brancaster, Norfolk, 422, 509
Brandlehow Woods, Cumbria, 12
Brandy Island, 69
Brandys rocks, Cornwall, 447
Branscombe, Devon, **468**

Brazil, Angela, 463
Brecon Beacons, Powys, **540–1**
Bredon Hills, Somerset, 100
Bredon tithe barn, Hereford & Worcester, **327**
Bremetennacum (Ribchester), Lancashire, 415
Brett, Captain, 180
Breweries and brewhouses, 81, 362
Brickworth Down, Wiltshire, 275
Bridestones Moor, North Yorkshire, **529**
Bridge House, Ambleside, 68
Bridgeman, Charles, 231, 239, 240, 241
Bridges, 364, 383–5
Bridgewater, Duke of, 46, 492
Bridgewater Monument, Ashridge, Hertfordshire, 492
Bridgnorth, St Mary's Church, 384
Brigantes, 396
Bristol, Temple Meads station, 364
Bristol, Earls of, 43, 125–7
Bristol, 4th Earl of (Bishop of Derry), 34, 125–7, 278–9
Bristol Cross, Stourhead, 256, 264
Bristol porcelain, 110, 111
Broadwood, John, 111
Bromley, Davenport, 46
Brontë, Charlotte, 466
Bronze Age, 395, 399, 400, 403, 404, 409, 432, 477, 488, 519, 538; hut circles, 468
Brook, Isle of Wight, 496
Broom Parc, Cornwall, 458
Broom Squires, 523
Brotherswater, Cumbria, 503
Brown, Lancelot ('Capability'), 63, 80, 98–9, 163, 172, 178, 221, 231, 232, 233, 239, 240, 250, 251, 513
Brown, Lt-Col., 381
Brown, Potto, 374
Browne family (of Townend), 200–1
Brownsea Island, Dorset, 424, 425, **478–9**
Brueghel, Pieter the elder, 207
Brunel, I. K., 359, 364, 365, 429
Brunel, Sir Marc, 364
Brussels tapestries, 60, 87, 136, 208
Bruton dovecote, Somerset, **288**
Buccleuch, Dukes of, 316
Buckhurst, Lord *see* Sackville family
Buckingham, Chantry Chapel, 310, **320**, 323
Buckingham, Dukes of, 40, 44, 87, 230, 280
Buckinghamshire, 2nd Earl of, 66
Buckinghamshire, NT land in, 430–1, 577
Buckland Abbey, Devon, 29, 37, 204, 312, **333–4**, 346; barn, 326, 334
Bugoty, dinner service by, 58
Bull Point, Devon, 475
Bumstead, William, 207–9
Bunyan, John, 290, 419
Burbage Brook, Derbyshire, 466
Burges, William, 128
Burghley House, 31, 40
Burlington, Lord, 43, 142, 151, 255
Burn, river, 372
Burne-Jones, Sir Edward, 71, 192, 222
Burnet, Bishop Gilbert, 31
Burney, Fanny, 176, 178

Burnham Overy, Norfolk, 363, 509; watermill, 360, 363, **372–3**
Burning Cliff, Dorset, 482
Burton Wood and Burton Point, Merseyside, 507
Burwell Fen, **431–2**
Bury, F., 182
Bury Castle, Somerset, 517
Bury, Lady Mairi, 149
Bury St Edmunds, Suffolk: Angel Corner, 586; Theatre Royal, 302–3
Buscot Park, Oxfordshire, 34, 48, **69–71**, 585; estate, **513–14**
Bustelli, 84
Butterfield, William, 291
Buttermere valley, Cumbria, **498–9**, 578

Cabal, The, 87, 115
Cade, Rowena, 448
Caerhayes Estate, Cornwall, 458
Caerleon, 397, 453
Caernarvon Castle, Gwynedd, 171, 416
Caldy Hill, Merseyside, 507
Calvert, Sir Harry, 86
Cambeak, Cornwall, 437
Camborne, beam-engines, Cornwall, 387–8
Cambridgeshire, NT land in, 431–2
Camden, William, 415
Camels Cove, Cornwall, 458
Campbell, Colen, 33, 192, 254
Campbell, Robert, 69
Canaletto, 44, 198, 208
Canals, 363, 380–3
Canning, George, 300–1
Canning Oak, The, 88
Cannock Chase, 180
Caractacus, 416, 491
Caratacus Stone, Somerset, 519
Carew and Carew-Pole family, 49–50
Carlin, Martin, 213
Carlisle, Bishop of, 321
Carlisle, Earl of, 46
Carlton Club, 160
Carlton House, 160
Carlton House Terrace, 284
Carlyle, Jane, 72
Carlyle, Thomas, 71–2
Carlyle's House, Chelsea, 36, **71–2**
Carminowe Creek, Cornwall, 450
Carne and Carne Beacon, Cornwall, 454, **457**
Carneddau area, Gwynedd, **536–7**
Carr, John, 155
Carrick-a-rede, Co. Antrim, **543–4**
Carrick Roads, Cornwall, 455
Carrington, Noel, 469
Carter of Piccadilly, 177
Carthusian houses, 312, 324–5
Cartmel Priory Gatehouse, Cumbria, 311, **320–1**
Castle Carra, Co. Antrim, 544
Castle Coole, Co. Fermanagh, 34, 72–5, 149
Castle Crag, Cumbria, 500
Castle Drogo, Devon, 36, **75–7**
Castle Howard, 38, 269, 280–1
Castle Ward, Co. Down, 34–5, 77–9
Castlereagh, Lord, 100, 149, 150
Castlerigg Stone Circle, Cumbria, **400–1**
Castles, 23, 307–9, 313–18

Catesby, Robert, 93
Catherine of Aragon, 209, 210
Catherine the Great, 40, 66
Cavendish, Earl of, 119
Cawdor, Earls of, 534
Cawley family, 65
Cearnach, Conal, 545
Celts, 395–7, 401, 408, 519, 545, 549
Cemlyn, Anglesey, Gwynedd, 422, 537–8
Cerne, Dorset: Abbey, 478; Giant, 411
Chalk Farm Roundhouse, 364
Chalon, Alfred Edward, 125
Chambers, Sir William, 236
Chapel Porth, Cornwall, 444–5
Chapels, 291–6, 310
Chapman, John, 343
Charlecote Park, Warwickshire, 26, 29, 37, 79–81, 229, 232, 233
Charlemont, Lord, 100
Charles I, 39–40, 44, 50, 54, 61, 80, 85, 101, 105, 130, 141, 367, 374, 445, 455, 461
Charles II, 36, 131, 133, 147–9, 154, 194, 228, 230, 400, 430, 478, 511
Charlotte of Wales, Princess, 240
Charnwood Forest, Leicestershire, 506
Chartwell, Kent, 36, 37, 82–3
Château d'Asnières, 87
Chatham dockyard, 364
Chatsworth, 38, 40, 119, 120
Chaucer, Geoffrey, 306, 319
Cheddar Gorge, Somerset, 426, 516, 586
Chedworth Villa, Gloucestershire, 397, 412–3
Cheere, Sir Henry, 143, 255
Chelsea porcelain, 84, 110, 170, 208
Cheshire, NT land in, 432
Chester, 397, 414
Chesterton, G. K., 134
Chichester, Rosalie, 51–2
Chick, The, Cornwall, 442
Chiddingstone, Kent, 284–5, 310; Castle Inn, 268, 284–5
Ch'ien Lung ware, 329
Child, Francis and Robert, 35, 156, 207
Chillingham Park, 512
Chillington Hall, 148
Chiltern Hills, 54, 419, 434, 491, 514
Chinoiserie, 86, 170, 177, 263
Chippendale, Thomas: senior, 84, 141, 152, 153, 177; junior, 194
Chinese Chippendale style, 177, 182, 211
Chipping Campden, Gloucestershire: market hall, 268, 299
Cholsey tithe barn, Berkshire, 326
Christabel (Coleridge), 90
Christie, Mrs Mary, 479
Churchill, Lady, 83
Churchill, Lord Randolph, 83
Churchill, Sir Winston, 36, 82–3
Churchtown Farm, Fowey, Cornwall, 462
Churnet, river, 519
Chute, Chaloner, 209
Chute family, 209–211
Chute, John, 209, 211
Cigolo (Lodovico Cardi), 193
Cilgerran Castle, Dyfed, 307, 315–16
Cissbury Ring, West Sussex, 396, 401–2

Cistercian houses, 311–12, 321–3, 333–4
Clandon Park, Surrey, 25, 33, 37, 38, 83–4
Clare, Earl of, 239
Claremont, Surrey, 230–1, 239–41, 254
Clark, Sir Kenneth (Lord Clark), 22
Clatterbach valley, Worcestershire, 490
Claude (Lorrain), 40, 41, 43, 164, 230, 231, 254, 330
Claudius, Emperor, 396, 416
Clavichords, 111
Claydon House, Buckinghamshire, 34, 85–7, 281
Clent Hills, Hereford & Worcester, 489–90
Clevedon Court, Avon, 230, 308, 334–5
Clevedon, Sir John de, 334
Cleveland Way, 531
Cley nature reserve, Norfolk, 508, 509
Clifden, Viscount, 135, 137
Cliff castles, 407–8, 440, 449
Clifton Maybank, Dorset, 146
Clifton suspension bridge, 429
Clifton, William, 331
Clive, Lords, 172, 240
Cliveden, Buckinghamshire, 13, 25, 36, 37, 87–9, 230, 234
Cloud, The, Cheshire, 433
Clouds Hill, Dorset, 36, 89–90
Clumber Park, Nottinghamshire, 233, 291, 422, 425, 512–13; Chapel, 291
Coade, Mrs Eleanor, 233
Coalbrookdale Company, 57, 63; blast furnace site, 365; bridge, 63
Cobbett, William, 487
Cockermouth, Wordsworth's house, Cumbria, 36, 225–6
Cockshot Point, Cumbria, 506
Coke of Holkham, 181, 419
Colchester, 396; Bourne Mill, 371–2; Castle, 307
Coldrum Long Barrow, Kent, 393, 401–3
Cole family, 111–12
Coleridge, Samuel Taylor, 36, 90, 500; cottage at Nether Stowey, 36, 90
Coleshill, Oxfordshire: estate, 513–14; House, 514
Collacombe Barton, 204
Colleton Barton, 204
Coln, river, 412
Colston Bassett Market Cross, Oxfordshire, 310, 585
Comber, H. F., 234
Comber, J., 234
Commodus, Emperor, 411
Commons Preservation Society, 11, 420
Compagnie des Indes, armorial dishes, 71
Compton, Isle of Wight, 496
Compton Castle, Devon, 26, 37, 38, 308, 335–7; Castle Barton, 580
Coney Island, Lough Neagh, 548–9
Coneysburrow Cove, Cornwall, 454
Coneys Castle, Dorset, 480
Coniston Hall, Cumbria, 91–2
Coniston Water, Cumbria, 91, 499–500
Conrad, Joseph, 134
Conseiglio, Francis, 141
Constable, John, 45, 330, 360, 482
Continuing Purpose, The (Fedden) see National Trust, Past and Present

Conwy Gwynedd: Aberconwy, 590; Castle, 171; Aberconwy, 590; river, 235, 237, 384; suspension bridge, 364, 384–5
Conyngham family, 184
Cook, Ernest, 70, 147, 298, 513
Cook, Captain James, 266
Cook, Thomas (landscape gardener), 221
Coombe Hill, Buckinghamshire, 417, 422, 430–1
Coombe Valley, Cornwall, 435–6
Cooper's Hill, Surrey, 526
Copeland, Mr and Mrs, 256
Copley, John Singleton, 42
Coquet, river, 94
Cordell Almshouses, 143
Cordell family, 143–4
Cordell, Sir William, 143–4
Corfe Castle, 267
Cornish Engines Preservation Society, 365, 387
Cornwall, NT land in, 433–64
Cornwall Naturalists' Trust, 452
Cornwall, Richard, Earl of, 312, 322
Corry family, 72–5
Corry, Isaac, 100
Corry, Colonel James, 75
Corsham quarries and stone, 286, 340
Cotehele, Cornwall, 25, 26, 29, 30, 309, 337–9, 438
Cotswold Hills, 27, 186, 187, 235, 361, 489
Cotswold stone, 103, 299
Cotton, Charles, 464, 465
Cotton, Robert, 300
Coughton Court, Warwickshire, 26, 37, 92–4
Councils for the Protection of Rural England and Wales, 422
Countisbury, Devon, 474
Country House Scheme, 13–14
Countryside Commission, 422
County naturalists' trusts, 424
Coverack, Cornwall, 454
Cox, David, 564
Crackington, Cornwall, 436–7
Cragside, Northumberland, 36, 94–7
Craig, Edith, 185
Crane Castle, Cornwall, 445
Cranmer, Archbishop Thomas, 129
Crantock, Cornwall, 442
Craven, William, 1st Earl of, 55, 56
Creech Grange Arch, Dorset, 267, 273
Cregennan, Gwynedd, 538
Crespin, Paul, 127
Cressent, Charles, 213
Croft Castle, Hereford & Worcester, 28, 63, 97–9, 230, 308
Croft family, 97–9
Croft, Lord, 97, 98
Croft, Sir Richard, 98
Crome, John, 360
Crompton, Samuel, 361
Cromwell, Oliver, 189, 228, 269, 280, 295
Cromwell, Ralph, 318
Cromwell, Richard, 209
Croome Court, 236
Crowlink, Sussex, 527
Crummock Water, Cumbria, 499
Cubert, Cornwall, 442–3

Cubitt, Thomas, 169
Cuckmere, river, 319
Cuddy Crags, 414
Cullen, Sir Rushout, 207
Culloden, battle of, 218
Culver Down, Isle of Wight, 417, **493**
Cumberland, Earl of, 130
Cumbria Naturalists' Trust, 501
Cumbria, NT land in, 498–506
Curzon of Kedleston, Marquess, 313, 318
Cushendun, Co. Antrim, **544–5**
Cuthbert, St, 418, 511
Cuyp, Albert, 53, 164, 170, 330
Cwm Idwal, Gwynedd, 537

Dahl, Michael, 42, 164
Dall, Nicholas, 181
Dalton, Dr Hugh (Lord Dalton), 14
Dalton Castle, Cumbria, 308, **316**
Dalyngrigge, Sir Edward, 313, 314
Damage Barton, Devon, 475
Danbury Common, Essex, **483**
Dance, George, 149–50
Danes, 390, 524
Danvers, Sir Thomas, 139
Darby, Abraham, 359, 365, 527
D'Argenville, 232
Darling, Grace, 511
Dartmoor, **468–9**
Darwin, Charles, 421
Dashwood family, 218–21
Dashwood, Sir Francis, 218–21
Daubeny, 2nd Lord, 331
Debdon valley, 94
De Bray, Henry, 306
De Burgh, Hubert, 307, 317
Defoe, Daniel, 420
De Grey family, 341
De Hesding, Erwulf, 340
Deirdre of the Sorrows, 545
De Jongh, Clement, 70
De Lamerie, Paul, 127
Delaney, Mrs, 77–8
Delftware, 104, 106, 115
De Marisco family, 471
De Mohun, Lady Joan, 100
De Mohun, Thomas, 462
De Mohun, William, 100
Derby: cotton mill, 362; porcelain, 110, 208
Derbyshire, NT land in, 464–7
Derbyshire County Council, 15
Derry, Bishop of: see Bristol, 4th Earl of
Derrymore House, Co. Armagh, 38, **99–100**
Derwent Estate, Derbyshire and South Yorkshire, **464**
Derwent, river, 225
Derwentwater, Cumbria, 12, **500–1**, 578
De Staël, Madame, 523
Destailleur, Gabriel-Hippolyte, 212
Deverel-Rimbury culture, 404
Devil's Frying Pan, Cornwall, 453
Devil's Punch Bowl, Surrey, 421, 523
Devis, Arthur, 206, 208
Devon and Somerset Staghounds, 518
Devon, NT land in, 468–77
Devonport dockyard, 364
Devonshire, Dukes of, 30, 37, 104
Dewerstone Rock, Devon, 469

De Wint, Peter, 315
Dickens, Charles, 297, 299
Dilettanti, Society of, 180, 219, 264
Dinas Gynfor, Anglesey, Gwynedd, 407, 590
Dinton, Wiltshire; Philipps House, 34, 37, **166–7**
Disraeli, Benjamin, 36, 71, 124–5
Disraeli, Coningsby, 124
Disraeli, Mary Anne, 124–5
Dizzard, The, Cornwall, **436**
Dobson, John, 215
Dockyards, 363–4
Dodman, The, Cornwall, 407, **458–9**, 462
Dolmetsch, Arnold, 111
Dolmelynllyn, Gwynedd, **539**
Domesday Book, 100, 307, 340, 353, 484
Donowell, John, 219, 220
Doom Bar, Cornwall, 441
Dora's Field, Cumbria, 506
Dorset, Earls and Dukes of, 130–1
Dorset, NT land in, 424, 477–82
Dorset Naturalists' Trust, 479, 480
Dove, river, 417
Dove Valley, Derbyshire, 425, **464–5**
Dovecotes, 270, **287–90**, 310
Dover Castle, 307
Dover Patrol Memorial, Kent, 497
Down, Co., NT land in, 549–50
Downhill, Co. Londonderry, 125, 265, 278; Mussenden Temple, 265, **278–9**
Downing, Sir George, 329
Downs Banks, Staffordshire, **519**
Doyden, Cornwall, **440–1**
Drake, Sir Francis, 29, 334, 336
Drewe family, 75–6
Drewsteignton, Devon, 75, 76
Druids, 416
Dryden, John, 130, 278
Duckpool, Cornwall, **435**
Ducros, Louis, 193
Duffield Castle, Derbyshire, 307, 579
Dugdale, Sir William, 92
Du Maurier, Daphne, 460
Duncombe family, 280–1
Duncombe Park, Yorkshire, 280
Dunham Massey, Greater Manchester, 139, **582**
Dunkery Beacon, Somerset, 102, 425, 518
Dunlap, John, 386
Dunluce, Co. Antrim, 547
Dunseverick Castle, Co. Antrim, **545–6**
Dunstable, 306, 576
Dunstanburgh Castle, Northumberland, 307, **510**
Dunster Castle, Somerset, 36, **100–2**
Dürer, Albrecht, 40
Durgan, Cornwall, 454
Durham, Bishop of, 216, 217
Durham Cathedral, 162
Durham, 1st Earl of, 265
Duse, Eleanora, 185
Dyer, John, 279
Dyfed, NT land in, 532–4
Dyrham Park, Avon, 32, 33, 48, **103–4**, 229
Dysart, Earls of, 37, 115
Dysart, Lady: see Lauderdale, Duchess of

Eadgar, King, 325
Eashing bridge, Surrey, 380, 587
East Pool mine, Camborne, Cornwall, **388**
East Riddlesden Hall, West Yorkshire, **105–6**; barn, 106, 326
Eastlake, Sir Charles, 39
Eastnor Park, 491
Easton-on-the-Hill, priest's house, Northamptonshire, 310, 585
Ebbor Gorge, Somerset, **516–17**
Ébénistes, 54, 170
Edale, Derbyshire, 464, 467
Edgcumbe family, 337–8
Edgehill, 209; battle of, 80, 85, 367
Edward the Confessor, 305, 307, 351
Edward I, 307, 308, 381, 416
Edward III, 139, 306, 313, 315, 358, 367
Edward IV, 309
Edward VI, 153, 168
Edward VII, 169
Egerton family, 196–7
Egremont, Baron (John Wyndham), 163, 164
Egremont, Earls of, 163–5
Elgar, Sir Edward, 491
El Greco, 208
Elizabeth I, 30, 79, 81, 92, 130, 140, 144, 153–4, 277, 335, 336, 341, 344, 353
Elizabeth, Empress of Russia, 213
Elizabeth, Queen of Bohemia, 55
Elizabeth the Queen Mother, 169
Elizabethan style, 29–30, 263, 345, 353
Ellys, Sir Richard, 66
Elmbridge Borough Council, 240
Elsheimer, Adam, 164
Elswick Works, 95
Elterwater, Cumbria, 502
Elton family, 334
Elton ware, 334
Emes, William, 107
Emmerson, H. H., 97
English Gardener, The (Meager), 139
Enniskillen, Earls of, 111
Ensor, George, 50
Enterprise Neptune, 15, 424, 426, 436, 468, 470, 477, 480, 482, 496, 506, 527
Eolwin, Ealdorman, 325, 373
Erddig, Clwyd, **106–8**, 229
Essex, NT land in, 483–4
Esthwaite Water, Cumbria, 506
Ethelwulf, King, 524
European Architectural Heritage Year, 117
Euston Station, 364
Evelyn, John, 103, 104, 117, 227, 228, 420, 522
Eworth, Hans, 101
Exeter, 5th Lord, 40
Exmoor, Somerset, 100, **517–19**
Eyam, Derbyshire: Riley graves, 266, 579
Eyre's Folly: see Pepperbox, The

Fairfax, General, 280
Fairfax-Lucy family, 79
Fairhaven, Lord, 235, 329, 526
Fal, river, 256, 455
Falkner, J. W., 482
Falmouth, 454
Faringdon Collection, 70

Faringdon, Lords, 69, 70
Farne Islands, Northumberland, 418, 421, 424, 426, **511–12**
Farringford, Isle of Wight, 496
Fedden, Robin, 13, 37
Felbrigg Hall, Norfolk, **108–9**
Fell Foot, Cumbria, 502, 506
Fenton House, Hampstead, **109–111**
Fenwick family, 214
Ferguson's Gang, 301, 376
Fermanagh, Viscount: see Verney family
Fetherston, John, 158, 159
Fetherstonhaugh, Sir Harry, 206–7
Fetherstonhaugh, Sir Matthew, 205–6
Feversham, Earls of, 280
Field of the Cloth of Gold, 209
Field Studies Council, 424, 523, 530
Fiennes, Celia, 37, 466, 522
Fife, Mrs Ronald, 154
Figsbury Ring, Wiltshire, **403**
Firebrace, Sir Cordell, 144
Firth, Cecil, 332
Fishing Cove, Cornwall, 445
FitzWimarc, Robert, 307
Flatford Mill, 424, 586
Flat Point, Ilfracombe, Devon, 475
Flaxman, John, 126, 127, 165
Fleming, William, 91
Flint Cottage, 522
Flitcroft, Henry, 192, 255
Florence Court, Co. Fermanagh, 34, 111–12
Folkestone Beds, 406
Follies, 273–5
Fonthill sale (1823), 81, 187
Fontmell Down, Dorset, **481–2**
Ford, Ford Madox, 134
Ford, Richard, 47
Forde, Edward, 205
Foreland Point, Devon, 474
Forestry Commission, 514, 529, 539
Forfarshire, wreck of, 511
Formby, Merseyside, 422, 425, **506**
Forrabury, Cornwall, 438
Forster, E. M., 89
Fortin, Master (engineer), 307
Fosse Way, 412, 416
Fountains Abbey, 530
Fouquet, Jehan, 208
Fowey, Cornwall, **461–2**
Fownes, Henry, 102
Fox, Alfred, 241
Fox family, 242
Fox, Dr Wilfrid, 261–2
Fox Talbot Museum, 343
Fox Talbot, William Henry, 343
Francini brothers, 215
Francis I of France, 209
Frankenthal ware, 110
Frederick, Elector Palatine and King of Bohemia, 56
Frederick the Great, 72
Frederick, Prince of Wales, 87
Frenchman's Creek, Cornwall, **454**
Freshwater Cliffs and Bay, Isle of Wight, 495–6
Friar's Crag, Cumbria, 501
Frindsbury tithe barn, Kent, 326
Frobisher, Sir Martin, 336
Froe Creek, Cornwall, 457
Froggatt Wood, Derbyshire, 466

Frontinus, Julius, 416
Furness Abbey, 308, 316, 357, 505
Fürstenberg ware, 110, 170
Fuseli, Henry, 165

Gainsborough, Thomas, 39, 43, 53, 70, 81, 104, 107, 126, 133, 164, 172, 213, 330
Gannel river and estuary, Cornwall, 203, **442–3**
Garrick, David, 133, 185
Gawthorpe Hall, Lancashire, **112–14**
Geertgen tot Sint Jans, 40
General Enclosure Act (1845), 419
Gentileschi, Orazio, 40
George I, 40, 130, 133
George II, 66, 130, 132, 136, 153, 175, 176
George III, 37, 87, 220
George IV, 44, 160, 166, 206, 297, 526
George V, 75, 246
George VI, 169
George Inn, Southwark, 268, **299–300**
Georgian Group, 38
Georgian Society of East Yorkshire, 142
Gerard, John: Herball, 190, 371
Germaine, Lady Betty, 132
Gerona, Spanish Armada galleass, wreck of, 547
Getty, Paul, 381
Giant's Causeway, Co. Antrim, **546–7**
Gibbet Hill, Hindhead, Surrey, 523
Gibbon, Edward, 250
Gibbons, Grinling, 32, 33, 62, 141, 163, 164, 193, 195, 196
Gibbs, James, 50, 111, 112, 218, 269
Gibside, Tyne & Wear: Chapel, 269, **292–3**; Hall, 292
Giffard family, 148
Gilbert, Adrian, 335, 336
Gilbert family: (Compton Castle), 28, 335–7; (Trelissick), 256, 443
Gillan Creek, Cornwall, 454
Gilling Castle, 61
Gillow (furniture maker), 104, 197
Gilpin, William, 43, 233
Girardon, François, 234
Glamorgan Naturalists' Trust, 424, 586
Glastonbury Tor, Somerset: St Michael's Chapel, 310
Glencoyne Wood, Cumbria, 421, 502, 503
Glendurgan, Cornwall, 235, 241–2, 454
Gloucester, Earl of, 491
Glyder Fawr, Gwynedd, 426, 536
Glyndwr, Owain, 315, 419
Gobelin tapestry, 147, 157
Godalming Navigation, Surrey, 380
Godrevy Point, Cornwall, **444–5**
Goethe, 21
Golden Cap estate, Dorset, 426, **479–80**
Golden Hinde, 336
Goldsmith, Lieutenant, 449
Goncourt frères, 47
Good Samaritan, wreck of, 442
Goodameavy, Devon, **468–9**
Goodhart-Rendel, H. S., 122
Goodman, Joseph, 374
Goodwood, Sussex: Shell House, 267
Goose Green, West Sussex, 191
Gordale Scar, Yorkshire, 530

Gorran Haven, Cornwall, 459
Gosford, N. Ireland, 161
Gosse, Sir Edmund, 134
Gower Peninsula, 424, **541–2**
Grand Tour, The, 43, 46, 108–9, 122, 205, 211, 219, 254
Grand Union Canal, 383
Grantham House, Lincolnshire, 114–15
Grasmere, Cumbria, 501, 502, 578
Grattan, Henry, 100
Gray, Thomas, 41, 43, 209, 211, 266, 500, 539; monument at Stoke Poges, 266, **282–3**
Gray's Printing Press, Strabane, Co. Tyrone, **386–7**
Great Chalfield Manor, Wiltshire, 13, 309, **339–40**
Great Coxwell tithe barn, Oxfordshire, 326, **328**
Great Exhibition (1851), 89
Great Gable, 421
Great Hangman, The, Devon, 470
Greater Manchester, NT properties in, 484–5
Green, Frank, 203
Greenwich, Painted Hall, 118
Greg, Samuel, 378–9
Gregory, Lady, 180
Grenville family, 333, 334, 435
Grenville, Sir Richard, 29, 333–4, 435, 437
Gresham, Sir Thomas, 156, 157
Greville, Charles, 206
Greville, Mrs Ronald, 36, 169–71
Grey of Fallodon, Lord, 512
Grey of Werke, Lord, 205
Grey's Court, Oxfordshire, 309, **341–2**
Gribbin, The, Cornwall, **460**
Griffith family, 168
Grime Moor, Yorkshire, 529
Grimes Graves, 401
Grinshill ashlar, 56
Grottoes, 267
Guardi, Francesco, 44, 208
Gubbay, Mrs David, 37, 84
Guildford, Surrey, Tower Mill, 380; Weir House, 587
Guildhalls, 310, 358
Gummer's How, Cumbria, 506
Gunby Hall, Lincolnshire, 13, 32, 584
Gunpowder Plot, 93
Gunwalloe Church Cove, Cornwall, **451**
Gurney family, 159
Guzzle Holes, West Glamorgan, 541
Gwent, NT land in, 525
Gwynedd, NT land in, 536–40

Hadrian's Wall, Northumberland, 397, 413–14
Hagley, 230, 231, 291, 292, 489
Hailes Abbey, Gloucestershire, 312, 321–3
Hall Walk, Fowey, Cornwall, 461
Hallstatt culture, 403
Ham Hill stone, 27, 199, 331, 355
Ham House, Surrey, 30, 31, 37, 115–17; garden, 230
Hamilton, Lady: see Hart, Emma
Hamps valley, Staffordshire, 521
Hampshire and Isle of Wight Naturalists' Trust, 494

Hampshire, NT land in, 484–8
Hampstead, Fenton House, 109–11
Hampton Court, 345
Hanbury Hall, Hereford and Worcester, 32, 117–18
Hancock family (Eyam), 266
Handbook (Ford), 47
Hardenclough Farm, Derbyshire, 467
Hardwick Hall, Derbyshire, 25, 26–7, 30, 37, 48, 112, 118–20
Hardy, Thomas, 36, 121, 437, 481; cottage at Higher Bockhampton, 36, 121
Haresfield Beacon, Gloucestershire, 421
Harewood House, 152
Harford, John, and Harford family, 271, 284
Harlestone, Northamptonshire, 306
Harley, Thomas, 63
Harman family, 472
Harpsichords, 111
Harrison, John, 153
Harrock Wood, Merseyside, 507
Hart, Emma (Lady Hamilton), 32, 206, 276
Hartley Wintney, Hampshire: West Green House, 218
Hartsop Hall, 503
Harvey's of Hayle (engineers), 387, 388
Harvington Hall, 94
Hasted, Edward, 350
Hastings, Warren, 203
Hatchlands, Surrey, 35, 122
Hatfield forest, Essex, 483–4; Old Doodle Oak, 484; Shell House, 267, 483
Hatfield House, 38, 65, 97
Hatley, Robert, 111
Hauduroy, S., 33, 103, 104
Havering, Essex, 306
Hawker, Rev Stephen, 434–5
Hawkins, Sir John, 336
Hawkshead, Cumbria, 579: Court House, 310, 357; Grammar School, 414
Hawksmoor, Nicholas, 32, 103
Hawksmoor, Staffordshire, 519–20
Hawkstone, Salop: grotto, 267
Hawley, General Henry, 218
Hayle, Cornwall, 496; Copperhouse Foundry, 388
Hayward, Jack, 472
Heathcoat, John, 127–8
Heathcoat-Amory family, 128
Heaton Hall, 73
Heaven, Rev Hudson, 472
Heddon's Mouth, Devon, 469–70
Heelis, William, 123
Helford River and Passage, Cornwall, 235, 241–2, 454
Hell's Mouth, Cornwall, 445
Hemmick beach, Cornwall, 458
Henderson, Sir Alexander, 70
Henrietta Maria, Queen, 105
Henry I, 306
Henry III, 312, 317, 322, 342
Henry IV, 309, 324
Henry V, 358
Henry VI, 114, 318, 357
Henry VII, 92, 337, 348
Henry VIII, 81, 92, 101, 129, 153, 168, 187, 202, 209, 210, 289, 290, 305, 306,

311, 324, 330, 331, 341, 343, 345, 346, 358, 455, 461, 478
Henry, Prince of Wales, 39
Herball, (Gerard), 190, 371
Herbert family, 172
Hereford and Worcester, NT land in, 488–491
Herefordshire Beacon, Malvern Hills, 490
Hertburn, William de, 216
Hertford, Marquesses of, 44, 47
Hertfordshire, NT land in, 491–2
Hervey, Frederick Augustus, *see* Bristol, 4th Earl of
Hesketh family, 349, 350
Heveningham Hall, 73
Heyden, Jan van der, 53
Hicks, Sir Baptist, 299
Hidcote Manor, Gloucestershire, 200, 235, 242–3
High Cliff, Cornwall, 437
High Ham windmill, Somerset, 369
High Peak, The, Derbyshire, 466
Highdown Hill, West Sussex, 404
Higher Bockhampton, Dorset: Hardy's Cottage, 36, 121
Higher Tregantle Cliff, Cornwall, 463
Highmore, Joseph, 208
Hill, Abraham, 350
Hill, Frances, 498
Hill, Octavia, 11, 18, 498
Hill, Sir Rowland, 181
Hill Top, Sawrey, Cumbria, 123, 506
Hinchingbrooke House, 325
Hindhead Commons, Surrey, 420, 523
Historic Buildings Council, 14, 15, 38, 260
Hoare family, 192–4
Hoare, Henry (II), 192, 193, 231, 255, 256, 264
Hoare, Sir Henry Hugh Arthur, 193
Hoare, Richard Colt, 192–3, 235, 256, 400, 410
Hoare, William (of Bath), 193
Hobart, Sir Henry, 65
Hobart, Sir John, 65
Hobbema, Meindert, 44, 53, 164
Hobbes, Thomas, 190
Hobson, Thomas, 329
Höchst ware, 110
Hogarth, William, 41, 208
Holbein, Hans, 39
Holdstone Down, Devon, 470
Holkham, 38, 40
Holland, Henry, 36, 63–5, 240
Hollybush Hill, Malvern Hills, 406
Holman Brothers of Camborne, 388; Engineering Museum, 388
Holman Hunt, William, 221, 222
Holnicote estate, Somerset, 518
Holworth, Dorset, 482
Holy Island (Lindisfarne), 137, 138, 308
Holywell, Cornwall, 442
Hondecoeter, Melchior d', 104
Honthorst, Gerard van, 56
Hoogh, Pieter de, 170
Hoogstraeten, Samuel van, 104
Hope, Thomas, 71
Hope Woodlands Estate, Derbyshire and South Yorkshire, 464

Hoppner, Thomas, 36, 160–2, 429
Hoppner, John, 133
Hornyold-Strickland family, 184
Horsey, Norfolk, 584; windmill, 360
Horst, G. W., 164
Hotwells Spa, Avon, 430
Houblon family, 483
Houdon, Jean Antoine, 217
Houghton, Norfolk, 38, 40, 67
Houghton Mill, Cambridgeshire, 360, 373–4
Housesteads, Hadrian's Wall, Northumberland, 397, 413, 414
Howard, Henry, 165
Howden Moor, 421, 464
Hoy Monument, Isle of Wight, 494
Huddleston, Father John, 148, 149
Hudson, Edward, 138
Hudson, Thomas, 50, 136
Hudson, W. H., 468
Hughenden Manor, Buckinghamshire, 36, 124–5
Huicke, Robert, 153
Hull, Humberside: Maister House, 142–3
Hull, Richard, 524
Hunter, Sir Robert, 11
Hunter's Inn, Devon, 470
Hussey, Edwin, 234
Hussey family, 249
Hyde Parker family, *see* Parker family (Melford)

Ickworth, Suffolk, 25, 34, 125–7
Ilam, Staffordshire, 465, 521
Ine of Wessex, King, 481–2
Ingestre, Staffordshire, 169
Irish Lady rock, Cornwall, 447
Iron Age, 401, 404, 407, 408, 411, 466, 476, 482, 488, 491, 520, 538, 539; forts, 401, 407, 440, 449, 476, 480, 490, 512, 514, 516, 517, 520, 541
Irving, Sir Henry, 185, 186
Isle of Wight: NT land in, 493–6; West Wight, 495–6
Isle of Wight Natural History and Archaeological Society, 494
Itchen, river, 377
Ivinghoe, Buckinghamshire: Beacon, 491, 492; windmill, 360
Ivory, Thomas and William, 66

James I, 65, 130, 146, 189, 341
James II, 132, 154, 172, 207
James, Henry, 41, 48, 134–5
James, William, 135
Jekyll, Gertrude, 158, 234, 242, 331
Jellicoe, Geoffrey, 89
Jenner, Sir Walter, 344, 345
Jersey, Earls of, 156, 207
John, Augustus, 180
John, King of England, 317, 525
John Lewis Partnership, 425, 479
John of Gaunt, 306, 307, 510
John of Padua, 81
John of Waverley, 311
Johnes family, 98
Johns, Rev C. A., 452
Johnson, Dr Samuel, 133, 176, 521, 547
Johnston, Major Lawrence, 235, 242
Jones, Inigo, 31, 112, 210

Josephine, Empress, 58
Joules family, 519
Julius Caesar, 390, 396, 418
Julius Frontinus, 416
Juniper Hall, 424, 523

Kahn, Herman, 22
Kändler, Frederick, 110, 127
K'ang-Hsi ware, 53, 111, 115, 170
Kauffmann, Angelica, 152
Kay-Shuttleworth family, 114
Keating, The Misses, 539
Keats, John, 109, 401
Keen, Henry, 206
Keiller, Alexander, 400, 409
Keith, Sir Arthur, 403
Keld Chapel, Cumbria, 310, 323
Kelmscott Manor, 222
Kempe, Charles, 221, 222, 291
Kempe, Margery, 312
Kenilworth Castle, 80, 306
Kennedy, President John F., 526
Kensington Palace, 236
Kent, Fair Maid of, 324
Kent, NT land in, 496–8
Kent, Weald of, 36
Kent, William, 43, 230, 231, 239, 240,
    241, 254, 281
Kete, Dyfed, 422, 532
Ketton, John, 109
Ketton-Cremer, R. W., 109
Kew Gardens, 236, 259
Kiberick Cove, Cornwall, 458
Kilkhampton, Cornwall, 435
Killerton, Devon, 235, 244–5
Killigerran Head, Cornwall, 422, 457
Kinder Scout, Derbyshire, 464, 466
Kingsley, Charles, 435, 472, 530
King's Lynn, St George's Hall, 310, 583
Kingston, 1st Duke of, 340
Kinver Edge, Staffordshire, 490, 520
Kinwarton, Warwickshire: dovecote,
    270, 288
Kip, Johannes, 104, 228–9, 260
Kipling, Rudyard, 27, 59–60, 134
Kirckman, Jacob and Abraham, 111
Kirkstone Pass, 503
Kit's Coty, 402
Kneller, Sir Godfrey, 42, 130, 136, 172
Knight family, 98
Knight, Richard Payne, 99, 233
Knights Hospitallers, 311, 350–1
Knights Templar, 471
Knightshayes Court, Devon, 127–8, 235
Knole, Kent, 25, 26, 29–30, 37, 48,
    129–33, 309
Knole and the Sackvilles (Sackville-
    West), 132
Knollys family, 341, 342
Knollys, Sir Francis, 341
Knowles Farm, Isle of Wight, 493
Knutsford Lodge, Tatton, Cheshire, 199
Knyff, Leonard, 228
Korean ware, 111
Kutani ware, 184
Kymin, The, Gwent: Round House and
    Naval Temple, 266, 276
Kynance Cove, Cornwall, 452

Labellière, Major Peter, 266
Lacock, Wiltshire, 270, 285–6, 310;

Abbey, 13, 28–9, 78, 311, 342–3
Lady Holme, Cumbria, 506
Lafayette, Marquis de, 217
Laguerre, Louis, 32, 118, 164, 196
Lainé, Louis, 214, 234
Lake District Defence Society, 11
Lake District, NT land in, 498–506
Lamb, Charles, 36, 90, 334
Lamb House, Rye, East Sussex, 36,
    133–5
Lamb, James, and Lamb family, 133–4
Lambert's Castle, Dorset, 480, 581
Lambeth ware, 149
Lambsowden Cove, Cornwall, 458–9
Lamerie, Paul de, 127
Lamledra, Cornwall, 459
Lancashire, NT land in, 506
Lancaster, Osbert, 31
Lancaster, Thomas, Earl of, 307, 510
Lancret, N., 47
Landmark Trust, 435, 472
Landor, Walter Savage, 334
Land's End, Cornwall, 407, 417, 425,
    446, 447, 448
Landseer, Sir Edwin, 182
Lane, Jane, 149
Laneham, Robert, 25
Lang, Archbishop, 458
Langdales, The, Cumbria, 427, 500,
    501–2, 505, 579
Langland, William, 491
Langlois, 84
Langton, Archbishop Stephen, 528
Lanhydrock, Cornwall, 26, 30, 135–7,
    230, 577
Lansallos, Cornwall, 461, 462, 577
Lanscroon, 172
Lanteglos-by-Fowey, Cornwall, 461, 462
Lantic Bay, Cornwall, 462
Lantivet Bay, Cornwall, 462
Lanyon Quoit, Cornwall, 405
Largillière, Nicolas, 94
Laud, Archbishop William, 209
Lauderdale, Duke and Duchess of, 31,
    115–16
Lavenham, Suffolk: Guildhall, 310, 358
Law, Bishop Edmund, 321
Lawrence, T. E., 36, 89–90
Lawrence, Sir Thomas, 170
Learmont, Mrs J. B., 175
Leasowes, The, Hereford & Worcester,
    230, 231, 490
Le Blond, Alexandre, 348
Lee, Thomas, 52, 283
Lees-Milne, James, 34
Legh family, 37, 139–41
Legh, Sir Peter, 113
Leicester, Earl of, 25, 93
Leicestershire, NT land in, 506
Leicestershire Trust for Nature
    Conservation, 506
Leigh, Dr, 152
Leigh Woods, Avon, 424, 429, 430
Leith Hill, Surrey, 524–5
Lely, Sir Peter, 40, 42, 115, 116, 164
Lemon, river, 332
Le Nain, L., 164
Le Nôtre, André, 228, 230, 254
Lenox-Conyngham, Capt. William, 189
Leoni, Giacomo, 33, 38, 83, 87, 88,
    140–1

Leopold of Saxe-Coburg, Prince, 240
Lesceave Cliff, Cornwall, 450
Lethieullier, Sarah (Lady
    Fetherstonhaugh), 47, 206
Letocetum, Wall, Staffordshire, 396, 414
Levant Mine engine, Cornwall, 388
Lévi-Strauss, Claude, 22
Levy, Mr Kenneth, 84, 117
Lewyn, John, 307
Lichfield, Earls of, 181
Lightfoot, Luke, 34, 86
Limoges enamel, 171
Lindisfarne Castle, Northumberland,
    28, 76, 137–8, 308, 512
Lindsay, Lord, 47
Lingwood Common, Essex, 483
Linnell (furniture maker), 104
Liszt, Franz, 297
Little Moreton Hall, Cheshire, 28,
    138–9
Liverpool, Albert Dock, 363
Liverpool, Earl of, 133
Lizard peninsula, Cornwall, 451, 452,
    462
Lizard Serpentine Company, 453
Llanberis Pass, 426
Llanborth Farm, Dyfed, 532
Llanrwst bridge, Gwynedd, 384
Lleyn Peninsula, Gwynedd, 416, 533,
    539–40
Llyn Idwal, Gwynedd, 537
Lochtyn, Llangranog, Dyfed, 532, 533
Loder, Gerald W. E., 259
Loe Bar and Loe Pool, Cornwall, 450–1
Logan Rock, Cornwall, 408, 449
Londesborough Park, 142
London, George, 104
Londonderry, Marchioness of, 149, 235,
    245
Long Crendon, Buckinghamshire: Court
    House, 310, 358
Long Melford, Suffolk, 143
Long Mynd, The, Salop, 421, 515–16
Longespée, William de, 342
Longleat, 31, 38, 112
Longshaw, Derbyshire, 466
Longstone lighthouse, Farne Islands,
    Northumberland, 511
Lonsdale, Earl of, 501, 579
Lookout Hill, East Sussex, 527
Lord's Seat, Derbyshire, 467
Lothian, Marquesses of, 13, 65, 67
Lotto, Lorenzo, 53, 208
Loughrigg Tarn, Cumbria, 502
Loughwood meeting house, Devon,
    293–4
Louis XIV, 137, 154, 254; furniture,
    136, 212
Louis XV style furniture and panelling,
    54, 87, 172, 182, 212, 329
Louis XVI, 203; furniture, 152, 182,
    203, 212, 213
Louis Philippe, 240
Love, Nicholas, 312
Loveden family, 69
Lower Brockhampton, Hereford &
    Worcester, 308, 343–4
Loweswater, Cumbria, 499
Lowland Point, 454
Lowry-Corry family, 73, 74
Luca di Tommé, 170

Lucas family, 371–2
Lucas, Sir Thomas, 371
Luccombe, Somerset, 518
Lucretius, 278
Lucy family, 37, 79–81
Lucy, Sir Thomas, 79–80
Ludshott Common, Hampshire/Surrey, 422, 582
Lugger, Lieutenant, 462
Lundy, Devon, 470–72; Marisco Castle, 471; Millcombe House, 471
Luttrell family, 100–2
Lutyens, Sir Edwin, 36, 75–7, 138, 526
Lyd, river, 472
Lydford, Devon; castle, 472: Gorge, 472–3; Bridge House, 580
Lyke Wake Walk, 531
Lyle, Col. A. A., 331
Lyme mastiffs, 141
Lyme Park, Cheshire, 30, 33, 37, 38, 139–41
Lyminge, Robert, 31, 65
Lynmouth, Devon, 473–4
Lysicrates, Choragic Monument of, 198, 282
Lyte family, 344–5
Lytes Cary, Somerset, 308, 344–5
Lyth, The, Selborne, 486–7
Lyveden New Bield, Northamptonshire, 276–7

Macadam, John, 364
Macartney, Lord, 190
McDonnell family, 544, 546
MacQuillan family, 546
Madocks, William Alexander, 539
Madox Brown, Ford, 70, 221
Maen Castle, Cornwall, 407
Maenease Point, Cornwall, 459
Maer Cliff, Cornwall, 436
Maes, Nicolas, 53
Maggotty's Wood, Cheshire, 16, 577
Magna Carta, 342, 525, 526
Maiden Castle, 396
Maister, Henry, 142
Maister House, Hull, Humberside, 142–3
Malham Tarn and Cove, North Yorkshire, 424, 530
Maltings, 362–3
Malvern Hills, Hereford & Worcester, 406, 419, 489, 490–1
Mam Tor, Derbyshire, 466–7
Manacles Rocks, Cornwall, 454, 456
Mander family, 221–2
Mander, Theodore, 221, 222
Manesty, Cumbria, 421, 500–1
Manifold Valley, Staffordshire, 425, 521
Manners, Lady Marjorie, 169
Mantegna, Andrea: Triumphs, 40
Mantua, Duke of, 40
Maratta, Carlo, 193
Marconi Memorial, Poldhu, Cornwall, 451
Margaret of Aragon, wife of Henry VI, 357
Margaret, Princess, daughter of Henry VII, 114
Maria Carolina, Queen of Naples, 57
Marie Antoinette, 213
Marlborough, Duke of, 220, 300

Marsden Moor, West Yorkshire, 530–1
Marshall, Ben, 208
Martineau, Denis, 145
Martock, Somerset: Treasurer's House, 310, 355
Mary of Modena, Queen, 172, 184
Mary, Queen of Scots, 93, 348
Mary Tudor, Queen, 168
Masefield, John, 519
Massingham, H. J., 468
Mawnan, Cornwall, 422, 454
Maximilian, Emperor, 330
Mayon, Cornwall, 447–8
Mazzini, Giuseppe, 72
Meade-Fetherstonhaugh, Sir Herbert and Lady, 207
Meager, Leonard, 139
Medlock Vale, Greater Manchester, 484–5
Medmenham, Lodge Farm, 577; Monks of, 218, 219
Medway valley, megalithic tombs, 393, 402–3
Meissen porcelain, 110, 117, 208, 211
Melford Hall, Suffolk, 26, 143–4, 229
Meller, John, 106–7
Melville, Viscount, 300
Memling, Hans, 207
Menabilly, Cornwall, 460
Menachurch Point, Cornwall, 436
Menai Strait, 167; bridges, 364
Mengs, A. R., 193
Meredith, George, 522
Merewether, Dean, 400
Merrill Trust, 118
Merton Abbey, 311
Mesolithic period, 391–2, 526, 530–1
Messel family, 234, 247, 248
Methley, Richard, 312
Metsu, Gabriel, 207
Mevagissey, Cornwall, 460
Michel Dene, East Sussex, 527
Middle Littleton tithe barn, Hereford & Worcester, 328, 328
Middlesex, Earl of, 130
Midsummer Hill, Malvern Hills, 406, 491
Miereveldt, Michiel van, 56
Mieris, Frans van, 53
Mill, Sir Richard, 346
Millais, Sir John, 214, 222
Millais, Lady, 221
Milldale, Derbyshire, 465
Miller, Sanderson, 78, 209, 343
Millet, J. F., 164
Milton, John, 351, 420
Minack Theatre, Cornwall, 448
Minerva Britanna (Peacham), 66
Ming ware, 53, 111, 329
Modern Painters (Ruskin), 221
Mohun family, 100, 461, 462
Mole, river, 522
Mompesson family, 144–5
Mompesson House: see Salisbury
Mona 'marble', 161
Monasteries, 311–12
Monk Coniston, Cumbria, 123, 499
Monkwearmouth: railway station, 364
Monnow, river, 317
Mont-Saint-Michel, 351, 355
Montacute, Somerset, 27, 30, 37, 145–7, 229, 236

Monuments, 276–283
Moore, Hugh Armytage, 234, 248
Moore, James, 141
Moore, Rev. John, 248
More, Hannah, 67
Morgan, William de, 221
Morland, George, 360
Moreton, family, 28, 139
Morley, Earls of, 176
Morris, William, 180, 191, 216, 221–2; firm, 97, 191, 192, 222
Morrison, Vitruvius, 150
Morte Bay and Morte Point, Devon, 474–5
Mortlake tapestries, 60, 104, 136, 141
Morton, Cardinal John, 129
Morwenstow, Cornwall, 433, 434–5; Rectory Farm, 434
Moseley Old Hall, Staffordshire, 36, 147–9, 230
Mottisfont Abbey, Hampshire, 29, 30, 209, 236, 311, 345–6
Mottistone, Isle of Wight, 496
Mount Edgcumbe, Cornwall, 338, 463, 464
Mount Grace Priory, North Yorkshire, 312, 324–5, 531
Mount Stewart, Co. Down, house, 149–51; garden, 149, 221, 234, 245–6; Temple of the Winds, 149, 246, 265
Mountflorence, Lord (John Cole), 111
Mow Cop, 267, 274
Moyser, Colonel James, 151
Muchelney, Somerset: priest's house, 310, 586
Mullion Cove, Cornwall, 451
Murat, Caroline, 58
Murgatroyd family, 105–6
Murillo, Bartolomé Esteban, 70, 104
Murlough Nature Reserve, Dundrum, Co. Down, 549
Museum of Childhood, Sudbury Hall, Derbyshire, 194
Mussenden Temple, Co. Londonderry, 34, 265, 278–9
Mutual Households Association, 38
Mwnt, Dyfed, 533
Mynydd Mawr, Gwynedd, 536
Mynydd-y-Graig, Gwynedd, 539

Nare Head, Cornwall, 457–8
Nash, John, 57, 271, 284, 458
National Portrait Gallery exhibitions, 147
National Trust Act (1907), 12, 425
National Trust Act (1937), 13
National Trust for Scotland, 327
National Trust, Past and Present, The (Fedden), 13, 37
Natural History and Antiquities of Selborne (White), 486
Natural History Museum, 391, 480
Nature Conservancy, 424, 430, 509, 517, 539, 542
Nature reserves, 424, 431–2, 480, 494, 506, 508, 509, 517, 519–20, 529, 537, 549
Navax Point, Cornwall, 445
Neale family, 340
Neanderthal man, 406

Near Sawrey, Cumbria, 123, 506
Needles Point, 477, **495**
Nelson, Horatio, Viscount, 144, 206, 276, 279
Nene, river, 159
Nennius, 414
Neolithic period, 392–3, 394, 400, 401, 402, 403, 408, 432, 483, 501–2, 527, 538, 547, 548, 549
Nesfield, W. A., 234
Nesfield, W. E., 96
Nether Alderley Mill, Cheshire, 374
Nether Stowey, Somerset: Coleridge Cottage, 36, **90**
New Forest Act (1964), 485
New Forest Commons, **485–6**
Newark Priory, Surrey, 381, 582
Newburgh, Earl of, 267
Newcastle, Dukes of, 133, 239, 240, 291, 513
Newcastle-upon-Tyne: railway station, 364
Newcomen, Thomas, 387
Newquay, Cornwall, 442
Newton Cliff, St Mawes, Cornwall, 456
Newton, Sir Isaac, 36, 224–5
Newton Links, Northumberland, 510, 585
Newton, Lords, 139, 141
Newtown, Isle of Wight, **494**; Old Town Hall, **300–1**, 494
Nicholson, Francis, 193
Nicolson, Sir Harold, 235, 252, 253
Nicolson, Nigel, 15
Niewe Herballe (Lyte), 344
Nightingale, Florence, 11, 86, 87
Nightingale, Parthenope: *see* Verney
Nonsuch Palace, 311
Nore Folly, Slindon, West Sussex, 267, 528
Norfolk and Norwich Naturalists' Society, 509
Norfolk, Duke of, 525
Norfolk Museum Service, 189
Norfolk, NT land in, 508–9
Norfolk Naturalists' Trust, 424, 509
Norreys (Norris) family, 353
Norreys, Sir William, 353
North Bere Place, 354
North Cliff mine, Cornwall, 445
North Wales Naturalists' Trust, 538
Northcote, James, 165
Northcott Mouth, Cornwall, 436
Northern Ireland: NT land in, 543–50
Northumberland, Earls of, 48, 162–4
Northumberland, NT land in, 509–12
Norton, Sir George, 430
Nostell Priory, Yorkshire, 35, 1.1–3
Nottinghamshire, NT land in, ; 2–13
Nunnington Hall, Yorkshire, 15 –4
Nymans, West Sussex, 234, **247**–
Nymphenburg figures, 84, 110
Nyon ware, 170

Oast-houses, 362–3
O'Cahan family, 546
O'Casey, Sean, 180
Offa's Dyke, 489
Oisin (Irish poet), 544
Olcan (first Irish bishop), 545
Old Soar, Kent, 308, 583

Old Stone Age: *see* Palaeolithic period
Oldbury Hill, Kent, **406–7**
Ombersley, Abbot, 328
O'Neill, Moira, 544
O'Neill, Shane, 544
O'Neills of Tyrone, the, 546
Onslow, Thomas, 2nd Lord, 33, 83
Opie, John, 165
Ordovices, 416
Orleáns, Duc d', 46, 213
Ormesby Hall, Cleveland, **155**
Osmington, Dorset, 482
Ostade, Adriaen and Isaac, 53, 170
Osterley Park, London, 25, 35, 37, 152, **156–7**
Oswald, St, 325
Otway, Lady Elizabeth, 68
Otway, William Young, 46–7
Oudry, Jean Baptiste, 330
Ould, Edward, 221
Ouse, river, 373
Overbeck Museum, Devon, 476
Overbeck, Otto, 250
Overbury, Sir Thomas, 341
Overton Hill, Wiltshire: The Sanctuary, 399
Owen, George, 533
Owletts, Cobham, Kent, **157–8**
Oxburgh Hall, Norfolk, 25, 26, 37, 234, 309, **347–8**
Oxford, 4th Earl of, 63
Oxford, 15th Earl of, 358
Oxfordshire, NT land in, 513–15

Packwood House, Warwickshire, 30, **158–9**, 229
Padstow, Cornwall, 441
Paget family, 168
Paine, James, 108, 151, 152, 214, 269, 392
Palaeolithic period, 390–1, 406, 528
Palladian style, 23, 33–5, 39, 86, 126, 140, 142, 151, 181, 192, 211, 218, 220, 263, 292
Palmer, Charles John, 189
Palmerston, Lord, 493
Paradise Cove, Cornwall, 457
Paris, Matthew, 306
Park Head, Cornwall, **441**
Parker family (of Melford), 144
Parker family (of Saltram), 43, 144, 176, 178
Parnell, Sir John, 100
Parr, Catherine, 187
Parry, Gambier, 46
Passavant, Johann, 39
Patrick, St, 542, 549
Paxton, Sir Joseph, 198
Paxton, Sir William, 279
Paxton's Tower, Dyfed, 266, **279**
Paycocke, Thomas, 348
Paycocke's, Coggeshall, Essex, 37, 309, **348**
Peacham, Henry: *Minerva Britanna*, 66
Peak District, The, 464, 465
Pearce (Pierce), Edward, 195, 196
Peckover House: *see* Wisbech
Peckover, Jonathan, 159
Pedn-men-an-mere, Cornwall, **448**
Pedn-vounder beach, Cornwall, 448
Peel, Sir Robert, 44

Pele towers, 183, 308, 316
Pelham, Thomas, 239
Pembrokeshire Coastal Path, 534
Pen Hill, Somerset, 517
Penare, Cornwall, 459
Penarfynydd Rhiw, Gwynedd, 605
Penarvon Cove, Cornwall, **454**
Penberth Cove, Cornwall, **448–50**
Pencannow Point, Cornwall, 436
Pencarrow Head, Cornwall, **462–3**
Pendarves Point, Cornwall, 441, 577
Pendennis Castle, Cornwall, 455
Penderel family, 147–8, 149
Pendower beach, Cornwall, **457**
Penhale, Cornwall, 443
Penn, John 283
Pennant, G. H. Dawkins, 160
Pennine Way. 464
Penny Post, The, 181
Pennyman family, 155
Penrhyn Castle, Gwynedd, 36, **160–2**
Penrhyn, 1st Lord, 162, 537
Penrose Estate, Cornwall, 450
Penshaw Monument, Tyne & Wear, 265, 588
Pentewan stone, 50
Pentire, Cornwall, 421, **440–1**
Pentireglaze, Cornwall, 440
Penwith group of megaliths, 405
Pepperbox, The, Wiltshire, 275
Pepys, Samuel, 104, 147
Percunning Cove, Cornwall, 458
Percy family, 162–3, 340
Persia, Shah of, 97
Peter the Great, 66
Pettifer (plasterer), 195, 196
Petworth House, West Sussex, 25, 30, 32, 33, 37, 48, **162–5**, 233
Peyvre, Paulin, 306
Phelips family, 27, 145–7
Philip II of Spain, 147
Philipps House, Dinton, Wiltshire, 34, 37, **166–7**
Phillips, Thomas, 164
Picts, The, 390
Pigeon-houses, *see* Dovecotes
Pike Low, Derbyshire, 464
Pike Pool, Derbyshire, 465
Pilgrim Trust, The, 225, 409
Pines, The, Putney, 222
Pitstone windmill, Buckinghamshire, 367, **370**
Pitt, William, 381
Place, Cornwall, 457
Plas-yn-Rhw, Gwynedd, 539, 540, 591
Plas Newydd, Gwynedd, **167–9**
Platel, Pierre, 27
Plym Bridge Woods, Devon, 469
Plymouth porcelain, 110
Plympton Priory, 456
Polcreek Cliff, Cornwall, 457
Poldhu Cove, Cornwall, 451
Pole, Sir John and Reginald, 49
Polesden Lacey, Surrey, 13, 30, 36, 37, 48, **169–71**
Polfreman, Joseph, 141
Polperro, Cornwall, 460, 461, **463–4**
Polridmouth, Cornwall, 460
Polruan, Cornwall, 461, 462
Poltesco Cove, Cornwall, 453
Polzeath, Cornwall, 421

Pompadour, Madame de, 87, 213
Pont and Pont Pill, Cornwall, 461, 462
Pope, Alexander, 130, 171, 230, 254
Port-Eynon Point, West Glamorgan, 424
Porth Farm, Cornwall, 422
Porth Joke, Cornwall, 442
Porth Ysgo, Gwynedd, 540
Porthbeor beach, Cornwall, 457
Porthcadjack Cove, Cornwall, 445
Porthcurno, Cornwall, 448
Porthleven, Cornwall, 450
Porthmellin Head, Cornwall, 457
Porthscatho, Cornwall, 457
Portloe, Cornwall, 458
Portquin, Cornwall, 440
Portreath, Cornwall, 444
Portsmouth dockyard, 363–4
Portway (Roman road), 516
Portwrinkle, 463
Potter, Beatrix, 123, 499, 501, 502, 506
Potter, Joseph, 168
Poussin, Gaspard, 193
Poussin, Nicolas, 40, 42, 43, 193, 230, 231, 282
Povey, Thomas, 104
Powis Castle, Powys, 28, 32, 63, 171–3, 229, 236, 307
Powis, Marquesses and Earls of, 171–2
Powys, Mrs Lybbe, 220
Powys, NT land in, 540–1
Praxiteles, 165
Predannack, Cornwall, 452–3
Prehistoric sites, 399–410
Pre-Raphaelites, 70–1, 215, 216, 221–2
Preservation, principle of, 16–17
Preston, Lord, 154
Price, Dr, 200
Price, Sir Henry, 259
Price, Sir Rose, 258
Price, Uvedale, 99, 233
Prideaux and Prideaux-Brune family, 441
Priests' houses, 310–11
Prince Regent: see George IV
Princes Risborough Manor, Buckinghamshire, 173–4
Printing presses, 386–7
Prior, Matthew, 130
Pritchard, Thomas, 63, 197
Pugin, A. W. N., 168, 265, 291, 347
Purbeck Hills, 273, 477

Quantock Hills, Somerset, 100, 586
Quarry Bank Cotton Mill, Styal, Cheshire, 359
Quebec House, Westerham, Kent, 36, 175
Queen Adelaide's Hill, Cumbria, 505
'Queen Anne' style, 32, 72
Queen's University, Belfast, 549, 550
Quiller-Couch, Sir Arthur ('Q'), 461

Radcliffe Camera, Oxford, 50
Radnor Mere, 374
Raeburn, Sir Henry, 170, 208
Raleigh family, 335, 336
Raleigh, Sir Walter, 93, 190, 335, 336
Rame Head, Cornwall, 452, 462, 463
Ramsey Abbey, Cambridgeshire, 373–4
Gatehouse, 311, 325
Ranelagh, 1st Earl of, 300

Ranelagh Gardens, 86
Ranmore Common, Surrey, 171
Raphael, 133, 220
Rashleigh family, 460
Rashleigh, William 460
Ratlinghope, Salop, 516
Rawnsley, Canon Hardwicke, 11, 12, 501, 505
Rayleigh Mount, Essex, 307, 581
Razumovski, Cyril, 213
Rebecca (du Maurier), 460
Rebecca, Biagio, 65
Red Book (Repton), 168
Red Earl's Dyke, Malvern Hills, 491
Regent's Park, 284
Reiss, Captain and Mrs F. E., 200
Rembrandt, 39, 70
Rennie, John, 381
Restowrack engine, 388
Revenge, The, 333
Revett, Nicholas, 219, 220, 221
Reynard's Cavern, Derbyshire, 465
Reynolds, Sir Joshua, 42, 43, 53, 70, 126, 130, 133, 155, 164, 170, 172, 176–7, 213, 216
Rhaiadr Dhu, Gwynedd, 539
Rhiw, Gwynedd, 539–40
Ribble, river, 415
Ricardo, Halsey, 122
Ribchester, Lancashire, 414–5
Richard Coeur-de-Lion, 377
Richard II, 306, 309, 313, 324
Richard III, 337, 352
Richardson family (of Derrymore), 100
Richardson, Jonathan, 170
Richest Man, The (Shanks), 15n
Richmond, 2nd Duchess of, 267
Richmond, Sir William, 136
Riesener, Jean-Henri, 213
Rievaulx Terrace and Temples, North Yorkshire, 265, 280–1
Rigg, 'Chairy', 68
Riley graves, 266
Ringstead, Dorset, 482
Rinsey Cliff, Cornwall, 450
Robartes, Richard, 1st Lord, 135–6
Roberts of Oxford (plasterworker), 341
Roberts, Thomas, 132
Robinson, Sir Thomas, 86, 280
Robinson, William, 234
Robinson's shaft engine, 388
Rocaille, 264, 267
Rochester Castle, 270, 287, 315
Rochford, Earl of, 172
Rocking Stone, Derbyshire, 466
Rockport, Co. Antrim, 544
Rode Hall, 267, 274
Rodin, Auguste, 180
Rollos, Philip, 127
Roman and Romano-British sites, 401–2, 411–16, 433, 470, 528; pottery, 404, 521
Romney, George, 53, 136, 144, 165, 172, 208, 213
Ross Castle, Northumberland, 512
Rose, Joseph: senior, 73, 86, 152, 177
junior, 152, 182
Rose, Thomas, 108

Rosemergy Cliff, Cornwall, 447
Rosemullion Head, Cornwall, 455
Rossetti, D. G., 70, 192
Rother, river, 313–4
Rothschild family, 36, 47, 48, 53–4, 212–14, 221, 234
Rothwell Market House, 277
Rousham, 230, 231
Rowallane, Co. Down, 234, 235, 248–9
Rowse, A. L., 435
Royal Academy, 42, 45
Royal Horticultural Society, 227, 231
Royal Institute of British Architects library, 228
Royal Military Canal, Kent, 363, 381–2
Royal Society, The, 206, 225, 350
Royal Society of Arts, 310
Rubens, 39, 40, 44, 103, 154
Rudhall, William, 117
Rufford Old Hall, Lancashire, 29, 309, 349–50; Philip Ashcroft Folk Museum, 350
Ruisdael, Jacob van, 44, 164, 170, 207
Rumps, The, Cornwall, 407, 440, 441
Runnymede, Surrey, 425, 525–6
Rupert, Prince, 55, 330
Rushton (Triangular) Lodge, 266, 277
Rushup Edge, Derbyshire, 467
Ruskin, John, 214, 221, 222, 501
Russell, Mr and Mrs Gilbert, 346
Rutland, Earls of, 280
Ruysdael, Salomon van, 45, 164, 170, 473
Rydal Water, Cumbria, 506
Rye, Sussex: Lamb House, 36, 133–5
Rysbrack, Michael, 84, 193, 256, 330

Sackville family, 130–3
Sackville-West, Victoria, 131, 132, 235, 252–4
Saenredam, Pieter, 207
St Agnes, Cornwall, 443; Beacon, 443–4
St Aidan, 137
St Aidan's Dunes, Northumberland, 512, 585
St Albans Abbey, 308
St Anthony Head, Cornwall, 456
St Anthony-in-Meneage, Cornwall, 454
St Anthony-in-Roseland, Cornwall, 456
St Aubyn family, 352
St Austell, Cornwall, 460, 462
St Brides Bay, Dyfed, 533, 534
St Catherine's Point, Cornwall, 460
St Catherine's Down, Point, Hill and Oratory, Isle of Wight, 310, 493–4
St David's Head, Dyfed, 533–4
St Endellion, Cornwall, 439
St Gennys, Cornwall, 436
St Herbert's Island, Cumbria, 501
St Ives, Cornwall, 446
St John's Jerusalem, Sutton-at-Hone, Kent, 311, 350–1
St Juliot, Cornwall, 437
St Just, Cornwall, 388, 446, 447
St Just-in-Roseland, Cornwall, 456
St Kilda sheep, 199
St Levan, Cornwall, 448
St Levan, Lord, 352
St Margaret's Leas, Kent, 496
St Martin-in-the-Fields, London, 50

St Mawes, Cornwall, 456, 457
St Michael's Mount, Cornwall, 28, 37, 259, 311, **351–2**, 435, 450
St Minver, Cornwall, 439
St Oswald, Baron, 152
St Oswin, shrine of, 308
Salcombe, Devon, **475–6**; Sharpitor House, 475
Salisbury: Joiners Hall, 589; Mompesson House, 32, **144–5**, 342
Salisbury, Ela, Countess of, 342
Salomon (gardener to Henry I), 306
Salop, NT land in, 515–16
Salthouse Broad, Norfolk, 424, 509, 583
Saltram House, Devon, 25, 35–6, 48, 144, **176–8**, 236
Salvator Rosa, 43, 231
Salvin, Anthony, 36, 102, 164, 194, 250
Samphire Island, Cornwall, 445
Samwell, William, 108
Sandham Memorial Chapel, 269, **294**
Sandymouth, Cornwall, **436**
Sandys, Francis, 125
Sandys, 1st Lord, 29, 209–11, 346
Sargent, J. S., 135, 185
Sarto, Andrea del, 53
Savage family, 144
Savonnerie carpets, 213
Saxons, 404, 407, 520, 521, 524
Saye and Sele (William Fiennes), Lord, 129
Scafell Pike, **503–4**, 505, 579
Scarth Wood Moor, North Yorkshire, **531**
Scheemakers, Peter, 281, 282
Schmitz, J., 182
Scolt Head, Norfolk, **509**
Scotney Castle, Kent, 28, 234, **249–50**
Scott, Sir George Gilbert, 291, 320
Scott, Sir Walter, 233, 384
Scott, William Bell, 215
Seal Hole mine, St Agnes, Cornwall, 443
Sederbach (Austrian sculptor), 343
Segontium, Gwynedd, 396, **416**
Selborne and Selborne Hill, Hampshire, 424, **486–7**
Selworthy, Somerset, 517
Serres, Dominic, 144
Seven Sisters, East Sussex, 527
Severn, river, 233, 326
Severn suspension bridge, 384
Sèvres porcelain, 171, 208, 213
Shaftesbury, Lord, 41
Shakespeare, William, 80, 299, 341
Shalford Mill, Surrey, 360, **375–6**
Shanks, Edward, 15n
Shap Abbey, 323
Sharington, Sir William, 28, 285–6, 342
Sharow Cross, 310
Sharpitor, Devon, **250**, 475, 476
Sharrow Grot, Cornwall, 463
Shaugh Bridge, Devon, 469
Shaugh Prior, Devon, 468–9
Shaw, Charlotte, 180
Shaw, George Bernard, 36, 178–80
Shaw, Norman, 36, 96, 97
Shaw's Corner, Ayot St Lawrence, Hertfordshire, 36, **178–80**
Sheerness dockyard, 364
Sheffield, Lords, 250

Sheffield Park, East Sussex, 17, 235, **250–2**
Sheldon tapestry, 348
Shelley, Percy Bysshe, 473
Shellwork, 267, 483
Shelmerdine, Mr & Mrs, 375
Shenstone, William, 230, 490
Sheridan, Richard Brinsley, 169, 170
Shinto temples, 198
Shirley family, 295–6
Shirley, Sir Robert, 164, 269, 295
Shrewsbury, Elizabeth, Countess of ('Bess of Hardwick'), 26–7, 118–20, 348
Shrewsbury flax-mill, 362
Shudi, Burkat, 111
Shugborough, Staffordshire, 25, 33, 37, 180–2, 221, 264–5, 281–2; park and garden monuments, 246, 281–2
Shute Barton, 308, 581
Shuttleworth family 112–14
Siam, King of, 97
Siddal, Elizabeth, 221, 222
Siddons, Sarah, 185
Sidney, Sir Henry, 336
Silures, 416
Sir Richard Grenville of the Revenge (Rowse), 435
Sissinghurst Castle, Kent, 26, 131, 235, **252–4**, 363
Sitwell, Sir Osbert, 46
Sizergh Castle, Cumbria, 28, **183–4**, 308
Skenfrith Castle, Gwent, 307, 317,
Slater Foundation, 241
Slindon estate, West Sussex, 267, **528**
Smallhythe, Kent, 36, 185–6, 309; priest's house, 310–11
Smallman family, 223
Smith, Mrs E, 368
Smith, Joseph (consul), 198
Smythson, Robert, 27, 112, 119
Snake Road, Peak District, 464
Snape, Suffolk; maltings, 363
Snowdon, 162, 237, 416, 426
Snowshill Manor, Gloucestershire, 27, **186–8**
Snyders, Frans, 164
Soames, A. G., 251
Soane, Sir John, 52, 65
Soane Museum, 143
Soar Mill Cove, Devon, 476
Soay sheep, 199
Society for the Protection of Ancient Buildings, 191, 360
Soho tapestries, 211
Somerset, 6th Duke of, 163, 164
Somerset, Earl and Countess of, 341
Somerset, NT land in, 516–19
South Crofty mine, Camborne, Cornwall, **388**
Southdown Farm, Dorset, **482**
Southey, Robert, 226, 384, 473
Southground Point, Cornwall, 460
Southwark, George Inn, **268**
Sow, river, 180
Spanish Armada, 547
Sparrow, Lady Olivia Bernard, 374
Speke Hall, Merseyside, 13, 27–8, 29, 30, 309, **353**
Spencer, Stanley, 269, 294
Spinets, 111

Springhill, Co. Londonderry, 34, 38, **189–90**
Stackpole, Dyfed, **534**
Stafford, Marquess of, *41*, 46
Staffordshire, NT land in, 519–21.
Staffordshire pottery, 84, 111
Standen, West Sussex, 190–2
Stane Street, 522, 528
Stanford University, 87
Stanley Smith Horticultural Foundation, 117
Stanley, Thomas, 375
Stapleton, Michael, 51
Staunton Harold Chapel, Leicestershire, 269, **295–6**
Steed, Wickham, 180
Steen, Jan, 45, 53, 207
Steeple Point, Cornwall, 435
Stennuit, Robert, 547
Stephenson, George, 359
Stephenson, Robert, 359, 364
Steuart, George, 56, 233
Steventon, Oxfordshire: monastic grange, 311
Stewart, Alexander, 149
Stewart, Sir Malcolm, 147
Stickells, Robert, 277
Stockbridge, Hampshire, **488**
Stockman, Henry, 236
Stoke Poges, Buckinghamshire: Gray's Monument, 266, **282–3**
Stokeleigh Camp, Somerset, 429
Stokesay Castle, 344
Stone Age, 390–4, 408, 517, 526, **530–1**, 547
Stoneacre, Otham, Kent, 309, **354**
Stonehenge, 393–5, 399, 409–10, 422, 589; Cursus, 393
Stonor family, 69
Storck, Abraham, *45*
Storr, Paul, 58, 71, 127
Stow, river, 192
Stourhead, Wiltshire, 17, 33, 43, 48, 57, 192–4, 231, 235, **254–6**, 264
Stowe, 86, 230, 231, 239
Stowe Barton, Cornwall, 435
Strabane, Co. Tyrone: Gray's Printing Press, **386–7**
Strafford, Thomas Wentworth, Earl of, 61, 164
Strangford Lough, 77, 78, 79, 149, 234, 235, 246, **549–50**; Wildlife Scheme, 424, 550
Strangles, The, Cornwall, 437
Stratford-upon-Avon canal, 363, **382–3**
Strathmore, Earl of, 392
Strauss, Johann, the elder, 297
Strawberry Hill, 187
Streatfeild family, 285
Street, G. E., 291
Streetly stone, 291
Strickland family, 183, 184
Strode, Essex (M.P. for Stockbridge), 488
Strode family, 331
Stroud valley, 361, 582
Strutt, Jedediah, 362
Stuart, James ('Athenian'), 149, 246, 265, 281, 282
Stubbs, George, 42, *44*, 53, 151, 208
Stukeley, William, 225, 400, 401

606